GEORGE ALEXANDER LENSEN

Balance of Intrigue

International Rivalry in Korea & Manchuria, 1884 – 1899

Volume II

Foreword by
JOHN J. STEPHAN

A FLORIDA STATE UNIVERSITY BOOK
UNIVERSITY PRESSES OF FLORIDA
TALLAHASSEE

University Presses of Florida is the central agency for scholarly publishing of the State of Florida's university system. Its offices are located at 15 NW 15th Street, Gainesville, FL 32603. Works published by University Presses of Florida are evaluated and selected for publication by a faculty editorial committee of any one of Florida's nine public universities: Florida A&M University (Tallahassee), Florida Atlantic University (Boca Raton), Florida International University (Miami), Florida State University (Tallahassee), University of Central Florida (Orlando), University of Florida (Gainesville), University of North Florida (Jacksonville), University of South Florida (Tampa), University of West Florida (Pensacola).

Library of Congress Cataloging in Publication Data

Lensen, George Alexander, 1923–1979
  Balance of intrigue.

  Bibliography: p.
  Includes index.
  1. Korea—Foreign relations—1864–1910.
  2. Soviet Union—Foreign relations—East Asia.
  3. East Asia—Foreign relations—Soviet Union.
  4. East Asia—Politics and government. I. Title.
  DS915.37.L46   327.4705   81-16287
  ISBN 0-8130-0722-4   AACR2

Typography by G&S Typesetters
Austin, Texas

Printed in the U.S.A. on acid-free paper

Contents

Volume I

Contents

Volume II

Sixteen

The Russo-Chinese Alliance

The relations between Russia and China have always been different in character from the relations between China and the other Western states. Russia, by
virtue of her contiguity and size, could not be ignored or offended. Thus
while China refused to conclude a treaty with Great Britain until forced to do
so in 1842, she had signed treaties with Russia in 1689 and 1727, and had done
so willingly, while negotiating from a position of strength. From the late
seventeenth century until the middle of the nineteenth century the Russians
enjoyed commercial, religious, and educational privileges, as well as access
to Peking, denied to other Westerners.[1] Although Russia secured from China
large territorial concessions north of the Amur River and east of the Ussuri
River in 1858 and 1860, she did so by diplomatic means rather than by direct
force of arms as did the British in the case of Hong Kong and Burma, and the
French in the case of Annam.[2] The territorial dispute between Russia and
China in Central Asia was solved amicably in 1881, with Russia returning the
Ili region she had occupied during the rebellion of the Muslim inhabitants
against the Manchu conquerors. The settlement strengthened Chinese self-
confidence and removed any fear of Russia.[3] Reporting from Peking in 1888
that the official relations between Russia and China were good in the sense
that St. Petersburg strove to avoid anything that might lead to a conflict with
China, Brandt remarked that Russian obligingness had made the Chinese
more intractable than ever.[4] It was the Russians who were worried about a
conflict with the Chinese more than the other way around. Giers wanted Russia either to strengthen her position in East Asia or to give it up. He was
concerned not only by the steady buildup of the Chinese forces in Manchuria,
but by the apprehension that the Chinese living on the Russian side of the
Ussuri River remained under the influence of Chinese officials, whom they
obeyed more than the Russian authorities.[5]

Li Hung-chang boasted to a number of persons that China had no reason to fear Russia because of the latter's extreme weakness along their lengthy border. He threatened Russia with war should she violate Korean rights.[6] The thoughts expressed by Li concerning the weakness of the Russian border and the vast region adjacent to China alarmed Zinoviev, the director of the Asiatic Department at that time, who feared that the spread in the Far East of the conviction that Russia was weak would soon confront the latter with immense questions which, like an ocean wave, would inundate everything in their path. Li's words impressed on Zinoviev and on Lamsdorff the need to strengthen the Russian Far East by the construction of a Trans-Siberian railroad.[7]

The construction of a Trans-Siberian railroad had been discussed since the 1850s. The decision to go ahead with the project was prompted in 1890 by the Chinese government's dispatch of English engineers to seek a route for a railroad through South Manchuria from the Russo-Chinese border to Tientsin and the laying of a line from Tientsin to Shanhaikuan. It was made possible by the influx of French millions. Although Witte was to assert that the primary function of the railroad in connecting the Amur Region with Russia was economic, its original objective had been strategic—to assimilate the "Siberian colony" and strengthen its security.[8] The Crimean War had shown how exposed Russia's eastern shores were to foreign naval attacks, and the flood of Chinese settlers into Manchuria threatened to block Russian acquisition of an ice-free outlet to the sea.[9]

The reluctance of the Manchu government to suppress the distribution of inflammatory anti-Christian treatises by Confucian literati and the procrastination of the authorities in proceeding against the ringleaders of the disturbances persuaded the foreign representatives that no faith could be put in the assurances of the Chinese government. In a joint protocol on September 9, 1891, the tsarist representative along with his colleagues of Belgium, France, Germany, Great Britain, Italy, Japan, Spain, and the United States agreed that the situation in China was exceedingly serious, if not critical, and that unless the foreign powers demonstrated their will to protect their nationals and enforce the observance of the treaties, further outrages and attacks of mounting severity were bound to follow.[10]

In spite of the feeling of approaching doom, the powers did not puncture the spirit of defiance which inflated China. The Russians did not wish to be prominent in any coercion of the latter. They were alarmed by what they regarded as Chinese encroachment in the Pamir region and did not wish to antagonize Peking. As Giers told the British representative in St. Petersburg, the Chinese were a "most tenacious race" and "as Russia had them for neighbors along he did not know how many thousand miles, he had to be careful how he dealt with them." [11] The German state secretary of foreign affairs, Baron Marschall, confided to the British ambassador, Malet, that Germany would not participate in any action against China unless Russia was persuaded to join, for to proceed without her would place the coercing powers in a "disadvantageous position." [12] Hatzfeldt, the German ambassador in London, also expressed the fear that the international coercion of China without Russian participation would leave St. Petersburg in a position "to establish an influence over the Chinese Government, especially in respect to its northern provinces, which would not be consistent with the independence of China." [13] Apart from the above, Marschall and Hatzfeldt had general reservations about the wisdom of weakening the Chinese government. Hatzfeldt saw "extreme danger" to European interests, should excessive Western pressure lead to the overthrow of the Manchu dynasty. [14]

On February 24, 1892, Giers warned Hsü Ching-ch'eng, that Russia would send troops to the Pamir region and expel the Chinese troops who had penetrated there, if they did not withdraw promptly. The Chinese pulled back, conscious of their own weakness in the borderlands. [15]

The myth of the China market was as strong in Russia as in the United States. Actual trade between Russia and China was insignificant. In 1881 it had amounted to only two and a half percent of China's foreign trade. Yet by 1891 it had doubled and the Russians were hopeful that with the construction of the Trans-Siberian Railroad Russian participation in the China trade would grow substantially. [16] Thus they were loath to alienate the Chinese for economic as well as for political reasons.

If the above relations fell short of "historical friendship" in that both sides remained suspicious of each other and made accommodations out of necessity rather than out of desire, they were a shade better—certainly no worse—than the relations of China with the other European powers. Thus Li Hung-chang's appeal for Russian mediation at the time of the Sino-Japanese War was not as surprising as believers in a "historical enmity" between Russia and China might think. [17] With the retrocession of the Liaotung Peninsula the Russians became heroes in Chinese eyes even though the intervention had been tripartite. [18] The fact that by defending Manchuria against Japanese invasion or annexation Russia had become a rampart not only of China but of the Manchu dynasty had added to the good image of St. Petersburg in Peking. [19]

By the unequal treaties imposed on China by Great Britain in 1842–1843 and adopted by the other powers as a model for their agreements with Peking China had lost the right to fix her own customs duties. The five percent ad valorem tariff set by the treaties could be increased only by mutual agreement. [20] An attempt by the Chinese government to obtain the funds for paying the indemnity due Japan by increasing the tariff rate was blocked by England, who would have been most affected by the change. Nor did Sir Robert Hart allow the boosting of the already high salt tax. Unable to raise the money at home, the Chinese government had to seek foreign assistance.[21]

Desirous of balancing their commitments so as not to give undue advantage to any power, the Chinese first approached bankers in Berlin and London, but they eventually accepted a loan from a Russo-French syndicate, whose terms were more favorable. The idea of lending money to China had not originated in St. Petersburg, which itself was in financial straits due to the construction of the Trans-Siberian Railroad, stepped up since the Sino-Japanese War, and the aftereffects of the famine of 1891–1893. It had been suggested by Paris which had a surplus of capital. France had offered to work with or through Russia not only because the latter was a good credit risk in view of her increased gold production, her recovery from the depression of 1893, and the high reputation of Witte, but because the tsarist government alone was in a position to give a prompt guarantee of the huge loan without parliamentary debate, thereby holding down the rate of interest.[22] Thus China borrowed from the Russo-French syndicate the large sum of 100 million gold rubles (400 million gold francs) at ninety-four percent face value and only four percent interest.[23]

The Germans, who had played a major role in the Tripartite Intervention, were deeply offended at having been left out. So bitter was Marschall about the Franco-Russian agreement, that Martin Gosselin concluded from the tone of his observations during a conversation on June 14 that "the joint action of the three Powers in the Far East is already a thing of the past." Since the loan had been secured on the customs of the treaty ports, it would be difficult to raise additional money to pay off the balance of the indemnity. The Russian government had "stolen the cream," fumed Schwabach, the correspondent of Messrs. Rothschild in the German capital.[24]

Aoki reported from Berlin on June 11, 1895, that the "intrigue" to raise sixteen million pounds sterling in France for China under the guarantee of Russia had caused "political uneasiness" in Germany and England. It was assumed that Russia sought to take a slice of Manchuria and to make Port Arthur the terminus of the Trans-Siberian Railroad; Russia could then station troops in Manchuria under the pretext of guarding the railroad. In case of China's default France would be in a position to occupy southern China. "To frustrate this scheme and also to maintain our prominence in Corea against Russia, we must secure [the] support of England and Germany, taking advantage of disunion and jealousy among [the powers]," Aoki telegraphed. Decrying the irresolution of his government, he asked that the Japanese minister to

Great Britain and he himself be given freedom of action to "liberate Germany from the triple concert" and bring about the "counteraction of England and Germany against [the] Russian scheme." [25]

When Nishi inquired in St. Petersburg about the motives behind the projected Russian loan, Lobanov replied that the sole aim of the tsarist government in offering the money to China was to enable the latter to meet the indemnity payments to Japan and thus to bring about the peaceful settlement of the Far Eastern conflict as soon as possible. Lobanov denied that there was any substance to the rumors that Russia was to obtain some concessions in Northern Manchuria or at Port Arthur in return for the loan. [26]

Nishi anticipated that China would "virtually come under the influence" of the tsarist government as a result of the loan. Since the loan covered merely the first payment to Japan and it was generally believed that it would be difficult for China to raise additional funds in the future, he recommended to his government that in case it decided to retrocede the Liaotung Peninsula, it make Peking "guarantee full payment of the whole indemnity." [27] Similar advice, with broader implications, was given to the Japanese government unofficially by the British foreign secretary through the Japanese minister in London. Arguing that the raising of the proposed loan guaranteed by Russia on the security of the Chinese customs might hinder the procurement of funds to meet the necessary payments, Kimberley suggested that it might be to Japan's interest "not to proceed to the evacuation of the Liao-tung Peninsula, without adequate security that the whole indemnity would be provided for." However, when Kato asked whether the British government would give Japan moral support to resist anticipated Russian pressure to withdraw immediately, Kimberley was unable to give any assurance in view of the resignation of the cabinet. [28]

It had been China herself who had approached Russia to lend her the money for the first payment of the indemnity to ensure the prompt evacuation of the Liaotung Peninsula even though European bankers and the German government had already made overtures to her, Montebello reported from St. Petersburg. Russia was the only country who could give a prompt guarantee by the will of the emperor without parliamentary debate and approval, [29] and had done so, enlisting the financial resources of France. Russia wished above all to exclude England from the combination, partly because she feared her rivalry, partly because she felt that having abandoned the other powers when an element of risk had arisen she should not profit from the financial, political, and commercial opportunities deriving from the intervention. Russia also desired to keep Germany out of the operation. Germany, Montebello explained, had joined Russia and France in their common action in the Far East in order to play the role of grand power and to prevent Russia and France from being alone in their diplomatic success or from solidifying their union. Russia and France had not been able to reject German support, and German participation had indeed contributed to the success of the démarche. But Russia did not see sufficient reason in this for remaining tied to Germany indefinitely. In a question where German interests were not involved to the same degree as the interests of Russia and France, who had common boundaries with China, Russia wished to preserve for the two powers all the benefits which were now in their grasp.

Lobanov foresaw that the exclusion of London and Berlin from the loan was bound to arouse their profound discontent when he insisted on the need to conclude the agreement before competition got too heated. Germany was trying to persuade China that she would become Russia's vassal if she accepted her guarantee; she had succeeded in shaking the resolution of the Chinese government somewhat. In a long interview with Hsü in the presence of Witte, Lobanov remonstrated that all such insinuations were without foundation. He assured Hsü that the Chinese government was free to turn to anyone it wished if it had found an arrangement as advantageous as that offered by Russia; the tsarist government stood by its proposal and·was waiting for a definitive answer from China.

Denying the allegations made by the Germans and the British that Russia intended to extend the Trans-Siberian Railroad to Port Arthur and take possession of that fortress, Lobanov assured Montebello in the most formal and official manner that the negotiations between Russia and China in connection with the loan were purely financial; there was no thought of a political or territorial arrangement. Lobanov had expressed the hope that in a few years Russo-Chinese relations would be such as to permit a modification of the northern boundary. France in turn might wish to seek certain benefits in the region of Tongking; their mutual cooperation in all Far Eastern matters at this time should facilitate such future arrangements. But for the moment, Lobanov had reiterated, there was absolutely no idea of any political or other engagement under the cover of the projected loan.[30]

As the foreign press continued to wonder about the advantages Russia expected to obtain from China in return for her guarantee of the low-interest loan and speculated regarding the construction of a railroad through Manchuria and the acquisition of an ice-free seaport, Lobanov told Lascelles that there was a simple answer to these suppositions. "The frontier between Russia and China was longer than the frontier between any two States in the world, and, thanks to the friendly terms on which these two States had been for upwards of 300 years, it had not been necessary for the Russian Government to take any serious military precautions for protecting the frontier. The Russian forces in Siberia did not exceed 50,000 men, but ten times that amount would not suffice if the frontier had to be guarded in the same way as the western frontier of Russia. This, he thought, was a sufficient reason for the Russian Government to wish to maintain their friendly relations with China, and to offer her their assistance." [31]

In accordance with instructions from London, O'Conor tried to dissuade the Tsungli Yamen from concluding the loan agreement with Russia. During an interview on June 12 he dwelled on the danger of such a course. He challenged the ministers to explain why Russia, who had always been a borrowing country herself, should now wish to lend money to China. The motivation, he suggested, was political rather than commercial. He warned that it was unprecedented for an independent state to effect a loan on the guarantee of a foreign power. No European country would do so lest she fall under the protectorate of the guarantor; he cited illustrations from history, including the case of Egypt, where political independence was lost in the wake of financial subservience. Although the ministers of the Tsungli Yamen denied that Russia planned to route the Trans-Siberian Railroad through Chinese territory to a Chinese open port and asserted that they would reject such a proposal if it were made, O'Conor foretold that they would find it difficult to refuse once they had placed themselves in Russian hands. He alleged that the construction of a Russian railroad through Chinese territory would be tantamount to the establishment of a Russian protectorate.

The ministers of the Tsungli Yamen said little in reply. Though they admitted that they could not understand why Russia insisted on making the loan, they asserted that they could not refuse the offer. They contended—without much conviction, it appeared to O'Conor—that the transaction would be purely financial and give Russia no right to interfere in China's internal affairs.

During a second interview at the Tsungli Yamen, attended by Prince Ch'ing, on June 15, O'Conor asserted that the issuance of a prospectus for the loan before the final consent of the Chinese government constituted an affront to Chinese dignity. He added that if China now borrowed money on the guarantee of a foreign power, she might find it impossible in the future to procure additional funds elsewhere.

Ch'ing retorted that Hsü had been instructed to seek the removal of the guarantee clause.

O'Conor did not confine his appeals to the Tsungli Yamen. He sent a private memorandum to the Chinese president of the Board of Works, supplying him with arguments for a strong protest against the Russian guarantee.

O'Conor and Schenck insisted that a Russian guarantee would be derogatory of China's national dignity.[32]

The Tsungli Yamen was flustered by the warnings of the British and German ministers. While it realized that their allegations might be due to jealousy at Russia getting the entire advantage, it admitted that the fact that Russia was borrowing the money to lend to China without any financial profit for herself and that she had requested China to keep their negotiations secret did give rise to some doubts. Noting that if it broke off the loan negotiations, it would lose what it desired, while if it silently concluded them, it might be preparing disaster, the Tsungli Yamen directed Hsü to communicate to the tsarist government that the German and British ministers had declared that China would suffer great disgrace if she borrowed from Russia and that "some other means must be found of carrying out her friendly offers." Further consideration could be given to the matter once it was seen how Russia replied. "The question is of the greatest importance, and must be handled with care and prudence to prevent future regret," the Tsungli Yamen cautioned.[33]

Lobanov reiterated to Lascelles on June 13 that the only object of the tsarist government in connection with the loan was to hasten Japanese evacuation of the Liaotung Peninsula and thereby to secure permanent peace in East Asia. He was convinced, he said, that Japan would not again seek territory on the mainland.[34]

While the Russians urged the Chinese to accept their proposal in order to ensure the early retirement of the Japanese troops from the Liaotung Peninsula,[35] Germany and England delayed the conclusion of the loan agreement by pressuring China into asking for the deletion of the Russian guarantee.[36] Their intervention was very active. As Staal related to Courcel, while Germany sought to lure China away from Russia with a more advantageous financial arrangement, though not backed by a governmental guarantee, O'Conor menacingly represented the Russian guarantee as a veritable seizure of China and an alienation of her independence. O'Conor threatened that Russia was preparing to partition the Chinese empire and demand the cession of Manchuria for herself.

Lobanov ordered Cassini to combat these maneuvers by denying positively any intentions of the sort on the part of his country and by referring the Chinese ministers to the text of the proposed agreement which contained no mention of any territorial cession whatsoever. Lobanov impressed on Cassini the need for absolute discretion in the affair, which had reached such a delicate stage. Only Gérard, whose cooperation the tsarist government valued, could be kept abreast of developments.[37]

At British and German urging, the Chinese asked and obtained a modification in the wording of the Russian guarantee. Instead of guaranteeing the bonds of the Chinese loan directly, Russia pledged to provide the contracting banks with the required funds in the event that the installments could not be met out of Maritime Customs receipts. ("Instead of A guaranteeing C directly, he guarantees B, who guarantees C," Hsü explained to the Tsungli Yamen.)[38] This permitted the Chinese to counter continued British and German objections with the declaration that they had no official cognizance of the guarantee given by the tsarist government to the French bankers and that the matter, therefore, did not concern them.[39]

On July 6 Hsü and the representatives of six French and four Russian banks signed the loan agreement in the office of the Russian foreign minister in the presence of both Lobanov and Witte.[40] On the same occasion Hsü, Lobanov, and Witte signed and exchanged declarations pertaining to the conclusion of the Chinese loan. The Chinese government committed itself to set aside for the payment of the percentage and amortization a portion of the Maritime Customs revenue remaining at its disposal after the payment of prior loans. The new obligation was to have priority over all claims, no payments to be made annually from the Maritime Customs receipts on loans concluded hereafter until full payment of interest and amortization had been made on this loan. In the event that the loan payments were stopped or delayed for whatever reason, the tsarist government, in agreement with the imperial government of China, assumed toward the contracting banks and commercial houses the obligation on its part to compensate and put at their disposal in good time the sums necessary for the payment of coupons and securities of the said loan on condition that the Chinese government would subsequently give to the Russian government supplementary security. The conditions of the supplementary security would be the subject of a special agreement, to be concluded by the two governments through their representatives in Peking. In view of the loan, the Chinese government declared that it would not grant to any foreign power any rights or privileges of any sort concerning the inspection or administration of any revenues of the Chinese empire. In the event that the Chinese government were to concede such rights to any country, they would be extended to the Russian government as well. The said declarations were to have the same force and significance as a treaty.[41]

The Chinese were pleased to have received the low interest loan and valued, rather than feared, the willingness of the tsarist government to guarantee the payments. Their gratitude toward Russia was increased,[42] notwithstanding the fulminations of the German and British representatives. The recriminations of Schenck and O'Conor became increasingly offensive to them. Schenck told the ministers of the Tsungli Yamen that they had been wrong in accepting such an "embarrassing" arrangement with St. Petersburg; they should have kept the matter strictly financial. He accused them of having given up China's independence and warned that they would suffer heavily for this sooner or later; they would have done far better had they allowed the Japanese to retain the Liaotung Peninsula, he declared.[43] O'Conor was so carried away by his fury in a stormy session at the Tsungli Yamen that he allowed himself a number of disrespectful remarks about Emperor Kuang-hsü himself. In a step unprecedented in Chinese diplomatic history, the Tsungli Yamen demanded the British minister's recall. London complied, but promoted O'Conor to the position of ambassador to St. Petersburg![44]

The signing of the loan agreement and the role played by the tsarist government in its conclusion was announced by the *Journal de Saint-Pétersbourg* on July 8. Addressing itself to foreign speculation regarding the motives of Russia in being of such singular service to China and to the charges that the great Asian empire risked becoming a vassal of Russia by accepting the latter's guarantee, the paper declared that the explanation of the Russian offer was quite simple. It was indicated by the geographical position of the two powers and by the relations which had existed between them continuously for over three centuries. It was but "the logical consequence of a perfectly clear situation," it wrote. The immensely long frontier between the two states required the cultivation of good-neighborliness and amity. "How many men would they have to maintain to guard this frontier if the relations between the two empires had not been such as they are in reality?" the *Journal de Saint-Pétersbourg* queried. Asserting that friendly relations between Russia and China were in the general interest as international trade throve on durable peace, the paper pointed out that Russia had never sought to interfere in the internal affairs of China, nor to exploit her riches for her profit. But neither had she ever refused to lend China her strong assistance when political circumstances confronted her with cruel difficulties, the journal added. Besides, when the Japanese government, in deference to the "amicable counsels" of Russia, France, and Germany, had expressed the "wise resolution" to renounce the permanent possession of the Liaotung Peninsula, it had been only natural for Russia, the initiator of the tripartite intervention, to trouble herself with the financial measures which had remained outside the accord, but on which depended the realization of the pledges obtained. Was not the facilitation of as advantageous a loan as possible for China in line with Russia's traditional relations with the great neighboring empire? And it hastened the liberation of Chinese territory, the objective pursued by the three powers, the journal concluded.[45]

To facilitate the work of the consortium Witte proposed the establishment of a Russian bank in China. Russian tea merchants, whose large transactions were handled by British banks, had already appealed to the Finance Ministry for the founding of a Russian institution. But the project which Witte advanced on July 6 on the occasion of the signing of the loan agreement was conceived in broader terms. He envisioned a bank which would not only carry out the usual commercial and industrial functions, but would strengthen Russian economic influence in China as a counterweight to the enormous influence which the British had acquired, mainly due to their "practical seizure" of the Maritime Customs administration. For this reason the bank was to have extensive rights: trade; the transportation of goods; any operations in the service of the Chinese treasury, notably the collecting of taxes and the issuance of currency; concessions for the construction of railroads anywhere in China; and the stringing of telegraph lines.

As in the case of the loan, the French were asked to put up most of the initial money without obtaining an equal, not to say controlling, voice. After months of negotiations they agreed to the arrangement, because the guarantee of the bank, as of the loan, by the tsarist government made the investment relatively safe.

The negotiations with the French were concluded in October of that year. The statutes of the institution, named the Russko-Kitaiskii Bank (Russo-Chinese Bank), were drawn up in St. Petersburg. They were signed by the French founders in the tsarist embassy in Paris on December 5 and approved by the Committee of the Trans-Siberian Railroad, which sponsored the bank, on December 22.[46]

The conclusion of the loan agreement had revived press reports of a secret treaty granting Russia the right to station her fleet in Port Arthur and to construct and administer railroads along the Nerchinsk-Tsitsihar-Vladivostok and Tsitsihar-Port Arthur routes. Russia was also said to have received exclusive commercial advantages.[47] Though the allegations were officially denied by the Russian government[48]—Lobanov called them "all nonsense"—suspicion persisted among the diplomatic circle in St. Petersburg. Deeming it possible that such an arrangement had been made in spite of the denials, Nishi bitterly told W. E. Goschen, the British chargé d'affaires in St. Petersburg, that if it was true that Russia had obtained the right for her fleet to anchor at Port Arthur, it was "a piece of very sharp practice." "The Russian Government would not allow Japan to stay there on the plea that from that position she would dominate Peking on the one side and Corea on the other, and now they were working to take up that very position themselves."

Goschen believed that no definite agreement to the above effect had been concluded and that Lobanov's statement was strictly correct, yet that the construction of railroads was being contemplated in the near future, parties of

Russian engineers being engaged in surveys in China. The activity of the Russian engineers had probably given rise to the notion that the use of Port Arthur by the Russian squadron would follow necessarily. "The Russian press has, of course, taken up the matter with its usual warmth," Goschen reported, "and the gist of its articles on the subject is that, if the report is not true, it ought to be true, and that, whatever is the case now, it certainly will be true in a very short time." [49]

No doubt Witte's desire to reroute the Trans-Siberian Railroad through Manchuria had been a factor in his conception of the Russo-Chinese Bank. Four days after the signing of the bank's charter he submitted a project to this effect to Nicholas and recommended that funds for the customary "gifts" (*podnosheniia*) to Chinese officials close to the emperor be put at the disposal of the Russian minister in Peking. [50] But if the annexation of Manchuria for this purpose or the acquisition of a naval base had been Russia's objective at this time, she would have made common cause with Japan instead of thwarting her ambitions. Implicit in St. Petersburg's denial of the Liaotung Peninsula to Japan had been the decision to form an alliance with China.

The idea of such an alliance was not one-sided. The failure of Chinese attempts to involve the powers in averting the Sino-Japanese War had brought into question the traditional Chinese policy of "fighting barbarians with barbarians." Li Hung-chang and many other key officials had become convinced that Chinese security might be maintained most effectively by reliance on the protection of one great power—Russia. [51]

Li Hung-chang had long been pro-Russian and anti-Japanese. British failure to intervene during and after the war on China's behalf had bolstered his conviction that China must rely on Russian assistance. Such prominent officials as Liu K'un-i, governor general of Liang-Kiang (Kiangsu, Kiangsi, and Anhwei), who had commanded China's armies during the closing phases of the war, and Chang Chih-tung, acting governor general of the same region, had urged the Tsungli Yamen to seek Russian protection from further Japanese and Western aggression. Chang Pai-hai, secretary of the prestigious Hanlin Academy, Wang Chih-ch'un, special envoy to Russia at the time of the funeral of Alexander III, and Grand Councillor Weng T'ung-ho advocated reliance on Russia. [52] Hsü Ying-k'uei, vice president of the Finance Ministry, who had once looked to England as defender against Russia, memorialized the throne in favor of a defensive alliance with Russia. As before, he regarded Russia and Great Britain as rivals. But England had turned away from China and was seeking Japanese support against Russia. As Japan was China's enemy, Russia, the enemy of Great Britain, was the obvious ally for China, Hsü reasoned. [53]

An alliance with Russia seemed perfectly logical at the time. China could not face the rest of the world singlehandedly. Japan had aroused her deep hatred; England had let her down; France had recently been at war with her and aggressively supported Roman Catholic subversion; Germany had no common boundary with China and thus could not offer effective military aid; and the United States eschewed direct involvement in the affairs of other countries. Russia seemed to be more powerful than Japan, by which China had just been humiliated. The cost of Russian friendship was bound to be lower than the cost of Russian enmity, which might well be incurred if Peking rejected St. Petersburg's outstretched hand. "Some people have compared Russia to a tiger or a wolf, believing that we might be injured if we interfered with it, and could not even imagine our avoiding being mauled once we let it into our house," Hsü Ying-k'uei remarked. "But the thing that must be noted," he argued, "is that China's military power has not been able to cope with that of Japan. How then can China afford to indulge hostile feelings toward Russia?" [54]

In Russia as in China the conclusion of an alliance was regarded not as an end, but as a means to an end. The main objective, from the Russian point of view, was to obtain a shortcut for the Trans-Siberian Railroad through Manchuria. The route projected originally formed a right angle and involved great engineering difficulties. The straight line through Manchuria promised substantial savings in time and money, access to abundant natural resources, and an improved strategic position. [55]

By no means everyone in the tsarist government concurred with Witte's proposal. Kapnist, director of the Asiatic Department, and Sergei Mikhailovich Dukhovskoi, governor general of the Amur Region, both of whom were directly concerned with Asia and the Russian Far East, argued that the Manchurian railroad should go to Blagoveshchensk, not to Vladivostok. They foresaw that the construction of so long a line as Witte wanted through foreign territory would entail more political risk than economic benefit. [56]

In a lengthy memorandum, dated January 11/23, 1896, Dukhovskoi contended that the Manchurian line must not be built in place of the Siberian or Amur line, but in addition to it. China was not likely to object to the projected Manchurian line, he thought, as the Russian proposal was only too favorable for her: millions of Chinese subjects would benefit therefrom without any expenditure on her part. Help from Russia would be facilitated in the event of new danger from Japan, while China would have many opportunities, should the friendly relations with Russia waver, to interrupt the service of the railroad. Yet the moment Russia took steps to establish herself more firmly in Manchuria, China's attitude was bound to become less favorable and she

Lieutenant General Sergei Mikhailovich Dukhovskoi, governor-general of the Amur region, 1893–1898. (*Vsemirnaia illiustratsiia*, 1893, 24.)

might be forced by Russia's Pacific rivals to join them in tripping the "inevitable and natural cause of events," Dukhovskoi warned. How to prevent such a turn of events and prepare for a fitting repulse must be considered in working out the project, he insisted.

The original scheme sent to Cassini had been worded in economic terms only, but the enormous enterprise begun by it entailed the honor and dignity of Russia and her future strength in the Far East, Dukhovskoi declared. This was not a concession for the construction of a line within the state, he noted. Here political, military, and administrative considerations were more important than economic ones.

Since the success of the enterprise would depend to a large extent on the support given by the Amur Region of which he was governor general, Dukhovskoi touched on the condition of Russian forces and resources in the Amur Region and on the general state of affairs in the Far East. Although less than thirty years had passed since the opening of the Suez canal, the Pacific shores had been transformed from unknown and legendary lands into a thriving international arena. Within one generation Western Canada, California, Japan, the colonies of France and other nations, as well as the large economic interests of England and Germany had grown stronger and developed. The results of the Sino-Japanese War and the position occupied by Russia with the construction of the Trans-Siberian Railroad had given an impetus to local life. Advances in science and technology had brought gigantic steamers and long railroads to recently lifeless seas and regions. Even sluggish China was evincing readiness to penetrate her depth with such railroads and had begun to strengthen and develop her might in the provinces bordering unto Russia.

The pace of developments in the half of the globe which previously had been of little interest to anyone was rapid. What a few years ago had not been worthy of attention or had been unthinkable was becoming of primary importance and inevitable, Dukhovskoi continued. Had it been long ago that Russia had begun the colonization of the Amur Region and the establishment of military forces there? Had it been long since the thought of the Trans-Siberian Railroad had first occurred? he asked rhetorically. The road had not yet been completed when it had become necessary to go beyond, to speak of the further development of military forces and the strengthening of Russian life in the borderland. "Was it long ago that we looked calmly at the characteristics of our Chinese frontier, while now we feel strongly not only its disadvantages, but its dangers and must seriously consider its rectification, remembering from historical examples that what can easily be achieved today sometimes demands because of delay extraordinary efforts, enormous expenditures and even bloodshed, with heavy responsibility on the part of the preceding gener-

ation before the following one. And all this is very natural, going parallel with
what is being done in general on the Pacific shores," Dukhovskoi wrote.

Yet the colonization and military strengthening of the Amur Region could
not be carried out as quickly as circumstances demanded and the Amur Region
would remain very weak temporarily, Dukhovskoi noted. Had the tripartite intervention led to war, the entire colonization effort of Russia would have
collapsed, railroad transport and construction would have come to a halt, and
much time and enormous difficulties and expenditures would have been required for the repair of damage.

Dukhovskoi warned that Japan, freed from her operations in China and
becoming ever stronger, could challenge Russia within the next few years to
great sacrifice, not so much in a military sense as in the supplying and improvement of the Amur Region, which had suffered from the mobilization of
1895. Was there any guarantee, he asked, that Japan, who now was angry at
Russia, might not under some simple pretext rush headlong at her, deeming
herself all-powerful. "The weakness of our position is perfectly known to our
Pacific rivals and they well realize that if they let the next few years pass, the
odds will shift too drastically to our side," Dukhovskoi observed. Leaving
aside France and Germany, he saw possible dangers not only from England
but from China herself with her "weak and treacherous government," for
even her passive resistance, in response to Japanese and English pressure,
could cause Russia much trouble. "Gratitude for a good deed can easily turn
into hatred," he pointed out.

"A diplomacy which would painstakingly remove the slightest causes for
stirring up the Far East within the next four to six years would render a great
service to Russia," Dukhovskoi remarked. It would take that long, he explained, to supply and prepare the Russian forces and bring closer the railroad
from Siberia. "Once this period is over, we shall be able to start talking
already in a different language," Dukhovskoi penned. ("This is true," Nicholas noted in the margin.) To protect herself against any eventuality during
these critical years, he continued, Russia must have a formidable fleet in the
Pacific Ocean, and in Turkestan the threat most felt by Russia's principal
rival, England—the forces and means of action against India. (This paragraph
was marked off by the tsar.)[57] Furthermore, Dukhovskoi reiterated, Russia
must not drop the originally planned Russian railroad through the Amur Region. Even in the unlikely case that all of Manchuria were to come easily and
soon under Russian sovereignty and Russia were able in constructing the
Manchurian railroad to guard it at the same time not only by military strength
but by Russian settlements with the establishment of Russian authority in the
entire region, the Amur line would retain its great colonizing and base-build-

ing importance. Without it, colonization, gold mining, and the great rise in Russian life would all be set back. Since the quick Russification of Manchuria was unthinkable, the domestic, purely Russian Amur line was to be also of great military importance to Russia for many years to come. Would it not be a great historical mistake, he asked, to run a 2,000 verst section of the Great Siberian Railroad through territory which for a long time would be foreign to Russia.

But Witte had Nicholas's ear and the tsar dismissed Dukhovskoi's vital question with a curt "*net*" (No) in the margin.[58]

The idea of railroad construction in northern China was no more exclusively Russian than the notion of a Russo-Chinese alliance. The Chinese, who for years had dreaded railroads as funnels of imperialist penetration, themselves had gradually come around to thinking of railroad construction as a part of national defense and economic development. But though they considered extending the T'angshan-Tientsin line to Manchuria in order to connect the Chinese forces inside and outside the Great Wall, they lacked the funds for doing so.

Li Hung-chang was a railroad enthusiast. Some 200 miles of track had been laid during his administration as governor general of Chihli. While his argument that the construction of railroads by China would facilitate and improve relations with Russia did not win many converts in the 1880s, it found a receptive audience following the Sino-Japanese War.

As Hsü Ching-ch'eng had predicted from St. Petersburg, Cassini approached the Tsungli Yamen on October 14, 1895, about the possibility of connecting the Trans-Siberian Railroad with China's Manchurian lines. Cassini's request that Russian surveyors be permitted in Manchuria was granted and Chinese engineers were sent to accompany the Russians. The Tsungli Yamen instructed Hsü to inform the tsarist government that it was feasible to join the Russian and Chinese lines, but that China would undertake the task by herself.

Hsü deemed it a mistake for China to agree to the construction of a connecting line even with the qualification that she would do so by her own effort, because it would expose her to further Russian demands. His misgivings were justified, for when he communicated the views of his government to Witte, the latter asked that China's Manchurian line be constructed by a Russian stock company. Hsü rejected the request, convinced that it would mean Russian control of the trans-Manchurian railroad.

A variety of routes were advocated by Chang Chih-tung, Li Chia-ao, and other officials, but there was general agreement among them that the construction of some line to connect with the Trans-Siberian Railroad would not only relieve Russian pressure, but would be in China's own economic and strategic interests. There were those who warned that Russia might seize the Manchurian railway as a means of invading China, but as an article in the Chinese newspaper *Shen-pao* countered, "And might we not, on the other hand, also be able to do the same with an enemy's line?" [59]

To settle the railroad question and to conclude an alliance with Russia the Manchu court appointed Li Hung-chang as its delegate to the coronation of Nicholas and Alexandra.[60] Li tried to decline on the grounds of ill health and old age, but the Chinese government insisted that he go.[61] The underlying purpose of Li's mission was kept secret, but there was general expectation of a Russo-Chinese alliance. The *North China Daily News* went so far as to publish the reputed provisions of a treaty of alliance, ratification of which Li was said to be carrying to St. Petersburg.[62]

The court ordered Li's second son, Ching-shu, to accompany him in view of his advanced years and ill-health, but Li insisted that his adopted son, Ching-fang, who was more experienced in foreign affairs, come also as his right-hand man.

Li assembled an impressive retinue. In addition to his sons, there were his own secretary (Yü Shih-mei), three interpreters of Russian, French, and English (Tak'oshihno, Lien-fang, and Lo Feng-loh), five secretaries, six foreign advisers of varying nationality from the Chinese Maritime Customs Service (Detring, A. Mouilleseaux de Bernières, E. B. Drew, Victor Grot, and James H. Hart, brother of Sir Robert Hart), a doctor, and thirty-five servants. In vain Witte hinted to Hsü Ching-ch'eng that the mission should be reduced in size to avoid arousing attention and suspicion.

Li left China in March 1896 for Russia, Western Europe, and the United States. Fearing that he might not survive the long and exhausting journey at the age of seventy-three, Li took along a dismantled teakwood coffin. With the Trans-Siberian Railroad not yet completed, Li had to travel from Shanghai to Moscow by sea via the Suez canal. Prince Esper Esperovich Ukhtomskii, president of the Russo-Chinese Bank who had visited Li at Tientsin the preceding year, and a Foreign Ministry official by the name of Radunovskii waited for him at Port Said and accompanied him on the Russian steamer *Rossiia* to Odessa and thence by special train to St. Petersburg, partly to establish good personal relations with Li, partly to prevent his stopover in other countries en route to Russia, lest he be exposed to "various intrigues on the part of European statesmen." [63]

The mission of Li Hung-chang to the West ushered in a new period in Chinese history. It ended the policy of "splendid isolation" heretofore pursued by the Middle Kingdom. Gérard, in his memoirs, likened Li's odyssey to the peregrination of Peter the Great in Western Europe toward the beginning of the eighteenth century.[64]

The study of the technical feasibility of routing the Russian railroad through Manchuria had been completed in February. While Li Hung-chang was on his way to Russia Cassini sought the Tsungli Yamen's permission for such a venture. He did so on April 18 by appealing to the good will of China, pointing out that the construction of such a railroad would be of advantage not only to Russia but to China herself. It would stimulate the economic development of Manchuria and facilitate its military defense against Japan or any other power. In transmitting numerous political and economic documents in support of the Russian request to the Tsungli Yamen, Cassini added that the extension of the Trans-Siberian Railroad through her territory would not cost China anything and that it was understood that out of respect for Chinese sovereignty the line through Manchuria would be constructed and operated not by the tsarist government but by a commercial company whose organization would be agreeable to both countries.

Despite Cassini's reassurances and amicable tone, Prince Ch'ing and the ministers of the Tsungli Yamen were stupefied by the grave and novel proposition. Ch'ing replied that the Tsungli Yamen must carefully study the voluminous file and that he himself would have to consult with Prince Kung and receive the orders of the emperor. It would take twelve days to prepare a suitable reply. Cassini did not press the issue and stayed away from the Tsungli Yamen until the thirtieth to give the Chinese time for reflection.

Meanwhile two compatriots joined Cassini to assist in the negotiations with the Chinese—Dr. Talpigo, a Vladivostok engineer who had been charged with studying where to build the line, and Dmitrii Dmitrievich Pokotilov, one of the directors of the Russo-Chinese Bank at Shanghai, who had been a Chinese language student at Peking (1891–1893) and subsequently was to become tsarist minister to China (1906–1907). But the day after his arrival Talpigo was struck dumb and paralyzed by an attack of hemiplegia and aphasia. Although Pokotilov had brought detailed instructions and although he enjoyed the full confidence of Witte and Ukhtomskii, he could not by himself furnish all the necessary technical assistance to Cassini.[65]

The reply which the Tsungli Yamen gave to Cassini on April 30 was negative. China had decided once and for all not to grant such concessions to any foreign power or to any foreign company and was willling to agree merely to construct a Manchurian railroad herself as soon as possible with the aid of Russian engineers and materials. In vain Cassini remonstrated that such a reply would make the most painful impression on the tsarist government.

"China has no regard for friendly international relations," Cassini complained. "We will affiliate ourselves with Japan, and seek other solutions," he threatened.

Weng T'ung-ho pointed to the great length of the railroad which, he alleged, would not be of the slightest benefit to China. "For us to extend our efforts to complete it—this is having regard for friendly international relations," he declared. "You are an official minister; have you no regard for principle?" he chided.

The outburst stunned Cassini. After an awkward silence he declared that the railroad through Manchuria must be completed in six years or it would be of no use in a crisis.

Weng nodded in agreement.[66]

With the arrival of Li Hung-chang in St. Petersburg that very day, the negotiations between the two countries shifted to Russia.[67]

Foreign Minister Lobanov had not wanted Li to come to the Russian capital on the eve of the coronation. He had wanted him to tarry in Odessa or to proceed to Moscow and there wait for the festivities. But Finance Minister Witte had received the tsar's permission for Li to come directly to St. Petersburg to begin the negotiations, for which there would be very little time during the coronation festivities. At Witte's suggestion a military honor guard greeted Li at Odessa when he set foot on Russian soil on April 28. Continuing his journey the following morning, Li reached St. Petersburg, as noted, on April 30, three weeks before the coronation.

Since Lobanov knew and cared little about the Far East, the task of hammering out a Russo-Chinese alliance, which Gérard called "the most important and most decisive act of the period begun by the Sino-Japanese War and the Treaty of Shimonoseki," had been entrusted by Nicholas to Witte. The secret meetings lasted from the end of April until the beginning of June and were divided between St. Petersburg and Moscow. Their length was due not only to the interruption of coronation business, but to the realization on the part of Witte that haste was regarded as bad form by the Chinese, who did everything slowly and with appropriate ceremony.

When Li entered Witte's reception room on the first occasion, Witte came out of his office to greet him, dressed in his official uniform. After exchanging deep bows, Witte led Li to a second reception room to drink tea. Witte and Li were seated; all others remained standing. When Witte asked Li if he would like to smoke, Li emitted a sound not unlike the neighing of a horse. Two Chinese rushed in from the adjacent room, one with a water pipe, the other with tobacco. Then began the ceremony of smoking. Li sat completely still—all he did was to inhale and exhale the smoke—as the pipe was lighted, held, and taken out of his mouth and put back into it by the Chinese attendants with

Arrival of Li Hung-chang in St. Petersburg. (*Vsemirnaia illustratsiia*, 1896, 462.)

a show of great awe. "By such ceremony Li Hung-chang clearly wished to make a strong impression on me," Witte recalled in his memoirs. "I remained, of course, very placid about it and made believe that I did not pay any attention to it." [68]

No business was mentioned during the courtesy call. Witte and Li merely inquired at length after the health of their respective emperors and empresses, their children, and all their nearest relatives. As Li got to know Witte better during the next meeting and saw that all the ceremony had little effect on the latter, he dropped some of the formalities. By the time they got to Moscow, the two statesmen talked to each other informally. [69]

While Witte and Li Hung-chang were still exchanging ceremonial courtesies, A. Iu. Rothstein, the chief business figure and actual director of the Russo-Chinese Bank, broached the subject of a "private company" for the construction and exploitation of the Manchurian railroad to Grot, one of the Maritime Customs officials who had come with Li. Grot, who was entrusted with financial matters, was a Russian subject and had been recommended to Witte by Cassini. Although Grot, as a representative of the Chinese side, at first objected to Rothstein's notion that the company be Russian and proposed instead that it be Chinese, a one million franc bribe persuaded Grot to look with favor on the idea of a Russo-Chinese joint-stock company in which China would have some representation. [70]

On May 3 Witte and Li got down to business. Witte, who had called on Li, began by telling him that China had remained whole due to Russian action, that the Russians had proclaimed the principle of the territorial integrity of China and would themselves always abide by it. But in order to be able to support the principle, the Russians would have to be put in a position where they could really give assistance if something happened, Witte pointed out. They could not show such help until they had a railroad to bring troops from Europe, where most of their forces were, as well as from the Amur Region and Vladivostok. During the Sino-Japanese War the Russians had dispatched some units from Vladivostok in the direction of Kirin, but in the absence of rail communication the men had progressed so slowly that the war had ended before they could reach their destination. To extend the Trans-Siberian Railroad as originally planned would require enormous time and expense. The quickest and shortest route to Vladivostok—through the northern part of Mongolia and Manchuria—was necessary, therefore, to provide the Russians with the means of supporting the integrity of China. It would lessen the danger to be expected from Japan, Witte specified. He added that the railroad was necessary also for economic reasons. It would raise the productivity of both the Russian and the Chinese regions through which it would run. The construction of the railroad, Witte proposed, should be entrusted to a private Russian company, for past experience showed that if China were to undertake the project by herself, it would run into countless delays and not be completed even in a decade.

Li, whom Witte found to be a man of remarkably sound mind and common sense, countered that the construction of the railroad by such a company would be tantamount to entrusting the road to Russia, "who would assume the rights and privileges of China." He feared that this would be objectionable to many powers and would precipitate more troubles than the railroad was supposed to eliminate.

Witte disagreed. He did not expect particular resentment against the construction of the railroad. Japan, who had years ago adopted European technology, could only welcome such a railroad, he thought, because it would connect her with Western Europe. Witte predicted that if China did not grant the concession for the railroad now, it would never be built.

Li rebuffed the railroad proposal, which was similar to that made by the tsarist government through Cassini and rejected by the Tsungli Yamen. Believing that Li might be more responsive if approached by the tsar, Witte arranged for a special audience. The customary reception during which Li presented his credentials to Nicholas on May 4 was confined to diplomatic courtesies. But the private meeting which Witte had arranged without public notice on May 7 was different in nature.

Having sent for Li Hung-chang confidentially through Li Ching-fang on the pretext of wanting to see the gifts brought for the coronation, Nicholas broached the subject of the railroad, holding out the prospect of Russian protection of China. After asserting that Russia, who had much land and few people, had no designs on foreign territory and that relations between their two countries were "extremely intimate," the tsar declared that the "true reason" Russia desired a Manchurian railroad was to be able to convey troops to China in the latter's defense. He assured Li that in granting the right of construction to the Russo-Chinese Bank, China could safeguard her control. Many countries had such an arrangement. If England and Japan would cause trouble again in the future, Russia could send troops to China's aid, Nicholas reiterated.

Since one of the charges laid upon Li by his government had been the conclusion of an alliance with Russia, the reference made by Nicholas to the armed support of China appealed to Li more than what Witte had voiced so far. When Li met with Witte and Lobanov the following day, on May 8, he tried to pursue the subject of an alliance, while the Russian statesmen continued to dwell on the railroad. Lobanov stated that he had no instructions from the tsar regarding the offer of military help, but promised to obtain them by the eleventh. He himself thought in terms of mutual assistance, either country coming to the aid of the other. The question was one of priorities. Lobanov proposed that a secret treaty of defense be concluded between Russia and China once the railroad convention had been ratified. Li, on the other hand, wanted the question of mutual defense resolved prior to the discussion of the railroad concession.

To protect himself, Li sought instructions from his government. "The two matters are closely bound up," he telegraphed. "Should the treaty of alliance be made first or the contract of the [railroad] company?"

The reply sent by the Chinese government following deliberations by the Grand Council in the presence of Emperor Kuang-hsü and discussions between Grand Councillor Weng T'ung-ho and Chang Yin-huan consisted of an imperial edict proposing three points as the basis for a secret alliance: (1) In the event of war Russia and China were bound to aid each other; (2) the Sungari and Hunt'ung rivers were to be opened to navigation; and (3) China was to invest five million taels in the Russo-Chinese Bank.

Li had indicated that he would proceed to Moscow for the coronation ceremonies on the sixteenth and the above telegram was to reach him there that day. But before this happened, while Li was still in St. Petersburg, Lobanov and Witte presented to him a Russian draft treaty of alliance and the contract for the founding of the railroad company.[71]

Witte and Li had worked out an oral agreement before Lobanov had composed the draft treaty on the basis thereof. The version on which Witte and Li and then Witte and Lobanov had agreed specified Japan as the object of the defensive alliance, but the draft Lobanov gave to Witte after submitting the proposal to the tsar called for mutual aid in the event of an attack by whatever side on China or the Maritime Region. Witte prevailed on Nicholas to restore the original wording, lest Russia find herself someday in the impossible position of defending China against Great Britain and France or lest she arouse against herself many European powers should the alliance become known.[72]

The Russian draft treaty consisted of a preamble and six articles. The first article declared that the treaty would take effect "in the event of an invasion by Japan or by a State allied to Japan of the territory of Russia in Eastern Asia, or the territory of China, or the territory of Korea." (The Russians themselves, in line with Witte's objections, deleted reference to an ally of Japan on the nineteenth.) Russia and China committed themselves to assist each other with all available land and sea forces in case of Japanese aggression and to provide whatever supplies possible. The second article stipulated that once common action had begun, neither power could make a separate peace without the consent of the other. Article three opened all Chinese seaports to Russian warships during the military operations and promised whatever help they might need. Article four provided for the construction of a railroad through the Chinese provinces of Heilungchiang and Kirin to Vladivostok in order to facilitate the rapid transportation of Russian troops and their supplies to endangered locations. At Li's suggestion, the stipulation was made that the construction of the Manchurian railroad would not be used as a pretext for encroachment on Chinese territory or infringement of Chinese sovereignty and that the terms of the contract for the Russo-Chinese Bank, which was to be entrusted with both the construction and the exploitation of the railroad, would be determined between the two governments. (Between the Chinese minister in St. Petersburg and the Russo-Chinese Bank, it was specified later.) The fifth article gave Russia the right to transport troops, provisions, and munitions by that railway "whether in peace or war." The sixth article stated that the agreement was to be effective for fifteen years from the date on which the railroad contract had been ratified by the Chinese emperor. (The Russians had originally thought in terms of ten years, but Li asked for the longer period.) Six months prior to the expiration of the treaty the two sides were to negotiate again concerning its extension.

The draft treaty reached Peking on May 16. It was followed by a telegram in which Li expressed his preference for the Russian draft. It contained nothing, he thought, to which objection could be made, because Russia was motivated by the desire for friendly relations with China. On the other hand, the rejection of the draft would be resented by Russia and might jeopardize the alliance China desired. Li reported that Witte had given him a draft contract for the Russo-Chinese Bank, including the provision that the railroad would revert to China after fifty or eighty years.

The Chinese government, after considerable discussion, proposed in a telegram to Li on May 21, that the last two articles be deleted from the Russian draft, in effect breaking the tie between the military alliance and the railroad; at the same time it wished to broaden the defensive commitment by seeking specification of the manner in which Russia would aid China in the event of trouble in the south or west, that is to say in case of conflict with England or France.

The Russians had told Li on May 19 that there could not be an alliance without the railroad concession. They rejected the counterproposal of Peking, which Li had received on the twenty-third, declaring that the six articles must remain intact. Russia would not commit herself to come to China's aid if England or France picked a quarrel with her, they explained, because it would affect the entire European and Asian situation. They agreed to editorial changes in wording, which emphasized the military character of the railroad as an instrument of mutual defense.

Word from Li that negotiations would be broken off unless the Russian treaty proposal was accepted *in toto* reached Peking on May 26. The following day the officials of the Tsungli Yamen—Weng T'ung-ho, Chang Yin-huan, Wu T'ing-fang, Li Hung-tsao, Jung-lu and the Princes Ch'ing and Kung—assembled to discuss the matter. After studying the secret telegrams received from Li Hung-chang, they agreed to the Russian terms and drafted an edict. The plenary powers for Li to sign the treaty were handed down by Emperor Kuang-hsü on the twenty-eighth and put into telegraphic form and dispatched by Weng T'ung-ho with Chang Yin-huan's assistance on the twenty-ninth. The imperial edict arrived in Moscow on May 30. The revised treaty text, sent out several hours later, was received on June 1.

During the coronation ceremonies, which had meanwhile taken place in Moscow, on May 26, Li Hung-chang had been assigned the chief place in the congratulating procession. As no particular attention seemed to be paid by the Russian authorities to Marshal Yamagata, the special envoy sent by the Meiji emperor, Li was convinced that Russia had estranged Japan and was determined to develop ties with China.

On June 3 Li Hung-chang, accompanied by his two sons Ching-fang and Ching-shu and by Lo Feng-loh and Lin I-yu, went to the house in which Lobanov was staying during the coronation festivities to sign the treaty. As the two sides looked at the handwritten copies of the document, Witte discovered to his shock that the first article had remained unaltered. When he called Lobanov aside and pointed out that the clause requiring Russian assistance against powers other than Japan had not been deleted, Lobanov exclaimed that he had forgotten to tell the secretaries to make the change. As it was already shortly after noon, Lobanov interrupted the proceedings and announced that dinner would spoil if they did not eat right away. While the Chinese delegation, unaware of the Russian embarrassment, joined Lobanov and Witte in the dining room, the two Russian secretaries painstakingly recopied the treaty with the necessary deletion. After dinner Lobanov, Witte, and Li signed the fresh text, Li affixing also his seal in the Chinese manner.[73]

The signing of the secret alliance, whose text was not revealed until after its expiration,[74] did not end the negotiations, because its ratification was contingent on the conclusion of the railway contract which had not yet been resolved. As arrangements had been made for Li to visit other countries, the Chinese minister to St. Petersburg and currently to Berlin was left to discuss them with Rothstein, Witte's closest associate in financial affairs. Since Hsü Ching-ch'eng had not participated in the negotiation of the alliance and had no powers to commit his government, he had to consult repeatedly with the Tsungli Yamen and with Li.

On June 13, the day that Li Hung-chang left for Berlin, the Chinese government received a lengthy dispatch from Hsü, containing a draft contract for the Russo-Chinese Bank and a draft agreement for the establishment of a Russo-Chinese Railroad Company.[75] The draft contract consisted of a preamble and a dozen articles. The preamble stated that the Chinese government would invest five million taels in the Russo-Chinese Bank and that it entrusted the construction and operation of a railroad line connecting the city of Chita and the Russian South Ussuri Railroad to the bank on the conditions enumerated in the twelve articles. It was stipulated that a company, to be known as the Chinese Eastern Railroad Company, was to be established by the Russo-Chinese Bank for the construction and operation of the railroad. Construction was to be begun within one year of the approval of the contract and completed within six years of the definitive determination of the route and acquisitions of the right of way. The wide gauge of Russian railroads was to be used for this line. The local Chinese authorities were to furnish whatever materials, labor, and transportation possible. The company had the right to employ as many foreigners or natives as it deemed necessary, criminal cases and lawsuits in the territory of the railroad to be decided by the local authorities in accordance with international treaties. The lands required for the construction, operation, and protection of the railroad and for the procurement of sand, stone, and the like, were to be turned over to the company free of charge if they belonged to the state; if they were private property, they were to be sold or leased at current prices. The lands belonging to the railroad company as well as its income and receipts were to be tax-free. The company had the absolute and exclusive right of administration of its territory. Passengers' baggage and goods in transit from one station to another were exempt from all imposts. Merchandise imported from Russia into China or exported from China into Russia by the railroad would pay one third less than the regular duties collected by the Chinese Maritime Customs. The railroad with all its appurtenances was to pass to the Chinese government free of charge eighty years after its completion.

The interlocking of the bank, in which the tsarist government had a dominant voice, and of the railway displeased Weng T'ung-ho. "Destestable! Dreadful!" he fumed. After due deliberation by him and members of the War Council and the Tsungli Yamen, the Chinese government proposed four modifications in a telegram to Hsü on July 4: the use of the narrow, Chinese gauge (which would mean that passengers and goods would have to change trains at the border); the taxing of the company income from mining operations; the imposition of duty at half the normal rate on goods shipped through Manchuria from one Russian station to another; and the transfer of the railroad to China after only thirty-six years.

The tsarist government retorted that it would rather forego the secret alliance than agree to the narrow gauge. It left the question of the taxation on mines for further discussion. It expanded the draft article on impost-free passage of baggage and goods from one Russian station to another, adding the stipulation that they pass through Chinese territory in special cars, sealed by Chinese customs officials. The article transferring the Chinese Eastern Railroad to China free of charge in eighty years was modified to the effect that the Chinese government would have the right to buy it thirty-six years from the day the entire line was completed and in operation, upon payment in full of "all the capital involved, as well as all the debts contracted for this line, plus accrued interest."

As the Chinese discussed the Russian reply at a joint meeting of the War Council and the Tsungli Yamen on July 21, the gauge question aroused primary concern. The wide gauge would link the railroad with the Russian network, the narrow gauge with the Chinese network. In the event that Russia lost the desire to check Japanese encroachment and turned against China instead, the wide gauge would facilitate Russian troop movements, the narrow gauge Chinese troop movements. From an economic point of view, China stood more to gain if the gauge was narrow, Russia if the gauge was wide. There was the additional danger that the adoption of the Russian gauge might form a precedent for other powers to insist on different gauges. Since Russia linked up her railways with the narrow gauge lines of Germany and Austria, why could she not do so with those of China, the ministers argued. It was decided, therefore, to seek the views of Li Hung-chang, who was by then in Paris, and to instruct him to take up the gauge question with the Russian side, even though it was sensed that his efforts would be fruitless.

Li replied that the linking of the German and Austrian railroads with those of Russia was not a matter of national defense. Use of the narrow gauge would offer China little protection, for the Russians could make the necessary technical adjustments for transporting their troops along the narrow gauge track in a couple of hours. Once China obtained the railroad, she could change the gauge. Li called Witte stubborn and impatient, but did not think that the treaty of alliance should be sacrificed because of him.

The ministers of the Tsungli Yamen were displeased with Witte's conduct. The treaty of alliance had become the source of "continuous extortions," Weng complained. The ministers were irritated as well by Li's reluctance to fight for the narrow gauge. It was he who had first advocated the adoption of the narrow gauge as the standard track for all of China and now he seemed willing to accept the wide gauge for the northeast. The officials doubted that China would be able to do anything about changing the gauge if she bought the railroad after thirty-six years. They directed Li to make a final effort to sway the Russian side.

By this time Li was in London and unable to negotiate with the tsarist government directly. He entrusted the representation of Peking's views to Grot, who had remained in Russia, unaware that Rothstein had secured the collaboration of the latter. As the negotiations between Hsü and Rothstein dragged on into August without progress, Rothstein recommended that the empress dowager be informed that if China did not sign the contract, Russia would resort to "other combinations" and the alliance with China would fail to materialize. A similar warning came from Li. He feared that Chinese procrastination might have induced the Russians to look for an alliance with someone else and expressed the apprehension that Yamagata might have maneuvered Russia into a political combination with Japan.

A meeting of the War Council and members of the Tsungli Yamen on August 13 reaffirmed the desire that Hsü seek the adoption of the narrow gauge. But when Witte rejected the demand categorically on the seventeenth, the opposition of the Chinese government collapsed. On August 28 the agreement concerning the Russo-Chinese Bank was signed at Berlin, where Hsü was posted part of the year. The signing of the Chinese Eastern Railway contract followed on September 8.[76]

The railroad contract became part of the Russo-Chinese alliance, whose ratification had been held up pending its conclusion. The exchange of ratifications took place at last on September 28 at the Russian legation in Peking. Cassini represented the tsarist government, Prince Ch'ing, Weng T'ung-ho, and Chang Yin-huan the Chinese government.[77]

In the spring of 1897 Ukhtomskii was sent to Peking to repay the mission of Li Hung-chang to the coronation and to present return gifts from the tsar to the Chinese emperor.[78] Ukhtomskii departed for China on the evening of March 26, accompanied by Prince Aleksandr Volkonskii of the Horse Guard, Captain Étienne Andreevskii of the Hussar Guard, Court Councilor Léon de Zabiello, secretary of the Ministry of Agriculture, Ziegler de Schaffhausen, one of the administrators of the Chinese Eastern Railroad Company, and Sergei Syromiatnikov, correspondent of the *Nouveau Temps* of St. Petersburg. Ukhtomskii had given some thought to resigning his position as president of the Russo-Chinese Bank before going on this official mission so as not to arouse Chinese suspicions, but then had decided against it; in fact, he announced his intention of inspecting the branch office of the Russo-Chinese Bank.[79]

So excited were British officials, merchants, and journalists about the special mission and so grave were their predictions of harm to their empire's interests from it, that Ukhtomskii was assured of making a profound impression even before he set foot on Chinese soil. As the German minister in Peking, Edmund von Heyking, remarked, the English allegations strengthened the belief in the superiority of Russian influence in China and since in the case of prestige that becomes true what people believe, the Russian position in China would indeed be profited thereby. "The Russian influence in Peking is very great, but still far from so great and unlimited as her embittered opponents deem it wise to depict," he wrote.[80]

Ukhtomskii was received with extraordinary honors when he reached China in May. As the bearer of letters and gifts from Nicholas to the emperor and empress dowager he was due respect. But the fact that he had gone to Port Said to meet Li Hung-chang and had taken him to St. Petersburg at the time of Li's voyage to Russia had made a deep impression on the Tsungli Yamen. Furthermore, it was assumed that Ukhtomskii was related to the imperial family, whereas in fact the title *kniaz'* (prince) had no such meaning or importance in Russia.[81] The British press had also been spellbound by the word "prince" and wrote of the Russian "princes" who had been dispatched to China.[82] Li Hung-chang could not help but wonder, therefore, why two princes (Volkonskii and Ukhtomskii) had been sent on one mission at the same time.

As the mission approached Shanghai on the German postal steamer *Prinz Heinrich*, the highest officials of the city met the Russians at the mouth of the river and had them transfer to a Chinese government steamer. As they passed Wusung, festively decorated Chinese warships greeted them with the gun salute customary for ambassadors. A triumphal arch had been erected at the landing place in Shanghai and an honor guard of Chinese troops lined up. The Russian guests were housed at state expense in the residence of the *taotai* of Shanghai. A banquet with a Chinese theater performance, to which the consular corps was invited, was given in their honor the following day.

A Chinese steamer, redecorated for the occasion, took the Russians to Tientsin,[83] whence they proceeded by the recently completed railroad to Peking on May 21. A banquet hosted by the secretaries of the Tsungli Yamen awaited the tired and dusty travelers in a tent at the terminal. From here they were accompanied by a Chinese military escort to the Russian legation, where they were to live during their visit.[84]

The tsarist legation was already very crowded. In addition to the regular staff, which consisted of two legation secretaries, three interpreters, a doctor, and a guard of ten Cossacks, there lived in the legation Pokotilov, the director of the Russo-Chinese Bank, an assistant of his, two teachers who were perfecting their Chinese for subsequent use in one of the Russian schools opened in North China, a lieutenant of one of the regiments stationed in Siberia, who dressed alternately in Chinese and European garb, and the postmaster, a Buryat from Lake Baikal by the name of Gomboev who was very influential in northern China, partly because his brother was revered as a Living Buddha, partly because he lent money to Mongol chieftains at high interest.[85] Two military attachés were assigned to the legation, but did not live in Peking where little of military value was to be seen.[86]

In a building vis-à-vis the legation, the Russians had established a post office, with a double-headed eagle in front of the door. (The first step in converting Peking into a Russian district city, Heyking remarked maliciously.) They had purchased a large piece of land next to the post office for the construction of a fine building for the Russo-Chinese Bank. On a nearby farmstead belonging to Badmaev, postmaster of the Russian border station at Kiakhta, European homes and sheds had been erected for the storing of goods or, if necessary, the housing of several hundred Cossacks.[87]

No sooner had Ukhtomskii arrived at the legation than Li Hung-chang came to welcome him. The following day, on May 22, Ukhtomskii and his entire entourage were received at the Tsungli Yamen by Prince Kung and all his ministers. On the twenty-third Li Hung-chang hosted a banquet at the temple in which he was residing.[88]

The extraordinary reception accorded to Ukhtomskii was the more remarkable, because he had not been officially appointed as the representative of the tsar by his government. But like the hero in Nikolai Gogol's satire "The Inspector General," Heyking asserted, Ukhtomskii made no effort to decline the role which the Chinese had assigned to him and to explain to the people that he was not in truth what they regarded him to be.[89]

On May 24 the gifts from Nicholas to Emperor Kuang-hsü and the Empress Dowager T'zu-hsi were carried to the Tsungli Yamen and from there to the imperial palace.[90] Gérard described them as "sumptuous and magnificent," Heyking as surpassing in costliness and extent anything ever presented in China. There were forty-eight crates of treasures, including large vases of lapis lazuli, golden drinking vessels with Russian enamel work, a diamond diadem, a silver dressing table, and a gramophone. But what impressed the Chinese more even than all the products of Russian artistic handicrafts or the three costly fox furs for the emperor of China was the munificence of the tsar in bestowing on every member of the Tsungli Yamen a large diamond for their headgear, Li Hung-chang receiving a particularly big one.

"One cannot deny that these gifts and honors of tangible value have been chosen with true understanding of the Chinese character and are probably intended to give the Chinese a high impression of the might and wealth of their Russian friend," Heyking observed. "It is difficult for any other state to compete with the cornucopia of splendor and generosity showered on the great of China." The diamond-framed miniature of Queen Victoria, which the new British minister, Sir Claude Maxwell MacDonald, had been instructed to present, looked paltry compared with the Russian gifts. Nor could the presents of the French Republic measure up to those of the Russian empire, particularly because, to the misfortune of the French, the Chinese took great offense at one of their gifts, a tapestry depicting a mythological subject—a naked woman and four monkeys in the corners of the border. "The Chinese unfortunately read only their own classic writers; one can hardly assume, therefore, that they are acquainted with the saying '*timeo Danaos et dona ferentes*' [Beware of Greeks bearing gifts]," Heyking concluded.[91]

On May 26 Ukhtomskii was received by the emperor. All tsarist officials who could be reached, including consuls and military attachés from Tientsin and Chefoo, were assembled for the occasion, so that twenty-two Russians were ushered into the imperial presence.[92]

The British and German ministers disliked the extraordinary attention shown to Ukhtomskii and resented the latter's unwillingness to call on them first on the ground that his position, as an ambassador, was superior to theirs.[93] MacDonald had visited Li Hung-chang several days before Ukhtomskii's audience with Kuang-hsü in order to explain to him that Prince Ukhtomskii was neither an imperial prince nor an ambassador. Except for Gérard and the Belgian minister, Baron Carl de Vinck de Deux Orp, the foreign representatives in turn refused to call on Ukhtomskii first, lest their own position be lowered in Chinese eyes.

The conduct of Ukhtomskii toward MacDonald was downright rude. O'Conor, who now was posted in St. Petersburg, had given Ukhtomskii a letter of introduction to his successor. Instead of taking the letter to MacDonald in person as was the custom, Ukhtomskii had mailed it to him from Tientsin and had sent word through Pavlov that he would not be the one to make the first visit. Meanwhile, before this communication had been made, Lady MacDonald had written to Pavlov inviting him to bring his guests to the ball in celebration of Queen Victoria's birthday on the twenty-fourth. Not a single member of the Russian mission appeared at the British legation because, as Volkonskii explained to an Italian acquaintance, the Russians were at "drawn daggers" with the English.

Nor did Ukhtomskii call on Heyking, who had extended a dinner to the members of the Russian mission through Pavlov several days prior to their arrival. Pavlov was visibly embarrassed by the development. Although he had promised to invite all ministers to dinner when Ukhtomskii came, he refrained from doing so, apparently for fear of meeting with refusals on their part.[94]

The younger members of the Russian mission were dejected at their consequent isolation by most of the foreign community.[95] Not so Ukhtomskii. He had deliberately avoided relations with the diplomatic corps in order to be freer to pursue with Li Hung-chang and other Chinese officials the negotiations and arrangements which were the main object of his visit.

Gérard, who got to know Ukhtomskii well, described him as young, educated, thoughtful, alert, and enthusiastic. Ukhtomskii showed no desire for the manners of a diplomat or a courtier, but was interested above all in the great questions facing his country and in the management of the newspaper *Peterburgskie vedomosti*, of which he was editor-in-chief. He had always had a passionate curiosity about the Far East, particularly Tibet and Mongolia, where he looked for certain origins of Russia. Throughout the duration of his embassy, Ukhtomskii searched for everything that could put him in touch with the indigenes, notably the Mongols, their priests and their chiefs, including the Living Buddha of Urga. Thanks to the special knowledge and qualifications of Grot, the Russian employee of the Chinese Maritime Customs, Ukhtomskii was able to collect a large number of Mongolian and Tibetan objects. Gérard admired the "curious personage" that Ukhtomskii was. "Journalist, archaeologist, president of a bank, [and] administrator of a railroad company, such was the man who with the confidence of the tsar and under the direction of Monsieur Witte had been called upon to continue and extend in the north of China the work of assimilation and absorption begun of old by Admiral Putiatin and General Ignat'ev," he wrote. After the mariner and the diplomat, it was the financier and entrepreneur, the man of economic and industrial realizations who appeared on the scene to gain the confidence of the indigenes by the most proper means of action and persuasion, Gérard reflected. In the choice of persons and in the conception and execution of the program there had certainly been "much art, prudence, and *savoir-faire*" he added.[96]

On May 27 Ukhtomskii presided over the formal opening of the head office of the Russo-Chinese Bank in Peking in the buildings and grounds of the old Korean legation, made available for this purpose by the Chinese government. The speeches and toasts pronounced in Russian and Chinese, as well as the flags and the music gave the ceremonies a Russo-Chinese flavor, though the presence of Gérard and the members of his legation was a reminder of the role played by French capital in the venture.[97]

Among the gifts and decorations from the tsar was the lady's order of St. Catherine for the empress dowager. The number of diamonds gracing the precious decoration had been enlarged by the substitution of a diamond-studded double-headed eagle for the picture of the saint.[98] Ukhtomskii had asked for an audience with T'zu-hsi to present the order to her directly, but this had been refused in accordance with Chinese custom. A second imperial audience was arranged instead on May 28, during which Ukhtomskii handed the decoration to Prince Kung.[99] During the course of the audience the emperor rose at the mention of the empress dowager. He did not get up to thank for his own gifts. When MacDonald presented to him the miniature of Queen Victoria several days later, Kuang-hsü remained sitting. The fact that the emperor, for whatever reason, had stood during Ukhtomskii's reception but not during that of his British colleague greatly enhanced the prestige of the former. "Everything in this happy period for Russia, all circumstances, even those which had been neither foreseen nor premeditated, turned to the advantage of our ally," Gérard recalled in his memoirs.[100]

Ukhtomskii and his companions left Peking on the morning of June 30, after a stay of over one month in the Chinese capital.[101] Accompanied by Grot, they headed for Urga with presents from the tsar for the Living Buddha and certain lamas. Thence they were to proceed to Irkutsk to return to European Russia by the Trans-Siberian Railroad.[102] As the foreign representatives speculated about the accomplishments of the Ukhtomskii mission,[103] it never occurred to them that one of its objectives had been the delivery of an overdue payment of one million rubles to Li Hung-chang.

Money has always been a weapon of international intrigue and a lubricant of business deals. The seduction of Grot, a Russian subject, by his compatriots has already been mentioned. More startling was the remuneration of Li Hung-chang himself by Witte from the Special Fund for Covering Expenses Connected with the Granting of a Concession for the Chinese Eastern Railroad—the Li Hung-chang Fund, as it was called by the tsar.

In the files of this fund rather than in the files of the administration of the Russo-Chinese Bank, there was kept a revealing document, dated May 23/June 4, 1896 (the day after the signing of the treaty of alliance). Written on plain paper and bearing no seal, it had been penned by Rothstein, with corrections in Witte's hand. It bore the signatures of Ukhtomskii, Rothstein, and Privy Councilor P. A. Romanov, director of the general office of the Finance Ministry. At the top of the document Witte had put "*Soglasen*" (I approve), with the knowledge of Nicholas. The protocol declared that the administration of the Russo-Chinese Bank had allocated a sum of up to three million rubles in paper (*Roubles Credit*) for discretionary expenses. One third or one million rubles in paper would be available when the (Chinese) Imperial Edict conferring the concession of the line to the Russo-Chinese Bank and a document from Li Hung-chang stipulating the principal conditions of this concession had been obtained. The second million could be dispensed after the concession had been signed and legalized and after the routing of the line had been definitively decided and confirmed by duly empowered Chinese authorities. The remaining one million rubles could be drawn when the construction of the line would be completely finished. The sums in question were to be put at the full disposal of Ukhtomskii and Rothstein who could obtain them, provided they observed the above conditions, against a simple receipt on their part, without any responsibility for the money. The amounts in question, the document concluded, were to be debited to the new Chinese Eastern Railroad Company as construction expenses.[104]

Upon the issuance of the imperial edict and the signing of the railroad contract Rothstein and Ukhtomskii were ready to make the first payment, lest the Chinese begin making difficulties. As the transfer of a million rubles to Shanghai in the name of Li Hung-chang would have compromised the latter, Ukhtomskii decided to go to Shanghai, take money out himself, and give it to Li. In a telegram to Witte at Yalta on September 14, Ukhtomskii asked for the preliminary release of one million rubles from the state bank. Witte replied not to make haste until construction had begun. As for the withdrawal, it should be made from the Chinese bank, which could receive a loan for this from the state bank to be repaid eventually with interest by the Chinese Eastern Railroad Company. Not until March 26, 1897, did Witte seek the permission of the tsar for transfer of the one million rubles from the special fund to China for the use of Ukhtomskii, who was leaving for there. The same day Witte addressed a letter to the administration of the Russo-Chinese Bank, informing it of the obligation of the administration of the company to put three million rubles in a special account of the minister of finance and advising it to release one million of that sum to Ukhtomskii. (The fact that the protocol of the railroad company administration regarding the transfer of three million rubles to the account of the finance minister was dated March 27 underlined the dominant role that Witte played in this affair.)

It was summer before Li received the million rubles from Ukhtomskii, who met with him repeatedly, both alone and in the company of Pokotilov, the director of the Russo-Chinese Bank, or of Iugovich, chief engineer of the Chinese Eastern Railroad.[105] The old man had worn himself out waiting,

Ukhtomskii reported upon his arrival in China. In January 1898 the administration of the railroad suggested to Witte that the next one million rubles be released for Li. Once more Witte chose to delay the payment. As Russia and Great Britain competed for another loan to China, money from the special fund seemed needed for new bribes. (The English too offered substantial sums to Chinese officials.) 250,000 rubles from the special fund went to the Buryat adventurer Petr Aleksandrovich (Zhamsaran) Badmaev, who hoped to lure Mongols, Tibetans, and Muslim Chinese away from Manchu China and into the Russian fold.[106] As will be seen, 609,120 rubles and 50 kopecks were paid to Li Hung-chang, 51,171 rubles and 1 kopeck to his colleague Chang Yin-huan in conjunction with the Liaotung lease.[107] But Li never saw the other two million rubles promised to him for the contract and construction of the Chinese Eastern Railroad. Witte had delayed the second payment until his own projected visit to the Far East, but the Boxer upheaval in China and the resultant destruction of much of the railroad nullified some of Li's promises and gave Witte the excuse for withholding payment.[108]

That Li accepted large sums of money from the Russians is incontrovertible. Whether it constituted bribery or "squeeze" is less certain. Witte and the Soviet historian B. A. Romanov who uncovered the compromising protocol in the Russian archives believed that the payments purchased Li's compliance with the Russian railroad scheme. The impression was left that by bribing the Chinese negotiator, the Russians forced the Chinese to let them construct a railroad through Manchuria against their will. Yet did the Russians really get the better of the Chinese or was it a matter of the Chinese letting them build a project which they wanted, but could not finance?

Li was a man of fabulous wealth, who had repeatedly used his official position for personal enrichment. Natural as it would have seemed to him to share in the profit that the Russians hoped to reap from the Chinese Eastern Railroad, it is doubtful that three million rubles would have meant enough to him in spite of his notorious cupidity to agree to something which he genuinely opposed. The great impression made on Li, who at that point had not yet been elsewhere in the West,[109] by the arsenals, shipyards, and warships the Russians showed him may have been more significant in his determination to collaborate with the tsarist government. Li was a strong advocate of railroad development and may well have used the Russians to do China's work.

As the Chinese historian Hsu Yung-tai argues persuasively, "It is only too likely that Sino-Russian relations in 1896 would have followed the same course if someone else had performed the mission in his stead." Not only did the Manchu government regard the Chinese Eastern Railroad concession as a means of purchasing Russian military assistance, but the treaty was in line with China's evolving strategy of relying on foreign aid in the expansion of the railway network. The Admiralty Board had for years been trying to construct a railroad in Manchuria, but had been unable to raise the necessary funds. Its inability to do so for lack of money—and not any bribe—had persuaded Li and other officials that the construction of a Manchurian line connected with the Trans-Siberian Railroad at Russian expense would turn Russia's efforts to China's economic advantage.[110]

As Heyking reported in March 1897, Li Hung-chang had related in the presence of many other members of the Tsungli Yamen that Nicholas had promised to him personally in St. Petersburg that Russia would not demand any territorial concessions from China and would protect the latter from potential new attacks by Japan. Though Li did not say so, Heyking was convinced that the tsar's pledge had been made in exchange for the permission to construct the Siberian railroad through Chinese territory. Heyking concurred that for some time to come at least, the Chinese had nothing to fear from Russia. The only enemy whom they dreaded and hated were the Japanese. Perhaps the most fatal side-effect of the overreliance which the Chinese placed on the promise of Russian protection was that it gave them a false feeling of security, as the result of which many Chinese deemed it possible to deny and forget the need for reforming their own army. "During the last New Year's audience," Heyking recalled, "Li Hung-chang contemplated with a woeful mien the row of Japanese officers who had accompanied the chargé d'affaires and told them in the presence of European diplomats: 'In the next war we shall be beaten by you again in the same way as last time.'"[111]

Seventeen

Reform Efforts

The setting of the hill-ringed capital of Korea was picturesque, but the city itself was dirty and malodorous. Except for two major arteries, the roads were narrow and winding; the houses with their thatched roofs were poorly built and in disrepair; open sewers ran alongside the streets. In summer the air was infested with all the microbes hostile to man.

The king was sympathetic to modernizing Seoul and his court. Though he still received the traditional prostrations from his officials, Kojong had settled for the three traditional bows customary before Western royalty from the foreign representatives. He had introduced electricity and modern weapons in his palace and had employed a number of foreigners. However, he had failed to heed most of their advice, partly because his energies were exhausted by public functions, partly because the counsels had been frustrated by "base intrigues" at his court. So great were the contradictions between the various factions that Frandin, the French consul, had described Korea back in May 1893 as on the verge of revolution, possibly bloody revolution.[1]

Japan had gone to war with China ostensibly in defense of the independence of Korea. She was determined at the same time to introduce such reforms in the adminsitration of the country as would deprive contending political factions of pretexts to disturb the public peace and to create crises which invited foreign intervention.[2] On July 23, 1894, Japanese troops occupied the royal palace and reinstated the taewongun in his old position.[3] In a lengthy circular note, dated July 28 and delivered after midnight on the twenty-ninth, Foreign Minister Mutsu informed the Russian minister, Hitrovo, that the king had charged the taewongun with the supreme administration of Korea and the inauguration of reforms. Mutsu alleged that Otori, the Japanese minister, had been called to the royal palace by a message from Kojong and had been assured by the taewongun that he would be consulted by him on all questions of

The city of Seoul in 1894. (*Illustrated London News*, 1894, 105: 204.)

reform. There was no need for the moment to discuss the independence of Korea or the equal treatment of China in commercial and political relations, he wrote, because the Japanese government would be able to regulate these matters directly with Korea. As China had rebuffed Japanese offers for concerted reform measures and had dispatched a large number of troops across the border as a hostile demonstration against Japan and Korea, Mutsu declared, his country did not intend to wait for the collaboration of China in effecting the reforms.[4]

Mutsu was pleased with Otori's success and instructed him to seize the opportunity "to effect the most radical reforms in [the] Corean Government in [the] shortest possible time." But he was disturbed by the disarming of all Korean troops in and around Seoul by the Japanese army, remarking in a note to Ito that Japan had intervened in Korea to reform her maladministration, not to infringe on her independence. He warned that such violation of Korean independence by Japan would arouse the suspicion of the powers and might prompt their intervention. The arms were duly returned, yet Mutsu found it necessary to remind his colleagues and underlings subsequently that Korea must be treated as an ally rather than an enemy, lest she appeal to the foreign powers, notably Russia, for support.[5]

To ensure her collaboration, Japan imposed a formal alliance on Korea.[6] She pressured the Korean government into asking her to drive out the Chinese troops it itself had invited and then declared that the Japanese expulsion of the Chinese soldiers from the peninsula on behalf of the Korean government necessitated the "mutual assistance both offensive and defensive" of the two countries. In the military alliance which was signed on August 26 by Otori and the president of the Korean Foreign Office, Kim Yun-sik, Korea undertook "to give every possible facility to Japanese soldiers regarding their movements and supply of provisions."[7] When Kim, who had signed the convention against his will, balked at notifying the foreign representatives of the alliance, the Japanese government simply published the text of the agreement in the Official Gazette (*Kampo*) on September 11. No special notification of the foreign representatives was necessary, Mutsu informed Otori, though the Korean government must be made to publish the treaty in a suitable manner.[8]

Informed by Hitrovo of the conclusion of the Japanese-Korean convention, Giers inquired in a secret cable on September 26 about the significance of the agreement. Hitrovo responded in a secret telegram on the twenty-eighth that it constituted first of all the legalization (*oformlenie*) of the state of affairs in Korea. "But in addition to this," he wrote in a dispatch on October 13 in which he enclosed a Russian translation of the text of the convention, "it has in my opinion special significance as a new, solemn declaration of the Japanese Government of its disinterested intentions toward Korea and of its striving merely to strengthen *the independence of this kingdom.*"

To the dissatisfaction of the other powers, Japan notified only the tsarist government of the convention she had concluded. Hitrovo regarded this as "an act of fully correct consideration" toward Russia on the part of the Japanese government, which, as he put it, showed "constant concern to reassure particularly us, as a neighboring power, concerning its intentions regarding Korea." When Foreign Minister Giers tried to ascertain the attitude of Great Britain toward the new development, the Foreign Office responded to Chargé Butenev that it had received no such communication.[9]

In accordance with his instructions, Otori prodded Kojong to appoint a seventeen-member reform council, which proclaimed a series of drastic innovations, such as the selection of officials according to ability rather than birth, the punishment of individual criminals rather than the entire family, the prohibition of slavery and of early marriage, and the right of widows to remarry. But while most Korean statesmen admitted the need for reforms, the government organs did not implement them, partly because petty intrigues still prevailed, partly because Korean officials did not know how to proceed. Frustrated by the disruptive disputation between the party of the taewongun and the adherents of the queen, on one hand, and the members of the Office of Military and Governmental Affairs, on the other hand, Mutsu wondered in mid-September whether Japan should try to impose a settlement by force. Toward the beginning of October he reminded Otori to try "by every possible means" to prevent the intrigues of Korean officials. No opposition to the invitation of the Japanese army to Korea could be brooked in view of the treaty of alliance; the memorialists who had made accusations in this regard should be punished, Mutsu instructed.[10]

The Japanese press bemoaned the dilemma confronting the imperial government. Prominent statesmen, to whom political intrigue had become second nature, seemed interested only in self-aggrandizement, while individuals prone to collaborate with the Japanese had an unsavory reputation. "More than once during the past fourteen years the desire for reform has been translated into action by Corean patriots, but so thoroughly Corean were the treachery and ferocity of their methods, that failure was always accompanied by disgrace," the *Japan Mail* lamented. "Yet the men thus discredited and attainted are the only Coreans that had proved the earnestness of their reforming purpose. They are precisely the persons whose services Japan must enlist for the achievement of her programme, and, at the same time, they are precisely the persons whose association with any programme provokes keen opposition on the part of those that were formerly their intended victims."[11]

So difficult yet important to Japan was the task of reforms in Korea that Tokyo decided to recall Otori and to send in his stead a more influential and experienced statesman, Count Inoue Kaoru, former foreign minister and currently home minister, who had assisted Lieutenant General Kuroda Kiyotaka in the conclusion of the first Japanese treaty with Korea in 1876 and who had negotiated in Seoul as minister plenipotentiary during the crisis of 1885.[12]

In view of Inoue's high position at home, Premier Ito wanted him to go to Korea in the capacity of special high commissioner for two or three months. But Inoue himself offered to serve in the lower position of envoy extraordinary and minister plenipotentiary, lest the attention of the foreign powers be unduly aroused by the special assignment. Inoue was convinced that the scheme upon which Japan had concerted for Korea required "not only great tact and delicate management, but constant supervision during some time and looking out for opportune moments," something that required the services of a regular minister.[13]

Sugimura Fukashi, first secretary of the Japanese legation in Seoul, was instructed to inform the Korean government that the Meiji emperor had appointed "such high and able personage as Count Inoue whom His Majesty would have otherwise never allowed to leave his side," in order to promote "the good understanding between the two Governments as well as all interests of Japan and Corea at this critical moment." To the foreign powers Japan explained simply that the successful and smooth reform of the Korean administration could best be secured by "the moral cooperation" of a person of such great ability and experience as Inoue. Besides, Mutsu argued realistically, the presence in Korea of a Japanese military commander of the highest rank necessitated the residence of an equally exalted personage as minister in order to maintain good relations between the Japanese civil and military authorities in that country.[14]

Otori had tried to diminish the authority of Kojong in view of the latter's hostility to innovations by supporting the taewongun, who seemed better disposed toward Japan. But the latter had refused to become a tool of Japanese policy and had encouraged his son not to abdicate his rights. Only reforms introduced by the Koreans themselves could succeed, the taewongun argued, for no one but they could determine what measures would be applicable to their country.[15] Finding the taewongun "still very insolent" and obstructive,[16] Inoue turned his back on him. As Queen Min, who was very influential, also appeared opposed to administrative reform,[17] he concentrated his efforts directly on Kojong, whose weak character was well known.

In a private audience with the king and his ministers on November 20,

Inoue presented a twenty-article reform plan designed to free Korea from the vassalage of China and to implant her independence. The Articles of Reform and National Policy were progressive. They transformed Korea from an absolute to a limited monarchy. Although they stated that the king was to have sole control of the government without interference by the taewongun or the queen, they stipulated that he must render the final decisions after full consultation with the ministers of the various departments. Laws and regulations were to be published and had to be observed by the king himself. The articles called for the management of the royal family by a Household Department; the definition of the functions of the cabinet and of the various departments; the fixing of taxes by law and their administration by the Board of Finance; the preparation of an annual state budget, with expenditures limited to income; the earmarking of a certain portion of the income for the training and maintenance of the army; the unification and lawful use of the police; retrenchment in the personnel and outlays of the Royal Household and of the government departments; the drawing up of a new legal code, modified on the basis of foreign laws adapted to Korean needs; the centralization of government and the systematization of personnel management; the limitation of the powers of the Council of State, with laws and regulations to originate in the various departments; the employment of experts as advisers in the departments; and the training of able young men in foreign countries.[18] So lengthy were Inoue's advice and admonitions, which the queen and the taewongun had been invited to hear from a separate room, that he could not complete his presentation in one afternoon, though the audience lasted from 1 P.M. until dark, and he continued his explanations from 2 until 6:30 P.M. the following day.

Kojong and the ministers agreed to implement the Japanese reform project.[19] But when the king several days later, on November 28, exercised his authority without first consulting the Japanese minister and made several modifications in the personnel of the departments, naming a number of officials unsympathetic toward the Japanese as vice presidents, Inoue proceeded to the palace and complained bitterly about the appointments. The king did not appreciate the good that Japan was doing for his country, Inoue lamented. Here she had gone to war with China to make Korea independent, strong, and prosperous, and Kojong did not deign to take the advice of her representative in naming vice presidents of the ministries. What ingratitude!

Kojong acknowledged that he had been wrong and made honorable amends. As a token of his goodwill he acceded to Inoue's demand that the conspirators Pak Yong-hyo and So Kwang-pom, who together with the late Kim Ok-kyun had played leading roles in the émeute of 1884, be given high posts in the government. (By a decree of December 17 they were appointed minister of the interior and minister of justice respectively.)[20]

Noting that Pak was presently in Seoul, whither he had been smuggled by Otori in July disguised as a Japanese, and was living near the Japanese legation guarded by Japanese sentries, and that So was expected to arrive from Japan shortly, the British consul-general reflected: "The Coreans are timid and long-suffering, but they are also cruel and vindictive, and know how to bide their time. It says much for the courage of these two that they are willing to take office, knowing, as they must know, that, sooner or later, they will fall victims to the vengeance that is waiting for them; but, if I may be permitted to say so, it says little for the sagacity of the Agents of the Japanese Government who are posing as the friends of Corea, that they should be anxious to thrust forward men whose appearance in public life will be an outrage on the feelings of the King and the large following who are loyal to him." [21]

In private audience on December 8, Inoue made it plain to Kojong that the Japanese would support and protect him, as well as the queen and the crown prince so long as they behaved as bidden. The queen promised never again to interfere in politics, and the king mustered a show of enthusiasm for the reforms.[22] Kojong pledged in writing that all the participants in the revolt of 1884 would be pardoned, that neither the taewongun nor the queen would henceforth be involved in public affairs, that no relations of the royal family would be employed in an official capacity, and that the multitude of eunuchs and palace ladies would be dismissed.

Harem life was oppressive. The women were not allowed to marry and literally could lose their head if they strayed from the path of virtue or, in the eyes of the jealous queen, aroused too much interest on the part of the king. The reduction of the seraglio promised financial as well as moral benefits, for it entailed a corresponding decrease in the staff of the palace and a cut in the kitchen and dressmaking expenditures. Yet the reform measure constituted a bitter loss for Kojong. So lonely had he felt when the palace ladies had departed shortly after his acceptance of Inoue's reform list on November 21 that he had ordered them back the following morning under pain of decapitation. But Inoue had persisted and had forced Kojong to agree to the removal of the women from the palace.[23] "I am in the saddle," Inoue was able to boast in a telegram to Mutsu on December 25.[24]

The implementation of reforms was not merely a matter of authority or persuasion, however. The dismissal of the courtesans was less a symbol of modernization than of lack of funds. Korea was in desperate need of money. "How can they organize [a] new army while present soldiers remain unpaid

Japanese legation guard in Seoul. (Angus Hamilton, *Korea*, 131.)

for the last five [months]? How can they establish [an] efficient police while it is barely sustained by voluntary contributions of ministers out of their own salary?" Inoue asked rhetorically.[25] He wanted Japan to extend a loan of five million yen at a favorable rate of interest to Korea. He bristled at the suggestion that Korea be charged ten percent for the money. "To exact ten per cent on [a] national loan is inconsistent with our apparently paternal declaration to help out this poor nation to independence and development," he remonstrated.[26]

On January 5, 1895, Inoue presented to Kojong a fourteen-article reform plan, for which he had already obtained the approval of the Korean cabinet. It included the main provisions of the twenty-point proposal and stated specifically that Korea was to give up all thought of dependence on China.[27]

On January 7, Kojong repaired to the ancestral tombs accompanied by Queen Min, Crown Prince Yi Ch'ok (subsequently known as Sunjong), the taewongun, the royal princes and ministers and vice ministers of state. There he solemnly inaugurated the new polity in a festive declaration, announcing an end to the old subjugation to China, the independence of Korea, and the introduction of the administrative reforms. He repeated the same oaths at the shrine of his ancestors the following day.

Reporting the above, Inoue commented that he had succeeded in establishing the independence of Korea in name; he could not make it a reality without money. He recommended strongly that the five million yen loan which he had requested be paid out of Japanese army funds, because the war had been undertaken for the purpose of Korean independence. Besides, he added, it was an investment which could be recovered.[28] When Mutsu responded that the Japanese government was now discussing the matter with leading banks "not without hope of success," Inoue shot back that he did not care whence the money came so long as a speedy settlement was reached. He could not stay in Korea any longer if he did not get a definite answer, he warned.[29]

In another telegram, on January 16, Inoue reverted to the dilemma he faced, having "just roused [the Korean government] to life from slumber" and not having the funds to effect the necessary reforms. At the same time he declared that as long as he remained in his present position he could not "morally allow" the Koreans to contract a loan on such unfavorable terms as the ten percent desired by some Japanese bankers. He insisted that the interest be less than eight percent, because loans that Korea had obtained from China and England at a time when anarchy had reigned in the country had not cost that much. "Just think how inconsistent we are to charge such high interest considering that this government is now practically in our hand, that we are dealing with reforming Corea, and above all that we are helping their independence," Inoue telegraphed. "Besides," he added, "it is my object as well as yours, I suppose, to take the whole financial power into our hands." He warned that if the Japanese insisted on ten percent interest, British bankers might underbid them and wrest financial control from Japan.[30]

On January 26 Inoue acknowledged receipt from his government of draft treaties for constructing railways and telegraph lines and for opening new ports in Korea for trade. Reserving his views until thorough study of the documents, he refused to open negotiations concerning the above before the loan question had been settled.[31]

The pressure exerted by Inoue in Seoul was bound to arouse foreign misgivings and in turn feed the apprehensions of the Japanese government about foreign reaction. On May 15 the Japanese minister in St. Petersburg inquired of the Russian foreign minister whether there was any truth to the rumor that his government was going to advise Japan to act in Korea strictly in conformity with the latter's independence. Lobanov denied the veracity of the rumor, but stated that word received from Seoul several days before to the effect that there was discontent throughout Korea because the Japanese government was audaciously interfering with the administration of the country, pressing for the appointment of Japanese officials and securing privileges in mining, railway, and other enterprises, had made a "generally disagreeable impression."

Nishi could give no positive assurances regarding the above for lack of information, but he expressed his confidence that there must be some misunderstanding. The Japanese government, he said, was earnest in its endeavors "to organize the administration of Corea and to make sound her independence." In his report Nishi warned Mutsu that Japan must be most careful in her actions in Korea, lest the said rumor become reality.[32]

Informed by Mutsu of Nishi's interview with Lobanov, Inoue cabled back that he was alive to Russian susceptibility to Japanese doings in Korea. It was the action of the Japanese government in raising questions concerning the building of railways and telegraphs and the opening of new ports that had received "undesirable prominence." As Mutsu well knew, he himself was fervently against such possibilities. Japanese advisers had been placed into all Korean ministries except, purposely, the Royal Household and Foreign Affairs. "Many things have been carried out in the presence of foreign jealousy and many yet remain on the table, some becoming [the] subject of joint protest by foreign representatives," Inoue remarked. Despite Japanese efforts the Korean government had not attained stability. There were constant plots and counterplots, as one ministerial crisis was followed by another. He did not know what could be done. "[The] Coreans are smart enough to see that as soon as peace has been declared, Japan alone cannot have free play," Inoue said. "If [Japan should] interfere with and give pressure on either party, they will surely look for help to foreign representatives." "Both parties are equally wrong," he added, "they merely strive for personal ascendency. Such being the case, I am quietly looking [at] what is passing. Interference [is] impossible without anticipating [the above] consequences." [33]

The prospect of Russian intervention worried Mutsu. "It appears that Russia will strongly remonstrate against Japan's action in Corea, but under the present circumstances Japan is not in a position to resist it successfully to the bitter end," he cabled to Kato Takaaki, the Japanese minister in London. "Since it is deemed advisable to stand against [a] Russian demand in a most becoming manner and, moreover, as I think domination of Russia in the East is not compatible with the best interests of England, and since England proposed in October last [a] joint guarantee of Corean independence by the powers, I intend to approach [the] British government on the subject of such [a] guarantee," he revealed. Mutsu asked Kato if he thought Japan could count on English support in such a proposal. If yes, he would send him the necessary instructions. Kato was to reply at once by cable, giving his own opinion without consulting the British government. [34]

Kato responded that he could express no definite opinion without sounding out the British government, because the situation had changed completely since October. He thought it possible, however, that the British government might assume a waiting attitude for the moment, "especially because [the] proposed arrangement may not be acceptable to Russia, who has ulterior designs against Corea and consequently to [against?] her present allies." "Knowing this," Kato speculated, "[the] British government may not be disposed to enter into [the] field until Russia shows her hand in [the] way of active interference in Corea." [35]

In detailed draft instructions for Kato, submitted meanwhile for the approval of Premier Ito, Mutsu declared that the independence of Korea had been the object of Japan's war with China and contended that the cession of the Liaotung Peninsula had been demanded principally for this reason. "No immediate danger need be apprehended from China, but that the integrity of Corea is seriously menaced cannot be doubted and [the] occupation of Corea and [the] consequent domination of [the] Yellow Sea by [a] strong military and naval power must be viewed with general alarm," he wrote. "The abandonment of [the] Fengtien [Liaotung] Peninsula will make Japan's future aid to Corea less effective than it otherwise would be."

In October of the preceding year Britain had inquired if a guarantee by the powers of the independence of Korea would be acceptable to Japan as part of the peace terms. The time had now arrived in Japan's judgment when such a guarantee would perpetuate Korea as an independent state, Mutsu stated. He pledged that if such a guarantee could be obtained, Japan would consent at once to withdraw her forces from Korea. One of the reasons given by the three powers for recommending Japanese renunciation of the permanent possession of the Liaotung Peninsula had been the fear that it would render Korean independence illusory. He felt, consequently, that they "could not logically refuse to join in the proposed guarantee." Kato was to inform Foreign Secretary Kimberley that Japan had not approached any other power on the subject and would not do so until it had received an answer from Great Britain. In approaching the British government most confidentially about the above, Kato was to convey also that Japan deemed it a "natural and necessary complement" to her renunciation of the permanent possession of the Liaotung Peninsula to demand assurance from China that "no portion of the abandoned territory shall ever be ceded to any other power."

Kato was to argue that the interests of Britain and Japan were identical and to propose that the two governments concert measures for approaching the other powers. He was to press for early action by London on the ground that "[the] Japanese Government have reason to think that Russia will shortly approach them on [the] subject of Corea and they would like to be in [a] position to reply that [the] question is under consideration." [36]

In preparation for a possible international guarantee of the independence of Korea, Mutsu drew up a draft declaration. Asserting that Japan had taken up arms against China to withdraw Korea from her injurious influence and that this objective had been fully realized by the conclusion of the Treaty of Shimonoseki, the document stated that the perpetuation of Korean independence was "a matter of common concern." Japan did not deem it necessary to shoulder the duty and responsibility of this independence singlehandedly. Expressing its readiness to cooperate with the other interested powers in any measure for the amelioration of the condition of Korea, the Japanese government announced its intention to base its future relations with Korea upon its convention rights. [37]

Worried about Russian intentions, [38] the Japanese sought English reassurance. On instructions from Saionji, [39] who had succeeded Mutsu as foreign minister, Kato asked Kimberley on June 24, whether the British government considered that the assurances given by Russia to China in 1886 not to encroach on Korean territory were still binding. Kimberley answered in the affirmative. He related that at the beginning of the Sino-Japanese War Russia had officially asked England whether she would agree with the former in maintaining the independence of Korea. Britain had replied yes, and Russia was precluded, therefore, from taking any part of Korea, Kato reported.[40]

On July 12 Ito told Chargé Lowther that it was his intention at an early date to propose to Salisbury "some understanding for the establishment of a joint guarantee on the part of the Powers for the independence of Corea." "The present moment when Russia, France, and Germany were apparently so harmoniously working together would not be a good one," Lowther relayed, but Ito hoped to solicit Salisbury's views on the subject later with a view to frustrating Russian plans.[41] Ito alleged that while it was generally assumed that the ambitions of Russia were directed merely to the acquisition of an ice-free port and a part of Manchuria, Russia really aimed to establish a protectorate over Korea. He asserted that there were many indications that she would move in this direction, although he conceded that he had no proof and that Russian declarations were contrary to it.[42]

When the British minister in Peking asked his Japanese colleague whether he had heard the rumor that a Russian military force of some 60,000 men was moving from Irkutsk towards the Korean frontier, Hayashi replied that he had no information to this effect. If it were true, he said, the General Army Staff in Tokyo must know of it, for it had secret agents in all the districts the Russians must traverse. Declaring that if the Russians were to invade Korea war between Russia and Japan would be brought very close, Hayashi voiced the conviction that the Japanese would be victorious on land. But on the sea, the Russians had decided superiority. The Japanese could not match the three strong ironclads of the Russians now in the China Seas. "Japan, however, was strong in torpedo boats, and had plenty of docks and coaling stations," O'Conor paraphrased Hayashi. "Their policy would be to carry on what he called a naval banditti warfare, surprising and harassing the Russian fleet, and coming upon them at unexpected places."[43]

Japanese misgivings were fed by the strengthening position of Russia in Korea despite the Japanese occupation. As the British consul general in Seoul reported in mid-July, Russian influence was "greatly on the increase" at the Korean court. While his own Korean interpreter was invited infrequently by the king, the Korean interpreter of the Russian legation was said to have had daily interviews with Kojong during the past few weeks. Hillier believed that the appointment of General LeGendre, a naturalized American citizen who some time ago had been dismissed because of his anti-Japanese sentiments, as private tutor to the king's son and adviser to the royal household had occurred at the instance of Waeber, who was on intimate terms with LeGendre. He had

heard that Nikolai Aleksandrovich Raspopov, secretary of the Russian legation, would become adviser to Kojong. Although he had not yet been able to
confirm the report, Hillier thought it very probably true, "as both M. Waeber
and the American Minister [Sill], who are close allies, have made no secret of
their objections to the imposition of so many Japanese advisers on this country, and of their intention to get them replaced by foreigners of other nationalities." "The present arrangement seems to me to present features which,
under the circumstances, are not altogether unsatisfactory," Hillier commented. "American *amour-propre* is satisfied by the employment of two advisers, though one (Mr. [Clarence R.] Greathouse) is not a very creditable
representative, while the Russians will also practically have two men devoted
to their interests, should Mr. Rospopoff's rumoured appointment prove
correct." [44]

The anticipated Russian complaint against Japanese arm-twisting in Seoul
came on July 31 when Hitrovo declared to Saionji on instructions from his
government that while Korea appeared calm and the king was disposed to
make the necessary reforms, Kojong feared that the interference of the Japanese authorities would lower his authority in the eyes of his subjects. The
tsarist government, therefore, reminded the government of Japan of the declaration it had made in the past regarding the independence of Korea in name
and in fact and expressed the hope that it would conform its acts to its
declaration.

Hitrovo supplemented the official statement with the personal observation
that he thought the Japanese government would do well, in order to avoid
misunderstandings, to come to an arrangement with the Russian government
concerning the Korean question and to give appropriate instructions to Nishi.

Saionji replied that for his part he shared Hitrovo's views regarding the
desirability of an entente with the Russian government to avoid future misunderstandings regarding Korean affairs, but that he could not form an exact
idea of what should be done until he had received reports from Inoue, who
had just returned to Korea, on the actual situation in Korea. [45]

Apprised of the above exchange, Inoue replied that the question of an understanding with Russia and its terms was "entirely for the government to
decide." If such an arrangement had been "necessitated by circumstances in
order to maintain the status quo with Russia," he cabled, "I will make it [a]
fundamental condition that neither of us would injure [the] territorial integrity
of Corea." It would be well, he added, to consider the reaction of England to a
Japanese entente with Russia. "If she could be persuaded to acquiesce in [the
arrangement] and look at [it as a] passing event, the object of which is only to

gain time for us, that may be all right, but if not, I cannot see [the] wisdom in letting off the weight that her present attitude lends to our foreign policy," Inoue cabled.[46]

Hitrovo touched on the Korean question also in the course of a conversation with Premier Ito. But Ito, like Saionji, parried his question about Japanese plans toward Korea with the retort that his government must wait for the reports of Inoue before reaching any decision.

Hitrovo complained to his German colleague about Ito's reserve (*Verschlossenheit*). He had given Ito the opportunity to express himself freely about the Korean question, which sooner or later was bound to be the subject of negotiations between Russia and Japan, but had been able to get absolutely nothing out of him.

Gutschmid believed that Japan still planned to withdraw from Korea. The only explanation he could find for the reserve of the Japanese government toward Hitrovo, he reported, was that it apparently wished to fulfill the promises it had made to Russia during the past summer regarding the independence of Korea without being enjoined to do so.[47]

The reforms initiated by the Kim Hong-jip cabinet under Japanese prodding exceeded the original purpose of providing Korea with a responsible form of government. Instead of concentrating on basic issues, the bureaucrats lost themselves in minutiae. They fixed the exact social position of the wives of officials and of the women of the harem. The wives were ranked as "Pure and Reverend Lady," "Pure Lady," "Chaste Lady," "Chaste Dame," "Worthy Dame," "Courteous Dame," "Just Dame," "Peaceful Dame," and "Upright Dame." The royal concubines received the titles of "Mistress," "Noble Lady," "Resplendent Exemplar," "Chaste Exemplar," "Resplendent Demeanor," "Chaste Demeanor," "Resplendent Beauty," and "Chaste Beauty."[48]

In their zeal to limit waste, the officials enacted petty sumptuary laws which aroused the indignation of the populace. They prohibited the traditional long pipes, which Koreans liked to smoke, shortening their stems. They regulated the cut and width of the sleeves of men's coats, the size and brims of their hats, the color of outer garments, and the number of servants who could attend sedan chairs. The measure which actually precipitated riots and turned most officials and commoners alike against the reform program as a whole was the prohibition of the topknot, the venerated traditional male hairdress, a compact twist about an inch in diameter and three inches long, which rose perpendicularly from the center of the top of the head. It symbolized not only tradition as such, for it went back at least five centuries, but it represented manhood and was connected with religious observances. The reformers' attack on the topknot, a foreign resident of Korea wrote, "was the 'last straw that broke the camel's back'—or when the relative strength and weight of the elements of the matter are considered it would be perhaps nearer to truth to say, it was the last camel that broke the straw's back."[49]

Meanwhile the uncertain international situation and the cost of the Sino-Japanese War kept the Japanese cabinet from providing the Korean government with the sort of funds Inoue demanded. Deprived of operating expenses and lacking popular support, the reforms withered on the vine. When Inoue, at his own request, returned to Japan on leave in June, partly because he wanted to consult with his government concerning the degree of Japanese interference in Korean affairs and Japan's future policy, partly because he was suffering from rheumatism in the Korean climate,[50] the Japanese newspaper *Nichi Nichi Shimbun* commented with resignation about the apparent hopelessness of his reform efforts in Korea and the seeming influence of Waeber at the Korean court. Conditions showed, the paper wrote, that Korea was incapable of self-reliance, even if her independence be guaranteed by the powers. There was nothing left to do but either, on the one hand, to annex the country or to make her into a protectorate, or, on the other hand, to leave her to her fate. Yet Japan had never harbored any intention to annex Korea and it was doubtful whether a protectorate would be in Japan's interest, the *Nichi Nichi* observed.[51]

In the wake of the Tripartite Intervention a new pro-Russian party had sprung up in Korea. This party supported the queen, who continued her machinations undeterred by everything that had happened. She managed to draw Pak Yong-hyo away from the taewongun and even from the Japanese, though he owed his position to the latter. When General Yi Chun-yong, the cherished grandson of the taewongun, was banished after Pak had accused him of plotting with the Tonghak to overthrow the king and assassinate the pro-Japanese cabinet minister, the taewongun vengefully brought charges of treason against Pak. As the latter, in July, once again fled for his life to Japan, the failure of Inoue's reform measures was exposed.[52]

By the time Inoue reached Tokyo, the Japanese government had decided to abandon the reform project. In a meeting on May 25, it had opted for a passive policy in Korea, "leaving off interference insofar as possible and causing Korea to stand up by herself."[53] When Inoue went back to Seoul in July, his line of conduct toward the Korean government differed accordingly. He meddled very little in domestic affairs of the country and let the king and his ministers rule more or less as they saw fit.

Inoue's replacement as minister at the beginning of September by a military man, General Miura Goro, aroused fears on the part of Kojong and his entourage that Japan might revive the policy of pressure and intimidation which

Otori and Inoue had pursued. But Miura assumed his duties with an air of great kindness toward the king and of noninterference in domestic affairs. It looked as if the Japanese had indeed abandoned, at least for the moment, the sort of tutelage which they had arrogated for themselves in the administration of Korea and by this change in policy sought to render the population more sympathetic toward themselves.[54]

Asked by Hitrovo when Japan intended to fulfill the promise she had given to Russia the preceding year to respect the independence of Korea, when, in other words, the independence of Korea would become a fact, Ito replied that Japan had every intention to evacuate Korea and to leave her to herself. The withdrawal of Japanese troops from Korea would take place immediately following the evacuation of the Liaotung Peninsula, except for two small detachments required for the protection of the Japanese legation, which would be stationed at Chemulpo and Seoul. Ito explained that it was necessary to retain several battalions in Korea until the withdrawal from Liaotung had been completed, lest the Koreans destroy the telegraph lines strung by the Japanese and interrupt communications between Japan and Liaotung; upon the evacuation of southern Manchuria the telegraph lines would be handed over to the Korean government, which would have to offer certain guarantees for their maintenance. Thereupon the evacuation of Korea would be set in motion.

Ito remarked to the German minister, that the whole Korean complication had been "a most unfortunate affair." It was impossible to perceive how Korea with her corrupt government, which did not even have an army to its name, could maintain her independence vis-à-vis her mighty neighbor (Russia), following the withdrawal of the Japanese troops. But this, he said, was a problem for the future.[55]

Eighteen

King, Queen, and Knave

Following the flight of Pak Yong-hyo, the queen and her relatives gave vent to their anti-Japanese feelings and increasingly sought the advice of Russian and American officials. Word that Queen Min was looking to Russia for support particularly alarmed the Japanese.[1]

Waeber, the tsarist representative, had nearly thirty years of experience in East Asia. He had been a language student at Peking from 1866 to 1870, vice consul and secretary in Hakodate from 1871 to 1873, vice consul in Yokohama from 1874 to 1875, consul in Tientsin from 1876 to 1884, and consul general and chargé d'affaires in Korea since 1885.[2] His familiarity with Chinese, Japanese, and Korean affairs and dealings commanded respect. His wife contributed to his success. A cultured and accomplished lady, she was popular not only in the foreign community,[3] but became an intimate friend of the queen.[4] Waeber's influence at court was enhanced further by the employment of a relative of his, a Mrs. Sonntag, to establish a school of handicrafts and to act as adviser on European cooking and table etiquette. The lady visited the queen frequently and discoursed with her for hours on various topics.

Queen Min's traditional hostility towards the Japanese, who in 1888 had tried to poison her with a birthday cake, had been exacerbated by Inoue's insistence on her noninterference in the affairs of government. Very intelligent, clever, and careful, she managed to survive Japanese intrigues so long as she relied solely on herself. But the attention Russia seemed to lavish on her and the assurances Waeber gave that she would be protected and that the Japanese, who had been forced to retrocede the Liaotung Peninsula, would not be allowed to dominate Korea, misled her into abandoning her usual caution, and she began to act as if the Japanese had already withdrawn from her country.[5]

The attempts of Queen Min to regain her former influence brought the

531

witch's brew of intrigue to a boiling point. "If the Japanese intervention in Korea had so far been of but very questionable use for the good and tranquility of this country, it had at least the advantage of removing from power the members of the family of the queen and to disencumber the country of greedy officials, who had fleeced the Korean people for so many years," the French representative observed. The freedom of action left to Kojong in recent months, however, tempted the queen to call back some of her relatives from the provinces and from China where they had taken refuge and to plot their reinstatement in the government. Lefèvre expressed the hope that the king would resist the solicitations of his spouse and in the interest of tranquility refuse to grant the premiership to one of her family members (Min Yong-ik), best known for his exactions. "To put at the head of affairs a man who oppressed the country for more than six years would constitute a detestable example for the officials of all ranks and would not fail to dissatisfy the population profoundly," Lefèvre wrote.

The French representative realized that the Japanese minister would not be indifferent to a nomination of this kind. It was one thing for Viscount Miura to desist from the practice of his predecessor to provide the king with hand-picked candidates for office; it was another thing for him to tolerate the appointment as premier of a personage known for his sympathies toward China and his hostility toward Japan. Lefèvre anticipated that Kojong's inability to stand up to his wife would prompt the Japanese legation to resume "after an appearance of reason, the policy followed previously by Count Inoue." [6] Not even he could conceive, however, of the sort of measures to which Miura would resort to remove the hostile influence of the queen once and for all.

The return of the old ministers implied, of course, the dismissal of their reform-minded successors, conceivably their execution. The disbandment of the Japanese-trained Korean troops, known as the *kunrentai*, demanded by the conservative party following fights between members of the *kunrentai* and the metropolitan police at the time of the mid-autumn festival and again on October 6, 1895,[7] would have left the anti-reform forces in full control.

Miura, who believed that the abandonment of reforms would endanger the independence of Korea and thereby threaten the security of his own country, was indignant at the seeming ingratitude of the court toward Japan. He was a military man without taste for diplomatic niceties. What was needed to solve the Korean question, he thought in his straightforward way, was prompt and vigorous action.[8] In a conference with Okamoto and Sugimura at the Japanese legation on October 3, he plotted the assassination of Queen Min. Her father-in-law had recently solicited Japanese patronage. Miura and his compatriots decided, therefore, to field the aged taewongun in another power play—to send him back to the palace at the head of the *kunrentai* and of Japanese adventurers,[9] supported by Japanese troops stationed in Seoul. To make sure that the taewongun would remain a pawn rather than an active piece in the game, they obtained written assurances on his part that he would not interfere directly in state affairs.

When War Minister An Keiju visited the Japanese legation on October 7 and broached the subject of the dissolution of the *kunrentai*, Miura and Sugimura decided to set their plot in motion that very night. They cabled Okamoto, who had gone to Chemulpo, to return at once, and they sent detailed instructions to Deputy Consul Horiguchi Kumaichi regarding the taewongun's entrance into the palace. Horiguchi was to meet Okamoto at Yongsan and to advance together with him. Miura ordered Umayabara Muhon, the commander of the Japanese battalion, to assist the taewongun by directing the disposition of the *kunrentai* soldiers and supporting them with his own men. Ogiwara Hidejiro was to lead the police force under him to Yongsan and consult with Okamoto about steps necessary to expedite the taewongun's entry into the palace. Miura asked Adachi Kenzo and Kunitomo Shigeakira to gather their cohorts and likewise rendezvous with Okamoto at Yongsan; they were to move into the palace together with the taewongun as the latter's bodyguard. Haranguing his countrymen to eradicate the evils which had plagued Korea for the past two decades, Miura instigated them to slay the queen. Sugimura meanwhile drew up and sent to Horiguchi for Okamoto a manifesto setting forth the reasons for the taewongun's return to the palace.

Horiguchi rode off to Yongsan followed by Ogiwara, who had ordered the policemen on duty to come also after changing to civilian dress and arming themselves with swords. Informed of the plans at Sugimura's behest, Li Shukwei, a Korean supporter of the taewongun, rounded up a number of compatriots and hastened to the taewongun's residence. Adachi and Kunitomo collected two dozen Japanese as bodyguards for the taewongun. About half of them were told of, and agreed to, the projected liquidation of the queen.

Okamoto duly rushed back from Chemulpo, meeting the fellow-conspirators and receiving the draft declaration and other documents at Mapho, rather than at Yongsan. After discussing the strategy of entering the palace, Okamoto led the group to the taewongun's residence outside Seoul. Here, in the early hours of October 8, as the party prepared to march, Okamoto exhorted the men to deal with the "fox" as exigencies might require. The hidden aspect of the mission now was revealed to most of the conspirators.

At about 3 A.M. the taewongun got into his palanquin and started out toward the capital, escorted by the motley Japanese body guard, by Li, and several other Koreans. They halted outside the west gate of the city, where the *kunrentai* joined them, to wait for the Japanese troops. Upon the arrival of the latter, the procession resumed its course, with the *kunrentai* as vanguard. On the way a number of additional Japanese swordsmen swelled the party.

The extensive grounds of Kyongbok Palace, which the conspirators reached toward dawn, were enclosed by a high outer wall. Inside there were many different buildings, most of them surrounded by lower walls of their own. The residence in which the royal couple was sleeping that night was between a quarter and a third of a mile from the main gate; it was close to the western outer wall with its side entrance.[10]

Although the palace was no longer occupied by the Japanese army, the soldiers having been withdrawn to the barracks outside the main gate, Japanese policemen had remained inside to guard the king. Regarding Kojong as a virtual prisoner in his own palace, the Russian and American chargés, Waeber and Allen, and the king's American adviser, Greathouse, had counseled him to invite Westerners to live at his court, and to protect him by their presence as witnesses of Japanese conduct. The three men who were asked to stay within the walls of the palace grounds and to supervise the royal guard were the American military instructors General William McE. Dye and Colonel F. J. H. Nienstead and the Russian architect A. J. Seredin-Sabatin, called Sabatin for short. They staggered their duties in such a way that two of them would always be inside the palace grounds. On the fateful night of October 7 to 8 General Dye and Sabatin "slept in."[11]

Dye was "a very charming old gentleman, skilled in growing apples," who in spite of his military position was not about to lay down his life in defense of his royal employers. Sabatin, in whose bosom beat a civilian heart, was likewise more concerned with his own safety than that of the king and the queen.[12]

The royal guard which defended the palace was under the command of Colonel Hyŏn In-tak, who had helped the queen escape in 1884. According to Sabatin the guard numbered about 1,500 men, but Dye, who was better acquainted with it, gives the figure as only about 800 men and these were there "on paper," about one third of them being customarily absent with their families.[13] The native officers of the guard were incompetent. The Chinese resident, Yüan Shih-k'ai, had frustrated Dye's efforts to secure the appointment and promotion of officers on the basis of examination in military science rather than as a reward for personal services. The royal guard had little training and experience as a cohesive unit. Following the occupation of the palace by the Japanese and their Korean collaborators in July 1894, no less than six different guard detachments, including Japanese and Korean policemen, all of them dominated by the Japanese, had operated inside the palace grounds like wheels within wheels. An attempt by Kojong and Dye to create an effective royal guard under the command of a nephew of the king and grandson of the taewongun was foiled by the Japanese who detained many of the picked soldiers as they ventured outside the palace ground walls to visit their families and replaced them surreptitiously with inferior recruits. Repeatedly the Japanese impeded any sort of drill by the guards, even mere manual of arms.

The Japanese, as will be recalled, had not only seized what artillery and ammunition they had found in the Korean capital, but had disarmed all Korean soldiers. When the Japanese government, partly in response to complaints by Kojong, partly because it wished to preserve the image of a Korean-Japanese alliance, had ordered the restoration of the weapons to the guard, the Japanese army produced about 400 rusty muskets, mostly without bayonets or rammers and many without locks or cocks. Even after a thorough cleaning and change of parts, these arms were little better than cornstalks. A few additional worthless weapons were found in the palace storehouse and in the lake, where they had been tossed during the Japanese attack the preceding year. The best fifteen or twenty guns, which Dye had put aside in his quarters for distribution to a reliable body of men in an emergency, were stolen when he was outside the palace one day. To make matters worse, the Japanese army did not return to the royal guard any ammunition. The few cartridges the defenders of the palace had were not reliable. They had come from three or four partially filled boxes which Dye had secretly recovered from a pond near his quarters.[14]

During the period from October 1 to October 6 the strength of the guard had been reduced sharply. Clashes in the city between members of the *kunrentai* and the police, whether spontaneous or prearranged, had drawn numerous detachments of the guard outside the palace grounds. The avenues leading to the royal quarters were denuded of sentries.[15] The policemen in the city also had been lured away from their posts to allow the conspirators to move up to the palace without challenge.[16] A Japanese adviser to the police administration of Seoul had let it be known that the *kunrentai* soldiers with whom the policemen had collided planned to attack them during the night of October 7 to 8 and had ordered them to assemble at their barracks in expectation of the assault which, of course, never came.[17]

A bright moon illuminated the fatal night. Sabatin saw nothing amiss when he made his customary rounds of the guard at midnight.[18] At 2 A.M. two members of the private police of the king reported to Colonel Hyön that they had observed some 200 Japanese soldiers move into the barracks in front of the palace. Soldiers of the royal body guard whom Hyön sent to the front gate verified the report, but the colonel took no further action at the moment.[19] At 4 A.M. Lieutenant Colonel Yi Ha-kun, a Korean officer of the guard, rushed into the building where Sabatin and Dye were sleeping and reported that Japanese and *kurentai* soldiers had assembled outside the palace gates. Sabatin and Dye hastened to the headquarters of the guard where half a dozen or more officers were supposed to be. They found it empty. Dye asked Yi to accompany them on an inspection of the gates as their interpreter, but Yi excused himself, saying that he had to go and see the king.

Sabatin and Dye proceeded to the northwestern gate alone. As they peered through its gaps, they espied between forty and fifty Japanese soldiers with fixed bayonets. When they challenged them and asked what they wanted, the soldiers silently moved away from the gate and hid from their view along the wall. Informed by messengers that between 200 and 300 *kunrentai* men were outside the northeastern gate, Sabatin and Dye hurried there, but they could see no one through the gaps in the gate. They did hear a rumble of voices, seemingly discussing something. At about 4:30 A.M. a Korean stepped up to the gate on the outside and demanded loudly that it be opened.

Sabatin and Dye returned to the headquarters of the guard and were debating what to do when, at 5 A.M., the sound of battering in doors reached them from the direction of the main gate of the palace in the south, followed by firing. Beyond the second northwestern gate someone intoned a speech, as if reading it. Loud cheers followed the words, and a few minutes later *kunrentai* soldiers began climbing over the palace walls from the backside of the courtyard and shooting at the guards, who left their posts and scattered, dropping their guns and shedding their uniform tops on the run.

As the palace guard retreated toward the headquarters building, Lieutenant Colonel Yi changed to civvies and disappeared. Dye managed to rally some 300 soldiers and eight officers and had them take up positions on the left side of the road leading from the little northern gate to the quarters of the king. No sooner did the *kunrentai* break through this gate and fire several volleys in the direction of the guards, however, than the latter resumed their flight. As they stampeded away in two different directions, some toward the residence of the Westerners, the others past the king's dwelling toward the queen's compound, they swept Dye and Sabatin with them. Since Dye and Sabatin had been standing on opposite sides of the road, they were involuntarily separated. Dye was carried to the relative safety of the Western quarters, Sabatin to the center of things. When the crowd pushed past the queen's compound, Sabatin held on to the gatepost and worked his way into the courtyard thinking that it would offer a haven of refuge.

As Sabatin stepped into the courtyard, he saw four Japanese sentries and two Japanese officers, as well as a platoon of *kunrentai*, all of them in a stationary position—the sentries manning two wicket gates, the *kunrentai* lined up in formation, their rifles at their feet. Near the *kunrentai* stood a well-groomed Japanese in European attire with a naked dagger in his hand. He seemed to be giving orders to between twenty and twenty-five countrymen of his, who had occupied the verandah of the main building and were rushing about in a state of great excitement. Like him most of them were garbed in Western dress, but were carrying one or two Japanese swords.

Fearing for his life, Sabatin went up to the Japanese lieutenant and addressing him in English sought to put himself under the protection of the Japanese army. The officer listened to him uncomprehendingly. When Sabatin switched to Japanese, the lieutenant hastened away. The sentries to whom the Russian thereupon turned were no more willing to become involved with him. In desperation Sabatin went up to the man who seemed in charge of the *soshi*.

"Good morning," Sabatin said in English as calmly as he could.

"What's your name?" the Japanese replied gruffly in the same tongue, ignoring his greeting.

"Sabatin," the Russian answered.

"What is your position?" the Japanese wanted to know.

"Architect," Sabatin retorted, carefully suppressing his connection with the royal guard.

Sabatin told the Japanese that he had come upon this scene by accident. He realized, he remarked in a steadied voice, that it was neither proper nor safe for him to be there in view of the excited manner of all the "gentlemen" on the verandah and asked him, as a man of obvious culture, to take him under his protection.

After reflecting for a minute, the Japanese replied dryly, "You are protected. Stand here and do not move."

Sabatin thanked him kindly, but asked as the Japanese started to walk away that he be assigned a soldier or two, because the other Japanese might not know that he had the pleasure of being under his protection.

The Japanese called over two of the *kunrentai* to stand on each side of Sabatin and went back to his business.

Rooted in place, Sabatin witnessed to his horror how the "gentlemen" began rushing in and out of the building through the windows, dragging out women by the hair of the head and hurling them from the verandah to the ground seven feet below, kicking them as they fell. The Japanese did so with much shouting and grunting, while the Korean court ladies in dignified con-

trast bit their lips and did not utter a sound, remaining limp and defenseless
like rag dolls. Four or five of the assassins had drawn their swords, but from
where he stood, Sabatin could discern no blood either on the unfortunate
women or on the blades of the weapons. As he was wondering how many of
the ten or twelve women he had seen defenestrated had survived the ordeal,
five particularly frenzied Japanese came screaming out of the building at such
speed that when they dropped the Korean woman whom they had dragged out
by the hair, they could not stop and ran smack into him. He parried their
startled questions by pretending not to understand any Japanese or Korean.
When a Korean who recognized him happened upon them and revealed Sabatin's connection with the palace guard, the five Japanese and then Sabatin's
protector interrogated him roughly regarding the queen's whereabouts. He
satisfied them that he did not know—and as a foreigner and a male could not
know—where she was hiding and was allowed to depart, even though the
Korean who had given him away pointed to the danger of leaving alive a
witness to their deeds.[20]

Meanwhile the *soshi* continued to search for Queen Min, who had concealed herself in one of the side rooms. To distract their attention and give his
wife time to escape, the king came out of the inner rooms of the building to a
front room and stood in the open doors in plain view of the Japanese. The
assassins rushed up to him, shook him by the shoulder, dragged him about,
and fired off pistols near him, but Kojong showed unexpected manliness and
would not betray the queen. Nor did the Japanese learn anything from the
crown prince whom they found in the inner rooms, though they roughed him
up and threatened him with their swords.[21]

Colonel Hyön was brought to the palace to identify the queen. He too,
however, refused to betray her in spite of continued beatings. "I do not know
where she is, even if you kill me," he told his tormentors.[22]

Queen Min was eventually given away by her most loyal supporter. When
the Japanese burst into the room where she was hiding in the midst of other
women, the minister of the Royal Household, Yi Kyöng-ik, stood with outstretched arms in front of the queen to shield her with his body, thereby
unthinkingly revealing her identity. As the assassin's swords cut into him,
severing both his hands and inflicting other grievous wounds, the queen made
a dash for freedom. She was overtaken and run through. As she lay on her
back on the floor in a pool of blood and faintly asked an attendant if her son
was safe, a Japanese jumped on her breast and pierced her again and again
with his sword.[23]

The assassins thereupon laid Queen Min on a plank, covered her with a silk
quilt, and carried her first to the courtyard and then to a pine grove in the

Apartments where Queen Min was killed. (*Vsemirnaia illiustratsiia*, 1896, 543.)

adjacent deer park. They arranged faggots of wood around the plank and without checking whether she was actually dead, poured kerosene over her body and set it afire. All that remained of the proud queen, whom a number of court ladies had been forced to identify at the pyre, were a few unconsumed bones.[24]

At about 6 A.M. Miura arrived at the palace, accompanied by Sugimura, an interpreter, and a strong guard. King Kojong had sent a messenger to Miura before dawn to inquire why additional Japanese troops were marching into the barracks at the front gate. In spite of the early hour, the messenger had found Miura, Sugimura, and the interpreter fully dressed and three sedan chairs waiting for them at the door. The sound of the attack on the palace carried to the Japanese legation while Miura was telling the messenger that he had learned of the troop movement from a Japanese colonel, but did not know its cause. By the time Miura reached the palace gates the Japanese troops and the *soshi* were still inside, but his arrival put an end to the violence, and the assassins dispersed.

Miura was admitted at once and saw the king who by then had proceeded to the audience chamber in an adjoining building. Present in addition to the Japanese minister were the legation secretary, the interpreter, the *soshi* leader (Okamoto) to whom Sabatin had turned for protection, and the taewongun. During the audience three documents were prepared and presented for Kojong's signature. They stipulated that henceforth state affairs would be managed by the cabinet; Prince Yi Chai-miun, the elder brother of the king, who had been escorted to the palace by Japanese troops, was named minister of the Royal Household; and a vice minister of the Royal Household was appointed. Subsequently ministers loyal to the queen were dropped from the cabinet and pro-Japanese officials who had been dismissed earlier in the year were re-appointed in their stead. Once the king had signed the documents, the Japanese troops were withdrawn, leaving the palace grounds in the hands of the *kunrentai*.[25]

The taewongun, who had tried to use the Japanese, was used by them instead. In a colorful proclamation issued over his signature that day, announcing his entry into the palace to aid the king in perfecting the government, the people were enjoined to go about their business and not to interfere with the reforms.[26]

Kojong had sent an official to the American chargé asking him to hasten to the palace at about the same time that he had contacted Miura. Although Allen had been awakened by the sound of gunfire at 5 A.M., he had not been dressed when the messenger had arrived. After getting ready, Allen stopped at the Russian legation to get Waeber to accompany him. There he met Sabatin, who was just reporting what had transpired. Allen and Waeber proceeded to the residence of Miura to enlist his cooperation, not realizing he was privy to the plot and already at the scene of the crime. It was shortly after 7 A.M. that the American and Russian representatives finally reached the palace.

As Allen and Waeber approached, they saw near the palace and inside its walls over thirty "evil looking Japanese with disordered clothes, long swords and sword canes" on their way out. Near Kojong's residence they met a "well-dressed portly Japanese," whom they recognized from Sabatin's description as the leader of the assassins.[27]

Prince Yi tried to turn Waeber and Allen away. He announced that the king was very excited and could not receive them. But Waeber pointed out that Miura's sedan chair was in front of the audience chamber and demanded that Kojong receive the representatives of Russia and the United States as well. After about an hour and a half, during which they interrogated General Dye and other Western employees, Miura came out and tried to mollify Waeber and Allen by offering to give the explanations they required to them and to the other foreign representatives at the Japanese legation. But Waeber and Allen persisted in their desire to see the king and assure themselves of his safety.[28]

They found Kojong in a pitiful state. He sobbed openly as he told them that he did not know what had happened to his wife. Surrounded by enemies, including his father, he was terrified that the *kunrentai* would harm him. He begged Allen and Waeber to have the Korean soldiers replaced, if need be, by a Japanese guard. He asked, furthermore, that the two Western representatives remain within call as long as Miura was in the palace. They did in fact wait for another half-hour and left only after Miura, whom they saw again briefly, told them that he was departing at once.

From the palace Waeber and Allen went to see their English and German colleagues and had them call on the distraught monarch to show him that he was not without friends. When Hillier and Krien arrived, Kojong looked "ill and worn." Afraid to speak frankly in front of his elder brother, he whispered to them as they left that he did not dare to ask openly for protection, but that he would feel more secure if a few Europeans could be kept in the palace near his room. (Dye and LeGendre stayed in the palace at night and were arranging for two or more Europeans to be in constant attendance, Hillier reported.)[29]

At Waeber's suggestion the five Western representatives—Waeber, Allen, Hillier, Krien, and Lefèvre—took up Miura's invitation and went to the Japanese legation that afternoon to hear what information he had to give regarding the events which had transpired in the palace.

Miura tried to cover up any Japanese involvement in the affair. The *kunrentai*, he alleged, had appealed to the taewongun for redress when jeering policemen had told them they would be disbanded the next day. The taewongun had agreed to intercede on their behalf if they accompanied him to the palace. Relating that he had been aroused by a royal messenger that morning, Miura contended that the official told him that a collision seemed imminent between the *kunrentai* on the one hand and the king's bodyguard and the police on the other hand and had appealed to him for the assistance of the Japanese army. Miura had thereupon dispatched Japanese troops to the palace and shortly afterwards had followed there himself, accompanied by Sugimura. Although the Japanese soldiers arrived too late to prevent the entry of the *kunrentai* into the palace, order had been restored by the time he reached the gate and the Japanese troops were drawn up close by. They had been warned strictly to shun hostilities, and whatever shots had been fired had been exchanged between the palace guard and the *kunrentai*. Who had pulled the first trigger, he did not know, Miura said.

Waeber, who as doyen spoke for all the foreign representatives, asked Miura to comment on eyewitness reports that Japanese troops had escorted the taewongun. Miura denied that Japanese soldiers had been with the old prince. When Waeber observed that there were no policemen in the palace grounds with whom the *kunrentai* could have come into conflict, Miura asserted that the police were stationed at the palace gates. Waeber thereupon charged that some fifty or sixty Japanese in civilian dress armed with swords had participated in the disturbance in the palace. Miura responded that it was possible that a few grooms and servants of the Japanese officers may have accompanied their masters into the palace grounds at daylight or that some of them, like the foreigners, may have gone to see what was happening, but he refuted categorically that they had taken any part in the disturbance.

Waeber retorted, and Allen confirmed, that he himself had seen some twenty or thirty armed Japanese civilians in the palace. When Miura reiterated that they must have been grooms plus perhaps some advisers and students, Waeber revealed that there had been an eyewitness to the events. He scoffed at the idea that civilians who had dragged the court ladies out of the queen's apartments, killing three or four of them in their search for the queen, had been grooms. He remarked that Japanese officers and soldiers had been seen at the scene in addition to a formation of *kunrentai*.

Miura protested that Japanese would not kill women. He had been assured by Japanese officers and men that no such outrage had been committed. Surely their word was more trustworthy than that of the Koreans, who were notorious for spreading absurd rumors, Miura argued.

Waeber shot back that the eyewitness was a European whose testimony was unimpeachable. Besides, the corpses of the women, seen by scores of people, were ample evidence of what had been done.

Reiterating his disbelief, Miura agreed to look into the matter further. Waeber challenged his suggestion that the investigation should be carried out in conjunction with the Korean government, noting that the accusations were levied against Japanese, not Koreans. It was in the interest of the Japanese government to get to the bottom of the affair, he declared. A thorough examination must be made both of the outrages committed by Japanese civilians and of the escorting of the taewongun by Japanese troops. The charges were too serious for a simple denial to be acceptable. The Japanese government, Waeber warned, had incurred "serious responsibilities" when it had set troops in motion.

Miura clung to the story that the troops had been sent at the request of the king and the Korean minister of war. He argued that the low casualties— only ten or twenty persons had been killed—spoke well for the discipline maintained.

Waeber informed Miura that Kojong had requested Allen and himself to try to get the *kunrentai* removed from the palace grounds. Did Miura deem it proper for the king to be guarded by mutineers?

The Japanese minister replied that he had no objection to advising their removal, but he asserted that he had no authority to remedy the situation. He could merely advise, not control.[30]

"Do you believe that no such disturbance will occur again?" Waeber queried.

"I am unable to give any assurance in the matter," Miura replied.

"If that be the case, everyone has to take care of himself," Waeber warned. "I regret such disturbance occurred in spite of the Japanese minister in Korea having under him sufficient soldiers to maintain peace and order in Seoul."[31]

There was ample evidence of Japanese involvement in the attack. General Dye had seen Japanese soldiers escort the taewongun's sedan chair, and the taewongun himself had told Waeber in front of Allen that he had been brought there by Japanese troops. The king's elder brother, who had been living in the city, confirmed the same to Hillier's interpreter, adding that he too had been carried to the palace by Japanese soldiers. He wanted Hillier to know, he said in confidence, that neither his father, the taewongun, nor he had been implicated in the murders that had been committed.

"No sane person can believe that this affair was unpremeditated," Hillier reported. He was confident that the taewongun would not have entered the palace at the invitation of the *kunrentai* "without promise of support from the

inside, and encouragement, if not compulsion, on the part of the Japanese."
To what extent the taewongun himself had been implicated in the murders
would probably never be known. "The protestation of innocence conveyed to
me by his son may possibly be true and [is] believed in by many Coreans,
who regard him as an automaton in Japanese hands," Hillier wrote; "but there
is also a prevalent suspicion that the Japanese civilians, of whose atrocities
Mr. Sabatin was a witness, were hired by the old Prince for the assassination
of the Queen, with whom he had always been at feud." [32]

When Hillier, who had known Prince Yi Chai-miun for a long time, told
him in a private interview at the palace on the afternoon of October 13 that he
and his father, the taewongun, were under the gravest suspicion of "being
implicated in, if not having instigated, the recent murder of the Queen and the
overthrow of the Government," the minister denied the charges. "We did not
know how far it would go," Yi declared in great agitation, twisting his hands
and perspiring profusely. "We got here after the real work was done. Do you
suppose we would join forces with these men who only last winter treated my
son and the grandson of my father with such base indignities, convicting him
of treason and banishing him?" he exclaimed rhetorically. "My father is now
lying sick," the minister continued. "He regrets the whole affair bitterly and
we would both leave the Palace but we fear the King would be murdered if we
go." "Today the King will ask you," he told Hillier, "not to come to see him
anymore. He is compelled to make this request, but he does not mean it. You
must decline and say that you or some other Representative will come daily."

"Now tell me frankly," Hillier inquired, "did Japanese troops attend you as
an escort to the Palace on the eighth?"

"I cannot answer you; it would cost me my life," Yi responded. "Go ask
any ten year old boy on the street what he saw. I cannot talk [any] longer; my
life is in danger."

At these words Hillier looked about and saw a Japanese writing down what
was being said. [33]

To cover his tracks Miura criticized the action of the *kunrentai* in a letter to
the Korean Foreign Office on October 9. He called for the strict punishment of
those guilty of mutinous and disorderly conduct and for the removal of the
kunrentai soldiers as guards in order "to dispell the suspicions of the inhabitants and others." [34] Kim Yun-sik replied that the king, "with a graciousness
as wide as the heavens, in his mercy and liberality," had pardoned the military
commander. He admitted that the action had not been "altogether right" from
the standpoint of "strict principles," and promised to convey Miura's advice
to the minister of war (who had been put into office by Otori the preceding
day) so that appropriate measures could be taken. [35] In a second letter to Kim,

Miura wrote about the allegation that a number of Japanese in plain clothes had entered the palace along with the *kunrentai*. Although he regarded the story as "a fabrication based on hearsay and unworthy of credence," he asked the foreign minister to confirm whether or not there was any truth to it.[36]

Kim replied that according to War Minister Cho Hui-yon some of the Korean soldiers had donned Japanese civilian dress in order to avoid a clash with the guards. He declared that "not a single Japanese had been present during the attack."[37]

Realizing that the Russian government would raise questions about the events in Korea, Saionji tried to keep Nishi informed. In a telegram on October 8 he cabled that one battalion of the *kunrentai*, alarmed at rumors of their disbandment, had forcibly entered the royal palace that morning, bringing the taewongun along as their head. No serious fighting had taken place because Japanese soldiers "rendered assistance to keep order." "Both the King and [the] Crown Prince are safe, but [the] whereabouts of [the] Queen [are] unknown," Saionji telegraphed.[38]

Saionji sent Nishi three follow-up telegrams the next day as more facts became available. In the first, he reconstructed the meeting between Miura and the foreign representatives, quoting some of the dialogue between Waeber and the Japanese minister.[39] In the second telegram Saionji stated that according to a later report by Miura the cause of the disturbance lay in the dissatisfaction of the *kunrentai* which had found support in the "ambition and vengeful spirit" of the taewongun. He echoed the assertion of Miura that the Japanese soldiers had proceeded to the place at the urgent request of the king and had exerted themselves to protect the palace and to preserve order. In view of the allegations that a few Japanese were implicated in the disturbance, a strict investigation was being made. He was confident, however, that even if it were substantiated, "there is no doubt that they are *soshi* who may have found their way to Corea in spite of stringent measures to prevent it and who may have obtained employment by the taewongun." Saionji instructed Nishi to refute in this sense any "erroneous reports" that might be published in St. Petersburg.[40]

The third telegram contained the text of a communication which Nishi was to make to the Russian foreign minister, expressing the "abhorrence" of the Japanese government at the news of the "unfortunate disturbance" in Seoul. It attributed the incident to "intrigue with the taewongun" and the desire for revenge on the part of the newly trained soldiers whose disbandment had been threatened by the Queen's party. Relating that a strict investigation had been ordered in view of the "rumor" that some Japanese had been involved in the event, the Japanese government promised any Japanese implicated in the affair would be "duly dealt with." It expressed the hope that "no misunderstanding should be entertained by [the] Russian Government regarding this regrettable event."[41]

As Lobanov was out of town, Nishi transmitted Saionji's communication to Shishkin, adding the supposition that the Japanese soldiers must not have learned of the unexpected disturbance in time to prevent it. Shishkin thanked Nishi for the information. The telegram received from Waeber had been too short to explain the situation and the tsar had ordered him to consult with Nishi regarding the affair just before he had come. He promised to convey the details to Nicholas shortly.[42]

On October 12 Saionji elaborated on the events in Seoul. Attributing the cause of the "disturbance" to friction between the Korean parties, he admitted that there was the possibility that some Japanese residents had been implicated and that the Japanese minister may not have taken all proper steps to halt it. In view of the fact that the foreign representatives had called at the Japanese legation and that Waeber in particular had attempted to condemn Miura in connection with the occurrence, the Japanese government had decided to investigate thoroughly whether any Japanese residents had indeed been involved and whether Miura had been remiss in his duties, "and if such be the case to punish them strictly." For that purpose, Saionji cabled, the head of the Political Affairs Bureau of the Japanese Foreign Ministry (Komura Jutaro), a prosecuting attorney, and army and navy officers had been sent to Seoul. Since he deemed it possible that Waeber had dispatched a "highly colored report" to St. Petersburg, Saionji instructed Nishi to convey the substance of the above to the tsarist government as far as he deemed it advisable and to ascertain privately and to telegraph both the actual nature of the report made by Waeber and the "attitude and intended action" of the tsarist government regarding the matter. He added that in view of the landing of Russian and American marines, he had issued strict orders to Miura and the Japanese consuls to take stringent measures to prevent any possible collision between Japanese soldiers or residents and the marines. "You will accordingly as your own suggestion request [the] Russian Government to issue similar instructions to [the] Russian Minister to Corea," Saionji concluded.[43]

In response to Saionji's telegram, Nishi called on the chief of the Asiatic Bureau and inquired what Waeber had reported from Seoul. Kapnist related that Waeber had communicated that the Korean minister of the Royal Household and two court ladies had been killed during the disturbance before the eyes of Japanese soldiers and that some Japanese had been implicated in the affair. Kapnist said that the Russian government was waiting for further information; it had no knowledge of the landing of Russian marines.

Nishi reported that although the general impression made by the incident was bad, the tsarist government was favorably impressed by the openness with which the Japanese government had broached the matter to it. No formal comment could be expected from St. Petersburg until the return of Foreign Minister Lobanov within two or three days.[44]

The Korean officials who had come to power with the aid of the Japanese conspirators and remained in office protected by the *kunrentai* lifted from the king all authority and ran the affairs of state as if he did not exist.[45] "He is so hedged in by his fears that he can do only what they wish him to do and must do things he abhors," Allen reported.

To assure Kojong of their sympathy and by their presence to show to his enemies that he must not be harmed physically, the American, Russian, and English representatives went to see him daily, their German colleague less frequently. The king could not speak to them freely, but he found occasion to whisper to Allen about his predicament.[46]

The officials who had seized the reins of government tried to eject General Dye against the wishes of the king. When Dye refused to leave, they moved Kojong away from his rooms. But Waeber and Allen, who visited the palace on October 14, selected new quarters for Dye, putting him once again close to the monarch "to the discomfiture of the assassins who surrounded him."[47]

The Korean cabinet ministers issued as royal decrees documents lacking the king's seal and signature. Among them was a decree, communicated by Foreign Minister Kim Yun-sik to the foreign representatives on October 11, whereby Kojong stripped Queen Min of her rank and degraded her to the position of a commoner for allegedly having caused all the ills of the kingdom and for having gone into hiding after having provoked the uprising of the soldiers.[48]

The pathetic decree deserves being quoted in full:

It is now thirty-two years since I ascended the throne, but my ruling influence has not yet extended widely. The Queen, Min, introduced her relatives into the court and placed them at my side, whereby she dulled my senses by their evil counsel. They oppressed the people and put my government in disorder by selling offices and titles. Hence tyranny prevailed all over the country and robbers arose in all quarters. Under these circumstances the foundation of my Dynasty was in imminent peril. I well knew the extreme wickedness of the Queen, but that I could not dismiss her was really owing to my lack of intelligence and my fear of her party.

In my desire to stop and to suppress her evil influence, I stated among other things in my oath taken at my ancestral temple in the 12th moon of last year, that the Queen and her relatives, as well as my own, should not thereafter be allowed to interfere in the affairs of State, hoping that the Min [Queen] might awake and mend her ways. But still she did not give up her old wickedness, and with her party and a crowd of mean followers she gradually came back to her old position, and watching my movements she managed to prevent the Ministers of State from having interviews with me and moreover she forced from me my decree disbanding the army of my Kingdom in order to instigate and raise a disturbance. When this disturbance actually arose, she left me and escaped as she did in the year Im-o [1882]. I have made enquiries as to her whereabouts, but she does not come forth, which convinces me that she is not only unfitted and unworthy of the Queen's seat, but that her crime is excessive and beyond compass. Therefore, as I, with her, cannot succeed to the virtues of my ancestors of the Royal Temple, I cannot but depose her from the Queen's seat and degrade her to the level of the common people.[49]

Baron d'Anethan, the Belgian minister in Tokyo, was outraged. Calling Kojong "a complete idiot," he fumed that the ludicrousness of this and companion decrees to a corpse revealed "the utter abjectness of this barbaric court."[50] But Lefèvre, the French consul general in Seoul, learned from a good source that Kojong had categorically refused to sign the edict, declaring defiantly: "You will first have to cut off the five fingers of my hand, then I shall sign, if I can do so."[51]

At a meeting of the diplomatic body, to which Miura had not been invited, it was decided that the decree published in the *Gazette* over the signatures of the cabinet ministers only, without the usual royal seal and signature, was not an act of the king.[52] Foreign Minister Kim nervously confided to Chief Commissioner of Customs Brown that this and related documents had not been written in his office. He had been forced, he said, by the five ministers in control of the government to attach his seal to them.[53]

The action of the Korean ministers in deposing the queen rather than proclaiming her death, which they took for granted, was motivated partly by the desire to avoid the traditional three years of mourning.[54] It also opened the possibility, by virtue of an ancient law, to set aside Yi Ch'ok as crown prince and leave Yi Kang, the son of the king by a concubine, as the only person in the way of the taewongun's grandson. (The taewongun had tried to seize Yi Kang, a bright young man popular with the foreigners, but the prince had managed to take refuge in the house of an American missionary.)[55]

Even Miura expressed his shock and distress in a letter to Foreign Minister Kim at the degradation of the queen for her failure to perform her "exalted duties." "I am aware that the august determination of His Majesty has proceeded from a thoughtful regard for his Royal line and the well-being of his people," he wrote. "Still in so unfortunate an event I cannot refrain from expressing my sympathy and sorrow for Your Excellency's Country." [56]

With the resignation of Pak Chong-yang as interior minister, the government had been left in the hands of the five conspirators who had been appointed to their posts while the bodies of the slain queen and her companions were still warm. They were a wanton lot. Yu Kil-chun, who took over as minister of the interior and had long been the key figure in the taewongun's party, had spent several years in prison for alleged complicity in the plot of 1884. A clever, vindictive, and cruel individual who would stop at nothing to advance his own interest, Yu exerted his influence mainly by manipulating the weak prime minister, Kim Hong-jip. Kim Ka-jin, the minister of public works and agriculture and chief of the Privy Council, was keen, cruel, and equally unprincipled; his most intimate friends suspected him of treachery. War Minister Cho Hui-yon was base and cunning. The secretary of the cabinet, Kwan Chai-hyun, was a better person, yet as guilty as the others of the recent troubles. As Allen noted, the above ministers had been put into office by Otori. Inoue had dropped them after getting to know them well, but Miura had reinstated them again. [57]

The Japanese dominated the Korean government through the cabinet ministers, whom Allen described as "facile tools" of Miura, [58] and through Japanese advisers placed in every department. But a few loyalists who had retained their positions kept the Western representatives privately informed of what was happening. Thus the diplomats learned that Miura had compelled the Korean Foreign Office through the Japanese advisers to write him a letter stating that no Japanese troops had come to the palace prior to those sent by him at the request of the king, even though he knew this to be untrue. [59]

The developments in Seoul had alarmed Nicholas. He remarked to Sir Frank Lascelles, the British ambassador to St. Petersburg, during his farewell audience on October 11 that order must be established in Korea. [60] As the landing of Russian and American marines to guard the legations gave rise to the expectation that foreign warships would once again be assembled at Chefoo, [61] Secretary of State Richard B. Olney warned Minister Kurino in Washington that Waeber, in his report concerning the participation of Japanese troops in the coup, had asked for the speedy dispatch of the Russian fleet to Korea. [62] "Lately one talks here with increased emphasis of the necessity of an armed intervention in Korea," Captain Lauenstein reported from St.

Petersburg in mid-October. The German military attaché remarked that most laymen had an exaggerated view of the forces which Russia had for this purpose in Eastern Siberia. However, the military administration was taking steps to increase the combat readiness of the troops in the Amur district and to beef up its units in the South Ussuri region and the Maritime Province.[63]

On October 17 Waeber went to the Korean Foreign Office in response to a long telegram received from St. Petersburg the night before. He demanded that the murderers and instigators of the slaying of the queen and of her ladies-in-waiting be brought to justice. He declared that he would recognize no act of the present Korean government; he would have no communication or intercourse with ministers appointed to the cabinet on the eighth of October.

Hillier, Allen, and Lefèvre shared Waeber's view that the horde of Japanese advisers to the Korean government should be removed along with Miura and that the Korean conspirators and the taewongun should be turned out of office as well. Inoue himself had referred to the Japanese advisers as "offscourings" of his country. There was general agreement among the foreign representatives that Kojong's royal powers should be restored, in so far as possible, to what they had been before the coup.[64]

As the participation of its diplomats and officers in the coup entailing the murder of Queen Min became evident, the Japanese government on October 17 recalled General Miura, Secretary Sugimura, Interpreter Kokubu, Student Interpreter Kusakabe, Military Attaché Major Kusunosuke, Police Inspector Hagiwara, and more than forty other persons. Distressed at having to avow the involvement of Japanese representatives in the foul crime, Saionji told Satow on the eighteenth that it was his hope the European powers would not suppose for a moment that the Japanese government had had a hand in the plot.[65]

On October 18 Saionji confirmed to Nishi that Japanese officers and private individuals had been implicated in the Korean "disturbance." Since the Japanese government had had no connection whatsoever with the affair, he telegraphed, Miura and other officers suspected of having been involved had been recalled and private individuals ordered deported from Korea. Any persons found guilty, Saionji asserted, would be punished regardless of their position. Komura Jutaro, chief of the committee of investigation in Seoul, had been appointed as minister resident in place of Miura. In the event that it be rumored in St. Petersburg that the Japanese government had designed or countenanced the events in Seoul, Nishi was to represent the above to the Russian government and to make use of "every means" to protect Japan.

Saionji added for Nishi's own information that the foreign representatives in Seoul had objected to the Korean foreign minister that the declaration of his government did not correspond to what they had learned about the events of October 8. They had insisted that those involved in the incident must be punished and that the royal decree deposing the queen could not be recognized as expressing the true will of the monarch. Relating to Nishi that the foreign representatives had furthermore protested against Kojong's intention to assume the title of emperor and to select a new queen and that they had questioned the justice of recognizing the present government on the ground that it had been organized against the king's will, Saionji declared that Japan's attitude regarding the above "does not much vary from theirs." [66]

Upon Lobanov's return to St. Petersburg on October 20, Nishi communicated to him the contents of Saionji's telegram in the hope of convincing him that the Japanese government itself had not been connected with the incident. He asserted that Japan's only desire had been and was the establishment of order in Korea on the basis of her independence.

Lobanov acknowledged Nishi's statement. Was it not advisable, he asked, for Japan to withdraw her troops from Korea because nothing worse could happen than the incident of October 8 and because the Korean people, who were said not to like the Japanese, were bound to become much more antagonistic towards them in consequence of the event?

Nishi countered that revolts would break out throughout Korea if the Japanese soldiers were withdrawn. He gained the impression that the argument swayed Lobanov, for the latter seemed to have doubts about the possibility of such an evacuation. It appeared to him that Lobanov had not yet decided what to do regarding the affair. However, the Russian press had begun attacking Japan that day, he reported. [67]

When Nishi learned from reliable sources that the tsarist government was not disposed to raise any questions regarding the Korean trouble for fear of arousing new complications of a grave nature, he called on the chief of the Asiatic Bureau on October 24 to ascertain whether his information was correct. Naturally he did not query him about this directly, but asked whether the time had not come to settle the matter of the exchange of decorations since the long-lasting political question had come to an end and since the trouble which had recently occurred in Korea could not possibly result in any difficulties between their governments as Japan was doing her best in this connection.

Kapnist responded that he had not forgotten about the exchange of decorations, but that he had been preoccupied lately with the Korean incident, "as it was at first reported and thought to be of serious consequence." Now that the matter had been cleared up, he would turn to the exchange of decorations, he said.

Probing further, Nishi asked Lobanov privately whether he thought that the recent Korean trouble would result in any difficulties between their countries. Lobanov replied that he did not think so. He reiterated, however, that it would be advisable for Japan to withdraw her troops from the country. Nishi in turn rechewed the argument that this would be impossible.

"Considering all these [points], I think [the] Russian Government will not raise any difficulties against us concerning [the] recent event," Nishi reported to Saionji. "The papers here have ceased the attacks, though one morning they wrote very strongly against Japan." [68]

Nishi's telegram crossed with Saionji's reply to his report of the twentieth, conveying Lobanov's query concerning the advisability of the withdrawal of Japanese soldiers from Korea. Saionji authorized Nishi to declare in response to Lobanov's suggestion that the Japanese troops were in Korea in order to guard the lines of communication, to maintain tranquility, and to protect the Japanese legation, consulates and subjects. In the absence of a cable between Japan and the Fengtien (Liaotung) Peninsula, it was essential for the Japanese government to have telegraphic contact with the occupied territory by way of Korea. Since some of the occupied points were inaccessible by sea, especially in winter, it was important also to maintain overland routes for transporting supplies. Past experience had taught that such lines of communication through Korea must be guarded at all times. Most of the Japanese troops in Korea were employed in such fashion. "It is [the] fixed intention of [the] Japanese Government immediately upon [the] evacuation of [the] Feng Tien Peninsula to make [an] understanding with [the] Corean Government regarding [the] future operation of these telegraphic lines and to forthwith recall the troops employed in maintaining [the] lines of communication," Saionji pledged.

In regard to the presence of Japanese troops for purposes of peace and protection, Nishi was instructed to express the hope of the Japanese government that in spite of the recent "deplorable incident," the Russian government might prove correct in the expectation that reforms having been set in motion, Korea herself would soon be able to maintain order and protect foreigners. In that event the Japanese government would gladly withdraw the troops stationed in Korea for that purpose, Saionji promised. Having secured the independence of Korea and having repeatedly and unreservedly declared in "unmistakable language" its recognition of her independence, the Japanese government could have no ulterior designs against the integrity of Korea and "would be highly gratified when it could safely recall all its troops from there," Saionji declared.

"In [the] present situation so far as administrative affairs are concerned, [the] policy of [the] Japanese Government is one of noninterference and they will share equally with [the] other Treaty Powers [an] attitude of expectancy only," Saionji telegraphed. "[The] Japanese Government do not doubt," he concluded, "but what these frank and loyal avowals will serve completely to remove all apprehensions of [the] Russian Government." [69]

Nishi took exception to Saionji's instructions. He cabled back that in his humble opinion such a declaration on the part of the Japanese government would at the moment be "unnecessary or at least premature." As he had reported already, even the Russian government appeared unable to make any difficulties for the present. It would not be too late, he thought, to issue the same declaration if any power formally proposed the withdrawal of Japanese troops. He would wait for further instructions, he concluded. [70]

Saionji responded that the purpose of the declaration was to define Japan's attitude toward Korea and to remove the suspicion of the other powers. ". . . we do not wish to create new complications," he assured Nishi. [71]

Meanwhile, on the morning of October 20, Kojong sent a private request to Waeber, Hillier, and Allen that they unite in sending him a guard of their respective soldiers for his personal protection. Waeber expressed willingness to telegraph his government about the matter if Hillier and Allen would do the same. Allen asked if they should not in propriety have the request sent also to the other representatives, including their Japanese colleague. Waeber and Hillier agreed that this would be the proper procedure, but they feared that Komura—who in view of his rank, was then dean of the Diplomatic Corps— might refuse to convene a meeting to consider the royal request. Allen there-upon asked that the issue be shelved until the return of Sill, who was on his way back from Japan, because Sill would take over as dean of the Diplomatic Corps and could be expected to give attention to the message from the king. Waeber and Hillier wished to comply with the king's request, but agreed to wait until Sill got back. [72]

The death of Queen Min had reduced the royal family to three persons: King Kojong, Crown Prince Yi Ch'ok, and Prince Yi Kang. The crown prince was "a young man of weak intellect." The twenty-year-old second prince, on the other hand, was "very bright and a general favorite." Born as an illegitimate son of the king, he had been made legitimate by royal decree in 1892.

As noted, the second prince had found safety in the house of an American missionary during the coup. He had been induced to leave his refuge with the promise that he would be appointed minister to Europe. He was duly ap-pointed minister to England, Russia, France, Germany, Austria, and Italy, but was instructed to go first to Japan to spend some time in study and to learn court etiquette. The king did not want the second prince to go to Japan, nor did the taewongun, who shared the apprehension that he might be kept there by the Japanese. (There was an indication in this, Allen reported, that the taewongun was breaking away from the Japanese and from the conspirators in power.)

The prospect of foreign soldiers entering the palace to guard the king excited the conspirators. On October 21 the minister of war warned Kojong that if foreign troops were to try to enter the palace, the Korean troops would be ordered to resist them to the death. It would be the last year of the conspirators' lives, Cho admitted, but it would be the last year of the king's life as well, he warned.

Despite the threat Kojong continued to urge the foreign representatives to send him a guard.[73]

Sill returned from Japan on October 23. He resumed his duties on the twenty-fourth. At the request of his Western colleagues he convened a meeting of the entire diplomatic body the following day, on October 25,[74] to discuss if there might not be some measures which they could take to assure the safety of the king who was in the hands of his enemies and whose life could be in danger at a given moment.

"What do you think?" Sill asked Hillier.

"I think that it would be proper to seek first the opinion of Mr. Komura," the British consul general replied.

"Having newly arrived in this country, I am not very much abreast of affairs, but I am ready to consider any suggestion made for the sake of assuring the security of the king," the Japanese minister remarked.

"It is clearly an anomaly to see the culprits of October 8 retain power," Waeber declared. "The only thing to do would be to restore matters to the state in which they had been before October 8."

"Viscount Miura acknowledged on October 8 that it was not just that the mutineers should guard the Palace and told us that he would suggest their removal [*renvoi*]," Hillier chimed in. "May I ask of Mr. Komura whether this was done?"

"I have no knowledge that a recommendation of this nature has as yet been made," Komura answered.

"Could not something of this sort be made now?" Waeber queried.

"The first thing to consider is the tranquility of the city, and one can ask oneself if in removing this guard the tranquility would be maintained," Komura countered.

"That would depend on the way the thing were done," Hillier observed.

"There is no danger of troubles in the city, but if things remain as they are, one may fear new troubles in the Palace," Waeber argued. "It is not admissible that one leave these people in possession of what they have taken by force of arms. One can remove them gradually. Besides, many have already saved themselves. I saw yesterday many less than previously."

"A conflict may take place when one removes them from the palace," Hillier interjected.

"One can have them go out without arms and to seize their arms once they have gone out and thus avoid a conflict," Waeber pointed out.

"The king is in a dangerous position; he is in the power of those who have killed the queen," Sill stated. "The motives which caused the assassination of the queen may lead to the doing away [*faire supprimer*] with the king and the crown prince." Turning to Komura, Sill continued: "I believe that an advice [on the part] of your legation would be necessary. Can't you do something to ameliorate this situation? Under the present circumstances even an arbitrary measure would be approved of. I hear that Count Inoue is en route to Korea. I hope that you can do something while waiting for his arrival."

"I am prepared to do all I can for the security of the king and the peace of the city and consequently to consider any proposition on this subject," Komura responded.

"It is no secret to anybody that the movement of October 8 was directed by someone, and that this someone was probably the present minister of war," Waeber observed. "If one dismissed this minister, the removal of the soldiers would be greatly facilitated."

"If one removed the present minister of war from power, the guard would make trouble," Komura objected.

"I must say that I have learned that last night soldiers of the guard went to find the Council of Ministers to demand that they take certain decisions, threatening to force them if they did not want to take these decisions. It seems thus that there would be danger in wanting to change them," Hillier remarked in support of Komura's contention.

"If you," Sill turned to Komura, "were to read to them the articles of law concerning uprisings, that would give them [cause for] reflection. I have great confidence in your power."

"The minister of war threatens all the other officers," Waeber added. "If Mr. Komura were to act energetically and would show them only thirty bayonets, these 300 or 400 soldiers would save themselves, but for this one must act with vigor. Minister of War Cho was at the head of the attack and he remains until now in power because no inquest whatsoever has been made regarding this affair."

"I am prepared to do everything possible for the peace of the Palace and to consider any suggestion on this subject," Komura repeated.

"In that case," Waeber retorted, "I would tell you: arrest the minister of war immediately; that would lead to the settlement of the question."

"Does this minister of war live continuously in the Palace?" Hillier inquired.

"He is sometimes in the Palace, sometimes outside," Waeber responded.

"This personage has so much power that if one were to arrest him, the soldiers would disband by themselves," Sill thought.

"There are also the two commanders of the troops who march in step with Cho," Waeber added.

"The arrival of Count Inoue may render these people determined to do anything; serious troubles may be imminent," Sill warned. "Arbitrary measures are necessary. Arrest them, while your soldiers placed outside prevent the Korean soldiers from entering."

"I would tell you," Waeber continued to Komura, "arrest Cho and the two commanders, make fifty men march through a gate and order the Korean soldiers to lay down their arms at another gate and to go to their barracks until all have left the Palace. Another question is to know the fate of the queen. If she is dead, where has she been buried? Koreans have told me at which spot she has been interred in the Palace. I cannot vouch for the correctness of the information, but this thing is generally believed, especially among the soldiers."

"It is necessary to know what has become of her," Sill agreed.

"Because of Mr. Cho and his friends all search is impossible," Waeber contended.

"This brings [us] back to the first question," Hillier interjected; "nothing can be done without this guard being replaced."

"One has talked lately of having the king change apartments; this has no doubt some connection with the remains of the queen," Waeber observed.

"The king does not ask for a change in residence," Hillier refuted; "he demands only one thing: that the present guard of the Palace be removed."

"The presence of the taewongun in the Palace may be of danger, but if one removes this guard very little power will be left to him," Waeber commented.

"Do you think," Sill addressed Komura, "that some of these suggestions would be feasible? Don't you fear the two or three individuals of whom one has talked? Do some of your soldiers direct and follow the change and prevent the king from falling victim of the same sort as the queen?"

"I regret the present state of affairs, but these remedies do not seem to me without danger," Krien observed.

"There is no danger at all," Waeber retorted. "With fifty men I would take upon myself to execute this operation."

"Me too," Hillier concurred; "I would take it upon myself. The representatives should be present on this occasion. But it is up to Mr. Komura to say whether this is feasible or not."

"I wish to do this in a peaceful manner and it can be made in such a way if one waits for the opportune moment," the Japanese minister responded. "We cannot do it now without employing force."

"Every delay may be dangerous," Hillier protested.

"I would take the necessary precautions that nothing would occur while we wait," Komura replied.

"There may be desperate persons among them who may prefer to be killed and to die together," Sill warned. "One must take precaution to prevent it."

"I understand well that Mr. Komura should not be prepared to act by force," Hillier declared. "He would want, no doubt, to examine this question and to inform us of his decision."

"That is understood," Komura confirmed.

"Could you not inform me of your decision tomorrow?" Sill asked.

"There is no immediate danger and I would take all the necessary precautions while waiting," Komura answered evasively.

"I think that I am expressing the views of my colleagues in saying that we have no objection to the taking of arbitrary measures to arrive at a satisfactory settlement of this question," Sill stated.

"I would be happy to learn the decision of Mr. Komura and to cooperate with him for the common safety," Hillier added.

"I'll let you know when I shall be ready," Komura responded.

"For the moment we rest on the assurance of Mr. Komura that the necessary precautions will be taken to prevent any danger to His Majesty," Hillier concluded.

As the representatives separated, it was agreed that Sill would notify his colleagues when Komura would inform him of his decision.[75]

The above conversation was remarkable for the reticence it showed on the part of the Western representatives to challenge Japan's dominant position in Korea despite the involvement of her subjects in the murder of the queen. Even Waeber called for Japanese restoration of order, rather than for action by his country alone or in conjunction with the other powers. It was ironical that Sill should have been pressing for "arbitrary measures" on the part of Japan, while the latter as the result of Miura's misdoings had withdrawn from his successor all authority over the Japanese troops in Korea.[76]

The Western diplomats looked forward to the arrival of Inoue Kaoru who had been dispatched on October 24 from the Japanese Court to the Korean Court as imperial representative[77] to convey the condolences of the emperor and the empress and their regrets that Japanese subjects had been involved in the plot of October 8.[78] "We expect that under Count Inoue's direction the conspirators will be put out of office and punished and matters restored as they were in so far as is possible," Sill telegraphed home.[79] "It is hoped that this envoy will have to offer to the king more than good words and that he will do what is necessary together with Mr. Komura to put an end to the abnormal situation in which this sovereign finds himself at present," Lefèvre remarked.[80]

Knowing that Inoue was to have an audience with Kojong on the afternoon of November 5, Sill, Waeber, and Hillier proceeded to the Japanese legation that morning. Speaking for himself and his colleagues as dean of the diplomatic corps, Sill told Inoue in the presence of Komura and Inoue's adopted son, Katsunosuke, that they had come to consult with him and Komura on the present situation, which he and his colleagues regarded as "very grave." With Inoue's permission, Sill read from a paper prepared by the three representatives. They had been informed, he recited, that at the audience which Inoue was to have with the king later in the day, Kojong would be made to say that no Japanese had been involved in the occurrences of October 8 and that none but the Korean officers of the *kunrentai* now in possession of the palace had been responsible for them. Such a statement would be untrue as the king well knew. If he uttered it, he would do so "under compulsion and threats of assassination . . . by members of the usurping cabal in the cabinet." There was "imminent danger," the representatives warned, of deeds being perpetrated in the palace on a par with and possibly worse than those which had occurred exactly four weeks ago. Surrounded by soldiers and officers who had gained their positions by mutiny, violence, and bloodshed, the king was terrified. He was in such constant fear for his life that he could not take his necessary food or rest. His anxieties and privations plus the knowledge that spies were watching his every move and word forced him to make statements which he and everyone else knew to be false.

"This condition of affairs, in which the Sovereign, whose word should be taken as law, is held a prisoner by a small faction who happen for the moment to command the movements [?] of the only efficient native force in the capital, and is constrained by them to do their bidding even to the extent of outraging his most delicate feelings in regard to his late Queen (who is universally believed to have been foully murdered) is most detrimental to the peace and reform of the country, and fraught with danger to its external relations," Sill read.

Deeply concerned as the foreign representatives were in the peace of Korea and the safety of the king, to whom they were accredited, Sill continued, they could not countenance the proceedings which had resulted in the present highly strained and dangerous situation and appealed unhesitatingly to Count

Inoue to cooperate in restoring the *status quo* and in giving back to Kojong "his personal liberty: his safety, and freedom of action." The only step necessary to attain that end was the removal of the mutinous troops and officials now surrounding the king and their replacement by guards in whom Kojong had confidence. "With the power now at the command of the Japanese legation the required change of the palace guard would seem to be a matter of no difficulty," the foreign representatives asserted. "We are ready to cooperate to the extent of our power, and if the change is not made, the responsibility for the consequences that may follow must, we fear, rest upon Japan." With the removal of the present guard from the palace and the restoration of Kojong's freedom of action and speech, they argued, it would be possible to discover the whole truth of what had happened, which was essential for the maintenance of future tranquility.

When Sill had finished reading, Inoue asked if he could consider the meeting to be informal in nature. Sill, Waeber, and Hillier agreed to regard it as such and to exchange views on the situation. Hillier remarked that he had joined in the gathering at the invitation of his colleagues in order to provide Inoue and Komura with any information in his possession which they might desire as well as in order "to offer his services and cooperation in the execution of any measures which might by common consent be considered to be advisable to secure the safety of the King," something he felt sure Inoue and Komura "had equally at heart with the other Representatives."

Inoue expressed his gratification that from what had been said, no suspicion was entertained of the complicity of the Japanese government in the affair of the eighth. When the three representatives confirmed the impression, Inoue went on to relate that since his arrival in Korea he had learned many facts which had altered his views of the situation. He recognized the danger to which Kojong was exposed and concurred with the general opinion that he must be relieved from the state of duress in which he was being kept. But unfortunately the conduct of Miura had aroused foreign as well as Korean suspicions of Japanese action, Inoue argued. If Japan were to remove the guard and restore the *status quo* without the cooperation of the representatives of the other powers in Korea her action might be misconstrued and criticized; joint action was, therefore, essential.

Sill responded that while he disapproved strongly of the many arbitrary acts which had lately been done in Korea, he was willing to assure Inoue of his full and unqualified support for arbitrary acts Japan might now think necessary in order to secure the end they all desired. Waeber replied in a similar vein; he offered to cooperate "to the full extent of his power." Hillier asked what Inoue meant by "joint action." Kojong had repeatedly asked the foreign representatives to join with the Japanese legation in sending in guards for his protection. Hillier had persistently refused to convey such proposals to his government, he said, unless it was spontaneously raised by Inoue or Komura. He would be glad to know, therefore, how far Inoue's recommendation for joint action was meant to go.

Inoue answered that by joint action he did not mean the direct participation of American, Russian, and British marines in the removal of the guards. This the Japanese garrison could do by itself. Unless each representative wished to take a few men for appearance's sake, he stated, what he desired was to be able to inform his government that all the representatives were agreed on the necessity of some action being taken and that they were working in unison. Sill, Waeber, and Hillier voiced their willingness to cooperate with Inoue in devising measures for the relaxation of the present tension.

Repeated attempts had been made by various members of the Korean cabinet to learn what he had proposed to do, Inoue continued, but he had evaded their questions by telling them that he was in Seoul simply as a special ambassador from the Japanese emperor to convey His Majesty's condolences to King Kojong. He asserted that he was glad to have been forewarned of the statement which the king was supposed to make under duress and would take care to provide no opportunity for such a statement. He would confine himself to presenting the letter and gifts which he had brought and would withdraw immediately thereafter.

The Korean prime minister, Kim Hong-jip, had asked for an interview with him the next day, Inoue revealed. He would sound him out about the views of the Korean government regarding the present situation. He would refrain from expressing any opinion himself except to inquire, in view of the fact that the Japanese government was putting Miura and other Japanese suspected of involvement in the recent plots on trial, what steps the Korean government was taking in a similar direction. He promised to convey the results of the conversation to the foreign representatives promptly.

With regard to the measures that were to be taken to relieve Kojong, Inoue declared, the removal of the taewongun seemed to him the first essential step, as the old prince was "the main-spring of the situation." From information in his possession, it appeared that it would not be difficult to convince the taewongun that his presence was undesirable; once he had been removed, the guards could be dismissed as well. Komura would confirm his opinion that no opposition to the entry of Japanese soldiers into the palace was probable, as it had already been suggested by the Korean minister of war, Inoue observed. But the sanction of the Japanese government must be obtained before anything could be done, he added.

The German consul, Krien, arrived at the Japanese legation at this point and raised the question what measures should be taken to protect the king while the transfer of the guard was being undertaken. It was agreed that it might be advisable for some of the foreign representatives to remain with Kojong during the process. It was "distinctly understood" that the Japanese occupation of the royal palace would last only until a fresh Korean guard, in whom the king had confidence, could be gotten together.[81]

The discussion of the Korean situation had been free and friendly, Komura and Inoue reported to Saionji in a joint telegram. They cabled that Sill, acting as spokesman for the foreign representatives, had urged the forceful removal by Japanese troops of the Korean minister of war and other chief officials as well as of the soldiers guarding the palace, but that he, Inoue, had opposed such unilateral action on the part of Japan for fear of creating new complications and had urged joint steps by all the foreign representatives. He had pointed to the need of beginning with the removal of the taewongun from the palace, but had reiterated that "recourse should not be had to forcible measures as far as possible," because another movement of Japanese troops was bound to arouse foreign suspicion. He had promised to inform the foreign representatives of the results of his conversation with the Korean premier the following day and they had agreed to consult further thereafter.

"Although it is our firm intention not to resort to forcible measures," Komura and Inoue telegraphed, "yet in the present situation we fear there is no other course open to us than ultimately guard [the] palace by our troops." They speculated that if this were done in response to both the request of Kojong and the recommendation of the foreign representatives, no serious consequences need be apprehended, and asked that the officer in command of the Japanese troops in Seoul be instructed to place them in the palace as guards upon the demand of the Japanese legation.[82]

When Inoue saw Kojong on November 5, he transmitted to him a letter from the Meiji emperor, expressing his profound regret that Japanese subjects had been implicated in the affair of October 8 and conveying his condolences. "In assuring you of my respect and my sincere affection, I wish you everlasting tranquility [*tranquillité sans fin*]," Mutsuhito wrote.[83] Inoue also presented some gifts from his sovereign. As he had promised to the foreign representatives, he did not touch on Korean affairs and the conversation was limited to polite platitudes.[84]

The interview which Premier Kim had with Count Inoue in the forenoon of November 6 lasted for several hours. Inoue evaded giving any advice on the Korean situation. He did strongly condemn the murder and subsequent degradation of the queen. While the act of assassination in itself had been a most infamous crime, the outrageous decrees defaming the dead queen had formed the blackest page in Korean history, Inoue declared. Why, he asked, had the premier put his seal to these infamous decrees? When Kim replied that he had been threatened with death if he did not comply with the demands of the officers in charge of the *kunrentai*, Inoue reminded him that he had repeatedly asserted his willingness to lay down his life for the king and queen. Why had he not taken this opportunity to demonstrate his loyalty?

He thought that he could serve the sovereign better if he was alive than dead, the premier replied lamely. He disputed the allegation that the tae-wongun was a constant menace to the life of the king and must, therefore, be removed from the palace. Being Kojong's father, Kim contended, the old prince wished no harm to the latter.

A man's character could be judged only from his past acts and deeds, Inoue rejoined. If a habitual thief said that he would not steal anymore, could one trust his words? Pointing to the "bloodthirsty tendencies" which the tae-wongun had displayed in the massacre of Christians in years past and recapit-ulating his repeated involvement in coups directed against Kojong and his late consort, Inoue insisted that he should be gotten out of the palace as soon as possible.

The premier responded that he knew a man who could remove the tae-wongun quietly if it was considered essential. In response to Inoue's query whether the minister of war could be removed as well, Kim answered that this would be much more difficult. Though Cho, like himself, had been the victim of compulsion, the officers who had forced him to accept the post would forcibly resist his arrest fearing that his dismissal would be their own death knell. Trying to exonerate the other members of the present cabinet as well, Kim asserted that they had gone along with the decree deposing the queen, caught between the threats of the mutineers and the fear that an acknowledge-ment of her death would lead to their own implication in the affair.

Asked why the palace guard had recently been doubled, Kim related that there was intimation of a plot to remove the king from the palace. A number of Korean officials had taken refuge in the American and Russian legations. A letter from one of them, in the Russian legation, asking Kojong to dress in common clothes sent in an accompanying parcel and to escape to the Russian legation had come into the possession of the taewongun, who had become alarmed and had doubled the guard.

Inoue dismissed the story as a stupid invention.[85]

On the morning of November 8 Komura came to the United States legation and requested Sill to communicate to the other foreign representatives that the Japanese government was unwilling to take the initiative in securing by force the dismissal of the present palace guard, the safety of the king, and his freedom from duress. Japan would act only if the other treaty powers approved in advance in writing the temporary occupation of the palace by her troops.

Sill called a meeting of the Western representatives that afternoon. They drafted a memorandum which Sill presented to Komura in reply that evening. They had already expressed their verbal opinion that it was essential for the safety of the king and the peace of the city for the present guard to be removed and the palace to be occupied by Japanese troops temporarily, the representatives stated. Noting that they had telegraphed home on the subject, they suggested that Japan refer to their respective governments for their opinions.[86]

"[The] Japanese are not moving to restore [the] status upset by themselves," Sill cabled to Washington in code. "The King is still in grievous peril and under [the] duress of [the] conspirators. The Representatives of England, Russia, France and myself are urging [the] Japanese to protect the King and restore [the] status by necessary force."[87]

The state of affairs in Seoul was growing worse by the day, Sill wrote on November 9. The king was a prisoner in his palace and was compelled to submit to various indignities by threats of bodily harm. The foreign representatives felt for him deeply; some of them called upon him daily to assure him of their sympathy. They had hoped that Inoue would right the wrong done by his countrymen, but the count had been in Seoul for ten days now and nothing had been done towards giving Kojong his liberty, restoring the *status quo*, recovering the remains of the queen, or punishing the guilty. "On the contrary," Sill reported, "the Japanese seem to feel a private satisfaction at the removal of the obnoxious Queen, and to have a secret desire to sustain the conspirators who are loyal to Japan, lest a new Cabinet might be pro-Russian in sympathy."

Aware of the Japanese attitude, the conspirators had grown increasingly bold in recent days and had arrested high officials who had been loyal to the queen. They had increased the number of policemen at the foreign legations and had doubled the guard about the king.

The sudden reluctance of the Japanese to intervene in Korean affairs when the foreign representatives asked them to do so made the case take on a very bad aspect, Sill observed, since things were left "altogether too favorable to Japan" as a result of the events of October 8. "The Russians," he noted, "have acted very favorably to Japan so far, but it is thought that if Japan shows no earnest intention to right the wrong she has done here, Russia may have to interfere."[88]

The reluctance of the Japanese to move against the guard occupying the palace and against the ministers implicated in the events of October 8 was understandable, the French representative reported. However much the current occupants of the Japanese legation might disapprove of what had been done, the guards were Japanese-trained and their officers, like the ministers, had been drawn from among the partisans of Japan. "To sacrifice her best friends in response to the demands of the foreign representatives must understandably appear very painful to the Japanese government . . . ," Lefèvre perceived.[89]

On November 9 Sill cabled in cipher that Japan would restore the status by "temporary force" if the foreign representatives concurred. Noting that the Russian government had already telegraphed its approval and that answers were expected from the other powers, he expressed the hope that the American secretary of state would wire his sanction.[90]

On the morning of November 12 the representatives of the United States, Russia, and Great Britain called on Komura at the Japanese legation to talk about the Korean situation. Although Sill as dean of the diplomatic corps normally spoke for the group, he declared that Waeber had some remarks of a personal nature to offer and asked him to open the conversation.

After reiterating that his comments were to be taken as the expression of his private opinion, Waeber began with the observation that in view of the fact that Russia was the nearest neighbor of Korea, her interest in the welfare of that country was "naturally as great as, if not greater than that of any other Power." The instructions which he had received when he had been appointed as the representative of the tsar at Seoul ten years ago, and to which he had adhered to the best of his ability, directed him "in general terms, to do everything in his power to promote peace and harmony and to further the best interests of the King and his dominion." The peace and harmony which his government wished to see preserved had been disturbed on no less than four occasions within the past fifteen months, Waeber pointed out: firstly, last July when the palace had been occupied by Japanese troops during a time of peace; secondly, when the taewongun had been taken from his seclusion and placed in power; thirdly when Pak Yong-hyo, who could not possibly have been a *persona grata* with the king or the government, was forced into office; and fourthly, on October 8, when the queen had been murdered with the knowledge and assistance of Japanese subjects, the Japanese legation itself having been implicated. Waeber reminded Komura that he had warned Otori of the danger of bringing the taewongun forward and of employing force in the introduction of reforms. He and Sill had likewise pointed to the peril of returning Pak to office. Count Inoue in his conversation with Premier Kim, had characterized the decree deposing the queen as one of the blackest pages in

Korean history, Waeber observed. The degrading, he noted, had been done by Korean ministers who had been brought to power by the Japanese legation. The attack on the palace by the subjects of another nation with the intention of murdering the queen, it seemed to him, "was perhaps a blacker spot on the history of that nationality than the degradation of the Queen, which Count Inoue so strongly and justly condemned."

In view of the fact that the various above-mentioned disturbances of peace and tranquility had been caused by the Japanese legation, Waeber continued, he had pointed out to Inoue, when the latter had come to the Russian legation several days ago to say that his government was not disposed to take military action to restore peace and tranquility unless specifically requested by the foreign powers to do so, that he thought that the Japanese government was under an obligation to take the initiative in putting matters straight. It was their duty also, he had stated, to redress the wrong done to Korea and especially to the king whose consort had been killed. "All the Governments of the world would look to Japan to take the first step in righting these wrongs, and would receive with surprise a request to invite the Japanese Government to take action and to assure it that its action would be approved," he had argued.

Meanwhile, Waeber related, he had telegraphed to St. Petersburg that it had been universally admitted at an interview with some of the foreign representatives that the safety of the king and the restoration of peace and order could be effected only by the adoption of strong measures and that it had been proposed that Japanese troops should enter the palace under certain conditions to protect Kojong. Since the dispatch of his cable, Komura had expressed the hesitancy of the Japanese government to take such measures for fear of complications with the foreign powers. He therefore begged to inform him now, Waeber declared, that he had received a telegram from the Russian government to the effect that it would acquiesce in any steps that might be taken, within the agreed limitations, for the restoration of order. In other words, Waeber assured Komura, if the Japanese troops were moved in the manner and with the limitations to which he, Waeber, had already agreed, no complications need be feared on the part of the Russian government. Stressing that in everything he had said he wished to convey his desire to see the securing of peace, order, and tranquility and the upholding of the authority of the king, Waeber asked, and expressed the hope that his colleagues would join him in asking, what steps the Japanese government intended to take in this direction. "The situation was critical," he underlined, "matters were not by any means quiet, and every day's inaction increased the danger."

Komura replied that he highly appreciated the friendly attitude of the Russian government and its readiness to support measures for the restoration of order and for securing the safety of the monarch. He wanted to know, he said turning to Sill and Hillier, whether their respective governments had also given their approval of this arrangement.

Sill responded that he had twice cabled to Washington that he and his colleagues strongly recommended the use of force if necessary to secure the restoration of order and the safety of the king. He had not received a reply, he admitted, but thought that silence meant approval. However, at the urgent request of Komura, he agreed to telegraph again and request an answer. He warned that he might still not receive a direct reply, but felt, he said, that the United States government would trust his discretion. Indeed, he went so far as to state positively that he had no doubt of his government's approval of the proposed action. Contending that Japan was going too far in demanding a request from every treaty power for her to act, Sill remarked that Komura surely did not mean to say that Japan was waiting for an answer from all the governments represented in Korea before she would take action. When Komura retorted that this was precisely the case, Sill uttered exasperatedly that then she would never act. He could not believe, he said pointedly, that the Japanese government was seriously expecting an authorization from all the foreign powers to redress a wrong for which its countrymen were responsible.

This would be tantamount to turning the tables completely, Waeber chimed in. "It was the duty of Japan to retrieve the situation and not to sit with folded hands until she was solicited to take action by more or less disinterested Powers," he declared. He made it clear that the Russian government had not "invited" Japan to act; it had merely stated that there would be no complication as far as Russia was concerned if Japan did what she was in duty bound to do.

Sill interposed that he had not asked his government to invite Japan to take action. Neither had he, Hillier declared. He too had informed his government of the suggestion made by the foreign representatives for Japanese occupation of the palace and of Komura's remark that he felt assured that such a step would not meet with the objection of the powers. Like Sill he felt that the absence of a reply from his government signified acquiescence. If the Japanese government wished to ascertain the views of his government it must do so either through the British minister in Tokyo or through the Japanese minister in London. It would be irregular for him in Seoul to solicit an opinion on behalf of the Japanese government.

Komura said that under the circumstances he would, with their permission, telegraph to his government that Sill, Waeber, and Hillier had voiced the opinion that the Japanese government should take the initiative in restoring order and securing the safety and freedom of the king by the temporary occupation of the palace with its troops. By "temporary," he explained, he meant until the guard was considered no longer necessary by the king or the foreign representatives.

A telegram in which Komura faithfully rendered the above exchange was drawn up and its wording approved by the foreign representatives.[91]

Waeber thereupon reiterated that the current situation was dangerous. The usurping cabinet, he warned, was getting bolder every day in the belief that the powers acquiesced in the inaction of the Japanese government and that it need not fear outside interference. Noting that it was freely stated that measures would be taken shortly to deny any access to the king, Waeber warned that "if any attempt was made to prevent him from entering the palace or from seeing the King, he would take in a guard of Russian sailors and the responsibility of any conflict arising from it would rest with Mr. Komura as it would be caused by circumstances which he had the power to prevent."

Sill echoed the implication that the Japanese government supported the usurping cabinet by not moving against it. He agreed with Waeber's contention that every day's inaction strengthened the latter and emphasized the danger of further delay.[92]

Informed of the views of the foreign representatives in Seoul and of the general concurrence of Komura and Inoue with these views, though they balked at the idea of Japan taking the initiative, Saionji replied that Japan must abide by the declaration she had recently made to the powers regarding noninterference in Korean affairs and that she could not resort to military action unless the powers freed her from all responsibility in the matter by making an open request to that effect.

Saionji telegraphed to Nishi and Hayashi that he had informally apprised the British, German, French, American, and Russian ministers in Tokyo of the above and that all but Hitrovo had appeared to agree with him. There was reason to suspect, he cabled, that the action of the foreign representatives in Seoul did not correspond with the views of their respective governments.[93]

Told by the Russian and French ministers that Inoue was the "prime mover" in the idea of having Japanese troops occupy the royal palace, Saionji sent him a careful warning. He expected to discuss the matter with him face-to-face shortly, as Inoue was about to return to make a personal report of the situation in Korea.[94]

Inoue and Komura denied that they had ever proposed the guarding of the palace with Japanese soldiers. They had merely ascertained the views of the

Russian and American ministers in Korea. Waeber, they reported, asserted that the purport of the telegram he had sent to Lobanov differed from what Hitrovo had shown to Saionji.[95]

Inoue had arrived in Seoul on October 31. As he was departing for Tokyo on November 16, he explained to the Western representatives that he was leaving so soon because he had come on a mission of condolence only. He had no power to restore or reorganize the Korean government and had to return posthaste to acquaint the Japanese cabinet with the exact condition of affairs in Seoul. He expressed the hope that upon hearing his account, the Japanese government might change its attitude and consent to the temporary use of Japanese troops to protect the king and secure his liberty. He was taking with him to lay before the cabinet copies of the memoranda and papers drawn up in regard to his talks with the foreign representatives.

Sill was not optimistic about the outcome of Inoue's discussions in Tokyo. The "most unusual reluctance" of the Japanese government to use its troops to repair the wrong which they had helped to perpetrate and the tenor of the Japanese press compelled him to believe, he wrote, that while the Japanese government "regret the manner in which the Queen was taken off, they are glad she is out of the way, and intend to support the usurping cabinet." [96]

Although the French consul general in Seoul had refrained from joining in the discussion concerning the occupation of the royal palace by Japanese troops[97] in the absence of instructions from his government,[98] he sympathized with his Western colleagues. Unsurprised as he was that Japan hesitated to remove from power Korean partisans of her own influence, Lefèvre regretted that the various démarches made by the American, Russian, and English representatives to the Japanese minister were not more fruitful. The populace of Seoul knew about the negotiations, and their lack of success, he feared, would have an adverse effect on the prestige of the Europeans in the country.[99]

Sill was mistaken in assuming that the American government would trust his discretion. In a telegram dispatched from Washington on the evening of November 11 and received the following night, that is to say after the interview at the Japanese legation, Secretary of State Olney reminded him curtly that intervention in the political concerns of Korea was not among Sill's functions and was forbidden by diplomatic instructions no. 64.[100]

Sill justified his action. He had been guided, he replied, by the mutual promise of the exercise of friendly offices stipulated in the treaty between the United States and Korea and by the instructions he had received on June 23, 1894, "to use every possible effort for the preservation of peaceful conditions." He had been doing what he could to ameliorate a situation which to this day endangered the life of the king, usurped his freedom of speech and

action, and imperiled the peace of Korea and especially of Seoul. In view of
the fact that, in so far as he knew, the United States had not expressed any
disapproval of the violent capture of the palace in July 1894 and of other
arbitrary acts by the Japanese in Korea, he had felt safe in telling Inoue and
Komura that he did not think that his government would object to the proposed temporary use of force to secure the safety and the liberty of the king.
Asking Olney to check him if he had gone wrong, Sill pledged to adhere to the
spirit of the secretary's latest instructions.[101]

"Confine yourself strictly [to the] protection of American citizens and interests," Olney telegraphed the same day. He reiterated that Sill was not to concern himself with the internal affairs of Korea and was to stay clear of démarches. "Your actions," he cabled, "[are] to be taken independently of [the]
other Representatives, unless otherwise instructed." [102]

On November 26 the foreign representatives were asked to come to the
palace without wearing their uniforms. After being received by Kojong in the
Audience Hall, they were led to a waiting room where Foreign Minister Kim
Yun-sik and Prince Yi Chai-miun brought to them the text of a decree signed
by the king and cosigned by all members of the cabinet except the minister of
war, announcing the restoration of the late Queen Min to her title and the
revocation of the decree which had deprived her of it. Following the reading
of the document the foreign representatives once more met with the king, who
informed them also that he had issued orders for the arrest of those guilty of
the crimes of October 8.

When Sill expressed satisfaction at Kojong's action and declared that he
had never recognized the decree of October 8 degrading the queen as coming
from the king, the interpreter asked whether he could say that the last remark
was made on behalf of his colleagues also. Before Sill could reply that he was
speaking for himself only, Komura burst out with a resounding "No!" But
Waeber backed up Sill and declared that he too had never recognized the
decrees of October 8. Hillier congratulated Kojong on the step he had taken
and expressed the hope that it might mark the beginning of a peaceful period
for him and his dominion. Krien and Lefèvre said nothing.[103]

The feeling on the part of the foreign representatives that the measures
taken by the Korean government meant a change for the better was shortlived.
An attempt by some thirty loyalists backed by about 150 soldiers to capture
the palace during the night of November 27 to 28 in order to restore to the
king his liberty and punish the usurping cabinet indicated that people had little
faith in the actions of the officials in power.[104]

The coup had been planned by several officers of the old royal body guard,
who believed that the queen was still alive and who wished to prepare the way

for her return to the palace.[105] Yin Cheu-son, who was employed in the royal household, forged a decree by the king ordering the soldiers of the old guard to come to the palace. Yi To-chol sought out the soldiers and put himself at their head.[106]

The American minister had learned of the plot at about 5:30 P.M. on the twenty-seventh. After consulting with Waeber and Hillier, who had hastened to the United States legation upon hearing similar stories, he had written a letter to Komura asking if he too had received word that an attempt was imminent to bring relief to the king. The Japanese minister had left for the palace and no reply was gotten from him until the following day. But the very fact that Komura had proceeded to the palace strengthened the portent of impending trouble.

For some time Sill had permitted, at Kojong's request, one or two American missionaries to sleep in General Dye's quarters at the palace to give moral support to the king by their presence. Because the British physician working at the Korean Government Hospital as an employee of the American Presbyterian Society had been summoned by Kojong, Sill allowed two American missionaries to accompany him to the palace. To assure their admission, he gave them his card and sent along one of the legation runners. When shots rang out during the night, the missionaries, toting revolvers in their pockets, hastened to the monarch's door. Kojong eagerly let them in and held the hand of one or the other during the remainder of the night, while General Dye supervised the defense of the palace.

The foreign representatives, who had gone to bed after instructing the legation guards to keep a sharp lookout, were awakened at 10:30 P.M. after three pistol shots had rung out, and again at 3:00 A.M. when great shouting was heard from the direction of the palace. Meeting in the lane at the back of their adjoining compounds, Waeber, Hillier, and Sill decided to go to the palace with their secretaries to see what was afoot. Waeber suggested that they take along a guard, but his colleagues objected, and they went without a military escort.

As the three representatives were starting for the palace, unsigned letters were handed to the servants of their legations announcing that the soldiers of the old royal body guard were gathering their forces "to kill the traitors of the Government and wash away their infamous names."[107] The missives asked the Western representatives not to be alarmed, but to come to the palace to support the king.

A longer letter, addressed to Komura, declared that "bent things necessarily stretch out and that false charges should be washed off." Accused unjustly of traitorous murder, the soldiers intended to kill the traitors of their country and by this action "wash off the foul name which has unjustly been given to them." Though the entire city be "crushed to pieces like fish flesh," the insurgents declared, they were determined to remove the stain on their honor. At the same time they asked Komura not to be anxious. The number of traitors they planned to kill did not exceed ten. Since Japan's aim was to aid reforms in Korea, they argued, Komura should pacify the minds of his countrymen and have them not stand in the way.[108]

As the Western representatives did not have an interpreter with them and the letters were written in a mixture of Chinese and Korean, they understood at the moment only the general drift that there was trouble, but that they should not be alarmed. At this juncture Vice Minister of Foreign Affairs Yun Chi-ho appeared and asked Waeber, Hillier, and Sill to do everything in their power to avert danger to the life of the king. The diplomats had already decided to proceed to the palace. Yun's appeal strengthened their resolve to avert a disturbance or at least try to preserve the king's life by their presence.

As they approached the rear gate of the palace accompanied by the vice minister, they learned that the insurgents had not gained access to the palace and that Kojong was safe. Believing that the conspirators might have been misled by indiscreet expressions of sympathy and interest on the part of the missionaries to count unduly on foreign support, the representatives sent word to the attackers through a follower of Yun that they were wrong in what they were trying to do and should disperse at once. They themselves went back to their homes immediately.[109]

The plot had failed, because the allies whom the loyalists believed to have inside had not opened the gates for them as arranged. When War Minister Cho arrived at the scene and forbade the soldiers accompanying the conspirators to fire their guns, the revolt collapsed. The leaders of the émeute were arrested without a single shot being discharged.[110]

Adherents of the king who had taken refuge in the American legation had not known of the conspiracy until just before Sill himself had learned of it. One of the refugees at the Russian legation may have been privy to this or some other plot. He had allegedly corresponded with an officer of the *kunrentai* who professed to be in sympathy with the insurgents. But whether out of fear or with malice aforethought, the officer had surrendered the correspondence and had failed to assist the attacking party.[111]

The Japanese government suspected that several Americans had been directly involved in the affair and that Sill and Waeber had either instigated the plot or given it their tacit approval.[112] Sill denied American involvement. The reports spread concerning the complicity of his compatriots posed a danger to the lives of the eighty American men, women, and children residing in Seoul.

"The Japanese," Sill complained, "seem to be making the utmost of any suspicions that can by any means be interpreted to the disadvantage of Americans and other foreigners in order apparently to call away attention from the horrors of the 8th October, which they have never yet seriously investigated."

The Westerners were now witnessing in Korea the reign of terror he had predicted, Sill wrote. The failure of the plot had strengthened the hand of the taewongun and his adherents. The old prince's word once again was law. He was said to have marked for death some 800 Koreans who had been especially friendly to foreigners. Two members of the government who had been educated in the United States—Minister of Education So Kwang-pom and Vice Minister of Foreign Affairs Yun Chi-ho—had already been arrested.[113]

Eight of the Koreans on the taewongun's list were refugees in the American legation. Waeber, who had granted asylum to a number of Koreans, had sent two refugees to Chemulpo, where they had been taken aboard a Russian man-of-war.[114] Sill wanted to do the same and get the Koreans in his legation abroad for a short time before the government demanded their surrender. Though no charges had been levied against the eight individuals, he feared that they might simply be taken away as witnesses and tortured to death in the process of examination. As the *Yorktown* was due to leave Shanghai shortly, Sill in a telegram of December 1 and again in his dispatch of the second requested Olney to authorize the commander-in-chief to grant them passage.[115]

Olney disapproved. Sill had no right to shelter refugees from arrest by officers of the *de facto* government and the proposed use of the *Yorktown* was "wholly inadmissible." "The Department," he reprimanded him on December 2, "sees with disfavor your disposition to forget that you are not to interfere with local concerns and politics of Korea, but are to limit yourself strictly to the care of American interests."[116] "Your course in continued intermeddling with Korean affairs in violation of repeated instructions noted with astonishment and emphatic disapproval," Olney telegraphed on January 11, 1896. He instructed Sill to cable any explanation he had to make and to answer whether he intended to comply with the instructions he had been given.[117]

Sill replied that he had unintentionally erred in certain points. Asserting that no harm had resulted in Korea, he promised that henceforth the secretary of state would have no cause for criticism. "I will act according to instructions scrupulously," he pledged.[118] In a subsequent dispatch Sill detailed that he had not sheltered the refugees from the officers of the *de facto* government, that he had warned them that he would have to give them up upon the proper demand of the authorities, and for that reason had wanted to get them out of the country before such a demand was made. He had gone wrong, Sill admitted, in alluding to the decree of October 8 even though the king had communicated directly to the American legation that it had been issued contrary to his wishes while he was powerless to resist. He had erred likewise, Sill continued, in hesitating with his colleagues to give full credence to the Foreign Office dispatch announcing the death of the queen. As regarded the accusation that he did not follow his instructions to act independently, however, he pointed out that it was his duty as dean of the diplomatic corps to call conferences of his colleagues and to submit conclusions on behalf of the body. "This may sometimes have given the impression of joint action when there was no previous intention of acting otherwise than independently," he contended. "I regret that the position of Doyen falls to me, since it often gives me a prominence of action that I would by no means seek or desire." Living in an atmosphere of "continued and often arbitrary and violent interference in Korean affairs," which occasionally threatened American interests and lives, he added, there was the temptation "to meet interference with counter-interference." He promised to make "no further errors in this direction" and to exercise "extra caution" to remain within his instructions.[119]

The fact that the abortive plot had been instigated by adherents of the queen[120] on the assumption that she was still alive prodded the government to acknowledge her demise. In a royal decree published in the official *Gazette* on December 1 and in letters written to the foreign representatives by Foreign Minister Kim the same day, it declared that it was now positively known that the queen had expired on the morning of October 8. Since the queen had been proclaimed dead once before, in 1882, and the people had mourned her loss for six weeks when she had suddenly reappeared at the palace one day, a large part of the population was convinced that she would show up again when her enemies were no longer in power. Even some of the foreign representatives were in doubt of the real facts, but when Komura stated that he was "very positive" that she was no longer alive, they agreed to accept the announcement and to express their condolences.[121]

The Korean populace was ordered to mourn for the late queen for a period of one year beginning on December 10. The funeral services were scheduled to take place in five months, because according to Korean custom seven months must pass between the date of death and the date of interment.[122]

On December 29 the *Official Gazette* announced the execution of three Koreans implicated in the events of October 8. Pak Sen, a young man in the employ of the Japanese, was convicted of seizing the queen by the hair and piercing her with his sword. The charges against Yun Suk-wu, a lieutenant of the old guard, and Yi Ju-hoi, former vice minister of war, were less specific. Yun was accused of having seen the burning of the queen's body and of having returned to the spot later to bury the charred bones of the queen's body secretly. Yi was charged with giving incredible explanations for his presence in the palace.[123]

The Korean scapegoats were comparatively insignificant individuals without influential friends to rally to their side. According to information the American representative obtained from a reliable and intelligent Korean in high position who had spoken with an officer of the court which had tried the hapless trio, the real reason for the execution of Yun Suk-wu was that he knew too much, having come upon the burning of the queen's body by the Japanese. As for the other two Koreans, there was no evidence that they had done anything at all.[124]

The real culprits fared much better. Though the Court of Preliminary Inquiries at Hiroshima reconstructed in detail the conspiracy of Miura, Sugimura, Okamoto and the other Japanese and the intrusion of the entire party into the palace, it released all the accused in its verdict of January 20, 1896, on the ground that there was insufficient evidence to prove that any of them had "actually committed the crime originally meditated by them." [125]

Nineteen

The Royal Guest

With the announcement of the death of Queen Min a temporary calm descended upon the land as preparations were made for her funeral. The relations between the king and the cabinet became if not very good, so at least reasonably satisfactory. Yet there was one issue that cropped up again and sharply divided Kojong and his ministers. The latter wanted him to issue an edict ordering the Korean people to cut their hair in the European style as of January 1, 1896. They contended that the masses would be unable to appreciate the advantages of reform and that the country could not be civilized so long as the Korean people clung to their traditional hairdo. Kojong retorted that instead of inclining the populace favorably toward reform, such a decree was bound to displease them. There were other, more urgent, matters to be taken up at this moment for Korea's welfare, he insisted.[1] As a compromise, the king issued a decree on December 30, 1895, in which he announced that he had cut his hair and that he invited his subjects to follow his example. "In an age when one travels on steamships and on railroads," he explained, "we cannot preserve our ancient habit of isolation. It is not for pleasure that we introduce the new innovations, but for the purpose of making the people rich and the army strong in order to save the State. It is impossible to risk losing the State in order to preserve our ancient customs." "We have already cut our hair," Kojong proclaimed; "none of our subjects will dare to refuse to imitate us, because in a realm one must listen to the King as in a home one must listen to the head of the household."[2]

The new regulations were strictly applied to government officials, policemen, and soldiers. Koreans in this category had to cut their hair or to leave office. The majority of employees conformed, but among those who chose resignation was Minister of Education Yi To-chai, an ultraconservative who treasured tradition.[3]

The inhabitants of the capital were more prone to accept new ways than their country cousins. Within a week after the decree had been issued, two thirds of the residents of Seoul had cut their hair and it seemed that the rest would follow suit in a few days.[4] But in the provinces, where the king's recommendation was mistaken for a general order applying to all Korean subjects, petty uprisings broke out. The government was compelled to send officials and troops to the trouble spots to quell the insurgents by moral persuasion if possible, by force if necessary.[5]

Abolition of the old coiffure was only one of the reforms proclaimed by Kojong. He directed the adoption of modern dress, the substitution of the Gregorian calendar for the Chinese calendar as far as the reckoning of days and months was concerned, and adopted the reign name "Kien-yang" or "The Establishment of Light" for designating the years of his rule beginning in 1896, so that January 1, 1896, became known as the first day of the first month of the first year of Kien-yang.[6]

The preceding autumn Waeber, who had been Russian consul general and chargé d'affaires in Seoul for a decade, had been promoted to envoy extraordinary and minister plenipotentiary to Mexico. He had been displeased by word of his replacement and had appealed to his government to be allowed to remain in Korea. Waeber's colleagues wondered along with him why St. Petersburg should have chosen to remove a person so conversant with the affairs of the country at a time when the post in Seoul was taking on increasing importance for Russia. Lefèvre speculated that the tsarist government had decided to take a more energetic attitude toward Japan in Korea and had felt that Waeber was too timid and too lacking in initiative to adjust to the exigencies of a new policy. It appeared to the foreign colony, furthermore, that St. Petersburg did not fully approve of the passive position Waeber had assumed toward the Japanese since their intervention in Korean affairs. "It is inevitable that the chargé d'affaires of Russia who was animated by very pronounced Japanophile sentiments had had for a long time a very reserved attitude toward the Japanese and had made but rather little effort to breach their influence," Lefèvre wrote. "This policy of neutrality, so natural for representatives of other powers, seemed to many persons extraordinary on the part of the agent of a country which borders on Korea and which is deemed to want sooner or later to absorb this small realm." Lefèvre had on numerous occasions heard Russian naval officers passing through Seoul express their astonishment at Waeber's policy in unflattering terms. Lefèvre added that upon receiving word of his replacement, Waeber had "sensibly" modified his conduct and, becoming more active, had tried to impede Japanese policy and to obtain for Russia "the legitimate share of influence to which she was entitled in that country." [7]

In December 1895 Waeber received orders not to leave Korea upon the arrival of his successor. Alexis de Speyer (Aleksei Nikolaevich Shpeier) reached Seoul on January 8, 1896. He assumed his official duties as chargé on the thirteenth. Although Waeber reported that his own continued presence pleased Kojong,[8] the unusual step by the Russian government, in the absence of an explanation, aroused much speculation in Seoul. Some guessed that Waeber would become an adviser to the Korean government, others that he would soon be sent to manage the Tokyo or Peking legations. "As Mr. Waeber knows the situation perfectly and has the confidence of the King and his party," Sill reported, "it is thought to be not improbable that Russia may take a very active part in Korean affairs in the spring—after the ice has cleared from the Vladivostok harbor." [9] Lefèvre was less alarmist. The explanation for the delay in Waeber's departure, he believed, was simply to provide him with the opportunity to brief Speyer fully on the situation in Korea.[10]

The person most distressed by Waeber's continued presence in Seoul was his successor, for the reins of Russian policy remained in Waeber's hands. A proud and restless soul, Speyer smarted under Waeber's direction, and asked for his recall. But when, as will be seen, the need arose for the temporary replacement of Hitrovo, it was Speyer who was sent to Tokyo and Waeber who was retained in Korea.[11]

Stopping over in Tokyo en route from Europe to Korea, Speyer had told the German minister, Gutschmid, that he intended in so far as possible to act in accord with the Japanese government and to remain in touch with the Japanese representative in Seoul. Neither he personally nor his government had any desire to treat Japan brusquely in the Korean question. His close to five years in Japan as secretary of the legation (from 1885 to 1890) had made of him a Japanophile, Speyer asserted; he loved and esteemed the Japanese nation. Since Speyer had not concealed his sentiments in St. Petersburg, Gutschmid commented, the Russian Government seemed to approve of his pro-Japanese feelings in appointing him as its representative in Seoul.[12]

On December 17, 1895, the Japanese government had honored Speyer with a banquet. Acting foreign Minister Saionji had expressed friendly feelings toward Russia and had revealed, as Speyer reported, that the Japanese government had begun to realize "the necessity of a rapprochement with Russia for the joint and amicable solution of the Korean question." [13] Saionji had suggested that Speyer and Komura begin to discuss the settlement of disputed issues.

Hitrovo had confided to Speyer his growing skepticism regarding Japanese assurances of friendship. Speyer himself saw upon his arrival in Seoul that Japanese actions in Korea did not correspond to Japanese assurances in Tokyo. Like Waeber, Speyer found that Kojong had been left with no more than the semblance of authority; Japanese advisers made all decisions of consequence. He reported to Lobanov on January 14, 1896, that the unceremonious way in which the Japanese threw around their weight in Korea was at variance with the assertions made by statesmen in Tokyo that the occupation of Korea had been "temporary and necessitated by force of circumstances" and that they were ready to enter into an amicable agreement with Russia concerning this question.[14]

In a conversation with the French representative in Seoul in the second half of January, Speyer gave some indications of the policy Russia would pursue toward Korea. Having heard that Lefèvre had on various occasions expressed the fear that the work of the Roman Catholic missonaries in Korea would be aborted if the country were annexed by Russia, Speyer conceded that in the event that Korea became an integral part of Russia, the propagation of Roman Catholicism would probably be prohibited there as it was in the other parts of the Russian empire. But there was no ground for envisioning such an eventuality, at least for the time being, he insisted. "I do not know, of course, what will happen in the distant future," Speyer admitted, "but as regards the present period, and by these words I mean the space of a generation, I can assure you that Russia has no desire at all [*n'a nulle envie*] of annexing this country, an intention gratuitously ascribed to us. Our designs on Korea are more modest," he assured Lefèvre. "It does not even enter into our aims to impose on this realm a protectorate based on a written convention. We simply want to eliminate the preponderant influence which the Japanese have taken in the direction of governmental affairs, to give to Russian influence the part to which we are entitled, and to establish little by little, order and tranquility in the country."[15]

When Speyer reported that Kojong was in the position of a prisoner and that the crown prince was to be sent to Japan against his will to receive his education there, the Russian Foreign Ministry instructed Hitrovo to bring Speyer's allegations to the attention of the Japanese government. Saionji in turn queried Komura, who denied the charge, asserting that the restraints on the king were the same as on other sovereigns in states with a cabinet system. It was Speyer who was a prisoner of Waeber and subject to the great influence of the taewongun on the Russian legation, Komura asserted. The rumor about the dispatch of the Korean crown prince to Japan seemed to be a fabrication, circulated by Korean refugees in the Russian and American legations, Saionji cabled to Nishi in St. Petersburg.[16]

The chief of the Asiatic Bureau of the Russian Foreign Ministry observed in a conversation with the Japanese minister in St. Petersburg that there seemed to be general dissatisfaction in Korea because the *de facto* power of administration was in the hands of the taewongun, with the Japanese minister in Seoul virtually running things. Nishi questioned the truth of the information on the ground that the Japanese government had no idea of interfering in the internal affairs of Korea. Informed by Kapnist that Hitrovo was to return to Russia on leave in February and that Speyer was to take over the legation in Tokyo as chargé d'affaires during his absence, Nishi urged Saionji to convince Hitrovo before the latter's departure of Japan's "peaceful attitude" toward Korea.[17]

Meanwhile domestic unrest continued to spread in Korea as a result of the haircut ordinance. As disturbances swept through the southern and eastern provinces of the kingdom, residents of the capital who had cut their hair did not venture beyond the outskirts of Seoul for fear of being attacked by the rural population. When the authorities of the city of Ch'ungch'ong tried to enforce the ordinance, the inhabitants rose *en masse* and murdered the governor and his suite, tearing them limb from limb. Notices by the Korean government that the abandonment of the traditional coiffure was a matter of choice, not of compulsion, failed to calm the population, and Korean troops with several Japanese officers were sent to disperse the insurgents.

So long as Japanese soldiers and policemen remained in Seoul, the capital seemed safe from attack, the English consul general speculated. But he saw no end to the state of disorder in Korea if the Japanese troops were withdrawn, because he regarded the Korean army as "little more than a farce."[18]

Yet with the failure of the loyalist attempt to restore the king to power and with the acquittal of Miura and his countrymen, the Japanese began to conduct themselves with ever less restraint. Their overbearing attitude and their association with the unpopular reformers fanned the embers of anti-Japanese discontent. As a Russian officer, Lieutenant Colonel Al'ftan, who toured Korea in December 1895 and January 1896 reported, "It was difficult to find anywhere in the country a corner where one did not speak of the Japanese with hatred and where one did not blame them for all the misfortunes which had befallen the native land, where there did not burn a fanatical hatred toward these uninvited strangers." The abolition of the topknot, a reform attributed by many to the Japanese, constituted the drop which filled the cup of patience to overflowing.[19]

By early February 1896 the Korean government had practically exhausted its military force in futile attempts to restore order in the countryside. Some of the insurgents were within a day's march of the capital. They had cut the telegraph lines and isolated Seoul.[20]

Waeber and Speyer concurred that the main objective of Russian policy must be the removal of the pro-Japanese officials from the Korean government. They favored restoring to the king the opportunity to appoint his own ministers, confident that this would result in a government with a pro-Russian orientation. Since experience had shown that the dismissal of Japanophile officials could not be achieved through agreement with Japan, Waeber and Speyer decided to extend support to the anti-Japanese party, which had solicited their backing.

Immediately upon Speyer's arrival—before he had officially assumed his post—Speyer had received a note from Kojong through Yi Pom-jin, who had taken refuge in the tsarist legation. Complaining about his fate, the king had declared that "he awaited help only from Russia and did not lose hope to see brighter days with her collaboration." In mid-January Kojong had asked Speyer to visit him. During the audience, which had been attended as usual by the pro-Japanese ministers, nothing of importance had been discussed. But as Speyer had been taking his leave, the king had slipped him a note in which he had asserted that the search for the queen was continuing and had expressed the supposition that she would be afraid to disclose her whereabouts "until the overthrow of the present government by the Russians."[21]

Clear as Kojong's hints were for direct Russian intervention, Waeber and Speyer could not respond to them on their own authority. Reporting Kojong's wishes to St. Petersburg on January 22, Speyer asked for instructions.

The tsarist government had been following developments in Korea with mounting concern. Speyer's very first telegram from Seoul, in which he had urged determined Russian opposition to Japanese policy in Korea, had evoked Nicholas's comment that it was time for the Japanese to give Russia an account of their outrages in Korea. But Foreign Minister Lobanov feared that direct intervention might lead to a collision with Japan and the other powers and might impede the strengthening of Russian influence in China, as well as in Korea. He cautiously sidestepped the request for instructions and on January 23 asked Speyer to obtain clarification "what was meant by the overthrow of the present regime in Korea and what means there are for this purpose." Lobanov warned Speyer not to lose sight of the fact that Russia did not want "to provoke new complications in the Far East at the present time."[22]

Speyer responded in the names of Waeber and himself that Kojong expected from Russia "the restoration of his power and the right to select ministers, as he himself did not dispose over the means to accomplish this, although the nation and the best people in Korea were with him." Speyer asserted that while conditions for the overthrow of the government were favorable in that everyone hated the Japanese yoke, no success was possible without Russian support, because the unarmed populace was powerless. He and Waeber felt, he warned, that Japan would swallow Korea if Russia refused to act.

"The solution of the Korean question by negotiations alone is unlikely," Speyer argued, because "Japan will not drive away the ministers and the father of the king, as this would be tantamount to renouncing Korea." The only successful means of assisting in the restoration of "the real independence of the country," Speyer telegraphed, was to bring to Seoul a detachment of Russian troops equal in number to that of the Japanese. There was little likelihood, he believed, that Japan, who had been weakened by her war with China, would venture on complications with Russia. "The quicker and the more determined our actions will be, the lesser the risk," he concluded.[23]

The query from Lobanov and Speyer's reply had been dispatched through Hitrovo.[24] Although the Russian minister in Tokyo by now harbored no illusions about Japanese designs on Korea, he was alarmed by the determined tone of Speyer's dispatch. Caution required, he deemed, first to explore all means of coming to an agreement with Japan in order to avoid arousing new complications. Although he forwarded Speyer's telegram, he took issue with his views in a cable of his own. He saw no special danger, he wired, in continuing the present, albeit unfavorable, state of affairs in Korea until such time as the Russian government found it possible to become more active. There was no need, he thought, to exert any pressure on the course of events in Korea now and insisted that nothing be undertaken in Seoul until his return to Russia, whither he planned to accompany the Japanese mission to the coronation of Nicholas II.[25] Since this was not to take place until later in the year, Hitrovo in effect advised his government to delay any action in Korea for at least three or four months.[26]

In St. Petersburg there was no objection in principle to the support of Kojong and the anti-Japanese forces in Korea. However, Speyer's proposal for the dispatch of Russian troops was rejected for fear of possible complications. Hitrovo's position was more in line with the policy of the tsarist government, and his recommendations were accepted. On February 1 Lobanov instructed Speyer that it was "inconvenient at the present moment to arouse in Korea questions purely internal in character" and that any decisions must be deferred until consultation with Hitrovo in St. Petersburg.[27]

The position of the Japanese in Korea was less secure, however, than the tsarist government or its representatives realized. The Japanese had aroused so much antagonism by their arbitrary conduct that the opportunity suddenly presented itself for the Russians to nullify the influence of Japan in Korea with little effort and practically no risk.

Upon the receipt of Lobanov's telegram on February 1, Speyer had cabled back a bleak picture of conditions in Korea. He had not repeated his proposal for the dispatch of a Russian detachment but had merely pointed to the difficulty of finding a way out of the situation, as the ministers surrounding the king would not tolerate a change in his position. He had described the disorders that were persisting north of the capital and had reported that the king was in fear for his life. But neither when he had proposed the use of Russian troops nor now when speaking pessimistically about the predicament of Kojong had the thought crossed his mind to shelter the king in the Russian legation and let him govern from there. It was an idea that was raised the next day for the first time by a member of the royal entourage.[28]

The acquittal of Miura and the other Japanese officials involved in the murder of the queen had shattered the composure of the king. His fears for his own safety increased momentously as it was openly stated that one or more of the conspirators would be brought back to Korea and given high posts in his government. The threat of an attack on the capital by topknot insurgents, information that the Japanese planned to force him to abdicate in favor of his younger and presumably more docile nephew Yi Chun-yong, and rumor of a plot on his life and that of the crown prince turned Kojong's mind to flight.[29]

On February 2 Kojong sent a note to Speyer through Yi Pom-jin, to the effect that he was surrounded by traitors and feared that now when there were disorders everywhere, they would take advantage of the situation "to destroy him and his son." "Together with the crown prince I intend to flee from the danger awaiting me and to seek protection in the Russian legation," the king wrote. "What do the two envoys think about it? If they agree, I shall take advantage of one of the coming nights to make my way secretly to the legation. I shall let you know of the day separately. I have no other way of saving myself. I hope deeply that both envoys are ready to show me patronage and protection."[30]

Even Speyer deemed the proposal too dangerous at first, and so told Yi. But the Korean dignitary persisted. He declared in the name of the sovereign that the latter was determined to run the risk if only the Russian representatives agreed to receive him, since it would be an even greater risk for him to remain in the palace. After brief deliberation Waeber and Speyer resolved to take the chance. The advantages for their country that the king's presence in the Russian legation could entail were enormous. They consented to offer asylum to Kojong following his flight from the palace.

This time the Russian Foreign Ministry approved of the plan and Nicholas decreed that a large Russian warship be ordered to Chemulpo. While the tsarist government had eschewed the dispatch of a Russian detachment to counterbalance Japanese influence for fear that it might have led to serious complications, it believed that the voluntary flight of the king from under the guard of individuals involved in the beastly murder of his spouse made any sort of military countermeasures on the part of Japan impossible.[31]

On February 3 Kojong sent Speyer his thanks for agreeing to grant him asylum. Thereafter he kept the Russian legation informed daily of the preparations for the flight. The plan was very simple. The king and the crown prince were to disguise themselves as court ladies and early in the morning, when the king and the crown prince were normally fast asleep, were to be carried out of the palace in closed sedan chairs of the type used by women. To dull the alertness of the guards, a number of court ladies were to ride out through the various palace gates every day for a number of days at the hour set for the escape.[32]

On February 7 Speyer was informed that everything was ready and that Kojong would proceed to the Russian legation the following morning. But on the eighth the king sent word that he regarded the legation guard as insufficient to guarantee his safety and had decided, therefore, to delay his flight. Speyer, who himself had desired the presence of a larger Russian force, took advantage of the king's message to request the commander of the cruiser *Admiral Kornilov* to send a landing party to Seoul.[33]

In a visit which Speyer paid to Krien that day, Speyer sought to reassure his unsuspecting colleague in advance by denying that Russia had any designs on Korea or any portion thereof. The interference of foreign powers—at first China, then Japan—in the internal affairs of the kingdom had been a misfortune for the country. "If one would leave the people alone, they would manage somehow," Speyer asserted.[34]

On February 10 several Russian naval officers and over a hundred Russian sailors with a Maxim gun were put ashore by the *Admiral Kornilov* and the *Bobr* (Beaver) at Chemulpo and proceeded to the capital.[35] As the Russian legation guard had been increased to forty men several days before, Hillier called on Waeber to inquire why such "apparently uncalled-for" reinforcements had been sent.

Waeber replied that both he and Speyer were alarmed at the gravity of the situation. The Korean troops were unable to cope with the insurgents, who could attack the capital any day. The Japanese government had assumed a stance of nonintervention in Korea.[36] If the insurgents overran the capital, the Japanese forces would be busy rescuing their own residents. Besides, he remarked, he did not wish to be beholden to the Japanese for protection. Waeber offered to help defend British subjects if anything happened, but he urged Hillier, as he had advised Sill, to send for guards of their own.[37]

Speyer, whom Hillier saw afterwards, echoed Waeber's remarks. He added mysteriously that he had reason to believe that there would soon be some startling events in Seoul.

Hillier thereupon went to see Sill. Not knowing what Speyer had in the back of his mind, the British and American representatives thought their Russian colleague was exaggerating the situation. They did not issue a direct call for marines, but as a precaution asked the commanders of their respective warships at Chemulpo to be prepared to send them "on demand."

When Waeber and Speyer dined with Hillier that evening, they repeated their advice in the presence of Komura, who was also at the table.[38]

Asked by Krien why so many Russian sailors had been landed, Waeber declared that they had come for the sole purpose of defending the Russian legation against the victorious insurgents. The precaution was the more necessary, he argued, because the American and British detachments had been withdrawn from the city. But Waeber's explanation did not ring true, Krien reported.[39]

Early in the morning on February 11 the king and the crown prince quietly left the palace through different gates. Between thirty and forty trusty attendants slipped out simultaneously through different portals. It was a dangerous undertaking and Kojong and his son, disguised as court ladies, crouched pale and trembling in the closed sedan chairs.[40] At about 7 A.M. the royal refugees and their retinue reached the Russian legation. Kojong and his son were promptly admitted and ushered into two spacious rooms prepared for them.[41]

Speyer immediately dashed off brief notes to his diplomatic colleagues, informing them that the king of Korea, "considering the present state of political affairs of this country to be very grave and his further stay in the Palace attended with serious danger for his personal safety," had taken refuge in the Russian legation, together with the crown prince.[42]

At about 10 A.M. Waeber called on his English colleague and told him that Foreign Minister Kim had been dismissed and replaced by Yi Wan-yong, formerly minister of education, who spoke English and had found temporary asylum in the American legation following the murder of the queen. He said that Hillier would probably be invited shortly to an audience with the king. When the British representative inquired how Kojong had gotten to the Russian legation, Waeber changed the subject.[43]

At 11 A.M. Sill, as dean of the diplomatic corps, received a letter from the new foreign minister asking him, on behalf of Kojong, to invite the foreign

The Russian legation in Seoul. (*Vsemirnaia illiustratsiia*, 1896, 542.)

representatives to visit the king at the Russian legation in uniform at noon that day.[44] Sill at once circulated the letter to his colleagues, and all the foreign representatives except Komura assembled at the Russian legation at twelve o'clock.

Speyer, who received them, apologized to Hillier that he could not have been more explicit the previous evening. As Hillier now saw, he said, he had grounds for his warning that something was in the air. Speyer related that the situation in the palace had become so intolerable that Kojong had requested Russian protection, which could not be denied. He revealed that the escape had been managed very quietly. Since the king's refuge in the legation, he contended, many high officials had come to offer their congratulations and to assure Kojong of their approval and continued allegiance. Speyer asserted that it was his hope that the king's stay in the Russian legation would be brief, for the soldiers and the police were loyal to him. But he reiterated the advice that Hillier send for marines to guard against any eventualities.

As Hillier looked about him, he saw the hall filled with Korean officials, among them ex-Chamberlain Yi Pom-chin, who had been in the Russian legation since October 8 and was said to have escaped to Shanghai on a Russian warship, Pak Chong-yang who had been deprived of the premiership on October 8, and An Keiju, who had been dismissed as war minister at the same time and recently had been condemned to imprisonment for involvement in the abortive plot of November 28.[45]

At 12:30 Sill, Hillier, Krien, and Lefèvre were ushered into the quarters of the king. Komura had not yet arrived, and Waeber and Speyer excused themselves on the ground that they had already met with the king.

"I feared danger at the Palace last night, and knowing that there were soldiers at the Russian legation, I came here early this morning with the Crown Prince, and have asked you to come and see me," Kojong announced.

"I am exceedingly sorry that any circumstances should make it necessary for Your Majesty to leave your home, and I hope you are safe and happy here," Sill replied.

"I hope Your Majesty is well and comfortable," remarked Hillier.

"I wish to say the same," declared Krien.

"I wish to say the same," Lefèvre chimed in.

"I also wish to say the same," echoed Sill.

"When will you come again?" Kojong inquired.

"When Your Majesty commands," Hillier promised.

Thus ended the audience, only minutes after it had begun.[46]

Komura had received the same written communication from Speyer as his

Western colleagues. Though he did not acknowledge it in writing until February 14,[47] he appeared at the Russian legation shortly after the departure of the other foreign representatives.[48] In an equally brief audience the king made the same terse announcement. All that Komura replied evasively was that he hoped that Kojong was in good health.[49]

Speyer reported that the attitude of his colleagues toward the accomplished fact had been sympathetic and that even the Japanese minister had tried to hold himself as correctly as possible and had appeared, outwardly at least, rather calm in regard to the new state of affairs.[50]

The question arises whether Kojong's flight to the Russian legation had occurred truly at his own initiative or whether it had been inspired by Speyer. According to the dispatches of Speyer and Waeber their role had been passive. Yet the Soviet historian Vladimir Petrovich Nikhamin voices the suspicion that the diplomats had played down their participation, because it had been in violation of their instructions not to interfere in Korean internal affairs.[51] The Korean scholar Synn Seung-kwon disagrees with Nikhamin's speculation, arguing that Kojong was more desperate than the tsarist representative and had really fled for his life.[52] However, a document in the French archives gives substance to Nikhamin's suspicion. In a confidential conversation with Lefèvre, Speyer admitted his initiative.

"Since my arrival in Seoul," Speyer told Lefèvre, "I was disagreeably surprised to see the state of affairs existing in Korea: on one hand a king without the strength to resist the unreasonable demands of his ministers, on the other hand ministers receiving their instructions from the legation of Japan. It seemed to me that such a situation could not be tolerated much longer and I looked for the means of remedying it. I thought that the simplest plan to adopt in order to knock the ministers from power would be to try to induce the king to leave his palace secretly and come to our legation. There, sheltered from all coercion, he could dismiss his ministers and freely form a new cabinet of his choice. I unbosomed myself of this scheme [*je me suis ouvert de ce projet*] to the king, but I found at first a certain hesitance on his part to venture on the undertaking. He was afraid of failing in this attempt and thereby rendering his situation still more painful [*penible*]. To induce him to take a decision, it was necessary for me on different occasions to represent to him his situation in the darkest light and to persuade him that by remaining in his palace longer, he daily ran the risk of assassination. The king, as you know, has a great fear of death. Hence, he was responsive to my arguments and ended by adhering to my plan."

Once he had felt sure of the king's adherence, Speyer related, he had telegraphed to St. Petersburg to inform his government of his project. But communications with Europe had been interrupted, and he had acted prior to receiving any response.[53]

When word reached Tokyo of Kojong's flight to the Russian legation, embarrassing questions and demands were raised in the Diet. The government prorogued the session of the Diet on February 15 to prevent the discussion of the Korean question. It informed the Russian military agent that strict instructions had been sent to the Japanese military commanders in Korea to prevent possible clashes with the Russian seamen.[54]

Kojong's first order of business upon reaching the safety of the Russian legation was to dismiss the Japanese-sponsored cabinet and to appoint a new government. He did so within hours of his arrival in consultation with Dr. Horace Allen, secretary of the American legation, rather than at the guidance of Speyer, who refused to become involved in the affairs of government. As a result, the new cabinet was more Japanophobe than Russophile in complexion and included several members of the American party: Acting Premier Pak Chŏng-yang, who seemed both timid and incompetent, Foreign Minister Yi Wan-yong and his brother, War Minister Yi Yun-yong. The dominant figure was Yi Pom-jin, concurrently minister of justice and chief of police, who had organized the king's flight. He had been associated with the Russians for a long time and was addicted to strong drink.[55]

A royal proclamation, signed by Pak, was posted at the front gate of the Russian legation and at a number of places in town. A penitent pronouncement in the Confucian manner, it heaped blame on the ruler's own head. "On account of Our unworthiness and maladministration the wicked advanced and the wise retired," Kojong confessed. The troubles that had befallen Korea during the past ten years due to his own fault made him "blush and sweat for shame."

Now, thanks to the righteous efforts of his loyal subjects there was hope that the state would be invigorated and calm would be restored, Kojong stated. Endeavoring to be merciful, he granted a general amnesty to all of his subjects except to "the principal traitors concerned in the affairs of July 1894 and of October 1895." "Capital punishment should be their due, thus venting the indignation of men and gods alike," he declared.

The proclamation assured the insurgents that no one would be compelled to cut off his topknot. The whole affair, Kojong alleged, had been precipitated by traitors, who had resorted to force and coercion. He called upon the insurgents to return to their respective places and occupations. His soldiers were to come back to Seoul upon receipt of their orders.[56]

A second proclamation, addressed to the army, was issued over the royal seal later in the day. It announced that evidence of another conspiracy had induced the king to seek refuge in the Russian legation. Calling the soldiers his children, Kojong promised not to hold them answerable for their participation in past troubles. "Come and protect Us," he appealed to them. At the same time he exhorted the soldiers to kill the principal officials who had conspired against him. "When you meet the chief rebels—Cho Hui-yon, U Pom-son, Yi Tu-hwang, Yi Pom-nae, Yi Chin-ho, and Kwon Hyong-jin— kill them immediately and bring their heads." [57]

The inflammatory proclamations were modified by a third royal edict the same day and by yet another one on the fourteenth. The above traitors were not to be decapitated outright, but were to be taken to the courts of justice for trial. [58] The action came too late to prevent the lynching of two members of the old cabinet. Arrested by the police in the Council Chamber inside the palace shortly after their dismissal on the forenoon of the eleventh, Premier Kim Hong-jip and Minister of Agriculture Chung Pyong-ha were hauled to the police station, where after a summary courtmartial by the police, they were sentenced to death and decapitated. As their bodies were thrown into the street, they were seized by an infuriated mob, who tied ropes to their legs and dragged them away, striking, kicking, and stabbing the corpses as they moved along.When the crowd reached the center of the city, it mutilated and disfigured the bodies and ripped them apart, strewing the pieces in the street. For the remainder of the day relays of people heaped nameless indignities on the remains of the two ministers, cursing them as the murderers of the queen and as the sponsors of the hair-cutting ordinance. [59] A third former cabinet member, ex-Finance Minister O Yun-jung, was slain several days later at a village southeast of Seoul as a matter of personal revenge at the instigation of someone who had been punished under his orders. [60]

Meanwhile, a number of Japanese had been killed in the interior of Korea in recent days. [61] Several hours after the lynching of Kim and Chong, a Japanese trader in the capital was stoned to death as he passed near the spot where the dismembered corpses lay exposed. [62] A flurry of apprehension swept through the Japanese colony, but the outbursts of 1884 were not repeated. [63]

A royal decree published in the *Official Gazette* on February 13 informed the general public of the king's presence in the Russian legation. Without going into details on the ground that the events of the eleventh were "too sad" to mention, Kojong announced his intention to return to the palace "in several days," and called on the people to remain calm and without fear. [64] In another pacificatory edict, printed the same day, Kojong spoke of being in fear day and night like a person "in danger of treading on the tail of a tiger," because his good intentions had not reached the people. As a token of his compassion for his subjects he decreed the remittance of all the arrears in taxes in the several provinces up to July 1894.[65]

The news that the king was in the Russian legation had come like a clap of thunder from the clear sky. "Is it true? If true, what does it mean?" the inhabitants of Seoul asked each other. "Will this be the beginning of an armed conflict between Japan and Russia?"[66]

The American minister telegraphed for a guard as soon as he learned of the new development, certain that "the city would be terribly and dangerously excited." Eleven men were to start out the following day. "Mob violence is more to be feared than anything else, though the large number of Japanese soshi in the city, whom Mr. Komura, the Japanese Minister, has but recently said he cannot control, are an element of danger," Sill reported. "It is idle to ask for Korean assistance," he reflected. "They cannot take care of themselves. . . ."[67] The British consul general similarly requested a naval guard. Commander Francis N. Pelly of the *Porpoise* landed Lieutenant Benson and sixteen marines at Chemulpo that very evening; they reached Seoul on the twelfth.[68]

Yet the city soon regained its calm. "The population of Seoul is so accustomed to palace revolutions and to coups d'état," Lefèvre observed, "that it ended by accepting, almost with indifference, events which, if they had occurred in Europe, would have turned the country upside down."[69]

On February 17 the Korean troops returned to Seoul as ordered. On the nineteenth the king received them in the Russian legation, personally thanked them for their service, and gave to each of the soldiers a small sum of money.[70]

Speyer was aware that the flight of the king was bound to give rise to the "wrongest commentaries." "One will probably say that he has escaped from the Japanese influence only to become a prisoner of the Russians," he told his French colleague. He assured Lefèvre that such a supposition would be "completely inaccurate." "Since he has been at the Russian legation the king of Korea has had absolute freedom of action [*a une liberté d'action absolue*]," Speyer declared. "He has invited to see him whom he desired and has chosen his new ministers without my having tried in any fashion to influence his choice. In a few days, when he will have received news from the interior of the country and when he will know how the news of these events will have been received there, he will leave the Legation and we shall let him govern in all freedom with his ministers, without our meddling in anything in the administration of the affairs of the realm. It suffices for us to have removed him from Japanese influence and to have rendered to him his freedom of action." "As for the Japanese," Speyer concluded, "I hope that they will have the wisdom to accept with good grace the new state of affairs."

Lefèvre was not enthusiastic about Russian restraint. Tsarist policy toward Korea was "no doubt very generous," but hardly practicable. "The Koreans are absolutely incapable of governing themselves and need a strong hand to direct them," the Frenchman reported. "To leave them free to their own devices is to condemn the country to remain eternally in disorder and anarchy." [71]

The success achieved by Russia as a result of the flight of Kojong to the tsarist legation and the fall of the Japanese puppet government was so great and unexpected that the Russians themselves were bewildered. Within a matter of hours they suddenly found themselves in a position to run the country. Although the escape of the king from under Japanese domination met with general approval in Korea, neither the statesmen in St. Petersburg nor their representatives abroad had any illusions about the degree to which Russia could exploit the situation. They realized that the growth in Russian influence would be matched by mounting opposition on the part of Japan. Any attempt to impose a protectorate on Korea or to make the country in any other way dependent on Russia was bound to lead to a collision with Japan, something for which their country was not prepared and which she could not afford because of her military weakness in the Far East. British opposition too could be expected should Russia behave as arbitrarily as Japan had done. Furthermore, popular approval would quickly turn into popular hostility if Russia tried to take undue advantage of the presence of the royal guest in her legation. It was a situation which called for the utmost of tact, patience, and self-possession on the part of the Russian representatives.

Speyer and Waeber evaluated the situation correctly and conducted themselves with moderation. Learning from the Japanese experience, they sought to exert and retain their influence while leaving Kojong and his ministers freedom of action; they interfered as little as possible in the internal affairs of the kingdom. Lest Korean suspicions and antagonism be aroused by the king's stay in the Russian legation, Speyer and Waeber hinted to Kojong as soon as the new government had been formed that it would be desirable for him to return to the palace shortly.

Kojong demurred. "The king," Speyer reported on February 19 with budding frustration, "listens with unconcealed fear to our protestations that it is necessary for His Majesty to return to his palace as soon as possible to calm public opinion, which will, of course, fail to understand a long and inexplicable stay of the king in the imperial legation, and declares every time in response to this advice that unfortunately he cannot follow it if the palace will not be guarded by a detachment of our troops."

Kojong believed that the Japanese were determined to regain their position and only waited for him to leave the protection of the Russian legation. Unable to silence his fears so long as Japanese troops remained in Korea and unwilling to turn him out against his wishes, Waeber and Speyer let the king tarry, though they realized that the Japanese would make use of his continued presence in their midst to undermine his authority. Thus the decision for the prolonged stay of Kojong in the tsarist legation was taken at his own behest against the advice of the Russian representatives.[72]

With the king in her pocket, Russia was confronted with the question whether to take advantage of the fortuitous situation and impose a protectorate on Korea or even annex the peninsula outright, either of which would court serious complications with Japan and other powers, or whether to rest satisfied with the shift in influence that had occurred and to regulate Korean affairs by an agreement with Japan, making some concessions to the latter, but retaining Russia's dominant position in Seoul. Kojong invited direct Russian involvement in Korean affairs. He asked the tsarist representatives as soon as he had moved into the legation to inform St. Petersburg that he was prepared to entrust the fate of his kingdom to Russia, the only country whom he trusted completely. It was his hope, he said, that Russia would deem it useful, both out of sympathy for Korea and out of political considerations, "to have on her Far Eastern borders a completely independent state, tied to her by unbreakable bonds of gratitude" and would aid Korea against enslavement by Japan. By Russian aid the king meant, Speyer reported on February 19, "that the imperial government entrust the role of guide and mentor [*rukovoditelia i nastavnika*] of the Korean ministers to some agent [*doverennoe litso*], who as chief adviser of the cabinet would be present at all its meetings and would direct the activity of the Korean dignitaries." Stressing the importance of financial advice, Kojong hinted that he required monetary assistance. He also spoke of the need for a Korean army and expressed the desire to leave its organization in Russian hands.

Speyer supported the establishment of a Russian protectorate, to which Kojong's proposals amounted. Anticipating objections on the part of St. Petersburg, he argued in a dispatch on February 28 that for the Russians to shun assuming the role of defenders and patrons of Korea for the sake of avoiding complications in the Far East would not bring about the desired result. Such an intolerable situation would be created in Korea if the tsarist government remained aloof that the latter would find it necessary to intervene eventually, but by then would be doing so without profit for itself. On the other hand, if Russia now decided irrevocably to take up the fortunes of Korea, who was throwing herself into her embrace, she would not only weaken thereby the serious nature of the impending complications, but would undoubtedly strengthen her position on the shores of the Pacific Ocean. As for Japan,

Speyer thought, it would not be difficult to come to an agreement with her if one offered her various trade benefits and the leading role in the financial organization of the Korean state.[73]

Speyer was not alone in feeling that Russia should take advantage of the situation to further her national interests. Regarding Korea as far more suitable than Manchuria for the acquisition of an ice-free port, the General Staff officer Al'ftan urged the establishment of a Russian protectorate over Korea "without any sort of philanthropic feelings toward the Korean people and their unfortunate fate." Lieutenant General N. I. Grodekov, acting commander of the Amur military district, agreed that Korea must be secured by Russia lest the Japanese do so and turn the Japan Sea into an inland sea whose entrances would be in their hands.[74]

Speyer's telegram with Kojong's above-mentioned proposal was dispatched from Seoul on February 15, but in view of the interruption of direct communication with Tokyo it was delayed en route and not relayed from there to St. Petersburg until a week later, on February 22. Without a reply from their government, neither Speyer nor the more cautious Waeber dared to make any commitments to the king. Kojong, whose personal safety was at stake, worried about the delay in response. On February 21 Speyer queried Lobanov again about the requests of the monarch, noting that Kojong considered Russian support of vital importance.[75]

When Speyer had proposed the dispatch of a large Russian force to match that of the Japanese, Hitrovo had opposed the recommendation, contending that Russian diplomacy did not have the power to prevent the Japanese from manipulating puppets behind which they hid. Nor was it desirable, he thought, for Russia to make the attempt, because the activity of these marionettes did not threaten the future of Korea. Hitrovo doubted that there was any danger to the person of the king, since his weakness of character made him the most acceptable figure for the Japanese. Noting that legally Russia could demand the withdrawal of Japanese troops, he counselled against doing so, for Korea would be left in a state of disorder. Russian insistence on the joint occupation of Korea, on the other hand, might lead to the intervention of third powers. Hitrovo consequently advocated the preservation of the *status quo*. To put the brake on Speyer's proposal, Hitrovo had reiterated that there was no urgent need to exert pressure on the course of events for the purpose of achieving an advantageous solution of the Korean question.[76]

Hitrovo took issue likewise with Speyer's new recommendations. He warned his government that it was premature to raise the question of an official Russian adviser and of Russian military instructors. Any step in this direction would force Japan to adopt an adventurous policy and might lead to

N. I. Grodekov, acting commander of the Amur military district. (*Vsemirnaia illiu-stratsiia*, 1898, 59: 370.)

the undesirable involvement of other powers just when the Japanese government was almost convinced of the necessity of an agreement directly with Russia and the latter would be able to achieve everything without arousing the hostility of Japan. Hitrovo saw no need for Russia to make haste concerning Korea, confident that she would not get away from her anyway (*vse ravno ona ot nas ne uidet*).[77] The military attaché, Colonel Wogack, cautioned the Russian General Staff by cable the same day that the appointment of a Russian adviser and of military instructors would outrage the Japanese who until now had regarded the events in Korea with relative calm. He too feared that Russian haste might push the Japanese into rash action.[78]

The tsarist government had decided what course to follow as soon as it had learned of the events of February 11. Believing that its objective of preventing Japanese domination of the peninsula had been achieved by the coup, it deemed it more important to regulate relations with Japan than to chance a collision with the latter by obtaining special rights and privileges in Korea. Lobanov consequently rejected the proposals conveyed by Speyer. He telegraphed on February 24 that the tsarist government was ready to give advice to the king, but that in view of the troubled state of affairs, it judged it "premature to raise the question of an official adviser and military instructors."[79]

Speyer made an honest effort to stay clear of the internal affairs of Korea, but there were occasions when he felt compelled to exert a moderating influence. For example, although Kojong had granted an amnesty to everyone not directly involved in the murder of the queen, a number of individuals not cited in the decree had been arrested and interrogated under torture on the suspicion of having been implicated in the affair. As rumors feeding on the government's breach of faith spread panic and many Koreans fled from the capital, the Russian chargé intervened with the members of the cabinet, impressing on them that while it was natural for them to try to shed light on the events which had led to the death of the queen, they must respect the word given by the king and limit the arrests to those individuals mentioned by Kojong.[80]

On March 1 Speyer left for Japan to replace Hitrovo, who was returning home on leave. In a farewell visit to his German colleague on February 29, Speyer explained that Kojong did not dare to leave the Russian legation for the time being out of fear both of Japanese *soshi* and of regular Japanese troops, whom he had come to know all too well in 1882, 1884, and again in recent years. Speyer expressed the conviction that Japan would not let it come to war with Russia. He contended that Russia and Japan were the two powers above all others called upon to reform Korea, but that the Japanese were unable to overcome the three hundred years of hatred which the Koreans felt for them. Even the good which the Japanese brought turned in the eyes of their neighbors into the opposite, not to mention the many mistakes and blunders which they had committed in recent years. Japan had nothing to fear from Russia in the further cultivation of her commercial interests in the kingdom, because Russia was not a commercial nation, Speyer argued. On the other hand, Russia would not let Japan continue to "civilize" Korea as she had done up to now.

It was necessary first of all, Speyer confided to Krien, to establish a small army of about 3,000 men, which would be able to suppress robberies and other unruliness, because one would not hear soon again of *political* uprisings. He thought his government would be willing to assist Korea in this task. Relying on these troops, the king would then be able to rule independently, as he deemed proper for him to do. Secondary reforms which Japan had introduced, Speyer continued, should be retained and expanded, but without haste and at first only the most essential ones, as he had told Kojong during his last audience. Korea could not afford luxury in this respect, he remarked. For example, in view of her limited finances it was too early to think of the construction of a railroad from Seoul to Chemulpo; an ordinary highway would suffice for the time being.

Waeber, who had resumed sole charge of the legation, remarked to Krien the following day, on March 1, that Japan found herself in the miserable position of a man who had illegally broken into a strange house and then was ejected by legal means.[81]

Waeber now signed himself as envoy extraordinary and minister plenipotentiary.[82] Sill suspected that the elevation of Waeber, who thereby once again became dean of the diplomatic corps, indicated "a determination on the part of Russia to put an end to Japanese management of Korean affairs."[83] However, as noted, Waeber had already been promoted to that rank in connection with his appointment to Mexico and may have used the new title simply for that reason. True to his instructions, Waeber left Kojong and his ministers freedom of action, influencing their decisions indirectly with care and great skill.

The Japanese military instructors were ordered back to Japan and the contracts for Japanese advisers were not renewed. Talks concerning a Japanese loan and a Japanese railroad concession were broken off. Yet no haste was shown by Russia to take over the role of Japan. While sending Korea a gift of 3,000 rifles, Lobanov warned Waeber that "the conciliatory agreement with Japan in Seoul must not be disturbed by the release of these arms."[84]

The American and British representatives in Seoul confirmed in separate dispatches that Kojong showed little inclination to leave the Russian legation, where his cabinet met daily for the transaction of business. "That the King is now enjoying greater peace of mind and a sense of personal security, to which he has long been a stranger, is testified to by all who have seen him lately," Hillier wrote. "I am told that His Majesty looks a different man to what he did a few weeks ago; that he has put on flesh, is cheerful in manner, and has lost the hunted and anxious look that was previously noticed by all who came in contact with him." [85]

With the exception of Prince Yi Chai-sun, Yi Chai-miun's successor as minister of the Royal Household, who occasionally went home to sleep, the other members of the cabinet did not venture beyond the reach of Russian protection. When they were not with the king, they stayed either in one of the rooms of the Russian legation adjoining the royal apartments or in a house two of them had rented in an American missionary compound next to the Russian grounds. [86]

The fears of Kojong and his ministers were not without foundation. The insurrection continued and though it was directed primarily against remaining officials appointed by the late cabinet and against Japanese residents, disorder prevailed. The situation was exacerbated by the presence of many lawless Japanese who would not be curbed by their own authorities. Incensed by the recent turn of events, they were ever ready for trouble. The local Japanese newspapers sought to fan popular discontent by suggesting that Kojong be dethroned for having insulted the country by deserting the palace. [87]

In reply to a query from Secretary of State Olney whether Russia was practically governing Korea through the king and abolishing the reforms instituted by Japan, [88] Sill replied in a telegram written on March 2 and sent by steamer to Pusan that no Japanese reforms had been abolished, except that hair cutting was no longer compulsory, and that there was no evidence of interference by Russia. "[The] Russian Minister earnestly disclaims such interference," Sill cabled. "[The] English Consul is satisfied with Russia's conduct so far. I only know that the King and [the] cabinet defer to Russian opinion in matters of consequence."

Reporting that the minister of justice was proceeding with the investigation of the murder of the queen, Sill noted that it had been due to Waeber that Kojong had provided for the presence of the American legal adviser, Greathouse, to insure the fairness of the trials and to avoid the customary cruelties. [89] "I think I see plain indications that the present policy of Russia is to suggest the appointment of intelligent and reputable foreign advisers to the new Government from nationals other than her own," Sill added in a dispatch sent the same day. [90]

As his American colleague had reported correctly, the British representative was not apprehensive about Russian interference in the internal affairs of

Korea. Noting that while Waeber continued to disclaim any responsibility for the acts of the Korean government, there were indications that he was proffering advice to Kojong and his ministers, Hillier commented: "Rightly so, in my opinion, for it is absolutely hopeless to expect that the King, or any Minister he may select, can govern the country without foreign advice, enforced, if necessary, by insistence." He was pleased that Kojong, at Waeber's advice, had sent for MacLeavy Brown and had instructed the minister of finance in his presence that every order for money issued by the Treasury must be countersigned by Brown. That this should have been done at the tsarist minister's spontaneous suggestion, Hillier wrote, was "a confirmation of the assurances of the latter that he has no intention of using the influence he now possesses for the pursuit of an exclusive policy." [91]

In a conversation with the French chargé d'affaires in St. Petersburg in April 1896, Lobanov asserted that Russian views regarding Korea had never changed. As the tsarist government had made clear to the government of Japan from the outset of the Sino-Japanese War, it wanted an independent Korea and it would not let any country place her under her protectorate. "The recent developments are without doubt very regrettable," Lobanov remarked to Vauvineux, "but in view of the mores of the country, one should not exaggerate the importance thereof; I hope that order can soon be reestablished in the peninsula without intervention by anyone." As for the intention attributed to Russia of acquiring a port somewhere along the Korean coast, Lobanov declared that the tsarist government entertained no such project for the moment. He did not conceal, however, that its point of view might change with the completion of the Trans-Siberian Railroad.

Lobanov's language, Vauvineux confirmed in his report to Hanotaux, was analogous to that used by Giers in September 1894. [92]

The reforms inaugurated by the Japanese in the summer of 1894 had curtailed the privileges of the Korean aristocracy, such as the monopoly of the Home Office on all civil service appointments in the provinces, in an attempt to create a modern administrative system. Upon the decline in Japanese authority following Kojong's flight to the Russian legation, the aristocrats sought to revert to the old ways. When MacLeavy Brown requested Waeber's assistance in obtaining a royal decree reaffirming the reforms, Waeber assented, but he did not exert due pressure on Kojong.

"M. Waeber's action, or rather inaction, is not altogether intelligible, as whatever mistakes or self-seeking may with justice be imputed to the Japanese, there can be no doubt that the reforms introduced were in the main to the advantage of Corea, and that a return under Russian sanction or acquiescence to the former abuses would hardly redound to the credit of the Russian

Representative," the British consul general reported. "I am myself inclined to believe," Hillier commented, "that in the absence of definite instructions from his Government he is often at a loss to know in what direction to exert his influence, while at the same time his good nature is too often worked upon by schemers like the present [Home] Minister [Nam Yon-ch'ol]." [93]

Reviewing the situation that prevailed in Korea following "the sudden and complete overthrow" of Japanese predominance, the American minister wrote: "Russian policy seems to be to make the least possible show either of force or of prevailing influence. She keeps a comparatively small guard, sixty or seventy men, at her Legation in Seoul, and plenty of ships at Chemulpo and in neighboring seas. The indications are that, having come into possession, by act of the King, of great power in Korean councils, she will hold with characteristic tenacity to what she has secured, making no exhibition of force unless she is compelled to do so." "The Russian Representative, Mr. Waeber," Sill reported, "says the King is his guest and that he will not suggest his departure from the shelter of the Legation, but that he is free to go whenever he deems it safe and advisable to do so, and it is definitely understood that Russia will not furnish a guard to protect him elsewhere. Meanwhile His Majesty feels a sense of personal security unknown to him since the seizure of the palace on July 23, 1894, until he sought and obtained the present asylum on the 11th of February 1896. And I believe he will be slow to leave his present quarters until he has a sufficient native guard, satisfactorily trained and commanded, to protect him and his court."

"This determination is not necessarily chargeable to timidity on His Majesty's part," Sill commented, "for his life will need special protection so long as the old Taie Won Kuhn [taewongun], the abettor of those who murdered the Queen, and the author, during the last half century, of countless murderous intrigues, lives and is at liberty to plot and to conspire with others for the destruction of the present government. I understand," Sill continued, "that he is in a great rage and eagerly awaiting a favorable opportunity to rally his formidable following for the murder of the King and the Crown Prince. The murder of the Queen in which he gladly acted a conspicuous though subordinate part has, it is said, made him more eager than ever before to put out of the way of his favorite grandson Ye Chun Yang [Yi Chun-yong], every obstacle to the Korean throne. There will never be peace in Korea until this incarnation of intrigue and remorseless cruelty takes final possession of the beautiful burial place which he has prepared for himself in the suburb of Seoul in sight of the Han river." [94]

The Russian newspaper *Novoe Vremia* was sharply critical of Waeber, alleging that the "extraordinary apathy" of the tsarist legation under his guidance had encouraged Miura to embark on the dastardly coup which had led to the murder of the queen. It accused him of having "nearly lost" Korea. In contrast, Speyer, who had replaced him, had "surveyed the diplomatic field of battle with his eagle eye" and had facilitated the flight of the king "under the mighty protection of the Russian eagle." Now that Waeber was once again in charge during Speyer's absence, the paper worried, "all the good which Speyer has done in a short time will again be spoilt by his *locum tenens*, although he has received strict instructions to avoid a repetition of his former mistakes." Admitting that it was impossible for Russia to proceed without compromise, *Novoe Vremia* argued that the situation in Korea demanded "extreme caution and an intelligent spirit of enterprise." It expressed the fear that Waeber might develop a policy injurious to Russian interests, "not by reason of malicious intentions on his part, but on account of his superfluous and inordinate love for the Coreans."

"Mr. Waeber has lived too long among the Coreans not to feel a certain sympathy for them," the paper explained. "It even seems to us as if his whole heart were wrapped up in their interests. If the Russians require any concession, Mr. Waeber considers, before all things, the interests of the Corean Government. He does this quite unselfishly and in an academic spirit, with the childlike conviction that it is proper for him to act thus. . . . But a policy of benevolence is no national policy. . . . In order to help the Government of Corea out of difficulties he liberally dispenses Russian money, without asking for any compensation. . . ."

Conceding that Russia was "bound to assist the Coreans in regaining their legs, and to introduce civilization into the country," the newspaper argued: "In doing so, we must not make a show of benevolence and altruism, inasmuch as we have the right of demanding compensation for every service rendered. Our relations must stand thus: We give you, but you pay or compensate our trouble by other means. Only under such conditions will Russo-Corean relations become normal, and not raise suspicions of mysterious Russian designs against Corea." [95]

Needless to say, the Japanese appreciated Waeber's low profile. They too thought that in all of Russian diplomacy they could not find a man so Korean in the heart as Waeber. They too regarded him as indecisive, lacking foresight, and as being taken in tow by events. [96] Japanese newspapers called for his retention in Seoul as the only man fit to preserve the peace of the Far East. [97]

The American charge d'affaires, on the other hand, was displeased with the weakness Waeber showed in his dealings with the Korean government. Reporting a change for the worse in the political situation, Allen wrote:

"Mr. Waeber, the Russian Minister at Seoul, has abstained from interfering in the details of Government as much as possible, and has given the conservative party so much liberty that they have now begun, through the King, to make changes in the Cabinet—a thing Mr. Waeber had declared he would not allow." It was confidently affirmed, he reported, that Hong, the unpunished murderer of Kim Ok-kyun, was to be named foreign minister! "It is understood that all these changes, and others that are prepared, are objectionable to Mr. Waeber, and that they have been made against his urgent protest," he related.

It looked to persons in Seoul, Allen continued, that Waeber did not have the full support of the tsarist government in his plans and actions. Prince Min Yong-hwan, who had been appointed minister of war, had brought back from St. Petersburg the news that a party in the tsarist government desired Waeber's removal and his replacement by a more vigorous representative, such as Speyer. Word of dissension among the Russians, circulated by a number of Russians as well as by Min, may have prodded the Korean conservatives into action. The Council of State, organized by Waeber, was not working at all, Allen complained. All the Council had done was to memorialize Kojong to leave the Russian legation.[98]

Twenty

The Russo-Japanese Entente

Preliminary conversations concerning a Russo-Japanese entente antedated Kojong's flight to the tsarist legation. As noted, Saionji had referred to a possible agreement between the two powers during his talk with Speyer on December 17, 1895. In the second half of December the Japanese government had tried to impress on Hitrovo that it was prepared to exercise moderation on Korean affairs and to settle all disagreements by means of negotiation. "In the Korean question," Hitrovo reported, "the Japanese government is inclined and forced toward moderation and tractability [*k umerennosti i sgovorchivosti*]." [1]

In January 1896, as the situation in Korea deteriorated, Tokyo became more persistent in seeking to persuade St. Petersburg of its sincere desire for negotiation and compromise in an attempt to forestall Russian action in the peninsula.

At the beginning of January, in the first of a series of meetings, Saionji assured Hitrovo that the Japanese minister in Seoul had been ordered not to interfere in the internal affairs of Korea. When Hitrovo asked whether Japan recognized the Korean government, Saionji replied evasively that Japan neither recognized nor disputed the present government of Korea, but like the other powers conducted business with the current ministers. Saionji declared that Japan wished to avoid in Korea any incidents which might lead to misunderstandings with Russia and he repeated several times that new instructions would be sent to Komura directing him "to try to maintain the sincerest relations with Mr. Speyer and to act jointly with him in all questions which may arise." [2]

Not satisfied with the vagueness of some of Saionji's answers, Hitrovo went to see Ito several days later. He accused the Japanese government of insincerity toward Russia in regard to Korean matters and tried to raise the question of the abnormal relationship between Kojong and his government.

Like Saionji, Ito avoided getting into a discussion of the basic issues, yet

602

dwelled even more persistently on the need for a Russo-Japanese entente. He had long ago come to the conclusion, Ito told Hitrovo, that in the Korean question Japan could find a way out of the difficulties of her present situation only by means of a direct and all-embracing agreement with Russia. He talked at length about the advantages of such an agreement. At the same time, however, Ito made no concrete proposal, saying that he did not formulate Japanese policy alone. Besides, he said, Japanese public opinion, which regarded any arrangements concerning Korea with suspicion, would have to be prepared before he could begin negotiations.

When Hitrovo argued that the initiative for an entente must come from Japan, because she was responsible for the new state of affairs in the Far East, Ito insisted that all he could do for the present in view of the above considerations was to instruct Komura to reassure the Russian representative by all means, to maintain the most amicable relations with him, and to confer with him in all cases of importance. A direct and comprehensive agreement would have to be concluded later. Ito expressed the hope that the dispatch of Prince Fushimi to the coronation of Nicholas II might provide the opportunity for such an agreement and confided that he himself was trying for that reason to be selected by the Meiji emperor as a member of the mission.

Hitrovo gained the impression from his talk with Ito that the Korean question essentially touched "the strings of national pride" far more than "the real interests of the country" and that the emotion aroused by the Korean question was based on historical myths. "Many Japanese," he reported, "are beginning to realize that the material interests of Japan in Korea are not all that significant, that a struggle to the death over Korea would entail excessively large risk and sacrifices and that in essence the skin is not worth currying." It was Hitrovo's belief, therefore, that Japan might be willing to compromise on Korea and that it would not be surprising if the Japanese government, having conclusively convinced itself that it could not make do without a direct agreement with Russia, would any day now turn to the latter with a suitable proposal. Hitrovo advocated a cautious and moderate Russian policy in regard to the Korean question so as not to deter Japan from seeking a solution through agreement with Russia, particularly since he apprehended that any Russian complications with Japan in Korea might lead to the intervention of third powers.[3]

The Seoul Memorandum

On February 11, 1896, before news of Kojong's flight to the Russian legation had reached Tokyo, Ito visited Hitrovo and conferred with him for two hours

about various aspects of the Korean situation.[4] Ito expressed satisfaction that
Speyer would replace Hitrovo during the latter's absence and promised to
summon Komura upon Speyer's arrival in order to decide what should be done
in Korea. Not knowing of the dramatic changes which had occurred in Seoul,
Hitrovo declared that in all justice the Japanese government ought to restore
the situation which had existed before the October coup and give back to the
king his freedom of action. Ito replied that Japan would assist in restoring
Kojong's freedom gradually, but that to make too drastic a change would be
dangerous in view of the internal struggle in Korea. If Russia wished, Ito
offered, Japan would be willing to remove the taewongun (who by this time
had been edging away from the Japanese). He was willing to consider other
changes in the Korean government as well, Ito remarked, but gradually and
eventually. To give the king complete freedom would be dangerous, Ito argued, as he could not handle himself, and a cabinet chosen by him would not
be capable of surviving.

Hitrovo countered that to deny the king the freedom to choose his own
cabinet contravened the recognized principle of the independence of Korea.
Ito conceded that Japan had gone further in Korea than expected, but that her
action had been compelled by circumstances. "We had been sincere when we
had expressed the opinion that Korea could exist by its own means, but experience has shown us the opposite," Ito contended. "We must recognize that
Korea cannot exist without suitable outside support." Hitrovo questioned Ito's
sincerity. The moment that the Japanese government had come to the conclusion that Korea could not exist as an independent state, it should have notified
Russia of its change of heart in order to come to an agreement with her, if she
shared the Japanese point of view, concerning the character, means, and
amount of support to be given to Korea. Hitrovo reiterated that the initiative
for an agreement between their countries must come from Japan as the one
responsible for the situation in Korea. Ito responded that the matter required
further study. Only after the views of Speyer and Komura had been heard
could the Japanese government start working out the bases for an entente.[5]

Conscious of the fact that rival factions in Korea tended to play Russia and
Japan against each other, Hitrovo warned Saionji that Kojong appeared to be
"a man having no fixed views, giving utterances to many self-conflicting
things, as they seemed convenient to [the] party to whom he speaks." They
should, he said, keep this in mind and guard against being misled. At his
suggestion, Saionji instructed Komura "to maintain close understanding"
with the Russian representative in Seoul.[6]

As word reached Tokyo of the flight of the king and the crown prince to the
Russian legation and of the appointment of reputedly Russophile advisers,

speculation arose that the Russian minister to Japan had somehow been behind the coup. Hitrovo had received permission in January to return home on leave. Passing over the legation secretary, Vollan, Lobanov had named Speyer, of whom he apparently thought more highly, to replace Hitrovo. Hitrovo's son, who served as an ensign aboard one of the Russian warships in the Pacific Ocean, had also received leave and was to accompany his father to Russia. There were those who charged that Hitrovo had simulated his furlough to hide his game in Korea and to lure the Japanese into a false sense of security.

Although Hitrovo's past tempted European diplomats to assume that he must have had at least an indirect hand in the developments in Korea, and although the events of February 11 must have revived fond memories of Balkan intrigue in him,[7] the German minister was prepared to accept at face value Hitrovo's assurance that news of the coup in Seoul had come as a complete surprise to him. Negotiations which he had conducted with Saionji and Ito during the preceding months had convinced Hitrovo, Gutschmid reported, that the Japanese government seriously endeavored to act in full agreement with Russia and to avoid any conflict. The Russian minister had consequently advised Lobanov not to press the Japanese for the moment and to leave them time to withdraw from Korea with honor. St. Petersburg had concurred with this policy and Lobanov had instructed the Russian agents in Seoul to exercise moderation and restraint. Hitrovo had thus made his travel preparations with complete peace of mind. Gutschmid was inclined to believe that this was true, particularly since it was impossible to direct such coups from a distance. "It appears to me far more likely," Gutschmid wrote, "that Mr. Waeber had been intent, with the help of the amenable Mr. von Speyer, to make up for the reversal of October 8 of last year and to bring about a *restitutio in integrum* [a full restoration], to be sure, minus the queen."

When Gutschmid called on Hitrovo on February 14 to inquire whether he had any telegrams about the recent events in Korea, the latter replied that so far he had received nothing, because the telegraph between Seoul and Fusan was out of commission. He did expect to hear something soon, however, since dispatches could be carried by courier from the Korean capital to Fusan and be cabled from there, as the Japanese had done. Hitrovo related to Gutschmid that informal *pourparlers* had recently taken place between him and Marquis Ito regarding Korea. As recently as two days ago, the premier had visited him to discuss certain points with the aim of collaborating with Russia and reaching an understanding between the two governments regarding this delicate question. Hitrovo had made no secret, he told Gutschmid, that the independence of Korea promised to Russia would remain a dead letter so long as the king would not be in a position to choose his own counsellors and to govern independently of foreign, that is of Japanese, influence. Ito had given to understand that he seriously desired to consider Russian wishes, but he had made no definite declaration.

The events which had just occurred, Hitrovo reflected, placed the Japanese in a very difficult position. Since they had declared the preceding year that though they disapproved of the upheaval of October 8, they could not intervene, they must now pursue the same policy.

When Gutschmid remarked that it would come finally to a Russian protectorate over Korea, Hitrovo retorted lively: "That is precisely what we do not want! [*Gerade das wollen wir nicht!*]" ("The ripe fruit is supposed to just fall into the lap and Korea is to be left to herself until conditions there become so unstable that Russia, once Japan has withdrawn militarily, can intervene directly and annex [the country]," Gutschmid surmised.)

"No one wants to hinder Japan in the development of her commercial relations with Korea, we least of all," Hitrovo stated to Gutschmid. "We have only political interests there. Hence the pretext of the Japanese that they must retain military forces there for the protection of their trade is completely invalid. They are so hated in Korea that the retention of their troops of itself harms their trade interests!" Yet Hitrovo realized the difficult position in which the Japanese government found itself vis-à-vis its own public in view of the historical ties between Japan and Korea.

Hitrovo said that the recent events might compel him to postpone his departure, set for February 23, by about two weeks, as he anticipated new negotiations with the Japanese government and as Speyer might prove indispensable in Seoul at present.[8]

Premier Ito told the German minister on February 15 that although he had as yet only the most meager information and no evidence for his suspicions, he thought that the palace revolution must have been the work of Waeber and Speyer. He conceded that Komura had apparently had no inkling whatsoever of the coup which, he admitted with frank admiration, had been executed with great skill.

Ito reiterated that Japan would adhere to the principle of nonintervention in the internal affairs of Korea. As regarded the withdrawal of Japanese troops from the peninsula, against which Berlin itself had advised, it could be carried out only gradually. For the moment it was absolutely necessary and a dictate of elementary prudence to retain sufficient military forces in the land to protect at least the telegraph lines. As for the probable and direct consequences of the coup, he could as yet make no comments.

Although Ito was aware of the danger posed by the presence of almost 200

Russian marines in Seoul, Gutschmid reported, he implied that strict orders had been sent to the Japanese commander to remain absolutely neutral and to avoid any cause for friction.

In response to Gutschmid's searching remark that he hoped that the confidential negotiations which Ito had conducted recently with Hitrovo had led to an at least temporary agreement regarding the mutual stance of the two powers in Korea, Ito stated that *all* that had been decided was for the Russian and Japanese representatives to communicate to each other their observations, particularly the remarks which the king would make to them, because Kojong was in the habit of saying something quite different to the Russian chargé and to the Japanese minister. As a result, in the past, the two representatives had informed their representative governments in the opposite sense giving rise to misunderstandings and tensions between the two governments. Such an *ad hoc* arrangement was all that had been concluded, Ito repeated. The future of Korea and the ways and means for a definitive agreement had not been the subject of the conversations. Nor could Japan make any definite promises in this direction at the present time, Ito declared. The situation in Korea was too unclear, and he must reserve the right for his government to act in accordance with circumstances. The recent events had shown that the complete independence of Korea was an impossibility, Ito observed. The Korean government had once again resorted to foreign help.

Ito revealed that he had conveyed to Lobanov through Hitrovo the most binding assurances that the Japanese government had no intention of taking hostile action against Russia or Korea. He told Gutschmid that he had just prorogued the Diet for ten days to prevent the spread of agitation, produced by the recent events in Korea, from the speaker's platform throughout the land and the press. In questions of foreign affairs, Ito contended, the Japanese people were still so immature politically that free discussion thereof must be strictly suppressed in every way as dangerous to the internal peace of the country.

At a dinner in the imperial palace that evening Acting Foreign Minister Saionji took the German minister aside and asked him whether he thought that the Russian cabinet had known of and sanctioned the recent coup in Seoul. When Gutschmid replied without hesitation that he was convinced that this had not been the case and that Hitrovo too had probably had no foreknowledge thereof, Saionji looked greatly relieved. He promised to keep Gutschmid informed of further developments.[9]

Because his visit to Ito had been noted by the Japanese press, Gutschmid called on his Russian colleague on the afternoon of the seventeenth, lest bearers of false tales seize the opportunity to sow mistrust between them. Ito had told him, he relayed to Hitrovo, that Japan would continue to adhere to the declaration she had made to the powers on October 26 of the previous year that she would let Korea go her own way and would refrain from interfering in her internal affairs, though she could not withdraw her troops until the security of communications had been assured. Hitrovo seemed to listen with particular pleasure to Gutschmid's account of the genuine admiration which Ito had shown for the *mise en scène* of the recent coup.

Hitrovo observed that the Japanese press had reacted rather well to the surprising news from Seoul and that the attitude of the Japanese government was very circumspect. Gutschmid gained the impression that Hitrovo had some apprehensions in this regard and the care with which the police guarded the tsarist legation since the receipt of the first telegrams from Korea suggested that the local authorities too had reckoned with the possibility of an anti-Russian outburst on the part of certain circles of the population. It now was Hitrovo's belief, Gutschmid reported, that the events of February 11 would actually contribute to a "speedy understanding" between the powers concerned regarding the Korean question.

The restoration, Hitrovo noted, had been very peaceful according to Speyer's telegrams, and the king had received the Japanese minister resident in the Russian legation. There had been no change in plans, Hitrovo added, in regard to his own replacement during his imminent absence. Speyer would still come to Tokyo. Waeber was familiar enough with Korea to be left there on his own again, and Speyer could no doubt contribute much in Tokyo to reaching an understanding after having studied the situation in Korea personally.[10]

Relating his conversation with Gutschmid to Satow on the fifteenth, Ito expressed doubt at Hitrovo's assertion that he had no news from Korea. Satow remarked that Zinovii Mikhailovich Polianovskii, a Russian language student, had told him the night before that Hitrovo was delaying his departure because of the troubles in Korea. It was the experience of the British in Central Asian affairs, Satow asserted, that the Russian government constantly assured them that nothing would be done, then some zealous officer on the spot did that very thing, and the government said that it could not avoid a *fait accompli*. When Ito noted that his only fear was that some of his younger countrymen in Seoul might create a disturbance, Satow concluded that the Japanese government had accepted the inevitable and would not resist what had been done.[11]

Asked by Saionji on February 17 whether he thought that the Russian government had known beforehand what was going to transpire in Korea, Satow repeated that in cases of this sort the Russians refused to undo a *fait accompli*, "so it came to the same thing." When Korean visitors told Satow on the nineteenth that they feared Russian annexation of Korea and asked if England would not help them, Satow replied that there could be no question of the British interfering to turn out the Russians, "especially as the King had put himself in their hands voluntarily, and had right on their side." He did not think that Russia wished to destroy the independence of Korea, he said, only to prevent the Japanese taking possession of the country.[12]

An attempt by Nishi on February 15 to learn the intent and future policy of Russia in Korea proved futile, as Lobanov himself was not yet fully informed about events in Seoul.[13] The following day, on February 16, Lobanov showed Nishi three telegrams—all that he had received from Seoul since the coup. Two of them, dated February 11 and 12 respectively, had arrived only the preceding day in view of the partial interruption in telegraphic communication. The information contained in the three cables was too meager for Lobanov to be able to take a stand on the situation. It appeared, he remarked, that the king had appealed for rescue to the Russian representative and that the latter had offered him all possible assistance. When Nishi wondered whether Speyer had taken an active part in the affair, Lobanov replied that he did not think so, but he admitted candidly that he did not know for sure because of lack of information. He assured Nishi that the Russian government desired the early establishment of tranquility in Korea without any foreign interference.

Nishi came away impressed, he reported, that Lobanov truly was not well acquainted with the events in Korea and that the Russian government had had no foreknowledge of them.[14]

The Japanese government debated for a whole week how to react to the events in Korea. Premier Ito and Foreign Minister Mutsu, who were most influential in shaping Japanese foreign policy, spoke up in favor of involving other powers beside Russia and Japan in an agreement regarding Korea.[15]

On February 17 the Japanese minister in London communicated to the British foreign secretary what information he had received about the dispatch of the Russian forces to Seoul and the subsequent flight of the king to the Russian legation. He voiced the suspicion that the two events were related and that Kojong's move had been prearranged with the Russian minister. On February 19, in accordance with instructions from Saionji, Kato asked Salisbury point blank what opinion the British government had formed regarding the developments in Korea. Salisbury responded that his government had as yet insufficient information to form a judgment. Even if Kato were right that there had been a Russian plot, the small number of men landed suggested that the affair was not important enough for Britain to raise a diplomatic question about it. He would be curious to know the views of the Japanese government "as [the] most interested party," Salisbury remarked.

Kato inquired what Salisbury thought regarding Russia's desire to obtain an ice-free port in the China Seas. Salisbury replied that as long as Russia merely sought a commercial outlet and tried to acquire it by peaceful means such as by purchase, Her Majesty's Government could not object, but that it would be an entirely different matter if Russia strove to create a fortified harbor or to occupy territory which did not belong to her.[16]

In response to a question by Sir Ellis Ashmead-Bartlett in the House of Commons on February 20 whether the agreement made by the Russian government not to occupy any port in Korea when Great Britain withdrew from Port Hamilton was still binding, the Foreign Office replied in the affirmative. It still held Russia to the pledge made in 1886 "not to occupy Corean territory under any circumstances whatsoever."[17]

The Japanese minister in Berlin tried to sway the views of his English colleague. Contending that the Russian naval force in the Pacific had been extended to such an extent that it would be hopeless for Japan to put up any resistance alone, Viscount Aoki fished for assurances of British support. It was to be foreseen, he declared, that the Russians would deflect the Trans-Siberian railroad to Port Arthur and would incorporate the Liaotung Peninsula into their empire. When Lascelles voiced doubt that England would go to war over Port Arthur, Aoki pointed out that Russian acquisition of the Liaotung Peninsula would completely change the situation in China and would ultimately lead to the annexation of at least part of Korea. That would be a calamity for Japan and would, he presumed, affect also Great Britain. He suggested that the latter take the initiative in bringing about an understanding between England, Japan, and China in order to stop any further Russian advance.[18]

Aoki found the German government equally lukewarm to his overtures. When he had pointed to the utterance of Kimberley that not only the independence of Korea but also her integrity must be preserved and had asserted that Germany, in view of her treaty relations with Korea, must wish that at least as much as Britain, the German foreign minister had agreed with him. "My opinion is that [the] German Government, having made [a] political mistake in [the] triple intervention, will not act rashly," Aoki telegraphed. "At any rate their attitude toward Japan is favourable," he added in consolation.[19]

The Italian undersecretary of state told the Japanese chargé d'affaires that Italy was disposed to act in accord with the other European powers. But Italian newspapers speculated that there was little hope after a recent speech by

Arthur James Balfour, leader of the House of Commons and deputy prime minister, that England would act vigorously against Russia and that Japan would probably have to stand up to Russia alone.[20]

The Austrian foreign minister, Count Agenor Goluchowski-Goluchowo, Jr., declined to give a direct reply to the inquiries of Kurino Shinchiro on the ground of the absence of Austrian interests in the Far East and his lack of information about the intentions of the European power. He did express the hope that Japan would maintain her position as "an important factor of peace in the East" by pursuing a policy of "prudence and common sense."[21]

Paris was preoccupied with parliamentary questions. As Foreign Minister Pierre Eugène Marcelin Berthelot told Sone Arasuke, he had not yet received an official report from Lefèvre and had not had the opportunity to examine the Korean question closely.[22]

Secretary of State Olney likewise told Kurino that he had no knowledge of the true aims of Russia. Having no particular policy in Korea, the United States had formed no opinion and would take no action, he declared. Personally he regarded the events in Korea as "too high-handed" an act on the part of Russia and tantamount to the seizure of the country. He strongly warned Japan to do everything possible to avoid a collision.[23] When Kurino, on instructions from Saionji, called on the secretary of state again several days later to sound the attitude of the United States, Olney repeated that while he personally considered Korea to be practically under Russian occupation, the policy of his government prevented any steps beyond the protection of American citizens. "He says [the] United States are greatly interested in [the] welfare of Japan and, if required, are willing to offer good offices at any time," Kurino reported.[24]

The negative replies which Tokyo received strengthened the position of the advocates of a bilateral agreement with Russia. Marshal Yamagata Aritomo, the "father" of the Japanese army, was the most influential figure in this group. After a conversation with Yamagata, who visited him privately, Hitrovo cabled on February 19 that Yamagata favored the solution of the Korean question "exclusively by means of a complete agreement with the Russians" and that he was trying to win the cabinet over to this idea. Former Premier Matsukata Masayoshi, who shared Yamagata's point of view, also called on Hitrovo. He berated past Japanese policy in Korea for its insincerity and stressed the need for a direct agreement with Russia.[25] Even Komura, the Japanese minister in Seoul, favored at least a temporary arrangement with Russia. As he had written to Mutsu on February 13: "Under the present circumstances the situation can be restored only by the use of armed force. Such an attempt will without fail lead to a collision with Russia, yet it is too early for us, I am deeply convinced, to quarrel with her. I consider it necessary, therefore, to adhere to exclusively peaceful steps." [26]

"The Japanese government reacted to the Korean events most sensibly, tactfully, and reasonably," Hitrovo reported. "It has understood that thanks to the former mistakes of its policy in Korea, its game is lost and that it ought to avert at all cost possible complications with us, that this was the only way out for them from the present difficulties." Should the recent events in Seoul pass without complications, Hitrovo remarked, it would be due first of all to "the sober prudence which in these critical circumstances triumphed in the highest counsels of the [Meiji] emperor over the feelings of Japanese chauvinism." [27]

As Hitrovo wrote in a private letter to Lobanov, he believed that the impotence which China had revealed in the war with Japan was bound to lead to her partition sooner or later. Consequently, he argued, Japan constituted for Russia the only large and serious quantity in the Far East and Russia's full attention must be focussed on Japan as the sole major political and military factor in the Far East which Russia must take into account and take into account seriously. In order for Russia to be able to do anything in the Far East, Hitrovo stated, she must be completely secure from the side of Japan and this could be achieved most readily by a timely, all-embracing agreement between the two powers. It was Hitrovo's belief that there were no conflicting interests between Russia and Japan except for the Korean question and that every effort must be made, therefore, to resolve the latter. He did not think this to be particularly difficult, because he was under the illusion that, as he put it, "the majority of right-thinking people in Japan herself are satisfied that Korea will become our property one way or another sooner or later." [28]

Hitrovo's interpretation of Japanese policy irritated Waeber. He complained to Lobanov that "sometimes Japanese policy is appraised on the basis of the amiable appearance of the Japanese spokesmen rather than on the basis of its actual content." [29]

On February 19 Nishi told Lobanov that he was afraid that if the "abnormal" state of affairs in Korea were allowed to continue, "serious consequences" would result. He inquired when, in Lobanov's opinion, the Korean government would be restored to normal by the return of the king to the palace. He urged the foreign minister to send appropriate instructions to the Russian representative in Seoul.

Lobanov conceded that he too was concerned that complications might develop, as the British and other powers were said to have landed marines. However, he was unable at present either to state how long Kojong would remain in the Russian legation or to send instructions to Speyer, because he had insufficient information about the actual situation due to the interruption of the telegraph line.

Nishi was not certain whether Lobanov's ignorance of details was due to "insufficient reports so far made on purpose" by Speyer or whether he had deliberately granted great liberty of action to the latter. Russian newspapers, he cabled, contained little or no intelligence about the events in Korea. General feeling appeared to be sympathetic toward the bold action of the Koreans in consideration of the affair of October 8 of the preceding year.[30]

Saionji conferred with Hitrovo in Tokyo the same day, on February 19. Referring to a telegram he had received from Nishi on the seventeenth, Saionji expressed gratification that the coup in Korea had occurred apparently without the foreknowledge of the tsarist government, although the landing of the Russian marines suggested that its representative in Seoul had been aware of approaching events. He voiced confidence that the tsarist government too did not desire the abnormal situation in Seoul to continue, because, as Nishi had cabled, it wanted the restoration of order without foreign intervention. Saionji declared that no misunderstanding should be created between their two countries by any mistakes on the part of their agents in Korea and that the best means of preventing such a misunderstanding, as Hitrovo had had occasion to suggest to Ito and himself, would be to establish an entente between their two governments. The Japanese government, therefore, wished to know the views of the Russian government on this subject and its intentions regarding the present situation of the king, who, Hitrovo would admit, could not stay forever in a foreign legation with his ministers.

Hitrovo stated that he too believed that the coup in Seoul had occurred without the knowledge of his government. He told Saionji that the instructions from Lobanov to the Russian representative in Korea had passed through his hands. They had specifically directed Speyer to refrain from provoking any new incident, but the coup of February 11 had occurred before the directive had reached Seoul. The Russian government was waiting for his own return to St. Petersburg in order to confer with him.

Hitrovo promised to telegraph to St. Petersburg what Saionji was saying and expressed confidence that the tsarist government would gladly entertain the proposal for an understanding. Hitrovo ventured the opinion that it would be up to his own country to take the initiative in remedying the abnormal situation of the king reigning from the Russian legation. On the other hand, as the prime cause of the present development lay in the doings of Japan, it would be up to the latter, he thought, to take the initiative for an understanding between their countries regarding their future attitude towards Korea.

Saionji retorted that if the two governments would agree in principle to enter into an understanding, the question of who should take the initiative would not meet with much difficulty. He suggested that Japan and Russia avoid future misunderstandings by informing each other of the purport of instructions concerning important questions of common interest prior to their being sent to their agents in Korea.

Hitrovo observed that he personally was convinced that an entente between Russia and Japan was very desirable and that such an agreement could be achieved, since neither of the two governments had any aggressive designs on Korea. "What Russia wants," Hitrovo asserted, "is that Korea not be a weapon between the hands of a power against Russia." Russia had no objection to the reforms that Japan wished to make in Korea, he continued, but he believed that Korea was really incapable of being independent and that the two governments must take this into consideration. It was necessary, therefore, to find a *modus vivendi* for allowing Korea to exist. Such a *modus vivendi*, according to Hitrovo, could be found only if the governments of Russia and Japan came to an understanding.

Hitrovo praised the notion of sending common instructions to their respective representatives as an excellent measure. It would be very salutary, he remarked, to show to their representatives in Seoul that the two governments were in agreement on the Korean question and this would pour, as the saying went, a little water into the wine, and calm the too pro-Korean sentiments of Waeber, who seemed convinced that Korea could really be independent.

Hitrovo opined that being more distant from the theater of action, one could judge the question more coldly from Tokyo and see things in their true light.[31]

In a telegram to Nishi on February 20, Saionji asserted that there had been no foundation for the allegation which someone had made to Kojong in order to entice him out of the palace and into the Russian legation that some of his cabinet ministers had been intriguing with Japanese soldiers to dethrone him. The Japanese government was confident, he telegraphed, that the king had nothing to fear from its troops. Saionji authorized Nishi to inform the tsarist government of the above, should he deem it necessary to avoid a misunderstanding.[32]

On February 23 Hitrovo communicated Lobanov's reply to Saionji. Due to the interruption of telegraphic communication, the Russian government still had no details about the changes which had occurred in Korea or their causes, the Russian foreign minister cabled. He entirely shared Saionji's view on the advisability of entering into an understanding concerning the instructions to be issued to their respective representatives in order to prevent future incidents. Lobanov desired to know, therefore, the general sense of the instructions which the Japanese government intended to send to its minister in Seoul.[33]

On February 24 Saionji handed to Hitrovo the Japanese proposal for the instructions. The Russian minister promised to telegraph it home together with his own observations. He requested that the text be conveyed also by the Japanese Foreign Office to Nishi for submission to the tsarist government directly. This was done on the twenty-fifth.

The gist of the Japanese memorandum was as follows: (1) The situation in Seoul now being calm, the Japanese government thought that it would be "convenient" for the king to return to his palace. It desired consequently that the Russian government instruct its representative in Seoul to take the necessary measures to that end. If Kojong was really apprehensive about the conduct of Japanese troops, the Japanese government was prepared to give assurances to the Korean government that the Japanese troops stationed in Seoul would be used merely for the protection of the legation, consulate, and subjects of Japan and, in case of necessity, also of the king. (2) The Japanese government desired that Russia and Japan instruct their representatives in Seoul to advise Kojong that he appoint impartial men in the event a new government had to be formed. (3) It was customary in Korea for those in power to inflict the most cruel punishments on their political opponents, thereby perpetuating a spirit of vengeance detrimental to the tranquility of the country. The Japanese government proposed, therefore, in the interest of everyone that the Japanese and Russian representatives in Seoul be instructed to counsel the Korean government to abstain from such inhuman penalties in the present instance.[34]

On February 25 Saionji communicated to Nishi for his own information that the foreign representatives in Korea all recognized the present situation as very critical, but had merely telegraphed an account of recent events to their governments and were waiting for instructions. None of them dared to urge the king's return to the palace for fear that Russian troops would be assigned to guard it, though Waeber himself hesitated to send Russian soldiers to guard the palace.

Saionji cabled that the attitude of the Korean people had changed suddenly since the coup and that anti-Japanese feeling prevailed everywhere. Messages from Seoul were greatly delayed, he added, because rioters had cut the telegraph lines between Seoul and Pusan and between Seoul and Gensan (Wonsan).[35]

Saionji believed and Lobanov concurred that the purpose of the contemplated agreement between Waeber and Komura in Seoul was to adjust the most acute questions which had arisen in connection with the changed circumstances in Korea—to arrive at a temporary *modus vivendi*. The negotiation of a broader and more permanent understanding was to take place in Russia, when the Fushimi mission would attend Nicholas's coronation.[36] Although Premier Ito, who had originally suggested the mission, would have been the logical person to accompany the prince and confer with Lobanov, the Japanese government named Marshal Yamagata in his stead. When the appointment elicited surprise in St. Petersburg, Saionji informed Nishi that Ito's presence was indispensable in Japan at this time.[37] The recent events in Korea had given to the opposition in the Diet new ammunition against the government and the premier had to remain in Tokyo to defend the policies of his administration.[38]

Nishi had asked to be recalled, but Saionji insisted that his continuation in the Russian capital was essential. Requesting Nishi to do his best to secure the assent of the tsarist government to the nomination of Yamagata, Saionji offered to obtain, if necessary, the intercession of the Russian minister in Tokyo with his government.[39] Hitrovo was pleased with the choice of envoy. In a dispatch written several days earlier, on February 20, he had speculated that the Japanese government had selected the marshal because Ito had for a long time opposed or at least delayed an agreement with Russia, while Yamagata had favored a Russo-Japanese entente all along.[40] "The appointment of Marshal Yamagata instead of Marquis Ito as envoy extraordinary is of the utmost significance and proves that the view of the necessity of a direct full agreement with us has definitely triumphed in the highest government spheres," Hitrovo asserted on February 27. Because of Yamagata's conciliatory attitude, Hitrovo anticipated that the marshal might make recommendations agreeable to the Russian side and would accept everything that the latter would propose.[41]

St. Petersburg was less optimistic than Hitrovo. It concurred nonetheless that in the process of hammering out an agreement in Seoul, negotiations be begun concerning a more general settlement of Korean affairs.[42] When Nishi explained the motive behind Yamagata's mission, Lobanov replied that the marshal would be received with due courtesy. Expressing his desire for a Russo-Japanese understanding, he asked for a few days' time to give a decisive answer.[43]

On February 27 Saionji telegraphed to Nishi that the Japanese government thought it possible that Russia might demand sooner or later that Japan withdraw her troops from Korea, as Sone had warned in a report from Paris. It was a subject that had to be approached "most cautiously" in view of the political situation inside Japan. Saionji instructed Nishi to endeavor to persuade Lobanov that except for such phases as required urgent treatment, the Korean question be left in the *status quo* until Yamagata arrived in St. Petersburg and could discuss the matter personally with Nishi. "It is plain that any sudden change in affairs of Corea before an understanding is entered with Russia would be conducive to evil results," Saionji cabled; "for instance, [the] immediate withdrawal of our troops from Corea at this juncture would not only augment disorder, but [would] seriously endanger [the] lives and property of Japanese in Corea." [44]

On February 28 Lobanov cabled a counterproposal to Hitrovo. [45] As he communicated to Nishi on the twenty-ninth, the Russian government shared the desire that the king return to his palace, expressed in the first point of the Japanese proposal, and it accepted the second and third points of the same proposal. It wished, however, to add two points of its own: that the representatives in Seoul were to examine whether it was necessary for foreign troops to protect the telegraph lines in Korea and that the points at issue be discussed in a conciliatory manner. When Nishi tried to pin Lobanov down on the first point and asked why he could not instruct the Russian representative in Seoul to let the king return to the palace, Lobanov retorted that Kojong had sought assistance because of danger to his life; hence it was very difficult as a matter of hospitality to drive him out of the Russian legation. Nishi remarked that in view of the tranquility which now reigned in the capital, Kojong might be persuaded by the Russian representative to return to his palace without violating the hospitality extended to him. Otherwise, he feared, serious consequences might result, because many Japanese residents in Korea had to be embarrassed by constant disorders in the interior as long as the present abnormal state of affairs continued.

Lobanov seemed to recognize this, Nishi reported, and said that he was waiting for further information from Hitrovo. Lobanov assured Nishi that the matter in Seoul could be settled without difficulty if the representatives of Russia and Japan would confer in a perfectly conciliatory spirit. [46]

On March 2 Hitrovo presented Lobanov's reply to Saionji. It consisted of five points: (1) The king was always free to return to the palace when he judged it possible and the Russian chargé would certainly not oppose it. (2) The representatives of Russia and Japan should aim to recommend moderate ministers to the king and to induce him to show clemency toward his subjects. (3) The two representatives were to study the question whether foreign troops were still necessary for the protection of telegraph lines and if so, which lines and in what number. (4) They were to come to an agreement also, if the occasion arose, regarding measures to be taken for the protection of their respective legations and consulates. (5) The above negotiations were to be conducted in a reciprocal spirit of conciliation. [47]

The following day, on March 3, Saionji formally accepted the Russian counterproposal. He told Hitrovo that he would send the necessary instructions to Komura and asked that the tsarist government send similar instructions to its representative in Seoul.[48]

In his telegram to Komura, dispatched the same day, Saionji communicated the text of the Russian counterproposal to which he had agreed. Directing Komura to confer with Waeber, he indicated the position he was to take on the five points: (1) Because the return of the king to the palace was very necessary, Komura was to make every effort to that end. (2) As for recommending to Kojong the appointment of moderate ministers, it was sufficient for Komura to establish the fact that they were being appointed as the result of consultation of the representatives of Japan and Russia, "thereby reserving ground for a voice in [the] future in regard to the action of such Ministers." He need not go so far as to dispute the personality of any particular individual with his Russian colleague. (3) Komura should consult most fully with the Russian representative concerning the king's show of clemency toward his subjects. (4) The stationing of troops in Korea for the protection of telegraph communication was still necessary at present. Since the Russian government did not seem to have any particular objection to this, Komura was to press for the continuation of such protection. (5) He need not take the initiative in discussing measures of the protection of the legations and the consulates. If Waeber brought up the subject, Komura was to explain to him fully the necessity of keeping Japanese troops in Korea in the present state of the country.

Before coming to a final understanding with the Russian representative, Saionji concluded, Komura was to report the results of the negotiations to him and await further instructions.[49]

On March 4 Nishi transmitted to Lobanov Saionji's acceptance of the Russian counterproposal. "He said that he is very glad to hear it and asked me to convey his satisfaction to you," Nishi telegraphed to Saionji. Lobanov stated that he had not yet received word from Hitrovo, but that he would send the required instructions to Seoul as soon as he heard from him.[50]

Upon receiving Hitrovo's confirmation of the acceptance of his counterproposal, Lobanov immediately directed him to send appropriate instructions to Waeber. The path was clear at last for reaching an agreement on the spot. Or so it seemed at the moment. The vagueness of the instructions sent by both sides allowed Waeber and Komura too much latitude. As they could not come to terms with each other, their governments were forced to intercede in order to rescue the negotiations.[51]

In a lengthy conversation with Ito at the latter's official residence on March 5, Hitrovo reiterated that the "regrettable" events in Korea had come as a surprise to his government, which had specifically directed its representative in Seoul to abstain from giving rise to any new incident, because Russia desired no fresh complications in the Far East. The interruption in telegraphic communication, he repeated, had unfortunately delayed the arrival of the instructions until after the king had received asylum in the Russian legation.

Ito replied that he too had been much surprised by what had happened, but that he was pleased at recent reports that calm had been restored in Seoul. He expressed satisfaction that their governments had been able to arrive at a certain understanding, thanks to Hitrovo's kind cooperation.

Hitrovo responded that he also was glad that the two governments had been able to come to an understanding regarding the instructions for their respective representatives in Korea. However, these were only provisional measures. As he had told him in a previous conversation, Hitrovo continued, it would be very desirable to have an understanding on the Korean question in general. He thought, he ventured, that Yamagata was entrusted with this task, and since he himself was due to go to Russia at least a month before the marshal, he desired to know the general points of the latter's mission, so that he could pave the way for him.

Ito confirmed that Yamagata was charged with a special mission to that effect. It was his hope, he said, that an entente between the two governments could be reached following an exchange of views between Yamagata and Lobanov. Reminding Hitrovo of a conversation the latter had had with Saionji, Ito declared that he too thought that Korea was incapable of existing by herself and required the aid of others. It was desirable, consequently, that Japan and Russia come to an understanding to that effect. What were Hitrovo's views on the subject, he inquired.

Hitrovo answered that in his opinion too, as he had already told Saionji, Korea was incapable of being independent by her own effort and that it was desirable to find a *modus vivendi* by means of an entente between Russia and Japan, permitting Korea to continue to exist. As he had declared to him several times, what Russia desired regarding Korea was that the latter not become a weapon against her in the hands of other powers.

If such were the real intentions of Russia, Ito retorted, it should be readily possible to reach an understanding between their countries, for as he had conveyed to Hitrovo previously, Japan had no aggressive intentions against Korea; nor did she desire to have exclusive influence in that country.

Hitrovo concurred that an understanding between their states was very possible. The Korean question, he noted, could not be separated from the Far Eastern question in general. Since here the interests of Russia and Japan were not in conflict (*n'ont rien de contraires*), one should be perfectly able to come to an understanding on the Korean question.

Ito agreed with Hitrovo. Nothing divided Japan and Russia apart from the

Korean question and since there was no disagreement on fundamentals in the latter, one should be perfectly able to reach an understanding on details. Ito asked Hitrovo to do all he could upon his return to St. Petersburg to bring success to Yamagata's mission.

Hitrovo answered that he had always acted in this sense and would continue to do so. Alluding apparently to the question of the withdrawal of Japanese troops, Hitrovo stated that there were certain measures which his government and that of Korea would like to see Japan take and toward which, in their view, the Japanese government itself was not ill-disposed. Yet he himself understood that such measures would offend national feeling and would greatly embarrass the Japanese government. Such questions must, therefore, be approached with caution and the delicate domestic position of the Japanese government must be taken into account. Since he himself was familiar with the situation, his presence in St. Petersburg should be useful.

It was for this reason, Hitrovo asserted, that he had asked for leave to return home at this time, even though the tsarist government had wanted him to remain in Japan a while longer.[52]

On March 6 Hitrovo wrote to Saionji that he had promptly transmitted the latter's acceptance of the Russian counterproposal and that he had just received a telegram from Lobanov ordering him to communicate the five points on which they had agreed to the Russian representative in Seoul and instruct him to adhere to them in his conduct. Hitrovo took the opportunity to inform Saionji that Speyer had arrived in Tokyo that morning.[53]

On March 12 Komura inquired of Waeber if he had received authorization to negotiate with him. When Waeber replied that he had, Komura proceeded to sound his views about the first four points of his instructions from Saionji.[54]

Ten days later, on March 22, Komura presented a draft memorandum to Waeber proposing the following: (1) The Japanese and Russian ministers, after first consulting with the other foreign representatives in order to secure their moral support, would jointly advise the king to return to the palace. The Japanese representative was to remove the Japanese troops from the barracks in front of the palace and give assurances as to the control of Japanese troops and of Japanese *soshi*. (2) Since a firm and efficient government was necessary to restore and maintain peace and order, the Japanese and Russian ministers were to endeavor at all times to induce the king to appoint moderate men as ministers and to see to it that justice was not made subservient to vengeance by one party against the other. (3) The Japanese troops in Seoul were to be reduced to two companies of 200 men each. These forces, plus one company at Pusan and one company at Gensan (Wonsan) were to be maintained until the complete restoration of tranquility in the interior. (4) Japanese troops for the protection of the telegraph line between Seoul and Pusan were to be withdrawn as soon as the insurgents along the line had been dispersed; they were to be replaced by gendarmes (*kempei*) numbering not more than 200 men.[55]

In his proposal Komura deviated from the instructions on which the two goverments had agreed. Touching the return of the king to the palace, he reiterated the first point of the original Japanese draft instructions, which had been rejected by Lobanov. In the question of the retention of Japanese troops, he ignored equal rights on the part of Russia.[56] Speyer, to whom Saionji showed the Komura proposal in Tokyo on the twenty-sixth,[57] judged it acceptable as a temporary measure. He did not catch the deviation from the joint instructions, perhaps because he did not attribute much importance to the talks in Seoul, believing that only through direct negotiations between the two governments could a lasting foundation be laid for the new state of affairs in Korea.

Saionji beamed with pleasure at Speyer's approval. In view of such a "loyal attitude" by the Russian representatives toward the business at hand, he declared, an agreement between Russia and Japan regarding the Korean question was bound to be concluded in the near future.[58]

Saionji's satisfaction was premature. Waeber rejected the Komura proposals, believing that the return of the king to the palace against his will prior to the formation of a reliable guard, along with a change in the composition of the government and the legalization of the presence of Japanese troops only, would change the balance of power in favor of Japan and thereby complicate the discussions which were to take place in Russia. In the counterproposal which Waeber submitted to Komura on April 6, he in turn advanced demands not envisaged in the joint instructions.[59]

Waeber reminded Komura that the flight of the king had been due to the usurpation of power by the cabinet, which contained persons involved in the murder of the queen, the establishment of a guard under the control of persons hostile to him, and the removal of high officials in whom he had confidence. Since Kojong had sought refuge in the Russian legation out of fear for his life, Waeber argued, the main condition for his return to the palace must be the assurance of his safety. He proposed, therefore, in regard to the first point that the king himself be left to decide when to go back to the palace, stating that he would be glad to advise him to do so when no doubt remained about his future safety. Waeber agreed to the withdrawal of the Japanese troops from the vicinity of the palace and the strict control of the *soshi* in order that the king could feel secure. In regard to the second point, Waeber tried to nullify Komura's suggestion that the government must be changed and that mercy must be shown to the defeated supporters of Japan. The present cabinet, he wrote, had been appointed by the king out of his own free will from among ministers who were known to be progressive and liberal and who had served repeatedly in the government. The king and the ministers had shown great clemency, the recent trial having been conducted fairly, without resort to torture. Concerning point three, Waeber demanded that the Japanese troops guarding the telegraph line between Seoul and Pusan be replaced as soon as possible by gendarmes. He agreed to the use of up to 200 gendarmes, but stipulated that they be withdrawn gradually from places where peace and order had been restored by the Korean government. Exceeding his instructions, Waeber proposed that the Japanese give up their ownership of the telegraph line.

"The Russian Minister feels it his duty to point out that the holding of a telegraph line by the Japanese Government in an independent country is an anomaly," Waeber wrote. "It would be in the interest of the peace of Korea if the Japanese Government were to abolish this anomaly by selling the telegraph line or by taking it off entirely in case the old Korean line is restored or no arrangement can be effected between the Korean and Japanese Governments as to the price for the transfer of this line."

In regard to the fourth point, Waeber wrote that the Japanese could station two companies of troops at Seoul, and one each at Gensan and at Chemulpo. He did not object to the temporary retention of Japanese soldiers, partly because he felt that the present royal forces were unable to cope with the continued disturbances, partly because he hoped to obtain an analogous right for his own country. It was to be "at the discretion of the Russian Government," he proposed, to keep a guard for the protection of its legation and consulates.[60]

Waeber's reply complicated the negotiations. Foreign Minister Mutsu, who returned to the helm of the Foreign Ministry on April 3 although still quite ill,[61] told Speyer that a number of modifications were essential. He demanded the deletion of the provision that the telegraph line between Seoul and Pusan be sold or removed, asserting that this was a matter which Japan would have to take up with Korea at her own initiative. He wished to put a limit on the number of Russian troops and on the period of their stay in Korea to equal the limitations placed on the Japanese.

Speyer regarded the differences in the proposals as insignificant and did not deem it necessary to consult St. Petersburg. He promised to convey the objections to Waeber and expressed the hope that the latter would make the appropriate changes in his memorandum.[62]

In a conversation with Gutschmid on April 8, Mutsu expressed the feeling that while Russia had been impatient with Japan in the wake of the murder of the queen, Lobanov had adopted a wait-and-see attitude, more favorably disposed toward Japan following the flight of the king to the Russian legation. Mutsu accepted Waeber's assurances that he had advised Kojong to return to the palace and that the latter himself was willing enough to do so, but was dissuaded by the intrigues of those surrounding him.[63]

In a talk with the English minister on April 16, Mutsu related that he had told Speyer not to attach too much importance to what he read in the local press, which exaggerated the significance of events in Eastern Asia. It was beyond the resources of Japanese newspapers to maintain a competent staff of correspondents in Europe and America, he explained. Ignorant of European world-politics, Japanese journalists busied themselves almost exclusively with the affairs of nearby Korea, where they could go at little cost. His own earnest wish, Mutsu assured Satow, was to keep things quiet in Korea. One could not hope for perpetual peace, he said, but Japan absolutely required peace for the next five years. She must trust that something favorable might develop during that period.[64]

On April 22, Komura presented a modified proposal to Waeber. In spite of pressure from Speyer, Waeber demurred. He did not wish to yield on the telegraph line, nor was he willing to limit the number of Russian troops in Korea. On April 30 he suggested to break the deadlock by signing forthwith the first two points, which had been approved by their governments. When Komura pressed for the limitation of Russian troops, Waeber replied that he could not assume the responsibility and must consult St. Petersburg.[65] On May 1 he telegraphed to Speyer about the disagreements and asserted that their resolution must be left to direct negotiation between the two governments.[66]

The delay irritated Mutsu. He prevailed upon Speyer on May 1 to telegraph Lobanov his dissatisfaction with "the intransigence of Waeber in the most insignificant questions."[67] To increase the pressure, Mutsu instructed First Secretary Omae Taizo, who was in charge of the Japanese legation in St. Petersburg while Nishi was away, to complain directly to the tsarist government that Waeber suddenly contended that some of the points he had been discussing with Komura did not admit of modification as they had been agreed upon by the two governments. When Komura had reminded Waeber that he himself had offered some modifications of these very points in his counter-memorandum, the latter had retorted that he had done so mistakenly due to a misconstruction of his instructions. As a result, the negotiations in Seoul seemed to be delayed. The Japanese government, Mutsu cabled, deemed it very important that an understanding be effected as soon as possible. He ordered Omae to request the tsarist government to issue instructions to Waeber "to the end that negotiations may be brought to [a] satisfactory and speedy conclusion by the exercise of conciliatory spirit."[68]

On May 3 Omae communicated Saionji's telegram to Lobanov and received his promise that the negotiations would be concluded soon in a conciliatory spirit.[69] The following day he left a memorandum with Kapnist, the chief of the Asiatic Department, reiterating the desire of the Japanese government for a speedy agreement. At the same time, as a token of Japanese good faith, Mutsu informed Speyer that his government was about to issue a decree limiting the emigration of Japanese subjects to Korea.[70]

Mutsu had revealed to Gutschmid that discussions were under way in Seoul between the Japanese and Russian representatives to arrive at a *modus vivendi*, to be formalized in all likelihood by an exchange of notes.[71] Komura and Waeber had confirmed this to Krien in Seoul, the former asserting that there had been only oral discussion so far, the latter admitting that an attempt had been made to reduce their respective views to writing.[72] When Speyer confided to Gutschmid about his differences with Waeber, the German minister wondered how genuine the controversy was. He suspected that it was a calculated gambit, with or without the knowlege of St. Petersburg, to temporize by sending the Japanese government, so to speak, "from Pontius to Pilate."[73]

The tsarist government, which was in a hurry to conclude the talks in Seoul because of the pending consideration of Korean affairs with Yamagata, was not as sensitive as Waeber concerning the remaining disagreements. In spite of the fact that Nicholas had made the marginal comment "*ne beda*" (no calamity; it doesn't matter) next to Mutsu's complaint about Waeber, the Foreign Ministry instructed the latter on May 5 "to conduct the negotiations in Seoul in the most friendly sense" and keep in constant touch with the Russian legation in Tokyo in order to avoid complications "most undesirable at this time."[74]

On May 5 Mutsu instructed Komura to seek the following amendments to Waeber's proposal: (1) That the Japanese minister too should advise the king to return to the palace. (2) That in case of cabinet changes in the future, the Japanese and Russian ministers jointly counsel the king to appoint moderate men. (3) That the entire point regarding the telegraph line be deleted or, if this could not be achieved, that they strike at least the words "or no arrangement can be effected between the Korean and Japanese Governments as to the price for the transfer of this line." (4) That Japanese troops be stationed also at Pusan, that the number of Russian troops in Korea not exceed the amount of Japanese troops there, and that they too be withdrawn when order was restored.[75]

Upon his return to St. Petersburg on May 7, Nishi called on Lobanov to ask what he had done to expedite the conclusion of the negotiations in Seoul. Lobanov told him about the instructions he had sent to Waeber on the fifth. When Nishi asked that Waeber be directed specifically to comply fully with the modifications contained in Mutsu's telegram to Komura of May 5, Kapnist suggested that they wait and see whether the above instructions had not led already to the settlement of the differences.[76]

When a telegram arrived from Waeber seeking guidance on the matter of limiting the number of Russian troops to be stationed in Korea, Lobanov directed him on May 11 to consent to all of the points, reminding him that the agreement was temporary in character.[77] Waeber bowed to his government and on May 13 reported that the final text had been worked out.[78]

On May 14 the Waeber-Komura agreement was signed at last after almost two months of haggling. Drawn up in the form of a memorandum, it contained the following provisions: (1) While leaving the matter of Kojong's return to the palace entirely to his own discretion and judgment, the representatives of Russia and Japan would advise him amicably to return to the palace when no doubts concerning his safety there could be entertained. The Japanese representative, on his part, gave the assurance that the most complete and effective measures would be taken for the control of Japanese *soshi*. (2) The present cabinet ministers, appointed by the king of his own free will and holding, most of them, ministerial or other high offices during the past two years were known to be liberal and moderate men. The two representatives would always aim to recommend to the king that he appoint liberal and moderate men as ministers and show clemency to his subjects. (3) The Russian representative agreed with his Japanese colleague that the present state of affairs in Korea might require the stationing of Japanese guards at some places for the protection of the Japanese telegraph line between Pusan and Seoul; these guards now consisting of three companies of soldiers should be withdrawn as soon as possible and replaced by gendarmes—fifty at Taiku, fifty at Kaheung, and ten each at ten intermediary posts between Pusan and Seoul. The distribution was subject to change, but the total number of gendarmes should never exceed two hundred men, who would be withdrawn by degrees from places where peace and order had been restored by the Korean government.[79] (4) For the protection of the Japanese settlements at Seoul and the open ports against possible attacks by the Korean populace, two companies of Japanese troops could be stationed in Seoul, one company at Pusan and one at Gensan [Wonsan], each company not to exceed two hundred men. These troops would be quartered near the settlements and should be withdrawn as soon as the danger of such attacks had ceased. For the protection of the Russian legation and consulates, the tsarist government could also keep guards not exceeding the number of Japanese troops at those places; they were to be withdrawn as soon as tranquility in the interior was restored completely.[80]

The Seoul memorandum showed concessions on the part of Japan on almost all points made in the original proposal of March 22. Japan backed down on her demands for the immediate or fixed return of Kojong to the palace, the dismissal of the anti-Japanese government, and Japan's exclusive right to maintain troops in Korea. Although she succeeded in the temporary retention of Japanese soldiers to guard the telegraph lines, she had to acknowledge the right of Russia also to station troops in Korea. In short, Komura's signature signified Japanese acceptance of the state of affairs brought about by the events of February 11.[81]

On May 20 Komura called on Waeber and informed him that Japan had removed the barracks and reduced the garrison as agreed. The telegraph line guards were being withdrawn, the *soshi* were under control, and the prohibition on Japanese going to Korea was being enforced. It was time, therefore, to discuss the return of the king to the palace.

Waeber replied that the Korean government had appealed to him in the wake of the incident of February 11 for the protection of the palace by Russian troops. He had recommended to St. Petersburg that the request be declined as contrary to custom. Yet he did not deem it safe for Kojong to return to the palace at this time, as unrest was still rife in the land due to the agitation of the taewongun.

Komura argued that the return of the king to the palace was vital and that they should discuss ways of facilitating it, but Waeber refused, saying that other foreigners familiar with the situation agreed with him.[82]

The newly appointed French chargé, V. Collin de Plancy, whose first audience with the king took place in the Russian legation,[83] had misgivings about the Waeber-Komura agreement. He worried that although the reduction of the effective forces of Japan by removing some of the troops from Seoul to Pusan and Wonsan might spare the pride of the Japanese government by letting it believe that it was not a question of evacuating the kingdom, the arrangement presented grave disadvantages. It put in the provinces isolated men whose conduct could not be supervised and whose very presence sufficed, considering the frame of mind of the population, to create new difficulties. "One feels, in view of these half-measures, the repugnance experienced in Japan in accepting unreservedly the consequences of the promises which had been made regarding the integrity of Korea," Plancy remarked. "But one must hope that the good sense of the Japanese statesmen will easily get the better of these hesitations."[84]

In April Minister Resident Komura was promoted to envoy extraordinary and minister plenipotentiary.[85] Unlike Plancy, Komura hesitated to have his first audience with the king in the Russian legation and did not transmit his letter of accreditation until Kojong received him at the Myeng-yi (Kyong-un) Palace on May 16.[86] Two weeks later, on May 31, Komura departed for Japan, leaving Secretary Kato Masuo in charge of the legation. It was explained that he had to take care of some personal matters in Tokyo, which he had not had time to arrange when he had suddenly been sent to Seoul to replace Miura. But Plancy suspected that the real reason for Komura's return home was to confer with Mutsu about the negotiations he had been conducting with Waeber.[87] Komura did go to the Russian legation for his farewell audience with the king, calling it a private meeting.

During a conversation with Krien, who visited him on May 29, Komura related that he had heard that ten Russian officers and the same number of noncommissioned officers would arrive in Seoul in June to train Korean troops. He had gained the impression during his last conversation with Waeber that these officers would live in the palace to which the king would return. Komura declared that his government would not tolerate the permanent presence of the Russians in the palace, since the Japanese military instructors had not lived there either. Even the stay of the king in the Russian legation would be preferable to that.

Komura stated that Russia would in a few months obtain a much better harbor than Port Lazarev, particularly if Japan made no objections. Actually, he remarked, his government would not be opposed to Russian acquisition of a commercial harbor in Korea, even if the terminal point of the Trans-Siberian Railroad were moved there. But it would not tolerate the fortification of this harbor or the establishment of a Russian naval base in Korea, even if it meant going to war over it. Komura laughed as he added that Japan could easily risk war with Russia. While the Russian fleet in East Asia was much stronger than that of Japan, he said, Japan had the great advantage of a nearby base of operations. In addition to the 48,000 troops who were stationed in the Amur provinces, the Russians had soldiers whom Count Muraviev had called "Cossacks," but these, he sneered, consisted largely of half-breeds and were of little military value.[88]

The Moscow Protocol

Both Hitrovo and Speyer advocated an agreement between Russia and Japan. Hitrovo went so far as to suggest in a private letter to Lobanov that the attainment of a close entente, if not of an alliance, with Japan should be Russia's

main objective in the Far East. But while Hitrovo regarded Korea as a secondary question in which concessions could be made for the sake of the primary
objective, Speyer considered the securing of Russian interests in Korea as the
sole goal of a Russo-Japanese agreement. Speyer favored a joint protectorate
of Russia and Japan over Korea, with Russia having control of the government and the army, Japan of the finances.

The Waeber-Komura memorandum had been concluded while Yamagata
was en route to St. Petersburg. Japan looked forward to a new agreement in
the hope of compensating herself for the concessions she had made at Seoul;
Russia who had fared well at Seoul was not as eager for a new agreement for
that very reason. Yet she was willing to conclude one in order not to impair
her relations with Japan.[89]

Nishi busied himself with preparations for the visit of the special mission.
"I tried hard to get suitable rooms in hotels of Moscow for the residence of
Marquis Yamagata but without success, as at present almost all nice rooms are
engaged already and those remaining are not only extemely dear but unsuitable for his residence," Nishi reported. He had been forced to rent a furnished
house both for the special embassy and the legation, at a cost of 8,000 rubles.
The two carriages he was about to engage for Yamagata and his suite would
probably cost another 2,000 rubles. He asked Saionji to communicate to Yamagata that he would make every preparation for him, but to warn him that at
the time of the coronation other living expenses in Moscow would be just as
high as the rooms and carriages.[90]

Nishi reported that although he had been informed that the Russian government would pay for the visits to the coronation of foreign princes only, he had
recently heard that the same treatment would be extended to Li Hung-chang.
When he had questioned Lobanov about this, the latter had answered evasively that the matter had not yet been decided by the Imperial Household,
though it was possible that Li might receive some special treatment. "Thus it
is probable that Li Hung-chang will be treated exceptionally, while even [the]
Special Ambassador of France will come at his own expense," Nishi telegraphed. "I bring this to your notice in order not to give any dissatisfaction to
Marquis Yamagata on his arrival."[91]

In its instructions to Yamagata, the Japanese government noted that Russia
and Japan agreed on the independence of Korea. Korean maladministration
and lack of discipline had resulted in internal unrest and in such incidents as
those of October 1895 and February 1896. Inasmuch as Russia and Japan both
desired Korean independence, they had a common interest in maintaining
peace and order in the country. The Japanese government concurred with
Hitrovo that it was desirable for Russia and Japan to discuss the Korean ques-

tion, because the kingdom was unable to maintain its independence without foreign assistance. Yamagata was directed to take the matter up with the tsarist government and to express Tokyo's willingness to conclude a political agreement that would insure the independence of Korea. Japan was prepared to collaborate bilaterally with Russia or to come to a broader understanding involving other countries. Since Russian and Japanese interests in Korea coincided, it was the expectation of the Japanese government, the instructions asserted, that if Yamagata frankly revealed Japan's position, Russia would be equally open, and "eternal peace" could be maintained in the Far East.

In secret instructions which supplemented the above, the Japanese government reiterated that Russia and Japan both desired the maintenance of Korean independence. It pointed out that Kojong was a man without a definite political ideology and that his inability to control the administration of the country effectively had given rise to a family quarrel. There was the danger that the controversy would spread, with the various factions soliciting foreign support. Some factions were known as the Japanese party, some as the Russian party, the Chinese party, and the American party. As a result, the family quarrel adversely affected relations between the powers. It had been the experience of the Japanese government that when the so-called Japanese party came to power in Korea, it did nothing to profit Japan; it merely used Japan for its own purposes as a weapon against its opponents. Hence it was not worthwhile for a power to arouse the suspicion of the other countries by supporting Korea. Inasmuch as Russia and Japan were the two states most directly involved, it was desirable that they confer with each other concerning the maintenance of public peace and social order in that country.

It was Tokyo's view that the Korean government should be reorganized without regard as to whether certain individuals belonged to the Russian party or the Japanese party. The expenses of the royal family should be reduced so that expenditures did not exceed income. A foreign loan would have to be floated to meet the needs of government until the necessary financial reforms had been implemented. Although the Japanese government had been involved in the reformation of the domestic administration since 1894, the work had not been completed. It was urgent for the Korean government to organize an army and a police force strong enough to suppress disturbances without foreign assistance. Russia and Japan, jointly or singly, would have to station troops in Korea until such time as the Korean authorities were able to cope with insurrections by themselves, for the Korean people were fond of riots and were apt to have more. It was inconceivable that Japan and Russia should station troops in Korea to protect their citizens and not concern themselves with the security of the country. In the event that Korea was attacked by another power, Russia and Japan must share equally in her defense. If Russia and Japan sent troops to protect the public peace and security of Korea, the instructions continued, the forces should be stationed in clearly defined areas and their barracks kept apart.

Yamagata was directed to keep his government informed not only of the general progress of the negotiations, but of every item proposed by the Russians. He was to consult with Nishi and with Tokyo. The Japanese government held out the possibility of another conference between plenipotentiaries appointed by the two powers following the settlement of the above issues. Should negotiations with a third power be necessary, Yamagata was to seek further instructions from the Foreign Office.[92]

Setting out from Japan on March 15, 1896, by way of the United States, Yamagata reached Moscow two months later, on May 17. As the attention of the foreign powers and the general public was riveted on the coronation, which was to take place on May 26, Yamagata opened secret negotiations with the Russian government. Nishi interpreted for him.

During his first confidential interview with Lobanov on May 24, Yamagata made the following draft proposal: (1) Russia and Japan would mutually guarantee the independence of Korea. (2) In view of the extremely difficult financial position of Korea, Russia and Japan would try to eliminate unnecessary expenditures and balance the budget. In the event that in their view financial or economic reforms required resort to foreign loans, the two governments would cojointly render the necessary assistance. (3) Russia and Japan would try, to the extent that Korean finances permitted, to let Korea create and maintain armed forces and police sufficient to deal with internal disorders without recourse to foreign assistance. (4) Telegraph lines belonging to Japan would continue to be managed by the latter until the Korean government would be in a position to purchase them. (5) In the event that the tranquility or order of the country was seriously disturbed or threatened, be it for internal or external causes, and if either the Japanese or the Russian government, by mutual consent, found it necessary to render assistance to Korea by sending troops in addition to those already there for the protection of their respective citizens and telegraph lines, they would, in order to forestall a clash between their forces, delimit the areas of the country into which each would dispatch her forces in such a way that one power would send troops into the southern part of the country, the other into the northern part of the country, a certain distance being left between the soldiers of the two powers as a precaution. (6) In the event that the agreement needed clarification or new circumstances requiring concerted action arose, the two governments would renew negotiations, which would be conducted by competent representatives of both powers in a spirit of conciliation.[93]

Lobanov remarked that the mutual "guarantee" of Korean independence amounted to a joint protectorate over the country. Yamagata replied evasively that the first article merely introduced the five others. Lobanov queried Yamagata about the financial aid involved and about the amount that Japan was prepared to give. In regard to the third article, he noted that Kojong was afraid of the Japanese army and because of its presence refused to return to the palace. He recommended that the Japanese troops be withdrawn.

Yamagata dwelled at length on the Korean situation to justify the retention of Japanese soldiers. Lobanov had revealed recently, he said, that Russia, in response to a request from the Korean government, had decided to send enough noncommissioned officers to Korea to organize an army of 3,000 men. Several tens of Korean officers were also being trained in Japan. It was necessary to see to it that these various officers did not become a source of conflict between their countries in the future.

Lobanov concurred with the idea of taking precautions to prevent a collision between their countries and to preserve friendly relations. He asked in regard to the fifth article, whether delimiting the areas where Russia and Japan were to send troops in case of necessity meant to draw a boundary line, that is to say, to partition Korea. Yamagata smiled in reply and Lobanov, according to Japanese sources, smiled also.[94]

The Japanese proposals were acceptable to Lobanov as a basis for negotiation. He did deem it necessary to make a number of changes and amplifications designed, on one hand, to confirm the Seoul memorandum of which Yamagata's draft made no mention and, on the other hand, to deprive Japan of the possibility once again to interfere in the internal affairs of Korea.[95]

At the second conference, on June 6, Lobanov had the wording of the first article changed from the "guarantee" of Korean independence to its "recognition," lest the provision be interpreted as a Russo-Japanese protectorate over Korea, which would have been at variance with her independence. He proposed the addition of another article to the effect that until such time as the Korean government was able to rely on its own troops, Russia should organize and train the royal guard. Russia wanted to get out of the current abnormal situation, Lobanov stated, but Kojong was afraid of the Japanese army and would not return to the palace unless Russia organized and trained his guard.

Yamagata countered that the guarding of the palace by Russian soldiers would arouse ill-feeling in Japan, where the public would think that Russia was about to occupy Korea. He warned that if they got involved in a discussion of this question now, they would endanger the conclusion of a cordial understanding on general principles. The sixth article provided for the negotiation of other problems at a later time; why not postpone the matter of Russian military advisers? He added that the king was unstable and listed the many ways in which Japan had helped his country in the past two or three decades.[96]

Lobanov insisted on the deletion of the provision in the fifth article for the delimitation of areas in northern and southern Korea to which their respective troops might have to be sent. He regarded the proposal as a masked offer for the partition of Korea, an eventuality which he did not consider to be in Russia's interest either politically or militarily, even though he had returned Yamagata's smile comprehendingly.[97]

That day, on June 6, Yamagata and Nishi were feted at a banquet in the imperial palace. In a conversation after dinner Nishi told Kapnist that he could never accept Lobanov's proposal for Russian training of the royal guard in Korea. Kapnist replied that Japan had guarded the palace and drilled the *kunrentai*. Why could not Russia do the same? As Yamagata and Nishi insisted that the matter be shelved for the time being, the exchange became so tense that the Japanese gave thought to postponing the entire negotiations.[98]

At the third conference, on June 7, the Russians presented a counterproposal in the form of a draft agreement in two parts, consisting of five public articles and two secret ones. The public articles stated in substance: (1) The governments of Japan and Russia recognized the independence of Korea. (2) In view of the serious financial condition of Korea, the two governments would advise the Korean government to eliminate unnecessary expenditures and maintain a balanced budget. If the governments of Japan and Russia agreed that it was necessary for Korea to float a foreign loan to reform her economy and finances, they would cooperate in providing the necessary aid. (3) To the extent that Korean finances permitted, the governments of Japan and Russia would let Korea maintain her own army, necessary and sufficient for the suppression of riots without resort to foreign assistance. (4) The telegraph lines presently in the possession of the Japanese would remain so until the Korean government was able to purchase them for the benefit of the country; Russia in turn could erect telegraph lines from Seoul to the Russian border. (5) In the event that a conference would have to be called to work out the details of the above provisions, the representatives of both sides must be conciliatory enough to come to an agreement. The secret articles stated in substance: (1) In the event that disorders arose due to internal or external causes and it became necessary for Japan and Russia to send troops in addition to those already there for the protection of their respective citizens and telegraph lines, the two governments must delimit the areas reserved for their operations, leaving enough space between their armies to prevent a collision. (2) Until the organization of an indigenous royal guard, the assistance of foreign instructors would be allowed.

When Yamagata objected to the provision for foreign instructors, because it was merely a euphemism for Russian instructors so long as the king resided in the tsarist legation, Lobanov added the clause that the temporary agreement signed by Komura and Waeber concerning the rights of Japan and Russia to maintain the same number of troops in Korea would remain in effect until the organization of the Korean army, with Russia extending protection to the king until such time.[99]

At the fourth conference, on June 8, Lobanov himself made several alterations in the Russian counterproposal. He deleted, for example, the clause in the fourth article "until the Korean government was able to purchase" the telegraph line. When Nishi proposed to insert "of a third country" before "foreign teachers" in the provision for military instructors in the second secret article, Lobanov objected on the ground that no interference by other powers should be tolerated upon the conclusion of the agreement. As Nishi continued to oppose the mention of foreign instructors unless Japan received equal rights with Russia in this respect, the subject was dropped. Nishi did not like the modification Lobanov had made in the first article, changing the guarantee of Korean independence to mere recognition thereof. Arguing that such a statement would be ineffective, he proposed that they substitute "to support" the independence of Korea. After debating the issue for some time, the two sides agreed at the suggestion of Yamagata to delete the article altogether.[100]

On June 9 Lobanov and Yamagata at last signed the Moscow Protocol. It contained the following provisions.

Public Articles

1. The Russian and Japanese governments, with a view to removing financial difficulties of Korea, will advise the Korean government to curtail superfluous expenditures and to establish a balance between expenditures and revenues. If, as the result of the urgency of some reforms, it will be necessary to resort to foreign loans, the two governments will assist it by common efforts.

2. The Russian and Japanese governments will try to leave it entirely up to Korea, insofar as the financial and economic condition of the country permits, to form and maintain indigenous armed forces and

police in a number sufficient for the maintenance of general order without foreign assistance.

3. In order to facilitate communication with Korea, the Japanese government will retain the management of the telegraph lines now in its hands.

The establishment of telegraphic communication between Seoul and her own border is granted to Russia.

These lines can be redeemed by the Korean government when it will have the necessary funds for it.

4. Should the above require more exact and detailed definition or if other questions arise requiring negotiations, the respective representatives of the governments will be instructed to come to an amicable agreement regarding such matters.

Secret Articles

1. Should the tranquility and order in Korea be disturbed or seriously endangered as the result of some internal or external cause and should the Russian and Japanese governments, by common accord, judge it necessary to come to the aid of the local authorities by means of sending troops in addition to the number necessary for the security of their nationals and the protection of their telegraph lines, the two imperial governments, desirous of preventing any collision between their armed forces, will determine the sphere of action reserved for each in such a way as to leave a space free of occupation between the troops of the two governments.

2. Until the formation in Korea of the necessary forces, mentioned in article 2 of the public clauses of the present protocol, the provisional arrangement signed by State Counselor Waeber and Mr. Komura regarding the rights of Russia and Japan to maintain an equal number of troops in the kingdom remains in force. As for the personal security of the king, the procedure established for this purpose will likewise be preserved until the formation of an indigenous detachment especially intended for this service.[101]

The protocol remained silent on the question of military instructors necessary for training a Korean army. Nor was provision made for the employment of foreign advisers. Hence the agreement was not as comprehensive as originally contemplated. Lobanov admitted to Speyer in a cable on June 15 that the protocol dealt with the existing situation and not with the future.

The protocol established the jurisdictional equality of Russia and Japan in Korea and mutually enjoined the two powers not to take separate action. The only, but important, exception was the confirmation of Russia's right, stipulated in the Waeber-Komura memorandum, to guard the king, a provision which gave Russia an edge over Japan. Yet the agreement did curb the expansion of Russian influence to some extent. For example, while Russia was not supposed to negotiate a loan to Korea without involving Japan, the latter was already a creditor of Korea.

The two agreements did not impose a joint Russo-Japanese condominium over Korea. Their main significance, from the Russian point of view, was the renunciation of Japan's exclusive influence in Korea and the preservation of the territorial integrity and independence of Korea. As Lobanov summarized to Speyer: "All in all, we were guided by the sincere desire to maintain good relations with Japan without violating the principle of Korean independence, which, in view of the hatred prevalent among the Korean population against the Japanese, corresponds completely to our interests." [102]

The Russians did not think in terms of sharing power with the Japanese.[103] To them the principle of independence meant that Kojong and the Korean government had the right to decide independently on the employment of military instructors and advisers. It was Lobanov's view that if Russia were asked by Korea to assist in this matter, she could do so without prior consulation with Japan, as she would have to do if the initiative were her own. "Korea, as a fully independent country," Lobanov wrote to Waeber on July 14, "retains complete freedom of action in all questions of internal and external policy, not subject to any limited conditions concerning the selection of foreign advisers and military intructors, to whose service she might resort."[104]

Neither the Seoul memorandum nor the Moscow protocol were made public at the time of their conclusion, although their existence and general nature were revealed confidentially to the diplomatic representatives.[105] Lobanov wanted to keep them secret, but agreed in principle to the publication of the ostensible articles provided the Japanese government gave Russia prior notice to allow simultaneous announcements in both capitals. When the Japanese government toward the end of the year sought Russian assent for revealing the public articles of the agreements, no reply was received from St. Petersburg, which was without a foreign minister due to the sudden death of Lobanov on August 31.[106] As pressure by the opposition in the Diet mounted and a question was raised on the floor of the lower house about the Moscow protocol, Okuma instructed Motono on February 16, 1897, to notify the tsarist government that the Japanese government would make public the ostensible articles of the Lobanov-Yamagata protocol in response to the above query on February 24. It would continue to keep secret the Waeber-Komura memorandum.[107] In a follow-up telegram on the twentieth, Okuma explained that while the Japanese government shared with the Russian government the general disinclination to publish such an understanding as the Lobanov-Yamagata protocol, the putting of the question in the Diet made it "absolutely necessary" for it to publish the document. Okuma expressed preference for revealing the Moscow protocol only, but was willing to make public both agreements on the twenty-fourth if Russia objected to this.[108]

Chargé Motono Ichiro replied on February 22 that the tsarist government agreed to the publication of both documents on February 24.[109] For once St. Petersburg acted with greater dispatch than Tokyo. While Okuma exposed the text of the public articles of the Lobanov-Yamagata protocol and the text of the Waeber-Komura memorandum in the course of a speech to the House of Representatives on February 26, the Russian government published them in the *Official Gazette* on the twenty-fourth, the date set by Okuma. It printed the documents along with a preamble in which it stated that it had made the arrangements in order to avoid any difficulties with Japan and assured that the Moscow Protocol did not in any way injure the principle of Korean independence laid down in the Treaty of Shimonoseki. It called the Seoul Memorandum a necessary supplement to the Moscow Protocol designed to show the intention of withdrawing the foreign troops from Korea.[110]

On March 2, 1897, Kato Masuo, who had succeeded as Japanese minister resident in Seoul on February 23,[111] sent Foreign Minister Yi Wan-yong copies of the Moscow Protocol and the Seoul Memorandum. In a covering letter he asserted on the basis of a telegram from the Japanese Foreign Office, dated February 26, that the object of the above agreements was to "strengthen and consolidate" the independence of Korea. He expressed the hope that the Korean government would not fail to appreciate this intention.

On receipt of the note the Korean Council of State sought the opinion of several foreigners, including McLeavy Brown, how to respond to it. After much deliberation it was decided unanimously to acknowledge receipt of the information with thanks, but at the same time to stipulate the reservations of the Korean government. In a brief reply on March 9, Yi declared that as his government had not joined in concluding the agreements between Japan and Russia, its freedom of action as an independent power could not be restricted by their provisions.[112]

Although Waeber held that Japan had no reason to be pleased with the results of the Seoul Memorandum and the Moscow Protocol considering how much she had originally asked and how little she had received in the end, Kato seemed well satisfied. The slaying of Queen Min had so compromised his country as to paralyze her activity in Korea. The agreements with Russia had revived her position by recognizing her right to intervene in the peninsula, even if only jointly with Russia. The mere fact of being associated with Russia in the decision of the Korean question had boosted Japan's prestige, Kato believed. There could be little doubt, the consul general of Great Britain, J. N. Jordan, wrote from Seoul in March 1897, that for the moment the Japanese had largely rehabilitated themselves.[113]

They had done so at Russian expense. "The secrecy which was maintained respecting these arrangements, and the circumstances under which they were signed, have caused a temporary revulsion of feeling against Russia, and against M. Waeber in particular, who has always been regarded as the friend of Corea," Jordan reported. "That he should have signed such a document while the King was a guest under his roof without His Majesty's knowledge seems to the Coreans entirely contrary to their conception of his character, and scarcely less objectionable is the action of the Russian Government in negotiating with Marquis Yamagata, and keeping the Corean Representative in Moscow in entire ignorance of what was going on."[114]

Twenty-One

Return to the Palace

The general public and the officialdom in Korea did not favor the prolonged stay of the king in the Russian legation. Petitions were circulated requesting his return to the palace.[1] Popular agitation was stilled by Kojong on August 12, 1896, when he issued a decree announcing his intention to move out shortly and ordered the prompt renovation of one of the palaces.[2] While the phrase "return to the palace" continued to be used in the discussions and dispatches pertaining to Kojong's departure from the Russian legation, there was no question of his going back to the Kyongbok Palace, which despite the meaning of its name, "Shining Happiness," was full of tragic memories and lay exposed to renewed attack. It was understood that he would proceed to the newly enlarged and fortified Kyong-un Palace within the security of the legation quarter of the capital.

The Kyong-un Palace (known at various times as the So-gung, Chong-nung, Myeng-yi, and presently the Toksu Palace) was five minutes by foot from the Russian legation and was surrounded by foreign dwellings, among them the consulate general of Great Britain, the Customs Office, and the legation of the United States.[3] The rebuilding of the palace, the expansion of its grounds, and the erection of protective walls took time and, of necessity, extended the period of Kojong's residence in the Russian legation.

On June 25 Speyer had handed to Saionji a verbal note informing him that the tsarist government had been requested by Kojong to guarantee his personal safety after his return to the palace. He had asked for assurance that the Japanese government would abstain from menacing the Korean king after his move to the palace. Saionji had given the required assurance by a verbal note the same day, commenting that the question seemed to have been settled by the Waeber-Komura memorandum and the Lobanov-Yamagata protocol.[4]

On August 21 Speyer represented to Saionji that the tsarist government, deeming it undesirable for the king of Korea to remain in its legation much longer, had repeatedly advised him to return to the palace, but that Kojong persisted in refusing to do so unless Russian soldiers would guard the palace. The tsarist government was willing to detail twenty soldiers to ease the king's mind and effect his departure. It inquired whether the Japanese government had any objection to this arrangement.[5]

Foreign Minister Lobanov was preparing to go abroad on August 25 and Nishi himself the following day, yet they made time for a meeting on the twenty-fourth. Nishi objected to the proposal of the Russian government conveyed by Speyer as contrary to what had been discussed and agreed upon in Moscow. He recommended that the representatives of both countries in Seoul be directed to take steps jointly to effect the king's immediate return by some other way.

Lobanov assured Nishi that he did not wish to undertake anything disagreeable to Japan. In issuing the instructions to Speyer he had meant, he said, for the chargé to consult with Saionji at a favorable opportunity, now that the Japanese public seemed to be calmer. He wanted to wait for Saionji's answer to the Russian proposal, he added, since its acceptance would offer a simple solution.

In his report Nishi advised Saionji not to agree. "I recommend you to insist upon my said opinion," he telegraphed.[6]

On August 28 Saionji replied to Speyer that the Japanese government was as anxious as the Russian government for the speediest possible return of Kojong to his palace, but that since the Moscow Protocol stipulated that the organization of a royal body guard should precede any change in the state of affairs regarding the king's personal safety, it thought that the two governments should first of all settle by common accord the question of the organization of a military force.

Speyer retorted that in his opinion it would be best to leave the lengthy discussion of this issue until after Kojong's return to the palace. However, if the Japanese government disagreed, he wished to know Saionji's views on the method of organizing the Korean army.

Saionji replied that he personally felt that it should be trained by both Japanese and Russian officers.

Speyer expressed the desire that the negotiations regarding army organization be held in St. Petersburg.[7]

Following the assassination of the queen, the cabinet which had seized control in the wake of her death had selected a site and made preparations for the burial of her remains. But the flight of the king to the Russian legation, the formation of a new government, and the continuity of disturbances and conspiracies had delayed interment.[8]

In an ordinance on August 19 Kojong recalled that six months had passed since he had left the palace and that he was grieved to think that the remains of the late queen were so far from him. He commanded that her coffin be moved to the Kyong-un Palace in two weeks. On August 26 it was announced that the king would proceed to his new abode on September 4 and that the remains of the queen would be deposited there at that time.[9]

The reconstruction of the palace and the building of wide roads leading to it necessitated the removal of hundreds of houses. The costly project greatly improved the general appearance and sanitary conditions of that part of the city, but it took longer than expected, even though work continued day and night. The temple destined to shelter the remains of the queen and the annexes where the sacrifices were to be performed were sufficiently ready for the solemn transfer of the coffin as scheduled on September 4, but the apartments of the king were not completed in time and Kojong, after spending the day at the palace, had to return to the Russian legation for a while longer.[10]

In a decree on November 1, Kojong announced his determination to move to the palace and ordered that the furnishing of the new royal residence be completed as soon as possible. According to Koreans well informed of court affairs, Kojong had been deeply impressed by the advice of Min Yong-hwan, who had recently returned from St. Petersburg as envoy extraordinary and had insisted on the urgency of such a step in order to put an end to a state of affairs incompatible with royal dignity.[11]

Everything seemed ready for the king's move to Kyong-un Palace toward the end of November when a plot was uncovered on the eve of the set date to gain control over him. Preliminary inquiries suggested that the persons involved had planned to escort Kojong to the old palace rather than to the renovated one. It was revealed during their trial the following year that they had wished to compel the king during his next visit to the new palace to remain there and to issue several proclamations drawn up by them. Their scheme included the murder of several progressive cabinet ministers and other high officials. But their primary motive, as the American minister put it, was "the one that generally governs, when Koreans combine for intrigue and violence, namely, to secure offices for themselves, their friends, and backers."

The officers who had hatched the conspiracy had hoped to exploit the discontent of those Korean soldiers who had not been chosen for training by the Russians and who were jealous of the favors reserved for the special battalion. They had approached the Japanese authorities for aid and sympathy, but had been turned down distinctly, although a private Japanese promoter who had been trying unsuccessfully to get a railroad concession from the Korean government became involved with them.

After a patient trial, kept fair by Greathouse, the American adviser of the Department of Law, five of those arrested were convicted and banished from the capital for varying terms. The affair had no serious consequences, except that the departure of the king from the Russian legation was postponed again.[12]

It was on February 20, 1897, that Kojong finally left the Russian legation, escorted by an honor guard commanded by Russian noncommissioned officers. Other members of the new battalion lined the street from the legation to Kyong-un Palace. At the king's request, the Russian officers and noncoms were housed within the palace walls, not far from his own quarters.[13] Thus the palace was guarded by Korean troops under Russian command.[14]

Noting that Kojong's move from the Russian legation to the palace gave "great satisfaction," the American minister asserted that his Russian colleague had neither advised nor opposed the king's departure. It was his understanding, Sill wrote, that Colonel Putiata, chief of the Russian military mission which had arrived at Kojong's bidding, had assured the monarch without prior consultation of Waeber that he could protect him.

On February 21 the Western representatives called on Kojong at his invitation and congratulated him that the peaceful conditions in his country had permitted him to return to the palace in safety.[15]

The remains of the queen had been moved in accordance with Kojong's command. Many elaborate sacrifices had been offered to her spirit in Kyong-un Palace. But her interment was postponed repeatedly in the expectation that the king would assume the imperial title and that his beloved consort could be buried thereupon as an empress, with due inscription being made on the funereal tablets.[16]

The question of Kojong's elevation to emperor dated back to October 1895, when several members of the new cabinet, a fortnight after the assassination of the queen, had urged the king to don the imperial mantle. The idea had orginated apparently with their Japanese mentors, who wanted to regain Kojong's confidence. Asserting that the title *wang* (king) was not merely inferior to that of *wang-chei* (emperor), but implied the tributary status of the country, they argued that Kojong's adoption of the name of emperor would offer proof of Korea's independence. "No emperor, no independence," was their watchword. One or two brave individuals in the assembly disagreed, pointing out that what Korea needed in order to gain the respect of her neighbors was good government and military strength, not a more exalted title for her ruler. But the majority was prepared, as the *Korean Repository* put it, "to use the argument of force in case the force of argument failed," and the coronation was scheduled for October 26, 1895.[17] The coronation did not take place, however, because of "friendy opposition" on the part of the foreign representatives, notably Waeber.[18]

In 1897 agitation for the assumption of the imperial title was revived by the Koreans themselves. In September popular appeals were conveyed to Kojong and at the beginning of October a multitude of government officials, led by the prime minister, after fasting and washing knelt in the courtyard of the palace for three successive afternoons and petitioned the king to accept the calling of emperor. "To assume the highest title because of the greatest merits has been the practice of all holy and illustrious rulers, and is agreeable to heavenly principles and human laws," they wrote in their memorial. Asserting that Kojong far excelled other monarchs in wisdom and bravery, had a disposition "like that of heaven and earth," and was "as great and as penetrating as heaven" in "lofty virtues" and "clear judgment," they begged him to grant their petition and accept the imperial title in compliance with "the will of heaven and the wishes of the people."[19]

In accordance with tradition, the memorial was submitted nine times, Kojong modestly declining eight times and yielding with a show of reluctance the ninth time round. Actually he himself had wished to become emperor, and for weeks preparations had been under way to build a new Altar of Heaven for the ceremony.[20]

Speyer was not behind the idea of making Kojong emperor, as is often assumed. He hesitated to support the move for fear that it would be unacceptable to the great powers. But Kojong persisted, contending that he needed the imperial title to thwart renewed efforts by the taewongun to impose his parental authority on him. He did not demand that Russia recognize the new title, he told Speyer; she could address him as before. He merely asked that the tsarist government not object to the change publicly.[21]

At a meeting on October 9 the diplomatic representatives discussed how to react if they were invited to attend an "imperial audience." Most of them thought at first of declining, because they did not know the attitude of their governments toward the change. The German and English representatives themselves did not like it. But Allen, who had taken over as the United States minister the previous month, pointed out that in the Chinese text of the American treaty with Korea there was mention only of "the chief ruler of the country"; he doubted that it made much difference what Kojong chose to call himself. Speyer proposed that they accept the invitation provided it did not imply that it was for the purpose of recognizing or congratulating the "emperor." To this everyone agreed and accepted the invitation when it arrived the next day, even though some of the representatives were annoyed that its wording was exactly as suggested by Speyer.[22]

The day selected by the astrologers as most auspicious for the coronation was October 12; the "lucky" hour, 3 a.m. The mourning costume worn by officials in memory of the late queen was doffed for the occasion, and as the king and the crown prince proceeded to the Altar of Heaven on the afternoon of the eleventh to inspect the oxen, sheep, and pigs that were to be sacrificed, the wide street leading to the altar was like a sea of color. Ancient costumes and weapons—wooden clubs, gilded hammers, rusty spears, and flintlocks—mingled with modern uniforms and rifles with fixed bayonets.[23]

In quaintness and uniqueness the ceremony on October 12 surpassed the coronation of Nicholas the preceding year and the Diamond Jubilee of Queen Victoria in June, the *Independent* declared. To begin with, no European potentate ever thought of holding a coronation ceremony at three in the morning.

At the appointed hour the king and the crown prince once more went to the Altar of Heaven. The altar was a circular mound built of stone, divided into three terraces, each one nine steps high. It had been constructed in twenty-one days by a force of 1,000 men on the former site of the reception hall where the king had at one time entertained Chinese envoys and performed the marks of vassalage to China. Sacrificial food had been arranged on tables on the upper terrace, where a circular awning of yellow had been erected.

The king bowed and the grand master of ceremonies read a prayer asking Heaven to bestow its blessings and guidance on the ruler as he assumed the mantle of emperor. Following the offering of the sacrificial animals, Kojong changed from his red royal robe to a yellow imperial one. At 5 a.m. he formally assumed the title of Whang-chei of Dai Han, Emperor of Great Han. Taking a seat, he received the congratulations of the ministers of state and of other officers, who had arranged themselves on the different terraces in accordance with their rank and kotowed to him nine times.

The ceremony was marred by a rainstorm, which penetrated through the awnings and drenched the silk robes of all the participants, who shivered in the cold of the autumn morning.[24]

The foreign representatives proceeded to the palace in the late afternoon of the thirteenth, dressed in full uniforms and accompanied by their suites. They were received by Kojong separately. Minister Resident Kato as dean of the diplomatic corps was the first to enter the audience chamber, together with his secretaries, consul, and naval and military attachés. Then went Allen with five naval officers from the U.S.S. *Boston*, and after him Speyer with a large staff of secretaries and attachés.

Kojong personally announced his assumption of the imperial title, though formal notification thereof was made to the representatives by the foreign minister with the request that they convey the information to their governments. The American minister could not tell Kojong how his government would regard the change in title. He did not congratulate him, but merely expressed the best wishes for his happiness and for the prosperity of his country. He pointed out that the United States as a republic did not look upon titles in the same way as some other powers. Kojong sought to assure Allen that he had not acted out of a desire for personal aggrandizement in becoming emperor. It had been his wish, he implied, to put an end thereby to being "talked down to" by neighboring China and Japan, both of whom had emperors.[25]

The first edict issued under the imperial seal on October 14 proclaimed that Korea was to be known henceforth as Dai Han or Great Han in honor of the three Han states which had been absorbed into the kingdom in ancient times (in place of Chosen, which was associated with vassalage to China). The beginning of a new year period was announced, 1897 constituting the first year of Kwang-mu. The late queen was raised to the rank of empress, the crown prince to imperial prince. A list of thirteen points mitigated by one degree the punishments imposed on all except those guilty of rebellion, murder, adultery, robbery, swindling, or stealing; it promoted by one rank all officials below the seventh rank as well as all officials above the age of 80 and private citizens above the age of 90; it threatened with punishment any official, irrespective of rank, who took bribes, broke the law, or oppressed the people; and it promised substantial considerations for the families of soldiers stationed in the interior and relief from unjust taxes for all persons, and special protection on the part of the local authorities to the helpless and unfortunate. "Ah! we ascended the royal throne by the grace of heaven and have assumed the imperial title according to the wishes of the people," the edict declared. "Our desire is to abolish old abuses and to introduce what is new, making good government and wholesome customs prevail."[26]

The Korean foreign minister informed the foreign representatives on the sixteenth of the imperial edict and of the change of name of the country.[27] The semi-official agent of the Chinese government, T'ang, confided to his English colleague that he was pained more by the ingratitude now shown deliberately by Korea to her former suzerain than by the treatment his country had received at the hands of Japan.[28] It was understood, the American minister reported, that the assumption of the imperial title by Kojong put an end to the pending negotiations for a commercial treaty with China.[29]

At the weekly reception of heads of legations in Tokyo on October 14, Okuma told the new Russian minister, Baron Roman Romanovich Rosen, that he had just received a telegram from Kato Masuo in Seoul informing him of the proclamation of Kojong as emperor of Korea. When Rosen asked him whether the Japanese government would recognize the new title, Okuma replied that no formal decision had yet been made, but that he foresaw no obstacles to it.[30]

The tsarist government had made no immediate response to the official notification of the Korean government regarding the change in title, but when Nicholas thanked Kojong on December 19 for the name day congratulations he had received from him, he addressed him as "His Majesty, the Emperor of Korea." "I express my deep thanks and sincere wishes that the cordial relations between Russia and Korea be ever tighter and stronger," Nicholas cabled.

The "imperial" party in Korea was greatly elated at the evident recognition of the new title by Russia. Kojong promptly informed the American minister of the telegraphic exchange.[31]

The Japanese government sought to clarify Russian policy. On October 22 Okuma cabled to Hayashi: "Confidentially ascertain and telegraph at once what action [the] Russian Government propose to take in the matter."[32]

While Russia procrastinated with a formal reply, Japan recognized the imperial title of Kojong in the first part of November. St. Petersburg followed suit, its agreement being communicated by Speyer on December 31.[33] The United States and subsequently Britain at first adopted the new title in their correspondence with Korea without formally recognizing it, the way Russia had done. By spring 1898 they too gave in and notified Korea of their recognition of the imperial title, as did France.[34]

In the cycle of life the mourning ceremonies for the late queen were interrupted when a son was born to Kojong on October 21 by his concubine, Om, with whom he had been living since his flight to the Russian legation.[35]

With the elevation of the late queen to empress in October 1897, preparations had been resumed for the burial of her remains. The fact that little had been rescued from the fire—only a small bone from one of her fingers, according to what the American minister had heard[36]—did not lessen Korean zeal. Although two extensive cemeteries and temples had already been prepared for the queen's remains at great cost, another, even larger, site commensurate with her imperial status was chosen, six miles east of the city.[37] For weeks before the final interment there were daily sacrifices in the royal palace, with special sacrifices offered on the first and fifteenth of each month.

On the morning of Sunday, November 21, the imperial remains, placed in a large catafalque, were borne to the grave in a motley procession, impressive to the Koreans, but grotesque and disorderly in Western eyes. Down the street moved high civil and military officials, some of them on horseback, 650 policemen, and 5,000 soldiers. Hundreds of scrolls recounting the virtues of the deceased, silk banners, small painted chairs with floral designs containing one of the souls of the dead, enormous white, gray, and lavender wooden horses on carts for use in the spirit world, and 4,000 lanterns, each carried by one man, brightened the sad occasion.[38]

The foreign representatives had repaired to the imperial palace before dawn. After a tedious wait in the cold they had seen the bier leave and had paid their respects to Kojong, who had remained behind. At 2 p.m. they called at the Foreign Office to accompany the emperor to the grave, but Kojong had already left and they followed on their own.

At the cemetery the foreign representatives were quartered in small paper rooms, four persons per room. When they were served dinner, Kato Masuo was placed in such an undignified position that he was forced to complain about it. Allen ascribed the incident to "lack of order and arrangement,"[39] but in view of Japanese involvement in the murder of the deceased whose remains were about to be buried one wonders whether the slight had indeed been unintentional.

Praying and wailing continued before the bier in the temple in front of the tomb throughout the night. At 3 a.m. on November 22 the emperor and the crown prince arrived in sedan chairs, each attended by a Russian officer. At 4 a.m. the diplomatic body returned to make their final bow of respect to the spirit of the dead empress. The large catafalque was then carried up the steep side of the mound. Kojong and his son followed to the top and it was in their presence that the coffin was lowered into the inner tomb with tears and wailing at the break of dawn in the eastern sky.[40]

At 10 a.m. the foreign representatives had a formal audience with Kojong. They remained at the cemetery for the rest of the day, returning with him in the evening, except for Allen who had caught a cold and had gone home following the audience.[41]

In his account of the funeral ceremonies, Allen noted that four Russian noncommissioned officers had remained constantly by Kojong's chair and that no one had been allowed to approach him without permission. He added that the obsequiousness of the officials in charge toward the Russian and French representatives had been very conspicuous. The attitude, he thought, may have been due partly to the general lack of order and system in Korea, partly to the desire of the officials to ingratiate themselves with those in power. "A short time ago, we saw the matter reversed," Allen recalled, "and the Russian Representative was neglected by these same officials, who then devoted themselves to the Japanese Minister quite as enthusiastically as they waited upon the Russian Chargé d'Affaires at this funeral."[42]

Twenty-Two

The Question of Russian Aid

The coronation of Nicholas II provided the Koreans, as it had the Japanese and the Chinese, with the opportunity for secret negotiations with the tsarist government. St. Petersburg had rejected Kojong's request for military instructors and for government advisers following his flight to the Russian legation. The coronation gave the king the pretext for sending a mission to Russia without arousing the suspicion of Japan and the other powers in order to re-open the question of Russian aid. Two sets of credentials were supplied to the special ambassador—one empowering him to attend the coronation as the representative of the king, the other empowering him to seek clarification of issues arising from the increasingly close relations between Russia and Korea.[1]

The Korean embassy was headed by Prince Min Yong-hwan, a cousin of the late queen. He had been appointed minister to Washington in the fall of the preceding year, but had been prevented from assuming that post by the murder of the queen and subsequent events.[2] Unlike other members of the Min family, the prince was known for his integrity, and his appointment by Kojong had been applauded by everyone.[3] Dragoman Evgenii Fedorovich Stein (Shtein) of the tsarist legation in Seoul, who accompanied Min Yong-hwan when he left from Chemulpo for Shanghai on a Russian gunboat on April 1, 1896,[4] characterized the prince as tactful, calm, and sympathetic to Western innovations.

Min Yong-hwan had been assigned 40,000 yen for expenses, and the diplomatic community, which did not know of the secret aspect of his mission, expected him to continue from Moscow to Western Europe and the United States.[5] Instead, he proceeded to St. Petersburg after the coronation festivities to enter into negotiations with Lobanov.

On June 5, 1896, several days prior to the signing of the Lobanov-Yamagata protocol, Min presented to the Foreign Ministry an *aide mémoire* with an attached mémorandum enumerating the proposals of the Korean government. The *aide mémoire* opened with the assertion that many years ago Korea had concluded a "secret treaty" with Russia, which bound the two countries together in close friendship. Alleging that Korea had not assented to all the demands posed by Japan in the hope of Russian assistance, the document contended that the Japanese had murdered the queen because of this resistance and because of Korea's friendly disposition toward Russia. By portraying Japanese deeds as a reaction to Korean sympathy toward Russia, Min tried to pin on the latter some of the responsibility for subsequent events. Having learned of the negotiations with Yamagata, Min warned in his *aide mémoire* that any agreement between Russia and Japan to exert joint influence on Korea would lead to conflict and would bring about a "new national calamity" for Korea. He expressed the hope that the proposals in the attached memorandum would be accepted without delay.

The proposals made by the Korean government were in essence a repetition and elaboration of the requests voiced by Kojong in February. They consisted of five points: (1) The protection of the king by Russian forces until the creation of a trained Korean army; (2) the sending of a sufficient number of Russian instructors for the training of the Korean army and the police; (3) the furnishing of three Russian advisers: one to the imperial household, one to the cabinet, and one for the direction of industrial and railroad enterprises; (4) the granting of a Russian loan of three million yen; and (5) the establishment of telegraphic communication between Korea and Russia.

The proposals were but an outline of the requests detailed in Min's instructions. The instructions stated that because it was impossible to trust Japanese instructors, Korea was forced to ask for Russian ones. Qualified instructors were wanted to train an army of 3,600 men and to organize attached cavalry, sapper, quartermaster, and veterinary units and military band, as well as a reliable police force. The three advisers were to be used in such a way that the main one would counsel the king himself; the second one was to direct the administrative and political activities of the government; the third adviser was to be in charge of opening mines, building railroads, and carrying out all other public works. In regard to the establishment of telegraphic communication between Korea and Russia, the instructions spoke of connecting the north Korean line with the Siberian line and of running, with Russian help, a line between Shanghai and Mokpo or between Chemulpo and Kiaochow. Russia was to be asked to send a specialist for the construction of the telegraph line from Seoul to the Russian border. But the receipt of military instructors was regarded as of primary importance. The attainment of this objective alone would crown the mission with success even if all the other requests were rejected, the instructions stated. Since Korea was on the verge of bankruptcy, Min was to strive also to obtain agreement, at least in principle, on a Russian loan, leaving the details for future deliberation.

The Korean proposals put the tsarist government in a delicate position. To carry them out would have been tantamount to establishing a Russian protectorate over Korea, something it neither desired nor could effect for fear of a collision with Japan and possibly with Great Britain. On the other hand, St. Petersburg hesitated to turn down the Korean proposals completely, lest its influence in Korea be destroyed. Since Min was pressing for a specific reply as to whether Russia was willing to take Korea under her exclusive protection, Lobanov apprehended that unless he assented partially to the requests, Kojong might seek the help and support of other powers. If Russia, in view of her military weakness in the Far East, could ill afford war with Japan over Korea, neither could she allow Japan to entrench herself in the peninsula bordering unto her realm by forfeiting her own influence. Unable either to accept fully or to reject outright the Korean proposals, the tsarist government resorted to a policy of half-promises and procrastination.[6]

Of the five requests made by Min only the one concerning the establishment of telegraphic communication between Korea and Russia did not threaten complications with Japan, as it had been authorized in the Lobanov-Yamagata protocol, and the Russian foreign minister agreed to it in his first meeting with the special ambassador. Although Russia was protecting Kojong during his presence in the legation, Lobanov refused to provide a Russian guard for the palace out of fear of antagonizing the other powers, especially Japan. He was willing to give merely a "moral guarantee" (*nravstvennoe ruchatel'stvo*) of the king's safety if he returned to the palace. Min consequently pressed for the dispatch of a large number of Russian military instructors. He asked for a minimum of 200 men, arguing that any other power would heed such a request without hesitation. But Lobanov and Kapnist evaded a definite answer on this issue and on the question of a Russian loan.

As the Korean mission lingered in St. Petersburg awaiting a formal reply to its requests, the Russian officials were at a loss how to occupy the delegates once all the sights of the capital and vicinity, including Kronstadt, had been exhausted. "Prince Lobanov in particular would be glad to see the departure of these people from the Far East," the German chargé Tschirschky reported on August 10. "The less they are otherwise occupied, the more they honor the minister with their visits, which in accordance with Oriental custom they always drag out considerably. Prince Lobanov complains that they approach him with all kinds of political requests which in most cases cannot be taken seriously at all, but which, in spite of all his efforts to dissuade them, the Koreans present anew again and again with tiresome stubborness." [7]

Almost a month passed before Min was handed a point by point reply to the Korean proposal on July 2. The Russian position had been formulated by Lobanov and approved by Nicholas. It stated: (1) The king was being protected by a Russian guard during his stay in the Russian legation. He could remain in the legation as long as he himself deemed necessary and convenient. Once he returned to his palace, the tsarist government could assume a moral guarantee of his safety. The Russian detachment now in the legation would remain there at the disposal of the Russian minister and, in case of necessity, could even be reinforced. (2) The tsarist government would soon send a high-ranking and experienced officer to Seoul to negotiate with the Korean government concerning the question of Russian instructors. He would concentrate first of all on the organization of the royal body guard. An equally experienced person would be dispatched to study the economic situation of Korea and determine what financial measures need to be taken. (3) The question of furnishing Russian advisers to the Korean government was solved by the preceding point. The above-mentioned agents would act as such advisers in the military and financial realm under the direction of the Russian minister. (4) The conclusion of a loan by the Korean government would be considered as soon as the economic condition of the country and the needs of the government became clear. (5) The tsarist government agreed to the connection of its telegraph lines with those of Korea and would give due assistance in this matter. [8]

Dissatisfied with the vagueness of the Russian reply, Min tried to obtain a more specific commitment. On August 7 he submitted a new proposal for an agreement between Russia and Korea, calling for mutual consultation and the pledge of the tsarist government to protect his country from any attempts on the independence of Korea by a third power. Lobanov rejected the proffer, assuring Min merely of "the aspiration to maintain friendly relations between the two governments." He left unanswered Min's assertion in a final plea on August 18 that Russia took upon herself to send the advisers for the Korean government and the military instructors, to provide the loan, and to run the telegraph line.

Meanwhile Lobanov had moved to implement some of the provisions of the five-point reply. On June 30 he had sent to Witte copies of the protocol he had concluded with Yamagata and of the agreement with Korea with a covering note, in which he asked that an agent of the Finance Ministry be sent to Seoul to study the matter of a loan. At the beginning of August Court Councilor [9]

Dmitrii Dmitrievich Pokotilov, who had studied Chinese as a language student attached to the Russian legation at Peking in the early 1890s and now was director of the Russo-Chinese Bank at Shanghai, was sent to Korea as temporary representative of the Finance Ministry. He was not empowered to negotiate a loan, merely to acquaint himself with the economic situation in Korea and find out which sources of her income could be used to pay for the interest on a loan.[10]

On June 30 Lobanov also requested Minister of War Vannovskii to send an agent to Seoul to negotiate concerning military instructors and the organization of a royal body guard and simultaneously to serve as military adviser of the Korean government. The Ministry of War named Colonel Putiata of the General Staff, who had been assigned to Marshal Yamagata during his visit to Moscow and at one time had served as military attaché in Peking.[11] The appointment was confirmed by Nicholas II at the beginning of August.

The Military Instructors Controversy

Prior to his departure, Putiata recommended that Russian troops be dispatched to Korea in the same number as those maintained there by Japan, as authorized by the Moscow protocol, in order to facilitate the guarding of the king and the instruction of Korean soldiers. Vannovskii approved of Putiata's proposal, but Lobanov vetoed it. In agreeing to the dispatch of a military representative to Seoul, Lobanov commented, the Foreign Ministry had not intended to decide the very delicate military questions in advance, but, on the contrary, to postpone them until they had been examined on the spot. However, several weeks later, when Putiata began to insist from Vladivostok, which he had reached together with Min Yong-hwan, that a group of drill instructors be sent to train the royal guard, the Foreign Ministry did not object. A proposal made by Japan in August for the joint training of the Korean army by both Russia and Japan may have curbed its opposition in the expectation that prompt action might preclude the need for sharing military influence in the peninsula.[12] On September 5, 1896, Vice Minister of Foreign Affairs Count Vladimir Nikolaevich Lamsdorff telegraphed an explanation for the Japanese foreign minister to Speyer, but the latter did not hasten to transmit it, taking advantage of a change in cabinets in Tokyo.[13]

The first contingent of Russian military instructors arrived in Seoul together with the returning special envoy, Min, on October 21 of that year. It consisted in addition to Colonel Putiata, who was in overall command of the military mission, of first Lieutenant Afanas'ev I, Second Lieutenant Sikstel', ten noncommissioned officers, and a doctor.[14] The party was met at Chemulpo by Chargé Waeber and several Korean dignitaries and was escorted to Seoul with pomp and ceremony.[15]

The Korean War Ministry wanted the instructors to start at once with the drilling of all its troops, some 2,200 men. Waeber would not let them begin, however, until he had received official authorization from St. Petersburg. Meanwhile the instructors were to study the condition of the Korean army and to map out a training program.

The Russians wished to form a separate battalion of 800 men, station it apart from other battalions, and arrange everything in the Russian manner. The Koreans resisted the idea for a long time, wanting the Russians to train all of the widely scattered units. They asserted that the soldiers not selected for the special battalion would be disgruntled at not being taught and might mutiny.

On October 27 the necessary confirmation was received from St. Petersburg. Acting War Minister Yi Ju-hoi agreed to the selection of 800 men for the special battalion, and on November 4 the winnowing process was begun. Most soldiers seemed eager at this time to become students of the Russians. Afanas'ev, who had been appointed commander of the special battalion, had the impression that some of the men were "feeble-minded," but he thought that their enthusiasm would make up for their lack of intelligence. Dr. Charvinskii picked out those who looked relatively young and healthy. (Most rejections were due to trachoma, which was widespread.) A list was made on the spot of the soldiers selected for training by the Russians, and Yi ordered a red seal affixed to their trouser belts so that they could not change places with others, that is to say, to sell their membership in the elite unit.

The task of training the troops was complicated by the language barrier. There was only one interpreter at first—a Korean officer who spoke some Russian badly—and the instruction had to be conducted mostly by example and mimicry. It was difficult to accustom the Koreans to pull in their stomachs and not to squat, smoke, fall out, or relieve themselves upon the command "Rest!" The long hair of the soldiers detracted from their military appearance. In view of the disturbances which had wracked the country in the wake of the hair-cutting ordinances, the Russians hesitated to give direct orders for hair cuts. But when some of the soldiers developed abscesses on their heads, they pointed out that the infections would disappear if the hair was cut short and washed more frequently. The afflicted men heeded the advice and eventually most of their comrades followed suit. Above all, the rifles were too big and heavy for the small Koreans and a great deal of practice was necessary for them to be able to handle them effectively. Yet by mid-December the soldiers had been trained sufficiently for guard duty to be able to assume the protection of the palace under the command of Russian noncommissioned officers.[16]

During the long voyage back from Moscow Min Yong-hwan had made a favorable impression on the Russian instructors who had accompanied him. Believing that Min had acquired a certain experience in Europe and was open-minded toward the reforms required by the military organization of Korea, they secured his appointment as minister of war.[17] Waeber aroused the hostility of the Russian military men when he opposed the appointment. Dissatisfied already with his generally slow and cautious methods, they agitated against him, favoring his replacement by Speyer from whom a more "spirited" policy could be expected.[18]

The fall of the Ito cabinet had been precipitated by the failure of the Japanese policy in Korea. Public opinion reproached Ito for having compromised Japanese prestige in the peninsula. Yet, as Plancy reported, the situation of the Japanese was not as bad as the press pretended. They occupied part of the country with their troops, were arrogant in speech, and did not disguise their intention of opposing Russian entrenchment in the peninsula.[19]

The Japanese representation in Korea had undergone successive changes. Komura had departed from Seoul on May 30, leaving Secretary Kato as chargé d'affaires ad interim.[20] On June 11 Komura was named vice minister of foreign affairs, exchanging posts with Hara Takashi, better known as Hara Kei, who became envoy extraordinary and minister plenipotentiary in Korea.[21] Before becoming vice minister of foreign affairs Hara had served successively as consul in Tientsin, secretary and chargé d'affaires in Paris, and director of the Foreign Ministry. He was, in Plancy's words, "intelligent, distinguished, but very reserved."[22] He was a "harmless being," Speyer found, and Gutschmid agreed.[23] Hara arrived in Seoul at the beginning of July, but did not present his credentials to Kojong until the sixteenth, refusing, as had Komura, to do so in the Russian legation.[24] Meanwhile Consul Uchida Sadadzuchi had left on furlough, Kato taking his place.[25] Having been sent to Seoul by Mutsu, Hara was recalled at the beginning of October, shortly after Okuma Shigenobu took over as foreign minister. Secretary Kato once again took over as chargé d'affaires.[26]

When Hara had questioned Waeber about Russian training of the force of 800 men, Waeber had replied that the detachment would form the royal palace guard and as soon as it would be ready for guard duty, the king would be able, if he so desired, to move from the Russian legation. Although there was the risk that the presence of a Russian-led drill force would give the Russians continued domination of the king, the Japanese government was so eager for

Russian military instructors and their Korean cadets. (Isabella Bird Bishop, *Korea and Her Neighbors*, 2: 263.)

him to leave the tsarist legation that it accepted Waeber's explanation and raised no further questions about the training of the royal guard.[27]

It had been expected in Japan that the Okuma cabinet would pursue a strong policy in Korea in order to correct some of the blunders of the Ito administration. But the chauvinistic aspirations did not survive the collision with reality, Speyer reported in mid-November. Conditions in the Foreign Ministry and the long way Japan had yet to go to recover from the victorious war with China convinced Okuma "that the energy and severity so dear to his party were hardly appropriate for the foreign policy of this young empire." "He could not realize," Speyer wrote, "that the policy of Japan must also at the present time, perhaps at the present time more than before, be extremely careful and circumspect and by no means disdain necessary compromises and concessions."[28]

Contrary to what Waeber had told Hara, Putiata did not limit his efforts to the organization of a royal body guard. Soon after his arrival in Seoul, he drew up a plan for the establishment of a Russian-led Korean military force of 6,000 men and its increase over a period of three years to an army of 40,000 officers and men. He proposed that 150 instructors be sent to Korea for that purpose, with the stipulation that only Russian military instructors be used. Putiata's proposal was supported by Waeber, who obtained approval from the Korean side, and by War Minister Vannovskii.

Foreign Minister Muraviev was worried that such action might bring complications with Japan.[29] Informed by Vannovskii on January 16, 1897, of Putiata's proposals, he instructed Waeber not to make haste in this matter and to exercise caution. Although Speyer like Waeber replied favorably to his queries about Putiata's proposal, Muraviev continued to fret. Not until March 8, after several reminders, did he answer Vannovskii's letter.

Muraviev agreed in principle that the reorganization of the Korean army under the leadership (*rukovodstvo*) of Russian instructors was very desirable for St. Petersburg from a military and political point of view, yet he insisted that implementation of the proposal be postponed. Noting that Japan would challenge Russia's right to the exclusive training of Korean troops, Muraviev proposed to delay the question until the scheduled replacement of the Russian representatives in Tokyo and Seoul in several months. Even then, he directed, only 3,000 men should be trained and Russia ought not to insist on a commitment that only Russian instructors be employed. It was desirable, he reiterated in the instructions of Baron Rosen, the newly appointed minister to Tokyo, that the question of a Korean army not arouse Japanese dissatisfaction.[30]

Putiata was disgruntled by the situation in which he found himself. As Waeber gave him only limited backing, the relations between the two men

Count Mikhail Nikolaevich Muraviev, counselor of the Russian embassy in Berlin, 1884–1893; tsarist minister to Denmark, 1893–1897; director of the Foreign Ministry in St. Petersburg, January–April 1897; and Russian foreign minister, April 1897–1900. (*Illustrated London News*, 1897, 110: 141.)

became so strained that Putiata resolved to communicate with Waeber only in writing. At the same time War Minister Min did little to facilitate contact between the Russian military mission and the native authorities. As the old habits of negligence and temporizing persisted, the officers and noncoms were not issued their modest salaries regularly and had to remonstrate every month to get paid.[31] This plus a large number of incidents—some of them minor, others more serious—led to threats on the part of Putiata to quit the thankless post.[32]

In spite of Waeber's differences with Putiata, he agreed that procrastination, not to mention refusal, in the matter of training the Korean army would be construed in Seoul as a sign of Russian weakness and would lead to a further decline in Russian influence. On March 19 Waeber inquired of Muraviev how the tsarist government thought to assist in the reorganization of the Korean army and whether he should continue to negotiate concerning the subject. He himself favored immediate and determined action as the best means of paralyzing growing Japanese influence.

Speyer shared Waeber's point of view. Referring to the agitation and demands in Tokyo that Japan participate in the organization of the Korean army and side with England against Russia, he urged on March 24 "to remove the importunities of England and Japan" and to solve the question of the military instructors immediately, presenting Japan with a *fait accompli*. The War Ministry likewise decried delays in the training of the Korean army. Yet Muraviev might have persisted in his procrastination had the Japanese not tried to seize the initiative.[33]

On March 17 Chargé Motono transmitted a note to the effect that the Lobanov-Yamagata protocol had left open the question of the organization of a Korean army. Recalling that the Japanese government had expressed the desire in August of the preceding year to settle the issues by means of an agreement with St. Petersburg, he explained that Tokyo had not wished to deal with the matter while Kojong was in the tsarist legation. Now that the king had left, Japan wanted to know whether Russia was disposed to open negotiations concerning her proposal.[34]

The idea of joint Russo-Japanese guidance of the Korean army had already been dismissed by the tsarist government the previous year. The renewal of the proposal prodded it to shelve whatever qualms remained and to undertake the training of the Korean armed forces by itself.[35] It informed Waeber in response to his query on the nineteenth that it had been decided in principle to assist Korea in the organization of her army and that while it would take some time to study all the details, he was to assure Kojong of Russia's willingness to proceed with the matter.[36]

When Muraviev[37] replied to Motono on March 24 that article 2 of the Loba-nov-Yamagata protocol had left the question of the organization of the Korean army and of military instructors up to the discretion of the Korean government and that St. Petersburg had the right to furnish instructors if asked to do so by the latter, Motono countered that the Russian position was contrary to article 4 of the above-mentioned protocol, the organization of the Korean army hav-ing been left to further negotiation. Ill acquainted though he was with the course of the negotiations in Moscow, since he had been in office only briefly, Muraviev thought that article 2 clearly allowed Korea to build an army and that Russia must proceed on the basis of Korea's independence. If the Jap-anese government wished to invoke article 4, which provided for future exam-ination of details and points on which general agreement had been reached or for the deliberation of new problems, it could do so in Tokyo with Minister Rosen, who was due to arrive at the beginning of June, or in St. Petersburg by submitting written proposals.[38]

Although Muraviev promised to examine the military instructors question upon the receipt of specific proposals, Motono was left with the impression that the tsarist government was "resolved not to open negotiation." Foreign Minister Okuma, therefore, reiterated through Motono that the Japanese gov-ernment attached "great importance" to the question and considered its settle-ment by Russia and Japan as "highly desirable in giving effect to their mutual understanding respecting Corean affairs." However, he agreed to defer nego-tiations until the arrival of Rosen in Tokyo.[39] Muraviev concurred.[40]

In a confidential letter to Waeber on April 8, Muraviev reiterated that desir-able as it was to solve the military instructors question as soon as possible, the execution of the project must await the arrival of Rosen in Tokyo and of the new Japanese minister in St. Petersburg. Muraviev was prepared to renounce the points in the Putiata proposal to which the Japanese objected most strongly, but he was unwilling to share the training with the Japanese, for this, in his view, would frustrate the building of an army that could insure the independence of the Korean government and the internal development of the country. Muraviev instructed Waeber to use all means of persuasion and his personal influence to obtain Kojong's secret promise to leave the organization of the Korean army exclusively in Russian hands.

Ignoring Muraviev's injunctions to delay the instructors project, Waeber and Putiata attempted to conclude the negotiations with the Korean War Min-istry as soon as possible in order to forestall Japanese opposition. But they made no headway due to dissension among the Korean leadership and due to the machinations of Japan, supported to some extent by England. In mid-April Waeber cabled that notwithstanding the favorable attitude of the king and the war minister, it was impossible to predict whether the agreement would be realized.[41]

Informed by Kato that as the result of a meeting between Waeber, Kojong, and Min, the latter was about to engage secretly some 160 drill instructors for a period of five years at a total annual cost of almost 100,000 yen, the Japanese government renewed its opposition.[42] Asserting that the adoption of the Russian proposal would virtually place Korea into Russian hands, Kato sought on April 25 to enlist his English colleague's support in warning the Korean government of the grave risks entailed in the employment of Russian military officers. But Jordan refused to become involved, insisting that the question of the violation of the Moscow protocol was a matter between Tokyo and St. Petersburg. He did promise to give as his personal opinion if his advice was sought that such an extensive military organization was neither necessary nor warranted by the financial condition of the kingdom.[43]

The following afternoon, on April 26, Kato had a long private audience with Kojong. He urged him to reject the Russian proposal if he cared for his dynasty and country. Pointing to the history of the Japanese army as proof of the fact that a strong military force could be built with relatively little foreign help, he warned of the "serious evils" which the employment of so many Russian officers would entail for Korea.

The king revealed that the engagement of the Russian officers was the result of a secret arrangement made by Min Yong-hwan while in Russia the preceding year. He had no choice, he asserted, but to carry out the agreement.[44] Kojong admitted that he and his government had approved of the venture at the time, but he alleged that they now regretted having done so. He declared that in view of the opposition of his ministers it was his intention, even though the draft contracts had already been handed to Waeber, to restore harmony in his cabinet by halving the number of officers to be employed.[45]

Kato objected to half measures. Reiterating the extreme danger of the arrangement, he urged Kojong to take back the draft contracts.[46] Hopeful of being able to frustrate Russian plans if the king, who had a deep sense of personal obligation to Waeber, were to maintain a neutral attitude, Kato finally succeeded in eliciting from him the promise that he would leave the decision entirely up to the cabinet.[47]

As Kojong said different things to different people, playing one side against the other, his actual sentiments were unclear. He told Plancy, the French chargé, that he was displeased with the engagement of the many Russian officers, but had not dared to resist it openly because of the pressure exercised on him. He had agreed to it formally, but hiding behind the ministers whom he was supposed to consult, had conveyed to them his true feelings; hence the almost unanimous opposition of the cabinet. According to Plancy, the most active resistance to the arrangement came from Foreign Minister Yi Wan-yong, even though the latter had been supported until then by Waeber and owed his position largely to him. But in this case, Plancy remarked, his feelings of patriotism were presumably stronger than his scruples of gratitude. Yi had offered his resignation because the acting minister of war had taken it upon himself to negotiate with Waeber, but Kojong had refused to accept it.

The opposition of the Korean cabinet to the employment of Russian instructors provided the Japanese with the opportunity to try to arouse the concern of the other powers. When Kato asked the French chargé's assistance in trying to maintain the *status quo*, Plancy replied that his advice to the Koreans, should they solicit it, would be for them to exercise the greatest prudence and not to provoke a conflict between Russia and Japan, since they would be the first to suffer its consequences.[48]

Immediately after Kato's audience on April 26, Waeber saw the king for two hours. On the morning of the twenty-eighth he had a long consultation with the Korean Foreign Office. That evening Kojong sent a private messenger to Kato requesting his views. Kato again stressed the undesirability of engaging so many Russian officers. A cabinet meeting held the same night could not reach a consensus. "From present indications it is probable that the project will fall through," Kato reported home.[49] But after a stormy debate on April 30, the Korean cabinet agreed to invite a small number of Russian instructors.[50]

That day, on instructions from Okuma, Motono demanded that the tsarist government defer the training of Korean troops until the general question of the organization of the Korean army had been resolved between the Japanese government and Rosen.[51] Muraviev replied that he would give an answer after making a detailed investigation.[52]

While the Japanese demand for the joint resolution of the question of the organization of the Korean army had been rejected by St. Petersburg firmly the preceding month and had precipitated the attempt to hasten the conclusion of an agreement concerning the instructors, Motono's objections met with a different reception now. The determined stand taken by Japan again confronted Russia with the dilemma whether to invite new complications by insisting on the realization of the Putiata proposal or to give in and conclude an agreement with Japan. Had the negotiations in the Korean capital been faring well, Muraviev might have rebuffed the Japanese pretensions once more, but since there was not prospect for a speedy settlement of the issue in Seoul, he adopted a conciliatory approach. Rejecting the advice of Speyer, written on March 24, that Russia ignore Japan's position and act more energetically, a memorandum prepared by the tsarist government on May 2 pointed to the dangers that such a policy would entail. It warned that in view of the determined tone of the Japanese note and of the increase in expenditures for the Japanese army and navy following the revelation of the Putiata plan, Russia must be prepared, should she insist on the realization of the project, "to meet such serious obstacles (and in the very near future) that it will no longer be possible to remove them by diplomatic explanations." Such a result would be incommensurate with the benefits that would accrue from an excessively persistent line of action in this question, the memorandum concluded.[53]

On May 4 Muraviev telegraphed Waeber to halt any negotiations concerning the organization of the Korean army until the receipt of new instructions.[54] The following day he informed Motono that he had directed Waeber and Speyer not to decide anything pertaining to the engagement of the Russian officers by Korea until the arrival of Rosen in Tokyo.[55]

But Waeber, who had not yet received the cease-and-desist orders, had continued his efforts on behalf of the agreement. In vain Kato had tried to bolster the king's opposition by telling him that there was no need to fear Russian threats—Japan would support him if necessary.[56] As noted, the cabinet had agreed to the engagement of a small number of Russian advisers. On May 4 Kato reported that Kojong had sanctioned the employment of Russian officers. A contract was being drawn up to be handed to Waeber the following day. "I am doing my best to stimulate [the] minister[s] opposed to the scheme and to persuade the Minister for Foreign Affairs to refuse to sign it," Kato telegraphed.[57] On May 5 he told Kojong of the discussions that had taken place in St. Petersburg and contended that it would be fruitless for him to invite any Russian instructors, because the tsarist government had renounced its plans for the organization of the Korean army.

That very day Putiata went into action. It is possible that he had heard that orders to terminate the negotiations were on their way and wanted to give the matter one last try. At any rate, he falsely informed the Korean minister of war that the squadron which Rear Admiral Evgenii Ivanovich Alekseev was assembling at Pusan and Vladivostok would shortly arrive in Chemulpo with reinforcements for the Russian legation guard so that the Korean government could act without fear of Japanese reprisals. The stratagem worked, for that evening Waeber was handed an official request for Russian instructors. Attached to the letter were a draft agreement for the organization of a Korean army of 6,000 men, embodying practically without change the major points of Putiata's proposal, and the terms of the contract to be concluded with the Russian instructors.[58]

Rear Admiral Evgenii Ivanovich Alekseev, assistant chief of the Russian naval general staff, 1892–1895; commander of the Pacific fleet, 1895–1897; commander of the Black Sea squadron, 1897–1899; commander-in-chief and commander of the troops in the Kwantung region and of the naval forces in the Pacific, 1899–1903. (*Vsemirnaia illiustratsiia*, 1895, 53: 188.)

According to Waeber and Putiata the orders from St. Petersburg to halt the negotiations concerning military instructors did not arrive until the following day, May 6. Waeber regarded this as fortunate, because he believed that abandonment of the project would have dealt a serious blow to Russian prestige not only in Korea, but in Japan. He attached great significance to the successful outcome of the talks, arguing that Japanese opposition had transformed the issue of Russian military instructors into the question of who could henceforth exert political dominance in Korea. Any concessions on the part of Russia in the matter of instructors would have strengthened the position of Japan and simultaneously would have undermined that of the king, who sided with Russia.[59]

Speyer assured the German chargé d'affaires, C. G. von Treutler, on May 6 that Russia had not yet responded definitively to Korea's appeal for military instructors; the current complications in Europe (the Cretan insurrection and the war between Greece and Turkey) precluded the creation of new entanglements in the Far East. At any rate, Waeber had been instructed not to commit himself to the realization of the arrangement. With remarkable candor Speyer added that if it had not been for the situation in Europe, Russia would probably have carried out the agreement and England, according to experience, would have calmly accepted the *fait accompli*. Without British support, the opposition of Japan would hardly have been cause for concern, he concluded.[60]

The United States minister in Seoul did not share the alarm of his British and Japanese colleagues about the proposed military training program. Ever since his arrival in Korea, the country had been in varying degrees of disorder. American interests, which by now were considerable, required above all the maintenance of peace and order. Yet the troops available for this purpose were "utterly incompetent." Whenever they proceeded into the provinces to suppress the recurring insurrections, their lack of discipline made them "vastly more dangerous to the safety of the country than the marauders" against whom they were sent. It was essential to organize an effective armed force and this could not be done without foreign aid. "No one who knows Korea and Koreans will gainsay this for a moment," Sill underlined.

Since the Japanese had made no objections when Russian instructors had come to train the royal body guard the preceding autumn and since Okuma, following the publication of the Moscow protocol, had defended the Russian action against critics in the Diet, Sill assumed that Russia and Japan were in agreement on the training of the Korean army as well, and supported the venture. "When it became known a short time ago that it was proposed to begin the extension of the drill to soldiers outside of the royal guard, I was rejoiced to hear it," Sill reported, "for I believed that such extension was vitally important for all concerned . . . I spoke favorably of it, as occasion served." Thus he urged Foreign Minister Yi Wan-yong through Allen on April 23 to agree to the completion of the contract with Russia drawn up at the king's request.[61]

Learning of the advice which Sill and Allen were giving to Yi, Okuma telegraphed to the Japanese minister in Washington, Hoshi Toru, that the assistance they were rendering to Waeber seriously undermined the position of the Korean foreign minister. Believing that the actions of Sill and Allen were not consistent with American policy in Korea, Okuma instructed Hoshi to complain to Secretary of State John Sherman, who had succeeded Olney on March 6.[62]

Taken to task by Sherman, Sill explained that he had acted without supposing that he was "antagonizing any interests." Not until his return on April 29 from Chemulpo, where he had gone on official business for several days, did he learn of Kato's protest to Kojong three days earlier against the employment of additional Russian instructors. From that moment, he assured the secretary of state, he had remained "studiously silent on the subject."

Upon receipt of Sherman's query, Sill had called on Kato to remove any misunderstanding that might have arisen between them. Kato asserted that he did not know where Tokyo had obtained the information. Neither he nor any member of his legation had as much as mentioned him or Allen in their dispatches concerning this question. They had communicated nothing, Kato said, to give ground for the complaint lodged in Washington.[63]

As Japanese and English newspapers in Tokyo began to spread the story that the tsarist government had assured Motono of its desire to calm Japanese feelings in the matter of the military instructors, Speyer inquired of Muraviev by telegraph how to conduct himself. Muraviev replied that he had decided to "suspend" the dispatch of military instructors to Seoul.

At the same time Speyer received a telegram from Waeber asking for information concerning the conversations he was said to have had with Okuma on that subject. "Count Okuma has never opened his mouth to me about it," Speyer retorted, asking in turn about the position of the Korean minister of war and what Waeber had stated to Kato. "They never said a word about it to me," Waeber echoed.

Convinced that the political views of the Japanese cabinet published in the local press came from an official source, Speyer was certain that an understanding had been reached in St. Petersburg between Motono and his English and American colleagues to deter Muraviev from the venture, which like all actions of this sort entailed some danger along with the many advantages. The about-face of the tsarist government irritated and discouraged Speyer and the officers of the Russian squadron. They made disparaging remarks about Muraviev. Speyer grumbled that the progress of Russia in Korea had been set back by ten years.[64]

When Motono, whom Muraviev informed on May 19 of the agreement concluded by Waeber in Seoul, asked whether it was "definitive and unalterable," Muraviev responded that although the contract had already been signed, it would not be implemented until an understanding had been reached between the Japanese government and Rosen. Since the Korean minister to Russia had arrived two days before, Motono inquired whether he had made any application about Waeber. Muraviev answered that he had not; the transfer of Speyer back to Seoul was still contemplated.[65]

The assent of Muraviev to defer the question of the Russian military instructors until the arrival of Rosen satisfied the Japanese public, whose anger had shifted to the Formosan and Hawaiian questions.[66]

Motono saw Muraviev again on May 24. The Russian foreign minister remarked that the telegram he had received from Waeber was too vague for him to say anything more than what he had told him already until he received a detailed report. But this was not important, he pointed out, because the matter was to be arranged after Rosen arrived in Tokyo.

The director of the Asiatic Department with whom Motono also had a confidential conversation read to him Waeber's telegram of April 12, concerning the desire of the Korean minister of war to engage twenty-one Russians. Kapnist related that Waeber had consented to the request in the name of the tsarist government, but expressed doubt that a special convention had been signed. He asked Motono to keep the above confidential.[67]

News of the "victory" in Seoul had been received in St. Petersburg with mixed feelings. Nicholas had expressed his satisfaction on the copy of the telegram sent by Waeber on May 6, convinced that the question which he regarded as the major means of strengthening Russian influence in Korea had finally been solved. Muraviev had seemed inclined at first thought to follow up the unexpected success and quickly carry out the agreement. But others had warned that Japan might use the occasion as a pretext for military action against Russia, possibly with English support. The Foreign Ministry had decided to delay the matter in order to avoid complications with Japan. It revealed its tactics in supplementary instructions sent to Rosen and Speyer on May 21.

Rosen was informed that the tsarist government was prepared to organize a Korean army of 3,000 men—half the number contemplated by Putiata—for which instructors already in Korea would suffice. The dispatch of additional instructors would be deferred until their need was established. The organization of the Korean army was to be postponed indefinitely, Russia committing herself to carry it out when it was deemed necessary to do so. Thus Muraviev sought, on one hand, to avoid a conflict with Japan by shelving the military project for the time being and, on the other hand, to insure that no other power gained control of the Korean army.

Speyer, who was to return to Seoul shortly, was instructed to exercise extreme caution in anything that might complicate relations with Japan. He was warned that important as the consolidation of Russian influence in Korea and the exclusion of the influence of third powers from the peninsula might be, the benefits of even exclusive Russian domination of weak and poor Korea could not at present make up for the harm which the exacerbation of relations with Japan could bring to Russia.

In a letter to Vannovskii on May 26, Muraviev noted that inasmuch as every Russian step in Korea aroused the natural suspicion of Japan, who was arming strongly, "the continuance of such actions will unavoidably provoke an armed conflict with Japan in the very near future." Since war with Japan was contrary to Russia's political interests, Muraviev thought it most desirable to maintain in the Far East a "peaceful temporizing posture in order not to exasperate Japan needlessly" and proposed to refrain in Korea from such actions as might do so.

Waeber was notified that the tsarist government deemed it best to postpone the implementation of the Korean plan for the organization of the army under Russian guidance. He was instructed to tell Kojong and his cabinet at the same time that St. Petersburg regarded the invitation as a commitment on the part of the Korean government not to solicit instructors of other nationalities. Secret instructions sent to Waeber immediately after the dispatch of the above telegram repeated that he must discontinue all negotiations concerning the Korean army until the assumption of their posts by Speyer and Rosen.[68]

Waeber was appalled by Muraviev's intentions, which threatened to turn his hard-won agreement into a scrap of paper. No sooner had he learned of the decision to postpone the dispatch of instructors than he had cabled to Muraviev on May 22 that any concessions in this respect would seriously affect Russian influence and would undermine the position of the king and those ministers who had voted for the invitation. Waeber's objections, echoed by Speyer, found support in the War Ministry and with the tsar himself, who on June 24 authorized the dispatch of a new group of instructors. A month later, on the evening of July 29, the second group of instructors, numbering three officers and ten noncommissioned officers, arrived in Seoul and the following day were introduced to Waeber by Putiata.[69]

The Japanese were irate at the violation of the assurances given to them in

May and, as Muraviev had feared, reacted promptly and with determination. The day that the Russian officers and men landed at Chemulpo, Kato called on Kojong to inquire whether rumors of the imminent arrival of the new party of instructors were true. The king confirmed that a number of Russians were coming at the request of his government.

Two days later, on July 30, in accordance with instructions from Okuma, Kato addressed a note to Waeber protesting against the signing of an agreement with the instructors. He alleged that Waeber had demanded the agreement from the Koreans contrary to the assurances given in St. Petersburg. Waeber denied the accusation, saying that the instructors had come solely at the invitation of the king.[70] In a written reply he stated that the three officers and ten noncoms had arrived in response to a request by the Korean government in early May for twenty-nine military instructors.[71]

On August 3 Kato inquired of Foreign Minister Yi Wan-yong in a note on what grounds the Russian instructors had been invited. Yi responded that Korea had the right to invite instructors of any nationality. "In this we are fully independent," he declared. Dissatisfied with the reply, Kato refused to accept it in an attempt to intimidate Kojong and his cabinet.

Kato's task was facilitated by the fact that during the past three months doubts had grown in Korea about Russian readiness to counteract Japan. Russian efforts to avoid a collision with the latter looked like weakness in Korean eyes. Kato's firm position, on the other hand, impressed the Korean government. On a plea of financial difficulties, it refused to begin the reorganization of the army and made no use of the freshly arrived instructors.[72]

Kojong told the French representative on August 7 that he was at a loss what position to take in regard to the Russian instructors who had arrived. Should the Korean government sign a contract with them and entrust the training of its soldiers to them or would it be a danger for the kingdom to have almost its entire army in the hands of the Russians? Moreover, should one not fear the protests of the Japanese government? If the employment of the Russian instructors threatened to provoke international complications might it not be best to indemnify them and ask them to return to Vladivostok? On the other hand, would this not arouse the dissatisfaction of the Russians?

Asked for his opinion, Plancy sympathized with Kojong's dilemma in not wishing to antagonize either the Russians or the Japanese or perhaps both at the same time. It would be better, he said, to seek an arrangement which would be agreeable to both, but he was not in a position, he declared, to give him any advice in this matter. When Plancy inquired about the conditions under which the Russian officers had been called to Seoul, Kojong asserted that the tsar, upon learning of the military situation in Korea, had deemed it useful to aid the country in the organization of her army; he alleged that Korea had never asked for military instructors. Plancy was aware that the king was not telling him the truth and did not expect to be consulted in the matter again.[73]

Informed by Kato of Waeber's attitude, Okuma instructed Hayashi Tadasu, the new Japanese minister in St. Petersburg, to request of the tsarist government that, inasmuch as Waeber did not seem to understand its real intentions and a formal contract for the employment of the Russian officers might be signed at any moment, it remind him to postpone all action until the necessary arrangements had been concluded in Tokyo upon the arrival of Rosen.[74] Hayashi transmitted the text of Okuma's telegram on August 5. Muraviev, Hayashi reported, "spoke evasively, but on pressure promised to give [a] decisive answer after mature consideration." [75]

The Russian reply, handed to Hayashi later in the month,[76] looked conciliatory. It stated that in response to Motono's request Waeber had been instructed already in April to discontinue negotiations concerning the reorganization of the Korean army. Yet it refused to issue any orders pertaining to the newly arrived instructors on the ground that they were supposed to have left Korea in April, but had been detained merely by unforeseen circumstances.[77]

As Hayashi did not think that the tsarist government would give any positive answer and there was no practical advantage to be gained by pursuing the discussion further in St. Petersburg,[78] particularly since Muraviev had held out the settlement of the instructor question in Tokyo upon Rosen's arrival, the Japanese Foreign Office instructed Kato to halt his démarches in Seoul.[79]

Efforts by Waeber to implement the military contracts came to naught. Although he obtained the dismissal of Foreign Minister Yi when the latter refused to sign them, neither Min Chong-muk, who had served as president of the Foreign Office several years before and now succeeded as foreign minister, nor anyone else dared to put his name to the contracts because of the opposition of the majority of the cabinet. As a result the services of the newly arrived drill instructors were not utilized pending the return of Speyer to Seoul.[80]

Baron Rosen, until whose arrival Speyer had to remain in Tokyo, was familiar with Japan, where he had served for six years as chargé d'affaires in 1877–1883. His German colleague in Belgrad, his previous post, had found him to be a very calm individual, not given to any sort of bluff. Witte described Rosen as an honest, reasonable person with a German way of thinking, by which he meant "noble stubbornness." [81] In contrast to Speyer, who had been preoccupied almost exclusively with the Korean question, Rosen realized that the latter must be settled in terms of the broader Far Eastern

Balance of Intrigue

question and of general Russian relations with Japan, war with whom must be avoided at all costs.[82]

On his way through Paris Rosen confided to Foreign Minister Hanotaux that the tsarist govenment was in absolute ignorance of events in Korea, because Waeber had abstained from transmitting any information about the situation in the country since his appointment as minister to Mexico, even though he had remained in Seoul. Rosen told Hanotaux that his government vividly desired to maintain good relations with Japan in the belief that English influence was not preponderant in Tokyo at the moment; he was armed with formal instructions prescribing him to work for a rapprochement and even an alliance with the latter. Although Rosen was aware of the ambitious aims of Japan, Hanotaux noted, he did not share the view of certain statesmen who believed in the impending breakup of the Chinese empire and were preoccupied with the advantages that Japan could derive therefrom.[83]

Rosen arrived in Tokyo on August 16. He was received by the Meiji emperor and his spouse on August 24. The return of the imperial couple to the capital and the arrival of Rosen had long been expected. When some of the Japanese newspapers linked the two events, Treutler scoffed that this was naive and too flattering to Rosen. Nonetheless the utterance was revealing, he thought, of the anxiety which careful analysts of Russo-Japanese relations could no longer suppress. Treutler testified that Rosen studiously displayed Japanophile feelings, admired the progress which had been made during the seventeen years since his departure, and benevolently attributed the inconveniences which dealings with the Japanese authorities now frequently entailed to the justified pride which the Japanese could take in the changed status of their country. Yet he suspected that Rosen's friendliness was "outward," intended to make Russian policy, which was "somewhat bitter for Japan's continental plans," more palatable.[84]

Desirous of good relations with Japan, Rosen had personal qualms about the idea that Russia organize the Korean army. At the time of his departure for Japan from St. Petersburg he had been told of the promise made to the Japanese government to postpone the military instructors question until he had a chance to discuss it in Tokyo. He was distressed to learn upon his arrival of the change that had occurred in Russian policy during his voyage and of the appearance of the new group of officers and men in Korea. On August 25 he cabled to Muraviev that the dispatch of the instructors had aroused great alarm in Tokyo. He requested clarification, because this action contradicted the instructions he had been given.[85]

On August 26 Rosen had an interview with Okuma. After explaining the situation in Korea, Okuma asked that the tsarist government direct Waeber to postpone all action regarding the engagement of the Russian officers until "the necessary arrangements" had been concluded between them in Tokyo shortly. Rosen promised to do so at once.[86] During the lengthy exchange, Okuma assured Rosen that Japan was willing to conclude an agreement with Russia in the belief that this would be "the best guarantee for peace and tranquility in the Far East." He promised to make concrete proposals in this regard at the beginning of September. Okuma blamed Waeber alone for the problems that had arisen in connection with the arrival of the instructors, expressing the belief that the tsarist government was ill informed about his activities. Conveying his satisfaction that Waeber was being replaced by Speyer, Okuma stated that Kato had been instructed to seek a friendly understanding with the latter.

As there had not been time for a reply to his telegram of the preceding day seeking an elucidation of Russian policy, Rosen remained noncommittal in his response to Okuma, saying vaguely that Russia too desired an agreement with Japan. But he warned, in line with the instructions which he had received in March, that the organization of a military force in Korea must remain Russia's responsibility.

Rosen's personal reservations concerning the dispatch of the military instructors were not heeded in St. Petersburg. Nicholas scribbled on his telegram of August 25: "What has been done, cannot be undone. Japan still maintains her forces in Korea, while we have none there. And you cannot conquer a country with instructors." Muraviev consequently replied to Rosen on August 28 that the presence of the Russian instructors should not arouse the fears of the Japanese, since they had troops in the country.[87]

To Hayashi, who had been instructed by Okuma to talk to the Russian foreign minister in the same sense as he himself had spoken to Rosen,[88] Muraviev contended on September 2 that the newly arrived instructors had been sent in response to a pledge made to the Koreans before he had promised to Motono on May 19 that the question of the organization of the Korean army would be postponed until the matter had been discussed between the Japanese government and Rosen; their arrival had been delayed by circumstance of travel. He dismissed the affair as of no importance, assuring Hayashi that no new arrangements would be made until an understanding had been reached between the Japanese government and Rosen. "Now, in the absence of proof as to the actual words [the] Russian Minister for Foreign Affairs fully employed in speaking to Motono, all discussions are in vain," Hayashi cabled.[89]

As Rosen parrotted Muraviev's explanation in an interview with Okuma on September 7, Okuma realized that it would be fruitless to belabor the issue. But it would be unwise, he thought, for Japan to give the impression that she

concurred entirely with the Russian understanding of the situation. Consequently he instructed Hayashi on September 9 to address a polite note to
Muraviev to the effect that it had been the impression of the Japanese government that Russia had agreed that the question of the employment of Russian
officers in Korea be deferred until the arrival of the Russian minister.[90]

Rosen himself disagreed with the line of action he had to follow. He tried to
convince the tsarist government that Russia must come to an agreement with
Japan, if need be by withdrawing from Korea. The results of a collision with
Japan, he understood, would not be worth the casualties and outlays even if
Russia were to emerge victorious, something he had the courage to doubt. He
noted that Japan had proceeded to rearm following the Sino-Japanese War and
that she had redoubled her efforts as soon as Russian intentions in Korea had
become clear. He warned against the illusion that the state of Japan's finances
would not allow the completion of the contemplated rearmament program.
Rosen was particularly alarmed by the growth of the Japanese navy, which in
his estimate was already more powerful than the Russian fleet in the Pacific
and was in a much better strategic position. He foresaw that the Korean controversy might offer the basis for an Anglo-Japanese rapprochement, which
would further complicate Russia's position in the Far East. Urging the tsarist
government to come to an immediate agreement with Japan by means of
serious concessions, Rosen pointed out on September 13: "If we shall not
wish to give to Japan that share of influence to which she believes herself
entitled after the victorious war fought precisely over this question, all that
will be left for the Japanese government [to do] will be to resort to force."
Rosen insisted that utmost care be taken to avoid provocative measures, lest
Japan be pushed into separate action on her own.[91]

The pending return of Speyer to Seoul had given rise to diverse speculations. Alarmists predicted that it signified the complete Russification of Korea
and, after a brief delay, the end of the ruling dynasty. Others depicted Speyer
as Japanophile and expected a conciliatory policy from him.[92] Speyer himself
had confided to Treutler in mid-June that his pleasure at going back to Seoul
soon had been greatly diminished by the deterioration of Russia's position in
the peninsula. He attributed the development to the complications in the European East—the Cretan insurrection and the war between Greece and Turkey—which had deflected the attention of his government from Korea. Even
a brief relaxation in one's vigilance could have the worst consequences in the
Far East, he pointed out. All had been undone (*tout est abîme*), he alleged,
and asserted that it would be very difficult if not impossible to regain what had
been lost.

Treutler did not take Speyer's plaint seriously. Speyer himself had spoken of the bad position of the Japanese in Seoul and had remarked that they would act more statesmanlike if they withdrew imperceptibly from political involvement in Korea. Treutler suspected that Speyer's remarks were designed to cast approaching events in the peninsula in the most harmless light for Russia. He looked forward with suspense to the much delayed arrival of Rosen, who was said to be carrying important instructions and was expected to visit Peking and Seoul before assuming his post in Tokyo.[93]

Speyer reached Seoul on September 2.[94] The very next day—before he officially relieved Waeber[95]—Speyer demanded of Kojong a prompt settlement of the instructors question. When the monarch blamed War Minister Sim Sang-hun for the confusion which had developed, Speyer suggested that he be removed. Sim was retired, yet in spite of continued negotiations the contracts remained unsigned, partly because of Japanese pressure on the Korean government.

Undeterred by such a "formality," Speyer declared that the Russian officers, once they had come to Seoul, would not leave without carrying out the functions promised to them by Sim.[96] At his insistence, the picking of soldiers for a new battalion was finally set for September 24. But the Koreans were masters at passive resistance.

In the days of Waeber the Russians had tried to form a second guard battalion of 1,000 men out of the five battalions of the War Ministry. As they had attempted to select the men on July 7, the five battalions together had totalled less than 600 persons, the authorities moving the soldiers of the same battalion from barrack to barrack to give the appearance that several times that number were on hand. With the formation of a special guard battalion frustrated, the Korean minister of war had proposed several days later that the Russians begin the training of the five battalions simultaneously, an impossible task which Waeber had to decline because of the small number of Russian instructors and the scattered disposition of the battalions.

Now, on September 24, when the Russian officers gathered again to form a separate battalion out of four or five battalions of the War Ministry, they found that the battalion commanders were not present, that their subordinates could not assemble the men, and that no one had come from the Ministry of War, as arranged the night before.

When Lieutenant Afanas'ev I, who had replaced Colonel Putiata, reported the above to Speyer, the latter rushed to the palace fuming. He threatened Kojong that if he was forced to inform St. Petersburg of what had transpired, a "cooling of friendly feelings toward Korea" might result. Kojong promised to take immediate steps to man the new battalion. On the twenty-seventh and twenty-eighth 991 men were laboriously chosen, but instruction did not get under way until mid-October as the reluctant recruits feigned illness and on other pretexts absented themselves to avoid service in the foreign-trained unit. "In the process of selection it was evident," S. Grudzinskii recalled, "that the soldiers had been inspired to try in every way not to be chosen. Many made pitiful grimaces, many claimed to be ill or old, many simply fled from the ranks and had to be chased out of the barracks."[97]

The attitude of the recruits must have exasperated the instructors. The beating of soldiers was still common in the tsarist army, and stories spread of the mistreatment of Korean troops by Russian drill sergeants. One Russian officer was said to have struck a Korean colonel over the head with his sword for a minor offense.[98] But talk of mutiny died down as members of the Japanese legation advised the "hot-heads" to wait until Japan could be in a position to assist them.[99]

The success achieved by Speyer in putting the instructors to work without the signing of the contracts, against which the Japanese protests had been directed, reinforced the feeling in St. Petersburg that there was no need to come to an agreement with Japan concerning the organization of the Korean army. It was decided to abandon plans for the future expansion of the Korean army rather than admit Japanese participation in the venture.

On October 15 Rosen was informed that Nicholas wanted no discussion with Japan of the joint training of Korean troops. He was instructed to consider the military training question as closed. He was to parry any Japanese protests with the retort that the engagement of Russian instructors could be considered as a rather weak compensation for St. Petersburg in view of Japan's military occupation of the peninsula.[100]

The Issue of Financial Control

The apparent resolution of the military instructors controversy in its favor emboldened the tsarist government. Turning a deaf ear to the cautions of Rosen, it sought to establish control over the finances of Korea as well.[101] The groundwork had already been laid the previous year with the dispatch of Pokotilov to Seoul to investigate the practicability of a Russian loan to Korea. As a special agent of Witte and a member of the diplomatic corps, Pokotilov had been charged with gathering both financial and political information.[102] Pokotilov had arrived in the Korean capital in mid-August 1896 and was staying as a guest in the Russian legation. In November of that year Witte had offered to the Korean government through Pokotilov a loan of three million dollars to enable it to repay a Japanese loan of the same amount contracted in March 1895. Although the matter of a Russian loan had been initiated by the

Korean government, it did not jump at the proposal, because of the proviso that the Customs revenue be pledged as security. It replied evasively that Korea would avail herself of Russian assistance in the event that the money would be required.[103]

More touchy than the matter of a loan was the appointment of a Russian financial adviser, requested by Min Yong-hwan at the time of the coronation of Nicholas II. Aware that the dispatch of a "financial adviser" might arouse opposition on the part of the other powers, Witte had suggested to Muraviev on May 31, 1897, that Senior Counselor of State Kir Alekseevich Alekseev, whose nomination as financial adviser had been approved by Nicholas, be given the inoffensive designation of "commercial agent." Muraviev had agreed with Witte's cautious approach, remarking that Alekseev's influence would depend largely on his tact and his ability to take advantage of opportunities that presented themselves. But by the time Alekseev arrived in Seoul with several secretaries on September 30, Speyer was back in control of the Russian legation. Flushed by his recent success in the military instructors question, Speyer pressed for Alekseev's employment as "chief adviser of all financial and related customs affairs of the kingdom." He did so without first consulting St. Petersburg, determined to strike "while the iron was hot."[104]

It was generally expected that Alekseev would replace Brown as chief commissioner of customs and as adviser and virtual comptroller of the treasury. Brown had done much to improve the economic condition of Seoul and the state of the Korean treasury, but in the process of conserving revenues he had angered many Korean officials. Although the British government planned to oppose Brown's removal, he himself was on the verge of giving up. He had felt for some time, he confided to Allen, by then the American minister resident, that his work in demonstrating that Korea could be self-sustaining and stand alone was really injurious to the country as a whole, because it bolstered the "corrupt" government from which no good could be expected. The lot of the people would be vastly improved if a strong power, willing and able to enforce order throughout the land, would come in and put an end to squeeze and other forms of corruption. "He said," Allen reported, "that looking far ahead he felt sure that Korea must in time go over to Russia, since Japan, the only one interested in preventing this, was impotent in the matter; therefore he felt no inclination to place obstacles in Russia's path now."

Krien, who had been the German consul at Seoul for the past decade, agreed that Korea must evidently have some stronger nation as her overlord. China was not equal to her great opportunities; Japan had failed in the task; and Britain did not care to assume the responsibility. Like Brown, Krien thought that the guidance of Korea seemed to fall naturally upon Russia.[105]

In an effort to thwart the dismissal of his countryman, Consul General Jordan asked for an audience with the ruler. An audience was promised, then declined as Kojong contracted a diplomatic illness. Fearing that Jordan might sway the weak monarch, Speyer had demanded that he receive him first. During their meeting, Speyer advised Kojong to insist firmly that Alekseev had come at his bidding. Kojong assented and told Speyer to present a note to the Foreign Office notifying him officially of Alekseev's arrival and asking when he could take up his duties. Speyer did so on October 6, without first consulting his government. In the letter, addressed to Min Chong-muk, Speyer stated that Alekseev had been dispatched by Nicholas in response to the request Kojong had made through Min Yong-hwan for an official of the Russian Finance Ministry to supervise and control the finances and customs revenue of Korea.[106]

Neither the Korean authorities nor the Western diplomats whom they acquainted with the missive conceived that Speyer had acted in violation of his instructions.[107] As the foreign representatives learned of the content of the note, they began to inquire whether a secret agreement had indeed been concluded by Min Yong-hwan in St. Petersburg. Former Foreign Minister Yi Wan-yong, whom the American minister questioned, asserted that while his name had been attached to the request for aid, he had not signed it and had not known of its existence until recently. "I am told that the document bears no seals, which are considered so necessary in Korea for the authentication of any document," Allen reported.[108]

Waeber had assured Brown that Alekseev would not supplant him, but was coming as an adviser to the Household Department. When Speyer insisted that Alekseev take charge of the Korean customs revenues and finances, the recently appointed minister of the treasury, Pak Chong-yang, threatened to resign. As Jordan repeated his request for an audience with Kojong, Kato informed him that he had been instructed by the Japanese government to cooperate with him in attempting to block the removal of Brown.[109]

On October 13 Jordan addressed a very strong letter to Foreign Minister Min Chong-muk in which he demanded a personal audience with Kojong before the general audience scheduled for that day. Min rejected the demand, but in view of the smallness of the audience hall and the large suites of each representative the legations were received separately. Jordan took advantage of the opportunity and after exchanging a few remarks about the imperial title which Kojong had just assumed, he complained of his inability to obtain a private audience to deliver a message from his government. When the foreign minister tried to silence the interpreter, the emperor ordered him to leave the room. When Min stalled, the crown prince pushed him out. Thereupon Jordan read the telegram from the British government in support of the retention of Brown. Kojong called Min back to hear the message. Turning to Jordan, he said that they would try to work out a satisfactory arrangement, but the British representative countered that nothing would be agreeable other than the fulfillment of Brown's contract.[110]

On October 18 Min sent to Speyer a copy of a letter from Pak Chong-yang to himself respecting the proposed employment of Alekseev. The letter pointed out that Brown had been engaged on instructions from the throne as chief commissioner of customs and adviser of the Finance Department in October 1895 for a period of five years; his term of office had not yet expired. As proof, Min forwarded a copy of the contract, which Pak had enclosed.

Speyer refused to accept the above documents as an answer to his request that a date be fixed for the commencement of Alekseev's duties. In a letter to Min, dated October 19, he threatened that unless he received a clear reply to his original demand the following day, he would report to St. Petersburg "the refusal of the Corean Government to give effect to a request that was made spontaneously by it to the Russian Government."[111] When no response was made in the allotted time, Speyer fired off another stiff note.

On October 22 Min Chong-muk apologized for the misunderstanding that had occurred. Asserting that the information from the Finance Ministry transmitted by him had not been intended as a reply, he assured Speyer that Alekseev would, of course, be employed after the conditions had been discussed with the Ministry of Finance. But Speyer, on the twenty-fourth, rejected this reply too as unsatisfactory, because it did not specify when Brown would be dismissed and when Alekseev could take up his duties.

Knowing through the Korean interpreter of the Russia legation, Kim Hong-yuk, who was close to the ruler, that the latter had repeatedly complained about the slowness of his ministers, Speyer obtained an audience with Kojong to resolve this "simple question" promptly. Confronted by data which Alekseev had managed to obtain about conditions in the customs administration, which cast Brown in an unfavorable light, and pressured by Speyer's decisive tone and argumentation, rendered in threatening and abusive language by Kim, Kojong caved in and promised to take the necessary steps for the dismissal of Brown.[112] But Jordan and his superior, Minister MacDonald in Peking, rejected Min's efforts to buy up Brown's contract.[113]

A complaint by the British chargé, W. E. Goschen, to the director of the Asiatic Department about the demand for Brown's dismissal aroused consternation in St. Petersburg. Kapnist assured Goschen that while the tsarist government had sent a financial expert at the request of the Korean government, it had given absolutely no instructions to Speyer for the removal of Brown. In a telegram on October 30 Muraviev inquired of Speyer whether there was any truth to the British allegation.

Speyer confirmed the facts in a telegram on November 2. He sought to justify his conduct with the argument that it was necessary to free the Korean Customs Service from the British Customs Service in China. He asked that his steps be supported as the deed had already been done and any concession at this time would be detrimental to Russian interests. Muraviev was angered by the unauthorized actions of Speyer and might not have approved them had the tsar not intervened. But Nicholas was delighted with the victory Speyer appeared to have achieved. "*Shpeer molodets*" (Good for Speyer!), he acclaimed, prodding the Foreign Ministry to uphold the chargé in the conflict over Brown. Goschen was told that the dismissal of the latter had probably been the result of the completely voluntary invitation by the Korean government of Alekseev as financial adviser and that Speyer as the representative of Russian interests in Korea naturally had had to assist Alekseev.

When Brown refused to give up his post and Min Chong-muk delayed signing the agreement worked out by Speyer and approved by Kojong concerning Alekseev's duties and obligations, Speyer obtained Min's dismissal from office. Cho Pyong-sik, who was simultaneously minister of justice and president of the Council of State, was appointed foreign minister in his place.[114]

Cho Pyong-sik acted with dispatch. On November 4 a contract for Alekseev's employment was readied in the form of an agreement between the governments of Korea and Russia. It was signed the following afternoon, on the fifth, by Cho and Speyer. Reiterating that Alekseev had been supplied by the tsarist government at the request made by Kojong through Min Yong-hwan, the contract gave Alekseev far wider responsibilities than customary for foreign employees. As chief adviser of the Finance Department and as director general of Maritime Customs, Alekseev was not only to prepare and submit to the Korean government, in consultation with the Korean finance minister, annual estimates of the revenues and expenditures of the country, but he was to receive and control at his own discretion all revenues accruing to the Korean government.

The contract was for an indefinite term. It could be dissolved supposedly at any time by the mutual consent of the two parties. Although it envisioned the replacement of Alekseev should the Korean government find an official of its own with sufficient financial knowledge to fill the post, the agreement stipulated that "no person, other than a Russian or Korean, shall be engaged in that capacity."[115]

Since Cho Pyong-sik had signed the agreement with Speyer without the customary discussion by the Council of State, there was considerable dissatisfaction in Seoul. Finance Minister Pak Chong-yang refused to recognize the agreement and on November 7 handed to the emperor a memorial accusing Cho of "anti-patriotic policy." But Speyer once again applied pressure, and Kojong asked for Pak's resignation.[116] Kojong appointed Minister of Public Works, Agriculture, and Commerce Chung Nak-yun, "a nice old gentleman known to be very weak," concurrently acting minister of finance and decreed on November 15 that Alekseev enter upon his functions.[117]

Word of the agreement signed by Speyer and Cho on November 5 aroused concern in the Russian Foreign Ministry. Muraviev telegraphed to Speyer on November 9: "I deem it necessary, in any case, that you exercise extreme caution and do not lose sight of the undesirable consequences which the strong excitement of the government of Great Britain may entail." As the attention of St. Petersburg was absorbed increasingly by Manchuria, Muraviev wanted Russia to pursue a policy of restraint in Korea, satisfying herself with the gains that had been achieved. When Witte continued to press for the support of Alekseev in the conflict with Brown, Muraviev retorted that this was not the time for demanding that the Korean customs service be put under Alekseev.[118]

Predictably, the English press in Japan expressed indignation and alarm at the replacement of Brown by Alekseev. Yet it could not conceal its grudging admiration for "the consummate skill with which Russia shapes a policy and the tenacity with which she pursues it until her objects are attained."[119]

Convinced that British representations would foil Russian plans, the Japanese had been slow to react. On first hearing of Speyer's efforts to obtain the engagement of Alekseev, Okuma had instructed Kato "to maintain ostensibly an attitude of noninterference." But when Kato reported that the contract had been signed, Okuma's successor as foreign minister, Nishi Tokujiro, telegraphed the contents of the document to Hayashi in St. Petersburg. Observing that the agreement, especially the latter portions thereof, was inconsistent with the Lobanov-Yamagata Protocol, he instructed him on December 16 "to represent the matter to [the] Russian Government in [the] form of [a] memorandum and invite careful reconsideration of the question."[120]

Hayashi did so on the twenty-third. What bothered his countrymen, he explained to Muraviev, was not so much the replacement of Brown by Alekseev as the stipulation that only a Russian or a Korean could fill the position of financial adviser. Declaring that his government regarded such restriction as a violation of the Moscow Protocol and in conflict with assurances given by Russia, Hayashi voiced the hope that the tsarist government, "moved by friendly feelings for Japan," would reexamine the Alekseev agreement.

Hayashi's representation aroused a flurry of activity in the Russian Foreign Ministry. Two telegrams were sent to Speyer that very day. In the first Muraviev communicated Hayashi's demand for the revision of the agreement and though he himself had formerly approved it, now demanded that Speyer explain how he could have signed the document without direct instructions from the ministry. He asked Speyer to suggest what serious and weighty arguments could be made in response to the Japanese statement and reminded him that present political circumstances made it absolutely necessary for Russia "to preserve friendly relations with Japan." In the second telegram Speyer was instructed not to relinquish the results achieved, yet to be more cautious than ever in all Korean affairs "in order not to elicit complaints and protests on the part of England and especially of Japan."

Speyer responded that he had acted for fear of losing the favorable opportunity; he had put his career on the line rather than allow this to happen. He recommended that Hayashi be informed in reply that Alekseev had come at the request of Kojong, whose freedom of action had been acknowledged in the Moscow Protocol. Believing that if the Japanese had accepted the presence of Russian military instructors, they would also put up with the role assumed by Alekseev, Speyer advised that the Japanese representation be rejected firmly. He did not think that Russia risked violating her good relations with Japan by showing firmness.

As Alekseev and Witte supported Speyer's arguments and the tsar sympathized with his actions, Muraviev went along with what he had done. With Nicholas's approval, he informed Speyer that the Foreign Ministry could not reprimand him and that it did not intend to relinquish the beneficial results he had achieved, albeit without authorization; it merely reminded him of the need for utmost caution.

In accordance with Speyer's recommendation a reply to Hayashi was drafted, declaring that Kojong was free to choose his advisers and could terminate the services of Alekseev at any time. But the rebuff was never transmitted, partly because Japan had readied her armed forces for action, partly because she suggested in Paris the possibility of a Russo-French-Japanese understanding concerning Korean and Chinese affairs. The answer that was handed to Hayashi was mild. Reiterating that the contract with Alekseev was not in contravention of the Lobanov-Yamagata Protocol, it expressed hope that the Japanese legation would see in the Russian explanations the sincere desire to study the Alekseev question "in the spirit of friendly agreement."[121]

While Speyer had been pressing for the dismissal of Brown, Alekseev himself was willing to retain his services as chief commissioner of Customs. At Alekseev's request Brown drew up a memorandum by which he agreed to a modification of his original contract with the Korean government, the stipulation being added that all members of the Korean Customs Service, regardless of their nationality, must be wholly in the service of the Korean government and receive all of their salaries from it alone. Brown accepted some additional demands in an informal and personal arrangement with Alekseev. When Alekseev pressed for the inclusion of all the modifications in a fresh contract between Brown, as chief commissioner, and the Korean government, Jordan "strongly advised" Brown not to enter into any new contract as such action would virtually recognize Alekseev's position. Eventually the clause pertaining to salaries was appended to Brown's original contract. The memorandum was signed by Brown and the new Korean finance minister on January 19. By preserving the original contract the status of the Korean Customs Service was left intact and the principle of noninterference with Brown maintained on paper, even though in fact Alekseev had superseded him in the position of financial adviser.[122]

On January 27 Speyer notified Cho Pyong-sik in writing that with the permission and direct participation of the tsarist government a bank by the name of Russko-Koreiskii Bank had been founded for the purpose of developing trade between their countries; it was to open for business shortly. He asked Cho to communicate this to the Korean government, especially to the ministers of finance and of agriculture and commerce.[123]

The Russo-Korean Bank was housed temporarily in one of the many foreign buildings recently constructed in Seoul; more extensive premises were to be built eventually on a site secured in the vicinity of the tsarist legation. The bank had a capital of 500,000 rubles, half of it guaranteed by the Russian government, half of it subscribed by the Russo-Chinese Bank of which it formed a branch. The amount of funds at its disposal promised to be much larger, however, as the Russo-Korean Bank was to serve as a Korean state bank and to receive the revenues of the Korean government.[124]

Although Cho Pyong-sik had collaborated in the installation of Alekseev and had faithfully carried out the directions of Speyer, the latter grew impatient with Cho's slowness and circumspectness and gradually detached himself from him. The other officials, who had been jealous of Cho's position, seized the opportunity to impede his work. Kojong himself had taken umbrage at Cho's ties with the Russian legation and surreptitiously encouraged the malcontents. When the discord between the officials had been sufficiently established, he named two functionaries—Yi To-chai and Yi Yong-in—to take over the portfolios of foreign affairs and justice respectively. Speyer did not impede Cho's removal.[125] In a conversation with Allen, he actually took credit for the change, claiming that he had initiated it, because Cho had "gone over to the Japanese," promising them the concession for the Seoul-Pusan railroad.[126]

The Case of Kim Hong-yuk

Speyer lacked the tact and the flexibility of his predecessor to cope with the delicate situation in which Russia found herself in Korea, in which, on one hand, she had to preserve her prestige as a power fit to maintain the independence of Korea and, on the other hand, had to be willing to make concessions, particularly in matters of secondary importance, and to refrain from crude pressure on the Korean government. Regarding every procrastination by Korean officials toward his demands as a personal affront and overestimating the importance of the concessions he had gained, Speyer thought he could ride roughshod over Korean feelings. His actions inevitably aroused mounting opposition.[127] As Jordan reported: "M. Waeber always showed a studious regard for native susceptibilities, and quietly furthered schemes Russian under the guise of Corean sanction, but his successor openly threw off the mask, and, although he may have effected more, has done it at the cost of alienating such public opinion as there is in the country."[128]

Public opinion in Korea was voiced by the Independence Club, which had about 2,000 members, the most vocal of whom had been educated in the United States. At a large meeting of the club and its sympathizers on February 20, 1898, a memorial to Kojong was drawn up and signed by 135 prominent members, including Yi Wan-yong, the former minister of foreign affairs who had sacrificed his position rather than consent to Russian control of the Korean army, and Yi Chai-yun, the able, English-speaking governor of Seoul, who had spent several years in Washington as chargé of the Korean legation.

Noting that an independent and sovereign state "must not lean upon another nation nor tolerate foreign interference in the national administration," the signatories expressed the "great disappointment and constant discontent" of the Korean public at the "giving away" to foreigners of the authority of administering the national finances and controlling the Military Department. They called upon Kojong to cooperate with his subjects and elicit their loyal support in the cause of independence. "We would rather be shot through our hearts, or have our abdomens cut open for the sake of the country and our Sovereign, than to prolong our unworthy lives with the shame and humiliation of neglecting our duties and shifting our inherent responsibilities," they proclaimed.[129]

Kojong issued a brief reply: "What you have expressed in language must be put to actual practice."[130]

The emotion generated by the meeting and the vague but seemingly receptive response of Kojong inflamed xenophobic feelings against Koreans working for foreigners. Kim Hong-yuk, the interpreter of the Russian legation, was particularly hated. A former water coolie in the streets of Seoul, he was a very common and uneducated man who could not read or write the classical Chinese used in official correspondence in Korea. He had been employed by the Russians, who did not speak Korean, because he had been born near the border and therefore spoke Russian. He had made himself indispensable to the Russian legation, serving not only as an interpreter, but as a mouthpiece, counselor, and general informant on Korean affairs. As he had risen from the lowest position to one of great influence, Kim had squeezed money from his countrymen and had treated them high-handedly and unscrupulously.[131]

For the past two years Kim Hong-yuk had seen Kojong almost daily. Since Speyer's return to Seoul, Kim had repeatedly threatened that the Russian officers and noncoms would be withdrawn from the palace if Russian wishes were not satisfied. When the question of a Russian coal depot on Deer Island had arisen, Kim had gone so far as to menace that if Kojong did not comply with the demand, he would be spirited away to Vladivostok. It was on this occasion that Prince Yi Chai-sun, late minister of the Household Department, was said to have remarked to those around him that he would give much— according to some reports $10,000—if someone would free him from Kim.[132]

Yi Chai-sun had been made minister of the Household when Kojong had fled to the Russian legation. He had been a firm friend of Waeber. When Kim had become more domineering under Waeber's successor, Kojong had instructed Yi to inform Speyer that he would prefer to deal with a different interpreter. When Speyer and Kim resented the suggestion, Kojong fearfully denied that it had been made at his behest. From that time on Yi and Kim were bitter enemies.[133]

On the night of February 22, as Kim was returning from the palace to the Russian legation accompanied by two policemen, three Koreans set upon them in the lane between the British consulate-general and the Russian legation. Two of the men grabbed the bodyguards and threw them down the bank, while the third attacked Kim with a sword.[134] Kim parried the blow with his cane and fled toward the little back gate of the palace. The assassin followed and struck the interpreter from behind, but he himself and his companions turned tail when Kim's screams brought out Korean soldiers and policemen from the palace and shortly thereafter British marines quartered in a small house at the nearby Customs office.

Kim's wounds were not serious—he had been cut on his right ear and shoulder—and he was expected to recover. The *Independent* called for the capture and punishment of the culprits to the fullest extent of the law. "The revival of the contemptible practice of assassination must be nipped in the bud," the paper proclaimed. But Jordan reported that "the only feeling which the incident has produced amongst Coreans, with whom political assassination is a familiar expedient, is one of almost universal regret that it did not succeed." [135]

In a note to Acting Foreign Minister Min Chong-muk, who had succeeded Yi To-chai in mid-February, Speyer expressed outrage at the "impudent" attempt on the life of his "meritorious" interpreter. He asked that the incident be reported to the emperor and that a search be made for the conspirators. He called for the punishment not only of the actual culprits, but of the instigators of the crime, however high their position might be. [136]

Speyer's note elicited an imperial edict. "How is it that police authorities permit the swords of an assassin to appear in the darkness of the night? Is there anything more startling than this? If the police perform its duties in such a careless manner, what is the use of maintaining the so-called Police Department?" Kojong asked rhetorically. He ordered that the culprits be captured within three days and warned that the commissioner of police himself would be severely punished if this was not accomplished. The Household Office too was commanded to make special efforts to track down the perpetrators of the crime. [137]

The attempt on the life of his interpreter had excited Speyer. He had been chafing for some time at mounting anti-Russian agitation, revealed in the hostile attitude of Yi To-chai toward the tsarist legation, and in the memorials of the Independence Club, which was composed, as Plancy put it, of "partisans of Anglo-American influence and above all of malcontents, people without official functions who made opposition only to obtain positions [for themselves]." [138]

On February 24 Speyer called on Allen and charged that three American citizens—Dr. Philip Jaisohn (So Che-pil), General LeGendre, and Colonel Nienstead—had instigated the Independence Club memorial, which he regarded as an attack upon his government. Allen countered that Nienstead had long been confined to his house with a fatal illness, while LeGendre, who had lived in the United States for only a few years, was affiliated more with the French and Russian legations than with the American one. He admitted that Jaisohn, a Korean with American citizenship who was a prominent member of the Independence Club and editor of the *Independent*, had expressed his sympathy for the memorialists, but there was nothing that he himself could do about it. It was true that the three men were American citizens, but they were all advisers of the Korean government and as such were free to advise it; it was not up to him to judge the character of their counsel.[139] In a telegram to Muraviev the following day, on the twenty-fifth, Speyer accused also the German consul of having participated in the anti-Russian agitation. But Foreign Minister Count Bernhard von Bülow assured Ambassador Osten-Sacken that such conduct on the part of Krien was contrary to instructions, and that he would be so informed.

Speyer's dispatches aroused serious concern in St. Petersburg, and the War and Navy Ministries were informed of the developments. At the same time, Speyer was directed to respect the full independence of Korea and was reminded to exercise extreme caution.[140]

On February 25 the three Korean assailants were apprehended. During the interrogation Yu Chin-kin, the ringleader, stated that he had been incited to the deed by Prince Yi Chai-sun. The commissioner of police, who owed his position to Kim Hong-yuk, promptly dispatched twenty policemen to the residence of the prince and had him thrown into jail and subsequently taken before the Supreme Court on a charge of having bribed a number of persons to perpetrate the crime. The action outraged the royal family, for Yi Chai-sun was a nephew by adoption of the late King Ch'olchong and not subject to arrest without prior imperial sanction. A special meeting of the Council of State was convened at which the commissioner of police was dismissed and the Law Department asked to punish him severely. There was even talk of executing him without a trial. The proceedings against the commissioner, who fled for his life to the Russian legation, in turn offended Speyer, who regarded it as a direct insult to himself and as an attempt to shield the assassins.

On February 27 one officer and 42 seamen of the gunboat *Gremiashchii* had arrived from Chemulpo at Speyer's request to reinforce the Russian legation guard, boosting its number to two officers and 100 men. While threatening to haul down his flag unless he obtained satisfaction for the incident, Speyer confided to Allen that he saw in the attack upon his interpreter an opportunity to crush agitation. "Two very pleasant things occurred to me on the same night," he told his American colleague while at his house; "one, the death of the Emperor's father removed an enemy, and the other, the attempt on the life of my Interpreter, places this Independence party right in my grasp." "I will push this matter to the farthest limit," he declared.[141]

Upon learning of the possible involvement of the monarch himself in the attempt on the life of Kim Hong-yuk, Speyer demanded that Kojong personally call on him at the Russian legation and tender a suitable apology for the attack on his interpreter.[142]

Speyer was convinced, he told Plancy, that the functionaries of the Anglo-American party who surrounded the emperor were endeavoring to persuade him at Jordan's inspiration to seek refuge in the British legation to escape Russian exactions. Once he had done so, they planned to enthrone in his stead one of his nephews, a young son of the regent presently in London. Speyer related that he had warned Kojong of the above and that Kojong had replied that he was aware of the maneuvers and would do everything in his power to foil them.[143]

Jordan reported meanwhile that according to messages he and several of his colleagues had received directly from the palace, Kojong was being urged by the Russian interpreters to escape from his present troubles by returning to his quarters in the tsarist legation. In view of the emperor's "weak and unstable character," Jordan wrote, "it would not greatly surprise us if he eventually yielded to these solicitations."

Jordan related that Kojong had been thrown into "his usual state of consternation and alarm" and kept sending messages to him and to the other foreign representatives that he was in great danger and expected to be carried off by force to the Russian legation. "He asked me to strengthen the guard of this Consulate General," Jordan recounted, "but I explained to His Majesty that I could not accede to his request as there was no danger to British subjects with which the present guard could not effectually cope, nor did it appear to me that his safety was likely to be in any way imperilled."[144] Accusing the Russians of wanting to get the emperor back into their legation, Jordan dismissed as "entirely groundless" the rumors that some of the other legations sought to give refuge to Kojong. He alleged that such stories were being circulated "industriously" to form the pretext for the emperor's removal to the tsarist legation.

Jordan described the situation into which Kojong and his officials had boxed themselves. "There is a wide-spread belief," he wrote, "that both the Emperor and many of his former Ministers, irritated beyond measure by the coercive methods of the Russian Legation as exercised through the Interpreter, indirectly encouraged, if they did not actually connive at, the attack upon the man, and now that it has failed they find themselves in an awkward predicament between satisfying the demands of the Russian Chargé d'Affaires on the one hand and keeping faith with the supporters of the anti-Russian movement on the other."[145]

Speyer stirred up a hornet's nest of opposition when he pressed Kojong to appoint the dismissed commissioner of police as minister of justice. On Sunday, March 6, placards appeared in the streets of Seoul denouncing Kim Hong-yuk for having overstepped his functions as interpreter by interfering in affairs of state. "His deportment has been most outrageous towards both the high and the low, and his language insulting in the extreme," the posted memorial charged. "The government is ruled by this one Kim, and other Ministers of State have become his hired men. He has openly sold Government offices to the highest bidders, and has caused the dismissals of those Ministers who were not subservient to him. His immoral character shocks the hearts of all decent men. He has manufactured Imperial Decrees to suit his own advantages and delivered them to the judicial officials in order to imprison dignitaries of State to revenge his personal grievances. He has been in control of the Palace, so that no other official could have access to the Palace without obtaining this man's silent permission." Asserting that no country could administer justice when such an "outlaw" controlled the state and that "wickedness, deception, and underhandedness" were driving out "straightforwardness, patriotism, and manliness," the memorialists declared that their forbearance could not endure this state of affairs much longer. They proclaimed their intention of appealing to the emperor to drive out "all these pesterous insects" from the palace and to show to the world that the Korean nation was not all composed of such characters.

The document bore the signatures of six prominent Koreans.[146] Several thousand more were expected to sign it by the time of its scheduled presentation to the emperor on the twenty-ninth of the month.[147]

On the night of March 11 Governor Yi Chai-yun, whose painstaking and fair judgments as chief of the city court had gained the respect of the foreign community, was summarily dismissed from his post and given a nominal position in the Household Department. Kim Hong-yuk was appointed governor of Seoul in his stead. Noting that the interpreter of the Russian legation knew neither English nor even the official Chinese characters, Allen branded him as "utterly unfit for such a post." It was expected, he wrote, that "as judge of the court to try the people suspected of the attempt upon himself," Kim would introduce a "reign of terror." The appointment was "so bad, and so unreasonable," Allen observed, that it was causing a "storm of opposition."[148]

Deer Island Depot

Meanwhile another issue was coming to a head—the above-mentioned desire of the Russian navy for a coaling station at Deer Island. Deer Island was a large, rocky island in the harbor of Pusan. There were three foreign settlements on the mainland at Pusan. The Chinese and the Japanese ones had been acquired and defined in a regular manner, but the so-called general foreign settlement between the other two had received no formal authorization. In 1889 Waeber had tried to persuade his colleagues of the need of reaching a formal understanding with the Korean government for the delimitation of a foreign settlement area at Pusan. The American representative, Dinsmore, had joined with Waeber in strongly favoring the placement of the foreign settlement on the north end of Deer Island, that is to say at the southern side of the harbor, but the British representative, Hillier, had hesitated to go along until he had received instructions from the British minister in Peking because Aston, who had preceded him, had spoken in favor of the site on the mainland, and the question had been dropped. When the Russian and American representatives obtained the greater and best portions of the small amount of foreshore available on the mainland for nationals of their countries in 1892 the establishment of a foreign settlement on the mainland was torpedoed. In August 1895 the Korean government notified the foreign representatives that it intended to reserve Deer Island for its own use and to deny foreigners the privilege of buying land on the island. The foreign representatives filed a unanimous protest and took advantage of the opportunity to ask the Korean government to delimit a foreign settlement area at Pusan. Brown, whom the Korean government sent to Pusan in September of that year, marked out a site for an "additional foreign settlement" on Deer Island, but the foreign representatives were not officially notified thereof. In the spring of 1897 the Russian naval authorities began taking steps to acquire a suitable piece of ground at the port of Pusan to serve the double purpose of drill ground and a place for storing coal and other naval supplies. When Jordan learned in August of that year that Secretary Kehrberg had arrived on a Russian torpedo cruiser at Pusan and had proceeded with the Korean superintendent of customs, known as the *kamni*, to Deer Island to select the site for a coal depot, he had asked Brown to telegraph to J.H. Hunt, the commissioner of Customs at Pusan, to be careful not to permit any encroachment upon the site of the proposed foreign settlement demarcated by himself and Brown in 1895. As it happened, the place selected by Kehrberg and the *kamni* lay almost in the center of the area marked out for an additional foreign settlement. Speyer, who was passing through Pusan en route to Seoul at the time, refused to recognize the additional foreign settlement because his legation had never been given due notice and supported Kehrberg's demand.

Jordan thereupon called on the Korean foreign minister and warned that the Korean government would find itself in an "awkward predicament" if it allowed the diversion to another use of the only ground practically available for the foreign settlement it had pledged to provide. On September 2 Min Chongmuk visited Jordan and assured him that he would under no circumstances permit the alienation of any part of the ground set aside for an additional foreign settlement.[149] Allen, Kato, and Krien secured a similar pledge.

On September 22 Vice Minister of Foreign Affairs Ko Yung-hui handed to

Secretary Kehrberg a protocol to the effect that the Korean government could not dispose of any part of the tract selected by Brown for a general foreign settlement in 1895 without a prior understanding with the foreign representatives in Seoul. It was perfectly willing, however, "to concede to Russia any other site which she may select outside the limits of the General Foreign Settlement."

Speyer ignored the unsigned paper as constituting merely Ko's view. He told Krien that the matter of the coaling station had been settled between Kehrberg and the local official at Pusan; he regarded the subject as closed. The hapless vice minister who had handed the protocol to Kehrberg was transferred to the obscure Education Department a few days later.[150]

As in 1889, rumors began to spread that Russia planned to occupy Deer Island, even though she demanded merely a regulated acquisition in conformity with the treaties and similar to the pretension made by all the other powers.[151] Yet when the British vice consul at Chemulpo, Joly, reported on October 23, 1897, that the Russians were making arrangements to establish a small depot for stores at that harbor, Jordan deemed it "a perfectly natural proceeding on their part, considering that they have a force of eighty sailors in Seoul who must draw their supplies to a considerable extent from Chemulpo."[152]

In November and December of that year a Russian squadron of eight vessels under Vice Admiral Fedor Vasil'evich Dubasov visited Korea. Dubasov inspected the coal depot site selected by Kehrberg. Traveling about the inner and outer harbors of Pusan, the Russian naval officers surveyed and photographed the region. On December 3 Dubasov visited Seoul, accompanied by fifteen officers and eighteen men. He told Kojong, who received him in audience without the usual formalities, of his strong desire for a coal depot on Deer Island. According to information obtained by the British representative, the monarch referred Dubasov to the foreign minister who intimated his willingness to accede to the Russian request.[153]

The American representative had heard that when Kojong had said that he would confer with the foreign minister on the subject, the vice admiral had declared that this was unnecessary since Kojong was the ruler and he would deal only with him. The monarch thereupon was said to have given his assent. At any rate, Cho Pyong-sik confirmed to Allen in the second half of December that a coaling station had been granted to Russia even though the formalities had not been gone through yet.[154]

On January 21, 1898, the Russian gunboat on which Kehrberg had come the previous July arrived at Pusan from Nagasaki for the purpose of buying and taking formal possession of the coal depot site on Deer Island. The captain tried to see the superintendent of customs, but the latter had left town for the Korean New Year holidays. He thereupon called on Commissioner Hunt and demanded his assistance, saying that instructions must have been sent to the *kamni* to issue the necessary title deeds, as Kojong had promised the site to Dubasov some time ago. He had brought along a hundred trees that were being planted and material to put up a fence around the site, and a Japanese contractor to make an estimate of the necessary buildings, the captain related. Hunt himself had not been kept abreast of the matter, but in view of the fact that the Russian captain spoke no Korean and was without an interpreter, he offered to inform the *taotai* of the purpose of his visit.

The *kamni*, upon his return to Pusan, did not dare to accede to the captain's demand on his own authority and telegraphed to Foreign Minister Cho Pyong-sik for guidance.[155] Although Cho owed his position to the influence of the Russian and French legations, he had incurred such unpopularity and opposition since his appointment in October of the previous year that he too tried to evade the responsibility of deciding the sensitive issue and contracted a diplomatic illness. It was the Korean vice minister of foreign affairs who instructed the *kamni* not to accept payment for the particular site, but to change it to another. "If the new site is the property of Coreans, we will buy it ourselves, and lease it to the Russians on the same terms as the Japanese coal depot," he telegraphed.[156]

Yi To-chai, who succeeded Cho as foreign minister on January 31, was no more inclined to yield to the Russian demand for the particular site, because it might be required some day for commercial purposes; he was prepared to substitute another place for a Russian coal depot. Yi's resistance was stiffened by the opinions offered by the British, Japanese, and American representatives that the selection of a suitable foreign settlement area should take precedence over the determination of a Russian coal depot site.[157]

As Yi would not bow to his wishes, Speyer drove him out of office after only two weeks by refusing to deal with him further. He declined to attend a meeting of the foreign representatives at the Foreign Office, returning Yi's letter of invitation unopened.[158] On February 16 Kojong granted "sick leave" to Yi and named one of Speyer's chief collaborators in the Korean government, Finance Minister Min Chong-mok, to take over as interim foreign minister.[159]

Min promptly agreed to the coaling station on the ground that an identical concession had been made to the Japanese. But the employees in his own office thought differently and refused to cooperate with him. Min could find neither official stationery for the dispatch nor a copyist to write it for him. The secretary who kept the Foreign Office seal disappeared. Thus it came about that Min agreed to Speyer's demand in a simple letter in his own hand.

Min's action provoked an immediate tender of resignation by the entire Council of State, which was composed of all the ministers and some other functionaries. In a vivid memorial to the emperor, the officials declared that they merely bore the title of councilors without exercising the prerogatives of the position. A proposal in regard to the Deer Island affair had been submitted to them by Foreign Minister Yi, but they had not been able to examine it in view of his absence. Now they learned that the interim minister had regulated the question without awaiting their decision. On the other hand, they had been informed that there would be established in Seoul a Russo-Korean bank which would receive special privileges from their government. The council had not been consulted in this matter either. If they were not competent to discuss the affairs, the officials concluded, it behooved the emperor to replace them, hence they asked to be relieved of their duties.

Min in turn wrote to the throne, justifying his actions. He asserted that he had done no more than follow precedent. The Council of State, he contended, had never been consulted in regard to concessions of this nature; he did not believe, therefore, that he had violated any laws or customs. Yet he could not bear the reproofs directed at him and asked the sovereign to accept his resignation.

Accepting Min's resignation from the post of *interim* foreign minister as well as from his position as finance minister, Kojong pointed out that the Council of State had been founded precisely for the purpose of deliberating on matters of interest to the country and that if such were not submitted to it, there would be no need for an institution of this sort. But at Speyer's urging, the emperor issued another decree naming Min *permanent* foreign minister. (A different person was appointed minister of the treasury.) This singular course of action did not calm the councilors.[160] They countersigned his reappointment in compliance with Kojong's wishes, then resubmitted their resignation. "Even if we are insignificant human beings, we cannot be inconsistent," they declared.

The emperor retorted that they had countersigned the reappointment. For them to send in again their joint resignation seemed neither consistent nor wise to him. "We are sorry because of your action," Kojong wrote. "You ought to understand Our reason of relieving him temporarily and reappointing him again."[161]

During this crisis the Independence Club held meeting after meeting and demanded that Min explain his conduct. Intimidated by the attitude of the assembly, Min replied that he had consulted with the Council. In view of the Council's assertion to the contrary, the answer elicited demands for another explanation. The Independence Club called upon Min to notify the Japanese government of the desire of the Korean court to recover possession of the land which had been conceded to her on Deer Island. Such a step, it reasoned naively, would remove the precedent to which Min had alluded and thereby would leave Speyer's demand without foundation.[162]

The Painful Query

As the excitement over Kim Hong-yuk and Deer Island gained momentum, there was danger of open violence. Noting that every Korean nobleman of a certain class had several hundred followers at his country place and that large bands of these were coming to the capital, the American minister speculated that the nobility might be on the verge of standing up for their rights with all the force they could muster. "The Russians are finding the Koreans very difficult to handle, as did the Japanese," he remarked with glee. "Kindness will accomplish much more with them than harshness, but above all strong measures must be backed by ample force." Since the Russians had only 100 marines in Seoul, Allen foresaw the possibility of an uprising which would temporarily drive the Russians out with great casualties. He thought the Koreans might be "foolish enough not to count the cost, and attempt some such course."[163] Jordan, to whom Allen related his fears on the ninth, doubted that the expectation of a massacre of the Russians and of a general attack on foreigners was "altogether justified." He believed that the Russian marines were strong enough to deter such an eventuality. Yet there was abundant evidence, he conceded, that the Russians themselves considered the situation as "very serious." Some of them spoke of the possibility of being obliged to quit Korea. The Russian advisers, he noted, bitterly criticized Speyer, attributing the situation to his unnecessarily harsh measures and highhanded conduct.[164]

Describing the movement which had arisen in Seoul during the past two months against Speyer and especially Kim Hong-yuk, the German consul observed that since Speyer's assumption of the affairs of the Russian legation, the progressive-minded officials who essentially represented the Korean intelligentsia had been completely excluded by the government at his behest. With the sole exception of Cho Pyong-sik, who was infamous because of his brutality and his extortions, the cabinet and the Council of State had been composed of nothing but "old, weak-minded and ignorant people primarily concerned with enriching themselves and obtaining lucrative official positions for their friends and relatives."

The anti-Russian agitation, Krien wrote, emanated from the unemployed officials, all of whom were members of the Independence Club. Relating the opposition of the officials to Speyer's demand for a coaling station site on Deer Island and to his having obtained the privileges of a Korean state bank for the Russo-Korean Bank, Krien explained that the deposit of Korean state funds in the Russo-Korean Bank was against the interests of the officials, because they feared that these monies might be removed from their disposal and, if it pleased the Russians, be withheld from them. The gruff behavior of the tsarist representative, the unruly conduct of his interpreter toward the Korean emperor, and the fact that the highest officials were dismissed if they hesitated to carry out Speyer's demands had contributed greatly to the anti-Russian mood. The ennoblement of Kim Hong-yuk, who was of low origins and could neither read nor write, had especially embittered officials and officers, he added. "While the Koreans were generally well disposed toward Russia so long as Herr Waeber represented the Russian interests," Krien wrote, "this attitude changed under Herr von Speyer gradually to the opposite, so that today the Russians are very hated, even though the successful work of Herr Alekseev and the military instructors deserves full appreciation." [165]

Jordan too attributed the main cause of Korean dissatisfaction not to particular issues—be they the demand for a coaling station at Deer Island, the connection of the Korean Treasury with the Russo-Korean Bank, or Speyer's desire to purchase large tracts of land as consular sites at the newly opened ports of Mokpo and Chinnampo[166]—but to the general conduct of the Russian chargé. "M. de Speyer's undisguised interference in the affairs of the Corean Government, and more especially his nomination and retention in office of Ministers who are put there simply to do his bidding has raised a storm of opposition which, in the opinion of many competent observers, may not disappear until some impotent attempt of a revolutionary nature demonstrates the futility of further resistance," Jordan reported.[167]

Although Speyer, like his interpreter, now moved about generally with an escort of Russian sailors,[168] he was blind to the nature of his own actions. As he reported the dismissal of the chief of police and the clamor of Independence Club members for the immediate withdrawal of all Russian instructors and advisers, he attributed the unrest to the ineffectiveness of his government's benevolent policy toward Korea. "We cannot remain calm observers of everything that is happening here for fear of completely losing our influence in the country," Speyer cabled to Muraviev on February 28, 1898. He saw no way out of the situation except to abandon the principle of Korean independence and to occupy the northern provinces of Korea with troops stationed in the Russian Far East.[169]

The tsarist government rejected Speyer's proposal, aware that its implementation would have led at best to the partition of Korea, which would have meant the entrenchment of Japan on the continent in dangerous proximity to the poorly defended Russian borders. The acquisition of Northern Korea could not compensate for the appearance of Japanese bases on the mainland. Far more important from the Russian point of view was the preservation of a weak, independent Korea as a buffer state. To follow Speyer's advice was to run the risk of war with Japan and Great Britain, just what tsarist diplomacy was trying to avoid. Desirous of an agreement with Japan, St. Petersburg drew a different conclusion from the events in Korea than had Speyer, who failed to consider the Far Eastern situation as a whole. Realizing that its hopes that Russian primacy in Korea would force Japan to yield in the question of military instructors and the financial adviser in exchange for commercial advantages had been dissipated by the erosion of Russian influence, the tsarist government was concerned primarily with the removal of obstacles on the way to an understanding with Japan.

In his reply on March 3, Muraviev instructed Speyer not to act rashly in the matter of Kim Hong-yuk and to diminish the consular sites at Mokpo and Chinnampo. He made it clear that Russia had no intention of violating the oft-repeated principle of the independence of Korea by occupying her northern provinces. In an attempt to cut the Korean knot with one blow, freeing Russia for an agreement with Japan while depriving the latter of leverage for unreasonable demands, Muraviev informed Speyer that inasmuch as judging from his reports most parties in Korea were hostile to Russia and there was reason to doubt even the loyalty of the monarch, the tsarist government deemed it impossible "to engage in further too active participation in the internal affairs of Korea," particularly as direct interference in the various branches of the government of the country had never been its task. The dispatch of the military instructors and the financial adviser had been undertaken at the time at the request of Korea herself for the sake of ensuring her completely independent development in the future. The growing hostility of the Korean government and of Kojong placed Russia in an intolerable position, especially because, as Witte pointed out, problems presently arising for Russia in the Far East demanded of her "full freedom of action and the preservation of friendly relations with Japan, as well as with England." Instead of wasting forces for the maintenance of dominant influence in Korea, where Russia's interests were less significant, the tsarist government desired to find "a way out with honor" (*vykhoda s chest'iu*) from the situation that had developed. Speyer was instructed to inquire personally of the emperor and the Korean government whether they deemed further Russian support of Korea necessary. If such aid was no longer required, the tsarist government would take appropriate steps, on condition that the Korean government would on its own defend the independence of the country from foreign encroachment.[170]

Although the instructions sent by Muraviev reflected the personal views of Nicholas, Speyer objected to the query he had been ordered to pose. In a telegram to St. Petersburg, he tried to convince the foreign minister of the imprudence of leaving the question of Russian aid to the free initiative of a bewildered government, which would make a snap decision without considering the situation or its reply carefully. It meant, he pointed out, to subordinate all the efforts made during the past six months to assert Russian influence in the peninsula to the incertitude of resolution which would be determined with infantile unconcern. To put an end to the anti-Russian movement, it would be preferable, he reiterated, to move troops to the frontier. He concluded by recalling the dangers to which Kojong was exposed by the present circumstances and proposed that the Korean emperor be advised, in case of necessity, to seek asylum in the Russian legation.

But Muraviev reaffirmed that Speyer was to inquire categorically whether or not the services of the tsarist instructors and of Alekseev were desired. He repeated that inasmuch as Russia wanted to preserve the independence and integrity of Korea, she did not wish to mount any military demonstration which could be interpreted as a menace to the latter; she desired at the present time above all to have full freedom of action and did not contemplate in any manner to aggravate the malaise brought about by the foreign rivalries in Korea.[171]

Yet Speyer persisted in his intrigues, obsessed by the thought that Russian passivity would terminate the influence of his country in Korea. The attempt of Speyer to lure Kojong back into the Russian legation, of which Jordan had complained, had occurred on March 3, before the receipt of Muraviev's telegrams. Two days later, on the fifth, Speyer once more tried to induce the frightened ruler to take refuge in the Russian legation, be it that he interpreted Muraviev's silence on this subject as implied approval or that he believed that the tsarist government would have to back him again if presented with a *fait accompli*.[172]

On the evening of March 7 Speyer addressed an official note to Foreign Minister Min. The remarkable document, whose plaintiff tone expressed the frustrations experienced by Russia in her aid to Korea, deserves to be quoted in full.

The latest deplorable events in Seoul and the senseless agitation against Russia of idle Korean politicians have naturally aroused extreme astonishment on the part of His Majesty the Emperor [Speyer wrote].
The dispatch to Korea of Russian instructors for the training of the

army and the maintenance of the palace guard and the appointment here of a financial adviser were measures undertaken by us at the request of the Emperor and the government of Korea and clearly pointed to our aspiration to secure for the Korean state neighboring unto us a completely independent development in the future.

Meanwhile the Korean Government, not appreciating apparently the significance of the services rendered by us to it, is itself creating obstacles to the realization of the objectives set by us in the interests of Korea herself.

We cannot further tolerate such a situation; in order to clarify it His Majesty the Emperor has graciously ordered me to inquire categorically of the Korean Emperor as well as of His Government whether or not they deem further support of Korea by Russia as essential for themselves. Should our aid in the form of instructors, palace guard, and a financial adviser appear superfluous in their opinion, we shall take measures to carry out their wishes, provided, however, that the Korean Government would by its own means attend to the further safeguarding of its independence.

I shall expect an answer from the Korean Government within twenty-four hours from the receipt by you of the present official communication and humbly beg Your Excellency to obtain for me at the earliest time an audience with His Majesty the Emperor in order to carry out the imperial command received by me.[173]

In directing Speyer to determine the wishes of the Korean government, Muraviev had not thought of applying pressure on Seoul. On the contrary, his telegram had implied that the tsarist government would welcome a negative reply as an honorable way out of the Korean morass. The above note was actually moderate in tone. What transformed the reasonable inquiry into another rash act of Speyer was the time limit he had set for reply, thereby giving the missive the character of an ultimatum.[174]

The Russian inquiry caught the Korean government by surprise. Foreign Minister Min responded with a request for more time. He asked for an additional three days to come up with a definite reply.[175]

Muraviev reprimanded Speyer as soon as he learned that he had demanded an immediate answer from the Korean government and that he had held out the possibility of renewed asylum for Kojong. The tsar was surprised at the initiative which Speyer had permitted himself to take in his counsel to the Korean emperor, Muraviev telegraphed. Nicholas did not comprehend, he cabled, how Speyer could have acted in such a way without specific orders to that effect.

In justification of his action, Speyer alleged that Kojong himself had wished to return to the Russian legation. He pledged to restrain him from doing so.

In an audience with Kojong on March 8, Speyer pressed for a decisive response to the query of the tsarist government. The emperor tried to evade the issue by talking of his sympathy for Russia, but eventually he agreed to give a clear answer in not less than three days, after consulting with Korean statesmen. He said that he personally wished to keep the assistance of the Russian military mission and of Alekseev and would try to persuade the members of the Council of State.

Speyer thereupon asked to talk to Kojong and the crown prince in private. After the various officials had withdrawn, Speyer revealed that he had exceeded his instructions in counseling the emperor to take refuge in the Russian legation in the event of peril; the advice must be considered null and void. Should the troubled situation force Kojong to leave the palace, Speyer related, he would have to obtain the assent of the tsarist government before being able to resume residence in the Russian legation. Visibly dispirited, Kojong recalled that when Nicholas had talked to Min Yong-hwan during the coronation festivities, he had promised him his support at all times and in all circumstances. He still counted on the goodwill of the tsar, Kojong said lamely.[176]

While the Korean government deliberated how to respond to Speyer's ultimatum, agitation grew to force the cabinet to reject the Russian military instructors and financial adviser. No longer was opposition confined to the Independence Club; similar views were voiced by the common people in meetings held in the open street.[177]

On the afternoon of March 10 some eight thousand persons assembled near the bell house on Main Street. One of the principal merchants of the city, Na Hong-suk, acted as chairman of the mass meeting. Speaking from the balcony of the Cotton Exchange, he and several speakers proposed to the crowd below a resolution calling upon Foreign Minister Min to relieve the Russian military instructors and financial adviser from their duties. The self-proclaimed Citizen Committee and the people in general remained orderly and moderate in tone at this meeting; any inflammatory outbursts were immediately suppressed by the leadership. As many foreign spectators including Speyer watched, the speakers argued politely that while they felt thankful for the kind feelings which Russia entertained for Korea's welfare, they were strongly opposed to foreign control of the Military and Finance Departments as detrimental to the independence of their country.

The resolution was unanimously adopted amidst much excitement and applause and was forwarded to Min.[178]

Another mass meeting on the twelfth passed less peacefully. It was directed against Kim Hong-yuk more than against the Russians themselves. Calling

Kim a traitor and a rebel, the participants demanded his death. The police tried to disperse this meeting, but were prevented from doing so by soldiers who sided with the demonstrators and threw stones at the police. Several Koreans who were recognized as being interpreters of the Russian officers were beaten, knocked down, and trampled.[179]

Meanwhile the proceedings against the assailants of Kim had taken an unexpected turn. Yu Chin-kin told the Supreme Court that he had been forced by the commissioner of police under torture to implicate Prince Yi, who actually had no knowledge of the assassination attempt. As a result the Ministry of Justice, on orders from the emperor, issued a warrant for the arrest of Kim, who was still holed up in the Russian legation, for having illegally arrested a member of the imperial family.[180]

The situation was so tense that Allen and his Japanese colleague thought for a time that a serious conflict was in the making. Kato conveyed his fears to Foreign Minister Nishi, who instructed him to observe an attitude of noninterference, yet to suggest to Speyer that he act with moderation. Nishi discussed the problem with Baron Rosen, who cabled a full report to St. Petersburg. Nishi approached the tsarist government also through Hayashi, ordering him to express the hope of his government that it would direct Speyer not to resort to extreme measures. The tsarist government assured Nishi through Rosen that it did not intend to let matters in Korea develop into a conflict.[181]

Meanwhile the Council of State to whom the foreign minister had referred Speyer's communication had sent it right back to him, refusing to have anything to do with Min Chong-muk. As the new deadline for a reply approached, Kojong convened the councilors on March 11 and urged them to keep the Russian military officers and Alekseev. Most of the dignitaries seemed to agree and Kojong sent a secret message to Speyer informing him that the matter had been resolved favorably. But once the Council had assembled again outside, free of any pressure from the throne, it decided on the opposite course.[182]

Kojong himself had hedged his bets. He had shown Speyer's note to the Japanese minister and had solicited his advice, which predictably had been for the return of the Russians home.[183]

On March 12 Foreign Minister Min penned a polite but firm reply to Speyer's ultimatum.[184] He expressed the gratitude of the Korean emperor and people for the refuge Russia had granted to Kojong in the wake of the murder of the queen and for the military instructors and the financial adviser whom the tsar had sent in order to strengthen the independence of Korea and lead her toward progress and enlightenment. Speyer's declaration that Nicholas had been surprised by the anti-Russian agitation in Seoul and wished to know, therefore, whether or not Korea wanted to retain the services of the military instructors and financial advisers had filled his emperor and government with a sense of shame. He pledged that the Korean government would be more careful in the discharge of its responsibilities so as not to give any further cause for anxiety to the tsar.

> Through your Sovereign's kind motives and your government's friendly disposition our military and financial affairs have made much progress [Min continued]. Both the adviser and instructors diligently and conscientiously discharged their duties so that the Imperial guard has been trained satisfactorily and the financial condition of the country placed on a systematic basis. These are all due to the unceasing efforts of your government and we will never forget your magnanimous spirit.
>
> Our government has decided that we will continue to manage our affairs according to the methods which your officials have so kindly introduced, though we must place the controlling power of these departments in the hands of our own countrymen. We will not employ any foreign military instructors or advisers. This decision was arrived at by the unanimous wishes of the old statesmen, the present government and the people at large, also through the enlightenment and independent spirit which your government has so diligently inculcated among us. I am sure that your Imperial Sovereign and your government will be glad to know that our people have become so progressive and enlightened as to desire to maintain their own sovereignty.
>
> Before we were able to manage our own affairs we had to solicit the assistance of the friendly powers but at the same time we must consider the advancement and maintenance of our independent and sovereign rights. My Sovereign and the people unanimously desire that the friendly relations between the two nations may become still closer and that no misunderstanding should exist. Your officials have accomplished their work and it is convenient for us to have them relieved from our service. I feel grateful to you for suggesting the idea of relieving these officials.

Min sweetened the rejection with another expression of his sovereign's thanks for Russian aid and communicated Kojong's intention to send an envoy to St. Petersburg with a personal message of gratitude to the tsar. He asked Speyer to inform the Russian government of the above decision, noting that it constituted the desire of the Korean emperor, the Korean government, and the entire Korean people.[185]

The Korean answer was delivered to the Russian legation at 6 A.M. At 8

A.M. the second interpreter of the legation arrived at the palace and demanded to speak to the emperor at once. The eunuch on duty replied that Kojong was asleep and could not be wakened under any circumstances. The interpreter explained, thereupon, that Speyer had not yet seen the note which had been brought early that morning, but that he would undoubtedly be very angry when he read it. He asked in vain that the reply be taken back in order to preserve the friendly relations between Korea and Russia.[186]

In view of Kojong's secret message, the answer came indeed as a shock to Speyer. He regarded the reply as unexampled in rudeness and attributed it exclusively to the impression of impotence left by the tsarist government's refusal to resort to drastic measures in Korea. In a telegram to Muraviev that day Speyer proposed that an ultimatum be handed to the Korean government demanding in view of its rejection of Russian assistance that all other foreign advisers be dismissed at the same time as the Russians and that the persons who had attacked Kim Hong-yuk be punished; the reception of an envoy bearing thanks should be refused beforehand. If one of the above demands were not met, the flag of the tsarist legation in Seoul ought to be lowered and Russian troops sent to occupy the northern provinces, Speyer urged. As things stood, Speyer believed, the weakness, cowardliness, and insincerity of Kojong prevented the Russians from ever counting on building anything lasting and stable in Korea; they would always run the risk of being subjected to unpleasantnesses and insults.

St. Petersburg agreed with Speyer's contention that a Korean embassy would be inappropriate, but it categorically rejected his aggressive proposals. Russia could only rejoice at Korea no longer needing her instructors, provided she could get along on her own, Muraviev telegraphed to him on March 14. He instructed Speyer to make no efforts to force the Korean government to retract its reply or to pose conditions for the recall of the military instructors and financial adviser. Alekseev was authorized to leave immediately; the instructors were to remain temporarily, not in the Korean service but as part of the legation guard in view of the uneasy situation in Seoul. To lower the flag and to occupy the northern provinces was not at all in line with Nicholas's thinking, Muraviev commented. Good relations must be maintained with Korea until she was able to defend her independence against foreign encroachment. "In the contrary case," Muraviev concluded, "we as a contiguous great power shall be able to safeguard our interests."[187]

Speyer criticized the policy of his own government in a conversation with the British consul general. But although he gave to understand that St. Petersburg was likely to withdraw the military instructors and the financial adviser on condition that the Korean government would not employ other foreigners in their stead, Jordan remained suspicious. "In their present excitable state the Coreans are disposed to accept these terms and allow the country to drift into a state of anarchy, but in the end it is very unlikely that Russia will seriously consent to abandon the position which she has been at such pains to secure for herself in Corea, unless it be for some ulterior purpose," he wrote.[188]

The Japanese minister in Seoul was pleased with the turn of affairs. The action of the tsarist government, Kato believed, had been prompted by protests from Tokyo and had been dictated by the desire to satisfy to some extent the wishes of his own country and possibly to gain her goodwill in view of Russia's more important preoccupations in China. He agreed with Jordan that the nature of the Korean reply had come as a complete surprise to Speyer.[189] Allen, with whom Kato also shared his views, reported that "the Japanese Government will expect to take a more active part in Korean matters hereafter."[190]

In accordance with instructions received from St. Petersburg on March 17,[191] Speyer informed Foreign Minister Min in a note written the same day that Nicholas considered the dispatch of a special Korean embassy to St. Petersburg "completely inappropriate." Russia did not need any expressions of thanks; she never imposed her good deeds on anyone. "Now that Korea considers that she can get along without the Russian instructors, officers, and adviser, dispatched by us at her own request," Speyer declared, "we can only congratulate her that she has so quickly reached that stage of independent development which can secure her full independence without any support from any military forces, instructors, and advisers." He had already made arrangements, he added, to terminate any further activity on the part of the Russian financial adviser and military instructors in Korea.[192]

Upon delivery of the above note to Min, Speyer asked the Russian officers to regulate their accounts with the Korean Ministry of War as soon as possible. The following day, on March 18, at high noon they gave up the command of their troops and ceased guarding the palace.[193] Alekseev too was ordered to wind up his affairs. The Russo-Korean Bank which had been in the process of negotiating the purchase of land for the construction of the necessary buildings halted its projects and waited for instructions from the tsarist Finance Ministry whether to continue or to abandon them.[194]

Speyer did not conceal his bitterness over the collapse of his strenuous efforts in Seoul. The telegram he had received from St. Petersburg contained only vague resolutions about the future. The tsarist government reserved the right to take measures to protect its interests if it saw that another power took too preponderant a position in the peninsula. Speyer complained that this showed that his government had found the burden too heavy and had taken advantage of the first occasion to shed it. "The march forward, which began six months ago, has been transformed into a retreat and according to her own utterances, Russia no longer seeks to play any role in Korea other than that devolving on the other powers," Speyer lamented to Plancy. "Seoul becomes a simple observation and information post where the agent of the tsar will have no initiative to take." "*Desinit in piscem* [It ends up in fish]," he grumbled.[195]

Speyer admitted to Allen that he had pursued his active course not only without authorization, but in the face of an urgent telegram from St. Petersburg to be cautious and to avoid creating difficulties. "He said that he was conscious that he would be made to suffer if he failed, but that he could not fail," Allen related. "His failure has apparently caused him to suspect every one; he has spoken to me so bitterly of every Representative here except our French colleague, that I have had to decline to listen to his remarks," Allen reported.[196]

The *Official Gazette*, published in the *Journal de Saint-Petersbourg*, reported that Russia had decided to withdraw the drill instructors and financial adviser from Seoul upon receiving assurance that Korea would do without any foreign assistance in the military and financial domains. Russia desired to abstain henceforth from any participation in the internal affairs of Korea "in the hope that strengthened by the aid which she had given to her up to now, the young state will be capable of safeguarding both her internal order and her full independence." Should the opposite prove to be the case, the communiqué stated, the tsarist government would "take measures to safeguard its interests and the rights which belong to Russia as a great power bordering unto Korea."[197]

Muraviev elaborated on the position of his government in conversations with the foreign representatives in St. Petersburg. He told Montebello that he saw the agitation in Korea as directed against the involvement of foreigners in general in the internal administration of the country and that he worried that it might erupt at any moment in an insurrection against the Korean emperor himself. The position of Russia in the peninsula had become "very delicate," he explained, because she had engaged herself toward Japan to respect and to maintain the independence of Korea. If a political upheaval had occurred while Russia still had military instructors in the Korean army and an imperial guard close to the sovereign, her responsibility could have been very heavy. It was for those reasons as well as out of the desire to forestall a movement which threatened to be mounted against her that Russia had asked Kojong if the presence of her military instructors and the financial adviser was still necessary.

"In insisting on the responsibility which Russia wished above all to shed and on her intention of faithfully executing her engagements in regard to the independence of Korea, Count Muraviev gave me to understand that he desired to act in these circumstances in perfect accord with Japan and that he envisioned even an occasion for joining the interests of the two countries for the eventuality a crisis were to erupt in Korea," Montebello reported.[198]

Muraviev admitted to O'Conor that he did not approve of the energy shown by Speyer in the matter of the military instructors and the financial adviser. However, Russia's decision to withdraw the officials in compliance with Kojong's wishes did not give the Japanese *carte blanche* to supplant them with men of their own, he declared. He had indicated to Minister Hayashi that whatever concessions Japan would obtain in this and in other matters would be required also by Russia. It was on this basis that Russia had agreed to abstain from direct intervention in Korea affairs, Muraviev pointed out.

Expressing satisfaction at Muraviev's renewed assurance that Russia desired only the maintenance of the independence of Korea, O'Conor remarked that the clause in the agreement concluded between Alekseev and the Korean government the preceding November stipulating that the financial adviser to the Korean government should be either a Russian or a Korean subject was in conflict with this assurance. Muraviev replied that he had already informed Hayashi that he had no objection to the modification of this clause.[199]

Muraviev had told Hayashi that while he did not insist on the maintenance of Alekseev in office, he would not consent to the appointment of any other foreigner, regardless of nationality, in his place. He had assured the Japanese minister, however, that he had no objections against the continued employment of foreigners currently in the Korean service.[200]

The London *Times* hailed the withdrawal of the Russian instructors and financial adviser from Korea as a triumph of Japanese diplomacy. It declared that the quiet but effective action on the part of Japan without fuss and ostentatious protestation afforded an admirable lesson for the British Government.[201] But the British consul general, who was painfully aware of Korea's ills, looked upon the departure of Alekseev and the drill instructors with mixed feelings. "In spite of his inexperience of Eastern affairs, and the great drawback under which he laboured in his ignorance of the language, M. Alexieff managed to exercise a fairly effective check on the expenditure, and apart from the political complexion his appointment assumed, his presence in the Finance Department had undoubtedly a good effect," Jordan wrote. Noting that the Russian instructors had trained an effective military force of about 4,000 men with "a fair measure of success," capable probably of coping with any foreseeable disorder, he worried that the great danger for the future lay in the inevitable deterioration of the financial administration now that no foreign adviser could be at the helm.[202]

The Russian press took issue with foreign newspapers which interpreted the withdrawal of the military instructors and financial adviser as a check received by Russian policy in the Far East. It was not a matter of a setback suffered by Russia, the *Gazette de Moscou* and the *Journal de Saint-Petersbourg* argued, but faithful adherence to her principle of nonintervention. "Russia does not impose her services on anyone, and she did not come to the aid of Korea except at the demand of the Korean government, lest that country risked being absorbed definitively by Japan. If now the government of a country by virtue of the independence which Russia did not and does not intend to impair declares that it can do without Russian assistance, Russia can withdraw calmly, as she has already done in similar cases [in Bulgaria and in Serbia]."

It was Russia's hope, the papers continued, that the young neighboring state would itself have the forces to ensure the internal order and independence of the country in such a way as not to impair Russia's interests in the Far East. "From the moment where it will be no longer a matter of the internal affairs of Korea but of Russian interests, Russia will certainly not remain inactive," the newspapers declared. "If, for example, profiting from the weakness of the Koreans, Japan would want to send new troops to Korea, Russia, on the basis of the treaty which guaranteed the independence of Korea, would also send Russian troops there to put them on a par with the Japanese military forces. Russia cannot tolerate that an element other than the Korean element fortify itself in Korea and there dispose of the resources of the country. It will be up to Korea [to see to it] that this reentry of Russia will not be necessary, the Emperor of Korea having declared that he will defend the independence of his empire without any foreign assistance." Pointing out that Russia's hands had been untied by the withdrawal of her officers from Korea and that she would now be able to follow developments in Korea guided solely by her own interests, the newspapers concluded that the situation in which Russia found herself was "incontestably advantageous."[203]

Sir Thomas Sanderson, permanent under-secretary of state in the British Foreign Office, attributed Korean opposition to Russia as well as to Japan to the attempts of the two powers to introduce reforms. The Koreans, he told the French representative, had little taste for the modern civilization that one wished to implant in their country. They got along best with the Chinese, Sanderson believed, because the Chinese left them more or less free to act as they liked. "Let us leave them alone so long as they do nothing to endanger the European interests," he declared.[204]

The quiet aquiescence of Russia in the decision of the Korean government and the prompt withdrawal of her officers from the Korean service and from their quarters in the palace made a deep impression in Seoul. "The perception and greatness of the Emperor of Russia, his magnanimous generosity and kindness, and, moreover, his absolute disinterestedness are shown by his ready assent to the wishes of the Corean Government. Our gratitude is engraved in our hearts and cannot be expressed in words," Min wrote to Speyer on March 18 in acknowledging his dispatch of the previous day. The Korean government was greatly indebted to Speyer for the promptness with which he had given effect to the tsar's command and had made the necessary arrangements of relieving the military instructors and the financial adviser of their duties, Min added. Although Nicholas had stated that it was not necessary for Kojong to send a mission of thanks to Russia, the Korean government had been so touched by the decision communicated by Speyer that it could not abandon the idea even if it wished to do so. "It is a duty incumbent upon Corea." [205]

Speyer replied in a brief note on the nineteenth that in view of the categorically expressed unwillingness of the tsar to receive a special Korean embassy, he could not raise this question again.[206] He also refused gifts of money which Kojong wished to offer to Alekseev and the military instructors.

Meanwhile the members of the Independence Club addressed a letter to the councilors of state and in the name of their twelve million fellow citizens expressed their approbation. The response which Min had made to Speyer regarding the withdrawal of the military offices and financial adviser had revealed the "divine sagacity" of the emperor and the "patriotic resolutions" of the councilors, they declared.[207]

Although Min's name had graced the exchange of notes by which the withdrawal of the Russian military instructors and financial adviser had been effected, the relations between the foreign minister and the state councilors had remained so bad that the latter seized the first opportunity to topple him from office. When it was revealed that the Italian and Austro-Hungarian ministers in Peking had never been notified of the assumption by Kojong of the imperial title, Min and the director of political affairs of the Foreign Office were dismissed for negligence bordering unto *lèse-majesté*. Minister of Education Cho Pyong-sik was named interim foreign minister. Since Cho, who had served as foreign minister on several previous occasions, had displayed a sharply hostile attitude toward the Russian legation during the six months that he had been a member of the new cabinet and had carefully abstained from any shows of courtesy toward Speyer, his appointment seemed to accentuate the scission which had occurred between the governments of Russia and Korea.[208]

Alekseev was transferred to Japan, where he was attached to the Russian legation in Tokyo as agent of the Russian Finance Ministry.[209] On the eve of his departure from Seoul, Foreign Minister Cho wrote to Speyer declaring that as Alekseev had been relieved of his duties as financial adviser to the Korean government, the agreement under which he had been employed should be cancelled and asked that Speyer return to him the copies of the agreement deposited in his archives.[210]

In November 1897 Speyer had been named to succeed Cassini as envoy extraordinary and minister plenipotentiary at Peking. He had remained in charge of the Seoul legation pending the opening of navigation on the Tientsin River.[211] Now that spring had arrived, Speyer looked forward to proceeding directly to the Chinese capital. But in the wake of the developments in Korea he was ordered to return to St. Petersburg.[212] Speyer had been ill for a long time. The worsening of his malady had made him increasingly nervous, a condition which may well have contributed to his gruffness and rash conduct.[213] At first Speyer consoled himself with the thought that the journey to Europe might improve his health,[214] but by the time he handed over the legation to Councilor of State Nikolai Gavrilovich Matiunin on April 12 he had heard that his appointment as envoy extraordinary and minister plenipotentiary to China had been revoked. As he bade farewell to his American colleague, he remarked that he did not know when he would return to the Far East, if ever.[215]

"The Russo-Korean bank, which opened with such éclat on March 1st, is closing up its affairs, and will be discontinued this week, the officials in charge of the same having been transferred to China," Allen reported. "The matter of the coaling-station on Deer Island at Pusan has not been finally settled; the deeds for the large tracts of land asked for at the new ports at Chinnampo and Mokpo by Mr. de Speyer have not been executed, and Russia has now nothing but the distrust of the Koreans to show for the vigorously aggressive course of its recent Representative during his stormy seven months' service in Korea."[216]

Twenty-Three

Russia and the Seizure of Kiaochow

Unified only in 1871, Germany had appeared relatively late on the Chinese scene. Yet her influence had risen rapidly. By 1895 Germany was second to Great Britain in the number of foreign firms and volume of business in China and as a source of Chinese imports, notably weapons and munitions.

The expansion of Germany's role in China had been facilitated by Li Hung-chang, who regarded Germany as the best military model for China and as a suitable counterweight in his policy of balancing the foreign powers against each other. The employment of many German officials by Li had been partly for the purpose of undercutting the monopoly of advisers the British had built up through their domination of the Chinese Imperial Maritime Customs.

Linking success in world trade and economic power with the development of a strong fleet, the German navy clamored for the acquisition of a sphere of influence with a major commercial depot in China.[1] Germany's participation in the Tripartite Intervention had been with an eye toward the opportunity of obtaining "appropriate compensation on Chinese territory" in the form of "one or more suitable coal or naval stations."[2]

On April 26, 1895, at the height of the intervention, the Kaiser thanked the tsar for the "excellent way" in which he had "initiated the combined action of Europe for the sake of its interests against Japan." Promising to do everything in his power "to keep Europe quiet and also guard the rear of Russia" so that nobody could impede the tsar's cultivation of the Asian continent and his defense of Europe from "the inroads of the Great Yellow race," Wilhelm solicited in exchange Nicholas's assistance in the procurement of a Chinese harbor by Germany. "I. . . hope," he wrote, "that, just as I will gladly help you settle the question of eventual annexation of portions of territory for Russia, you will kindly see that Germany may also be able to acquire a Port somewhere where it does not *gêne* [bother] you." [3] The tsar replied that he would not object to German acquisition of territory in East Asia. [4]

Vice Admiral Friedrich von Hollmann, state secretary of the German Naval Office, drew up a list of possible places: Chusan Island in the north and Amoy Island with Kulanghsü in the south; Kiaochow (Chiao-chou) Bay in the north and Mirs Bay in the south; the Montebello Islands at the southern tip of Korea in the north and the Pescadores in the south. [5] The Kaiser thought of occupying Weihaiwei if the Russians took a port in Korea, remarking that a *fait accompli* was always respected more by other states than mere recriminations. But when Chancellor Hohenlohe and Foreign Secretary Marschall pointed out that Weihaiwei was still in Japanese hands, Wilhelm dropped the idea. His primary concern, he explained, was that Germany respond immediately to the advance of England or Russia in those regions with the occupation of some point. [6]

Undersecretary of Foreign Affairs Rotenhan went over the list of possible acquisitions compiled by Hollmann. He eliminated the Pescadores, for they had become Japanese as a result of the Treaty of Shimonoseki, and Chusan because China had pledged to England not to cede it to a third power. He dropped Amoy since it was a treaty port; the other powers would not tolerate its seizure. Mirs Bay was undesirable due to its proximity to Hong Kong and its exposure to typhoons, while the same sort of Russian and Japanese opposition could be expected to the taking of the Montebello Islands as had been shown to the British occupation of Port Hamilton. Rotenhan, therefore, chose Kiaochow Bay, negotiation for whose acquisition offered the best prospects for success, because Germany would in this case deal with China alone, or so it seemed at the time. [7]

Kiaochow Bay, an inlet on the southern side of the Shantung Peninsula, was of great strategic importance. It formed a harbor that was not only large enough to hold all the fleets of the powers in Chinese waters, but that was, practically speaking, ice-free and open all year. A canal had formerly connected Kiaochow Bay with the gulf of Pechili. It was partially choked now but could be reopened at relatively small cost. Once this was done, the power holding Kiaochow Bay would be in a position to dominate the trade of both Peking and Shanghai. [8]

There was the danger that the occupation of a bay on the mainland could readily involve Germany in complications with China; on the other hand, it would enable her to protect and support her Catholic missionaries in Shantung Province. [9] On September 23 Wilhelm telegraphed to Marschall from Theerbude that according to the latest news general ferment in China was likely to develop into a major persecution of Christians. As events in Kwantung had led the British to assemble a large squadron, he ordered the dispatch of German naval vessels to the China Sea to guard especially the settlements on the Shantung Peninsula.[10]

Ever since the conclusion of the peace preliminaries between China and Japan the Kaiser had been worrying that the West might be overrun by Orientals if Japan succeeded in dominating, organizing, and stirring up the vast Chinese empire. Brooding over the danger which he envisaged for Europe and the Christian faith in the development of Asia, he made a rough sketch of the Yellow Peril, and had it drawn up expertly by Professor H. Knackfuss and lithographed for public distribution.

The engraving, which his military aide, Lieutenant Colonel Helmuth von Moltke, nephew of the late field marshal by the same name, presented to the tsar on September 30, depicted a group of women in ancient, Valkyrie-like costumes standing on a precipice and looking over a plain clovered with flowering cities, ship-filled streams, and cultivated fields. The female figures, above whom a bright cross shone, represented the European states. In the foreground was Germany, pressing close to her Russia, to the side France, then Austria and the others. Before them stood the angel of war, a flaming sword in his right hand. With the left hand he pointed into the distance where the smoke of a burning city was rising beyond a landscape that symbolized commerce, trade, European culture and civilization. The thick clouds of smoke joined in the shape of a dragon, which was advancing menacingly, while a seated Buddha rose from the flames. The picture bore the caption, in Wilhelm's own hand: "Völker Europas, wahrt eure heiligsten Güter" (Peoples of Europe, guard your most sacred goods).[11]

In a covering letter to Nicholas, the Kaiser summarized the meaning of the sketch: "It shows the powers of Europe represented by their respective Genii called together by the Arch-Angel Michael,—sent from Heaven,—to *unite* in resisting the inroad of Buddhism, heathenism and barbarism for the Defence of the Cross. Stress is especially laid on the *united* resistance of *all* European powers, which is just as necessary also against our common internal foes, anarchism, republicanism, nihilism."[12] The engraving, Moltke noted, portrayed the coming struggle for survival, the *Existenzkampf*, between the white and yellow races. He commented that the danger had been stemmed temporarily by the tripartite intervention.[13]

Desirous of Russian support in China, the German government eagerly watched the reaction of the tsar to the imperial sketch. When Ambassador Radolin telegraphed from St. Petersburg that the gift of the Kaiser had reportedly been framed with care, Marschall jotted at the bottom of the cable, "It is working! That's great!" (*Also es wirkt! Das ist sehr erfreulich.*)[14]

As the continued presence of a strong German squadron in the China Sea increased the need for a coaling station, Marschall instructed the German ambassador in St. Petersburg, Prince von Radolin, to sound out the tsarist government unofficially about German acquisition of such a coaling station. If direct cession of the territory could not be obtained, a lease would be sufficient, he added. Marschall asked Radolin, furthermore, to broach the same subject to the Chinese minister in St. Petersburg ostensibly on his own behalf. In speaking to Hsü Ching-ch'eng he was to stress in particular "how useful a strong German fleet in Chinese waters would be also from a Chinese point of view, in that it would constitute a counterweight to the endeavors of the other powers and this would effectively contribute to the maintenance of the balance in East Asia." Hsü had asked Radolin earlier in the month whether the German government would have any objections to the construction (by Russia) of a railroad through Manchuria to Vladivostok. When talking to the Chinese minister, Radolin was to give as his personal opinion that the imperial government could only rejoice if China improved her communications in the interest of trade.[15]

Radolin called on Hsü on October 29 and after an exchange of pleasantries turned to the question of a coaling station. He began by asserting that Germany had given China many a proof of unselfish friendship and was probably the only great power who had not demanded anything for herself. Germany desired merely to see her trade secured and for the sake of world peace watched over the maintenance of the European balance in Chinese waters. The presence of a strong German fleet must be a reassurance for China, Radolin argued. Yet Germany did not like to leave her costly ships, which could at a given moment be used as a counterweight against this or that great power in favor of China, in Hsü's distant seas without a secure shelter. It would seem to him, Radolin contended, that each of the East Asian empires should be glad to cede to a befriended unselfish power a suitable refuge, which after all would be to her own benefit.

Hsü replied in beautiful phrases how highly he valued German friendship and how he shared Radolin's views. But he feared, he said, that if China would meet the otherwise justified German wish which indeed would be of advantage primarily to China, the other powers would voice similar desires and claims or raise difficulties. Radolin denied this. Pointing to the construction by Russia of the railroad through Manchuria and hinting at the commercial concessions the French had received in southwestern China, he complained that Germany was the only one of the three powers who had received no consideration for her part in preserving the territorial integrity of China.[16]

The subject of a German coaling station was also raised in Peking the same day by the German minister, Baron von Schenck zu Schweinberg. The Tsungli Yamen officials whom he saw promised to submit the matter to Prince Kung. Their immediate reaction was the same as that of Hsü, namely that compliance with German wishes would trigger similar demands by the other powers.[17] As the Tsungli Yamen procrastinated, evading discussion of the issue under the pretext that it had not yet been possible to lay the matter before Kung, Schenck suggested to his government a month later that the island of Quemoy might be obtainable as a coaling station if an official request were made.[18]

On December 14 the Tsungli Yamen received Brandt, the former German minister to Peking, then on a tour through China. When the reception was over, Schenck, who had accompanied Brandt, took advantage of the presence of Princess Ch'ing and Kung and of Grand Councilor Weng T'ung-ho to raise the question of a German coaling station. He asked for the lease of an unspecified coaling station under Chinese sovereignty. Ch'ing and Kung refused to consider the request on the familiar but justified ground that it would expose China to similar demands by the other powers.[19]

On February 1, 1896, Hsü Ching-ch'eng, who served concurrently as minister to St. Petersburg and Berlin, reiterated to Foreign Secretary Marschall that the Tsungli Yamen feared that if China fulfilled Germany's wishes, other powers could express similar desires, which China in her weakness would not be able to resist. Which powers did the Tsungli Yamen have in mind, Marschall asked. England and France long had naval stations and Russia had recently been conceded one in Kiaochow Bay. Hsü replied that as far as he knew, Russia had been allowed the use of Kiaochow Bay only temporarily, for one year.

Marshall responded that Germany would be satisfied with the lease of a coaling station for a number of years. He alleged that Germany had given particular proof of friendship, in that in spite of China's present weakness, she had chosen the path of amicable agreement, though the failure of the Chinese government to carry out some of Germany's treaty-based claims would have provided her with full justification for the use of force. While repeating that China could see from this that Germany was well disposed toward her, Marschall made it clear that his country was determined to obtain a coaling station, even if only on lease.[20]

Back in St. Petersburg, Hsü told Radolin in strict confidence that the question of the ceding of an island could hardly be solved without the use of a "little force." Although Hsü was not prepared to back the German request officially for fear of being denounced as a traitor, he and Kreyer, his legation councilor, recommended that Germany take possession of the desired place and then begin negotiations.[21]

As the High Command, the Ministry of the Navy, and the chief of the East Asian squadron continued to clamor for the acquisition of a coal and naval station, Councilor Reinhold Klehmet of the German Foreign Ministry examined the seemingly favorable attitude of the powers toward such an eventuality. He noted that Nicholas, in his letter to Wilhelm, had accepted the German demand for a base in East Asia as a matter of course and that the Russian newspaper *Mokovskiia Vedomosti* recognized that Germany because of her East Asian trade and because of her services to China could demand a base on the Chinese coast. Referring to Hsü's hint that resort to force might be necessary, Klehmet observed that the German minister to Peking had repeatedly urged the same.

Heyking, who had succeeded Schenck that year, proposed that Chinese delays in meeting the complaints of German Catholic missionaries be used as a pretext for action. Further inaction, he warned, would seriously impair German prestige in China. Heyking and Bishop Johann Anzer both asserted that the authorities and inhabitants of Shantung had lost respect for their countrymen, scoffing that Germany made only empty threats. "Bishop Anzer stormily demands energetic action in the interest of his mission, in order to instill respect in the Chinese again. He indicates that his missionaries may otherwise press him to return under French protection, which would prove to be the more effective one," Klehmet recorded.[22]

In mid-June Li Hung-chang arrived in Berlin from St. Petersburg. He was received by Wilhelm on the fourteenth. He visited Prince Bismarck in Friedrichsruh and had two lengthy political discussions, each several hours long, with Foreign Secretary Marschall.

Although Li repeated a number of times how thankful he was for Germany's effective intervention in the Liaotung question and how everyone wished not only to maintain but to strengthen the friendly relations between the two countries, his gratitude was not unstinted. Li observed with a smile that Germany had been much more sympathetic toward Japan than toward China from the beginning and that this attitude continued to prevail. It was the only way that he could explain to himself that Germany had remained so passive at the outbreak of the war as well-prepared Japan had attacked completely unprepared China without any cause. He had been told in Russia, Li added, that the indemnity of thirty million taels which China had to pay for the retrocession of the Liaotung peninsula had been demanded by Germany and that Russia had given in to German pressure in this matter, though she had originally striven to obtain the return of Liaotung without compensation.

Marschall tried to shift the responsibility for German passivity on British shoulders, asserting that it was due primarily to the fact that England, who possessed the greatest interests in East Asia, had from the outset observed a policy of complete indifference. As for the assertion that Russia had played the major role in the retrocession of Liaotung and that its return would have been effected for free if she had had her way, Marschall continued sarcastically, it spoke well for the patriotism of the Russian who had made it; the latter must have stressed the indebtedness of China to Russia with the hind thought of securing Chinese compensation. Actually, Marschall contended, he himself could claim with far greater justification that "if Germany had not participated in the intervention, *Japan would never have given in at all in the Liaotung question.*" He had positive proof for this assertion, he said. He did not wish to pursue the matter further, but at any rate China must regard Germany along with Russia as the power to whom it owed the return of Liaotung. He knew nothing regarding the allegation that Germany had pushed for the payment of compensation on the part of China. From the beginning Germany had been of one mind with Russia and France that it was impossible to expect Japan to retrocede Liaotung without financial compensation. The Japanese had originally demanded a much higher compensation and it had been due to the joint efforts of Germany and Russia that it had been reduced to thirty million taels.

Marschall admitted that in Germany, especially in military circles, Japanese successes in the battlefield had been welcomed. This was simply due to the fact, he claimed, that they were regarded indirectly as victories of German military science. "The thought of the viceroy that we are partial toward the Japanese surprises me insofar as we have been accused in Japan on the contrary of partiality toward China," he declared. "It is evident from this fact that we have preserved complete impartiality."

Turning to the attack, Marschall pointed out that it was much easier to deal with Japan than with China, for whatever Germany had negotiated with the Tsungli Yamen in recent years had been dragged out incredibly. Promises had not been kept but withdrawn, and even in the question of the reform of the Chinese army by German instructors, which was of vital interest to China, the Chinese government had not conducted itself in a manner that would have left Germany with much inclination to take further steps in this direction.

Li Hung-chang conceded that the slowness of the Chinese authorities was a grave shortcoming. No one, he said with a smile, was more convinced thereof than he himself. But the Chinese clung so much to the old, that anyone who wanted something new had to proceed with extreme caution, lest the danger of revolution or even of anarchy be precipitated. The machine must be handled very gently and cautiously. As a man of reform he was already under attack. Were he to proceed without caution, it would be grist for the mill of his many, powerful enemies.

Marschall argued that the policy of Germany in the Liaotung question had emanated from the basic principle which she had repeatedly sought to apply in East Asia and which she had been the first to voice, namely the maintenance of the East Asian balance of power and of the territorial integrity of the Chinese mainland. He freely admitted that in establishing and carrying out this principle, Germany had thought first of all of her own interests, which required the maintenance of the East Asian balance. Nevertheless, he contended, it was of vital interest to the Chinese government for this principle to be championed by a European great power if the latter demonstrated, as Germany had done, that she was unselfish and interested primarily in maintaining and furthering her *commercial* relations with China. "That German policy could not be carried out in the long run without the possession of a firm base for our fleet as the natural champion and protector of our East Asian interests," Marschall asserted. Declaring that such a naval station was an "imperative demand" (*eine unabweisliche Forderung*) of Germany, Marschall explained that his country needed a station with a spacious harbor and terrain suitable for the establishment of a coaling station and for the construction of docks and fortifications for their defense; the present condition, where Germany had to obtain coal from others and in the event of repairs had to use foreign docks, did not correspond to German dignity or interests. He would be lacking in candor, Marschall told Li, if he hid from him that the possession of such a station constituted the "indispensable prerequisite" (*die unumgängliche Voraussetzung*) for entering into any negotiations and in general for upholding that East Asian policy, of which Germany had given China proof in the Liaotung question. It must be obvious to the Chinese government whether it would improve its position if it rejected such a demand and thereby would force Germany to be guided exclusively by her own interests, he warned.

Li Hung-chang replied that he was well acquainted with Germany's wish for a naval station in Chinese waters. The difficulty of carrying out the desire lay in the fact that if Germany received such a station, other states would make similar demands. When Marschall interjected that Russia already let her fleet anchor in Kiaochow Bay, Li countered animatedly that Russia had no rights to the bay, that China had let Russia use the bay for only several months. The viceroy asserted that during his recent talks in Russia the tsarist government had been absolutely unselfish. He himself, he alleged, had told the tsar that Russia might wish to acquire a port on the Korean coast, but Nicholas had rejected the suggestion. Not a word was said that Russia expected a concession for her assistance in the Liaotung question, Li declared.

Neither did Germany claim any compensation for her intervention in the Liaotung question, Marschall retorted; she was simply demanding what was essential to further her trade with China and to continue the East Asian policy inaugurated in the Liaotung question. Germany was just as unselfish as Russia, Marschall contended. If Russia did not attach great weight to the acquisition of a harbor as Li asserted, it was because she had one in Vladivostok and because she could easily acquire another on the Korean coast. Besides, the situation was different in that Russia was a neighbor of China and hence not dependent like Germany on sea routes. Marschall argued that the construction of the Trans-Siberian Railroad and its extension through Chinese territory would soon give Russia all that she needed to secure her interests, particularly the development of her trade with China, and that England and France already had bases in East Asia; only Germany had nothing. Such a state of affairs was intolerable for Germany, he declared. Once the Chinese government, as he expected, came to realize that it had indeed been Germany who had regained Liaotung for it, it would not be able to refuse Germany's demand, which was absolutely necessary to continue her balancing policy. "Far be it from me to accuse one of the powers interested in East Asia of selfishness," Marschall declaimed, "but I must accentuate that the 'unselfishness' of Russia, England, and France toward China would be considerably strengthened if Germany, supported by a naval station, would enter East Asian questions as an active factor. The Chinese government should realize whether it would be more advantageous for the Chinese government to grant to Germany the demanded naval station or possibly to forego that Germany continue the East Asian policy she has pursued up to now."

Interpreting Marschall's last remarks as a threat, Li retorted excitedly that Germany could perhaps pursue a policy hostile to China. He recognized, he said, that the cession of a place to Germany would be more than offset by the maintenance of friendly relations with Germany and asserted that he supported the German demand in Peking and would do so again in the future. He did want to know, however, whether in such an eventuality Germany would continue to support China actively.

Marschall replied that in this respect the interests of nations were stronger than any written agreement. "If we were to create for ourselves through the possession of a naval station, through the increase of our trade, [and] through the participation of German money in Chinese railroad enterprises and other things a heightened interest in the preservation of the integrity of the Chinese empire, we would naturally intercede in the maintenance and protection of these interests," he expounded.

Li commented that this argument would be most effective in China, and he invited Marschall to stress this point. He promised to write Peking in the same sense, but asked Marschall to reflect how difficult it was for China at this moment, after the unfortunate war, to give up a piece of her territory.

Marschall countered that the Germans were willing to be flexible about the form of the cession. He suggested that a harbor and sufficient land for the construction of docks and a coaling station be leased to Germany for a period of fifty years.

Li thought that an understanding could be reached on such lines and promised to do his part in achieving it. He explained why decisions of the Chinese government took so long. The audiences of the ministers, who in accordance with tradition had to make their reports to the emperor in a kneeling position at three o'clock in the morning, were limited to thirty minutes. Since the emperor frequently made no immediate decision, it took weeks for the same matter to be taken up again.[23]

When Admiral Alfred von Tirpitz, commander of the German cruiser division in the Far East, asserted in a conversation at Chefoo in August of that year that Russia no longer needed Kiaochow Bay because she could find suitable places in Korea and Liaotung, Heyking sounded out his tsarist colleague, an old acquaintance. Cassini replied that the Russians had so far not found a satisfactory harbor in Korea and that nothing was coming of Port Arthur either. Chefoo was unusable, so that the only possible acquisition remained Kiaochow Bay, which, he alleged, had been *officially* conceded to Russia by the Chinese as winter station for their fleet. Heyking consequently told Tirpitz to stop considering Kiaochow Bay as a German base.[24]

Yet German interest in Kiaochow persisted. In November 1896 Admiral Eduard von Knorr, commander-in-chief of the German navy, on personal orders from Wilhelm sought information about the character of the bay from Gustav Detring, the commissioner of customs at Tientsin and a protégé of Li Hung-chang for whom he had interpreted during the latter's visit to Germany. Detring replied that the bay was eminently suitable for acquisition by Germany. He asserted that the Russians may have been assigned Kiaochow Bay for the current winter and might be acting like masters of the bay by virtue of the frequent appearance of their ships, but that there was no question of a cession of the bay to Russia. He had the most binding assurances to that effect by influential persons, he said. Detring calculated that England would make no difficulties if Germany sought to lease Kiaochow Bay. He believed that

Britain's interests were identical with those of Germany and that she would welcome an increase in German influence in North China to counteract Russia. But the latter, Detring surmised, would hardly agree to the cession of Kiaochow Bay to Germany unless she herself received a similar good anchorage, such as Talienwan.[25]

On November 18 Hsü, who always spoke to his German colleague in St. Petersburg with great respect for Germany and professed the wish for the development of German influence in China, sent Kreyer to Radolin with a strictly confidential communication. He related that in a recent meeting with Marschall, Detring had tried to influence the German government to forego the idea of territorial gain and to confine itself to *moral* acquisitions, such as railroad concessions, because a base would be costly to fortify and difficult to defend against other powers and because its acquisition would impair German prestige by calling into question the unselfishness hitherto displayed by Germany. The Chinese had a very different mentality, Kreyer protested, as he had suggested already several months earlier. The concept of moral conquests was alien to them. The only thing the Chinese understood was force. If Germany did not take without ado what she desired or needed, the Chinese would regard this merely as a sign of weakness rather than as proof of noble unselfishness. The Chinese themselves, Kreyer continued at Hsü's behest, would be guided solely by what was best for them, and however much they might promise and whatever concessions they might give to German firms, they would break their word without compunction as soon as they realized that it was against their advantage or if another power granted them more favorable conditions.

Kreyer argued that in order for Germany to acquire in China a position similar to that of Russia, France, and England, she must seize a suitable harbor or at the very least force the leasing of a coaling and naval station; the "all too delicate manner" of Heyking in this question did not appear appropriate to the Chinese. Asserting that everything he was telling Radolin as a German was consistent with his duties as a Chinese official, Kreyer contended that the Chinese must know that such an acquisition would be in the interest not only of Germany but of China herself, who thereby would be protected from the excessive greed of the other powers, in that unselfish Germany by the presence of her sea power would maintain the balance in East Asia. To do this, he reiterated, Germany needed a harbor in which her ships could lie and move about freely and from where she could protect German trade. Minister Hsü fully recognized this, but he did not have the courage to advise Peking accordingly, Kreyer stated.

"The Russians, opined Herr Kreyer (or, I assume, strangely the minister who has sent him)," Radolin reported, "have found the only right way of dealing with the Chinese. First they took Pamir from them and thereby showed them their power, then they exercised leniency and returned Liaotung to them, and now they take in hand [the construction of] the railroad through Manchuria, which is probably tantamount to the conquest of the latter province. The Russians have demonstrated to the Chinese that they can do [*walten und schalten*] as they please, and this has impressed the Chinese." "If Germany, who up to now has not acquired anything there, will be guided by further considerations vis-à-vis China, the German reputation in the Far East will decline and China will not even be grateful for it," Radolin conveyed. "Not only Kreyer's but also the minister's—naturally strictly confidential— suggestions are directed at indicating to us that the inconsiderate protection of German trade interests is the only right way," he concluded.[26]

Wilhelm read Radolin's report with great interest. Taking issue with Kreyer's assertion that Detring had tried to dissuade the German government from acquiring a base in China, he jotted in the margin: "He told me the very opposite and was in full agreement with me and my navy about the point to be chosen." Next to the contention that the only thing the Chinese understood was force, the Kaiser scribbled, "Right, that is what Detring told me too." He welcomed the warning that further German inaction would lead to a decline in German prestige and that China would not even be grateful for German considerateness. "Right! That is what I have been preaching to the Foreign Office for the past two years without any success whatsoever! That is the same as what my admirals and commanding officers continuously report from China." Wilhelm noted that Detring too had told him that Heyking's delicacy was unsuitable. He agreed with a brief "*Ja*" that the acquisition of a German base would be in China's own interest and remarked after the observation that unselfish Germany would protect China from the excessive greed of other powers by maintaining the balance of power in East Asia: "All ideas which have been advocated by me for years."[27]

In a telegram from Altona, whither the report had been forwarded, Wilhelm reiterated to Hohenlohe that the views of Hsü conveyed by Kreyer were consonant with what he had been preaching for the past two years and that they confirmed the impressions and convictions expressed by his admirals and ship commanders in China. "We must now act quickly and with determination," Wilhelm cabled. "Amoy must be occupied at once. After the occupation has been effected, negotiations can be opened with China." He thought in terms of Amoy, Wilhelm explained, because England regarded it as already within the German sphere of interest. Whenever a German cruiser arrived in

Amoy, the English fleet left the harbor in order not to be in the way should it seek to occupy it.

Wilhelm agreed that the intended presentation of the order of the Black Eagle to the Chinese emperor be postponed. As Hsü had cautioned Radolin, the bestowal of the honor on the emperor before China had done anything concrete for Germany would be regarded as an act of incomprehensible obligingness or weakness. "Inconsiderate seizure [*rücksichtsloses Besitzergreifen*] of a seemingly suitable harbor—against which even the emperor of Russia had no objections—would appear completely natural to the Chinese, particularly since they would see in it protection on the part of Germany against the excessive tutelage of other powers," Hsü had reiterated. "It is depressing that it takes a Chinese envoy to make clear to us stupid Germans what we must do in China for our own benefit and advantage," Wilhelm fumed.[28]

At Hohenlohe's request Councilor Klehmet prepared a lengthy memorandum explaining that the acquisition of Amoy, which was both the hub of Chinese sea traffic and a treaty port, would arouse the energetic opposition of France, Russia, and England as well as of China. The consequences could not be foreseen. Germany would probably have to withdraw under the superior pressure of the other powers, suffering a fatal blow in prestige. China would certainly cancel her commercial orders, and Germany's competitors would see to it that the Chinese market would long remain closed to Germany, at least as far as government transactions were concerned. Germany must drop the idea of the occupation of Amoy, particularly without any justification, that is to say by naked force in violation of law, unless the other countries' power of action and consequently willingness to oppose was paralyzed by some unforeseeable complication. Nor could less sensitive places, such as Samsah Bay north of Foochow, be seized in the midst of peace unless China gave cause or at least pretext for such action by the violation of German rights. The naked breaking of law, Klehmet warned, would compromise German policy irreparably; not even the acquisition of a coaling station would be able to make up for that. All that Germany could do was to wait until China gave her cause for reprisal.[29]

Armed with Klehmet's memorandum, Hohenlohe made a report to the Kaiser, in the presence of Admiral Hollmann, on November 29. He persuaded Wilhelm to consider Kiaochow Bay rather than Amoy as a potential German base. Georg Francius, director of the harbor works at Kiel, and Captain Zeye, deputy commander of the East Asian squadron, were sent to the China coast to study the suitability of various places from both naval and commercial points of view.[30]

A Chinese legation had been established in Berlin in 1877. Since 1887, however, it had been directed by the Chinese minister in St. Petersburg, routine matters being left in the hands of a Chinese attaché in Berlin. Important matters between China and Germany had to be handled consequently either in St. Petersburg or Peking. Not only did the German government find the arrangement increasingly inconvenient, but Hsü Ching-ch'eng himself recommended that a separate minister be appointed for Germany. As he explained to his government in October 1896, the rivalry between Russia and Germany for economic benefits made it difficult for one representative to remain on good terms with the two powers simultaneously. The German government wanted the attaché, a Manchu by the name of Kingyintai, appointed as China's minister. But though the Manchu spoke German well, the Tsungli Yamen did not agree on the ground that he could not write his native tongue correctly. The fact that Kingyintai had a German wife may also have hindered his promotion. When it was rumored that Lo Feng-loh might be appointed minister to Berlin, the German government was pleased, because it believed that Lo could be bribed to agree to the concessions Germany required.[31] When the Chinese government nominated Huang Tsun-hsien instead, the German government declined to accept him in order to bring pressure on Peking.

On December 1 Heyking berated the Tsungli Yamen for the treatment accorded to Germany. He likened Chinese friendship to the offering of a glass of wine that someone else had declined because it had lost flavor. Switching metaphors, he threatened: "We Germans love music very much, but we have different kinds of music. One is very soft and pleasant, that is the melody of friendship, which China has heard until now. But we also have a music which sounds very sharp and loud, more or less like a military march. I hope that we shall not be given cause to play this music to China."[32]

On December 14 Heyking repeated the objections of his government to the appointment of Huang. He used the occasion to hold out German assent to an increase in Chinese customs duties in exchange for the leasing of a coaling station for a period of fifty years. Li Hung-chang would not hear of such a deal, but Chang Yin-huan, a prominent member of the Tsungli Yamen, replied that if Germany would guarantee that the other powers, notably France, would not pose similar demands, the matter could be examined closer. However, on December 27 Prince Ching officially rejected Heyking's proposal, repeating that China could not fulfill Germany's wish lest the other powers insist on similar concessions. He announced that Hsü Ching-ch'eng, who had been serving concurrently as minister to St. Petersburg and Berlin, would henceforth represent China in Berlin exclusively.[33]

Meanwhile Cassini, the Russian minister to China, who had returned from Peking to St. Petersburg overland toward the end of the year, encouraged German ambitions. Calling on Radolin a number of times, he spoke of the good relations which existed between himself and Heyking, who, he said, understood the Chinese and how to deal with them much better than his predecessors. Cassini expressed pleasure that their two countries were acting in such harmony and praised the plucky and always correct bearing of Admiral Hoffmann who had positioned his squadron alongside that of Vice Admiral Sergei Petrovich Tyrtov for common action when the Japanese had threatened to offer resistance. He did not understand, he told Radolin, why Germany had not demanded a justified reward for her services to China in the same manner as Russia and France had done. "While I and the French Minister [Gérard] sat at the Tsungli Yamen all the time and did not mince matters [*kein Blatt vor den Mund nahmen*] in order to demand the necessary payment for the services rendered, the German minister [Schenck] was never there, as if he did not care about the success," Cassini revealed in strict confidence. Asserting that the delicacy customary in Europe in the presentation of demands was not appropriate in China and would not be understood there, Cassini declared that there was room in China for everyone—for Russia, for France, and for Germany. He had never believed that the Germans, after the enormous services which they no less than the Russians had rendered to the Chinese, would satisfy themselves with such few claims, Cassini concluded.

Radolin had quietly listened to Cassini's "deduction," without making any comments. But he had been struck, he reported, that the latter's views coincided with those indicated by Hsü through Kreyer, namely that if one wanted to have anything in China, one had to demand it without ado and finally to take it.[34]

Informed of the Tsungli Yamen's rejection of Heyking's proposal, Marschall suggested in a letter to the Kaiser, who was then in Hubertusstock, that once the definite results of the investigations of the harbor building engineer were in hand, Germany should demand of the Chinese government determinately one last time the yielding of a naval station. If the Chinese did not agree, German warships might simply occupy a suitable place and present them with a *fait accompli*. In such a case the concessions now held out to the Chinese by Heyking would no longer be applicable.

Wilhelm disagreed that Germany should repeat her demand one more time. "No!" he scribbled in the margin. "That would be a humiliation after such a rejection! That was the *last time*." Next to the statement that a *fait accompli* might possibly be created through the occupation of a suitable place, he jotted

down "Yes immediately"; next to the assertion that in such a case the concessions held out by Heyking would no longer be applicable, he remarked "Certainly not." At the bottom of the document the Kaiser wrote: "No more inquiry! As soon as the place has been determined, to occupy it immediately."[35]

It was indecision about the sort of place Germany ought to obtain that
delayed action. As noted, the German Foreign Ministry had thought originally
in terms of a coaling station; the navy had enlarged the concept to a naval
station and then to a base for German commerce. Ultimately Germany sought
a place which would form the starting point for a German colony in China.[36]

On May 5, 1897, Heyking reported the impressions gained by the inspection team. Neither Amoy, nor Samsah Bay, nor the harbor of Changtao, which
was formed by two little islands slightly north of the Chusan Archipelago, had
satisfied Francius and Zeye. So far they had seen only charts of Kiaochow
Bay, but they agreed that it would probably be more suitable from a technical
point of view. Zeye confirmed the assertion made by Tirpitz that Admiral
Alekseev, the commander of the tsarist fleet in East Asia, had repeatedly and
unequivocally declared that Russia had no pretensions to Kiaochow Bay. It
was possible, Zeye suggested, that the Russians had come to realize that the
acquisition on their part of a naval station far from their base of operations
would lead to a splintering of their forces. Hohenlohe speculated that the
contradiction between Alekseev's assurances and the assertions made to himself by Cassini sometime ago probably meant that Cassini, in his proposals for
concessions to be demanded from China, had gone beyond the intentions of
his government.

Although the Chinese were said to be preparing Kiaochow Bay as a naval
port of their own, Heyking did not think that their sensitivities need be spared
when it came to determining whether the bay should be considered as a base
for the influence of Germany and for the spread of her economic interests in
East Asia. As the inspection team left for Kiaochow on the warship *Kaiser*, he
sent along Interpreter Krebs to simplify the task. If any foreigners were to ask
him for the reason of the *Kaiser's* journey to Kiaochow Bay, Heyking
reported, he would reply that it was of interest to the German navy to find
out how far the Chinese had gotten in the construction of the intended
fortifications.[37]

In the light of Heyking's dispatch, Rotenhan instructed Radolin on June 22
to ascertain inconspicuously, without revealing Germany's possible intentions, whether Admiral Alekseev's utterance that Russia had no pretensions
to Kiaochow Bay corresponded to the views of influential circles in St.
Petersburg.[38]

Radolin replied on July 3 that he had taken advantage of a conversation at the Russian Foreign Ministry concerning the mission of Price Ukhtomskii to Peking and the impending visit of Chang Yin-huan, who had represented China at the Diamond Jubilee of Queen Victoria and was traveling together with Cassini from London to St. Petersburg, to touch on the desired subject. Vice Minister Lamsdorff had replied that the Chinese regarded the harbor as their best and most important one and wished to fortify it, to which the Russians had no objections. To Radolin's "casual" query why the Russia squadron which had wintered in Kiaochow Bay had left the latter to the Chinese when it had such a good location, Lamsdorff had responded that the Chinese "*étaient maîtres chez eux*" [were masters in their own place]; besides, the distance from Vladivostok seemed too great to him for Russia to be especially interested in laying claim to this harbor.

Radolin promised to keep the matter in mind and at a favorable opportunity seek to obtain a still more positive expression from Count Muraviev himself without letting on what it was all about. In view of the influence which Cassini had on Foreign Minister Muraviev in matters pertaining to China, Radolin asked for permission to sound out the former. Cassini was to be in St. Petersburg at the same time as the Kaiser. Cassini would be receptive to possible German wishes, Radolin believed, particularly since he was to get a German decoration in honor of Wilhelm's visit.[39]

Upon reading Radolin's dispatch of July 3, Hohenlohe telegraphed to Rotenhan, who was taking his place while he was at Alt-Aussee, that it was his intention to settle the question of Kiaochow Bay directly with the tsarist government during his forthcoming visit to St. Petersburg. It must hence be prevented, he cabled, that during Radolin's discussions with Cassini and particularly with Muraviev any pronouncement be made by the Russian side that would complicate his negotiations.[40]

Meanwhile the arrival of Chang Yin-huan gave Radolin the chance to query Muraviev inconspicuously about Kiaochow Bay. Was it true, he asked in the course of conversation on July 7, that the Chinese, who placed large orders for arms, even wanted to fortify Kiaochow harbor where the Russian fleet had wintered? Muraviev replied that he was aware of the fortification of the harbor, yet had no objections to it. Insofar as he knew, he added, the Russian fleet still had the right to winter there if circumstances indicated it. If all this interested Radolin, Muraviev remarked, he ought to speak to Cassini who was better informed in all Chinese matters than he himself.

Since Cassini dined at his place that evening, Radolin turned the conversation to China. No sooner had he done so than Cassini related how graciously the Kaiser had received him in Berlin and how he had spoken at length about his desire for a Chinese harbor. Cassini remarked that he fully shared Wilhelm's view that Germany needed a good station in China for the protection of her interests and ships; it was only regrettable that so much time had been lost. The moment was less favorable now; the Chinese had become much less responsive than they had been immediately after the war. One would have to wait for a good opportunity because it was of cardinal importance in China to determine the right moment for action. Cassini observed that it should not be difficult to find a suitable harbor for Germany, because it did not matter to the latter if it was located a little more to the south. On the other hand, if Russia required such a harbor, which had become less urgent in view of the excellent icebreaker in Vladivostok, its distance from the latter would be a consideration. Kiaochow Bay was alright for occasional wintering, Cassini added; in view of the intimate relations between China and Russia the fortifications would be no obstacle to this.

Radolin did not pursue the subject further for fear of revealing Germany's serious interest in Kiaochow.[41]

From August 7 to 11 Wilhelm stayed with Nicholas at Petergof, near St. Petersburg. He was accompanied by Chancellor Hohenlohe and by Bernhard von Bülow, who was then still acting secretary of foreign affairs. In a tête-à-tête, Wilhelm asked Nicholas whether Russia had any designs on Kiaochow. Nicholas replied that Russia was interested in retaining access to this bay until she had the use of another harbor, further to the north, namely Pingyüan, not far from Port Arthur. When Wilhelm inquired whether Nicholas would mind if German warships, in the absence of a German naval station, anchored in Kiaochow Bay in case of necessity upon seeking due permission from the Russian naval authorities, the tsar assured him that he had no objections.

Wilhelm informed Bülow, who by now had become the regular foreign secretary, of the exchange of views, which was then reduced to writing by Chancellor Hohenlohe. Hohenlohe's formulation was read to Muraviev and then confirmed in a letter from Hohenlohe to Muraviev. (The letter gave the more northerly port on which Russia had her eye as Pechili.) Muraviev commented that Russia had no intention to retain Kiaochow Bay permanently, though he could not say as yet when she would evacuate it. He added that Russia would like Germany to have Kiaochow Bay after she withdrew from there, if for no other reason than that Great Britain not get hold of it.[42]

Heyking notified the Chinese government that Germany had arranged with Russia concerning the possible use of Kiaochow by her warships the following winter. He ignored Li Hung-chang's objections that it was not up to St. Petersburg to give permission; that the bay was Chinese territory.[43]

When Chargé Tschirschky called on Lamsdorff in mid-October to inform him that German vessels had entered Kiaochow Bay and that he regarded the notification which he now was making as fulfilling the obligation undertaken by Germany to give due notice to Russia of such an occurrence, Lamsdorff replied that there must have been a misunderstanding. The German government was assuming that China had put Kiaochow Bay at Russia's disposal permanently and definitely. This had not been the case. At the time of the Sino-Japanese War, when her fleet had not been able to winter in Japanese ports as usual, Russia had obtained from China the right to use the harbor the following winter, that is to say only temporarily, and if he was not mistaken, Russia had even promised to stop using it as soon as possible because the Chinese government had special plans for the bay. Hence she was not in a position, in his opinion, to make arrangements concerning the harbor. Furthermore, as he recalled, it had been agreed that the commander of the German squadron would seek *prior* permission of the local Russian authorities. No Russian vessels or organs had been in Kiaochow Bay since the war. He did not see how Russia could control the use of the bay so long as she herself had no ships there. Nor did he know what sort of face the Chinese would make when German vessels suddenly appeared in the bay.[44]

Lamsdorff's comments strengthened the feeling of the German government that there was no agreement between Russia and China regarding Kiaochow whereby St. Petersburg would have had the right to object to German use of the bay. Sir Claude MacDonald subsequently confirmed to Heyking that the Chinese government had made no arrangements with Russia concerning Kiaochow, although Li Hung-chang had promised without authorization that the Russians could use the bay in the event of a war between Russia or China and Japan.[45]

Determined by now to acquire Kiaochow Bay, Berlin waited for the right pretext to seize it. As the German government had displaced that of France as the official protector of all German Catholic missions in China and as Li Ping-hêng, a noted opponent of Christianity, had become governor of Shantung Province, it was merely a matter of time before a usable incident occurred. Rumors of the kidnapping of Chinese children by foreigners added to the explosive atmosphere. Germany's opportunity came on the night of November 1, with the murder of two German missionaries, Franz Nies and Richard Heule, in Kiachwang, a small village in southwestern Shantung, by members of the Tataohui, an anti-Christian secret society.[46]

As soon as Wilhelm read about the murders in the press, he telegraphed to the German Foreign Office that "abundant atonement" [*ausgiebige Sühne*] for the attack on the German-Catholic mission which stood under his protection must be effected by energetic intervention of the navy. He commanded that the squadron steam to Kiaochow immediately, occupy it, and threaten the

severest reprisals if the Chinese government did not forthwith pay high monetary compensation and punish the culprits. Angered by Chinese unwillingness
to lease a coaling station to his country and mindful of Hsü's contention that
the Chinese understood only the language of force, Wilhelm expressed his
determination to abandon Germany's hypercautious and weak policy in East
Asia and to show the Chinese "with full severity and if necessary with the
most brutal lack of consideration [*mit brutalster Rücksichtslosigkeit*]" that
one could not trifle with the German Kaiser and that it was bad to have him for
an enemy.[47]

Hohenlohe duly instructed Heyking to demand from the Chinese government sharply compensation for the murder of the missionaries as well as for
the stoning near Hankow by the Chinese populace of the commander and a
number of officers from the German gunboat *Cormoran*, and from one of her
boats. At the same time, Hohenlohe advised Wilhelm that he must seek Russian assent before occupying Kiaochow. Nor would it be wise, Hohenlohe
thought, to seize any other place without prior consultation. Should he try to
obtain Russian consent in St. Petersburg, Hohenlohe inquired of the Kaiser.[48]

Wilhelm regarded it as humiliating that the German empire should have to
seek permission in St. Petersburg to protect and avenge her Christian pro-
tégées in China and for this purpose to make use of a point which she had not
occupied three years ago out of excessive moderateness. Yet he did so for the
good of his country, as he communicated to Bülow. He sent the following
personal telegram to Nicholas: "Chinese attacked German mission Shantung,
inflicting loss of life and property. I trust you approve according to our conversation Petergof my sending German squadron to Kiaochow, as it is the only
port available to operate from as a base against marauders. I am under obligations to Catholic party in Germany to show that their missions are really safe
under my protectorate."

Nicholas thanked Wilhelm for informing him in person and expressed his
regret over the Chinese attack on the German Catholic missions under Wilhelm's protectorate. "Cannot approve, nor disapprove Your sending German
squadron to Kiaochow as I have lately learned that this harbor only recently
had been temporarily ours in 1895–1896," he cabled. He voiced concern that
severe penalties in the east of China might cause some excitement and insecu-
rity and widen the gap between Chinese and Christians.[49]

Wilhelm informed Hohenlohe that he had already contacted Nicholas himself and that the latter had replied that he could neither approve nor disapprove
of German use of Kiaochow. (He did not pass on the tsar's misgivings about
the counterproductivity of severe punishment in eastern China.) Wilhelm
communicated to Hohenlohe that in view of Nicholas's response he had in-

structed the Navy Department to send to Admiral Otto von Diederichs the telegram he had drafted himself ordering the prompt occupation of suitable points and places in Kiaochow by the entire German squadron. "We must make immediate use of this outstanding opportunity before another great power manages to incite or aid China! [It is] now or never," the Kaiser declared to Hohenlohe.[50]

Wilhelm had acted as soon as the Chinese had presented Germany with the long-awaited pretext, convinced that German regard, influence, and prospects for commercial development were on the line. "The eyes of everyone, of the Asians as well as of the Europeans living there, are upon us and everybody asks himself whether or not we shall stand for this," he explained to Bülow.

He did not share the concern of the tsar that stern measures might worsen the situation. "Thousands of German Christians will heave a sigh [of relief] when they will know the ships of the German Kaiser to be near them, hundreds of German merchants will rejoice in the knowledge that the German Empire has at last won a firm foothold in Asia, hundreds of thousands of Chinese will tremble when they will feel the iron fist of the German Empire heavily in their neck, and the entire German people will be glad that its government has done a manly deed," Wilhelm asserted. Informing Bülow that he had communicated the tsar's reply to Hohenlohe and had ordered Diederichs to proceed to Kiaochow, he remarked that the bay would now become German despite Li Hung-chang's intrigues and Cassini's lies. In this respect the decoration for Cassini seemed to have had some effect. "Russia, as one can see from this, puts great value to have us on her side in East Asia and to keep us in good humor," Wilhelm contended. "But let the world draw from this incident once and for all the moral," he declared, "that as far as I am concerned: 'Nemo me impune lacessit' [No one hurts me with impunity]."[51]

On November 7 Hohenlohe informed Wilhelm that the Chinese had given full satisfaction for the insult of the German naval officers. It remained for Germany to demand expiation only for the murder of the missionaries. As Heyking was away from Peking traveling, he proposed to take advantage of the unavoidable delay to make sure of Russia's actual position in regard to the occupation of Kiaochow. He asked permission to instruct Tschirschky to communicate to Muraviev that Germany would direct the action which had become necessary against Kiaochow Bay and its shore if Russia did not raise any objections. In this way, he thought, it would become clear whether or not there was substance to the rumor of a secret Russo-Chinese treaty regarding Kiaochow.[52]

On November 8 Rotenhan conveyed to Tschirschky the exchange of telegrams between the Kaiser and the tsar and the subsequent orders issued to

Diederichs to occupy Kiaochow and from there to negotiate energetically concerning the expiation for the outrages committed against the German missionaries. The German government appreciated Nicholas's obligingness, Rotenhan cabled. It believed that Russian interests would not be affected, particularly since the recent establishment of a Russian coaling station on Deer Island obviated the need for possible access to Kiaochow. Diederichs and Heyking would be instructed, Rotenhan assured, to avoid any unnecessary harshness and to concentrate on securing the lives and work of the missionaries, so that in this respect too the German government was taking into account the concern of the tsar regarding the inflaming of Chinese hatred against foreigners. He ordered Tschirschky to disclose the above to Muraviev or his deputy at once in strictest confidence.[53]

On November 10 the Russian chargé d'affaires in Berlin, von der Pahlen, orally communicated to the German Foreign Ministry the text of two telegrams he had received from Muraviev. In the first, dated November 8, the Russian foreign minister cabled that after the Kaiser had informed the tsar of the massacre of the German Catholic missionaries and the consequent dispatch of the German squadron to Kiaochow, he had instructed Cassini by order of Nicholas to support the démarches which would be made by the German representative to the end of obtaining the punishment of Chinese implicated in the massacres. At the same time Admiral Alekseev had been requested that in the event the German squadron entered Kiaochow, a part of the Russian squadron be sent there too, because Russia had priority of anchorage in the port since 1895. "We hope, however, that this incident will be settled amicably between Germany and China and will render the intervention of other powers for the same unnecessary," Muraviev concluded.

In the second telegram, dated November 9, Muraviev expressed the belief of the tsarist government that the explications of the Chinese government could satisfy Germany and make the dispatch of a German squadron to Kiaochow unnecessary. But should the latter take place, he cabled, it was understood that the Russian ships would enter there not for the purpose of taking part in any hostile action but solely to the end of affirming Russia's priority of anchorage. He pointed to the likelihood that the penetration of foreign vessels into a port which China considered as closed would induce other powers to seek to profit from the example.

Muraviev's views were elaborated in a telegram sent by Tschirschky from St. Petersburg the same day. Muraviev had stated to him, Tschirschky reported, that Russia had obtained from China at the time not only permission to use the harbor temporarily during the winter of 1895–96, but the right of *premier mouillage* (first anchorage), that meant the promise that if ever the

harbor were made available to another power, Russia would have prior refusal. To protect this right, Muraviev had reiterated, Admiral Alekseev had
been ordered to send Russian vessels into harbor the moment German ships
entered it; they would not participate in German action to exact atonement for
the murder of the missionaries. Muraviev deplored the step of the German
government, because, he said, the English and perhaps also the French would
now send ships to Kiaochow Bay without one being able to hinder their doing
so. Thereby would be achieved precisely what was against the mutual interest
of Germany and Russia: the harbor would be opened first of all to England and
then to all nations. It remained an open question, he added, how China would
react to the forcible occupation of the harbor. He stressed in conclusion that he
had not discussed the matter with anyone so far.

After quoting the above three telegrams, Rotenhan observed that Muraviev
had made it sufficiently clear that the tsarist government had no intention of
leaving the possession of Kiaochow to another power should China lose it, but
that it would take Kiaochow itself. In view of the change in the situation,
brought about by the unexpected Russian explanations, and because a break
with Russia lay outside the framework of the Kaiser's policy, Rotenhan asked
Wilhelm, who was then in Gross-Strehlitz, to determine whether his order
dispatching the squadron to Kiaochow should remain in force and whether
Heyking should be supplied with the appropriate instructions.[54]

Muraviev's pronouncements irritated Wilhelm. "*Unglaublich unverschämt*
[unbelievably impudent]," he jotted in the margin of Rotenhan's dispatch next
to Muraviev's assertion at the end of the first telegram that Russia hoped that
the incident would be settled amicably between Germany and China so that
the intervention of the other powers for the same would be unnecessary. When
he read of Muraviev's claim in Tschirschky's telegram that Russia had received the right of first anchorage, he wrote sarcastically: "This he kept secret
from us and apparently from his Emperor. Li Hung-chang has recently explained specifically that Russia has nothing to say in Kiaochow." Next to the
contention that the English and perhaps the French would send ships to
Kiaochow Bay, the Kaiser noted, "Yet only if Russia calls upon them to do
so." He put two exclamation marks where Muraviev alleged that the harbor
would be opened first of all to England and then to all nations. He did not
believe Muraviev's assurance that he had not discussed the matter with anyone. He would have talked about it to Hanotaux, Wilhelm surmised. Next to
Rotenhan's observation that the tsarist government itself would take Kiaochow before letting another power have it, the Kaiser scribbled that this was
the very opposite of what both Muraviev and Nicholas had told him in
Petergof.[55]

In a telegram to Foreign Secretary Bülow, who was then in Rome, Rotenhan pointed out that the instructions which Muraviev had sent to Pahlen on the ninth differed intrinsically from Nicholas's direct reply to Wilhelm on the seventh. While Nicholas had cabled that Kiaochow had been in Russian possession only temporarily in 1895–96 and that he could therefore neither approve nor disapprove of the dispatch of the German squadron to the harbor, Muraviev claimed *priorité de mouillage* (priority of anchorage). Muraviev conveyed that Admiral Alekseev was to send part of his squadron to the bay at the same time as the German vessels to guard that Russian priority, and that Cassini was to press the Chinese to give satisfaction to the Germans in order to contribute to a friendly resolution of the conflict and thereby make superfluous the intervention of other powers. Muraviev's communication revealed, Rotenhan cabled, that the Russian mediation which Germany had not solicited was already in operation and that the possibility was raised of the intervention of other powers in addition to Russia in the event the incident was not solved peaceably.

It was evident, Rotenhan telegraphed to Wilhelm, that Russia intended to hinder the permanent occupation of Kiaochow Bay by Germany. The arrangement which had been reached in Petergof between the Kaiser and the tsar made German action and the prolonged stay of her vessels in that harbor dependent on Russian agreement. The only choice open to Germany, therefore, was either to let the German vessels enter Kiaochow Bay together with a Russian squadron and there to wait until Cassini succeeded to obtain for Germany satisfaction from the Chinese without the use of force or to direct the action intended against Kiaochow against another point on the Chinese coast, where Germany was not bound by any arrangement. To be sure, Anzer, the Roman Catholic bishop of southern Shantung Province, had asserted that there was a general agreement between Russia and China whereby the former had undertaken to protect China against the seizure of Chinese territory by any third power. But in the occupation of any other point on the Chinese coast Germany would find herself in a better position vis-à-vis Russia than in the case of Kiaochow Bay. "In Kiaochow Bay, where by ignoring Russian exception we have put ourselves in the wrong from the very outset, the Russians have the agreed upon right to restrict or to hinder our action as they please. At all other points of the Chinese coast such obstruction would no longer be a question of right, but might," Rotenhan argued. He recommended that Germany select another point for her action, for example the harbor of Changtao Island, which had also been considered by the navy. Other points suggested by the navy, such as the Chusan Islands or Wusung had the disadvantage that their occupation would irritate English sensitivity at least as much as the occupation of Kiaochow that of Russia. Even Changtao was near Chusan, that is to say close to the English sphere of interest.

Rotenhan deemed that Wilhelm might be inclined to enter into another direct exchange of thought with Nicholas to interpret the latter's telegram of the seventh, but he doubted that anything positive could be gained thereby. It was likely that Muraviev's explanations of November 9 had been sent after the usual weekly audience with the tsar and thus constituted an authentic interpretation of Nicholas's telegram. The continued retention of Kiaochow as the object of operations thus would hardly be of practical use for Germany, Rotenhan concluded.[56]

"The note of Count Muraviev corresponds fully to the character of this mendacious gentleman," Wilhelm cabled in reply to Rotenhan on November 10. Muraviev's allusion in the first telegram to intervention by other powers was an "impudence" (*Unverschämtheit*), he repeated. Whatever material differences Germany had with China, she would settle them in consonance with her honor and advantage; she did not require the intervention of other powers. As regarded the second telegram, the Kaiser continued, it was not up to Count Muraviev to decide whether or not the Chinese explications satisfied Germany, but up to himself. He pointed out that in so far as he knew Muraviev had always spoken only of Russia's right to make temporary use of Kiaochow, never of a right of first anchorage. Certainly the tsar had not known thereof. "Either Count Muraviev lied to us at the time when he kept secret the right of *premier mouillage* or now when he asserts it," Wilhelm declared. He dismissed the idea that the English or French should seek anything in Kiaochow unless they were inspired to do so by Muraviev (*wenn er es ihnen nicht suppeditiert*).

Wilhelm noted that the German squadron was already under way. He declared that the admiral could calmly carry out his "requisitions" should the Chinese reply prove unsatisfactory; at any rate, Diederichs would remain in Kiaochow for the time being. He did not believe, the Kaiser cabled, that Russia wanted to keep Kiaochow permanently, because the tsar had pointed out to him the area at the Yalu, presumably the terminal point of the Manchurian railroad, as a future harbor. Likewise Alekseev had repeatedly stated to Diederichs that he had no pretensions to Kiaochow. The Russians did not want to entrench themselves there, since they would be too far from their base from a military point of view.

"One should try to come to an arrangement with Russia to obtain the right to Kiaochow, if need be by purchase," Wilhelm telegraphed. "Russia too will bow before absolute facts and certainly start no war over Kiaochow, because we are indispensable to her in the Orient. All this can be arranged diplomatically; what cannot be tolerated, however, is that Count Muraviev assume toward us disloyal action with a haughty protector-like tone. What is taking place is happening after the most loyal agreement and exchange of views with His Majesty the Tsar directly, and I rely on his words. If Count Muraviev has not informed his master properly or does not like the agreement, that is his business; it does not concern me. I think the price for Kiaochow will be somewhat high, but hardly exorbitant," he concluded.[57]

In a preliminary response to the Kaiser's telegram of the tenth, Hohenlohe pointed to the passage that the admiral who was on his way to Kiaochow Bay could carry out his requisitions in case the Chinese answer was unsatisfactory. He interpreted this to mean, he cabled to Wilhelm who was then in Silesia, that the Kaiser wished Diederichs to refrain from a proclamation and from the occupation of Chinese territory until the Chinese reply was received and was found to be unsatisfactory and asked for instructions whether to arrange for this through the High Command. In the event that the order was received too late and the admiral should have gone further, Hohenlohe requested permission to direct the latter to act in such a way as not to prejudice later diplomatic negotiations. Otherwise, he feared, the diplomatic negotiations would be doomed from the start.[58]

Wilhelm gave the desired approval, but as Hohenlohe had apprehended, it reached the Far East too late to deter Diederichs.[59]

In another, lengthy telegram later in the day, Hohenlohe communicated to Wilhelm the text of a statement that he was about to make to the Russian ambassador orally and in writing. "Never, since the beginning of world history, has a political question been handled more openly and loyally than the Kiaochow question on the part of our most gracious Ruler vis-à-vis the Kaiser of Russia," the note began. It related how Germany had obtained repeated assurances from Russia—from Lamsdorff, from the admiral in the East Asian waters, and finally from the tsar himself—that she had no rights or claims to Kiaochow Bay and how Diederichs had been dispatched there only following the exchange of views between the two sovereigns. Yet two days after the receipt of Nicholas's telegram, Muraviev depicted the position of Russia in regard to the Kiaochow question in a way which completely contradicted the communication of the tsar. "The personality of Count Muraviev suffices to dispel the suspicion that one had waited on Russia's part until our action had been initiated in order to confront us then suddenly and unexpectedly with the choice between a political *échec* [check] or a worsening of our relations with Russia," Hohenlohe stated to Osten-Sacken. "We are convinced instead that Count Muraviev did not know the text of the telegram of his emperor to ours when he made those assertions." He expressed confidence that Muraviev, upon learning of the said telegram, would understand that the Kaiser could not accept a political failure which would be difficult for his own position and that of his empire both internally and externally.

Having quoted the text of the statement he was about to make to Osten-Sacken, Hohenlohe commented to Wilhelm that he did not fear the imminence of a conflict with a European power. He did expect, however, that the Russians and the French would try to incite the Chinese against them, as had been done previously in the case of the Abyssinians against the Italians. He warned that the main result of an actual state of war with China would be to ruin German trade in that country for decades to the advantage of England.[60]

Hohenlohe's assumption that Muraviev may not have known the content of Nicholas's telegram at the time he made his assertions appears to have been correct. At least Muraviev told Radolin with some embarrassment in mid-December that a draft cable had been sent from Tsarskoe Selo to St. Petersburg for his perusal, but when one had not been able to find him right away, the tsar had dispatched the cable without his seeing it.

The Kaiser praised the text of Hohenlohe's note. In regard to the chancelor's apprehension that the Russians and the French might instigate the Chinese against the Germans as the Abyssinians had been set against the Italians, Wilhelm commented in the margin: "With the difference that the Chinese are no warriors. I fear nothing from China; [we must] only remain firm and tread firmly, what we have never yet done there and are now doing for the first time. I am thoroughly convinced that everything will end well. But 'landgrave become hard' like a boulder of bronze."[61]

In a telegram to Count von Hatzfeldt, the German ambassador in London, Hohenlohe speculated that Muraviev would not have dared to speak the way he did had it not been for Germany's bad relations with England. He asked Hatzfeldt to consider whether some outwardly useful step toward the improvement of Anglo-German relations could not be undertaken to shake Muraviev's confidence in this direction. Furthermore, if Germany, as he feared, would be forced to withdraw from Kiaochow upon the receipt of the demanded compensation, it would be highly desirable for her to consider the occupation of one of the other points on the Chinese coast proposed by the Germany navy, all of which lay near the British sphere of interest. A rapprochement with England would be of benefit from this point of view as well.[62]

In a subsequent telegram to Hatzfeldt, Hohenlohe pointed out that to his mind the danger in the near future lay not so much in a war between Germany and Russia, but in the possible price of an understanding between them. He therefore gave Hatzfeldt a free hand to suggest to the British premier, Lord Salisbury, in his own name that it would be to England's advantage to meet German demands somewhere, even in Samoa, at this time.[63]

On November 14 Osten-Sacken transmitted to Hohenlohe a telegram from Muraviev, dated the thirteenth, reminding him that the letter Hohenlohe had addressed to him from Petergof on August 10 and the secret note which Radolin had remitted to him on September 4 had recognized Russia's priority of anchorage and made the entry of German warships into Kiaochow Bay subject to prior agreement with the Russian naval authorities.[64]

Hohenlohe retorted that whatever pronouncements may have been made by either side prior to the dispatch of Nicholas's telegram were nullified by the imperial declaration.[65]

That day, on November 14, Diederichs arrived at Kiaochow Bay. Since the telegram ordering him to stay his hand until the Chinese reply to Heyking's démarche had been evaluated had not reached him, he proceeded to land 700 men and issued an ultimatum to the Chinese garrison to withdraw. As the numerically superior Chinese force pulled out without firing a shot, leaving behind all heavy weapons, Deiderichs raised the German flag over the Chinese installations and proclaimed the occupation of Kiaochow by his country.[66]

On November 15 Wilhelm presided over a conference in the palace of the chancelor, attended by Hohenlohe, Rotenhan, Commanding Admiral Knorr, Navy Secretary Admiral Tirpitz, Chief of the Navy Cabinet Admiral Baron Gustav von Senden und Bibran, and Adjutant General Hans von Plessen. It was agreed that the permanent seizure (Besitzergreifung) of Kiaochow Bay was intended.[67] Wilhelm remarked that he clung to the telegraphic assent of the tsar. Thankful for German support of Russian policy in East Asia, Nicholas had informed him already two years ago of his concurrence that Germany take a harbor in China. The Kaiser deemed that Kiaochow did not hold any special interest for Russia, because it lay south and outside of the Gulf of Pechili; besides, Russia could always send her fleet there. Consequently, he was confident that Russia would not go to war over the bay. At the same time, Wilhelm was convinced, the seizure of territory would be greeted with jubilation by the German public and the intervention for the protection of the Catholic missions would arouse the appreciation and support of the Center Party in the Reichstag. The conferees wished to determine, if possible within the next five or six days, whether any European power, notably Russia, would oppose in words or deeds the permanent seizure of Kiaochow by Germany. If not, a colonial force of 1,200 men was to be recruited and sent there at once as the warships could not leave their crews on shore for any length of time without harming maritime interests. Additional warships were to be dispatched as well. Until the political situation in Europe had been determined, the German intention was to be kept secret. Until then only such preparations were to be made in the ministries as could be undertaken without attracting attention. To prevent China from waging war against Germany, her sovereign rights were to be preserved if possible in the occupation of the territory, perhaps by taking the land merely as a long-term lease. "Our demands on China are to be set so high that they cannot be fulfilled and thus will justify the subsequent [seizure]," the conferees concluded.[68]

On November 16 Osten-Sacken communicated to the German government a telegram from Muraviev to the effect that the Chinese ministers had declared to Chargé Pavlov in response to the démarches which he had made that they would do everything to give to Germany immediately the fullest satisfaction on the basis of the precedents established in the case of similar demands made by France, England, and the United States, to wit, the capital punishment of the criminals, financial compensation to the families of the victims, and the exemplary punishment of the Chinese authorities, recognized as culpable of not having taken the necessary measures to prevent the massacres. The emperor of China had already published an edict in this sense.

Hohenlohe thanked Osten-Sacken for his communication in a brief answer. "It has not come to my knowledge so far that the minister of Germany who was traveling at the time of the massacre has already presented our claims to the Chinese government," he wrote.[69]

Heyking had indeed not done so yet and the Russian action was regarded in Berlin as premature, to say the least. Wilhelm was annoyed at the unrequested Russian intervention at Peking. When Chargé Tschirschky on the seventeenth relayed the assertions of Muraviev concerning the satisfaction given up by China, the Kaiser reiterated that it was not up to Muraviev but up to himself alone to judge German-Chinese relations and what was to be demanded and conceded.[70]

On November 17 Osten-Sacken transmitted to Hohenlohe a telegram from Muraviev, dated the sixteenth. It declared that Nicholas was "very much surprised" at the interpretation given to his personal reply to Wilhelm. In the tsar's eyes his cable had not changed the situation in anything. In accordance with declarations made by the Chinese government, Russia considered the port of Kiaochow closed to foreign squadrons, but the moment other foreign ships penetrated there, Russia's priority of anchorage remained in force.[71]

Submitting Muraviev's telegram to the Kaiser, Hohenlohe pointed out that its tone and content made it clear that the tsar had been brought to believe that Wilhelm wanted to make use of his direct reply unfairly to the damage of

Russian rights, which he had never intended to forfeit. Nicholas's self-love would find it difficult to overcome such an impression, Hohenlohe remarked. Under the circumstances, he recommended a dilatory approach: to point out to the tsar that the Russian fleet could, of course, stay in Kiaochow Bay and that Germany and Russia would without doubt come to an understanding about further matters. This would give Germany time to determine the position of the other powers, particularly of England.[72]

The Kaiser fully agreed with Hohenlohe's communication. "The infamous right of *premier mouillage* will in no wise be impaired by our occupation and subsequent seizure," he wrote. "The Russians can lie there and anchor until they become black or yellow. But this cannot hinder us from constructing there a coaling station and docks."

Wilhelm noted further that General Strykov, whom he knew well, had told him that day during dinner at the Alexander Regiment: "In the name of God remain there, you are our only sincere friend, we do not want to have other people near us! You would be like a sentinel vis-à-vis us and would aid us to defend our common interests against Japan above all. The Russian army loves you, it has confidence in you and it is in grief because of that fanfaronade with the French Republic; the army would be grateful to you for feeling on our side and supposes that you will remain for good and all at Kiaochow."[73]

The demands for compensation which Heyking presented to the Tsungli Yamen on November 20 were as follows: (1) the dismissal of Governor Li Ping-heng; (2) the construction of the cathedral begun by Bishop Anzer at the expense of the Chinese government and the erection of a board announcing imperial protection; (3) severe punishment of all culprits and full compensation; (4) a guarantee against the repetition of similar incidents; (5) compensation of the German empire for all costs arising from the event; and (6) the giving of priority to German entrepreneurs in the construction of a railroad with mining enterprises in Shantung Province.[74]

Prince Kung replied that there was nothing in the above demands concerning which the Chinese government could not negotiate amicably, but first Chinese territory must be evacuated. Then one could negotiate perhaps also about a naval station.

Heyking countered that evacuation was the one point which he could not discuss. He argued that no assault on China had taken place, as the Chinese government had allowed the continuation of amicable relations by voluntarily withdrawing its troops. The conversation was conducted in a friendly tone, and the Tsungli Yamen promised a written reply in several days.

Pavlov related to Heyking that he had communicated to the Tsungli Yamen that it was the hope of the tsarist government that the provisional German occupation would end soon, but that the Chinese government must pay just compensation. The Russians had advised Peking to grant if possible everything that Germany demanded so as to force the latter morally to withdraw. The Chinese, however, desired to obtain the evacuation first in order to concede as little as possible, Heyking reported. Germany must not agree to prior evacuation, he telegraphed.[75]

The Chinese demand that Germany evacuate Kiaochow as a precondition for negotiation concerning the compensation due Germany infuriated the Kaiser. "This impudence is bottomless!" he scribbled in the margin of a report from Hohenlohe. "Has been prompted by Muraviev and Hanotaux." It was the more important to hasten the dispatch of the vessels, he added.

Hohenlohe drafted a mild rebuff of the Chinese demand. The German government did not doubt the intention of the Chinese central government to do justice to the German demands, he wrote. But it was Germany's experience that the Chinese central government was not always able to force the provincial authorities to carry out such directives. Germany would prefer it, therefore, to watch herself over the execution of the pertinent orders and would hence remain in Kiaochow for the time being.

"One can always become more specific later," Hohenlohe remarked to the Kaiser. "For the time being all equivocations of whatever sort through which the Chinese government seeks to evade making reparations are still useful for our purposes, as we are thereby exempted from the necessity of showing our cards earlier than it suits us."[76]

Heyking reported on November 22 that the note received from the Tsungli Yamen declined negotiations concerning the demands for compensation until the German troops as well as ships had been withdrawn. He had learned from a reliable source, he telegraphed, that Pavlov and the French chargé d'affaires, Count René de Sercey, had advised the Tsungli Yamen to drag out the matter without yielding anything, as Germany would be forced to withdraw. He therefore asked for permission to declare to the Tsungli Yamen that until the settlement of the compensation demands the Germans would retain the occupied territory as security and would set up a provisional administration.

"*Ja*," approved the Kaiser.[77]

That day Rotenhan addressed to Osten-Sacken a reply to Muraviev's telegram of the sixteenth. The Kaiser, he wrote, wanted the tsar to be informed of a number of considerations. The most important of these—and the conversations and telegrams between Wilhelm and Nicholas regarding Kiaochow were recounted again—was that the Kaiser had dispatched the squadron only after the tsar's reply had revealed no reservations concerning such action. "It is fitting to recall here," Rotenhan declared, "that the government of His Majesty the Emperor of Germany had through a démarche made at St. Petersburg in March 1895 offered its cooperation and likewise had taken the initiative in the joint diplomatic action which had checked the progress of the Japanese in Korea and on the continent." As a result of the tripartite intervention Russia had been able to incorporate in the zone of her exclusive influence not only Korea but all the northern portion of China up to and including Peking and the inner part of the Yellow Sea. Germany, on the other hand, had seen her position in the Far East threatened, as evidenced by the series of affronts, insults and heinous crimes directed against the Germans—missionaries, seamen, and others. The only possible explanation for this phenomenon, Rotenhan suggested, was that hostile influences had cast doubt on the spontaneity of German cooperation in 1895 and had interpreted the disinterestedness shown by Germany since then as a symptom of weakness. Whatever the cause, he stated, it was patent that Germany found herself vis-à-vis China in an unworthy position which the Kaiser must remedy by all means at his disposal. "His Majesty believes that His Majesty the Emperor of Russia, whose policy he has backed in Asia as in Europe and whose opinion he had solicited in the present case before acting, will find himself in accord with him in the thought that at this time any modification made in the plan of action already under way would confirm the Chinese government and people in an attitude incompatible with the interests as well as the dignity of Germany," Rotenhan communicated. It was hardly necessary to add, he concluded, that the presence of the Germans in Kiaochow Bay would not constrain Russian vessels wanting to stay there so long as Russia did not have permanent establishments in the interior Yellow Sea.[78]

The same day, on November 22, Wilhelm swore in the navy recruits at Kiehl. At his invitation the officers and a detachment of men from the Russian cruiser *Vladimir Monomakh*, which was lying in the harbor, attended the ceremony. After the swearing-in, the Kaiser called for three hurrahs for the tsar. During the dinner which followed, Wilhelm drank to Nicholas as honorary admiral of Germany and to the *Waffenbrüderschaft* (brothers-in-arms relationship) of the Russian and German fleets in all seas. The Russians responded with enthusiasm. The Russian commander, Prince Pavel Petrovich Ukhtomskii, spoke warmly in English of the indissoluble friendship of the two fleets and of the honorable admiral of the Russian fleet, the German Kaiser. Asked by Prince Heinrich, Wilhelm's brother and chief of the Second East Asian Squadron, how the Kiaochow question was being regarded in Russia, Ukhtomskii responded that the Russians had neither designs nor interests there and were extraordinarily glad to have the Germans at their side in that bay.[79]

In the afternoon Wilhelm went aboard the *Vladimir Monomakh*. In the officer's mess Ukhtomskii toasted him first as Kaiser, then as "his" admiral. Wilhelm in turn gave a toast in Russian to the health of the tsar. When bidding farewell, he declared that Nicholas could rest assured that as in 1895 so at any time he could see his vessels at the side of his own when it came to warding off danger and distress from wherever it might come. He was proud, the Kaiser added, to see the admiral's flag, which Nicholas had bestowed on him when naming him Russian admiral during his visit to Petergof earlier in the year, flying from the main mast of a Russian ship for the first time.[80]

The Kaiser's evident purpose in all these public professions of friendship for the tsar was to incline the latter more favorably toward the Kiaochow question. And in this Wilhelm succeeded, for Russian policy hereafter became increasingly friendly.[81]

Meanwhile Yano Fumio, the Japanese minister at Peking, alleged that the Russian "minister"—he probably meant Chargé Pavlov—had promised to the Chinese government to rendezvous the Russian fleet in the China Seas and to protest against German occupation of Kiaochow Bay. The question remained, however, to what extent Russia would actually assist China. Noting that England, in spite of her sympathy with Germany, would not cooperate in any move, Yano ventured to suggest that Japan herself help China if Germany's occupation continued, so as to have sufficient ground in the future to protest against the cession of Chinese territory "near or remote from Taiwan" to any power. In view of Russian naval movements, Yano wanted Japan to dispatch her fleet to these waters as well as to watch whether the German occupation was to be temporary or permanent. The fact that the tripartite intervention of 1895 had forced the Japanese to retrocede the Liaotung Peninsula on the plea that the peace of the East would be endangered by the cession of a portion of the continent to another power offered a "good pretext" for a Japanese protest in the present case, Yano pointed out.[82]

But the Japanese government proceeded with great caution. Sharing the general belief that Germany would not have acted without a prior understanding with Russia, whose fleet had wintered at Kiaochow Bay, it hesitated to formulate a policy until it was certain of the extent of the German demands and of the attitude of the other powers.[83] It was premature, Nishi replied to Yano, to decide definitively in what way Japan could best assist China. It was "highly desirable" he pointed out, "not only for China and Japan, but for [the] peace of the East" that the Sino-German dispute be adjusted promptly and without recourse to arms. He instructed Yano to use every means at his disposal "to induce China to settle the matter accordingly."[84]

Yano called on Li Hung-chang at the Tsungli Yamen and spoke of amicable relations between their countries. Responding in kind, Li asked for his assistance in inducing the German minister to enter into negotiations with the Chinese government at once. When Yano conveyed Li's desire to Heyking upon his return from the Tsungli Yamen, the German minister appeared much pleased. He promised to advise Berlin to hasten negotiation.[85]

Muraviev told Hayashi that the German government had given notice to Russia of the probable occupation of Kiaochow Bay as a coercive measure, but that there was no further understanding between Russia and Germany. In his opinion, he said, the occupation was related to the Kaiser's policy to obtain the consent of the Reichstag for the augmentation of the German navy. He revealed that the tsarist government had instructed Pavlov to assist Heyking in obtaining satisfaction. He added that the Russian fleet had not used Kiaochow as a winter station since the preceding year.[86]

The Japanese chargé d'affaires in Berlin, like Muraviev, linked the occupation of Kiaochow with German domestic politics. As elections for the Reichstag were to be held the following year, the government wooed the public with a strong foreign policy and would probably embark on a program of naval expansion. "[The] present occupation, whether prolonged or terminated by [the] counter-action of [the] Powers, will be certainly used to arouse patriotic feeling," Miyaoka telegraphed.[87]

When Yano reported that most members of the diplomatic corps believed that Germany had asked for a monopoly on the construction of railroads and adjoining mines in Shantung Province,[88] Nishi replied that such a demand would be "highly objectionable to Japan." It was the desire of his government that China not agree to this or if she could not resist German pressure, that she limit the concessions to a specific railroad line and to mines in particular localities. In the event that the above concessions were granted, Japan wanted China to open Kiaochow to the commerce of all treaty powers. Nishi instructed Yano to suggest the above confidentially to Li Hung-chang. He asked Yano to exert his "best endeavors" toward that end, but cautioned him at the same time to take care that his action "may not be construed by Germany as interference on the part of [the] Japanese Government."[89]

Asked by Foreign Minister Hanotaux about the views of the tsarist government concerning the German action in China, Mohrenheim replied that one must make the best of a situation which one could not prevent. It was evident from the conversations he had had with Cassini and Admiral Alekseev, who were presently in Paris, Mohrenheim continued, that his government desired the departure of the German forces from Kiaochow Bay and was disposed to offer its support to Berlin in obtaining from China in exchange for Kiaochow Bay another point, not located inside the sphere of influence of Russia or close to her border.[90]

Witte raised the question of substituting another bay for Kiaochow in a conversation with Radolin on November 25. He voiced concern that the German occupation of Kiaochow would force Russia to take a Chinese harbor to the north of it, which in turn would induce Japan to entrench herself on the Chinese mainland, presumably in Korea, and this would then lead inevitably to a Russo-Japanese war, a war in which Russia could expect no more than moral help from Germany and France. Witte counseled, therefore, that Germany take instead of Kiaochow a harbor to the south of Shanghai, so that neither Russia nor Japan would be compelled to seek compensation.

Upon consulting Bülow, Radolin replied that far from damaging the Russian interests, the German seizure of Kiaochow offered to Russia the greatest imaginable security, for it forced Germany to rely more on Russia and consequently would compel also France to go along with Russia, just as in the tripartite intervention of 1895. Were Germany forced to take territory neighboring unto the British sphere of interest, the same logic of facts would point to her support of the Far Eastern policy of England.

Witte seemed persuaded by these arguments and made no further objections to the seizure of Kiaochow. He merely advised that it be carried out in a manner most bearable for China, such as by an apparent lease.[91]

Osten-Sacken discussed the Kiaochow question with Bülow on November 30 in a complaining and sad rather than irritated or even threatening tone. He lamented that the misunderstanding which had occurred between their governments might leave a residue of ill feeling. He could not understand, he said repeatedly, why Germany would not recognize Russia's priority of anchorage.

Bülow retorted that Germany had no objections to Russian warships also entering Kiaochow Bay occasionally, but that the alleged right of priority of anchorage advanced by Russia was not applicable to Germany. In his view there were two aspects to the Kiaochow question, an objective and a personal one. In regard to the first, Bülow reminded Osten-Sacken that Germany had been of great service to Russia for many years both materially and morally not only in the Near East but also in the Far East. Russia owed it to a large extent to the position of Germany that Japan had not entrenched herself in the Korean peninsula during the Sino-Japanese War. He was surprised, Bülow said, that Russia had not welcomed the German occupation of Kiaochow, for the action was in her interest; it would make it easier for Germany to stand by Russia's side against Japan and any other opponents. He reiterated that Germany could just as well have occupied another point on the Chinese coast, but that in such a case she would have had to seek cooperation with England. For the time being, Germany preferred to throw the weight of her might and influence to Russia rather than to another power.

As for the personal aspect of the question. Bülow continued, the Kaiser had proceeded most loyally. He could not conceive, he declared, that the Russian side or even the tsar himself could attribute to the Germans things which would impair their dignity and authority and thus would be completely unacceptable for them. He assured Osten-Sacken that Germany was prepared to continue the confidential exchange of views concerning the Kiaochow question in a friendly and loyal spirit and was sure that no trace of misunderstanding would remain in this regard. He hoped that the entire process would, on the contrary, lead to the strenghthening of good relations between their countries.

The overall impression which Bülow gained from the interview with Osten-Sacken was that Russia did not want to fall out with Germany over Kiaochow. It was evident at the same time that Muraviev found it very unpleasant that the fat morsel of Kiaochow, which he had wanted for his own land, had been snatched by someone else and that in this matter a contradiction between his views and that of the tsar had been exposed. Osten-Sacken thus faced the task of extracting Muraviev from this embarrassing situation fairly gently. "It seems to me," Bülow wrote, "that in this state of affairs we should remain in a calm but unshakably firm defensive position, yet on the other hand avoid to the extent that it is up to us what could needlessly embitter the director of the Russian policy; indeed we should make it as easy as possible for him to withdraw from his indefensible position."[92]

That day Wilhelm personally opened the session of the Reichstag. As expected, he pointed in his speech to the insufficiency of the imperial navy in protecting the growing commerce of Germany and declared that the federal government had come to the conclusion that the extent and speed of naval construction must be determined by legislation. When he related that the assassination of German missionaries and the attack on the mission house had compelled him to send his East Asiatic squadron to Kiaochow Bay and to land troops there to obtain full reparations and a guarantee against the repetition of similar events, the members of the Reichstag and of the Federal Council enthusiastically cheered "Bravo!"[93]

On December 1 Muraviev told Tschirschky that he had replied to diplomats who had asked him about the Kiaochow question during his interviews that day that Kiaochow had been a closed port and that Russia, in spite of her right of first anchorage, could make no objections to the entry of the German ships. To the further query what Germany's ultimate designs were in the occupation of Kiaochow, he had answered that he did not know.[94]

Although the German government did not agree with the reassertion of Russia's priority of anchorage, Bülow was pleased by the conciliatory tone of

Muraviev's remarks. Henceforth, he expected, less attention would be paid in the discussion of the Kiaochow question to the issue of the bay itself than to the "world-determining significance of good German-Russian relations." Germany, he telegraphed to St. Petersburg, would be glad at any time to equalize the advantages which she had gained in Kiaochow by reciprocal action in support of Russia.[95]

Radolin reiterated to Muraviev how important it was for both of their countries to cooperate and thereby to forestall any attempts to create complications out of the situation. It would be a significant advantage for the interests of Russia, he argued, if Germany became her neighbor in East Asia.[96]

In a brief speech in the Reichstag concerning the German navy on December 6, Bülow alluded to the Kiaochow question. "We do not want to put anyone in the shade," he declared, "but at the same time we demand our place in the sun. In East Asia as in the West Indies we shall strive, faithful to the traditions of German policy, to maintain our interests without unnecessary harshness but also without weakness."[97]

Lord Salisbury regarded the German proceedings at Kiaochow as violent and contrary to international usage even though the acquisition of a coaling station by Germany would not in itself injure British interests. What worried him, Salisbury revealed to Minister Kato, was that the actions of Germany might be emulated by other powers and thus entail serious consequences. Noting that the German attitude might be made clearer after the fate of the naval bill just presented to the Reichstag was decided, Salisbury held out the possibility that if Germany pressed China too much, he might offer terms to Russia and ask for her intervention.[98]

Muraviev told Chargé Vauvineux that he was not alarmed so far by the action of Germany in Kiaochow, believing as did Salisbury that it would be very difficult for her to occupy such an unsafe bay (*une baie aussi peu sûre*) permanently. "You can assure M. Hanotaux," he declared, "that, contrary to the assertions of the newspapers, there have never been exchanges of views between Russia and Germany on this subject. There has been no question of the occupation of the above-mentioned point except in the telegram addressed directly to the Emperor [Nicholas] by the Emperor Wilhelm. . . ." Muraviev characterized the German action as contrary to international law, but doubted that it could have grave consequences, because of its domestic orientation: the desire of Wilhelm to demonstrate to the Reichstag the need for an increase in the naval budget and to gain the Catholic vote by his support of the missions.[99]

On December 6 Radolin reiterated to Muraviev the arguments he had already presented to Witte. The foreign minister seemed equally receptive and spoke no longer of the right of first anchorage, but merely of the fact of the first entry of Russian vessels, which he called a "privilege" rather than a "right." The latter, Muraviev added, would presuppose a treaty stipulation with China to this effect.[100] Radolin once more stressed the importance for Germany and Russia as neighbors to stick together against common enemies.[101]

The Chinese had tried to break up the Russo-German combine. Li Hung-chang, who had become a member of the Tsungli Yamen upon his return from the West, had been sent to the tsarist legation on November 15 with a request for Russian aid. But St. Petersburg at the time had refused to dispatch a squadron to Kiaochow, asserting that it had entered into negotiations with Berlin in defense of China.[102] The Chinese government also appealed to Japan and Great Britain, but as neither seemed eager to intervene, the upper hand was gained in Peking by officials who questioned the advisability of soliciting foreign assistance. The traditional policy of using "barbarians" to fight "barbarians" was alright so long as China was strong, but when she was weak there was the danger that the user would become the used. China's only recourse, Chang Yin-huan argued, lay in self-strengthening and self-reliance. It was decided, therefore, to go ahead and negotiate directly with the Germans, Weng T'ung-ho and Chang Yin-huan being appointed imperial commissioners.[103]

On November 28 Weng and Chang informed Heyking that the Chinese government would for the time being not raise the issue of the evacuation of Kiaochow and that they could thus proceed with the settlement of the reparations question.[104] On December 3 they came to the German legation again to declare China's readiness to accept the German demands. They asked that the straitened financial position of their country be taken into consideration in calculating the compensation for the expenses incurred by Germany. The Chinese officials agreed that the occupation of Kiaochow was to continue until the fulfillment of the demands, including the completion of the cathedral and two other churches. They were willing, they said, to affirm the acceptance of the German claims in an exchange of notes.

As Heyking was evasive when Chang and Weng asked whether the Germans would withdraw from Kiaochow once all their demands had been met, the two mandarins pleaded that China was unable to offer any resistance; other powers would take advantage thereof following the German advance, and China would stand on the verge of destruction. They proposed, therefore, in strictest secrecy that the Germans evacuate Kiaochow and take another harbor in the south instead. "I answered dilatorily, but pointed out that it would be advantageous for China herself if Germany possessed a strong position in the north," Heyking reported.[105]

On December 7 Weng and Chang paid their third visit to Heyking.[106] Empowered by Emperor Kuang-hsü to conduct secret negotiations, they proposed that the cession of a naval station be considered separately from the missionary incident, with reference to the intervention regarding Liaotung.[107]

Heyking suggested, therefore, that after Germany had declared the missionary matter fully settled and had renounced compensation for the expenses she had incurred, Kuang-hsü hand over Kiaochow Bay to Prince Heinrich of his own free decision and out of gratitude for the return of Liaotung. The mandarins accepted the proposal in principle, but made a counter-offer: Kiaochow to be made a treaty port; China to promise that the latter would not be ceded to any other power; Germany to be granted a settlement and the right of railroad construction at Kiaochow and to receive in addition another harbor in the south. When Heyking insisted on Kiaochow, the officials did not say No, but asked that their proposal be submitted to the Kaiser since it would restore the prestige of China. The Chinese demanded that the Germans evacuate Kiaochow before any harbor be handed over and before Prince Heinrich arrived.

In his report Heyking expressed the view that the acceptance of a southern port together with the privilege granted in Kiaochow appeared to be more favorable for Germany. For the Chinese the advantage lay in maintaining the outward appearance and in securing Kiaochow against any claims. He added that the Chinese were pressing extraordinarily for the prompt conclusion of a settlement with Germany for fear, he believed, of territorial inroads by England or Japan.[108]

On December 8 Li Hung-chang, on his own authority, once again appealed through Pavlov for a Russian naval demonstration at Kiaochow, believing that the Germans could not be induced to pull out by words alone. When he informed the Tsungli Yamen of what he had done, Weng T'ung-ho complained to the emperor and Li was ordered to withdraw the request immediately. As Pavlov had already forwarded Li's plea, the Chinese minister in St. Petersburg was instructed to communicate to the Russian Foreign Ministry that China did not wish to create complications between Russia and Germany on her account and that no naval demonstration was necessary.[109]

The German Foreign Ministry, meanwhile, rejected the linking of the cession of Kiaochow with Germany's role in the Liaotung question. As Holstein wrote in a memorandum on December 8, Germany had acted at that time jointly with Russia and with France. Although the two powers had derived various benefits from the tripartite intervention, they had so far not demanded any territory as remuneration. Should Germany now suddenly, after almost three years, demand territorial advantages for herself alone, specifically as compensation for her participation in that action, Russia and France could thereupon choose either to seek corresponding concessions for themselves (something no longer desirable for Germany, he remarked parenthetically) or to object with apparent justification that Germany wished to derive from this common proceeding for herself alone advantages which Russia and France had renounced in order not to bear the responsibility for the collapse of the Chinese empire.[110] Nor did Berlin agree to take a southern port proffered by Peking, though this might have given her more than she had actually demanded. The German government suspected that the plan might not have originated in China and that (contrary to what it had repeatedly threatened to St. Petersburg) the possession of a southern port would push Germany into a permanent association with those powers which pursued an anti-British policy. (At least that was the explanation Bülow subsequently cabled to Hatzfeldt in London).[111]

Wilhelm decreed that no reference be made to the Liaotung action in the agreement concerning Kiaochow. Any other motivation would be preferable.

Bülow instructed Heyking on December 12 to convey to the tsarist representative in Peking that Germany was conscious that by entrenching herself below the Russian sphere of interest she would enter into a permanent community of interest with Russia and was prepared to proceed accordingly. In 1895 France had been averse to action against Japan for fear of worsening her relations with England, but had been drawn along by the unwillingness to let Russia and Germany operate alone. In the future too, Bülow held out, Russia would always be able to count on France against Japan and her friends if German participation was secured in advance. The German settlement in Kiaochow, he contended, thus at least doubled the Russian position in East Asia. On the other hand, he reiterated, were Germany to take instead a place next to the English sphere of interest, she would have to support English policy in compensation.[112]

When Heyking told the Chinese negotiators on December 15 that Germany was not willing to accept any harbor in place of Kiaochow, they replied that China would have been ready to cede the latter had MacDonald not demanded of the Tsungli Yamen a harbor for England as soon as one was yielded to Germany. Japan had allegedly made a similar statement, and demands from other sides would follow. The mandarins finally suggested that Germany be allowed to retain Kiaochow silently, without mention of any length and without a written agreement.[113]

Meanwhile the Germans continued to strengthen their military position. By early December they had occupied all the territory which surrounded the bay, including the Chinese administrative centers. On December 17 Prince Heinrich left Germany for Kiaochow with close to 1,500 marines and naval artillerymen, Wilhelm's farewell speech ringing in his ears: "Make it clear to every European there, to the German merchant and, above all things, to the foreigner in whose country we are . . . that the German Michael has set his shield, decorated with the imperial eagle, firmly on the ground. Whoever asks him for protection will always receive it. . . . But if anyone should undertake to insult us in our rights or wish to harm us, then drive in with the mailed fist and, as God wills, bind about your young brow the laurels which no one in the entire German Empire will begrudge you."[114]

On December 25 Chang and Weng called on Heyking to accept the German demands only to find that they had grown. Germany required a concession for the construction of a railroad from Tsingtao to Tsinan instead of the general provision for priority in railroad construction in Shantung Province. She also sought the lease of all Kiaochow Bay, not just one shore, as the Chinese desired. Heyking added that his government would not consider the missionary case closed until the Kiaochow lease had been granted.

The Chinese negotiators tried to modify the terms in another meeting on the twenty-eighth, pleading once again that other powers would present similar demands if China gave in.

Although the Chinese government had countermanded Li Hung-chang's recent request for a Russian naval demonstration at Kiaochow, Russian warships had arrived at Port Arthur ostensibly in response to Li's prior plea of November 15. Whatever hopes the Chinese may have had that further procrastination might lead to Russian eviction of the Germans from Kiaochow was undermined by Heyking, who told Weng bluntly that Pavlov's assurances to the contrary, the Russians had not come to defend China but to seize Port Arthur for themselves.[115]

Any doubt that the Chinese may have entertained about the allegation of the German minister was soon dispelled by St. Petersburg. In response to continued pressure from Berlin for the backing of the "moderate" German demands on the ground that a favorable and speedy conclusion of the German negotiations with China would not only have a calming effect throughout East Asia but would provide Germany with the possibility of giving Russia effective support,[116] Nicholas had agreed to assist the German leasehold claims as a practical manifestation of the "hand-in-hand policy" of the two powers. On December 29 Muraviev counseled the new Chinese minister in St. Petersburg, Yang Ju, to accede to the wishes of Germany who, he said, was fully in harmony with Russia. When Yang asked whether Russia would not then want a harbor too, Muraviev replied that Germany needed a harbor because of her enormous trade; Russia with her small commerce did not require one at the moment. Russia had one harbor (he undoubtedly was thinking of Vladivostok) and this was sufficient; two harbors would be too expensive.[117]

With every passing day the German demands seemed to increase. On December 29 Heyking conveyed to the Tsungli Yamen a draft lease agreement, which provided for a 99-year lease of both sides of Kiaochow Bay, including the city of Tsingtao and all islands within the bay. On the thirtieth he took advantage of the outbreak of new anti-foreign and anti-Christian disturbances to reopen the missionary case, whose conclusion had been held up by the Kiaochow question, and demanded a concession for the construction of a second railroad, running from Tsinan to the border of Shantung.

In discussions on January 1 and 3, 1898, Weng and Chang tried to whittle down the term of the lease to fifty years, and attempted to retain the southern shore. They also tried to modify the customs duties and regulations drawn up by the Germans. But Heyking rebuffed all suggestions and objections.

On January 4 Heyking descended on the Tsungli Yamen with his entire staff and declared that Kiaochow was and would remain a German port with or without a convention. If China refused to sign the lease, Germany would take what she wanted by force. Confronted with the naked truth, the Tsungli Yamen bowed to the ultimatum.

On January 12 a preliminary agreement regarding the missionary case and a separate convention pertaining to Kiaochow seemed to put an end to the haggling. But before the final documents were formally signed, the slaying of a German sailor in Shantung and the robbing of two German missionaries in Kwangtung led to further demands on the part of Heyking. Depressed and humiliated, Weng T'ung-ho asked to be relieved from the position of chief negotiator, and Li Hung-chang was appointed in his stead.

Unable to mobilize Russian support, Li Hung-chang could not beat back the German demands either. The agreements which were finally signed on March 6 gave Germany the right to build the railroads Heyking had desired, a German-Chinese company to be established for that purpose.[118] The Kiaochow territory, which extended for a radius of 50 kilometers, was leased to Germany for a period of 99 years, with China giving up the exercise of her sovereignty in that region for the duration of the lease.[119]

To sugarcoat the seizure the preamble of the treaty described it as an expression of "the grateful appreciation" on the part of the Chinese government for the friendship shown by Germany. It motivated it by the mutual desire of the two governments to strengthen the friendly bonds between their countries and to develop the economic and commercial relations between their subjects. The rights which the Germans received, including the right to have German troops march through the Kiaochow territory at any time, were described as being for the purpose of strengthening the friendly relations between China and Germany and at the same time increasing the military preparedness of the Chinese empire.[120]

Although Bülow assured members of the Reichstag that the occupation of Kiaochow would not disturb peaceful relations with the powers, because the bay was not too close to the respective spheres of interest of England, France, or Russia,[121] he revealed to Hatzfeldt that it was becoming difficult for the political leadership to block the military, who were clamoring for the dispatch of significant naval forces to East Asia in the light of the Japanese naval demonstrations and preparations, whose significance everyone could see but whose objective no one knew. The moment Germany would send reinforcements and commence naval armaments on a large scale the situation in East Asia would be exacerbated, Bülow realized. By showing that she might drop the role of observer and become an active participant, Germany would push France into a more active role for the same considerations as in 1895, assuming that France still wished to remain Russia's friend. Russia on her part would be induced to give a more decisive character to her East Asian policy as soon as she noticed that the rash policy of the Japanese facilitated her firm reliance on Germany and France. England too would then perhaps be faced with all kinds of serious considerations.

The German government would be ready at any time to accept the consequences of its actions, but it would not trigger these consequences unless absolutely necessary, Bülow telegraphed to Hatzfeldt. The need of strengthening the German fleet would remain unrefuted until it was clear to Germany that Japan was not arming against her. Bülow expressed doubt that England, even if she desired war, would recommend to the Japanese as prelude to the conflict a policy bound to strengthen and unify the opponents. He warned that from the moment Germany began to arm she would no longer have a free hand politically, but that she and the other powers would then be propelled by events.[122]

Twenty-Four

The Leasing of Port Arthur

As China appealed for Russian aid against Germany, Foreign Minister Muraviev wanted to take advantage of the request to secure for Russia the needed naval base in the Far East.[1] In a lengthy memorandum to the tsar on November 23, 1897, he observed that the complications which had arisen in the Far East in 1895 had prompted the Navy Department to look for a firm base in the Pacific Ocean for the Russian fleet, which until then had been using exclusively the ports of Japan for wintering, temporary anchorage, and other needs. He related that Vice Admiral S. P. Tyrtov, who had commanded the combined Russian naval forces in the Pacific at that time, had deemed Kiaochow Bay as suitable for a base in all respects. Prolonged stays by foreign squadrons had not been allowed in Kiaochow, a closed port, but the Russians had persuaded the Tsungli Yamen after lengthy negotiations to instruct the local authorities in Kiaochow to let the Russian squadron enter and stay in the port and to give every assistance to its crews. Although Tyrtov had been informed of this immediately, he had not made full use of the privilege. He had notified Cassini that his request for the opening of Kiaochow had been made only in case of need and that he would confine himself to sending but one vessel there, and that for only a few days.

When Germany, in view of Russia's disinterest, had occupied Kiaochow, the Navy Ministry had not bemoaned the loss of that bay, because it was too far from Vladivostok and completely cut off from Russia. But if St. Petersburg could look calmly on German action on the southeastern shore of the Shantung Peninsula, Muraviev continued, it could not accept the fact that Russia did not have in the Pacific a single completely convenient and equipped port to meet the needs of her navy. "Even if the acute crisis, which in 1895 had prompted Vice Admiral Tyrtov II[2] to seek the opening of Kiaochow, has passed—passed to such an extent that our vessels, as the director of the Navy Ministry reports, could again spend the winter of 1896 to 1897 in Nagasaki and other ports of Japan—the general state of affairs in the Far East, created as an consequence of the Sino-Japanese collision and our intervention in favor of China, not only has not changed, but is more and more taking on a definitive character which points to the absolute necessity for Russia *to be prepared for all eventualities*," Muraviev declared. To accomplish this, he argued, it was necessary for Russia to maintain a sizeable fleet in the Pacific Ocean and to have at her complete disposal a port which was convenient for wintering, was fully equipped and richly supplied.

Since Russia did not have such a port along her own shores, the question arose naturally where to seek one—in Korea, and if so on the eastern or western coast of the peninsula, or along the Chinese coast, and if so, exactly where. Yet to this urgent question there was as yet no clear answer on the part of the most interested department, Muraviev complained. To be sure, the Navy Ministry had recently appealed to the Foreign Ministry for the acquisition of a piece of land inside the port of Pusan in order to build a depot with a wharf for the Russian warships. Muraviev saw no obstacles to the speedy realization of such a project, but he questioned whether it could provide a reliable base for the Russian fleet. Connected with Seoul by a Japanese telegraph line guarded by Japanese troops, Pusan had long been craved by Japan. Before the war with China Kojong had promised that Japanese entrepreneurs would get a concession for the construction of a railroad from Seoul to Pusan, and now Japan was pressing for the realization of this strategically important undertaking. Under the circumstances there was the danger than any attempt by Russia, once she had acquired the piece of land, to establish herself more firmly at Pusan could lead to a collision with Japan. In view of its proximity to Japan's naval sphere of influence and its isolation from the Trans-Siberian Railroad, Pusan could not be a solid base for Russia's Pacific squadron. "In the absence of another suitable port in Korea, which would at the same time be not far from our operational base," Muraviev argued, "it would seem that we ought to pay attention exclusively to the Chinese coast and there seek a buttress [*opora*] for our squadron."

According to information recently furnished by the Russian consul in Chefoo, Andrei Nikolaevich Timchenko-Ostroverkhov, there were four separate, excellent bays in spacious Talienwan—Victoria Bay, Yunk Bay, Hand Bay and Odin Cove—all of which were ice-free and could accomodate vessels with a draught of twenty-two feet or more. Data obtained from other competent persons confirmed the virtues of Talienwan and its advantageous position compared with Port Arthur, which it could easily dominate. Besides, Talienwan had a number of strategic advantages over any other port on the eastern shore of Korea. If the Russian vessels had their sole base on the east coast of Korea, they would find themselves trapped in the Japan Sea and completely cut off from the main base of operations in the event of a break in relations between Russia and Japan and the latter's natural, immediate occupation of Pusan and the blocking of the Korean Strait. On the other hand, in case of the same hostile acts by Japan, if Russia had a port on the Liaotung Peninsula, her vessels would be free to exit through the Yellow Sea. Furthermore, Talienwan was less distant than Korean ports from the Trans-Siberian Railroad, considering the fact that it was planned to connect the main line with Kirin and Mukden. In the absence of other indications by the Navy Department regarding the acquisition of a reliable base in the Pacific and in view of events in Shantung, it behooved Russia, Muraviev thought, to proceed immediately with the occupation of Talienwan or another port, whichever the Navy Department preferred, provided the Russian squadron was presently strong enough to accomplish the mission and ward off possible complications. The fact that the Chinese government, according to telegrams from Pavlov, had solicited Russian protection from Germany in the Kiaochow question played into Russian hands. "We could, therefore, easily explain in Peking our occupation of Talienwan by our desire to have a firm buttress for our squadron in the eventuality of further developments unfavorable to China," Muraviev contended.

The foreign minister adduced additional considerations for the adoption of such a decisive course of action. "The experience of history teaches us," Muraviev penned, "that Oriental peoples respect above all strength and power; no representations and counsels, dissipated before the authorities of these peoples, attain [their] goal. And the conduct of the Chinese government for the entire recent period of time has fully confirmed the indications of history." He complained that despite repeated representations on the part of Pavlov and the most solemn promises and assurances of the Chinese ministers, Russia had to date failed to attain any of her demands. The southern routing of the final section of the Trans-Siberian Railroad had not been settled and the Chinese government was about to go back on the assurances given to Russia in regard to her construction of connecting and other branches to Kirin and Mukden. The regulations worked out by Russia concerning navigation on the Amur and Sungari rivers had not yet been accepted by the Tsungli Yamen, and the question of leaving military instruction in northern China exclusively in Russian hands was taking a very unfavorable turn for St. Petersburg according to Pavlov's latest reports.

Muraviev concluded: "All these circumstances, it seems, clearly indicate that henceforth we cannot and must not count on the friendly assurances of the Chinese central government, which, as the last telegram of Court Councilor Pavlov testifies, is impotent before the absolute power of its mighty governors general and heads of provinces. And while we shall uselessly and fruitlessly waste time on representations and friendly admonitions in the Tsungli Yamen, satisfying ourselves with the prolix promises of the Chinese ministers, all other European powers will attain what they want by the means which the German government used so successfully in the acquisition of a port convenient for its vessels in the south of the Shantung Peninsula." [3]

Nicholas agreed with Muraviev's reasoning. "*Vpol'ne spravedlivo*" (entirely true), he jotted on the document. In a note to Muraviev the same day, he wrote that there was no time to lose and that he was therefore calling a meeting for the afternoon of the twenty-sixth. He asked Muraviev to invite in his name the ministers of war and finance and the director of the Navy Ministry, sending them copies of the proposal and a plan of the region in question. "I have always been of the opinion that our future open [ice-free] port must be either on the Liaotung Peninsula or in the northeastern corner of the Bay of Korea," Nicholas added. [4]

In spite of the tsar's favorable disposition, Muraviev's proposal ran into strong opposition at the special conference, over which Nicholas himself presided. Witte pointed out that Russia had but recently, at the time of the coronation, concluded the Moscow treaty with China "in order to preserve the Asian continent from a new foreign invasion." China had voluntarily conceded to a Russian company the right of connecting the Trans-Siberian Railroad with Vladivostok via Manchuria; at the same time, Russia and China had committed themselves to defend each other and Korea in case of a Japanese attack on Russia's Pacific borders, on China, or on Korea. It was impossible to seize Chinese territory after such a treaty of alliance, Witte declared. He warned that if Russia did occupy a place in China and Japan then followed her example and did the same, Russia, by virtue of the treaty, would have to defend China against her. Instead of copying Germany, Russia should exert every effort to disincline the latter from the occupation of Kiaochow. Perhaps, he ventured, one should send the Russian fleet immediately to Kiaochow and have it remain there until Germany withdrew from the port. Russia must not seize Port Arthur because the Germans were seizing Kiaochow. If the occupation of Kiaochow did not matter to Russia, one ought to react to it calmly; if, on the other hand, it injured Russian interests, one should take action against Germany. It would be illogical, Witte argued, for the Russians to seek compensation in hostile actions against China because the Germans annoyed them by taking Kiaochow from the latter.

Muraviev retorted that the treaty obligated Russia to defend China against

Japan, not against European powers. Due to "special circumstances," Russia was unable at this time to hinder Germany from occupying Kiaochow. In his opinion, the treaty did not prevent Russia from occupying Talienwan and Port Arthur in view of the German occupation of Kiaochow.

Witte countered that the occupation of a part of Chinese territory by Russia involved great risk. There was no doubt, he argued, that the other powers would follow the Russian example. In the process, Japan might direct her lust not only against China but also against Korea, where Russia at the moment had preponderant influence. It was, of course, impossible to foresee how things would turn out, but it was clear to him that the step in question could entail very dangerous consequences. They had only just begun the construction of the railroad through Manchuria. The occupation of Port Arthur would require tremendous new sacrifices for the connection of the port with the main line of the Manchurian road. But aside from the enormous expenditures, the project would take several years to complete, during which Port Arthur would be cut off from Russia. This factor alone entailed such risk that one was forced to question the expediency of occupying Port Arthur.

Muraviev dismissed the likelihood of complications arising from a Russian move into Port Arthur. He expressed the fear, on the other hand, that if Russia did not occupy Port Arthur, England might do so in the wake of the German action.

War Minister Vannovskii remarked that there was general agreement that Russia needed an ice-free port in the Pacific Ocean. At one time Russia had selected Port Lazarev, but had found it to be inconvenient; then she had looked at Kiaochow and had found it inconvenient as well. The Germans meanwhile had liked the latter and had occupied it. An official of the Foreign Ministry and the commander of one of the Russian warships had inspected Port Arthur and had recognized it to be convenient. Vannovskii supported the idea of taking advantage of the situation and occupying Port Arthur if there were no weighty objections. He did say that the decisive voice in this matter must rest with the navy.

The director of the Navy Department, Admiral Pavel Petrovich Tyrtov, responded that the suitability of Port Arthur was questionable. Though it was impossible at the moment to acquire a port in southeastern Korea, it would be better, in the opinion of himself and the admirals, not to occupy Port Arthur, but to use Vladivostok for two or three years as the base for the squadron, preferring to acquire a Korean port in the future.

Witte concurred that it was highly desirable for the Trans-Siberian Railroad as well as for Russia in general to have an outlet to the Pacific Ocean and that Russia's eastward advance must result in the acquisition of such a port. But this took time and it was essential to attain the objective by a friendly agreement, not by force. Several years ago the routing of the Trans-Siberian Railroad through Manchuria had seemed not feasible, yet what had once appeared impossible had been realized through an absolutely peaceful and friendly agreement. Before starting something new one should complete what one had begun, namely the construction of the railroad through Manchuria to Vladivostok. Once this had been finished and Russia had preserved the amicable relations which had always existed between her and China, she would obtain from the latter, on the basis of economic interests, an outlet to the Pacific Ocean just as she had attained the construction of the Manchurian railroad. The European powers were newcomers in China, while the Russians were her ancient neighbors. What the Europeans did to China the Russians must not do, for their attitude toward China was completely different. The policy of Russia in the East had always been characterized by fairness, Witte contended. If Russia continued to abide by her traditional policy of friendship toward China and did not embark on a path of force and disregard for her interests, she would always achieve better results than Europe.

What with the support of the Navy Ministry, the views of Witte prevailed. The conference decided against the occupation of Port Arthur, both because of the treaty with China and in order to maintain the prestige of Russia in the East.[5]

Although Nicholas had originally expressed agreement with the Muraviev proposal, he had been swáyed by Witte's passionate objections and the views of the Navy Ministry. But when Muraviev, who resented Witte's role in the shaping of Russian Far Eastern policy and wanted to achieve something significant himself, shortly returned to the tsar with information that British warships were cruising near Port Arthur and Talienwan and repeated the warning that England might seize the bay if Russia did not do so first, the weak monarch changed his mind again.[6]

The decision of Nicholas to take Port Arthur and Talienwan distressed Witte. "Remember this day, Your Imperial Highness," he said to Grand Duke Aleksandr Mikhailovich, whom he met as he stepped out of the study of the tsar. "You will see what terrible consequences this fateful step will have for Russia." From Tsarskoe Selo Witte hastened to Counselor Tschirschky, who was in charge of the German legation while Radolin was on leave. He related to Tschirschky that during his visit to Russia the Kaiser had told him that if he ever wanted to ask him for anything or to express his opinion about anything he should feel free to do so directly through the German legation. Witte now requested that Tschirschky telegraph to Wilhelm that he asked and counseled in the interest of their two countries that Germany, once it had obtained the necessary punishments and financial compensation, withdraw from Tsingtao (Kiaochow), for its retention would lead to other steps with the most terrible consequences.

When Wilhelm replied several days later that Witte obviously did not know a number of essential circumstances due to which Germany could not follow his advice, Witte realized that an understanding must have been reached between the two sovereigns. As he noted in his memoirs, his efforts to dissuade Nicholas from following into German footsteps had been doomed to failure. With the foreign minister and the war minister both advocating the seizure of Port Arthur and Talienwan for the good of Russia, it had been only natural for the young and glory-craving tsar to heed their recommendations.[7]

Witte did not keep his annoyance to himself. He told O'Conor in a strictly private and personal conversation that the German occupation of Kiaochow was not only an "act of brigandage," but a "*bêtise*" (stupidity), because it alienated the tsarist government.[8] When Radolin, with whom Witte was on friendly terms, returned from leave and asked what he thought about events in China, Witte replied that it was a lot of "childishness." He was referring in his own mind to the Kaiser, who had precipitated the entire incident, but did not specify so, of course. The Russian Foreign Ministry, like other foreign ministries, was in the habit of deciphering the dispatches telegraphed by the foreign representatives. Shown the account of Radolin's conversation with Witte by Muraviev, the tsar took offense at Witte's words. When Witte visited him several days later, Nicholas received him with unusual coldness and when Witte took his leave hinted darkly; "Sergei Iul'evich, I would advise you to be more careful in conversations with foreign envoys."[9]

The occupation of Port Arthur was undertaken at the insistence of the Russian foreign minister and of the chief of the General Staff ostensibly after prodding by Peking that if Russia did not occupy the place, England would do so, Hayashi learned subsequently from a "reliable source" in St. Petersburg. Witte had opposed the occupation on four grounds, he was told. It would provide Germany with a pretext to make her own occupation of Kiaochow indefinite; Li Hung-chang had denied in a cable to him that the Chinese government had willingly consented to the occupation of Port Arthur; it was impolitic to injure the feelings of the Chinese at the very moment when it was essential for Russia to befriend them; and it would be too costly because of engineering difficulties to make Port Arthur the terminus of the trans-Manchurian line.

In reporting the above, Hayashi related that although the Kaiser had spoken to the tsar about the occupation of some part of China during his visit to St. Petersburg the preceding summer, Nicholas had forgotten to mention this to the foreign minister at the time and had remembered it only when the Germans had moved into Kiaochow. Wilhelm had sent two telegrams to Nicholas, Hayashi recounted. The first one had asked for the tacit consent of Russia to the German occupation. It had been answered in the sense that although Russia would not oppose the scheme, she considered it full of risks. The content of the second telegram, sent by the Kaiser to the tsar secretly, had been learned by Muraviev through a spy he had planted in the Telegraph Office.[10]

Muraviev's apprehensions regarding Port Arthur had been awakened by Admiral Dubasov, whose views did not coincide with those of the Navy Ministry. As soon as Diederichs had telegraphed him about his occupation of Kiaochow Bay on orders from Berlin, Dubasov had sent an urgent, secret cable to St. Petersburg asking for permission to occupy Port Arthur without waiting for the conclusion of the negotiations at Peking in order to forestall seizure of the port by English or Japanese vessels. The bureaucrats in the capital had not made haste with a reply, putting the telegram aside until Muraviev's regular audience at Tsarskoe Selo. As a rumor spread through the city of Nagaski and the roadstead where he was wintering that the English fleet was preparing to leave for Port Arthur in order to take up position at the entrance to the bay and bar access to the Russians, Dubasov lost patience. He sent a second, more decisive telegram directly to the tsar, asking for orders to occupy Port Arthur immediately.[11]

Dubasov did not reveal the gist of the imperial reply, which he deciphered personally. He ordered Rear Admiral Reunov to get his vessels under steam, but did not say where he was sending them. The destination was indicated only in the sealed, secret packet, which was to be opened at sea. As a cover for the real mission, Dubasov fabricated the rumor that new disorders had broken out in Seoul in reaction to Japanese intrigues and that the three Russian warships were being dispatched for the protection of the tsarist legation.

The stratagem failed to deceive the British captains. They slipped out of the harbor hours before the Russians did so and by the time Reunov's vessels reached Port Arthur two days later, they found the *Immortality* and the *Undaunted* lying athwart the passage into the port, blocking entry. Outraged, Dubasov called on his government to make energetic representations at London for the removal of the British ships from Port Arthur.[12]

Ambassador Staal did so twice, the second time with the implied threat that he hoped that the British would not make it necessary for the Russians to resort to more practical measures (*mesures plus réelles*) for the protection of their interests. Salisbury responded that the vessels had not been sent on instructions from London, but at the discretion of the admiral. They and other vessels would depart shortly if they had not done so already. He made it clear, however, that British ships of war had the right to visit Port Arthur and other Chinese ports in the vicinity. He objected to the announcement made by the Russian Telegraph Bureau that the British vessels had received orders from London to leave Port Arthur immediately as inaccurate and injudicious. "It was likely to arouse excitement and irritation in England and might entail inconvenient results."[13]

Reunov received word from Dubasov that the expected seizure of Port Arthur by Russia had aroused much excitement in Great Britain and that war could break out between the two powers. As if to underline the strained relations between their countries, the senior English commander refrained from making the customary courtesy call on Reunov.

Several days later the situation changed radically. Reunov was informed that the crisis had passed, that Britain had agreed to the Russian occupation of Port Arthur. The English commander belatedly made the traditional visit. A few days afterwards the British vessels left, and the Russians remained sole masters of the situation.[14]

Muraviev had telegraphed to Osten-Sacken on December 14 that the tsar, in view of the German occupation of Kiaochow and with the assent of the Chinese government, had ordered one detachment of the Pacific fleet to cast anchor in Port Arthur and to remain stationed there until further orders. Persuaded that Russia and Germany must and could go hand in hand in the Far East, Nicholas had charged Osten-Sacken to inform the Kaiser thereof, Muraviev had concluded.[15] Osten-Sacken had transmitted the above to the German Foreign Ministry at once.[16]

It is not clear whether Reunov reached Port Arthur before or after Osten-Sacken's communication. Sources differ widely regarding the exact date of his arrival.[17] The vessels entered Port Arthur sometime in mid-December, in all likelihood on or between the fourteenth and the seventeeth of that month. When Pavlov informed Li Hung-chang of the anchorage of the Russian vessels at Port Arthur and Talien, Li expressed confidence that Russia had no intention of seizing Chinese territory. As Pavlov gave oral confirmation, Li was visibly relieved; he offered the services of the Chinese authorities in supplying coal and said that the Tsungli Yamen would furnish an interpreter for the Russian commander. Reunov testified to the cooperation and goodwill shown by the local officials, who on December 18 turned away the British cruiser *Daphne*.[18]

On December 17 Bülow replied to Osten-Sacken that Wilhelm, to whom he had submitted his communication of the fourteenth, cordially applauded "the energetic as well as prudent measure" ordered by the tsar. "In effect," the Kaiser believed, "once the impregnable position of Port Arthur had been protected from a sudden attack, Russia could calmly watch the coming of events which will mark the slow but progressive *effondrement* [collapse or giving way] of the Chinese empire." Wilhelm agreed with Nicholas on the solidarity of their interests in the Far East and on the need to make common cause against a common danger.

Bülow added in this regard that there was no imminent danger of conflict with Japan, because the latter was preoccupied to a large measure with the difficulties which had arisen from the annexation of Formosa. He contended that the risk inherent in future events could be reduced considerably and the dangers which could result from prolonged resistance by the Chinese government could be removed if the tsarist representative at Peking were ordered to support the German claims for a long-term lease of Kiaochow Bay and related concessions.[19]

On December 19 the Wolffbureau, a German news office, forwarded to the Kaiser a telegram from the Russian telegraph agency announcing that Reunov had just entered Port Arthur with the full assent of the Chinese government in order to winter there. "This action is motivated exclusively by the need for a provisional wintering station and there can be no question of a forcible occupation and of any demonstration or hostile intention against China, Germany or any other power," the communiqué declared.

"Praise God, the other post on the Yellow Sea has now been mounted also," Wilhelm rejoiced.[20] "Please accept my congratulations at the arrival of your squadron at Port Arthur," he cabled to Nicholas that day in a personal telegram in English, signed "Willy." "Russia and Germany at the entrance of the Yellow Sea may be taken as represented by St. George and St. Michael shielding the Holy Cross in the Far East and guarding the Gates of the Continent of Asia," he raved. "May you be able fully to realise the plans you often unrolled to me; my sympathy and help shall not fail in case of need."[21] "Your enemies, whether they be called Japanese or English, now become my enemies; and every troublemaker, whoever he may be, who wishes to hinder your intentions by force, will meet the German squadron side by side with your warships," Wilhelm added in a message which he asked Osten-Sacken to convey to Nicholas.[22]

The German press, which since the occupation of Kiaochow had reiterated continually the friendly nature of relations between Germany and Russia, universally sympathized with the latter's occupation of Port Arthur. The Russian action could hardly have surprised German statesmen, an organ of the government observed, since the acquisition of the port by Russia had long been recognized as being merely a matter of time. It saw no violation of German interests in the move. Indeed, it interpreted the simultaneous occupation of Kiaochow and Port Arthur as the continuation of German and Russian cooperation in East Asia.[23]

Osten-Sacken was in a good mood when he called on Bülow during his reception day on December 21. He emphasized repeatedly that "the little cloud" which had cast a shadow on relations between their countries following the German occupation of Kiaochow Bay had disappeared. There could no longer be any question of a misunderstanding between their sovereigns; the relations between Russia and Germany were clear. He knew, Osten-Sacken said, that Russia could count on German support in East Asia. It was providential, he remarked, that Germany and Russia could walk side by side in Europe without antagonistic interests, while in East Asia they were forced to rely on each other. Osten-Sacken doubted that there was any direct danger from Britain. The English, he opined, would confine themselves to big words and would at most try to mobilize Japan against Russia and Germany the way they had attempted the preceding year to incite Greece against Turkey, twenty years ago Turkey against Russia, and thirty-three years ago Denmark against Germany.[24]

Osten-Sacken showed some concern about Japan. The present Japanese government was peacefully inclined, but he foresaw the possibility that it could be replaced by a more action-minded ministry. However, Baron Rosen was very conciliatory by nature and had been instructed specifically to act in a placating manner vis-à-vis the Japanese.

Bülow told Osten-Sacken that the quicker the Chinese government decided to accept the German demands the more likely the integrity of the Chinese empire, which Russia desired and for which it strove, would be preserved from premature partition attempts. The cabinet of St. Petersburg would substantially contribute to the prevention of an untimely collapse of the Chinese empire if it utilized its mightly influence in Peking to induce the Chinese government to go along promptly and smoothly with the German demands, Bülow stated.

Osten-Sacken responded that he shared Bülow's conception and had already written to St. Petersburg in this sense. He had no doubt, he said, that the tsarist representative in Peking had appropriate instructions.[25]

Russia informed Japan on December 17 of the dispatch of a unit of her Pacific squadron to Port Arthur for temporary anchorage. Rosen told Nishi that Nicholas had deemed the step necessary because the German squadron had occupied Kiaochow and was likely to remain there indefinitely. He said that the assent of the Chinese government had followed already. "Our amicable relations with Japan serve as a guarantee for us that the Tokyo Government will regard with trust the objectives which presently induce us to seek a safe anchorage near Shantung Peninsula," declared the Russian announcement which Rosen transmitted to Nishi.[26] Three days later, on December 20, Nishi made the following brief reply to Rosen: "[The] Japanese Government take note of the announcement of the Russia minister in Japan, with perfect confidence that the anchorage of a portion of [the] Russian squadron in Port Arthur will—as announced—be of a temporary nature."[27]

Nishi, who had served in St. Petersburg for over a decade and was sympathetic toward Russia, did not desire a conflict over Port Arthur. "I trust you will [exert your] best efforts to maintain [the] most intimate relations possible with [the] Russian Government and keep me constantly and fully informed regarding [the] attitude and prospective action of [the] Russian Government as well as [the] tone of the Press," he telegraphed to Hayashi.[28]

Yet Japan could take no chances and made extraordinary military preparations in spite of her involvement in Formosa in order to be prepared for any eventuality. As the Russians represented to the Germans that the Japanese actions were aimed at them, the Germans speculated that the Russians were saying so in an attempt to scale down the demands they had made on China and to secure for themselves German support against Japan before going along with Germany's acquisition of Kiaochow. Although Bülow made use of Russia to bring pressure on Peking, he hesitated to rely solely on her. He believed that Berlin should on one hand maintain contact with St. Petersburg and on the other hand remain on tolerable terms with London so that whatever might happen, all powers would have to reckon with Germany. At the same time Bülow tried to reassure Tokyo that the German and Russian moves did not constitute a prelude to the dismemberment of China.[29] He did authorize Chargé Treutler to tell Nishi as his own personal opinion, should Nishi bring up the future, that Germany had no objections in principle to Japanese expansion on the mainland.[30]

Treutler saw Nishi on December 30. Conveying that the emperors of Germany and Russia had no intention of effecting the partition of China by the occupation of Kiaochow and Port Arthur, he argued that when England had taken Hong Kong no one had entertained the idea that this would lead to the breakup of China. He said that the object which Germany had in view was "much less serious than the cession of Hongkong."[31]

Yano advised Li Hung-chang on December 18 as his personal opinion that China inform Japan officially of her consent to the temporary anchorage of the Russian fleet at Port Arthur. "I have ascertained from Chinese official sources that China did not so far grant to Russia use of fortresses and barracks at Port Arthur, nor did she grant landing of seamen," he reported.[32] Nishi replied that the Chinese minister in Tokyo had made the announcement suggested by Yano

to Li, but that "his exact meaning was almost incomprehensible." He instructed Yano to ascertain the actual situation from Li and other Chinese officials directly concerned with the negotiations as well as from his diplomatic
colleagues and keep him constantly and fully informed.[33]

Hayashi telegraphed on December 29 that despite the declarations of the
tsarist government that the occupation of Port Arthur was to be temporary, it
seemed from the general impression that it was intended to be permanent.
"The tone of the press is half intimidating and half explanatory towards Japan; but their venom is chiefly directed to England," he communicated, remarking that the newspapers had been cautioned by the government not to
attack the German occupation of Kiaochow. "As you are aware of, no report
on political matters either by press or otherwise can be implicitly trusted in
this country," Hayashi commented acidly.[34]

Tei reported from Tientsin that the motive for the Russian anchorage at Port
Arthur and Talienwan had been portrayed to him by a Chinese official as
"voluntary protection offered by Russia, of which China is unable to refuse."
The Russian consul had declared that the Russian vessels had come "for protection in accordance with [a] request from China," and would remain until
the German fleet evacuated Kiaochow. "It appears that [the] situation is very
critical," Tei concluded.[35] But Li Hung-chang assured Yano that the anchorage granted to Russia at Port Arthur was only temporary—until the question
between China and Germany had been settled. The Chinese government, he
said, had expressly made such a condition and was confident that it could be
effected. Neither England nor France had come forward so far with demands
of their own, nor were they likely to do so in the future if Russia duly retired
from Port Arthur, Li told Yano.[36]

Meanwhile, the Chinese were becoming increasingly alarmed by the
strengthening of German forces at Kiaochow. In response to repeated inquiries by Li Hung-chang, Pavlov declared, in accordance with instructions from
St. Petersburg, that the Chinese could count on Russian aid in the event of a
"large collision" with Germany, provided they settled satisfactorily all questions which had recently arisen regarding the Manchurian railroad and other
matters and if the Russian fleet were given the exclusive right to use several
harbors of China. According to Pavlov, the Chinese ministers were delighted
by his statement and agreed to carry out the Russian demands; they strongly
asked for effective Russian assistance in the removal of the German squadron.
They did solicit Russian aid on the terms laid out by Pavlov, but with misgivings rather than pleasure. Li's immediate reaction had been that he feared to
make any promises, as the Russians might not carry out their end of the
bargain in regard to assistance against Germany. Li's colleagues, in the report

to the throne, pointed to the danger of China throwing herself into the arms of Russia and counseled the avoidance of foreign aid and intervention. By the time the ministers had come around to the Russian demands, Nicholas had decided on the occupation of Port Arthur.

Lacking funds for the payment of the remainder of the indemnity to Japan and unable to raise them elsewhere, the Chinese government approached the tsarist government several days later, on December 14, through Li Hung-chang with the request that it guarantee a new loan for 100 million liang (taels), as it had done in the case of the loan of 1895. Witte instructed Pokotilov on December 16 to inform Li that Russia was prepared to arrange for such a loan under certain conditions. China must (1) give appropriate guarantees for the punctuality of her loan payments; (2) confirm unconditionally permission for the southern direction of the main line of the Chinese Eastern Railroad;[37] (3) commit herself not to allow any foreigners other than the Russians to construct railroads and exploit other commercial undertakings in all three provinces of Manchuria and in Mongolia; (4) remove forever all difficulties made by local authorities in regard to the alienation of land and the acquisition of materials for the construction of the Chinese Eastern Railroad; (5) give, in accordance with the concession agreement, free of charge all government land and materials necessary for the construction of the railroad; (6) remove all obstacles to the navigation by vessels belonging to the Chinese Eastern Railroad Company on the Sungari River and on all its tributaries; (7) give to the board of directors of the Chinese Eastern Railroad Company, at the time of the signing of the loan agreement, a concession for the construction of the railroad from the main line of the Chinese Eastern Railroad to whatever harbor would be selected for that purpose by the board of directors of the Chinese Eastern Railroad on the shore of the Yellow Sea to the east of Port Yingtze (Yingkow, the port of Newchwang); and (8) let Russia, after the selection of the said harbor, choose in it a place for the establishment of a port for the Volunteer Fleet, all vessels flying the Russian flag to have the right to enter that port. So sure did Witte feel of his position that he directed Pokotilov not to exert any pressure on the Chinese in regard to the loan, which they themselves had requested from Russia, and let the Chinese government propose in its own name the conditions he had dictated.[38]

"Russia has offered to China [a] new loan, evidently aiming to put the latter under her complete financial control; and to see the evacuation of our army from Weihaiwei realized as soon as possible," Yano telegraphed from Peking.[39]

On January 1, 1898, Count Osten-Sacken transmitted to Foreign Secretary von Bülow an unsigned and undated copy of a dispatch in French instructing him to explain to the Kaiser and to the German foreign minister the Russian action in northern China. "On the basis of the principle, virtually recognized by the German government, of our exclusive sphere of action in the provinces of North China, including all of Manchuria, the Province of Chihli and Chinese Turkistan, we cannot allow foreign political influence there, and all the efforts of the imperial government will be directed toward the affirmation and consolidation of this [Russian] influence in order to maintain good neighborly relations with the Chinese Empire," the memorandum declared. It argued that the above conditions "imposed" on Russia the "obligation" to preserve the Chinese troops stationed in the said provinces from any European influence and to oppose absolutely the admission in their ranks of foreign officers or instructors, the more so since the Chinese central government has assented to this in a formal agreement. However, because of the insubordination prevalent in the Chinese military administration, the commanders of various army corps had, in violation of their instructions, approached the representatives of different foreign governments at Peking about obtaining foreign instructors for their troops. Thus recently even more German instructors had appeared among the troops garrisoned within the Russian sphere of influence. In view of the declarations of the German government recognizing Russia's obligation to conserve her supreme political influence in the Chinese provinces bordering unto her own empire, St. Petersburg asked Berlin to take the necessary measures to prohibit German officers and soldiers from serving as military instructors in North China. Such service, the Russian government explained, not only constituted a violation of its interests, but gave to the other powers a ground for seeking the employment of their military instructors. It concluded that a firm promise by the German government to put an end to this prejudicial state of affairs in North China would be proof of its sincere desire to arrive at a friendly understanding (*une entente amicale*) with Russia regarding the questions of the Far East.[40]

Wilhelm, with whom Bülow discussed the Russian memorandum on January 2, agreed to receive Osten-Sacken in audience. He approved of the provisional reply that the discussion of individual questions must await the conclusion of the Kiaochow agreement. The German government counted in this connection on the decisive influence of Russia at Peking, because the realization of the German Kiaochow treaty would contribute more than anything to the pacification of East Asia and would offer the best guarantee against the premature crumbling of the Chinese empire; it would also offer the surest check to English attempts at intervention as well as to Japanese hostilities. Once China in the interest of herself, of Russia, and of peace had accepted the moderate demands of Germany, the latter would gladly accommodate Russia in all remaining details pertaining to East Asia.

In regard to the declaration in the Russian memorandum that not only Manchuria and Chinese Turkistan, but also the Chinese province of Chihli belonged to the Russian sphere of action, Wilhelm remarked that Russian entrenchment in Manchuria and Turkistan could only be desirable for Germany, but that the province of Chihli, which included Tientsin and Peking, would be a fat morsel. Nevertheless, if Russia loyally and successfully helped Germany in the rapid conclusion of the Kiaochow agreement and recognized her interests in Shantung, including the Hwang-ho (Yellow River) up to its bend to the north, Germany could let her have Chihli. The Kaiser likewise shunted aside until he knew the outcome of the Kiaochow question the demand for a secret understanding between Germany, Russia and perhaps France regarding the measures to be adopted to secure Japanese evacuation of Weihaiwei permanently once China had paid up the war indemnity. Wilhelm deemed it best, he told Bülow, not to scare Russia away from the idea of further collaboration with Germany until the Kiaochow agreement had been secured. The future would show how to act afterwards. Germany did not have a direct interest in weakening or even smashing Japan, because, circumstances permitting, she might be able to use her on her side, the Kaiser observed. "At any rate in this as in all other questions, '*do ut des*' [I give in order that you give] must remain our lodestar. Without appropriate equivalents we must give neither material nor moral help," Wilhelm declared. He expected the Russians to labor the harder for German support the stronger the Japanese were and the more unpleasant they made themselves toward the Russians and the French.

The Kaiser included the commercial and financial questions raised by Witte and Muraviev to Radolin among the issues to be settled by Germany with Russia accommodatingly after the conclusion of the Kiaochow agreement.[41]

In sending to Radolin a copy of the memorandum which Osten-Sacken had conveyed to him on the first, Bülow wrote that the German government had always stayed clear of the recruitment of German instructors for the provinces of northern China even though it had not known of a Russo-Chinese agreement, and that none of the military men in that region were any longer on active service with the German army. If, therefore, the Chinese government annulled their contracts, the German government would be duty-bound merely to see to it that the German subjects concerned received due compensation.[42]

On the morning of January 4 Osten-Sacken called on Bülow at the latter's invitation to discuss the memorandum conveyed by him regarding the German military instructors in North China. Bülow told him that the Kaiser would receive him at a time yet to be determined. He summarized the reply he had sent to Radolin and remarked that Wilhelm was in agreement with it.

Osten-Sacken did not deny that the Russo-Chinese agreement to which the memorandum referred was as yet unknown to Germany and admitted that the German military instructors who were in North China had not been engaged through the German government nor were they still in the service of the German army. He urged nonetheless that the German minister in Peking be instructed to prevent the further recruitment of German military instructors for North China. When Bülow countered that this matter and the understanding proposed by Russia regarding their mutual spheres of action would be handled obligingly by Germany as soon as China agreed to the leasing of Kiaochow, Osten-Sacken responded animatedly that it was of decisive importance not only for the future position of the Russian government but especially for the tsar himself that Germany leave no doubt that she had no intention of intervening from Kiaochow in the region to which Russia had been laying claim for herself since the conclusion of peace between China and Japan. It was vital for Russia (*eine Lebensfrage*) to be reassured in this respect. Russia could not tolerate any foreign influence in Chihli, he explained, lest all successes of Russia's past East Asian policy as well as the security of her East Asian frontier be put in question. Osten-Sacken alleged that Nicholas had reconciled himself to the German seizure of Kiaochow only because he had assumed as certain that Germany would not intervene from Kiaochow in the Russian sphere of influence (*Machtsphäre*). Otherwise German entrenchment in Kiaochow would prove to be a direct blow against Russia.

Bülow assured Osten-Sacken that German loyalty toward Russia was beyond doubt (*turmhoch über jeden Zweifel erhaben*). This could be seen from Wilhelm's recent telegrams to Nicholas as well as from the entire conduct of Germany in East Asia. Not only did Germany not want to be Russia's opponent in East Asia, but she felt that circumstances compelled the two powers to rely on each other there. But practical collaboration was possible solely on the basis of mutual full equality, Bülow declared. It was necessary, he argued, for Russia, who exerted great influence in Peking, first to help Germany effectively in the quick realization of the Kiaochow agreement so as to make it possible for Berlin to turn calmly to other questions.

In his record of the conversation Bülow noted that Osten-Sacken repeatedly reverted to the assertion that it was of utmost importance for Nicholas to receive assurances that Germany would not endanger the Russian position in the Gulf of Pechili and would recognize Manchuria and Chihli as belonging to the Russian sphere. He added that Osten-Sacken seemed impressed to a certain extent by the latest reports from London about English naval movements and plans of action.

The Kaiser read Bülow's account of the conversation with his usual skepticism. When he came to the passage that Osten-Sacken did not deny that the Russo-Chinese agreement was as yet unknown to Germany, he jotted in the margin; "*Ahem*! How could he thus have lied [that Germany] 'virtually recognized' what we did not know?!" Concerning the sphere on which Russia had an eye since the conclusion of the Sino-Japanese War, Wilhelm remarked that Nicholas had heretofore always referred to Manchuria, Mongolia, and Korea. When the Kaiser read about the security of the Russian frontier, he exclaimed, "That lies on the Amur and at Kiakhta! What does it have to do with Chihli?" In regard to the request for assurance that Germany would not interfere in the Russian sphere of influence, he wondered what region was meant. It was not possible to intervene from Kiaochow in the areas indicated to him by Nicholas. "*Aber, aber!*" (Come, come!), he scribbled next to the assertion that the German occupation of Kiaochow may have been a blow against Russia. "Behind this there lie Cassini and Gérard out of pique, and Hanotaux out of envy." He approved of Bülow's retort that German loyalty toward Russia had been beyond doubt and that Germany and Russia must rely on each other in East Asia. To the declaration that practical collaboration was possible only on the basis of mutual full equality, he added: "and absolute honesty." Regarding Bülow's observation that Osten-Sacken seemed impressed by English naval movements and plans of action, Wilhelm commented: "Even more probably by the agitation of Hanotaux and Gérard; these are afraid of clashes with England in Africa, [and] do not want to venture against her in Asia; yet, on the other hand, [they] do not want to leave us alone with Russia, as this would become dangerous for the [Franco-Russian] alliance!"[43]

The conditions which Russia had posed on December 16, 1897, for the loan that China needed had alienated erstwhile supporters of the Russo-Chinese alliance. Chang Chih-tung lent a willing ear to the notion of an Anglo-Japanese-Chinese alliance, proposed to him by two Japanese military officers, Kamio Mitsuomi and Utsunomiya Taro, seeing in it a means of counterbalancing Russia. In a series of telegrams which he and Governor Liu K'un-i sent to the Tsungli Yamen in December 1897 and January 1898, Chang advocated an alliance which would exploit the fact that while Russia plotted together with Germany, England was her enemy. In spite of the animosity left by the recent war with Japan, there were influential Chinese statesmen who favored an alliance with the latter. Resorting to the simile once used toward Korea, Governor Ch'en Pao-chen of Hunan Province declared: "Japan is to us as lips and teeth; we share both peace and danger." Reformers like K'ang Yu-wei and the censor Yang Shen-hsui supported the idea of an alliance with Japan in the belief that China must follow the example of the Meiji Restoration. Although Grand Councillor Weng and several other members of the Tsungli Yamen were in favor of cutting the bonds with Russia, the advocates of the old alliance—notably Li Hung-chang and Prince Kung—prevailed thanks to the backing of the empress dowager.[44] Rejecting Chang's proposal in a telegram on January 21, 1898, the Tsungli Yamen expressed the belief that "all nations are in awe and envy of Russia's brilliance, especially England and Japan." Judging others by themselves, the Chinese assumed that the British and Japanese wanted an alliance with them in order to use them as a "barrier." They had nothing to gain and much to lose from such an alliance, they thought. It would entail a break in Sino-Russian relations, of which Germany and France would take advantage. "The misfortune cannot even be considered," the ministers cabled.[45]

The cooperative attitude of the Chinese toward the Russians underwent a drastic change once it became evident that the latter had not come to oust the Germans. While the Chinese had ignored a warning by the British minister on December 19 that if China would grant various concessions to other powers, England would present demands of her own, they were more receptive when MacDonald returned with a protest against the Russian loan and offered his good offices for arranging a loan in England on better terms. The fact that British warships had assembled at Port Hamilton and Japanese warships at Tsushima bolstered the Chinese position vis-à-vis Russia. On December 29, 1897, the ministers of the Tsungli Yamen received Pavlov coldly and asked him for written assurance that Russia did not intend to retain Port Arthur and Talienwan.[46]

On the twenty-first Li Hung-chang renewed the request that the tsarist government hand to Minister Yang Ju a statement to the effect that the visit of the Russian vessels to Port Arthur and Talienwan was due to recent events and would be temporary. Li said that he was being accused of criminal credulity toward Russia and was being held responsible for her occupation of the ports. His future as a statesman and even his personal safety depended on the receipt of such a document, Li asserted.[47]

Informing his government of the Chinese demand, Pavlov recommended that it be carried out if the Chinese agreed in turn to put their acceptance of the Russian conditions of December 16 in writing. He warned that if Russia gave the written commitment without receiving a similar written assurance from China in exchange, the Chinese would interpret this as "cowardliness before Japan."

In accordance with Pavlov's advice, Muraviev instructed him on January 4, 1898, to declare to the Tsungli Yamen that Russia never had any territorial designs and would leave Port Arthur and Talienwan "when the political circumstances and the interests of Russia and China allowed it," a communication to this effect to be made to the Chinese minister in St. Petersburg; that in view of her friendship with China, Russia expected the Peking government to put at her use a well provided anchorage in the Pechili or Korea Bay to deliver Russia from the need of wintering in Nagasaki; and that Russia demanded a written commitment to carry out the oral promises regarding the instructor and railroad questions and the concession for a connecting branch line to one of the ports on the Yellow Sea.

When Pavlov communicated the above to the Tsungli Yamen on January 7, the ministers remarked that the only serious difficulty lay in the question of a line to the Yellow Sea, which the Chinese government would like to build itself. The following day, on the eighth, Li Hung-chang telegraphed to Witte that the mouth of the Yalu River would offer the best conditions for the construction of a port and that the Chinese government would like to build a branch line connecting such a port with the Russian railroad in Manchuria by itself with Russian assistance. But Witte no longer was satisfied with a line to Korea, though he himself had suggested it but recently, or with the demands of December 16. The guarantees which he now wanted for the Russian loan and which Muraviev stipulated in the instruction he cabled to Pavlov on January 11 included not only the revenue of the Maritime Customs but of the land customs at the Chinese Eastern Railroad and in the provinces of Manchuria in general, as well as the entire salt revenue. The loan proffer was made on a take-it-or-leave-it basis, the Russians refusing to haggle over the terms and demanding that it be signed within two weeks.[48]

The British were willing to provide a loan of twelve million pounds sterling at par, for fifty years, at four per cent per annum, not including the sinking fund. In return they demanded the opening of Talien as a treaty port, the opening of the town of Nanning in southwestern Kwangsi Province and Hsiangtan in northeastern Hunan to foreign trade, the right for foreign steamers to navigate the inland waters, permission to construct a railway from Burma to the Yangtze River, the abolition of the likin tax at the treaty ports, the pledge that no portion of the Yangtze valley would be alienated to any other power, and that in the event of default certain revenues would be placed under the control of the Imperial Customs.[49]

The ministers of the Tsungli Yamen, with whom MacDonald conferred at length on January 15, objected above all to the demand regarding Talien, asserting that Pavlov had strongly protested on instructions from his government against the establishment of an open port. He had warned them, they said, that such a step on their part would bring upon them the hostility of Russia. MacDonald retorted that Talien was the only port giving access to northern China during the winter. He challenged the Chinese to explain the attitude of St. Petersburg unless Russia harbored ulterior designs on Talien. Although the Chinese concurred that the opening of the port would protect it from annexation, they feared to become embroiled with Russia. All that Mac-Donald could do was to try to shame them by expressing his "astonishment" that China was not free to open a treaty port wherever she desired in her own territory.

"The Russian threat has evidently greatly frightened the Yamen, who see clearly the advantage of opening Talienwan, and had previously seemed to welcome the idea of doing so," MacDonald reported. "I stated that, according to my instructions, the offer of the loan depended upon the Chinese Government accepting this among other concessions, but I consider it probable that rather than incur the danger of reprisals on the part of Russia, the Yamen will relinquish the loan," he concluded.[50]

When Muraviev learned from the newspapers of England's demand for the opening of Talienwan, he reminded O'Conor that the British government had recently recognized in a public speech the right of Russia to have an open port. Since Talienwan was one of the few ice-free places on the north coast of China, Russia could hardly be expected to approve the British demand. Thought had been given to a port near the mouth of the Yalu River, Muraviev remarked, but the harbors in that region appeared to be frozen in winter; the choice was very limited.[51]

During the course of the conversation O'Conor observed that he had read in the papers that two Russian men-of-war had passed through the Suez canal en route to China. Muraviev acknowledged that this had probably happened; the hurried equipment and "suspicious movements" of the Japanese fleet had necessitated the reinforcement of the Russian Pacific squadron.[52]

As Salisbury agreed to a guarantee by his government of a British loan and MacDonald continued to woo the Chinese, Muraviev sent new instructions on January 20 in the event the Russian proposal was not accepted. Pavlov was not to adhere to the two-week time limit and was not to break off negotiations if the Chinese wished to discuss the Russian conditions. He was directed, furthermore, to propose to the Chinese "very carefully," so as not to damage Russian negotiations concerning the loan, to conclude a written agreement about the lease of the Liaotung ports, in view of China's impotence to prevent the "opening" by the English following the departure of the Russian vessels.

That day it was learned in Peking that the British had promised a substantial bribe to the Chinese ministers for arranging a loan with their country. A similar offer followed from St. Petersburg on the twenty-first, Pavlov being instructed to distribute secretly among the Chinese statesmen one million rubles for this purpose. Fearing that a British loan might rend the friendship between China and Russia, Witte telegraphed to Pokotilov on his own responsibility that if the million rubles did not suffice, the sum could be increased.

On January 23 Pavlov and Pokotilov invited Li Hung-chang to the Russian legation and offered him 500,000 liang (taels) for the arrangement of the loan. Li promised his help and gave to understand that if the Russians could arrange the loan at full face value, as the English offered to do, he could almost guarantee that their loan would be accepted. Pavlov was told the same at the Tsungli Yamen on the twenty-fourth. However, after a conference with Mac-Donald the same day the ministers instructed Li to ask Pavlov to agree to the discontinuance of the loan talks. This Li refused to do. On January 25 the Russians called Li again and promised to increase the one million ruble "reward" if he could arrange for the dispatch of Hsü Ching-ch'eng, the former minister to Russia and now honorary president of the Chinese Eastern Railroad Company, to St. Petersburg for the negotiation of the loan. Pavlov and Pokotilov also had a secret meeting with Chang Yin-huan that day, offering him 200,000 liang on the same conditions as the amount promised to Li. Finance Minister Weng T'ung-ho declined to see the Russians for fear of arousing suspicion as he had no personal contacts with any foreigners, but Pavlov was given to understand that he had come to a secret understanding with Li who would share his remuneration with him. But MacDonald tightened the screws. He warned the Tsungli Yamen that Britain would revive various old claims and act like Germany if her loan were not accepted. On the twenty-sixth Li broached the possibility of dividing the loan between England and Russia, but at this point France objected to the British conditions, favoring the negotiation of an international loan in which all interested powers, even Japan, could participate. On February 2 Yang Ju informed the tsarist government that China had decided not to obtain any foreign loan. However, as Pokotilov surmised, this was merely a subterfuge; China could not raise the money internally and would revert to the English loan after some time had passed.

Witte was taken aback by the military preparations the British were making in connection with the loan question. What had aroused the British was, of course, not the loan alone, nor the lease of Port Arthur, but the apprehension that Russia intended to seize a large part of the Chinese empire and to withdraw it completely from world trade.[53] Staal had contributed to the conviction during his protest against the presence of British men-of-war at Port Arthur and Talien when he had referred to the Liaotung Peninsula and then to Manchuria as a whole as Russia's "sphere of influence." Salisbury told the French ambassador, Courcel, that England, who had eighty per cent of China's foreign trade, would not let herself be pushed out from any part of the empire for any reason.[54] The chancelor of the exchequer, Sir Michael Edward Hicks-Beach, had declared in a speech that China was the most hopeful market of the future for the commerce of the world and that the British government was determined to see the door to the market kept open, "even at the cost of war, if necessary."[55] To avoid war with Great Britain St. Petersburg decided to abandon its loan efforts, to explore the possibility of working with England rather than against her, and to procure, with London's assent, the construction of a branch from the trunk line of the Chinese Eastern Railroad to Talien or another port on the Yellow Sea between Yingtze (Yingkow) and the mouth of the Yalu River, the port to be if not exclusively so at least largely in Russian hands.[56]

On February 20 Muraviev renewed the correspondence with Pavlov concerning the lease of the ports, offering to help the Chinese to extricate themselves from the difficult situation in which they found themselves by dropping Russian objections to the loan with Britain, in fact to use St. Peterburg's influence to soften English terms. China was to grant the lease of Port Arthur and Talienwan in exchange for Russian assistance in this matter, the secret agreement of 1896 forming the basis for the transaction. Pavlov was to broach the subject at a "favorable moment."

On March 1 the Chinese government concluded a loan for sixteen million pounds sterling at 4½ per cent for a period of forty-five years with British and German financiers through the Hong Kong-Shanghai and the German-Asiatic banks.[57] Two days later, on the third, Pavlov began the negotiations concerning the leasing of Port Arthur and Talienwan.

General Aleksei Nikolaevich Kuropatkin, who had become acting minister of war at the beginning of 1898—he became regular minister of war in July—[58] pressed for the retention of Port Arthur rather than simply the use of a port on the Yellow Sea demanded of China and the construction of a branch line of the Chinese Eastern Railroad to Talienwan. Although neither Muraviev nor Witte supported Kuropatkin, a special committee was formed to work out the details. It consisted of Grand Duke Aleksei Aleksandrovich, who acted as chairman, Witte, Muraviev, Kuropatkin, P. P. Tyrtov, Navy Chief of Staff Vice Admiral Fedor Karlovich Avelan and Army Chief of Staff General Viktor Viktorovich Sakharov. At a meeting in the second half of February the conferees agreed to demand of the Chinese government the leasing of the southern part of the Liaotung Peninsula up to a line running from Port Adams on the western shore through Adams Peak to the little place of Pitzewo on the eastern shore of this peninsula and the establishment of a neutral zone from the above line northward to a line running straight from the city of Yingkow on the western shore of the Liaotung Peninsula through the city of Takushan to the mouth of a river on the east coast of the peninsula. (They were prepared, in the event of Chinese opposition, to reduce the area by shifting the boundaries of the neutral zone as well as of the leasehold substantially southward.) No Chinese military forces, only policemen, were to be allowed in the leasehold eventually; a limited number of Chinese soldiers could be admitted at first at the discretion of the Russian authorities, provided they would be subordinate to the same Russian authorities. Permission was to be obtained from the Chinese government for the construction of a southern branch from the trunkline of the Trans-Siberian Railroad. Should there be difficulties in bringing it to Port Arthur, the terminal point of the branch line would be one of the most convenient points for this on the Liaotung coast, beginning with the city of Yingtze (Yingkow). A Russian unit was to be shipped at once from Vladivostok to Port Arthur to give muscle to the wishes of St. Petersburg.

On March 3 Pavlov read a memorandum with the above demands to the ministers of the Tsungli Yamen, adding that in view of the urgency of the matter he would like to have a reply in principle within five days; the details of the agreement must be decided in final form within two weeks, by the twenty-seventh. As the main argument for the presentation of the Russian demands was the inability of China to protect herself from outside attack, the Chinese retorted that China should be given a chance to try out her powers of defense, Russian occupation of Port Arthur and Talienwan and their connection with the trunk line of the Chinese Eastern Railroad to follow only in the event of further failures on the part of China. They met Pavlov's importunities with vague replies and excuses.

The Tsungli Yamen appealed to the English and Japanese legations for assistance. Complaining about the conduct of the Russians, the Chinese ministers pleaded for the issuance of a pledge on the part of Great Britain and Japan that neither of them would occupy Port Arthur and Talienwan if the Russians withdrew from there, so as to defuse the Russian argument for the preventive detention of the ports.[59]

The Chinese government, MacDonald reported, was "fully conscious of the absurdity" of the pretext that Russia needed the lease of Port Arthur and Talien "to assist China in resisting the aggression of other Powers on Manchuria." Yet it could not reject the Russian demands without foreign aid and thus solicited the above assurances from Great Britain and Japan even though Pavlov had not referred to any power in particular. When MacDonald warned

General Aleksei Nikolaevich Kuropatkin, director of the Russian war ministry, 1898–1904. (*Vsemirnaia illiustratsiia*, 1898, 59: 51.)

that if the Chinese yielded to the demands of Russia, similar claims would probably be made by other powers including his own country, the ministers of the Tsungli Yamen replied that that was why they were trying to resist the Russian demands.[60]

The publication in the London *Times* on March 7 of a telegram from its Peking correspondent to the effect that Russian demands made in consequence of the loan concluded at Peking included "sovereign rights" over Port Arthur and Talienwan and that Pavlov had threatened that Russian troops would advance into Manchuria if China did not comply in five days aroused concern among Englishmen and Japanese, particularly as MacDonald reported the same.[61] On instructions from Salisbury, O'Conor hastened to Muraviev, who had been down with small-pox for almost a month and had just returned to work, to ascertain whether the allegations were true.[62] Muraviev revealed to O'Conor that Pavlov was negotiating with the Tsungli Yamen for the right to construct a railroad to Talien or to Port Arthur via Kianchen on conditions similar to those laid down for the Chinese Eastern Railroad, as well as for the cession of these two ports for a certain number of years. He assured him that no demands had been made for sovereign rights over these places, nor had the dispatch of troops into Manchuria been threatened.[63] He explained that the acquisition of an ice-free port on the coast of China was of vital necessity for Russia, who could no longer count on being able to supply and repair her ships in safety in Japanese ports. Britain, Germany, and France had naval stations open all the year, while Russia was ice-bound in Vladivostok. Muraviev remarked that Russia was seeking the cession of both Port Arthur and Talienwan, because one would be useless without the other, yet Talienwan would be open to foreign trade like other ports in China. He reiterated that Russia was not demanding either sovereign rights or a perpetual cession, but hinted that her position might change if Germany received such rights at Kiaochow.

O'Conor could not resist expressing the apprehension that regardless of the assurances given to him by Muraviev and earlier by Vice Minister Lamsdorff that Port Arthur would not be reconverted into a military fortress, once Russia had taken over the fortifications would be repaired as a matter of course. He observed that the studding of the Gulf of Pechili with foreign fortresses could not be in the interests of British commerce and was bound to arouse the deepest concern of his government.[64]

MacDonald reported from Peking on March 10 that information he had obtained since his earlier dispatch showed that the *Times* telegrams had "exaggerated the peremptory nature of the Russian demands" and that, in his opinion, no immediate action on the part of Britain was necessary. Although

Russian naval strength would be greatly increased by the occupation and fortification of Port Arthur, he doubted that the balance of power in China would
be seriously affected thereby. "Her Majesty's Government," MacDonald telegraphed, "must, I think, face the fact that Russia is determined to make a
Russian province of Manchuria, and she has a similar design on Mongolia.
Much can be done to impede and delay her in the execution of these projects
by opposition, but as England cannot, unless she is prepared to go to war,
actually stop her, I think the best policy would be to refrain from opposing the
acquisition of Russia of a lease of Port Arthur and Talienwan, and to make the
best terms possible for our neutrality." [65] "The neutral attitude is not easy to
maintain for any length of time, and I hope the negotiations with the Russian
Government will soon reach a definite result," MacDonald remarked a week
later.[66]

While appealing to England and Japan for diplomatic weapons with which
to combat the Russian exactions, the Tsungli Yamen dispatched Hsü Ching-
ch'eng to St. Petersburg as special ambassador with instructions to induce the
tsarist government to withdraw its demands.[67] One of China's ablest diplomats, with more experience than Yang Ju in dealing with the Russians, Hsü
had been in Berlin conferring about the Kiaochow question.[68]

The Russians were determined not to let the Chinese use the dispatch of
Hsü as a means of delay.[69] On March 12 Pavlov communicated to the Tsungli
Yamen that he had informed his government of Hsü's appointment. The Foreign Ministry had replied that Nicholas would be glad to receive Hsü, but that
an immediate decision must be reached on the four basic principles: (1) the
lease of Port Arthur and Talien, (2) the retention of sovereign rights by China
over the places leased, (3) the erection of naval buildings and defense installations in the leaseholds at Russian expense, and (4) the right of constructing a
branch line from Talien to the main line of the Chinese Eastern Railroad on
the same conditions as the main line.[70] Details could be worked out later. He
demanded a categorical reply within two days. When the Chinese protested
that inasmuch as they had sent an ambassador extraordinary to St. Petersburg
they must wait for him to negotiate the question before giving an answer,
Pavlov remarked drily that Hsü could be set aside and the matter resolved in
Peking.

The Tsungli Yamen instructed Hsü to request an audience with the tsar to
sound out his views. It pointed out in another cable that when the Liaotung
Peninsula had been retroceded by Japan, China had promised not to let another power occupy it. If China now granted Russia a lease on Port Arthur and
Talien, Japan was sure to cause difficulties for China. "Your task is to exhort
the Foreign Ministry not to make trouble for both of us, but to have regard for

our feelings of friendship," the Tsungli Yamen cabled. It suggested that Russia use Port Arthur and Talien at her convenience for anchorage and storage of coal without a formal lease. "[Then] Japan and other countries naturally will not get to use this as a pretext to start another dispute, and the whole situation will benefit."

Muraviev received Hsü on the same day. Noting that the Kiaochow question had been settled, that England had received rights in the Yangtze region, and that French demands had been met, he declared that Russia consequently must be granted a lease on an ice-free port for her navy and for storing coal "to protect the rights of both countries." In vain Hsü pleaded that England, France, and Japan would be aroused if China gave such a lease to Russia. Muraviev insisted that the will of the tsar be carried out, though the extent of the lease might be negotiable. He did not agree to the Chinese proposal that the Russian vessels winter at Port Arthur without a formal lease, a small piece of land being set aside for them as a coal depot. "The intent of their words is very firm, much more so than before," Hsü telegraphed.

The following day, on the thirteenth, Muraviev handed to Hsü a map of the territory Russia wished to lease. "This is exceedingly unexpected," Hsü cabled. He reported that Ukhtomskii had seen Nicholas on China's behalf to explain the dangers facing her.[71]

Confronted with Pavlov's ultimatum, the ministers of the Tsungli Yamen made a reply by March 14, but studiously evaded the issues. They repeated that the results of Hsü's mission must be awaited.[72]

Received by Nicholas on the fifteenth, Hsü reiterated that England, France, and Japan would demand territorial compensation if China granted the lease to Russia. China would not be able to resist the exactions alone and the overall situation in the Far East would be disrupted. He urged the tsar to draw up a far-reaching plan respecting their friendly relations. "Upholding the peace and giving in will benefit both of our countries," Hsü argued.

Nicholas retorted that the leasing of the ports would be of mutual interest. Its purpose was to protect the two countries. He assured Hsü that he had no intention of acquiring more territory. "All reports and rumors of Russian troops entering Manchuria are incorrect," Nicholas declared. He expressed the hope that Hsü would convey to his government that it should agree to the lease as soon as possible "to make other countries know that our two countries have reached a decision on a friendly basis." "Only this will be satisfactory," the tsar insisted.

Hsü promised to telegraph the communication. When he remarked that the tsarist government must make some concessions for the sake of reaching an agreement, Nicholas said nothing.

The Tsungli Yamen's response was cabled to Hsü on the seventeenth. It disputed the justification advanced by Muraviev for the presentation of the Russian demands, arguing that the benefits received by the British in the Yangtze region did not include any territorial concessions and that France's demands had not and could not be met. It dismissed the notion that Port Arthur and Talien could be used by the ships of Russia and China simultaneously. The terrain at Port Arthur was too narrow and constricted for this; nor would it be convenient to have their forces placed together at random. The situation was different at Talien and could be discussed perhaps. Repeating the compromise it had offered that Russian vessels use Talien Bay for anchorage and storage of coal without a formal lease, the Tsungli Yamen tried to shame St. Petersburg into accepting it. "Formerly Russia promised to unite in mutual aid, but now she acts like a bandit chieftain and the chief plotter of military action, with harm to our friendly relations and a hindrance to the over-all situation," it stated. The Tsungli Yamen related that Pavlov was "extremely anxious to get results." It complained that his character was "perverse and obstinate" and that it was difficult to negotiate with him. Hsü should tell the Russian Foreign Minister, it concluded, "not to be so deceptively ambiguous."

Hsü reported on the same day that the tsar had appointed Chargé Pavlov as plenipotentiary special ambassador to negotiate the Port Arthur and Talien question and that the Russian Foreign Ministry insisted that China conclude the discussions at Peking punctually. In a telegram on the eighteenth, Hsü warned that if China did not accept the Russian demands by March 27, Russia would "carry out her own solution without regard to our alliance and friendly relations." Ukhtomskii had secretly told him that Nicholas had authorized the Foreign Ministry and the Army and Navy Departments "to work things out satisfactorily," Hsü conveyed in another cable. "There is nothing that can be done to bring about an understanding," he telegraphed. "I fear if we pass the [time] limit, there will be trouble. The situation is very tense." On March 19 Hsü reiterated that the Russian Foreign Ministry was resolute in its intention and insisted that the general principles be accepted at Peking without further discussion; details could be worked out later in a separate document. He repeated that the lease must be signed by the twenty-seventh to forestall hostilities.[73]

The confidence which Muraviev displayed in the negotiations with Hsü was rooted in his conception of the Chinese character. He regarded the Chinese as fatalists who would make only token resistance.[74] Meanwhile the Chinese efforts to enlist British and Japanese support against Russia came to naught. In contrast to the excited tone of the British daily press, the attitude of the

British government was very reserved.[75] In a "very confidential" telegram to
MacDonald on March 11, Salisbury conveyed that England was disposed to
raise no objection to a Russian railroad in the Liaotung Peninsula or to the
leasing of Port Arthur and Talienwan provided Russia threw no obstacle in the
way of the construction of a commercial railroad to be built by an Anglo-
Chinese company from Hankow to Peking.[76] The undersecretary of state, Sanderson, whom Kato saw when Salisbury was ill, said that Britain would not
give the assurance China had requested that she had no designs on Chinese
territory; she would not make such a declaration without being asked by Russia. Her intention had been publicly declared and that ought to suffice.[77] When
newspapers published on March 12 a Reuter's telegram to the effect that Mac-
Donald had lodged a strong protest with the Tsungli Yamen against Chinese
cession of Port Arthur to Russia on the ground that it would destroy the balance of power in the East, Salisbury remarked, "Of course this is entirely
devoid of truth."[78]

The Japanese government had been prepared to give the assurance desired
by the Chinese if the British government would enforce its decision of maintaining the integrity of China. Upon the receipt of Kato's report from London
regarding the views voiced by Sanderson, the Japanese government decided
not to give the desired assurance for the time being.[79]

England did seek affirmation from the tsarist government that it would
abide by the provisions of the Treaty of Tientsin at any port in the Liaotung
Peninsula or in any territory leased by China to Russia. In a private postscript
to a telegram to O'Conor, Salisbury remarked that Britain could not accept
any distinction in this respect between Port Arthur and Talienwan.[80]

Muraviev demurred. He insisted in a lengthy interview with O'Conor on
March 13 that only Talien could be opened to foreign commerce, though he
pledged that Chinese sovereignty would not be abridged in either port.[81]

In view of this, O'Conor deemed it his duty to warn Salisbury that evidently only a small part of the ultimate intentions of the tsarist government
toward China was covered by its official language and assurances. He predicted that once Russia had gained a cession by lease of Port Arthur and
Talienwan under the promise of opening one or both of the ports to foreign
commerce, she would reconstruct the defenses of Port Arthur and fortify one
of the three harbors of Talien Bay. While it was not yet clear whether the
terminus of the Russian railroad would be at Talien or at Yangchow, there was
little doubt, O'Conor contended, that the tsarist government looked forward
to being in possession of Manchuria before the expiration of the lease and that
Chihli Province would be virtually, if not actually, in Russian hands. "If the
effete Government of Peking is still in existence and not upset by a revolution,

which will hasten Russian action, it is probable, at all events, that Russian influence will be so great that they will be able to oppose successfully, and entirely nullify, the promise given by the Chinese Government, that the Inspector-General of Customs shall be a British subject," apprehended O'Conor, who had served in Peking prior to his appointment to St. Petersburg. Although the projects of Russia might be thwarted by a combination of powers, it was difficult to say who would unite with Britain in this aim. He suggested, therefore, to accept the Russian assurances "with a full appreciation of their real value" and to preserve the balance of power as well as British prestige and interests by obtaining in return the cession of a port in Chusan, perhaps Silver Island in the Yangtze River, as well as the right of connecting the Burmese railroad with the Anglo-Chinese lines. "I am aware that this is at the very least tantamount to recognizing spheres of influence, a policy which does not commend itself to Her Majesty's Government," O'Conor cabled, "but as the disintegration of China has unfortunately already commenced, it would secure to England a share, and a preponderant share, in the partition." "It is the policy of the Russian Government," O'Conor asserted, "to obtain their demands by what they term friendly negotiation, but, once they have effected their object, they will more or less take China under their protection, and then so strongly oppose any compensatory demands Her Majesty's Government may make as to bring the two countries to the verge of war, while Her Majesty's Government will be unable, save by force, and in direct opposition to China, to get a satisfactory settlement of their claims. On the other hand, the Russian Government will be able to advance its specious argument that all they did was with the consent of China."[82]

MacDonald meanwhile cabled in reply to Salisbury's telegram of the eleventh that he did not regard a promise on the part of Russia not to oppose the British railroad concession as an adequate *quid pro quo* for British nonopposition to Russian policy in Manchuria. He suggested the following conditions for a friendly attitude toward Russia: (1) that the tsarist government confine itself to "fair competition" in regard to any commercial enterprise the English might undertake and throw no obstacles in their way; (2) that the Russians not interfere with the position of C. W. Kinder, whose dismissal from the post of chief engineer of the Imperial Railway of North China would be a severe blow to British prestige; and (3) that Russia be given to understand that Britain regarded the Yangtze region as her sphere of influence. MacDonald observed that the maintenance of British rights under the Treaty of Tientsin would have to be guaranteed in a special arrangement with the tsarist government as the treaty had not envisioned the leasing of Chinese territory. "It should be distinctly understood that our freedom to ask similar leases in other parts of

China would in no way be affected by our abstaining from opposing the present demands," MacDonald concluded.[83]

The British government instructed O'Conor not to make the communication to the tsarist government proposed to him on the eleventh until he had seen MacDonald's reply.[84]

Kato gathered from opinion in the British press, speeches in Parliament, and private conversations that despite the dissatisfaction of the general public, the government of Great Britain would acquiesce in the domination of the Liaotung Peninsula by Russia if the latter guaranteed that the ports in question would be accessible to British trade in every respect. The inquiries addressed to Russia were intended to elicit a definite guarantee, as the pledges so far given by St. Petersburg were extremely vague. In the absence of such an assurance, Kato expected, the British government might be compelled to occupy some place itself in order to restore the balance of power and to appease public excitement at home. Yet Sanderson, to whom he had talked, had seemed at a loss what to occupy. In any case, it was unlikely that the British government would oppose Russian aggression by active force, Kato concluded.[85]

On March 13 Li Hung-chang had informed MacDonald that the tsarist government had refused to transfer the negotiations regarding Port Arthur and Talien to St. Petersburg.[86] On the fifteenth the Chinese Privy Council inquired of the British minister indirectly and confidentially how his government would receive a proposal for an alliance between England, Japan, and China. It also wanted to know whether he thought it advisable for the Chinese government to meet the Russian demands by opening Talien and Port Arthur and at the same time several commercial centers as treaty ports. MacDonald replied that he was not prepared to venture an opinion on the question of an alliance. As for the second point, he responded that the Privy Council was well aware that it had always been the policy of England that as much of China as possible should be open to world trade.[87]

Upon receipt of MacDonald's report of the above exchange, Salisbury telegraphed that it might be worthwhile for the Chinese government to suggest to Russia making Port Arthur and Talien both treaty ports, with special coaling and docking facilities for Russian ships of war. "The suggestion should not be put forward in the form of official advice from us, as Russia will almost certainly refuse," Salisbury added privately.[88]

That night, on the fifteenth, Muraviev informed O'Conor that he had seen the tsar in the morning and that Nicholas had authorized him to give O'Conor the assurance that both Port Arthur and Talien would be opened to foreign trade like other Chinese ports in the event the Russian government obtained a lease on those places. Muraviev assured O'Conor further in Nicholas's name that British rights and privileges in Chinese ports would be respected and that the sovereignty of China would not be impaired.

Muraviev repeated the assurances during his official reception at the Foreign Ministry on the afternoon of the sixteenth. He asked O'Conor, however, that the guarantees not be mentioned yet in the House of Commons, which was debating this issue, lest it be regarded as want of courtesy toward the Chinese government, which had not yet formally agreed to the lease. He suggested that instead of stating that the tsarist government would respect the rights and privileges of the Treaty of Tientsin, it would be better to apply the Russian assurances to the treaties between China and the foreign powers in general.[89]

On March 20 O'Conor had a more or less private conversation with Lamsdorff, who defended the policy of Muraviev. As Lamsdorff reiterated that the occupation of Port Arthur and Talien did not signify the partition of the Chinese empire and did not violate its integrity, O'Conor asked facetiously whether he would deem the integrity of Great Britain violated if Russian troops occupied Dover Castle, while leaving the police administration of the town to the English government. When Lamsdorff responded with a straight face that he would not regard this as a violation of British integrity, O'Conor declared that in such a case it was a waste of time for them to debate whether or not the occupation of Port Arthur constituted a violation of the integrity of China and the dismemberment of that empire. He did point out that it amounted to just that in the eyes of Europe and of every Chinese mandarin. Since the occupation by a foreign power of Port Arthur, which lay at the gate of Peking, had to be viewed as a menace to the Chinese capital and to the freedom of action of the emperor and his ministers, it was evident that this measure changed the entire policy of Russia toward China and that the tsarist government would not be able to appear any longer as her friend or protector, O'Conor argued. It was, he ventured, most dangerous to begin the dismemberment of China; Lamsdorff himself and other members of the tsarist government had deplored its initiation by Germany. Warning that it was hard to say where the partition of China would end once fairly started, O'Conor foresaw that "it was quite on the cards that when the Chinese really realized that the Central Government was quite powerless, an insurrection or revolution—induced perhaps directly by some accidental calamity, like famine or inundation—would break out which would bring the whole edifice of Chinese sovereignty toppling down before any country, not excepting Russia, was ready or able to take up even a part of the succession."

E. E. Ukhtomskii, with whom O'Conor had talked earlier, viewed the proposed occupation of Port Arthur as a grave mistake. He had pointed this out to

the tsar several times. Like O'Conor he feared that it would lead to the overthrow of the Manchu dynasty and that it was not in the interests of his country
"to hasten unduly the inevitable development of events." Ukhtomskii speculated that Muraviev desired the occupation of Port Arthur as a set-off against
the German occupation of Kiaochow. Right or wrong, Ukhtomskii and various "shrewd and influential" persons to whom O'Conor spoke on the subject,
believed that it was too late to turn back.[90]

On March 21 Hsü related to O'Conor that Muraviev had informed him that
he had given assurances to the British government to the effect that Russia
would respect all treaties existing between China and foreign countries and
that both Talien and Port Arthur would be opened to commerce in the event of
their lease.[91] Salisbury instructed O'Conor to communicate to Muraviev that
the British government noted with satisfaction the assurances that the tsarist
government had no intention of infringing on the rights and privileges guaranteed by the existing treaties between China and foreign countries nor on Chinese sovereignty. "Her Majesty's Government, on their part, would not regard
with any dissatisfaction the lease by Russia of an ice-free commercial harbor,
connected by rail with the trans-Siberian Railway which is now under construction," Salisbury telegraphed. But Russian control of a military port in
the immediate vicinity of Port Arthur would be objectionable as "a standing
menace to Peking and the commencement of the partition of China," Salisbury stated. The British government was prepared, he added, "to give assurances that beyond the maintenance of existing Treaty rights they have no
interests in Manchuria, and will pledge themselves not to occupy any port in
the Gulf of Pechili so long as other Powers pursue the same policy."[92]

As the Tsungli Yamen, confused by conflicting reports, sought clarification
whether or not England had come to terms with Russia concerning the proposed lease of Port Arthur and Talien, Assistant Undersecretary of Foreign
Affairs Bertie informed Lo Feng-loh on March 23 that the British government
concurred in the opinion of the Tsungli Yamen that Port Arthur ought not to
be leased to Russia. It had no objection to the leasing of Talien as a commercial port and the construction of a railroad to that place. If the Chinese government followed its advice in that matter, Britain would give a pledge not to
occupy Weihaiwei when it was evacuated by the Japanese, provided China
committed herself not to alienate or lease it to any other European power.[93]

When O'Conor saw Muraviev that afternoon, on the twenty-third, and re-
hearsed the arguments against the Russian occupation of Port Arthur, the
foreign minister remarked with some heat that it was England alone that made
difficulties and as usual stood in the way of Russia. No other government had
raised any official questions or shown any resentment against the proposed

action of his country. He reiterated that Talien was useless without Port Arthur, as Russia needed a safe harbor for her fleet, dependent neither on the elements at Vladivostok nor on the goodwill of the Japanese. "Every other Great Maritime Power had a naval station in the China Seas, and why should not Russia, whose fleet was now very considerable, and whose territory was conterminous?"

Muraviev did not like O'Conor's request that he put in writing the assurances he had given him in regard to the validity of the existing treaties and the sovereignty of China. After thinking about it for several minutes he agreed to do so, but he said that he did not see how he could formulate anything concrete until China had agreed to the Russian demands.[94]

On March 26 Hsü's interpreter called on O'Conor to seek confirmation of the assertion made by MacDonald to the Tsungli Yamen that O'Conor was negotiating with the tsarist government to prevent the leasing of Port Arthur to Russia. O'Conor replied that if Hsü had any doubts about the veracity of MacDonald's statement, he should inquire of Salisbury through Lo. While giving the interpreter to understand that the information was correct, O'Conor made it clear that he would not let himself be used as a "diplomatic buffer" by the Chinese.[95]

In a lengthy dispatch, which he asked O'Conor to read to Muraviev, Salisbury examined the potential impact of Russian policy on British interests. It was evident, he remarked, that the concessions demanded by Russia would profoundly and permanently affect the conditions of Manchuria. "For good or for evil, the social, political, and economic state of this region must inevitably be revolutionized when it is traversed by a railway under Russian management, connecting ports on the Pacific under Russian control with the commercial and military system of the Russian Empire." Salisbury reiterated that the British government was not dissatisfied with Russian claims for an ice-free port at Talien and its connection by rail with the general system of Russian railways, because this was in line with British policy of opening China to world commerce. Its objection to the military side of the Russian demands, namely the occupation of Port Arthur, was not to the acquisition of a naval base *per se*, but to the lease of this particular place, because of the political repercussions of international importance that it was likely to entail in the Chinese capital. Since the British government feared that Port Arthur would command the maritime approaches to Peking and give to Russia "the same strategic advantage by sea which she already possesses in so ample a measure by land" if the rest of the Gulf of Pechili remained "in hands so helpless" as those of China, it retained full liberty to take what steps it deemed best to protect its own interests and to diminish the "evil consequences" which it anticipated.[96]

Meanwhile, upon telegraphic confirmation by Hsü that Russia insisted that the convention pertaining to Port Arthur and Talien be concluded at Peking and that Pavlov had been named plenipotentiary for this purpose, the Tsungli Yamen had realized that it could no longer avoid negotiating with the Russian chargé.[97] Li Hung-chang confided to Yano on March 19 that the Chinese ministers did not know what to do. It was worthless to appeal to the foreign powers, Li said, because France and Germany would only welcome the opportunity to present further claims of their own.[98] Great Britain would not move easily and Japan was very cautious. It had been suggested that China acquiesce in the Russian demands and let the matter run its course. Anyway, Li concluded, China was helpless and had not decided on any definite step. "You will imagine [the] attitude of Germany, France and Russia, and the grave issue of the situation," Yano cabled to Nishi; "but above all, [the] Chinese Government look upon the Russian demand most seriously." [99]

Although the Chinese ministers invited Pavlov to a conference at the Tsungli Yamen on March 20, they continued to procrastinate. They were as evasive as ever during the meeting, pleading that their position was very difficult, for if they gave the concessions to Russia, similar claims were bound to be made by the other powers, which would be the beginning of the complete partition of China. They contended, furthermore, that Port Arthur was too crowded to satisfy Russia needs; Li Hung-chang urged Pavlov to go see for himself before the conclusion of a convention. Finally, the ministers argued that it was impossible to study such an important question in such a brief period of time.[100]

The ministers of the Tsungli Yamen saw no way out of the situation. On March 21 Li Hung-chang and Chang Yin-huan met with Liao Shou-heng, president of the Board of Punishment, in Weng T'ung-ho's study to discuss the draft treaty in detail. They criticized each other's words without proposing a course of action. "It was nothing but empty talk, so it was all over for us," Weng recorded in his diary. Prince Ch'ing, with whom Weng talked on the twenty-second, could devise no means of resisting the Russian demands, nor could Li Hung-chang and Chang Yin-huan who joined them. As they were conferring, news arrived of massive Russian troop movements at Port Arthur. "The various ministers all wiped away their tears. What sort of circumstance is this?!" Weng wrote in his diary. Ch'ing, Li, and Chang agreed that there was nothing they could do but grant the entire treaty. At this point an official by the name of Yang Yü-shang arrived with the idea of proposing to St.

Petersburg the conclusion of a four power alliance between China, Russia, Germany, and France to thwart the "greedy plots" of other states. The notion appealed to the others, yet they set it aside as impracticable. When his visitors left, Weng continued to think of what policy China should adopt. "On successive nights I did not sleep, nor in the morning could I rest peacefully," he noted in his diary.[101]

Witte had been so upset and offended by the decision to retain Port Arthur and Talien over his strong objections that he had broken off all personal relations with Muraviev. In view of his disagreement with the tsar's policy and the personal reprimand he had received, Witte asked Nicholas, when the latter returned to the Winter Palace, to be relieved of his duties. Nicholas did not accept Witte's resignation and assured him that he was satisfied with his work as finance minister. Declaring that the Liaotung question had been decided, wisely or not, Nicholas called on Witte to assist him in resolving the problem as successfully as possible. Since a landing party had been sent from Vladivostok to secure the territory by force if the Chinese did not agree to the lease, Witte applied the leverage of financial rewards for the Chinese negotiators in order to avoid bloodshed and prevent the shattering of friendly relations with China.[102]

The appointment of Li Hung-chang and Chang Yin-huan as plenipotentiaries to deal with Pavlov marked a turn in the discussions. Better informed than their colleagues with the realities of the situation, they recognized the futility of Chinese opposition in the face of Russian determination to occupy Port Arthur, if need be by force. Though they complained to Pokotilov in a confidential conversation on the twenty-first about the difficulty of their position in view of the excitement that had been aroused among the officialdom and the memorials that were being sent to Kuang-hsü urging him not to give in to the demands of St. Petersburg, they promised to take the Russian case to the country palace after he offered to each of them 500,000 liang if the Port Arthur-Talienwan question was settled within the time stipulated by the Russians and without extraordinary measures on their part.[103]

When Li sought to assure the emperor in the presence of Prince Kung and the empress dowager on March 22 that Russia had no hostile intentions toward China and that relations between the two powers were of a most friendly character, Kuang-hsü became very angry. "You all said that Russia could be depended upon and signed a treaty with her, giving her great benefit," he exploded. "Now, not only was she unable to prevent [Germany from taking Kiaochow], but she herself revokes the treaty and demands land. You call this showing friendliness?" Li and Kung took off their caps in a gesture of apology. As Li replied that the treaty of alliance would remain intact if China leased Port Arthur and Talien to Russia, Kuang-hsü shook with anger, but Tz'u-hsi silenced him with the query, "This time, then, do you want war?" [104]

On his visit to the Tsungli Yamen the following day, on March 23, Pavlov found the Chinese ministers cooperative. They discussed the substance of the Russian demands and accepted most of them. Nor did they raise any objections during a six-hour conference on the twenty-fourth. Indeed, the officials were very forthcoming in such matters as the compensation of the Chinese Treasury for the port installations at Port Arthur and decided not to include conditions to that effect in the text of the convention. [105]

Happy with the sudden smoothness of the negotiations, Pavlov telegraphed that the offer of a "reward" seemed to have produced the necessary action and recommended that the promised money be paid as soon as possible upon the signing of the convention on the twenty-seventh. [106] Witte instructed Pokotilov the following day, on March 25, to pay the one million liang when the matter was concluded successfully. He informed him that he had opened for him credit for another half-million liang in the event additional expenditures should prove necessary in this connection. He could spend the money upon agreement with Pavlov, seeking Witte's authorization if time permitted. [107] With Witte's permission, Pokotilov and Pavlov set aside between 250,000 and 300,000 liang as gifts to the authorities in Port Arthur and Talien. [108]

The negotiations for the leasing of Port Arthur and Talienwan lasted for two weeks—from March 3 until March 17. A Russian landing party had been readied at Port Arthur in the event the Chinese did not sign the lease, but no direct force proved to be necessary as the Chinese bowed to the Russian demands. As in the case of the Chinese Eastern Railroad lease, lucre had eased the way. But, as the loan question had shown, money alone could not have achieved results. Li and Chang made the best of a bad situation. They realized that the Liaotung Peninsula would go to Russia one way or another. Too weak to resist the exactions of any great power unaided, China gave in when Great Britain and Japan refused to intervene on her behalf. The Russian occupation of the Liaotung Peninsula was achieved with the "moral" support of France and Germany and the secret assent of Great Britain. The bribes were a minor, if colorful, factor. [109]

On March 26 Kuang-hsü endorsed a memorial from the Tsungli Yamen requesting imperial approval of the Russian demands. [110] The following afternoon, on the twenty-seventh, Pavlov, Li, and Chang signed and sealed the Russian and Chinese texts of the Peking convention, giving to Russia a twenty-five year lease on Port Arthur and Talien with adjacent territory and extending the concession for the construction of the Chinese Eastern Railroad granted in 1896 to the construction of a branch line to one of the ports along the shores of the Liaotung Peninsula. The preamble of the convention spoke in terms of further cementing the friendly relations existing between the two empires and of insuring the means for mutual support; the first article talked of providing a reliable base for the Russian navy on the shores of Northern China. The convention stipulated that the lease in no way nullified the sovereign rights of the Chinese emperor over the territory. It did not demarcate the leasehold, stating merely that it was to run north of Talien Bay for a distance necessary for the defense of the place from attack by land, leaving the drawing of a specific border and other details to a special protocol, to be concluded by Hsü in St. Petersburg. Upon the drawing of the line of demarcation, the entire leasehold and adjacent sea space were to fall under the full and exclusive use of the tsarist government. The twenty-five year lease term could be prolonged by mutual consent. During the period of the lease all military and civilian command in the leasehold and the adjacent waters were to rest completely in the hands of one Russian individual, who would, however, not bear the title either of governor or governor general. No Chinese land forces would be admitted into the territory. The Chinese inhabitants would be free to move out of the leasehold or to continue living there. Chinese who committed a crime would be taken to the nearest Chinese authorities for trial and punishment according to Chinese laws, as stipulated in the Treaty of Peking of 1860. To the north of the leasehold there was to be established a neutral zone whose borders were to be fixed by Hsü and the Russian Foreign Ministry. The civil administration of the neutral zone was to be completely in Chinese hands; Chinese troops, however, would be admitted only in agreement with the Russian authorities. Port Arthur, as an exclusively military port, was to be open only to Russian and Chinese vessels. At Talienwan one inner bay would be reserved exclusively for Russian and Chinese naval vessels; all other parts of the port would be open to foreign trade and to commercial vessels of all nations. The tsarist government assumed the cost of erecting in the leasehold all necessary installations for its sea and land forces. It undertook to build fortifications, maintain a garrison and to take all measures for the defense of the place from foreign attack. The tsarist government likewise undertook to place and maintain beacons and other warning signs necessary for the safety of navigation. The above-mentioned extension of the railroad concession provided for a connecting branch from one of the stations of the trunk line to Talienwan plus, should it prove necessary, from the same trunk line to another, more convenient, point on the shore of the Liaotung Peninsula between Yingtze and the mouth of the Yalu River. The permission for the construction of the railroad, the convention noted, must never under any circumstances serve as a pretext for the seizure of Chinese territory or for infringement on the sovereign rights of China. The convention was to take effect upon the exchange of ratifications in St. Petersburg.[111]

Pavlov had meanwhile informed Dubasov that the Chinese government had agreed to the cession of Port Arthur and that the time had come for Russia to receive the port from the local authorities. The admiral's staff issued operational instructions how to take the fortress and the port in the event of local resistance. Two divisions of Chinese troops stood outside Port Arthur. General Li, the commander of one division, had been paid 100,000 rubles by the tsarist legation not to interfere with the Russian occupation of Port Arthur. But somehow, due to a misunderstanding, nothing had been given to General Fu, the commander of the other division, and there was fear of opposition on his part.

Two volunteer ships arrived from Vladivostok with a regiment of infantry and two squadrons of Cossacks. Two large transports were loaded with coal. Everything was readied for the operation in expectation of word from Reunov that the British had departed. As the *Immortality* and the *Undaunted* left for Weihaiwei, Dubasov led the remainder of the Russian squadron from Nagasaki to Port Arthur. The vessels reached the roadstead on March 26 and made preparations to move into the harbor in the morning, with their crews at battle stations and the landing party in the cutters. There was no call for hostilities, however. As the two volunteer ships with the land forces spearheaded the entry on the twenty-seventh, the large crowd of Chinese common people and coolies who had gathered on the harbor wall ran onto the gangplanks with shouts of welcome and helped to guide the Cossack horses ashore. In view of the friendly reception, general quarters were secured on the squadron and the vessels with shallow draught entered the harbor one by one.

By evening it was learned that the Chinese divisions had withdrawn from the region of the Liaotung Peninsula conceded to Russia. A belated bribe of 50,000 rubles had greased Fu's retreat as well.[112]

The next day, on the twenty-eighth, the Russian flag was hoisted together with the Chinese flag. The simultaneous raising of both flags made a most favorable impression on the Chinese. Li in particular was delighted by the Russian gesture. But the commander of the Russian Pacific squadron protested that this was contrary to custom, and instructions arrived from St. Petersburg in April to lower the Chinese flag.[113] An official announcement by the tsarist government on March 29 asserted that the leasing of Port Arthur and Talienwan had been the "natural result" of the friendly relations established between the two neighboring empires, all of whose efforts must be devoted to the preservation of tranquility along the enormous expanse of their border regions for the mutual benefit of the peoples under their sway. It declared that the agreement in no way infringed on the interests of any foreign power, in fact gave to all the nations of the world the possibility of establishing contact in the near future with this hitherto closed region on the shore of the Yellow Sea. It predicted optimistically that the opening of Talien to all commercial fleets would create in the Pacific Ocean a new spacious center for the commercial and industrial undertakings of all powers by means of the Trans-Siberian Railroad which eventually would connect the extremities of the Old World. "Thus the agreement signed in Peking," the announcement concluded, "has for Russia a deep historical significance and must be joyfully welcomed by all who cherish the benefits of peace and progress on the basis of mutual relations between peoples." [114]

During the weekly reception at the Russian Foreign Ministry on March 30, O'Conor inquired why the official announcement had not mentioned the opening of Port Arthur to trade, of which Muraviev had assured him repeatedly. Muraviev answered that "the time was not opportune" to make the assurances public, but that he would confirm them if O'Conor addressed a note to him. However, when O'Conor did so on April 1, Muraviev contended that the statements he had made earlier had constituted a friendly exchange of views, not assurances. He communicated to O'Conor and to Salisbury through Staal that all he had pledged had been respect for Chinese sovereign rights and the treaties existing between China and foreign powers. Talien had been thrown open to the commerce of the whole world; elsewhere due respect for Chinese sovereign rights required the scrupulous maintenance of the situation that had existed prior to the lease of the two ports. "British ships of war and commerce would, consequently, be admitted to Port Arthur on the conditions prescribed by existing regulations, but Russia could not abuse the right of use accorded to her by China for the purpose of arbitrarily transforming a closed military port into an ordinary commercial harbor." [115]

Transmitting a translation of the above communiqué to Hanotaux, Montebello remarked on the "great importance" of the arrangement which Russia had concluded with China and on the "dazzling diplomatic success" which she had achieved. Recalling that Muraviev's policy had been criticized by several of his colleagues who saw in the sudden occupation of Port Arthur a premature measure which might kill Russian influence in China and might make difficult the peaceful accomplishment of Russian plans, Montebello observed that the outcome had given the lie to these predictions. "The operation was carried out most calmly, in the most amicable manner," he reviewed. "The special ambassador sent by the Chinese government to deal with this affair showed no ill humor; the negotiations were transferred to Peking and confined to a chargé d'affaires; Count Muraviev conducted them from afar;

one did not hear speak here of any pressure, of any menace, and China signed on the stipulated day the conditions posed by Russia." "Count Muraviev I must say here," Montebello continued, "has shown from the beginning an extreme confidence in the ultimate success; there was much talk for a number of days that all was not going as he desired; he let it be believed himself; but in his relations with me, he had never manifested the least apprehension. He had at his disposal irresistible arguments for making Li Hung-chang bow, and he managed to use them at the last moment. The minister of the Emperor of China did not show himself insensible this time again. The bill to be paid was perhaps a bit steep, but the object was undoubtedly worth some sacrifice." [116]

On April 5 Pavlov was received in solemn audience by the emperor of China in order to transmit a telegram from the tsar. In the cable, which Pavlov read out loud, Nicholas saluted Kuang-hsü and wished him a happy reign. The tsar declared that Russia attached "great historical significance" to the convention as it would undoubtedly strengthen the friendly bonds existing between the two neighboring empires for centuries and clearly corresponded to their reciprocal interests. Unprecedentedly Pavlov was allowed to ascend the steps of the throne to hand the tsar's telegram directly to the emperor, who raised himself slightly as he accepted it. Kuang-hsü expressed pleasure at the "profoundly amicable" message. "The sincere amity which has existed between our two states for over 200 years and which in recent times has been affirmed by a Treaty of Alliance will consolidate further in the future," he proclaimed. He echoed that the good of both nations would be served by this sincere friendship and their community of reciprocal interests. [117]

Since the Treaty of Alliance concluded between Russia and China in 1896 had remained secret, the publication of Kuang-hsü's response elicited a number of inquiries. Pavlov told MacDonald that the preamble to the convention recently signed regarding the lease of Port Arthur spoke of the better protection of the mutual interests of both countries and of the cementing of the good relations existing between them. As the Chinese used the same word for "treaty" and "convention," MacDonald was led to believe that the Chinese had construed the phrasing of the preamble as amounting to an alliance. [118]

As stipulated, the Peking Convention of March 27 was amplified by a supplementary protocol, signed by Hsü and Muraviev at St. Petersburg on May 7, as well as by a contract for the construction and exploitation of the South-Manchurian branch of the Chinese Eastern Railroad, signed by Hsü and the board of directors of the Chinese Eastern Railroad at St. Petersburg on July 6.

In the process of determining the southern border of the Russian lease, Dubasov, on his own authority, sent the *Dmitrii Donskoi* to occupy the Miao (Changshan) Islands at the entrance of the Gulf of Pechili. He issued proclamations to the local populace announcing the annexation of the islands to Liaotung. Only after the fact did Pavlov receive instructions to enter into negotiations with the Chinese government about the incorporation of the islands into the leasehold. But the Chinese refused to lease the Miao Islands, pointing out that they formed a part of Shantung Province, not of Manchuria; they were unrelated to the demarcation or defense of Liaotung and their occupation constituted the seizure of the entrance of the Bay of Pechili. All they agreed to do was to include in the protocol of the commission determining the boundaries of Liaotung the pledge not to cede the Miao Islands to any foreign power, not to give any commercial concessions or open any ports to foreign trade on these islands.[119]

It remained for Russia to determine the port which was to become the terminal point of the South Manchurian branch line. On June 10, following an inspection by the engineers Kubedz and Iugovich, the board of directors of the Chinese Eastern Railroad settled on Talien.[120] At Witte's suggestion Talien was renamed Dalny (Dal'nii), meaning "distant." The Academy of Sciences had favored an appelation which, like Vladivostok, would have expressed the glory of the Russian empire, but Witte did not want to offend Chinese sensibilities further and chose a name that sounded like the original.

The contract signed by Hsü on July 6 gave additional privileges to the Chinese Eastern Railroad Company. In order to facilitate the transportation of materials and supplies for the construction of the railroad, company vessels were allowed to navigate the Liao River and enter the port of Yingtze and several closed ports of the Liaotung Peninsula; the company received permission, furthermore, to run temporary branches from the South Manchurian line to these ports. The company was allowed to prepare timber and charcoal in Manchuria for its own use. A customs house was to be established at Dalny under the administration of the Chinese Eastern Railroad. Finally, the company received the right to operate its own steamship company in order to connect the terminal points of the railroad—Vladivostok and Dalny—with the major port cities of China, Japan, and Korea to insure the speedy transportation of passengers and freight between Russia and Western Europe and the Far East.[121]

A great deal of work was required to make Port Arthur into an effective naval base, particularly because it was still in the half-destroyed condition in which the Chinese had gotten it back from the Japanese. As a closed harbor with a basin and quays, Port Arthur could accommodate a fair number of vessels though it was very small. But vessels drawing more than twenty-four feet, such as battleships and large cruisers, could not enter the basin, and a long ship like the *Rossiia* could not swing in the harbor itself. It was necessary to lay permanent head and stern moorings in the harbor and dredge Port Arthur to obtain full benefit from its possession.[122] One also had to widen the large dock, repair the small one, deepen the eastern harbor and build a new one in the shallow western basin. And the machinery and the machine-tools in the shops had to be replenished.

Dubasov had many ideas for the creation of a new stronghold. He dispatched one of his naval officers, G. Tsyvinskii, to San Francisco to solicit American participation in the vast undertaking. Military engineers and artillery construction commissions from St. Petersburg set up well-staffed offices and prepared building estimates. They drew up plans for defensive works and for a whole new city on the shore of the western basin. In the office for the construction of the southern line of the Chinese Eastern Railroad, opened by Kubedz and Iugovich, Tsyvinskii saw completed plans for Port Dalny, with docks and a harbor, as well as plans for a railroad station and a wharf. "The projects for the creation of a 'new stronghold' were baked like blini [that is quickly, in large quantity] and plans and estimates in the millions [of rubles] were sent, seeking urgent appropriations for pressing defense works for the port and the fortress," he recalled in his memoirs. "But in Petersburg no one even thought of faraway [Port] Arthur; there one was occupied with 'current affairs,' cut the estimates, and the transfers of money were delayed by half a year," Tsyvinskii grumbled.[123]

The Japanese followed the Russian activities closely. In September 1898 a Japanese ex-soldier by the name of Fukuhara, who had been residing in China for two years, was arrested by the Russian army for making a plan of the fort at Port Arthur. He was released two months later on condition that he would leave Port Arthur forthwith after repeated protests by the Japanese government that it enjoyed full and exclusive jurisdiction over its subjects throughout China, except where "actual and absolute cession of territory" had been made, as had not been the case with Port Arthur. "[The] Japanese Government have not questioned [the] right of [the] Russian Government to take steps to prevent [the] commission of acts such as that complained of, but they are persuaded that [the] jurisdiction to punish any act committed in China by [a] Japanese subject especially in time of peace is vested exclusively in Japanese authorities," Foreign Minister Okuma explained.[124]

The entrenchment of the Russians in Manchuria elicited a proposal in the Privy Council of China that the capital be moved from Peking to Nanking. It was received as almost treasonable, because it involved the abandonment by the Manchu dynasty of its native land. "Were the ruling dynasty Chinese," MacDonald reflected, "it is very probable that the capital would be changed, and the step would certainly relieve the Government from much of the pressure they now feel from the north, but a Manchu dynasty could hardly take it without risk of a rebellion."

The warlike preparations made by Japan during the Russian negotiations with China had caused much uneasiness in Peking, as the Chinese wondered whether the Japanese were getting ready for war with Russia or for a fresh attack on them. "As far as I can gather from the Japanese Minister here, the Japanese Government are watching the Russian negotiations with greater coolness than might have been expected, though they must feel great irritation," MacDonald reported.[125]

Pokotilov had given to Li Hung-chang the promised half a million liang on March 28, the day after the signing of the convention.[126] Li was well pleased and asked that his gratitude be conveyed to Witte. Chang Yin-huan, on the other hand, stayed clear of Pokotilov so that the latter could not pay him off promptly. When Pokotilov did get a chance to talk to Chang confidentially on April 8, Chang said that he was very much afraid to accept the money now, as many charges of bribery had already been levied at him; he preferred to wait until the talk had died down. Pokotilov assured him that the promised sum would remain at his disposal. Only 10,000 liang had been spent in Port Arthur so far, he reported, as the persons to whom gifts had been promised had left town; payment would be made later.[127]

Chang had reason to be worried. In May a censor accused him and Weng T'ung-ho of having accepted large bribes in connection with the loan from the Hong Kong and Shanghai Bank Corporation. Weng was dismissed the following month, though on a different charge—alienation of the affections of Kuang-hsü and Tz'u-hsi. Chang remained in office until September, when his reform efforts on behalf of a national conscript army trained in the Western style, rather than his corruption, led to his downfall. On September 21 his house was surrounded by troops and an inventory of his property made preparatory to its confiscation. His arrest and banishment to Sinkiang (Chinese Turkistan) on the charge that "his actions were deceitful, mysterious and fickle, and he sought after the rich and the powerful" followed in short order.[128]

Stripped of his wealth, Chang turned to the Russians. In his urgent, ciphered telegram of September 21 about the surrounding of Chang's house, Pokotilov had remarked that he had not paid him anything yet.[129] On October 4 he reported that Chang has asked for the payment of an "additional" 15,000 liang. Pavlov backed the claim. "I deem it desirable," he telegraphed, "to fulfill Chang Yin-huan's request in view of the favorable impression which this will produce for us on the Chinese officials who had previously been with him and who may be very useful to us when an opportunity arises."[130] The payment was duly made to the exiled official, though the total he received was but a fraction of what he had been promised. While Li Hung-chang had collected on March 28 the equivalent of 609,120 rubles and 50 kopecks, Chang ended up with only 51,171 rubles and 1 kopeck.[131]

The strain of the negotiations and the penetrating cold of winter in St. Petersburg had taken a heavy toll of Hsü Ching-ch'eng's health. He had developed a racking cough, spat up blood, and had trouble sleeping. He had to recuperate in his native village for two months before he could proceed to Peking with a report of his mission. Upon his return to the Chinese capital, Hsü worked at the Tsungli Yamen and in high posts at the Board of Rites and the Board of Civil Office. He also lectured as a professor at Peking University. But Hsü's experience abroad and opposition to mounting xenophobia aroused the suspicion of ultraconservative officials. In July 1900 he and another official, Yüan Ch'ang, were publicly executed after having repeatedly memorialized the throne to suppress the anti-foreign Boxer movement.[132]

Twenty-Five

The Russo-Japanese Détente

The occupation of the Liaotung Peninsula by Russia, who in concert with Germany and France had denied the same region to Japan only two and a half years earlier, had aroused popular indignation in the island-bound empire. Yet it actually produced a détente in Russo-Japanese relations, because the Japanese government saw in the Russian move in Manchuria, where Japanese interests were as yet minor, a shift away from Korea, the area of primary concern to Japan. It strengthened its notion of *Man-Kan kōkan*, whereby Japan and Russia would exchange their rights to Manchuria and Korea somewhat like they had once exchanged their claims to Sakhalin and the Kuril Islands.[1]

The logic of a Russo-Japanese entente was perceived by many. Russia must desire to remain on friendly terms with Japan, lest she be forced to maintain substantial naval forces in the Pacific, which would fetter her action in Europe, Plancy pointed out in August 1896.[2] Kurino told Hanotaux in December 1897 that Japan regarded the Franco-Russian group as strongest and consequently desired an entente with the two powers to assure the normal development of her commercial interests in Korea and in China. Communicating to Hanotaux that he had been informed by his government that St. Petersburg was convinced that the entry of the Russian squadron into Port Arthur could not result in any misunderstanding or quarrel with Tokyo, he reiterated that his government harbored the most amicable sentiments toward Russia and France.[3]

Informed of Kurino's words to Hanotaux, Muraviev remarked to Montebello that he had never been worried about the attitude of Japan when China alone was involved. If he feared any complications, it was over Korea, where Russia would never permit that Japan establish herself too firmly, while Japan would not easily give up the position she had acquired.[4] He instructed Rosen to inquire whether Kurino's remarks had been personal or on instructions from Nishi.[5]

Kurino set down his reasoning in a cable to Nishi. While English journals hinted at the advisability of an Anglo-Japanese understanding, he did not believe that Great Britain would give Japan more than moral support or would ever oppose by force the advance of other powers in the East. Forcible intervention would mean war with Russia, France, and Germany, which would leave Britain totally isolated in Europe. Beside, the interests of England and Russia in the East were in different regions, so that London would not consider the risk of war worthwhile. He was convinced that if the Chinese question became more serious, a European concert would result notwithstanding the jealousies among the powers. Since Hanotaux seemed disposed to admit the equal participation of Japan in the Chinese question, Kurino deemed this to be "an excellent opportunity" to settle the Korean question with Russia once and for all.[6]

Nishi informed Kurino that Rosen had inquired whether the remarks he had made to Hanotaux had been his own and that he had replied that they had indeed been personal. "I trust you will bear in mind," Nishi telegraphed, "that [a] definite course of action to be pursued by Japan has not yet been determined and that you will govern yourself accordingly."[7]

The German naval attaché in St. Petersburg, Captain Kalau vom Hofe, reported that month that he had managed to learn from tsarist navy circles that the Russians had for the time being given up the idea of establishing themselves on the west coast of Korea and were concentrating their entire strength at Vladivostok. Fifteen million rubles had been assigned for the enlargement of the shipyards. The guiding motives of Russia in the near future were the absolute need for peace, avoidance of any arousal of military instinct on the part of Japan, as well as the desire not to fritter away her forces, because Russian military preparations had not kept pace with those of Japan.[8]

Informed of the above, Bülow attributed the "change" in Russian policy to the German occupation of Kiaochow. In the face of the Kaiser's action in East Asia, which naturally had to distract and share the attention the Japanese had heretofore concentrated on Russia, the latter had the choice either to side with Germany against Japan and her eventual friends or to withdraw and to prepare for the role of a spectator in a possible German-Japanese conflict. The communication revealed, Bülow wrote, that Russian policy, which was directed by Muraviev but inspired by his friend Cassini in Peking, leaned toward the second alternative.

Bülow concluded from everything that Muraviev had stated recently that while Russia would not oppose the East Asian policy of Germany, she would certainly not support it. (He believed that the Chinese proposals for the exchange of Kiaochow for a port further south were due to Russian inspiration.) Yet there was no danger of any intervention by European powers if Germany remained in Kiaochow, because France and England would be glad that Germany stayed away from their own spheres of interest and gladder still that the action would exacerbate relations between Germany and Japan, he thought. An acute conflict between Germany and Japan would benefit Russia, as Japan would not be able to spare the means to oppose Russian expansion into North China and Korea.[9]

Treutler reported from Tokyo that there was a strong Russophile tendency in a small but influential circle of the Japanese general staff. General Kawakami had repeatedly told the French military attaché during a journey to Formosa the preceding summer that it would be best for Japan, even at the cost of certain sacrifices, to work for an agreement with her mighty neighbor. "In view of the care with which the Russian legation under Baron Rosen cultivates friendly relations with influential Japanese, I am convinced," Treutler wrote, "that it will not miss also this favorable opportunity for making new contacts [*zur Aufknüpfung neuer Faden*]."[10]

On December 29 Mohrenheim communicated to Hanotaux a secret telegram from his government, dated the twenty-eighth and received that morning, that Russia was fully prepared to come to an accomodation with Japan on the Korean question through the friendly mediation of France. Noting that it would appreciate the participation of Hanotaux, the tsarist government remarked that Kurino would have to receive, of course, appropriate plenary powers.[11] Hanotaux agreed to pursue the matter, but directed Mohrenheim's attention to the personal nature of Kurino's remarks and to the ministerial crisis which had erupted in Tokyo.[12]

At his diplomatic reception during the first week of January 1898, Muraviev tried to draw out Hayashi on the subject broached by Kurino to Hanotaux without revealing, of course, the disclosure made to him by the French.[13] He told Hayashi confidentially that Nicholas had expressed to him the view that the continual friction between Russia and Japan in Korea was not in the interest of either power. Keeping in mind the fact that Japan's interest in Korea was greater than that of Russia, could they not reach an arrangement to avoid future complications? Noting that Japan had declared from the beginning her intention to uphold the independence of Korea and that Russia had always concurred with this objective, Muraviev said to Hayashi that he thought that there being agreement on this basic issue, all other matters could be arranged to their mutual satisfaction. It was his intention, he indicated, to make an overture along these lines shortly, after due consideration.[14]

Hayashi, who spoke only English and that with difficulty, did not respond as Muraviev had desired, whether because his personal sympathies were more toward Britain or because he had no instructions in this matter.[15] He replied vaguely that the Japanese government would always be willing to enter into an arrangement to smooth out whatever difficulties there might be between the two countries.[16]

Reporting the above conversation to Hanotaux, Montebello observed that while Kurino may have been somewhat ahead in developing his personal ideas, Muraviev had gained the impression from assurances Hayashi had given when talking of Marquis Ito and his probable return to the premiership that the new prime minister would be favorably disposed toward an understanding on many points. Muraviev had taken a lively interest in Kurino's words to Hanotaux, seeing in them to a certain extent a Japanese overture, for it was hard to believe that Kurino would have ventured to make such personal remarks without any authorization whatsoever. At any rate, he instructed Rosen to encourage the Japanese in any overtures they might make.[17]

Muraviev had asked Hayashi not to report the contemplated overture to his government until it had been officially announced, but the Japanese minister did so anyway in a special, confidential telegram. "When the overture is made," Hayashi cabled, "I can ascertain if their intention is to conciliate Japan, by leaving her more freedom of action in Corea, in order to carry out their scheme in Liaotung free from opposition. If it is found so, we might claim reasonable, but more solid compensation than mere influence in Corea." "I do not think it either necessary or advisable to attempt to check Russian progress in Liaotung," he commented, "because having already at least two great naval powers as our neighbors, one more addition will give us rather advantage than harm; while the attempt to check it lays upon us eternal burden without certainty of permanent success." Hayashi asked Nishi to acquaint him beforehand what compensation Japan should seek if he concurred with his views.[18] In a follow-up telegram on January 11, Hayashi asked for "immediate instructions how to meet [the] overture of [the] Russian Government."[19]

On January 15 Rosen called on Nishi and communicated to him that Russia was prepared to assist Japan as far as possible in her commercial and industrial interests in Korea. Nishi retorted that it would be difficult to reach a satisfactory understanding "unless Russia was ready to abandon her position on the subject of the drilling of the army and the engagement of the Financial Adviser."[20]

Informed by Nishi of the conversation with Rosen, Hayashi inquired on the twentieth whether in the absence of instructions, he could consider Nishi's

virtual declaration that absolute abandonment of the military drill and control
of the finances by Russia in Korea were a condition *sine qua non* for any
understanding to be the policy of the Japanese government and act accordingly or did Tokyo intend to arrive at some compromise eventually. He remarked that Muraviev's account of Rosen's interview with Nishi and Ito differed somewhat from the description Nishi had sent. According to Muraviev,
Rosen had responded to Nishi's objection against military instructors that their
employment was counterbalanced by the stationing of Japanese troops in
Korea. Muraviev had told him that Ito had promised to Rosen to discuss the
various matters again. Muraviev had asked him in the meantime to invite the
Japanese government to propose what it wanted with a view to coming to an
understanding. "I am anxiously waiting for [an] answer on the points," Hayashi cabled. "A Minister—most probably [the] Minister of Finance [he
added]—is reported to have said to his friend, that so long as [the] present
Minister for Foreign Affairs continues in his office, Japan has every reason to
be contented, stigmatizing thereby [the] weakness of his diplomacy." [21]

Still without a reply, Hayashi tried to prod Nishi into action. "[The] recent
attitude of [the] Russian Government plainly shows their desire to conciliate
us in order to make an enemy less, if not to make a friend more," he communicated in a strictly confidential telegram on January 27. "Under these circumstances," he argued, "we may frankly make them understand that it is
desirable to soften [the] irritation of the mass of Japanese people and military
class by a considerable concession in Corea regarding political influence as
well as material advantages. Negotiating on this base, we may try to obtain as
much as we can; but we cannot claim to exclude Russia entirely from [the]
Corean Government, as we have neither [the] right nor [the] might to enforce
such a demand. Therefore, we must make up our mind to be satisfied with
whatever we can obtain. Some persons may object to this from pure sentimentalism, and some from the vague fear of wounding English feeling; but after
[the] frequent failure of sentimental policy in Corea, it is time to give up
sentimentalism, and to confine our attention strictly to interest." [22]

Hayashi's cable crossed with the response that Nishi made at last to his
preceding telegrams on January 26. His immediate answer to Rosen regarding
the abandonment of military drill and financial control, Nishi revealed, had
been "merely for the sake of exchanging views and not with the object of
insisting irrevocably upon it." The alleged statement by Rosen that Russian
military training was counterbalanced by the stationing of Japanese troops in
Korea had never been made to him. He instructed Hayashi to tell Muraviev
that the Japanese government viewed "with satisfaction" the declaration
made by the tsarist government through Hitrovo to uphold the independence

of Korea and that it was "in perfect accord" with the tsarist government about the conclusion of a "definite understanding" between their countries on that basis. Hayashi was to declare that Japan's present commercial and industrial interests in Korea should be preserved; Japan would be willing to enter into understandings with Russia from time to time as the occasion might arise concerning the future promotion of these interests. The Japanese government would want Russia in turn to consult with it respecting her dealings in Korea. "In making the above statement," Nishi directed, "you will add that [the] Japanese Government desire [that the] Russian Government would consent to leave to Japan either the drilling of troops or the appointment of [a] financial adviser." [23]

Upon the receipt of Hayashi's telegram of January 27, Nishi responded that the views of the Japanese government were evidently in substantial agreement with those of Hayashi. He noted that the Japanese government had no partic-ular proposition to make at the moment beyond those he had mentioned and was "fully prepared to enter into [an] understanding with [the] Russian Government in a conciliatory spirit." Hayashi could act accordingly, he concluded. [24]

Hayashi meanwhile communicated to Muraviev on January 29 the state-ment telegraphed by Nishi on the twenty-sixth, adding on his own that it was necessary to appease the irritation of the Japanese public. Muraviev replied that the military instructors had been dispatched originally at the request of Kojong, who wished his body guards trained to defend him against his father, the taewongun. It was very difficult to recall them now. He admitted privately that the appointment of the financial adviser was not quite in accordance with the understanding between the two governments and might be arranged other-wise. He had learned from Witte, he said, that Japanese as well as Russians could be shareholders of the Russo-Korean Bank; there was no reason to keep it exclusively Russian. He promised to speak more definitely to Hayashi after seeing the tsar on Wednesday (February 2). [25]

When Muraviev received Hayashi again on February 2, he said that he wanted to wait another two or three days, because Rosen had telegraphed from Tokyo that Ito Hirobumi had promised to make some detailed proposi-tions. Reporting the above, Hayashi surmised that some mistake must have occurred. He inquired whether Nishi intended to insist strongly on Russian consent for Japanese military instuctors and the financial adviser. So far he had referred to the matter only orally, but he intended to transmit a written statement if Nishi was firm in his resolution. [26]

There was certainly a mistake concerning Ito, as no such promise had ever been made, Nishi answered. "Regarding [the] desire of [the] Japanese Government that [the] Russian Government would consent to leave to Japan either the drilling of troops or the appointment of [the] Financial Adviser," he clarified, "[the] Japanese Government do not intend to insist irrevocably upon the same, but desire to attain something, at this juncture, to appease national feeling respecting [the] action of Russia in Corea." [27]

On February 16 Hayashi presented the following proposal to Muraviev: (1) Japan and Russia pledged to maintain the independence of Korea; (2) the military instructors of the Korean troops would be designated by the Russian government; (3) the financial adviser would be designated by the Japanese government; (4) in matters relating to commercial and industrial interests, Japan and Russia, with a view to preventing any misunderstanding, must in the future consult with each other before undertaking any new measure. [28]

When the Foreign Ministry submitted the Japanese proposal to Witte for his decision, the latter remarked that while he deemed it highly desirable to find a means for reconciling Russian and Japanese interests, he could not agree to the removal of the Russian financial adviser from Korea. Firstly, the appointment of the Russian financial adviser had occurred entirely in response to the wishes of the Korean government and he had already entered upon the execution of his functions. Under the circumstances, his recall would harm Russian prestige in the Far East. Secondly, with the removal of Alekseev from Korea Russia would be deprived of the possibility of supervising Korean finances and of supplying Korea with the financial aid to pay off the loan concluded by her in Japan. Thirdly, the recently established Russo-Korean Bank could expect collaboration and support from the Russian financial adviser; if he were removed, the bank would have to close. Since it appeared that the chief commissioner of the Korean Customs, the Englishman Brown, was remaining in the service of the Korean government, the addition of a Japanese as chief financial adviser would place the entire finances, customs, and with them all economic influence in Korea in the hands of England and Japan, Russia's main rivals in the Far East. [29]

No reply was made by the tsarist government to the Japanese proposal for three weeks, as the Liaotung question and the matter of continued Russian aid to Korea were being worked out. Had St. Petersburg concluded an agreement with Japan concerning Korea prior to the leasing of Port Arthur, it might have lacked the leverage to prevent Japanese opposition thereto. Furthermore, once the recall of the Russian military instructors and financial adviser had been decided, an agreement with Japan could be approached in terms of mutual noninterference in Korean affairs rather than as the joint intervention projected by Japan, which was more likely to entail complications. [30]

On March 10 Muraviev told Hayashi that since the financial adviser and the military instructors had been engaged by the will of the Korean ruler, an independent sovereign, there was nothing the tsarist government could do about it. It was willing, however, to reconsider the term of the contract of the financial adviser and invited the Japanese government to suggest alterations. In reporting the above, Hayashi remarked that Russian policy seemed to have undergone a change since the recent turn of events in the East, for what Muraviev now said was nothing more than the acceptance of what the Japanese had demanded before he had made the overtures for an understanding and amounted to a virtual withdrawal of the latter. He asked to be informed of the general policy his government had adopted regarding Korea.[31]

On March 11 Muraviev informed Rosen of the tsarist government's decision to secure Port Arthur for a long period of time. He expressed the hope that Japan would trust Russia's peaceful intentions. To give proof of its "sincere readiness" to maintain "the best possible relations" (*vozmozhno luchshie otnosheniia*) with the Japanese government, the tsarist government was willing, provided that Russia received the use of Port Arthur, to enter into a friendly agreement regarding the proposals made by Japan, "but, of course, on the indispensable condition of the preservation of the full independence of Korea." The above was being sent to Rosen for his own information so that when the time came he could talk with Foreign Minister Nishi in this sense.

On March 14 Muraviev wrote to Nicholas that the Korean declination of further Russian aid had untied the tsarist government's hands in Korea, as a result of which it might be advisable to enter into negotiations with Japan in the spirit of the telegram to Rosen. That day Rosen was authorized to commence the discussion of Korean affairs on the basis of the previous cable. Noting that it had been impossible heretofore to reach an agreement with Japan because Russia had been committed to assist Korea in the military and financial fields, Witte observed that now that Russia had been freed of her obligations in this respect it was possible to consider the Japanese proposal, provided Japan had relinquished any claims for direct interference in the internal administration of Korea and had openly recognized the full independence of that country.[32]

Meanwhile, on March 8, Nishi had informed Hayashi of the attempt on the life of Kim Hong-yuk, the Korean interpreter of the Russian legation, and of the "urgent and threatening demand" that Speyer had reputedly made in this connection. Relating that he had instructed the Japanese minister in Seoul not to interfere in the matter, but merely to suggest to his Russian colleague the desirability of moderation, Nishi had ordered Hayashi to apprise the tsarist government of the above and to convey the hope of the Japanese government that it direct the Russian representative in Korea "not to resort to extreme measures."[33]

Nishi elaborated on the fourteenth that the demand to which he had referred had been Speyer's query, in the form of an ultimatum, whether or not Kojong and the Korean government regarded Russian aid as superfluous. He communicated the Korean reply, which deftly asked for the withdrawal of the military instructors and financial adviser.[34]

Muraviev gave Hayashi the same account of events in Korea, adding that he had instructed Rosen to communicate to Nishi that the tsarist government would not permit the engagement of any other foreigners by the Korean government after the Russian employees had been withdrawn. This ought to be agreeable to Japan, Muraviev contended, because it equalized the influence of their countries in Korea. When Hayashi remarked that there were nearly 20,000 Japanese residents in Korea and that his government must provide for the protection of their interests, Muraviev stated that the tsarist government would do whatever it found necessary in regard to protecting its subjects, as would Japan. Asked whether his remarks about the employment of foreigners applied to those already in the Korean service, Muraviev answered that existing arrangements might be left as they were, though the details might require further consideration. He expressed the hope that after this open dealing, Russia and Japan would try to be on friendly terms in Korea.[35]

Hayashi reported on March 18 that the tsarist government had agreed to the dismissal of the financial adviser and the military instructors. Alekseev would be recalled immediately; the instructors would remain temporarily with Speyer in view of the unsettled state of affairs. The tsarist government had declared its intention of refraining from active participation in the affairs of Korea in the hope that the "young country" which had been "consolidated by Russian assistance" would be able to maintain internal order as well as full independence by her own efforts. Should it prove otherwise, Russia qualified, she would act to protect her interests and rights as a great neighboring power.[36]

In making the above-mentioned communication concerning the withdrawal of the Russian employees from Korea, Rosen declared in the name of his government that Russia had not been able heretofore, because of the existence of the engagements with Korea regarding the financial adviser and military instructors, to come to a frank understanding with Japan about that country. Now that the causes for this inability had been completely removed through the termination of the engagements, the tsarist government was willing "to come to a perfect understanding with Japan, on the basis that Russia and

Japan should reciprocally engage definitively to recognize the independence of Korea and to abstain from all direct interference in the internal affairs of Korea." Rosen informed Nishi at the same time that the tsarist government had decided, "in view of the recent change in the situation in the East," to secure the lease of Port Arthur and Talienwan from China.[37]

Nishi spoke warmly of his desire to bring about a complete understanding with Russia, Rosen recalled in his memoirs. He said that hitherto Korea had been a bone of contention between their countries, because Russia needed an ice-free port. Now that Russia had obtained such a port in Manchuria, Korea need no longer be a source of friction between them. What did he think, Nishi asked Rosen, about the conclusion of a reciprocal engagement between Russia and Japan not to impede each other's policies in Korea and Manchuria respectively? Rosen encouraged Nishi to put the proposal in writing; he would be glad to telegraph it to his government, he said. (According to his memoirs, Rosen supported the idea fully and promised to urge its adoption. In his report to the Foreign Ministry, however, Rosen claimed to have made the qualification that Russia obviously could not relinquish all influence in the bordering state. He favored a division of spheres of influence, but not complete renunciation of Korea.)

The written proposal which Nishi transmitted on the evening of March 19 was in the form of a *note verbale*. It was accompanied by a personal letter in Russian, which Nishi had mastered during his studies at St. Petersburg University, expressing the hope that the tsarist government would receive the Japanese proposal favorably and thereby eliminate all possible causes of friction between their countries.[38]

The proposal itself read as follows:

The Imperial Government would not be indisposed to unite with the Imperial Government of Russia in a self-denying understanding, reciprocally engaging definitively to recognize the Sovereignty and independence of Korea, and to abstain from all direct interference in the internal affairs of that Government. At the same time, it is probable that occasions may actually arise for Korea requiring external advice and assistance; and in case the same should not be tendered by either of the two Governments, Korea might find herself compelled to apply to a third Power—which is certainly not desirable in the interest of both countries. Having in view such contingency as well as propinquity and existing interests the Imperial Government think that the duty of extending such advice and assistance should be left to Japan. Accordingly, if the Imperial Russian Government should share these views, the Imperial Government would consider Manchuria and its littoral as, in all respects, outside of their sphere of interest and concern." [39]

As Nishi commented in a telegram to Hayashi on the twenty-first, the Japanese government had availed itself of the opportunity to propose to Russia "a division of spheres of influence, according to the boundaries between Korean and Manchuria." So long as the situation in Eastern China had remained unchanged, Japan had been content with an equal share of influence with Russia in Korea, Nishi explained. But now that Russia was about to extend her activities to Manchuria and its ports and harbors, Japan could not look on with indifference, because of her past relations with that region. The continued maintenance of an equal position of Russia and Japan in Korea would only be conducive to misunderstandings and friction due to the different interests of the two countries and the conflicting sentiments of their representatives. As Russia achieved her aims in Manchuria, her interests in Korea would decline and it would become unnecessary for her to regard Korea as within her sphere of influence. Japan, on the other hand, could not neglect her interests in Korea, for they were incomparably greater than those of any other power commercially, historically, and in terms of "national sentiment" and were bound to increase and to expand further. "For those reasons," Nishi pointed out, "[the] Japanese Government desire that Russia whilst endeavouring to develop her new acquisitions and safeguard her immense interests in [the] future should consent to leave Korea entirely under the influence of Japan." He had assured Rosen and asked Hayashi to impress on Muraviev that in the event of a division of spheres of influence, Japan would uphold the independence of Korea and would refrain from direct interference in her internal affairs. The Japanese proposal, Nishi declared, had been made solely out of the desire "to avoid any possible irritation, which might perhaps result from [the] new state of things, and to remove, completely and for ever, all causes of misunderstanding and disagreement, which might prove detrimental to the ever increasing friendly relations between the two Empires." [40]

In a telegram to London Nishi justified the proposal a little differently. It had been made, he cabled to Kato, "in order to remove all cause of irritation, and to strengthen our position by throwing Russia back to a safe distance from our frontiers and to conserve our actual interests." [41] An advocate of Japanese collaboration with England, Kato voiced his displeasure at Nishi's proposal to Russia. He criticized it as inconsistent with Japanese motives. Russia would get absolute freedom in Manchuria, while Japan would receive not much more than Russia in Korea even if she got the right of giving advice. In view of Nishi's promise of strict noninterference, on which Russia would insist,

Japanese influence in Korea would be "illusory." "We should and could get perfect freedom in Corea, in view of the motives underlying [the] spontaneous withdrawal of Russia," he argued.[42]

Hayashi too thought that Nishi was giving away more than necessary. "As [the] Russians withdrew from [the] Corean Government by their free will, we are not bound to desist from our action in Corea, while to seek their consent and be refused will have the appearance of [being] morally bound to them," he telegraphed on March 23. It was his observation that Russia would not consent to the Japanese proposal unless Japan threatened to obstruct her in Manchuria in case she refused. Since Japan would be obliged to interfere in Korea whether or not Russia consented, he wondered whether it would not be better for Japan to act first and explain when necessary rather than to seek Russian approval beforehand. He dismissed the Russian threat to do in the future the same as Japan if Korea failed to preserve her independence. "I cannot see how this can be carried out," he argued, "if [the] Coreans are brought round to us."[43]

The Russian military were as opposed to the Japanese proposal as Kato and Hayashi, though for the opposite reason. They blocked Muraviev's intention of renouncing Russian interests in Korea in exchange for Japanese acceptance of the Russian position in Manchuria, insisting that the political domination of Korea by Japan would constitute a permanent threat to the security of the Maritime Province.[44]

The Russian counterproposal, telegraphed on March 29, two days after the signing of the Peking Convention, declared that the tsar was entirely in favor of an agreement between the two empires. It suggested the conclusion of a new protocol, to supersede all previous ones, on the following basis:

1) Russia and Japan definitively recognize the Sovereignty and entire independence of Corea, mutually engaging to refrain from any interference in the internal affairs of that country.

2) In case Corea should experience the need of assistance and advice of foreign Powers it would be most natural for her to seek them at the hands of the two neighboring Empires, in which case she would, as an entirely independent State, have the indisputable right of choosing between Russia and Japan.

3) Desiring to avoid every possible cause of misunderstandings in this respect, Russia and Japan mutually engage, in case Corea should apply to one of them, not to take any measures in the sphere of military, financial, tradal [sic] or industrial affairs without having previously come to a mutual agreement in respect to them.

The telegram pointed out that such a general agreement would correspond to the first and fourth points of the proposal presented by Hayashi to Muraviev on February 16; the second and third points were no longer applicable as neither Russia nor Japan had any military instructors or financial adviser in Korea. Noting that Russia had given clear proof of her full recognition of the independence of the "young" Korean empire by withdrawing the military instructors and financial adviser the moment the Korean government had indicated its desire of doing without them, the tsarist government declared: "Having in view that the Japanese Government consider Manchuria and her littoral in every respect outside the sphere of their interests and concern, we, on our part, will by every means amicably facilitate the relations of Japan with Corea; but nevertheless we cannot admit the exclusion as a matter of principle of all influence of Russia who cannot divest herself of all concern in the destinies of a State adjacent to her frontier." [45]

Muraviev gave Hayashi a copy of the above communication on March 30. To soften the negative reply, he underlined the willingness of his government to conclude a friendly agreement with Japan in the form of a protocol that would supersede all previous agreements. Expecting that the Japanese government would hear from Rosen before his telegram could arrive, Hayashi sent that day only a summary of the main points of the Russian counterproposal, adding that inasmuch as the tsarist government declared it impossible to renounce in principle its interests in Korea, it would be useless to attempt to define spheres of interest. [46] As Rosen for some reason did not submit the Russian counterproposal until April 2, there was much confusion in Tokyo, particularly because the document he conveyed differed from the brief summary Hayashi had cabled, and Nishi had to seek confirmation of the full text from Hayashi. [47] Embarrassed at not having sent the full text of the Russian proposal, Hayashi blamed Nishi for not having kept him sufficiently apprised of the situation. "I am afraid that want of information and precise instructions regarding pressing questions and tardiness of answer to inquiries lead to injurious result, beside making my position here very perplexing," he complained. [48]

The delay with which Rosen communicated the Russian reply may have been due to his bitter personal disappointment at its rejection of the division of influences, which he had supported. As he summed up the meaning of the answer in his memoirs, "the Russian Government took note with great satisfaction of the Japanese Government's declaration that it considered Manchuria with its littoral as being entirely outside the sphere of Japanese interests, but that it could not make a similar declaration in regard to Korea."

"When I read to Baron Nissi [Nishi] the text of Count Mouravieff's reply, he merely smiled sarcastically and said regretfully that it was plain that nothing further could be done about it, and the matter was allowed to drop," Rosen recalled not quite accurately.[49]

Kato protested from London on April 5 that the new Russian proposal was "quite as useless and fruitful of future conflicts" as the previous one. All it would do would be to give Russia time. "We have [a] plausible pretext to go far beyond your original proposal and [to] insist upon [the] complete withdrawal of Russia from Corea, leaving perfect freedom to Japan in every respect except the recognition of its independence," Kato telegraphed to Nishi. "If Russia refuses," he argued, "it is far better to reserve liberty of action and take such measures [as are] necessary to advance our interests in Corea now as soon as possible after the receipt of [the] Chinese indemnity." Convinced that the activity of Russia in Korea would recommence as soon as her position in Manchuria was consolidated somewhat, Kato warned of the inevitability of a "struggle" with Russia, if her ambition was not checkmated, under conditions that would be more disadvantageous for Japan. He contended that "energetic action or, to say the least even [a] show of firm determination" on the part of Japan might prevent such an eventuality. If the Japanese government was "determined to keep peace at any price and pursue [the] purely passive policy of trying to preserve Corean independence and integrity," he proposed that it at least induce England to join in the treaty as an additional check against Russian encroachment. In that case such matters as the right of giving advice to the Korean government might be omitted, he remarked, as they would "naturally follow precedents and influence in spite of treaty stipulations."[50]

On April 8 Nishi informed Rosen that the Japanese government consented to the conclusion of a definitive agreement with Russia. Leaving the first point of the Russian proposal unchanged, the Japanese side revised the second point to the effect that if Korea applied to Japan or Russia for advice and assistance, neither would nominate military instructors or financial advisers without prior mutual agreement in this regard. The third point of the Japanese counterproposal stipulated that Russia recognized the "preponderance" of Japanese interests in Korea in commerce, industry, and the number of Japanese residents and that she would support Japan in the promotion of these interests. Instead of substituting the projected agreement in place of those signed in 1896, the Japanese government deemed it "consistent with the idea of continuity" to declare in the new agreement that it was made in pursuance of the fourth article of the Moscow Protocol.[51]

In a memorial to the tsar on April 10 Muraviev noted that the Japanese reply on the whole corresponded to the Russian conditions and thus laid to rest rumors about the imminence of an Anglo-Japanese alliance against Russia. He urged that British attempts to lure Japan to her side be forestalled by the prompt conclusion of a Russo-Japanese agreement along the proposed lines. Nicholas agreed, and Muraviev instructed Rosen the same day to take immediate steps for the signing of an agreement. The third point of the Japanese counterproposal was modified. Instead of pledging her "support" of Japanese economic interests in Korea, Russia bound herself merely, "as far as possible not to impede the development of commercial relations between Japan and Korea." Rosen was authorized to alter the text further, depending on the position of the Japanese, but in such a way, Muraviev stipulated, "that the Japanese could not think that Russia was sacrificing to them her future commercial and industrial relations with Korea."[52]

Rosen intimated to Nishi on the twelfth that the articles he had proposed were acceptable to the tsarist government, except for the above-mentioned modifications.[53] On his own initiative and contrary to his instructions to conclude an agreement with Japan as soon as possible, Rosen tried to make the agreement concerning Korea dependent on a Japanese commitment concerning Manchuria. Nishi responded on the sixteenth that Japan could give a formal declaration regarding Manchuria and her littoral only if Russia in turn accepted the conditions of the first memorandum, which he had presented to him on March 19. If, on the other hand, Russia were satisfied with signing merely the proposed agreement pertaining to Korean affairs, the Japanese government would "connive" at her occupation of Port Arthur and Talienwan. Nishi assured Rosen confidentially that the Japanese government had no ulterior motives in making the suggestion and would not oppose Russia.[54] He said that Hayashi had been instructed to make a similar statement in St. Petersburg.

The Russian Foreign Ministry cabled to Rosen on April 19 that it had taken notice of the information that the Japanese government was prepared to recognize that Manchuria lay outside its sphere of influence. It did not consider it necessary, therefore, to insist on a special statement or to deal further with the question, which was extraneous to the contemplated agreement about Korea. When Rosen reported that the editing of the text of the agreement had been completed, Muraviev instructed him again, on the twenty-fourth, to sign immediately.[55]

The Russo-Japanese entente concerning Korea was signed by Nishi and Rosen in Tokyo the following day, on April 25, 1898. The final wording of the protocol was as follows:

Article 1. The Imperial Governments of Japan and Russia definitively recognize the sovereignty and entire independence of Corea, and mutually engage to refrain from all direct interference in the internal affairs of that country.

Article 2. Desiring to avoid every possible cause of misunderstanding in the future, the Imperial Governments of Japan and Russia mutually engage, in case Corea should apply to Japan or to Russia for advice and assistance, not to take any measure in the nomination of military instructors and financial advisers, without having previously come to a mutual agreement on the subject.

Article 3. In view of the large development of Japanese commercial and industrial enterprises in Corea as well as the considerable number of Japanese subjects resident in that country, the Imperial Russian Government will not impede the development of the commercial and industrial relations between Japan and Corea.

In accordance with Nishi's wishes, the preamble stated that agreement had been reached on the articles in pursuance of the fourth article of the Moscow Protocol signed by Lobanov and Yamagata in 1896.[56]

St. Petersburg was greatly relieved at the signing of the protocol. On Muraviev's note informing him of the conclusion of the agreement, Nicholas jotted: "I am happy at the conclusion of this ticklish business."[57]

The two governments had concurred to keep the Nishi-Rosen Protocol secret for the time being, but their hand was forced when incorrect versions of the agreement appeared in the press.[58] On May 12 the *Official Gazette* in St. Petersburg published the text of the agreement with a brief introduction, in which it mentioned the efforts of the tsarist government since the end of the Sino-Japanese War to assure the integrity and full independence of the Korean state. It asserted that the self-reliance Korea had achieved thanks to the assistance of the Russian military instructors and financial adviser had made it possible for Russia and Japan to proceed to an amicable exchange of ideas to determine in a clear and precise manner the relations between them in the face of the "newly created situation in the Korean peninsula." The conclusion of this amicable agreement, the paper declared at the end of the communication, enabled Russia "to direct all her efforts toward the accomplishment of the historical and essentially pacific task incumbent upon her on the shores of the *Grand-Océan* [Pacific Ocean]."[59]

The fact that all the "inspired papers" were busy with explanations in favor of the protocol led Hayashi to conclude that "not a few Russians" shared his dissatisfaction with it.[60] P. Tolstoy did indeed criticize the Nishi-Rosen convention in an article in *Russkii Trud* in June for what he regarded as a unilateral self-denial on the part of Russia. While Russia promised not to impede the development of Japanese commercial and industrial interests in Korea, Japan assumed no reciprocal obligation; and no restrictions whatsoever were placed on the activities of England and other powers.[61]

Transmitting a clipping from *The Independent* of May 24 with the text of the new convention between Russia and Japan, the American minister remarked that the second article was regarded in Seoul as the only one of importance. "The convention is not thought to be a matter of much moment here," Allen wrote. "The one of June 9, 1896, was found to be of no practical importance, and it is thought that this will be of much the same nature."[62]

The critics of the Nishi-Rosen convention did not know of the unofficial pledge Japan had given to Russia regarding Manchuria. More perspicacious observers had anticipated some understanding concerning Manchuria in connection with the Russian withdrawal from Korea. When Russia had accepted the Korean decision to do without the military instructors and financial adviser, the tsarist diplomats in Japan had argued that their government had thereby proven what it had always claimed but no one had believed, namely that Russia was being unselfish in according aid to Korea. Treutler did not think that the Russians were saying so in an attempt to make the best of a bad situation, because he was sure that Russia could have avoided the turn of events in spite of all the anti-Russian intrigues had she seriously wanted to do so. He was convinced that there was a direct connection between the Russian occupation of Port Arthur and the Korean episode. With the acquisition of an ice-free harbor in the Liaotung Peninsula, the Russification of Korea had become far less important for St. Petersburg, Treutler argued. It would be natural for Russia to concentrate for the time being on the enormous task confronting her in North China, particularly since the possessor of Vladivostok and Port Arthur and of the land connecting these two points would always be in a position to throw in a pregnant word in the Korean peninsula, where a strong friend would probably be needed again in the near future. "If one takes into consideration furthermore that Russia, at the instant when she releases Korea, cuts off the branch on which all the foes of Russia in Tokyo are sitting, one could well imagine that the events on the Korean stage may have been directed by an adroit hand from St. Petersburg," Treutler speculated. "It would be a superb exit, which would show the Russian friend voluntarily leave the position in Seoul, which only recently had been considered unassailable, in a halo of the most unselfish friendship, and the effect would be purchased not too dearly when the one who departed [from the stage] had Port Arthur, etc. in his pocket and a Russo-Japanese brotherhood [*Verbrüderung*] as inviting final scene before his eyes." [63]

The tsarist government marked the détente in Russo-Japanese relations with the dispatch on an official visit of Grand Duke Cyril, first cousin of the tsar and second in order of succession to the throne, who was then serving as an ensign on the cruiser *Rossiia*. During the four days that Cyril stayed in Japan he was received with particular cordiality. The Meiji emperor put Shiba Palace at his disposal and invited him several times to dine with him. He was entertained also by the various princes and by the Russian legation, where the diplomatic representatives of the powers braved the humid heat of Tokyo in their naphthalene-smelling uniforms to pay their respects to the tall and slender ensign of royal blood. The imperial family arranged festivities for Cyril, and Prince Kanin took him sightseeing. The cities of Tokyo and Kyoto and Kanagawa Prefecture presented him with valuable gifts and the Grand Cross of the Chrysanthemum, reserved for sovereigns and their families, was bestowed on him.

Rosen had dreaded the visit in view of the attempt on the life of Nicholas at Otsu in 1891. He had vainly pleaded with Muraviev to postpone the visit, believing that popular resentment against Russia had not been stilled sufficiently to guarantee the grand duke's safety. But the Japanese government took precautions on a vast scale and, to Rosen's relief, the venture turned out to be a great success. Prince Arisugawa made Cyril promise that on the next call of his ship at Yokohama, he would come and spend several days with him and the princess privately at their palace in Tokyo, "a pointedly intimate kind of hospitality such as had never yet been extended to any royal visitor by any member of the Imperial family," Rosen remarked in his memoirs. At any rate, as his French colleague observed at the time, the warm reception accorded to Cyril was destined to efface the last traces of the Otsu incident. [64]

Twenty-Six

The Anglo-Russian Arrangement

The occupation of Port Arthur and Talien by Russia evoked a countermove by Great Britain. "The best plan would perhaps be, on the cession of Wei-hai Wei by the Japanese, to insist on the refusal of a lease of that port on terms similar to those granted to Germany," Salisbury telegraphed to MacDonald on March 7, 1898.[1] Weihaiwei was a large bay whose mouth was open to the frequent northerly gales. An island across the mouth gave protection to a limited anchorage of some three battleships, three fairly large cruisers, and a considerable number of vessels of not more than eighteen feet draught, the British Admiralty estimated. Additional modern vessels could lie in safety, though not in comfort, in positions exposed to the sea. At the moment, the greater part of the bay was too shallow for shipping, but it could be dredged and made safer by the construction of breakwaters.[2]

Fearing the occupation of Weihaiwei by Germany,[3] Undersecretary of State Sanderson asked Minister Kato Takaaki during a conversation on March 12 whether Japan would evacuate Weihaiwei even to make room for that power. Kato answered that he saw no reason to believe that his government would break its treaty engagement. He asked "for the sake of argument" what the attitude of Great Britain would be if Japan did decide to retain Weihaiwei after the indemnity had been paid. Sanderson stated that he could not reply for his government, but that personally he did not have the least objection. He expected Germany and Russia to object to such action and did not know what support, if any, Great Britain would give Japan. "On my suggesting Great Britain might occupy the place by arrangement with Japan, in case of her evacuation, he smiled significantly, but gave no reply," Kato reported.[4]

Germany, meanwhile, supported Russian opposition to Japanese retention of Weihaiwei. Describing Japan as the "most bellicose element in East Asia," Foreign Secretary Bülow surmised that Foreign Minister Muraviev would be

acting in the interest of peace if he influenced Peking to make the payment of
the remaining 13 million pound indemnity dependent on the renewed assurance by Japan to evacuate Weihaiwei immediately upon receipt of the
sum.[5]

O'Conor reported from St. Petersburg that Hayashi had expressed the conviction that Weihaiwei would be evacuated by the Japanese forces in May.
O'Conor doubted that either Russia or Germany would endeavor to replace
them. "Japan might possibly not be averse to seeing England in possession of
Wei-hai Wei, and probably they would prefer England there to any other
Power; but, in any case, the persistent resentment of Russia would be incurred
by the Power that took it," O'Conor warned.[6]

Satow told Nishi that the Chinese government had suggested that Britain
might occupy Weiheiwei after the withdrawal of Japanese troops under the
same terms as the lease of Kiaochow. When he inquired whether this would be
agreeable to Japan, Nishi replied that in assuring China that Japan would
evacuate Weihaiwei after the payment of the full balance of the indemnity, the
Japanese government had expressed the desire that China hold Weihaiwei
herself, but that in case she would be unable to do so, it would not object to
the occupation of the place by "any Power disposed to support the independence of China."[7]

On March 25 Salisbury instructed MacDonald to demand a reversionary
lease of Weihaiwei on the departure of the Japanese on terms similar to the
Russian lease of Port Arthur on the ground that the cession of Port Arthur to
Russia had materially altered the balance of power in the Gulf of Pechili.[8]
MacDonald could assure the Tsungli Yamen, Salisbury cabled, that the British would provide the Chinese with all reasonable facilities for using the harbor. He was to point out that the British would not be asking for the lease if
the Chinese were able to maintain themselves at Weihaiwei unassisted; the
British demand hence was made in the interests of China at least as much as of
England. But Salisbury made it clear that the desire of China for British
friendship must not show itself by refusing the requests and advice of England
while granting those of powers "less anxious for her welfare."[9] "The lease of
Wei-hai Wei to us should include sufficient territory on the mainland to enable
us to dispose of the land defences as we deem best," Salisbury instructed
MacDonald. "It should not be for a specific term of years, but for the duration
of the occupation by Russia of any port on the Liaotung Peninsula."[10]

On April 1 Satow informed Nishi in strictest confidence of the presentation
of the British demand to the Chinese government for the lease of Weihaiwei
upon its evacuation by the Japanese. The British government assured Japan
that it did not seek to hasten the date of her withdrawal from Weihaiwei and

trusted, in view of Satow's reports, that the proposed step would receive "the concurrence and support of the Japanese government." In giving the concurrence—but not the support—of his government, Nishi expressed the expectation that Britain would in turn back Japan in the event she would find it necessary at any time in the future "to take similar measures in order to strengthen her defences or to promote her interests." [11]

The following day, on April 2, Minister Rosen intimated to Nishi under instructions from the tsarist government that Russia would be prepared to give her consent should Japan desire to obtain a pledge from China not to cede Weihaiwei to any other power after the withdrawal of the Japanese forces. Nishi replied that anxious as Japan was for China to hold the place herself, she was unwilling to attach such a consideration to her evacuation. [12]

Pavlov had instructions to urge the Tsungli Yamen to conclude a protocol with Japan in which China would pledge not to cede Weihaiwei to any other power after its evacuation by the Japanese forces. He too was to communicate that Russia was prepared to respect the obligations of such a protocol. [13] St. Petersburg also approached Berlin about the desirability of such a pledge on the part of Peking. [14]

The ministers of the Tsungli Yamen meanwhile agreed after much discussion to lease Weihaiwei to Great Britain on the same terms as Russia had received Port Arthur and until such time as Russia remained in occupation of the Liaotung Peninsula. The lease was to take effect when the Japanese pulled out. [15] The ministers asked in connection with these arrangements that special facilities be set aside at Weihaiwei for the training of Chinese naval officers and men by officers of the British navy. MacDonald supported the Chinese request. Since Russia had sent an officer of the imperial guard to drill and organize Chinese troops in the north, he telegraphed to Salisbury, Britain should agree to assist in organizing and training the Chinese navy. The British government should insist, he added, that the carefully selected officer on the active list would be given "full powers and a free hand." Salisbury replied to MacDonald that the British government fully sympathized with the desire of the Chinese government to reform its military and naval forces and would be glad to assist them "provided conditions were arranged which gave reasonable prospect of good results." [16]

Deputy Prime Minister Balfour telegraphed to Lascelles that he should tell the German government that the British demand for the lease of Weihaiwei had been forced by the Russian occupation of Port Arthur. Its sole object was to maintain the balance of power in the Gulf of Pechili; it should not give any umbrage to German interests in Shantung because it was impossible to make Weihaiwei into a commercial port. [17] The communication which Lascelles made on April 4 left the implication that Britain was stepping into the vacuum created by Japan's withdrawal in order to prevent the occupation of Weihaiwei by Russia.[18] But the Germans, with Russian encouragement, deemed the British action as directed also against them and demanded a specific pledge that Britain would not encroach upon their interests in Shantung, notably not build any railroads in this province.[19] As Wilhelm commented: "In Weihaiwei England gets two neighbors, of which one [namely Russia] is hostile to her. It will be that much more opportune for her to remain there on good terms with the other neighbor [Germany]." If England would guarantee to respect German interests in Shantung, which nature had separated from Weihaiwei by high mountain chains, and look upon Weihaiwei merely as a naval base and not a commercial point of attack, Germany could leave Britain a free hand in the Gulf of Pechili. "Our press should not needlessly publicize its malicious relish [*Schadenfreude*] at the newly created antagonism between England and Russia," Wilhelm warned, "as we shall thereby make the others mistrustful and ill disposed toward us."[20]

Metternich, who was with Wilhelm at Homburg Castle, commented that it was a venture of doubtful value from the English point of view for Britain to entrench herself in the Russian sphere of interest and eventual sphere of influence in an inferior harbor, which could be defended only at enormous cost and even then poorly. It could but suit Germany, on the other hand, if Russian and English forces were withdrawn from other points and sent to the Gulf of Pechili.[21]

Bülow concurred that the British demand for the leasing of Weihaiwei had been a mistake, committed out of the desire to save face. Referring to Osten-Sacken's communication about the desirability of a Chinese pledge not to cede Weihaiwei to any other power, Bülow remarked that the tsarist government had not proposed joined action by Russia and Germany in this regard. It had not reverted to the suggestion it had made toward the end of the previous year regarding a delineation of their mutual spheres of interest in China, even though Germany had declared herself ready to receive and discuss pertinent Russian proposals. As far as he could judge, the tendency of Russia was, now as before, to prod Germany into an isolated action without assuming commitments of her own for fear of impairing the attitude of France. Noting that Muraviev, in contrast to his earlier statements, had asserted to Radolin on April 6 that Russia did not regard the leasing of Weihaiwei to England as a danger but as an advantage in that it enabled Russia to act more freely at Port Arthur, Bülow remarked that the new position of Russia made it possible for Germany to reach an independent decision, motivated exclusively by her own interests. He had consequently delayed a reply to the Russian intimation, hoping that meanwhile an agreement could be reached with England on the basis of the guarantee regarding Shantung.[22]

Wilhelm agreed with the course of action proposed by Bülow and expressed the hope that the talks with England would attain the desired result.[23] As he explained, it could not be desirable for Germany in view of the "unsure, contradictory, and false attitude" of the tsarist government, if Weihaiwei would constitute a wedge driven between the Russian and German possessions, whose proximity might not be without danger eventually. He suggested that should the tsarist government approach Germany again, while her negotiations with Britain were still under way, Germany should play for time by asking for clarification to what extent France would be willing to make common cause with Russia against England over Weihaiwei. Once the agreement with England had been concluded, Germany could "openly" thank Russia for having warned her of the dangers inherent in the British leasing of Weihaiwei; Germany too had recognized the threat and had averted it by negotiations with England.[24]

Lascelles handed the desired assurance to Bülow on April 21. It formally declared that in establishing herself at Weihaiwei, England had "no intention of injuring or contesting the rights and interests of Germany in the province of Shantung or of creating difficulties for her in that province." It stipulated further that England would not construct any railroad communication from the Weihaiwei leasehold into the interior of the province.[25] The official announcement published in the *Reichs- und Staats-Anzeiger* on April 22 asserted that the British communication had been made to Germany "spontaneously."

Osten-Sacken swallowed the explanation concocted by Wilhelm.[26] He volunteered confidentially that the British occupation of Weihaiwei was directed more against his own country than against Germany. But Russia would not tolerate the presence of England in North China permanently, Osten-Sacken opined; she would take her revenge once the Siberian railroad had been completed and her position on the Indian border had been solidified.[27]

At MacDonald's urging, the negotiation of a definitive agreement respecting Weihaiwei had been deferred until the bay had been actually occupied by the British and the latter would be in a position "to insist on such boundaries and conditions as may seem desirable."[28] On May 7 the balance of the indemnity was paid by China. The withdrawal of the Japanese forces from Weihaiwei was ordered three days later and carried out on the twenty-third.[29] The Japanese had removed the guns and destroyed the fortifications, but not the buildings they had erected.[30] When the British took over on May 24,[31] they marveled at the excellent state of order and cleanliness of the quarters and at the large quantity of furniture which the Japanese had left behind for their use.[32]

The accord between England and China had caught Russia by surprise. Muraviev had been furious with "the weakness and duplicity" of the Tsungli

Yamen. Neither the Chinese minister nor the British ambassador had given him any inkling of the negotiations. The démarche which Muraviev had proposed to prevent the occupation of Weihaiwei by another power had been made useless.[33] He had been compelled, therefore, not to take any action against the proceedings of England.[34]

"The English must always and eternally intrigue against us and step into our path hinderingly," Nicholas II had told the German naval attaché, Commander Kalan vom Hofe. "But here [in Weihaiwei] they have gone completely astray." They had hoped, Nicholas asserted, to disquiet and intimidate Russia, but to no avail. Russia had paid no heed to all the clamor and had remained calm. The English government had probably allowed itself to be carried away by public opinion, Nicholas mused; it was a thoughtless action which Britain now regretted.[35]

The announcement by the British government of the Anglo-Chinese accord about Weihaiwei had indeed been received by Parliament "more with acquiescence than with enthusiasm."[36] There was growing doubt about the wisdom and necessity of continued Anglo-Russian rivalry. As the editor of the *Imperial and Asiatic Quarterly* had commented already in October 1896, the "alarmist stories" that were circulated periodically about "Russian designs" had failed to materialize. There was every reason to believe that Russia was acting "in a fair and conciliatory spirit" in Korea. There were indications, he wrote, "that British, if not Russian, statesmen are beginning to discover that the interests of both nations would be best consulted by, if possible, an amicable settlement, not only of Far Eastern questions, but also of all conflicts of interests which the now accelerated process of dissolution of the Turkish Empire and the march of events in Central Asia may speedily, but surely, bring to a head."[37]

Russia refused to give the same consideration to English views that she did to Japanese views in the formulation of her Korean policy, because the commercial stake of Britain in the peninsula was minor. When Undersecretary of Foreign Affairs George Nathaniel Curzon warned in the House of Commons on July 19, 1897, that if the Korean ports were used as *points d'appui* for operations which might threaten the equilibrium of the Far East, England would have to protect her own interests, *Novoe Vremia* retorted angrily: "Russia protects the independence of Corea, not England, and if such protection necessitates the continual presence of Russian ships of war in one or other of the Corean ports, Petersburgh cannot consult in London the views of the Minister of Foreign Affairs and of his assistant on the subject."[38] The Russian chargé in London, Pavel Mikhailovich Lessar, reminded the Foreign Office on August 13 of that year that Britain had failed to adhere to the intervention whereby Russia, France, and Germany had defended the independence of

Korea by thwarting Japanese acquistion of the Liaotung Peninsula. He made it clear that the defense of Russia's important interests in Korea was one of the principal objects of her Far Eastern policy.[39]

In China, on the other hand, Great Britain played a major role; an Anglo-Russian understanding there might well be of mutual benefit. On January 17, 1898, Salisbury instructed O'Conor, if he considered it practicable, to ask Witte "whether it is not possible for England and Russia to work together in China." "Our objects are not in any serious degree antagonistic; on the other hand, if we try, we can both of us do each other a great deal of harm. It is, therefore, better that we should come to an understanding," Salisbury telegraphed. "If we could regard Russia as willing to work with us, we would go far to further Russian commercial objects in the north," he concluded.[40]

Muraviev, to whom O'Conor conveyed the British overture, replied that his own views coincided entirely with those of Salisbury; the same, he felt sure, held true of the tsar to whom he would transmit them without delay. When O'Conor expressed the opinion that in order to achieve a "really effective understanding," their efforts should not be confined to the Far East but embrace their respective interests in general, Muraviev declared himself ready "to consider at once any proposal tending to create a closer understanding, or entente between the two Governments." Muraviev suggested that the British government should formulate its views on the subject; O'Conor hinted that it would be better for Muraviev to take the initiative. O'Conor thought the negotiations would progress more rapidly if conducted in London; Muraviev replied that he would prefer to carry them on in St. Petersburg. At any rate, Muraviev said, he was prepared to show his hand if Salisbury did the same.

"From my study of the political situation since my return," O'Conor reported, "I am led to consider the moment opportune for coming to a friendly agreement as to our respective interests both in China and elsewhere, as it appears to me that the Russian Government, and especially the Emperor, are most anxious to avoid any complications until the Siberian railway is finished." But it was necessary, he warned, to insure that the tsarist government would not be able to nullify the advantages Britain might receive as soon as Russia had gained her temporary objective.[41]

Witte, with whom O'Conor talked on the evening of January 22, tried to ascertain how far England would go with Russia. If their two countries could come to an understanding, he remarked, their ruling would be law in the Far East. O'Conor refrained from going into details. He stated broadly that it was Britain's "natural and necessary policy" to keep China open to foreign trade, to oppose prohibitive tariffs, and to prevent other powers from impairing her commercial interests and consequent political position. The object of his visit, O'Conor explained, was to find out whether Witte was still of the opinion that an understanding was possible and if so, whether he would support it. Witte replied that he favored an "alliance" between their countries; he was ready to back the "practical and commercial policy" of England if the latter did not impede Russian ambition in the north. Producing a map of China from a carefully locked desk, Witte drew his hand over the provinces of Chihli, Shansi, Shensi, and Kansu and said that he personally thought they would probably be absorbed by Russia eventually. The lower part of China, embracing the entire Yangtze region, on the other hand, would undoubtedly form the British sphere of preponderance, he anticipated. He remarked that Germany could be held in check between Russia and England.[42]

On January 25 Salisbury revealed what he had in mind. The governments of Turkey and China, because of the extreme weakness of these empires, were constantly guided by the counsels of foreign powers. The advice tendered by England and Russia threw the two powers into constant opposition to each other and their efforts were consequently neutralized much more frequently than justified by the antagonism existing between their respective interests. It would be of mutual advantage therefore to remove the antagonism, which was likely to increase otherwise, by an understanding between England and Russia. No infracting of existing rights was contemplated, nor any division of territory. All that the British government desired was a "partition of preponderance." In both Turkey and China there were large regions which interested Russia much more than England and vice versa. "Might not an arrangement be arrived at in regard to those territories by which, when the advice of the two countries is not in accord, the Power least interested should give way and render assistance to the Power whose interest is superior?" Salisbury suggested.[43]

Muraviev, to whom O'Conor communicated Salisbury's scheme, wrote in a memorandum to the tsar on January 31 that it was worthy of consideration as far as the delineation of spheres of influence in China was concerned. Under the present political circumstances and in view of the occupation of Port Arthur and Talienwan by Russian vessels, it would seem highly desirable for Russia to enter into an amicable agreement with England by the division of spheres of influence in China in the sense of Salisbury's proposal, that is to say, that the Russian sphere be bordered in the east by the Hwang-ho (Yellow River) and in the south by the English basin of the Yangtze River. Such an agreement would give Russia full freedom of action in the Gulf of Pechili and thereby offer the possibility of removing the English from any interference in the affairs of Northern China, Muraviev pointed out. With Nicholas's permission he would engage the British ambassador in further discussion concerning the Chinese aspect of Salisbury's proposal.[44]

At a court ball on the evening of February 1 Nicholas told O'Conor that he

favored an entente between Russia and England on the lines he had mentioned
to Muraviev.[45] The latter recapitulated to O'Conor during an interview on the
afternoon of February 2 the assurances given by the tsar. Nicholas had instructed him, he said, to inform O'Conor that he thought it desirable to come
to an understanding in the first instance regarding Chinese affairs because of
their urgent nature. Nicholas wanted Salisbury to clarify in what way and to
what extent the two governments should aid one another. When O'Conor
repeated Salisbury's proposal, Muraviev asked him to transmit the tsar's message anyway. The Russian government, he stated, would present its demands
upon receipt of Salisbury's answer; the negotiations would then continue until
they had reached a settlement. Muraviev suggested that they leave the definition of their respective spheres of influence in Turkey until a later time. He
added that both countries would gain when it was shown that English distrust
of Russian designs on India was a misconception.[46]

At another court ball on the evening of February 8 Nicholas expressed to
O'Conor his full sympathy with the proposal of the British government, remarking that at this time the consideration of affairs in the Far East was most
pressing. He voiced regret that the illness of Muraviev, who was suffering
from smallpox, would delay the negotiations. Yet Lamsdorff carried on and
asked O'Conor the following day, on the ninth, for a more precise definition,
if possible in writing, of the policy and interests of Great Britain, notably to
what countries the arrangement was to extend. While Lamsdorff reiterated
that it was more urgent at the moment to deal with the Far Eastern situation,
O'Conor nonetheless pointed to the possibility of an understanding concerning the Turkish East as well. England would be prepared, O'Conor related, to
recognize the complete legitimacy of Russia's striving to include in her sphere
of influence not only the Black Sea with its shores and the Bosporus, but an
outlet to the Aegean Sea, her own interests being now primarily on the Af-
rican continent.[47]

In the course of conversation O'Conor alleged that Russian threats to the
Peking government had thwarted the conclusion of a loan agreement between
China and Great Britain. Lamsdorff replied that too much credence should
not be given to the explanations made by the Chinese in London for the failure
of the British loan negotiations, because the Chinese ministers used the same
arguments vis-à-vis the tsarist representative in Peking, contending that England resorted to all kinds of means and threats to block a Chinese loan from
Russia. This was a good illustration, he remarked, of the sort of misunderstandings that could easily be eliminated if the agreement proposed by Salisbury were to materialize.[48]

On February 11 O'Conor informed Lamsdorff of the conditions on which the British government had agreed to make a loan to China. Lamsdorff in turn revealed to him the preferences of the Tsungli Yamen in this regard, as confided to Pavlov. He told O'Conor during the interview that it would be advisable to put on record in an official and confidential note the views of the British government and the stage reached by the negotiations concerning an Anglo-Russian entente.

O'Conor did so the following day, on the twelfth, in a note addressed to Muraviev. He began by recalling the communication he had made on January 19 on behalf of Salisbury regarding the reason why the British government considered an agreement between their governments desirable and the lines on which it should be based. It was evident, he pointed out, that there were large portions of both the Chinese and the Ottoman empires in which Russia and Great Britain had interests of varying degree and where some arrangement could be worked out whereby the power least concerned should give way and support the other. For example, the portion of the Ottoman Empire which drained into the Black Sea or the sea as far as the beginning of the Aegean Sea, as well as the drainage of the Euphrates up to Bagdad interested Russia much more than Great Britain, while the latter was far more interested in Turkish Africa, Arabia, and the valley of the Euphrates below Bagdad. In China, Russian interests were predominant in the north, British interests in the Yangtze valley. O'Conor noted that Muraviev had concurred with the views of the British government and that the tsar himself had told him on the twentieth that an arrangement of the sort suggested by Salisbury would be desirable. Salisbury, to whom he had reported the encouraging words of Nicholas, had suggested that the negotiations begin with the most pressing question, that is with China. Hence O'Conor had communicated to Muraviev through Lamsdorff the previous day the conditions on which the British government proposed to guarantee a loan for the Chinese government and in exchange had been informed what the Tsungli Yamen had told Pavlov in this connection. "The negotiations would now appear to have arrived at a point permitting the discussion, to the mutual advantage of each country, of the more definite issues at stake," O'Conor concluded; he had addressed the present communication to Muraviev in the hope of facilitating this aim.[49]

The note transmitted by O'Conor was "a document of primary importance," Muraviev wrote to Nicholas on February 14. Without limiting Russian freedom of action in any way, the British government stipulated in advance certain principal bases which could be of significance for Russia in the future. "I shall not fail to announce to O'Conor first of all," Muraviev declared, "that England, as is evident from the note of the ambassador, has quite correctly determined our right to predominant influence in the north of China, in consequence of which we on our part would be ready to admit [*dopustit'*] the influence of England in the south of the empire." [50]

In a secret telegram from St. Petersburg on February 22, O'Conor pointed out that hardly any considerations would deter Russia from holding on to Port Arthur and Talienwan. British objections would merely revive mutual distrust and jealousy. The Chinese would not heed the English unless they promised material help and Russian influence would increase in Peking at British expense in proportion as the Siberian railroad approached Peking. On the other hand, if Britain offered no opposition, the danger of complications would disappear and an understanding between Russia and England on a firm basis would be feasible. The matter had arrived at a stage, he thought, where the points of decision were either to acquiesce in the demands of Russia and continue the negotiations for an entente, or else to risk Russia getting what she wanted without British assent and break off the negotiations, engendering much bitter feeling. O'Conor deemed it advisable in case the first alternative was adopted to avoid pledging Britain in any definitive manner until she saw what Russia was prepared to do in the broader issues. [51]

That day, on February 22, O'Conor received a reply from the tsarist government to his note of the twelfth. It stated that Nicholas, to whom the note had been shown, had expressed satisfaction at the desire of the British government to enter into an entente with Russia in order to obviate misunderstandings between their countries in those parts of the world where their interests were at issue. Asserting that the tsarist government hailed the English overtures with pleasure, the document indicated that there was now a good opportunity for solving the China question, especially the matter of a foreign loan. [52]

The garnering of the Chinese loan by British and German bankers affected the Anglo-Russian negotiations adversely. Lamsdorff told O'Conor that Nicholas had been greatly disappointed by the conclusion of this loan just when the talks between their governments had been proceeding so auspiciously. The loan plus commercial advantages recently obtained by Britain in China had made such an unfavorable impression on the tsar that he did not seem inclined, Lamsdorff inferred, to pursue the discussion of the broader question for the time being. [53] When Muraviev resumed his weekly reception of the diplomatic corps on March 8, he said virtually the same to O'Conor. [54]

On the afternoon of March 24 Staal called on Balfour to ask how things stood between their countries in the Far East. Balfour replied that Britain had always looked with favor upon the idea of Russia obtaining an ice-free port on the Pacific Ocean, but the tsarist government, he alleged, had given "a most unfortunate extension to this policy" by its demand for Port Arthur, whose acquisition would affect the balance of power at Peking and thus was objectionable to the British government. Staal, who had not received any instructions from his government recently, retorted in his own name that Russia had found it necessary to obtain some guarantees in northern China, because Germany had modified the *status quo* in that country.[55]

When Staal complained about the continued friction between the governments of St. Petersburg and London in an interview with Salisbury on May 6, the latter attributed it to the unjustified occupation by Russia of Port Arthur which had forced England to obtain some security of her own. Staal retorted that he failed to understand how the acquisition of Port Arthur could have aroused British susceptibilities, since Salisbury had declared in a speech before the Primrose League that the port by itself was of no significance. Since Salisbury realized that the influence which Russia had over the court of Peking was due to her proximity to China rather than to the acquisition of Port Arthur, why had Weihaiwei been taken as a response to the Russian occupation of Port Arthur? It was a place of no importance except as a menace against Russia. Salisbury had known for a long time that Russia had an arrangement concerning Port Arthur. Russia had been forced to invoke the arrangement because the state of affairs had been changed by the German occupation of Kiaochow, against which Salisbury had raised no objections.

Salisbury shrugged his shoulders and said with a smile that the British government had been pushed by public opinion into doing something. It had chosen Weihaiwei, he alleged, because it had not known what else to take. What good did it do to revert to the question of Port Arthur and Weihaiwei, he asked rhetorically. "What is done is done, it is wiser not to talk of it further," he concluded.[56]

In a speech at Birmingham in mid-May Colonial Secretary Joseph Chamberlain declared that since England had been unable to come to an understanding with Russia concerning China, where great events were in store, she must maintain her influence there by abandoning her policy of isolation and seeking an alliance with those powers whose interests approximated her own.[57]

Chamberlain's attack on Russian policy aroused little emotion in St. Petersburg. The best response to make to such an excess in language, Muraviev told Montebello, was "the calmest indifference." It was with equanimity too that Russia could regard the British occupation of Weihaiwei, he remarked, because she aspired only to a strong defensive position in the Liaotung Peninsula; she had no aggressive ulterior motives. Besides, great effort and expenditure would be required for Britain to make Weihaiwei into an effective stronghold; it constituted imperfect compensation for what Russia had acquired. "The position which Russia today holds in the China Sea with a port where her ships will always be available, the proximity of her military establishments of the Amur, whose important forces will be ready at all times to advance overland or to be disembarked at any place, permit her to watch with calm the defense and development of her interests, while maintaining the good relations already established with Japan and preserving, as long as she will not be provoked, a pacific attitude, which is undoubtedly the rule of her policy in the Far East," Montebello reported.[58]

Not until June 14 did Muraviev refer to the public speeches made by Chamberlain and other British leaders and to the attacks on himself by the English press. Was there anything to be gained by all the abuse heaped on Russia, he asked O'Conor, who was retiring as British ambassador to St. Petersburg. The tsarist government desired to cultivate very friendly relations with Great Britain. It had assured the latter that it would respect all existing rights and privileges for the development of the China trade, in which Britain was so deeply interested, and had not opposed the important concessions England had recently received concerning Hong Kong. Russia regarded Hong Kong and the Yangtze region as Britain's sphere of political influence, but expected England to show reciprocity. He saw no justification for militant antagonism between their countries and assured him that Nicholas was most favorably disposed towards a cordial understanding with the British government.

O'Conor reported that Muraviev's language was "marked with more cordiality than on any previous occasion." He considered the change of tone to be an "auspicious omen" for his successor, although Muraviev had agreed with him that it would be best for the time being "to attempt very little, and to wait for a 'revisement' of public opinion."[59]

By August the tension provoked by the occupation of Port Arthur and Weihaiwei had markedly declined and the British press speculated about the negotiation of an Anglo-Russian understanding. The necessary talks were delayed, however, because the tsarist ambassador was on leave, the new British ambassador to St. Petersburg, Sir Charles S. Scott, had only recently reached his post, and the British, as Bertie confided to the French chargé, did not know what they wanted. On one hand, they were discontented with the policy followed by Salisbury, fearing a gradual loss of English commerce in China to foreign competitors; on the other hand, they sensed instinctively that war with Russia could entail risks and unknown factors. Yet it seemed desirable that the tension which still existed between the governments of St. Petersburg and London not be prolonged and an entente reached in a month or two, before the English politicians scattered to their electoral districts.[60]

On August 28 Scott wrote to Muraviev, who was in Moscow attending the unveiling of the monument of Alexander II, that Balfour had gained the impression from reading his confidential reports that Muraviev was about to make some definitive suggestion in regard to railroad concessions in China which might form the basis of a solution for the difficulties created between their countries by the opposition of Pavlov to the terms of a loan by the Shanghae and Hong Kong Bank for the construction of a railroad line to Newchwang. He invited Muraviev to make the suggestion before further obstacles were placed in the path of an agreement. In a private message Scott outlined the terms for a settlement suggested by the language of Muraviev to him and of Lessar to Balfour: that money from the British bank could be used for the construction of the Newchwang line, but that it was to be a Chinese line, under Chinese control, not mortgaged to any non-Chinese company; that Russia would refrain from participating in railroad concessions in the Yangtze basin, England to undertake a similar engagement concerning Manchuria.[61]

Upon his return to St. Petersburg on September 1, Muraviev had several conversations with Scott in which they talked about the conclusion of an agreement on the above-mentioned terms, but phrased at once more amicably and more concretely. They must take every precaution, Muraviev warned, not to allow the sincerity of the intentions of their governments to be compromised by any action of private enterprise.[62]

Since Muraviev's major objection to the British loan was the pledging of the projected railroad line to the Shanghae and Hong Kong Bank as security, Scott proposed in Balfour's name that the loan be guaranteed instead by the existing line west of the Great Wall, the Shanhaikuan-Tientsin line. This proved acceptable to the Russian side, because the line in question was already in British hands. But when Lamsdorff informed Scott of the tsar's approval and proposed that he draft appropriate notes, the ambassador replied that he did not have the authority to separate the railroad question from a general agreement concerning China.

The tsarist government did not wish to commit itself to an overall understanding until it knew exactly what regions Britain had in mind. On September 25 Scott clarified that the Yangtze region could be defined as the provinces bordering onto the Yangtze river plus the provinces of Hunan and Chekiang. The British regarded Manchuria as a clearly defined country and waited for a proposal from the Russian government considering the definition of its extent that should be included in the agreement.

On September 28 Scott elaborated on a general agreement restraining Russia and England from competing or interfering in the construction and financing of railroads in each other's spheres of influence. Witte disliked the restrictions. He would have preferred not to take prohibitive measures against foreigners in the Russian sphere if the Russo-Chinese Bank in turn could have received free rein in the southern part of China. But Muraviev countered that the tsarist government could not sacrifice political interests of primary importance to the state for questionable profits of private railroad companies and banks. If Russia gave free access to Manchuria and the northern regions of China in general to the English, he warned, American, Japanese, and other foreign entrepreneurs would follow unimpeded by virtue of the agreement. "We shall thereby grant them a primary role in the economic and political development of the country, which due to its close proximity along almost the entire Asian border of [our] state must be under the preponderant influence of Russia and, with the completion of the great railroad line enter into the closest rapprochement with Siberia," Muraviev objected.[63]

In an interview with Witte on November 1, Scott declared that although British trade and enterprise must retain equal opportunities anywhere in China "with a fair field and no favour," it should be quite possible to reconcile the respective interests of the private enterprise of both countries, active primarily in different regions, by mutual agreement and concessions without allowing their rival schemes to evolve into irritating diplomatic questions.

Witte concurred, adding that he very much desired the best of relations with Great Britain. There might be interests difficult to reconcile between Russia and Germany and between Russia and Austria, he said, but he was convinced that once "rightly understood," there ought to be no antagonistic interests dividing Russia and Great Britain in China or elsewhere. The views he expressed were neither platonic nor personal, but the result of his official position, he noted. As finance minister he had "absolute need" of a frank understanding with Britain, the greatest commercial nation.

In regard to the proposed railroad agreement, Witte expressed skepticism that any paper agreement could offer sufficient security for such a concrete question. He thought that a more solid basis for amicable relations between the two powers could be furnished by a general agreement whereby Russia and Great Britain would concur to submit to frank and friendly discussion any problem of potential conflict that might arise between them anywhere in the world "with a firm resolve to seek its satisfactory adjustment by a due regard to the legitimate interests of both." The issues in China could be settled under such a general agreement, he argued; he saw no great objection, for example, to acceding to the British demand for declaring Talien a free port.[64]

Lamsdorff shared Witte's apprehension that the terms of a specific agreement could be evaded or neutralized by private interests and would not offer sufficient guarantee for either side. He expressed the fear that too much latitude had been granted by its statutes to the Russo-Chinese Bank, four of whose six directors were non-Russian, in regard to taking railroad concessions in China. He echoed that there was no real antagonism between the aims and interests of the two powers in China, remarking that they were equally determined to respect her territorial integrity. He too favored a general agreement which would be applied to each case as it arose.[65]

Informed of Witte's views, Salisbury commented that admirable as the sentiments he had expressed might be, they would not gain in force by being made the subject of a convention. They were "amiable platitudes," not an engagement on either side. "What we desire is that railway concessions in the Yang-tsze region shall not be claimed from the Tsungl-li Yamen by Russia, nor shall she oppose our claims there; we undertaking, as regards Manchuria, to observe the same conduct towards her," Salisbury telegraphed to Scott. "If we do not obtain this I do not see that an Agreement is to contain anything of value to us," he remarked.[66]

In a free wheeling after-dinner conversation at Muraviev's house on November 25, Scott, Witte, and Muraviev sought to clear the ground for an arrangement. Muraviev began by endorsing the assurance Witte had given to Scott earlier that Nicholas and all his ministers earnestly desired a frank and satisfactory agreement with Great Britain. They were convinced, he said, that there was no real antagonism between the two powers anywhere; that their rights and interests could be reconciled by open discussion. He invited their comments on the form of the agreement to be concluded.

To avoid debating the "paternity" of the original proposal, the discussants agreed "to admit a joint paternity, or to regard it as fallen from the clouds." Witte and Muraviev deemed the clause pertaining to the construction of a Newchwang line satisfactory. There has never been any question, Witte stressed, of the right of the Shanghae and Hong Kong Bank to offer a loan for the construction of the line on the usual security; the opposition had been to China's violation of the pledge given to Russia "for valuable consideration" that such a line would remain Chinese, with its control not passing by mortgage or otherwise to any non-Chinese company or government. He pointed out that a loan could be taken from the British bank on any security which did not violate the pledge, such as, for example, on the security of the constructed portion of the line west of the Great Wall.

Turning to the recognition by both governments that their railroad interests lay in different geographical areas and to the proposal to define and protect them from mutual interference in a written agreement, Muraviev worried that such a division of spheres of interest might arouse fear on the part of China and other countries that Russia and Great Britain were preparing to split "a sick man's estate," whereas in fact they were equally interested in respecting the territorial integrity of China and preventing her dissolution. Whatever agreement they devised, Muraviev added, ought not to be secret and should be of a nature to assure China and the other powers that it was not directed against their interests.

Witte enlarged on the difficulty of making the Russo-Chinese Bank adhere to an agreement which would bar it from the richest part of China and confine its operations to the least important one. By such a stipulation the tsarist government would offend the pride not only of the influential foreign directors and stockholders of the bank, but of the private Russian investors and the general public. There was no intention on the part of Russia, Witte assured Scott, to acquire an exclusive sphere of influence or interest in China. All she had gotten and desired was what was absolutely necessary to protect the interests of the railroad through Manchuria to the outlet of Talienwan. The pledge regarding the Northern Extention had been exacted from China only because in foreign hands the railroad could easily tap the trade route and kill the Russian line by competition. The outlay involved in the construction of the colossal Trans-Siberian Railroad was so enormous that it was imperative for him, as finance minister, to make certain it would return a profit in the future, Witte explained. Declaring that he respected Britain's legitimate desire to keep the door open for her commerce in China, Witte observed that Russia had no foreign trade to compete with that of England and would not have any for the next fifty years; she did not produce enough to meet consumer demands at home. He required, Witte contended, a good and permanent understanding with Great Britain in order to attract British capital and enterprise to his country. He concurred with Muraviev's contention that Russia and Great Britain as the two largest empires in Asia could do great harm unto each other if they continued to work at cross-purposes; their cooperation, on the other hand, would further the interests of civilization in the East. Yet Witte warned against the conclusion of an agreement that would be so detailed that its terms might in the future cause disputes and litigation and thereby renew mistrust.

Witte and Muraviev elaborated on their alternative proposal for an exchange of notes in which the two powers expressed their conviction that no real antagonism existed between their interests and aims in China or the Far East, that they were equally desirous to respect the independence, integrity, and interests of China and each other's treaty rights there, and intended for the future to reconcile all their financial, commercial, and other interests on this basis by frank and friendly discussion. A separate settlement was contemplated for each difficulty as it arose, "*von Fall zu Fall*," Muraviev stated.[67]

While dissension in the tsarist government delayed a positive response to the British proposal, the prestige and self-confidence of England was bolstered by the withdrawal of the French from Fashoda in Egypt. A new toughness could be seen in the communication which Scott made on November 30. He asserted that while he regretted that the idea of delineating the spheres of influence by a written agreement was meeting with various objections, he was glad to learn that both Muraviev and Witte were in favor of an agreement which would respect both the independence of China and Britain's treaty rights, which, he remarked, did not permit the establishment by virtue of railroad concessions of any preferential tariff or exclusive regulations in regard to transit goods or passengers depending on nationality. He welcomed that Muraviev and Witte were prepared to recognize and observe the policy of the Open Door based on British treaty rights; that they did not intend to demand the creation in China of a sphere of exclusive Russian influence and interests; and that they were inclined not to go beyond those measures necessary for the defense of their Manchurian railroad. If the Russian side would find it possible to give a written engagement regarding the above, it would go far to dispel existing misgivings and suspicions, Scott declared. He would be willing, he said, to go along with the desire expressed by Muraviev and Witte for an exchange of notes to the effect that no real antagonism existed between the financial, commercial, and other interests of the two countries in China.[68]

The proposal that Russia give a unilateral written engagement to England regarding her obligations to China, an independent state, shocked the Russians. "In the entire history of all our assurances regarding Central Asian affairs there was never anything like it," fumed Lessar. "If we desired to increase our leasehold on the Liaotung Peninsula the way the English did in Hongkong, we would have to seek the consent of England as we would have committed ourselves before her to respect the integrity of China," he wrote in a private letter from London. "If some other power were to occupy the most important points of the Gulf of Pechili, we would not be able to obtain compensation from China without permission from England." The engagement Salisbury wanted would leave England as the judge of what was necessary for the security of the Manchu dynasty, with Russia forfeiting the right to deal directly with an independent country, Lessar pointed out. If they could not return to the original notion of dividing spheres of influence, it would be better for Russia to have no agreement at all than the one now proposed. It would be interpreted as giving in to English threats and would only lead to further demands. He doubted that a show of firmness on the part of Russia at this time would entail grave risk. It had been easy for England to beat France in her colonies; it would be a very different thing for her to war with Russia. In spite of the favorable turn of events for Britain and the rise in her prestige, her actual forces were not great. "If the English will see that they did not frighten us and if, at the same time, we shall pursue a very cautious policy in Peking, avoiding new questions, it will probably be possible to avoid serious complications even without an agreement," Lessar concluded.[69]

The reply that Russia gave at last on February 7, 1899, reverted to the original proposal, made to it almost a full year before. It had studied the various proposals for the conclusion of an agreement for the purpose of removing conflicts arising from the interest of their subjects in the economic affairs of China, which had gained such significance since the Peking government had decided to further the construction of railroads through its vast territory, the tsarist government wrote. But the questions raised had been too many and too complicated for it to be able to work out any concrete plans for the resolution of specific problems. Just the same, it did not wish to delay a general agreement which would testify to the mutual determination of their countries to avoid any sort of conflicts and to collaborate in the peaceable solution of all questions regarding the development of their industrial and commercial interests in China. It had come to the conclusion, therefore, that it would be best at the moment in regard to Far Eastern affairs to settle on the proposals of the British government outlined in the note of its ambassador in St. Petersburg on February 12 of the past year. If the government of her Majesty, the Queen, shared this point of view it would be possible now, without entering into premature discussion of specific questions and details which could be solved gradually as needed, to determine the general provisions of an agreement on the basis of the division of spheres of influence depending on their respective economic or geographical interests. In view of the fact that the question of greatest interest to both governments at the moment was the question of the construction and exploitation of Chinese railroads, it would be natural to reach an agreement on this question first. One could resolve that Russia would not obstruct any British railroad undertakings in the Yangtze region and that Great Britain on her part would not impede analogous Russian undertakings in the region north of the Great Wall. "To conclude such an agreement would be the easier," the tsarist government wrote, "because it would be in full accord with the proposal made to us by the British government a year ago and because it would correspond to the idea of the delineation of spheres of influence, an idea the ignoring of which in the negotiations being conducted so very recently evoked the regret of Marquis Salisbury." [70]

Confronted with mounting tension in South Africa and the imminence of military involvement there, the British government agreed to the narrowed phrasing of the China question. In a note handed to Scott on March 15, Muraviev fleshed out the skeleton proposal: Russia committed herself not to demand for herself or for her subjects any railroad concessions in the Yangtze region and not to obstruct either directly or indirectly any railroad demands in that region supported by the British government; England, on her part, committed herself not to demand either for herself or her subjects any railroad concessions in the region north of the Great Wall and not to obstruct either directly or indirectly any demands supported by the Russian government. He added in the note that the contemplated agreement was not to violate the rights of the Shanghae and Hong Kong Bank regarding the Shanhaikuan-Newchwang line, though there could be no question of the surrender of ownership or control of the same to the bank.

In supplementary correspondence during the second half of March and the first half of April the tsarist government assured the British that it recognized all the rights obtained by them to the Newchwang line and affirmed at the same time its own right to demand of the Chinese government a concession for the construction of a branch line from some point on the Chinese Eastern Railroad toward Peking.[71] On April 19 Muraviev transmitted to Scott the text of the identic notes he proposed to be exchanged by the two governments relating the respecting railroad concessions in China and the loan which had been contracted by the Chinese government with the Shanghae and Hong Kong Bank, acting on behalf of the British and Chinese Corporation. Salisbury, to whom Scott telegraphed the provisions, suggested one change which was incorporated in the final text, namely the specification that Russia and Britain could not support applications for concessions in each other's spheres of influence by other foreigners either.[72]

The exchange of notes took place in St. Petersburg on April 28, 1899. In identical language, except that the Russian note was composed in French and the British note in English and that each listed the commitment by his own country first, Muraviev and Scott declared that the two powers had arrived at the agreement animated by the desire to avoid all cause of conflict on questions where their interests met in China and considering "the economic and geographic gravitation of certain parts of that Empire." The agreement was confined to the two points mentioned above: (1) Russia engaged not to seek for herself or on behalf of her subjects or others any railroad concessions in the Yangtze basin and not to obstruct either directly or indirectly in that region railroad concession applications supported by the British government; (2) Britain, on her part, engaged not to seek for herself or on behalf of her subjects or others any railroad concessions north of the Great Wall and not to obstruct either directly or indirectly in that region railroad concession applications supported by the tsarist government. The contracting parties asserted that their agreement, which they would not fail to communicate to the Chinese government, did not infringe on Chinese sovereign rights or existing treaties. By averting "all cause of complications between them," they assured the world, the arrangement was "of a nature to consolidate peace in the Far East, and to serve the primordial interests of China herself."[73]

Additional identic notes exchanged at the same time stipulated that the general arrangement was not to infringe in any way on the rights acquired by the Shanghae and Hong Kong Bank acting on behalf of the British and Chinese Corporation in connection with the loan for the construction of the Shanhaikuan-Newchwang line. It stated that the Chinese government might appoint both an English engineer and a European accountant to supervise the construction of the line and the expenditures related to it, but the line was to remain Chinese in ownership and control. The branch line from Siaoheichan to Sinminting was to be built by China herself who might permit European, not necessarily British, engineers to inspect it periodically to insure that the work was being done properly. It was understood that the special agreement would not interfere in any way with the rights of the tsarist government, if it thought fit, to support the application by Russian subjects for railroad concessions running from the main Manchurian line in a southwesterly direction through the region in which the Chinese line terminating at Sinminting and Newchwang was to be constructed.[74]

The Anglo-Russian arrangement aroused little concern in Berlin, partly because it was regarded as simply the reduction to writing of the relative position which Britain and Russia had already established in China, partly because the German public did not share the optimism voiced in London and St. Petersburg that the agreement would pave the way for removing other causes of friction between the two old rivals.[75] The French, on the other hand, were distressed. Not only did the arrangement reserve for the English an industrial monopoly in the Yangtze valley in which their own entrepreneurs were increasingly interested, but it lessened chances for Russian backing at Peking of various French demands.[76]

The arrangement with England, Russia's major rival, on top of the agreements with both China and Japan, who were bitterly hostile toward each other, constituted a feat of tsarist diplomacy of which any juggler could have been proud.

Conclusion

The Policy of Russia in East Asia

The emergence of the U.S.S.R. as a super-power in the period since the Second World War and the spread of her military and political influence to the far corners of the earth have led to a psychological projection in American minds of the present into the past, resulting in an exaggerated view of the might possessed and exercised by tsarist Russia. The problem of determining the actual policy of Russia is complicated by the fact that the tsarist regime had as bad a press in the United States as the Soviet government. It too was depicted as despotic and as determined to enslave not only its own people but mankind as a whole.[1] Lumping the various ethnic groups together as at once "Russian" and "Oriental," the American mistrusted them one and all. They assumed that whatever Russian diplomats did, be it subtle or inept, had to mean something and that the vagaries of tsarist diplomacy must be connected by a continuous policy.[2]

Historians, like journalists and diplomats, have, with few exceptions, penned a distorted record of tsarist foreign policy. In light of the large number of scholars who depict Russia as a particular menace to her neighbors, one would think that there is a wealth of concrete evidence to that effect. On closer examination, however, one finds that most of the books are interrelated; they are based on the same few sources either directly or indirectly by quoting from each other. Thus historical myths feed on themselves.[3]

The root of the problem lies not in the deliberate falsification of history, but in the inability of most writers on international relations to read Russian and in the inaccessibility of Soviet diplomatic archives to the limited number of Western scholars who can handle the language. The widely known surveys of imperialism in East Asia published in English before the Second World War were based primarily on British sources, which were inherently hostile to Russia; repeatedly the speculations of British diplomats about what Russian

835

designs *might* be, crept into the accounts as the actual policy of St. Petersburg. The scope was broadened after 1945 by recourse to Japanese and Chinese materials, yet the latter tended to be no less anti-Russian, raising the specter of Russian aggression as justification for Japanese and Chinese actions. A multi-archival approach, including the digestion of Russian documents, is necessary to determine what actually happened and thereby lay the foundations for meaningful generalization. It is hoped that the above reconstruction of events and contemporary observations on the basis of thousands of documents from eight countries will have provided not only fresh and intimate detail, but a corrective to common notions about Russian objectives during the period under review.

Despite the fact that Russia had beaten the other powers by more than a century and a half in establishing diplomatic relations with China and had run a close race with the United States in the opening of Japan, she had reduced her pace to a jog on the Korean track. She did not want to lead for fear of initiating changes with which she was not prepared to cope. Even following the opening of the Hermit Kingdom by Japan and the United States, Russia lagged behind for many laps, mindless of the exhortations and expectations of others.

The expansion of Russia, eastward across the continent, had the outward appearance of a deliberate and massive effort on the part of the tsarist government. Actually, a handful of adventurers haphazardly made their way to the Pacific, extending the sway of their sovereign informally as they exacted tribute from the indigenes they passed. The penetration by Russia of the outer fringes of the Manchu empire, her advance down the Kuril stepping stones toward Japan, and her progress to the Korean border likewise looked like part of a master plan. Yet here too the authorities in the capital played a secondary role, at times legalizing, at times disavowing the arbitrary actions of individual subjects. One would think that the situation had drastically changed by the 1880s and 1890s, when the Age of Imperialism was in full bloom and China lay prostrate on the butcher block. However, the picture that emerges from our examination of this slice of history is still one of bureaucratic passivity, of lack of central purpose, and of disharmony in St. Petersburg, at variance with the popular image of an aggressive design for world conquest.[4] This is not to suggest that the Russians were more virtuous by nature than their rivals or that they were not given to expansion at all. Like the other powers of the day, the United States included, Russia intrigued, acquired territory, and controlled where she could, but in East Asia she was less the initiator of events than their exploiter, was drawn into situations as much as pushed her way into them, and generally was more occupied with defensive than with offensive measures. Russian policies were not aspects of a grand scheme and were not always pushed to their ultimate conclusions or successful when energetically applied. There was room for improvisation by the representatives of Russia abroad and the outcome was frequently a failure of their effort.

The amicable renegotiation of their frontier in 1875 had removed the major source of discord between Russia and Japan. Neither in Japan nor on the continent had Russian commercial interests developed sufficiently to undermine the harmony attained between the two states by decades of patient negotiations and mutual restraint. Nor had either country prior to the late 1880s reached a degree of military strength threatening to the other. Indeed, the position of Russia in the Far East had actually deteriorated. It is almost inconceivable how weak the great empire was within its own boundaries in the generation following the acquisition of the Maritime Province in 1858–1860.

The colonization of the eastern regions proved more difficult and less profitable than anticipated. The various groups of Russian settlers—families of Cossacks, peasant conscripts, convicts, exiles and, after 1861, liberated serfs—lacked the experience, resources and numerical strength to cope successfully with the rigors of Siberian existence. Instead of becoming the bread basket of the Russian Far East, the Amur valley swallowed up imports of grain and beef; the river itself, due to the sparseness of population and scarcity of transportation facilities, failed to metamorphose into the lifeline of the Russian empire. These factors plus the sale of Alaska (1867) and the decline in the fur trade along the Sea of Okhotsk, weakened Russia's interest in the eastern regions and undermined the foundations of her strategic position in the Far East. Russian vessels remained dependent on the facilities and supplies of Japanese ports—they had to use the dry dock at Nagasaki because there was none at Vladivostok. Russian military posts on the Pacific coast, on Kamchatka, on Sakhalin and in the Amur and Ussuri regions were drastically cut or completely abandoned. Meanwhile Korean, Manchu, and Chinese settlers moved into the Russian regions at a faster rate than Russian colonists and attained not only numerical superiority but, in the case of the Chinese merchants, commercial control of the area. Permitted by the Russo-Chinese treaties of 1858 and 1860 to retain their local administration, the Chinese extended their political influence over the natives and even collected tribute from them.

The creation of the Volunteer Fleet in the later 1870's facilitated communication between the European and Asian extremities of Russia, but it did so at the expense of both the Amur route and of travel by land, so that the Russian Far East was more like a colony than an integral part of the empire. As disappointment eroded interest, the Russian position in the Far East was weakened further by the assignment there of second-rate officials, who delegated much of their work to still less competent subordinates, and by the frequent reliance on foreign merchants as Russian consuls.[5]

Although Russia's commercial and political interests in China were greater than in Japan, they received surprisingly little attention from the tsarist government. The Foreign Ministry had a separate Asiatic Department, divided into a Near Eastern and a Far Eastern section, but the entire department occupied only two large rooms in the early 1890s. So underdeveloped were Russian interests in central and southern China at that time, that there was no permanent tsarist consulate in Shanghai. (The functions of an acting consul were carried out by a local Russian merchant of German extraction, Iulii Avgustovich Reding, who had such a gloomy countenance that the Russian sailors nicknamed him Sentiabr Oktiabrevich [September (son of) October].) The low regard in which St. Petersburg held the post of Peking was evident from the fact that Popov and Kumani had been merely consuls general in Marseilles before being appointed ministers to the Manchu court. Cassini too came from a relatively minor post; he had been consul general and then briefly minister resident in Hamburg.[6]

The primary motives for the construction of the Trans-Siberian Railroad were economic. Merchants and individual enthusiasts prodded a reluctant central government into the costly undertaking. That the internal development of Siberia rather than the speedy transportation of troops was the main consideration may be seen from the fact that early plans did not call for a through railroad, merely for separate lines to link up the waterways. Not until after the outbreak of war with Japan were the sections of the Trans-Siberian Railroad fully connected. The consolidation of the lines enhanced the economic impetus of the railroad. Besides serving as an artery of domestic growth, it promised to become the major route of trade between Western Europe and the Far East.[7]

Japanese business circles welcomed the construction of the Trans-Siberian Railroad. The Russo-Japanese Society (*Russko-Iaponskoe obshestvo*), founded in Tokyo in the summer of 1894, sought to promote commerce between the two countries. In a report to the Finance Ministry penned after the tripartite intervention, Hitrovo wrote that the eagerness of Japanese capitalists to invest in Russo-Japanese trade guaranteed that the Trans-Siberian Railroad would have a brilliant future; it was "destined to become the shortest trade route of Japan not only with Russia, but with Europe in general."[8]

As the international situation in the Far East deteriorated, increasing attention was paid to the strategic aspects of the railroad. But in looking to the Trans-Siberian Railroad for the transportation of troops, the planners neglected the buildup of the Volunteer Fleet, which traditionally had carried soldiers to and from the Far East. The Russian General Staff was painfully aware of the precarious position in which Russia would find herself prior to the completion of the Manchurian extension if a conflict with a naval power of greater strength cut her communications by sea.[9]

The Pacific squadron of Russia was weaker than outsiders realized. The arbitrary rule of Rear Admiral Alekseev, the illegitimate son of Alexander II, and of the ships' commanders had thoroughly demoralized the officers, some of whom had been at sea for over five years without relief. Lack of discipline, improper training and assignment, and general disorder characterized the squadron while Alekseev was in command from 1895 to 1897. When Rear Admiral Dubasov took over in 1897, the necessary repair of the vessels and replacement of the exhausted personnel left the squadron practically out of commission for about six months.[10] Until such time as the Russian fleet had been expanded and the construction of the Chinese Eastern Railroad completed, patience, prudence, and restraint were dictated for Russia.

Russian foreign policy was hamstrung by the inability of the Ministries of Foreign Affairs, Finance, Navy, and War to agree on common objectives in the Far East. While the Foreign Ministry aimed above all at avoiding an armed conflict with Great Britain or Japan, the Finance Ministry aspired to preserve an entente with China in order to develop Russo-Chinese commerce. The Navy Ministry's priority was a naval base, while the General Staff was more concerned with the development and security of the Russian possessions along the Amur River.[11]

Although Russia had acquired a common frontier with Korea in 1860, she did not seek to legalize the illicit trade that had ensued and left the opening of Korea to Japan and the United States. Her involvement in the internal affairs of Korea in 1885 was unpremeditated. It came in response to repeated appeals from Seoul made, the Russians believed, by the Korean government. Möllendorff, who had concocted the scheme of a Russian protectorate over Korea, was not a tsarist agent; his request for Russian aide was not a cover for Russian designs. The attempt of the German official in the Korean employ had emanated from his personal conviction that Russia was the only power in a position to preserve the independence of the peninsula from Japanese encroachment. The tsarist government declined the offer of a protectorate. It decided to send a number of military instructors to train a Korean army necessary for the maintenance of order in the land, but backed out quietly as soon as it learned that Möllendorff's plea did not represent the wishes of the Korean government. Not so Speyer, St. Petersburg's local representative, whose importance and influence would have increased with Russian participation in

Korean affairs. Miffed by the request for American instructors after King Kojong had hinted at a secret alliance with Russia, Speyer berated the president of the Korean Foreign Office for the perceived deception and insult of his country. His outburst, however, was not a true reflection of tsarist policy.

Allegations voiced in 1885 that Russia intended to take Port Hamilton because she needed an ice-free port were spurious. They were an excuse rather than the cause for the occupation of the very place by Great Britain. Although the Russian press urged the tsarist government to match the British move by the seizure of Quelpart Island, St. Petersburg chose to work for the withdrawal of the British from the Korean harbor. It threatened Peking and Seoul to exact compensation if the British occupation were sanctioned, but did so as a means of terminating the latter. There was no foundation to the rumors current at the time that Russia planned to annex Pusan or Port Lazarev. To secure the evacuation of Port Hamilton, the tsarist representative in China pledged that Russia would not move in upon Britain's withdrawal and that she would not heed a Korean request for a Russia protectorate. As can be seen from the draft treaty proposed by Ladyzhenskii to Li Hung-chang in the fall of 1886, Russia's main objective was the preservation of the political and social *status quo* and thereby of peace and order in Korea. She wished to do so at the time in collaboration with China, partly because the influence of Peking was then dominant at Seoul, partly because Peking was more conservative in outlook than reform-minded Tokyo.

Chargé Waeber, who had arrived in Seoul in the fall of 1885 with the ratified copy of the treaty of amity, applied the salve of mildness to soothe the feelings irritated by Speyer's abrasive personality. The aim of the draft proposal for an overland trade agreement which he conveyed to Kim Yun-sik the following year was to produce closer relations between the two countries and to regulate the intercourse of their subjects. Contrary to the belief of the Korean government that Russia wanted to lure more Koreans into her fold, she desired a halt in the influx of indigent indigens, who constituted a burden on the treasury of Vladivostok. The tsarist government declined a request made by Kojong in the fall of 1885 for the dispatch of Russian warships to strengthen his position vis-à-vis Yüan Shik-k'ai. It counseled the Korean monarch not to impair his relations with the Chinese, even though the latter used the Russian "menace" as a pretext for tightening their control over the kingdom.

Russian self-denial was governed by military and economic weakness. Russia had fewer warships than China in the Pacific Ocean and lacked as yet the means to rush large forces overland by rail. The acquisition of Korean territory would have been disadvantageous to Russia, because it would have required great expenditures and would have undermined her overall position. As the governor general of the Amur region and the director of the Asiatic Department of the Foreign Ministry reaffirmed in a joint report in the summer of 1888, Russia must not absorb Korea. Korea was a poor country of no commercial value, was too remote for effective defense, and her annexation would impair relations with China and Japan as well as with Great Britain. On the other hand, Russia realized that the domination of Korea by a strong China would seriously endanger her own position in the southern Ussuri region. Her weakness compelled her to eschew force. She did apply firm moral pressure in defense of Korean independence, convinced that Orientals respected only those who displayed self-confidence. To avoid difficulties with the other powers, she tried to stay clear of sole involvement in Korean affairs. She wanted Seoul to resort to the assistance of all the foreign representatives rather than just that of Russia if outside support was required. There was no substance to Japanese and Western speculations that year of the existence of a secret Russo-Korean treaty of defense.

Japanese opposition to Chinese control of Korea suited Russia so long as it remained moderate and peaceful. The prospect of Sino-Japanese collaboration was as disconcerting to St. Petersburg as war between the two neighboring states.

Although the tsarist representative in Tokyo had inquired of the Japanese Foreign Office what measures it was prepared to take to thwart the political intrigues of Kim Ok-kyun, Russia remained a silent observer of the macabre events surrounding his assassination. Nor did she take any measures upon the outbreak of the Tonghak rebellion beyond the reinforcement of her legation guards. Sympathetic as Speyer and Waeber were with the plight of the Korean masses, they chose to take no official notice of the misrule. Although Cassini and Hitrovo warned from Peking and Tokyo of the international embroilment that the Korean disorders might precipitate, St. Petersburg gave greater credence to the reports of Waeber on the spot that all was quiet in the land. The failure of the tsarist government to appreciate the seriousness of the situation was underlined by the fact that it allowed Cassini to go on furlough and Waeber to take his place, thereby leaving its legations in China and Korea without their permanent chiefs during the crisis. When word of the imminence of Chinese intervention was flashed by Waeber from Peking, Russia cautiously pried into the intentions of the Japanese government. She dispatched a gunboat to Korea, but merely to witness developments.

The request for Russian mediation of the intensifying dispute between China and Japan made by Li Hung-chang in June 1894 pleased Cassini, Foreign Minister Giers, and Tsar Alexander III. Aside from preventing a Sino-

Japanese war, such mediation stood to boost the influence of Russia through-out the Far East without any sacrifices on her part. But the conflicting claims transmitted by the tsarist representatives in China, Japan, and Korea were so confusing that the Foreign Ministry confined itself to supporting the requests of the Korean government for the withdrawal of both Chinese and Japanese troops from its territory. Though Russia warned Japan of the responsibility she would incur if she prevented the evacuation of Korea conjointly with China, she declined to undertake official mediation without Japanese assent. The tsarist government rejected Li's offer of direct participation in Korean reforms along with China and Japan, regarding the proposal as a ploy to draw Russia into the conflict on China's side. It was determined not to exceed the bounds of "friendly advice" in its representations to Tokyo.[12]

It was Great Britain who first raised the idea of international démarche, though she herself eventually did not participate. Despite its rejection of the three-cornered arrangement proposed by Li, which Britain sought to head off, the tsarist government did not support the English plan for a five-power inter-vention to bring about an agreement between China and Japan, lest London play the leading role. It agreed to a subsequent suggestion for a bilateral peace effort with England only after the word "assist" had been dropped. Russia, to whom China had appealed before turning to the other powers, was jealous of her priority; she was willing to collaborate, not to follow. As it turned out, the effort was in vain, for Japan did not heed the advice proffered by Great Britain and Russia to save the peace by the geographical separation of the Chinese and Japanese forces in Korea.

St. Petersburg had consistently ignored the pleas of its representatives in the Far East for a more active Far Eastern role. During most of the war Rus-sia's main concern was to keep the conflict from her borders and to prevent any agitation among the Koreans and Chinese in her realm. She merely re-fused to recognize the reforms imposed by Japan on Korea, notifying Seoul that she regarded them as temporary.

Contrary to what one might have expected in the light of subsequent action, the eventuality of a Japanese victory worried the tsarist government less at first than that of a Chinese one, because the extent of Japanese power was not yet understood. Giers trusted the assurances of Tokyo that the independence of Korea would be maintained; he doubted that Japan would want to become Russia's direct neighbor on the continent. He regarded a victorious Japan as a natural ally of Russia against China. A Chinese victory, on the other hand, Giers feared, might endanger the economy of the Vladivostok region, since China might be pressured into opening the ports of North Korea to European commerce.

Although the tsarist government refrained from issuing a formal neutrality declaration, it remained neutral throughout the conflict, waiting for future developments to dictate its policy. It withheld support from a British effort to bring multinational pressure to bear on the belligerents to halt the fighting; it hedged on a Chinese appeal for a collective intervention to acknowledge the independence of Korea and determine the amount of the war indemnity; and it rejected a British proposal for bilateral Anglo-Russian mediation on the ground that China had not yet proposed peace to Japan directly and the latter's demands were still unknown.

The unexpected strength displayed by Japan and the secrecy in which she shrouded her objectives, gradually produced a change in Russian attitude. St. Petersburg intimated to Tokyo "privately" that it expected the evacuation of Korea by Japanese forces after the war; it offered to assist in averting the intervention of other powers if Japan would exchange views with her; and, as she failed to elicit Japanese cooperation, she got Paris and London to join in individual warnings to Tokyo that operations against China must not be carried to the extreme. (Russia worried that the capture of Peking might precipitate revolution in neighboring China.)

Russia's preoccupation with the independence of Korea had left the impression that she would not act to block the acquisition of other territory, yet by February 1895 the tsarist government began to debate what to do in the event Japan would seek a permanent foothold on the Gulf of Pechili, not far from her own border. Russian indecision had been fostered by the illness and death of both Alexander III and Giers; it was protracted by the irresolute character of young Nicholas II and the unfamiliarity with Asian affairs of Lobanov-Rostovskii, who succeeded as foreign minister in mid-March.

The revelation of the Japanese peace terms in early April, on the eve of their acceptance, confirmed Russian apprehension that Japan had continental ambitions. It confronted St. Petersburg with the choice of accepting the change in the situation and making the most of it by joining forces with Japan and obtaining an ice-free port in Korea and a stretch of territory in Manchuria in compensation or of thwarting Japanese expansion to the continent and preserving the status quo in alliance with China. "Aggressive" as the second alternative may have looked to Japanese eyes, it represented a "passive" policy from the Russian point of view, for an alliance with China meant that St. Petersburg was satisfied with its position in the Far East and wished to do no more than to consolidate it. (The subsequent territorial gains were not premeditated by Russia as the fruit of siding with China; she did not want to initiate the breakup of the Manchu empire.) An alliance with Japan, on the other hand, would have been a vote for more aggressive obejctives. Paradoxically, it was the "passive" Far Eastern policy that involved greater risk of confrontation, a risk that Russia was not prepared to face alone. Prior to reaching any definite decision, therefore, she explored whether France, Great Britain, and Germany would join her in advising Japan in a "very friendly" démarche that the permanent occupation of the Liaotung Peninsula would impede the restoration of lasting peace in the Far East, because it would constitute a perpetual threat to the Chinese capital and would render the independence of Korea illusory.

The weakness of Russia—her inability and unwillingness to stand up to Japan alone—left her foreign policy subject to foreign influence. Germany in particular took advantage of the situation; "Willie" prodded cousin "Nicky" into the Far Eastern morass to get him out of his way in Europe and the Near East. Had it not been for Germany's enthusiastic endorsement of Russia's tentative inquiry, St. Petersburg might well have changed tack, for the tsar was inclined not to oppose Japan and at the special conference of April 11 Grand Duke Aleksei Aleksandrovich advocated a secret deal with the latter.[13] The support of Germany and France strengthened the position of Lobanov and Witte, who believed that war with Japan was inevitable and that denial to her of a beachhead on the continent was a strategic necessity—a defensive move to give Russia time to complete the Trans-Siberian Railroad and build up her armed forces before the ultimate encounter. Yet Russia did not want war with Japan. She was polite in her remonstrances during the Tripartite Intervention, forewent any territorial demands of her own, and made every effort to smooth ruffled feelings once Japan had agreed to the retrocession of the Liaotung Peninsula. With the threat to the security of her weak and sparsely populated borderlands removed, Russia slackened her military preparations. She once again thought in terms of amity with Japan as well as with China, unconscious of the scars her action had left in Tokyo.

That the tripartite intervention had not darkened the horizon of Russo-Japanese relations to the extent assumed by most historians is evident from a number of unpublished dispatches from the tsarist minister in Tokyo, who closely followed the rapidly shifting currents of opinion in the Japanese press. It was true that the intervention had aborted the sympathetic coverage which Russia had received in recent years as the construction of the Trans-Siberian Railroad had held out hopes of prosperous trade with Europe. "The newspapers burst out in the most unrestrained indignation concerning the purportedly perfidious line of action of the three powers and especially of us. Some of the papers in their chauvinism and Japanese conceit went to the absurd; they advocated taking the field against Russia and all but divided already the fruits of the forthcoming victories over her," Hitrovo reported. Yet in all this indignation against Russia, Germany, and France, Hitrovo discerned much that was "put on and hollow." He charged that the Japanese government partly supported the feeling in order to deflect public attention from its own mistakes. "I do not doubt," Hitrovo wrote in August 1895, "that all this belligerence on the part of Japanese public opinion and the press particularly toward us will abate before long, if foreign events will be conducive to this. The sensible understanding of the real interests of Japan will, of course, eventually win over the artificially inflamed outburst of passion, evoked by the momentary insult to Japanese national pride." Warnings were cropping up already in Japanese newspapers against the danger of placing too much hope on the unreliable support of England, Hitrovo observed. "Voices are even beginning to be heard which directly preach the necessity of a complete understanding and a close rapprochement with Russia," he noted. Such a campaign was being waged by the widely ready *Nippon* and *Kokumin* as well as by some other Japanese newspapers. Hitrovo directed attention especially to an article on Nicholas II published in *Kokumin*. Although it contained some ridiculous notions, the article was on the whole sympathetic toward the tsar and toward Russia. It recalled with praise that Nicholas had not blamed the Japanese emperor for the attempt on his life when he had visited the country in 1891. Turning to the tripartite intervention and Russian guarantee of a loan to China, the article skirted the question of the wisdom of these steps and applauded Russian diplomacy for the speed and brilliance with which it had executed its policies.[14]

Having blocked Japan's penetration to the mainland and thus having removed what had seemed to her a direct threat to her security, Russia desired to remain on good terms with Japan. At the imperial reception in St. Petersburg on New Year's Day 1896, Nicholas told Nishi repeatedly that he earnestly hoped that the friendly relations between their countries would become stronger.[15] To emphasize that there were no hard feelings between them as the result of the Triple Intervention, the Russian and Japanese governments bestowed decorations on each other's leading foreign ministry and legations officials.[16] Additional decorations were presented by Japan on the occasion of the coronation of Nicholas II to the tsar himself and to key statesmen.[17]

The German minister in Tokyo testified in January 1896 that Russo-Japanese relations were by then "normal and entirely friendly." The relief of Vice Admiral Tyrtov by Rear Admiral Alekseev as chief commander of the combined Russian squadron in the Pacific Ocean and the departure of Minister Hitrovo on an eight-month leave in February seemed evidence thereof.

Both Ito and Hitrovo had assured him that their governments were approaching the Korean question with mutual understanding and expected no cause for friction in its regulation.[18]

"The relations of Japan with Russia have recently improved markedly and must be characterized as nothing short of friendly," Gutschmid reported the following month. Hitrovo who was to depart for home on February 23 had told him that he was leaving Japan without any anxiety. He had gradually convinced himself, Hitrovo had said, that the Japanese government had decided on a frank and sincere attitude toward Russia and that particularly in Korea, "the barometer for the mutual relations," it wished to act solely in complete accord with the tsarist government. He had good grounds for the accuracy of his assumptions, Hitrovo had assured Gutschmid. The present tone of the Japanese press, with which he was very pleased, seemed further proof that Japan harbored no ulterior motives regarding Korea. On the basis of this conviction Hitrovo recommended to his government not to press the Japanese in order to give them some six to eight months time to liquidate [their involvement with] Korea, of which they seemed to have had absolutely enough.[19]

In guaranteeing the loan which provided China with the funds for the indemnity due Japan, St. Petersburg may have gotten a handle on Peking. But this was a byproduct, not the motivation for raising the money Russia herself lacked. Lobanov helped to keep both the indemnity and the interest on the loan as low as possible in order to expedite payment and thereby hasten Japanese withdrawal from the continent. The loan was not "virtually forced" upon China by Russia and France, as is commonly stated, but was the low bid made in response to a Chinese request.

The negotiation of a shortcut for the Trans-Siberian line through Manchuria was kopeck-wise and ruble-foolish. As Count Kapnist, the director of the Asiatic Department, and Governor General Dukhovskoi had vainly warned Witte, the construction of so long a line through foreign territory entailed more political risk than economic benefit. The secret alliance which Russia concluded simultaneously on June 3, 1896, was not imposed on China; on the contrary, it was demanded by Peking as a condition for granting the railroad concession. Considering the fact that the Chinese desired a railroad through Manchuria but lacked the means to build and operate it, the arrangement whereby Russia was allowed to do so for a limited number of years whereupon she was to hand it over for free, in exchange for the obligation to protect China against renewed attack by Japan, was less a matter of Russia "taking" China than of "being taken" by her. The Chinese felt safe in using the Russians, whose sparsely populated and ill-defended border regions posed no threat to them.

Incredible as it may sound to most Americans, who believe that given a free choice anyone would want to adopt their political, economic, and social system, the Russian model seemed more appropriate to Chinese reformers at the time. K'ang Yu-wei argued that although no country was as prosperous and contented as the United States and none as powerful and wealthy as England and Germany, their forms of government differed from that of China; the Russian autocracy, on the other hand, resembled the Chinese political system. K'ang advocated that Emperor Kuang-hsü follow in the footsteps of Peter the Great and use his monarchical authority to modernize the empire rapidly; he looked to Russia as an example for reshaping the institutions of China.[20]

While agreeing to assist China in the event of an attack by Japan, Russia sought to defuse potential trouble by courting an understanding with the latter concerning Korea. That Russia should have done so at the same time was cited by the Japanese defense during the War Crimes Trial in Tokyo following the Second World War as an example of Russian perfidy. However, St. Petersburg was sincere in its desire for good relations with Japan and was hesitant to challenge the latter's predominance in Korea. It was Japan who undermined her own position by the assassination of Queen Min, even though the Japanese minister and the hired swords had acted without the knowledge or approval of the central government. Despite this outrage the tsarist representative was reluctant to take advantage of the turn of events; Waeber joined his colleagues in calling upon Japan to restore order, bring the culprits to justice, and provide for the safety of the king. As the Japanese who had interfered too much leaned the other way and refused to disband the Japanese-trained royal guards or to remove Japanophile officials, Waeber and his successor, Speyer, wished to support the anti-Japanese party in Seoul. But Lobanov worried that direct intervention might lead to a collision with Japan and the other powers and might impede the strengthening of Russian influence in China as well as in Korea. He cautioned Speyer that Russia did not want to provoke any complications in the Far East.

The flight of Kojong to the tsarist legation offered the government of Korea to Russia on a royal platter. However, although Speyer himself may have been partly responsible for the king's escape from Japanese domination, he left him a free hand in forming a new cabinet. To the disgust of their Western colleagues and foreign residents, neither Speyer nor Waeber dictated policy. In fact, once the Japanese puppet government had been dismissed, Speyer urged

Kojong to return to the palace. Personally, Speyer favored the renewed appeal made by Kojong for turning Korea into a Russian protectorate, but the tsarist government deemed it more important to regulate relations with Japan than to chance a collision with the latter by obtaining special rights in Korea. It was willing to furnish the king with informal advice, not with an official adviser or military instructors.

The remarkable restraint exercised by the tsarist government in Korea may have been due in part also to its mounting preoccupation with China. As Nikhamin points out, the risks entailed in an aggressive policy were about even in both regions, but the potential benefits were much higher in Manchuria and China proper.[21] The withholding of financial and economic assistance was interpreted as Russian weakness by Korean officials, who began looking for help elsewhere, even from Japan.

The dramatic events in Korea underlined the need for a Russo-Japanese understanding. As Hitrovo explained to Saionji, all that Russia wanted was that Korea not become a weapon against her. She had no objections to the reforms Japan wished to make in Korea, but since the kingdom seemed incapable of governing itself, a *modus vivendi* must be found by their countries to allow Korea to exist. While Speyer considered the securing of Russian interests in Korea as the sole objective of a Russo-Japanese agreement, Hitrovo deemed the attainment of a close entente, if not of an alliance, as Russia's primary goal.

The Seoul memorandum concluded between Waeber and Komura in May 1896 was an interim compromise whereby Russia consented to join Japan in counseling Kojong to return to the palace as soon as this could be done safely; Japan agreed to withdraw some of her forces and recognized Russia's right to maintain the same number of troops in Korea as Japan to guard her legation and consulates. The Moscow protocol signed by Lobanov and Marquis Yamagata on June 9 established the jurisdictional equality of Russia and Japan in Korea and mutually enjoined them not to take separate action in economic, military and other matters. Although a secret article provided for the dispatch of additional troops by either side upon due consultation if disturbances broke out again, the two agreements did not impose a joint condominium on Korea. Their main significance, from the Russian point of view, was the renunciation of Japan's exclusive influence in Korea and the preservation of the territorial integrity and independence of the latter. The Russians did not think in terms of sharing power with the Japanese. To them the principle of independence meant that Kojong and the Korean government were free to employ whatever foreign military instructors and advisers they desired.

The request for Russian military and economic aid and advice tantamount to a protectorate, revived by Min Yong-hwan, who, like the special envoys of China and Japan, had entered into secret negotiations with the tsarist government on the occasion of Nicholas's coronation, placed St. Petersburg in a quandary. As before, it could not agree to anything substantial for fear of precipitating a collision with Japan and possibly Great Britain; yet to turn Korea down once again flatly might drive her into the arms of another power. As Min's persistence outlasted the procrastination of the Russian Foreign Ministry, the tsarist government on July 2 made a token commitment; it promised to assume a *moral* guarantee of the king's safety upon his return to the palace and to dispatch two individuals to Korea—a high ranking officer to discuss the military instructor question and an official to study the economic situation to determine what financial measures were necessary.

The matter might have rested there had Tokyo not proposed the following month the training of the Korean army by Japan and Russia conjointly. Dreading Japanese participation in the running of the Korean army, St. Petersburg shed its caution and sent a contingent of military instructors to Korea with the returning envoy. Renewed Japanese overtures for the joint guidance of the Korean army impelled Russia to intensify her efforts in an attempt to exclude Japan by presenting her with a *fait accompli*. The furor that this action aroused in Tokyo persuaded Foreign Minister Muraviev to backtrack and to shelve the reorganization of the Korean army under Russian guidance until the new Russian minister, Rosen, arrived in Tokyo and took the matter up with the Japanese government. But the War Ministry and the tsar himself were swayed by the objections of Waeber and Speyer and a second contingent of military instructors was dispatched in July 1897.

The fact that the instructors were put to work even though the Korean government, in response to Japanese pressure, did not sign the contracts for their employment, tempted the tsarist government to provide also the financial adviser Min had requested and to establish a Russo-Korean bank. Unaware of the arm-twisting in which Speyer was engaged, it acted in the belief that Korea genuinely desired Russian aid. When it learned from various sources that this might not be true, it instructed Speyer in March 1898 to seek clarification whether or not the Korean government wanted assistance from Russia. Muraviev made it plain that Russia did not wish to intimidate Korea; she desired her independence and integrity. As the Korean government took advantage of Speyer's inquiry, which he had rashly phrased in the form of an ultimatum, to sound a polite "Thanks, but no thanks," the tsarist government abided by the decision.

Two factors compelled St. Petersburg to revert to the policy of self-restraint in Korea, from which it had been lured by the intrigues of Korean officials and its own representatives in Seoul: the warnings of Rosen that Japan would resort to force if she was not given the share of influence due her in Korea, and the Russian occupation of Port Arthur. The acquisition of an ice-free port elsewhere decreased Russian interest in Korea; its leasing depended on the acquiescence of Japan and Great Britain, who were being antagonized by Speyer's antics.

Since the settling of her frontier dispute with China in 1881 Russia had been a proponent of the *status quo* in East Asia, reluctant to take any step that might precipitate the division of China for which she was not ready. It was the German seizure of Kiaochow which induced Russia to occupy Port Arthur. Nicholas had not objected when Wilhelm at the height of the tripartite intervention had solicited his assistance in case Germany required a Chinese harbor, and Cassini had encouraged German ambitions in 1897. Russia, whose ships frequented Kiaochow, wanted Germany to take a port to the south of Shanghai lest she herself be forced to venture into a harbor farther north, a move that could precipitate a dangerous chain-reaction. She dropped her objections upon being assured that her warships would be able to use the port as before and that the German seizure of Kiaochow would redound to her security in that Germany would be compelled to rely increasingly on Russia. Sidestepping an attempt by Li Hung-chang to invoke the Russo-Chinese alliance against Germany, the tsarist government counseled China to accede to her demands.

The leasing of Port Arthur and of the Liaotung Peninsula on which it was located in the wake of the German acquisition of Kiaochow compounded the mistake Russia had made in embarking on the construction of the Chinese Eastern Railroad. Although it was accomplished peaceably, by diplomatic pressure and bribery rather than by direct force of arms, it was a rash act of Muraviev, who had little understanding of the Far Eastern situation and was hell-bent on distinguishing himself. The lease was demanded in the name of the Russo-Chinese alliance—to give Russia the means of defending China—but Witte opposed the move strongly as a breach of faith toward the Chinese ally. Ukhtomskii, who was more familiar with Chinese affairs than Muraviev, tried to forestall the action by warning that it would contribute to the weakening and eventual overthrow of the Manchu dynasty. The occupation of the Liaotung Peninsula outraged Emperor Kuang-hsü, alienated what Chinese reformers had looked to Russia for inspiration, and contributed no doubt to the violent anti-foreign outburst that was to erupt in China the following year. It also brought Russia within Japanese striking distance.

The leasing of Port Arthur is generally represented as a step that made the Russo-Japanese War inevitable, because by taking the very territory she had denied Japan, Russia gave the lie to her earlier professions and infuriated the Japanese government. This was not the case. As Russo-Chinese relations deteriorated, Russo-Japanese relations improved. It had been for the sake of avoiding a collision with Japan that Russia had dropped the idea of acquiring an ice-free port in Korea and had chosen Port Arthur, to which the Manchurian line could be run more easily. The apparent retreat of Russia from Korea, indicated by the withdrawal of the military instructors and financial adviser and now by the selection of a port elsewhere, opened the door for a possible understanding between Russia and Japan.

The logic of a Russo-Japanese entente appealed to a number of statesmen on both sides, who regarded the economic and political interests of their countries as more complementary than competitive. By the agreement which Nishi and Rosen signed in April 1898, Japan connived at the Russian occupation of Port Arthur, while Russia promised not to impede the development of Japan's commercial and industrial relations in Korea; the two powers pledged not to provide any military instructors or financial advisers to Korea without prior agreement between them. But the arrangement fell short of the free hand Japan wanted in Korea to balance the expanding influence of Russia on the continent. Had the tsarist government taken up the offer made by Foreign Minister Nishi the preceding month for a division of spheres of interest—Korea to be within the Japanese sphere, Manchuria within the Russian one—history might well have run a different course. Muraviev had been inclined to go along with the proposal, but had been stopped by the military, who saw in the political domination of Korea by Japan a permanent threat to the security of the Maritime Province.

In a long conversation with his French colleague on November 17, 1899, Rosen expressed concern at the new direction which Russian foreign policy was taking and at the false impression that was being created about Russia's actual aims.[22] He was strongly opposed to the rigid and menacing attitude shown in a number of recent incidents by his government toward that of Japan, whose correctness and goodwill were undeniable. He attributed the conduct of St. Petersburg to the influence of young bureaucrats who could not sleep because of the laurels garnered by Speyer and who accused him of excessive Japanophilia in the knowledge or perhaps the imagination that the tsar personally did not favor a policy of waiting in Korea. He criticized Witte for envisioning the conquest of Korea by railroads and banks, means which the finance minister regarded as more modern and more effective than recourse to arms; such "puerility" on the part of an otherwise remarkable man astonished Rosen. A contributing factor in Russian excitations was the exaggerated ardor of Russian agents in Korea who wished, in Rosen's words, "to make their little Speyer" (*faire leur petite Speyer*) and in the combativeness of the navy people who looked for violent encounters to distinguish themselves. As far as Rosen was concerned, if one wished to conquer Korea, one should do so straightforwardly. But if one did not want to conquer her or even if one deemed it preferable to wait, the Russian demonstrations were not merely useless but profoundly detrimental; they attracted the attention of the entire world, made others believe in intentions which Russia did not have, and excited to no purpose the loud complaints of the English and the suspicions of the Japanese.

Rosen saw no point in an impetuous policy. He was persuaded that time worked to the advantage of Russia who would become the mistress of Korea by the force of circumstances; instead of interfering with the Japanese it would be better to let them install themselves in the peninsula without hindrance. They would soon find themselves beset with such grave financial difficulties and such disorders that their position would be weakened in a short time and they themselves would pave the way for a change in regime favorable to Russia.[23]

The incidents to which Rosen had referred, including a melee involving Russian and Japanese sailors and the arrest of a Russian naval officer by Japanese police, were resolved amicably in correspondence between Foreign Ministers Aoki and Muraviev, who were personally acquainted and on good terms with each other. Thus, as Rosen had hoped, cooler heads had prevailed and the détente between Russia and Japan was prolonged.[24]

The arrangement made by Russia with Great Britain in the spring of 1899 was designed to protect her interests in Manchuria. The initiative had come from London, where doubt had been growing for some time about the wisdom of continued Anglo-Russian rivalry. The sinister designs periodically attributed to Russia had proven exaggerated, and the cost of turning Weihaiwei into a useful stronghold underlined the wastefulness of matching lease with lease. The tsarist government eschewed the suggestion for a comprehensive settlement of the differences between the two powers in the various parts of the world in favor of a more limited, and more easily negotiable, division of spheres of influence in China. Neither St. Petersburg nor London wished to precipitate the partition of China; they merely wanted to guarantee their railroad monopolies. The outlay for the construction of the Trans-Siberian Railroad and its Manchurian extension had been so enormous that Russia could not tolerate its imperilment by foreign competition.

Russia needed peace to modernize her economy and to complete the construction of her railroad network. To give proof of her pacific intentions and to halt the arms race, Nicholas II had issued a dramatic call to the other countries the preceding autumn to convene a world congress for the maintenance of universal peace. The Russian press reported that the tsar's proposal was welcomed unanimously in Europe and was regarded as one of the most important acts of international policy of the nineteenth century. Although no one could take a public stand against peace and the first peace congress in history was convened at The Hague in the summer of 1899, the Russian peace offensive was in fact met with suspicion and derision abroad.[25] Refusing to believe that Nicholas may have been motivated by humanitarian considerations, foreign statesmen looked for selfish, if not evil, motives behind the appeal. They pointed out that Russia lacked the funds to match the artillery buildup planned by Austria, that there were conditions attached to the Russian concept, and that the recent acquisition of the Liaotung Peninsula cast doubt on Russian devotion to peace.[26]

The character of Russian expansion and the question of its persistence were widely debated at the turn of the century. The Austro-Hungarian finance minister, Benjamin von Kállay, regarded the acquisition of Port Arthur by Russia as the most momentous event since the fall of Napoleon Bonaparte or the unification of Germany. Thinking in terms of an irresistible Russian *Drang nach Osten*, he foresaw the "stretching out" of the immense Russian state, which already reached from the Baltic to Kamchatka, into a larger, Russified, Russo-Asian empire.[27]

Witte, who opposed further expansion as detrimental to the finances with which he was charged,[28] had a different view of history. He believed that having gotten the railroad connection to the open sea, there was no further territory for Russia to desire. The administration of distant provinces, even in the Caucasus and the Trans-Caspian region, cost the Russian Treasury more than she recovered from their exploitation. Instead of expanding or assuming new responsibilities, Russia must turn inward and consolidate what she had.[29]

The eminent Chinese scholar Liang Ch'i-ch'ao agreed that Russian expansion was finite. Attributing the fear of Russia to "tendentious illuminations of the historical past," he wrote in a preface to a Russian translation of his study of Li Hung-chang; "I see that our view of Russia's dealings with neighboring countries is one-sided. After all, historical drives are not limitless and have a definite goal. Once the goal has been achieved, all efforts are devoted to the development of the internal life of the state, to digest all that has been achieved."[30]

Yet the flood of allegations ascribing aggressive designs to the tsarist government continued unabated, even though it was privately conceded that Russia was too weak in the Far East to expand by force.[31] One reason was the lack of trust in what Russians said; another was the usefulness of the Russian "menace." Repeatedly the Russian bear was used as a bugbear by the various powers to intimidate and contain their rivals or to justify their own moves in the international balance of intrigue.

Notes to Volume 2

Chapter Sixteen

1. Maximilian August von Brandt, *Dreiunddreissig Jahre in Ost-Asien*, 143–44; Hsü, *Rise of Modern China*, 163–66.

2. Hsü, *Rise of Modern China*, 271–74; Dun J. Li, *The Ageless Chinese*, 2d ed., 414–18. The Russians regarded the acquisition of the Amur Province and the Ussuri region as a "peaceful conquest." See Boris Borisovich Glinskii, *Prolog russko-iaponskoi voiny*, 24.

3. Hsü, *Rise of Modern China*, 390–98. For details see Baymirza Hayit, *Turkestan zwischen Russland und China*; Maurice Jemetel, "La Chine et les Puissances Européenes," *L'Economiste français* 1882, 446–48; *Russko-kitaiskie otnosheniia 1689–1916*, 54–60.

4. Brandt to Bismarck, A. no. 77, Peking, Apr. 7, 1888, GA, FSU/China, 8/74.

5. Schweinitz to Bismarck, no. 144, St. Petersburg, May 31, 1888, GA, FSU/China, 8/74.

6. As Chinese newspapers predicted Chinese annexation of Korea with the removal of the Korean king and queen to Chinese territory and the dispatch of Marquis Tseng to Seoul as governor general or viceroy, Shevich warned Foreign Minister Okuma in February 1889 that the latter possibility posed for Japan the danger that Pusan might be converted into another Hong Kong or Gibraltar. Okuma did not believe in any bold action on the part of the Chinese and declared that the preservation of the *status quo* was essential. "In this respect our interests coincide with those of Japan," Shevich reported. Noting that in accordance with the Tientsin convention Japan had the right to do the same as China should the latter undertake something in Korea and that China had committed herself not to act in this respect without giving prior notice to Japan, Okuma promised to advise Russia of Chinese plans regarding Korea, providing China kept Japan informed. "This is highly interesting and not bad for us," Alexander III commented on Shevich's report (Shevich to Russian Foreign Ministry, no. 11, Tokyo, Jan. 26/Feb. 7, 1889, as summarized in *Dnevnik V. N. Lamzdorfa 1886–1890*, 181–82).

7. *Dnevnik V. N. Lamzdorfa*, 181–82.

8. F. A. Rothstein, *Mezhdunarodnye otnosheniia v kontse XIX veka*, 254–56.

However defensive such action may have appeared in Russian eyes, the prospect of a large buildup in Russian forces in Asia upon completion of the Trans-Siberian Railroad alarmed the other powers. It prodded Japan into trying to implement her continental aspirations before Russia could block them singlehandedly.

9. Robert Britton Valliant, "Japan and the Trans-Siberian Railroad, 1885–1905," iv.

10. Communicated by Count Hatzfeldt to British government, Oct. 28, 1891, EA, FO 405–52, pp. 119–22.

11. Henry Howard to Salisbury, no. 229, St. Petersburg, Sept. 25, 1891, EA, FO 405–52, pp. 96–97. While Howard refrained from getting involved in a discussion of the Pamir question, he remarked that in recent years the Chinese had been generally the invaded rather than the invaders, "although they had a wonderful faculty of Chineseifying their conquerors."

12. Malet to Salisbury, no. 196, Berlin, Oct. 17, 1891, "Very Confidential," EA, FO 405–52, p. 108.

13. Salisbury to Malet, no. 244, Oct. 20, 1891, EA, FO 405–52, p. 109.

14. *Ibid.*

15. Schweinitz to Caprivi, no. 76, St. Petersburg, Feb. 24, 1892, "Very Confidential," by Mr. Klos, message from Berlin, dated Mar. 5, 1892, and Brandt to Caprivi, no. 76, Peking, Apr. 4, 1892, GA, FSU/China, 8-2/74.

16. "O torgovle Kitaiia s Rossieiu," 1, 15. The balance of trade was unfavorable for Russia. Purchases from China amounted to 4% of Russian imports, sales to China totalled only 0.6% of Russian exports (*Ibid.*, 4).

17. While American authors tend to think in terms of "the long heritage of hate and conflict which weighs so heavily on Soviet-Chinese relations," (Harry Schwartz, *Tsars, Mandarins, and Commissars*, 7) Russian authors, both tsarist and Soviet, stress the friendship and relative lack of conflict which had characterized the centuries of contact between the two vast empires (see, for example, Glinskii, 23).

18. Hsü, *Rise of Modern China*, second ed., 422–23.

19. Gérard to Hanotaux, no. 128, Peking, Aug. 20, 1895, DDF, ser. 1, 12: 174–176.

20. Paul H. Clyde and Burton F. Beers, *The Far East*, sixth ed., 78.

21. Malozemoff, 69.

22. Malozemoff, 70; Hanotaux to Montebello, no. 149, tel., Paris, May 23, 1895, DDF, ser. 1, 12: 34–35.

23. Romanov, *Rossiia v Man'chzhurii*, 86–93; Malozemoff, 70–71; Irwin J. Schulman, "Sino-Russian Relations 1895–1896," 53–55; Marquess of Dufferin to Kimberley, no. 35, Paris, June 10, 1895, EA, FO 405–63, p. 232; Aoki to Saionji, no. 111, Berlin, June 11, 1895, JA, TEL 1895/0468–0469. A commission of ¼ percent on the value of the coupons and bonds was to be levied by the paying agencies. The general oversight of the syndicate loan was entrusted to the Banque Internationale de Commerce à Saint Petersbourg. The loan was to run until 1931 (Stanley Wright, 660).

24. Martin Gosselin to Kimberley, no. 144, Berlin, June 14, 1895, "Very Confidential," EA, FO 405–62, pp. 270–71; Kimberley to O'Conor, no. 76, tel., London, June 13, 1895, EA, FO 405–63, p. 244; Herbette to Hanotaux, no. 142, Berlin, June 15, 1895, DDF, ser. 1, 12: 87–88.

25. Aoki to Saionji, no. 111, Tokyo, June 11, 1895, JA, TEL 1895/0468–0469. Aoki told Gosselin that he was convinced that Russia would obtain "a very substantial *quid pro quo*" for the loan (Gosselin to Kimberley, no. 143, Berlin, June 14, 1895, EA, FO 405–63, p. 278). See also Kato to Saionji, no. 108, via Nishi, St. Petersburg, June

8, 1895, JA, TEL 1895/0465; Kimberley to O'Conor, no. 73, EA, FO 405–63, p. 213; Saionji to Nishi, no. 110, Tokyo, June 17, 1895, JA, TEL 1895/0733.

26. Nishi to Saionji, no. 52, St. Petersburg, June 12, 1895, JA, TEL 1895/0470–0471.

27. Nishi to Saionji, no. 56, St. Petersburg, June 21, 1895, JA, TEL 1895/0490.

28. Kimberley to Lowther, no. 53, London, June 24, 1895, EA, FO 405–63, p. 302. "China's excessive gratitude seems bent on putting on Russia's golden fetters: Russia insists, and all I can do is to stiffen China against accepting killing conditions," Robert Hart remarked (Hart to Campbell, no. Z/663, June 2, 1895, *The I. G. in Peking*, 1021–22). "China is drifting—no one knows where, and Britishers for the moment look on from the bank and are out of the swim completely," he complained (Hart to Campbell, no. Z/664, June 9, 1895, *Ibid.*, 1022–23). Switching metaphors, Hart wrote: "We appear to be like a colt tied to a post—cantering round till the rope tightens, dashing back till it is loose and pulls us up the other way, and mistaking circular movement for progress! China is fighting the word "guarantee" and its awful consequences and Russia is quietly substituting iron chains for hemp rope. . . ." (Hart to Campbell, no. Z/665, June 23, 1895, *Ibid.*, 1023–24).

29. The French government declined to join in the guarantee lest a parliamentary debate wreck the loan arrangement (Hanotaux to Montebello, nos. 164, 164 bis, tel., Paris, May 31 and June 1, 1895, "Confidential," and Montebello to Hanotaux, no. 124, tel., St. Petersburg, June 2, 1895, DDF, ser. 1, 12: 60–61).

30. Montebello to Hanotaux, no. 72, St. Petersburg, June 12, 1895, DDF, ser. 1, 12: 81–85. See also Montebello to Hanotaux, no. 124, tel., St. Petersburg, June 2, 1895, DDF, ser., 12: 61–62, and O'Conor to Kimberley, no. 67, tel., Peking, June 10, 1895, "Secret," EA, FO 405–63, pp. 231–32. To raise the funds for the loan to China Witte had turned first to Messrs. Rotschild in Paris, but the latter had declined to become involved unless Messrs. Rotschild in London were included. As the French government objected to the simultaneous issuance of a loan in Paris and Berlin, Witte had been forced to choose between the two. The exclusion of Germany thus may have been more a matter of necessity than of volition for Russia (Lascelles to Salisbury, no. 177, St. Petersburg, July 10, 1895, "Very Confidential," EA, FO 405–64, p. 71).

31. Lascelles to Kimberley, no. 164, St. Petersburg, June 19, 1895, "Confidential," EA, FO 406–63, p. 301. The Austrian ambassador to St. Petersburg, Prince Liechtenstein, told Lascelles that when he had alluded to the Chinese loan Witte had not concealed the hope that while Russia gained no direct advantage by the loan, China might fail to repay it punctually, thereby allowing Russia to interfere in the administration of her finances (Lascelles to Salisbury, no. 177, St. Petersburg, July 10, 1895, "Very Confidential," EA, FO 405–64, p. 71). However, the one time that China defaulted on the instalment payment—in December 1911 as the result of the Chinese October Revolution—the tsarist government advanced the funds to the syndicate without interference in Chinese affairs (Stanley Wright, 660).

32. O'Conor to Kimberley, no. 229, Peking, June 18, 1895, "Secret," EA, FO 405–64, pp. 91–92. In a telegram to Lowther on June 15 O'Conor suggested that if Japan informed China at once of her own motion that she would not ask any additional indemnity for the retrocession of the Liaotung Peninsula, China might be prodded into rejecting the Russian loan (O'Conor to Kimberley, no. 72, Peking, June 15, 1895, "Secret," and O'Conor to Kimberley, no. 73, Peking, June 15, 1895, "Secret," EA, FO 405–63, p. 253. See also Saionji to Nishi, no. 111, Tokyo, June 17, 1895, JA, TEL 1895/0733).

33. Tsungli Yamen to Hsü, tel., Peking, June 14, 1895, EA, FO 405–64, p. 96.
34. Lascelles to Kimberley, no. 156, St. Petersburg, June 16, 1895, "Confidential," EA, FO 405–63, p. 299.
35. Hsü to Tsungli Yamen, St. Petersburg, May 25, 1895, "Secret," EA, FO 405–64, p. 57; O'Conor to Kimberley, no. 61, Peking, May 27, 1895, "Secret," EA, 405–63, p. 177.
36. Henry Howard to Kimberley, no. 209, Paris, June 28, 1895, "Confidential," EA, FO 405–63, p. 308.
37. Courcel to Hanotaux, no. 149, London, June 23, 1895, "Confidential," DDF, ser. 1, 12: 92–95.
38. Hsü to Tsungli Yamen, tel., St. Petersburg, June 24, 1895, EA, FO 405–64, pp. 148–49; Kuo, 175–78; Stanley Wright, 660.
39. O'Conor to Salisbury, no. 253, Peking, July 5, 1895, "Confidential," EA, FO 405–64, pp. 147–48.
40. Malozemoff, 70; Romanov, *Rossiia v Man'chzhurii*, 90. The syndicate was composed of the following institutions: Hottinguer & Co., La Banque de Paris et des Pays-Bas, Le Credit Lyonnais, La Société Générale pour favoriser le développement du Commerce et de l'Industrie en France, Le Comptoir National d'Escompte de Paris, La Société Générale de Crédit Industriel et Commercial, Peterburgskii Mezhdunarodnyi bank, Peterburgskii Uchetnyi i Ssudnyi bank, Russkii dlia Vneshnei torgovli bank, and the Volzhsko-Kamskii bank (Cordier, *Histoire des rélations de la Chine*, 3: 307; Romanov, *Rossiia v Man'chzhurii*, 90 footnote 1).
41. *Sbornik dogovorov i diplomaticheskikh dokumentov po delam Dal'niago Vostoka 1895–1905*, 56–60; *Russko-kitaiskie otnosheniia 1689–1916*, 67–69; *Treaties and Agreements with and Concerning China*, 1: 35–40.
42. Hsü, *Rise of Modern China*, second ed., 422–23.
43. O'Conor to Salisbury, no. 253, Peking, July 5, 1895, EA, FO 405–64, pp. 147–48.
44. Cordier, *Histoire des rélations*, 3: 309–10; Gérard to Hanotaux, no. 53, tel., Peking, June 21, 1895, DDF, ser. 1, 12: 91; Stanley Wright, 660.
45. Extract from the *Journal de Saint-Pétersbourg* of June 26/July 8, 1895, enclosed in Lascelles to Salisbury, no. 175, St. Petersburg, July 8, 1895, EA, FO 405–64, pp. 69–71.
46. Romanov, *Rossiia v Man'chzhurii*, 90–92; Malozemoff, 70–71; Cordier, *Histoire des rélations*, 3: 310–12; Gérard, *Ma mission en Chine*, 72–74; Dufferin to Salisbury, no. 6, Paris, Jan. 7, 1896, EA, FO 405–70, p. 22. The French put up ⅜ of the original capitalization of six million rubles, yet had only three members in the central directorate; the Russians, who furnished ⅜ of the capital, had five directors and the chairman. Prince Ukhtomskii was the first person to preside over the board of directors (see Romanov and Cordier for further details). "Things look worse and worse and England is more and more out of the running: Russia and France are hauling in the line hand over hand and will soon be feeling the grip tightening," Hart reflected. He added: "Gérard's manner is the suavest possible and the method he follows the most *captivating* in every sense: and people would rather be duped politely than be taken by the neck and have their noses rubbed in their own interests" (Hart to Campbell, no. Z/681, Oct. 20, 1895, *The I.G. in Peking*, 1037–1038).
47. Dispatch of a Hong Kong correspondent published in the London *Times* on October 25, 1895, EA, FO 405–65, p. 10; Kato to Saionji, no. 128, via Nishi, St.

Petersburg, Oct. 26, 1895, JA, TEL 1895/0974; Gosselin to Salisbury, no. 239, Berlin, Oct. 26, 1895, "Confidential," EA, FO 405–65, p. 15.

48. Salisbury to W. E. Goschen, no. 319 A, London, Oct. 28, 1895, EA, FO 405–65, p. 16; Kato to Saionji, no. 130, via Nishi, St. Petersburg, Oct. 29, 1895, JA, TEL 1895/0985; Nishi to Saionji, no. 86, St. Petersburg, Oct. 30, 1895, JA, TEL 1895/0989.

49. Goschen to Salisbury, no. 254, St. Petersburg, Nov. 4, 1895, "Confidential," EA, FO 405–65, p. 36. Gérard attributed the origin of the rumors to the dispatch of the Russian engineers to Manchuria and to a harangue of the governor general of the Amur region made at Vladivostok. The tsarist legation at Peking had obtained the right for the Russian squadron to winter at Kiaochow, he noted (Gérard to Bethelot, no. 207, Peking, Dec. 21, 1895, DDF, ser. 1, 12: 363–64). Schenck did not attach great importance to the question of secret Russian concessions even though they might be contrary to the commitments undertaken by the three intervening powers not to seek special advantages for themselves, because the influence of Russia in the Chinese regions bordering unto herself was so great that she could anyway obtain concessions such as railroad construction there at any time. Besides, he thought the terrain too mountainous and unworthy of exploitation for Russia to route the Trans-Siberian line through Manchuria (Schenck to Hohenlohe-Schillingsfürst, no. A 277, Peking, Dec. 21, 1895, GA).

50. Romanov, *Rosiia v Man'chzhurii*, 92–93; Malozemoff, 71–72.

51. John E. Schrecker, *Imperialism and Chinese Nationalism: Germany in Shantung*, 28.

52. Yungtai Hsü, "Procedure and Perception in the Making of Chinese Foreign Policy," 24, 33–37; Schulman, "Sino-Russian Relations," 65–72; Hsü, *Rise of Modern China*, 423. For the text of a memorial by a group of Hanlin academicians proposing a secret alliance with Russia, see Sung-ping Kuo, "Chinese Reaction to Foreign Encroachment," 144–45, and Schulman, "Sino-Russian Relations," 64–65.

53. Chang Lung, *La Chine à l'aube du XXe siècle*, 111–12.

54. Hsü, "Procedure and Perception," 40–41.

55. For the gradual development of the idea of running part of the Russian Great Eastern Railroad through some portion of Manchuria, see Romanov, *Rossiia v Man'chzhurii*, 82–85.

56. Romanov, *Rossiia v Man'chzhurii*, 97–100.

57. "X" who translated this document in the *Chinese Social and Political Science Review* stated that "the sentence was underlined" by the tsar. The footnote published with the Russian text in *Krasnyi Arkhiv* reads: "*Etot absats otcherknut Nikolaem II.*" That "*absats*" means paragraph rather than sentence is immaterial, for the paragraph in question happens to consist of the one sentence. But the thrust of "*otcherknut*" is less clear. It is one of those frustrating words that can have opposite meanings. ("Underline" [*podcherknut*] is not one of them.) It could mean that Nicholas marked the paragraph for emphasis or for deletion! (See *Slovar' sovremennogo russkogo literaturnogo iazyka*, 8: 1690–1691.)

58. "Pervye shagi," 83–91; "First Steps," 272–81. For Witte's retort, dated March 31/Apr. 12, 1896, see "Pervye shagi," 91–102.

59. Hsü, "Procedure and Perception," 52–95; Schulman, "Sino-Russian Relations," 88–90.

60. In spite of its desire for an alliance with Russia, the Chinese government did

not have any specific proposal in mind. It may not have thought that any concessions on its part would be necessary (Schulman, "Sino-Russian Relations," 83).

61. Hsü could find no basis for the rumor that Cassini had bribed the empress dowager's favorite eunuch, Li Lien-yin, to dispatch Li Hung-chang to Russia.

62. Aoki to Saionji, no. 20, via Nishi, St. Petersburg, Mar. 5, 1896, JA, TEL 1896/ 0465. Aoki reported from Berlin that the news of the reputed alliance had excited great alarm in Europe and declared that it was high time for the Japanese government "to take definitive measures against further complication." Saionji sought clarification from Aoki. What was the nature of the alarm and what did he mean by "further complication," Saionji inquired (Saionji to Aoki, no. 14, Tokyo, Mar. 6, 1896, JA, TEL 1896/1017). He instructed Hayashi to ascertain in Peking if there was any truth to the report and, if so, to obtain the provisions. He offered to furnish him with "reasonable fund" for this purpose (Saionji to Hayashi, no. 33, Tokyo, Mar. 3, 1896, JA, TEL 1896/1013). Aoki replied that by "further complication" he had meant "complications which will result from those actions by Russia which are diametrically opposed to our [Japanese] interests." He reported that the main features of the supposed alliance gave Russia full use of Chinese harbors and arsenals, the liberty to buy horses and engage coolies and to provide military officers to China. Aoki related that Chancellor Hohenlohe had asked him what Japan intended to do and had offered to exchange views on the subject, as the Russian Mediterranean squadron was about to leave for the China Seas. "He assured me Germany is no longer engaged in triple cooperation in the Far East," Aoki telegraphed (Aoki to Saionji, no. 23, Berlin, Mar. 9, 1896, JA, TEL 1896/ 0487). Informed by Hayashi that as far as he could learn there was no definite alliance between Russia and China, (Hayashi to Saionji, no. 126, Peking, Mar. 10, 1896, JA, TEL 1896/0484) Saionji notified Aoki thereof and pointed out that the Japanese government consequently was "not yet in a position to form any views on the subject." However, he authorized Aoki to sound out the views of the German chancellor. "I like to know what he meant by saying Germany is no longer in triple cooperation in the Far East," Saionji cabled (Saionji to Aoki, no. 17, Tokyo, Mar. 13, 1896, JA, TEL 1896/1039). Nishi, whom Saionji had also contacted, reported that Lobanov had "absolutely denied" the foreign report of a Russo-Chinese alliance and had assured him that there had never been "even consultation" with the Chinese government regarding any concession in the ports of the Liaotung region. However, it was regarded as certain among the diplomatic circle in St. Petersburg, Nishi added, that Li Hung-chang would come with extensive powers to negotiate concerning railroad concessions in Manchuria up to Talien (Dairen) Bay (Nishi to Saionji, no. 24, St. Petersburg, Mar. 16, 1896, JA, TEL 1896/0512–0513).

63. Hsü, "Procedure and Perception," 96–102; Marcella Bounds, "The Sino-Russian Secret Treaty of 1896," 114–15; Schulman, "Sino-Russian Relations," 85; Hsü, *Rise of Modern China*, 423–24; Vitte, 2: 48, 50; Gérard, *Ma mission en Chine*, 124–26; Cordier, *Histoire des rélations*, 2: 340–41.

64. Gérard, *Ma mission en Chine*, 121.

65. *Ibid.*, 135–38; Efimov, *Vneshniaia politika*, 180; Romanov, *Rossiia v Man'chzhurii*, 104–5; Lensen, *Russian Diplomatic*, 41.

66. Schulman, "Sino-Russian Relations," 90–97; Romanov, *Rossiia v Man'chzhurii*, 104–5. Reports that Cassini had signed a secret agreement with China were false. The "Cassini Convention" published by the *North China Herald* in October 1896 was spurious, based in all likelihood on a copy of a preliminary outline prepared by Cassini before the meeting of April 18 (Romanov, *Rossiia v Man'chzhurii*, 135–39;

Malozemoff, 78). Robert Hart had questioned at the time the conclusion of a convention by Cassini, but had been confident that the latter carried home Peking's proposals or assurances to act in such a manner. He commented: "That China would be forced by circumstances into the arms of Russia and France has to me seemed a certainty all these last ten years: in the far-off end it will perhaps be best for China, and at the present moment it is the easiest way for the Government to throw off care and put its 'head' deeper into the 'sand,' but there will be a between time of trouble—if not chaos!" Hart thought it best for Great Britain to reach a "good understanding" with Russia, but warned that the latter had "specific designs in the far future" and that if England did not plan quite as far, she would eventually have the "experience" and Russia the "cake" (Hart to Campbell, no. Z/731, Nov. 8, 1896, *The I.G. in Peking*, 1090–91).

67. Schulman, "Sino-Russian Relations," 91–97.

68. Vitte, 2: 50–51.

69. *Ibid.*, 2: 52–53.

70. Romanov, *Rossiia v Man'chzhurii*, 107–10.

71. Schulman, "Sino-Russian Relations," 98–102; Hsü, "Procedure and Perception," 102–5, 109–10; Kuo, 190–92; Efimov, *Vneshniaia politika*, 183–86; Vitte, 2: 53–55.

72. Vitte, 2: 55–58.

73. Schulman, "Sino-Russian Relations," 103–9; Hsü, "Procedure and Perception," 106–13; Vitte, 2: 58–62; Bounds, 117–19. "The treaty was an act of extraordinary importance," Witte recalled in his memoirs. "Had we abided by that treaty it would not have been necessary, of course, for Russia to endure the shameful war with Japan and we would be standing with a firm foot in the Far East." The treaty was composed in French and Chinese. For an English translation of the French text, see Victor A. Yakhontoff, *Russia and the Soviet Union in the Far East*, 365–66; for an English translation of the Chinese text, see S. Y. Teng and John K. Fairbank (eds.), *China's Response to the West*, 130–31.

74. The full French text and a Russian translation thereof were published by the Soviet historian B. A. Romanov in the short-lived journal *Bor'ba klassov* in 1924 (Romanov, "Likhunchangskii fond," *Bor'ba klassov* 1924, 1–2: 101–4). The alliance was known as the Moscow Treaty of May 22, 1896 (old style). Romanov thought this to have been the first disclosure of the secret treaty, but Li Ching-mai had released an English version in the London *Daily Telegraph* on April 15, 1910, to vindicate his father from the accusations of his enemies. A telegraphic summary of the provisions had been filed by the Chinese delegation to the Washington Disarmament Conference in 1921 (Weigh, 64–65; Peter S. H. Tang, *Russian and Soviet Policy in Manchuria and Outer Mongolia 1911–1931*, 45 footnote 224). Gérard chanced upon the treaty in the spring of 1897 while thumbing through a notebook of other documents which Li Hung-chang had asked him to read (Gérard, *Ma mission en Chine*, 146). When Sir Claude MacDonald, the British minister to Peking, asked Li Hung-chang on June 10, 1897, whether it was true that China had come to an arrangement with Russia similar to the reputed Cassini Convention, Li admitted the existence of a railroad agreement, nothing else (MacDonald to Salisbury, no. 30, tel., Peking, June 11, 1897, EA, FO 405–70, p. 60). O'Conor learned of the military aspects of the treaty from "an entirely trustworthy source" in St. Petersburg in June 1898 (O'Conor to Salisbury, no. 244, St. Petersburg, June 16, 1898, EA, FO 405–77, p. 251).

75. Hsü, "Procedure and Perception," 113–14, 146; Schulman, "Sino-Russian,"

118–19. On May 30 Witte had submitted to Nicholas for his approval the draft of an agreement between the tsarist government and the Russo-Chinese Bank regarding the founding of a Russo-Chinese Railroad Association. By ensuring the tsarist government's complete influence over the construction and exploitation of the railroad, it placed the concession, for all practical purposes, into its hands. The fourth article, which was eventually excluded from the charter of the association but kept secret, stipulated that 700 out of the 1,000 shares of stock to be issued by the company were to be purchased by the tsarist government. The remaining 300 shares could also be acquired by the tsarist government if it so desired or upon the request of the Russo-Chinese Bank (Romanov, *Rossiia v Man'chzhurii*, 119–21).

76. Schulman, "Sino-Russian Relations," 119–23; Hsü, "Procedure and Perception," 114–19; Efimov, *Vneshniaia politika*, 190–91; Weigh, 65–73. For the text of the railroad contract, signed by Hsü, Rothstein, and Ukhtomskii but not published until 1916, see *Treaties With and Concerning China*, 1: 74–77; Weigh, 333–37; Yakhontoff, 366–70; and *Russko-kitaiskie otnosheniia*, 74–77. Weigh also gives the Statutes of the Chinese Eastern Railroad, dated December 4, 1896 (Weigh, 339–48).

77. Schulman, "Sino-Russian Relations," 109; Glinskii, 38. The Chinese officials affixed their personal seals rather than the seal of the Tsungli Yamen.

78. Gérard to Hanotaux, no. 76, Peking, June 5, 1897, and no. 81, June 13, 1897, DDF, ser. 1, 13: 421–22, 428–31.

79. Gérard, *Ma mission en Chine*, 217–18; Tschirschky to Hohenlohe-Schillingsfürst, no. 159, St. Petersburg, Mar. 25, 1897, GA, FSU/China, 8/4.

80. Heyking to Hohenlohe-Schillingsfürst, no. A. 66, Peking, Apr. 28, 1897, GA, FSU/China, 8/4.

81. Heyking to Hohenlohe-Schillingsfürst, no. A. 38, Peking, Mar. 14, 1897, GA, FSU/China, 8/4.

82. Heyking scoffed at the practice. He regarded Ukhtomskii and Volkonskii as "*Fürste*" rather than "*Prinze*."

83. Heyking to Hohenlohe-Schillingsfürst, no. A. 79, Peking, May 20, 1897, GA, FSU/China, 8/4.

84. Heyking to Hohenlohe-Schillingsfürst, no. A. 85, Peking, May 28, 1897, FSU/China, 8/4. There had been talk of an unprecedented reception of Ukhtomskii by Li and the members of the Tsungli Yamen at the city gates, but this had not taken place.

85. "One must not imagine among the Russians who appear on more or less mysterious missions in Peking figures of the sort one encounters on Nevskii Prospekt [Avenue] in St. Petersburg," observed Heyking. "Most of the subjects of this nation sent here are inconspicuous, little people, who look as if they had been selected because they would not appear too different outwardly from the Mongols and the Chinese." Coming upon a number of such persons and their correspondingly looking wives, Gérard once had not been able to suppress the remark, "*Voilà les races de l'avenir! Ce n'est past beau, mais ça pullule!*" (*There* are the races of the future! They are not beautiful, but they multiply rapidly.) (Heyking to Hohenlohe-Schillingsfürst, no. A. 63, Peking, Apr. 27, 1897, GA, FSU/China, 8/4).

86. Heyking to Hohenlohe-Schillingsfürst, no. A. 63, Peking, Apr. 27, 1897, FSU/China, 8/4. Colonel Wogack stayed mostly in Tientsin, occasionally in Shanghai; Colonel Konstantin Nikolaevich Desino resided in Chefoo.

87. "*Beeilen wir uns, ehe es zu spät wird!*" (Let us hurry up, before it will be too late!), Wilhelm scribbled at the end of Heyking's report.

88. Gérard, *Ma mission en Chine*, 218.

89. Heyking to Hohenlohe-Schillingsfürst, no. A. 79, Peking, May 20, 1897, GA, FSU/China, 8/4.

90. Gérard, *Ma mission en Chine*, 218. According to Heyking the gifts were taken to the imperial palace from the legation on the twenty-fifth (Heyking to Hohenlohe-Schillingsfürst, no. A. 85, Peking, May 28, 1897, GA, FSU/China, 8/4).

91. Heyking to Hohenlohe-Schillingsfürst, no. A. 79, Peking, May 20, 1897, GA, FSU/China, 8/4; Gérard, *Ma mission en Chine*, 218–19.

92. Heyking to Hohenlohe-Schillingsfürst, no. A. 85, Peking, May 28, 1897, GA, FSU/China, 8/4.

93. Russian interpreters and secretaries explained to their Western colleagues that Ukhtomskii felt that he would forfeit the position which he had in the eyes of the Chinese if he visited the foreign representatives (Heyking to Hohenlohe-Schillingsfürst, no. A. 107, Peking, June 30, 1897, GA, FSU/China, 8/4).

94. Heyking to Hohenlohe-Schillingsfürst, no. A. 85, Peking, May 29, 1897, GA, FSU/China, 8/4. Pavlov apologized to Heyking for Ukhtomskii's conduct and said that he had counseled the latter to pay a belated visit to Heyking. His advice, he said, had come to naught because of the counterinfluence of Gérard. ("*Hund!*" [Dog!], Wilhelm commented in the margin of Heyking's dispatch.) Pavlov had made the same allegation to the Italian representative, Marquis Giuseppe Salvago-Raggi. However, when Gérard heard thereof he compelled Pavlov to call on Heyking and Salvago and declare to them that he had erred, that it had not been Gérard who had determined Ukhtomskii's conduct. ("*Also kein Hund*" [Thus not a dog], Wilhelm remarked.) "I accepted the explanation silently, because I felt sorry for the poor man," Heyking reported. "Pavlov, as this event shows, is a very weak character; he hates Gérard thoroughly, but does not have the courage to resist him" (Heyking to Hohenlohe-Schillingsfürst, no. A. 107, Peking, June 30, 1897, GA, FSU/China, 8/4).

95. Heyking to Hohenlohe-Schillingsfürst, no. A. 85, Peking, May 28, 1897, GA, FSU/China, 8/4.

96. Gérard, *Ma mission en Chine*, 220–21. Heyking, who had been offended by Ukhtomskii's unwillingness to visit him, was less kind in his description of him. "Bad tongues could say that he reminds one of a subordinate, heavy coachman," Heyking wrote (Heyking to Hohenlohe-Schillingsfürst, no. A. 107, Peking, June 30, 1897, GA, FSU/China, 8/4).

97. Gérard, *Ma mission en Chine*, 221–22; Heyking to Hohenlohe-Schillingsfürst, no. A. 85, Peking, May 28, 1897, GA, FSU/China, 8/4.

98. Gérard, *Ma mission en Chine*, 218–19.

99. Heyking to Hohenlohe-Schillingsfürst, no. A. 85, Peking, May 28, 1897.

100. Gérard, *Ma mission en Chine*, 219; Heyking to Hohenlohe-Schillingsfürst, no. A. 107, Peking, June 30, 1897, GA, FSU/China, 8/4. Heyking pointed out that Kuang-hsü had risen not out of gratitude for the precious gift for his aunt or out of respect for the Russians, but because Chinese etiquette required that the emperor get up everytime the empress dowager was mentioned.

101. Heyking to Hohenlohe-Schillingsfürst, no. A. 107, Peking, June 30, 1897.

102. Gérard, *Ma mission en Chine*, 224.

103. Heyking expressed doubt that Russia had gained any practical results from the gift-bearing mission. At the same time, Germany's own position had been somewhat helped thereby, the Tsungli Yamen being a little more accommodating than usual in a

number of questions. "They will in time have to speak to us in another way," Wilhelm remarked (Heyking to Hohenlohe-Schillingsfürst, no. A. 107, Peking, June 30, 1897).

104. Romanov, "Likhunchangskii fond," 105–6.

105. *Ibid.*, 106–10; Gérard to Hanotaux, no. 76, Peking, June 5, 1897, and no. 81, Peking, June 13, 1897, DDF, ser. 1, 13: 421–22, 428–31.

106. Romanov, "Likhunchangskii fond," 110–12. For an account of Badmaev's fantastic schemes, see Malozemoff, 48–49. Witte and Ukhtomskii eventually broke off all relations with Badmaev (Vitte, 2: 49–50).

107. Romanov, "Likhunchangskii fond," 112. Witte gives a more equitable distribution of bribes in his memoirs: half a million to Li, a quarter of a million to Chang (Vitte, 2: 142).

108. Romanov, "Likhunchangskii fond," 113.

109. During his visit to New York Li Hung-chang met the son of General Ulysses S. Grant. "Are you rich?" he asked him. When Frederick Grant replied in the negative, Li was bewildered. "Do you mean to tell me," he marveled, "that your father was a General during a rebellion that lasted five years, and brought it to a successful conclusion, and that he was afterwards twice elected President of the United States, and that yet you his son are poor! Well! I do *not* understand how that could possibly be" (Mrs. Archibald Little, *Li Hung-chang His Life and Times*, 262–63).

110. Hsü, "Procedure and Perception," 107, 119–32. A shift in Russian policy following the German occupation of Kiaochow and the outbreak of hostilities between Russia and China in Manchuria in the wake of the Boxer uprising were to leave the Russo-Chinese alliance in shambles. Yet the turn of events had been foreseen by neither side. The bad faith shown by the tsarist government in the leasing of Port Arthur was the result of opportunism, not of premeditated deceit. Men like Witte strongly opposed the venture. The Russian railroad through Manchuria was to become a terrible financial drain and source of conflict with China and Japan for the tsarist regime and a "damned inheritance" for its Soviet successors, but that is another story (See Valliant, "Japan and the Trans-Siberian Railroad, 1885–1905," and Lensen, *The Russo-Chinese War* and *The Damned Inheritance: The Soviet Union and the Manchurian Crises 1924–1935*).

111. Heyking to Hohenlohe-Schillingsfürst, no. A. 34, Peking, March 9, 1897, GA, FSU/China, 20/4.

Chapter Seventeen

1. "Note sur Seoul," appended to Frandin to Develle, DP, no. 56, Seoul, May 22, 1893, FA, CP, Korea, 5: 86–90.

2. Excerpt from *Japan Mail* of Oct. 15, 1894, enclosed in Trench to Kimberley, no. 142, Tokyo, Oct. 18, 1894, EA, FO 405–61, pp. 248–49.

3. Conroy, *Japanese Seizure*, 261–63.

4. Mutsu to Hitrovo, July 28, 1895, enclosed in Hitrovo to Giers, no. 45, RA, AVPR, Iaponskii stol, 1894, delo 899.

5. Conroy, *Japanese Seizure*, 263–65.

6. Mutsu and Otori had recommended the conclusion of such an alliance to each other at about the same time—their telegrams crossed (Mutsu to Otori, no. 80, Aug. 13, 1894; Otori to Mutsu, no. 46, Pusan, Aug. 17, 1894; Mutsu to Otori, no. 85, Aug.

17, 1894, *Nihon gaiko bunsho*, 31: 333–35. See also Otori to Mutsu, no. 67, Seoul, Aug. 25, 1894, and Mutsu to Otori, no. 103, Tokyo, Aug. 26, 1894, *Nihon gaiko bunsho*, 31: 336).

7. Copy of treaty enclosed in Sill to Gresham, no. 38, Seoul, Aug. 3, 1894, *Korean-American Relations*, 2: 343.

8. Otori to Mutsu, no. 80, Seoul, Sept. 8, and Mutsu to Otori, no. 115, Tokyo, Sept. 9, 1894, Conroy, *Nihon gaiko bunsho*, vol. 27, pt. 2, pp. 338–39.

9. Hitrovo to Giers, no. 57, Tokyo, Oct. 1/13, 1894, RA, AVPR, Iaponskii stol, 1894, delo 899. When Giers had tried to ascertain the attitude of Great Britain toward the new development, the Foreign Office had responded to Chargé Butenev that it had received no such communication (Kimberley to Lascelles, no. 224, Foreign Office, Sept. 17, 1894, EA, FO 405–60, p. 274).

10. Conroy, *Japanese Seizure*, 268–69; Ro, 40–42; Mutsu to Otori, no. 142, Oct. 7, 1894, *Nihon gaiko bunsho*, vol. 27, pt. 1, p. 675.

11. *Japan Mail*, Oct. 15, 1894.

12. Trench to Kimberley, no. 142, Tokyo, Oct. 18, 1894, EA, FO 405–61, p. 248; Conroy, *Japanese Seizure*, 62–65, 159–61.

13. Mutsu to Nabeshima for Ito, Tokyo, Oct. 4, 1894, JA, TEL 1894/2978–2979; another Mutsu to Nabeshima for Ito, Tokyo, Oct. 4, 1894, JA, TEL 1894/2981; Ito to Mutsu, Hiroshima, Oct. 4, 1894, JA, TEL 1894/3401. In the telegraphic exchange which ensued between Mutsu and Ito, the former argued that if Inoue succeeded Otori as minister, he could act as he pleased and could be recalled whenever he had completed his work. On the other hand, if he were appointed commissioner, he would not be able to do anything officially; someone else would have to be sent as minister, and Inoue would have to work through him as *kuromaku* ("black curtain," that is to say, behind the scenes) (Mutsu to Nabeshima for Ito, Tokyo, Oct. 10, 1894, JA, TEL 1894/2998–2999). Ito thereupon decided to send Inoue as *tokuha benri taishi*, but Mutsu again objected. If Ito meant "resident ambassador" by that term, it was entirely against international usage to send such a high functionary to a small country; if he had in mind "special ambassador," it would arouse the suspicions of the powers just when England had proposed their intervention in the Sino-Japanese war. Noting that an envoy extraordinary and minister plenipotentiary could do everything that was required and that the appointment of Inoue to the special post seemed motivated by the desire merely to avoid the appearance of degrading him, Mutsu offered to go in the inferior capacity himself (Ito to Mutsu, Hiroshima, Oct. 9, 1894, JA, TEL 1894/3409; Mutsu to Nabeshima for Ito, Tokyo, Oct. 9, 1894, JA, TEL 1894/2995–2996). Ito countered that the dispatch of a member of the cabinet to Korea was likely to arouse the attention of the powers, regardless of the title under which he might be sent. But he left the decision regarding the position to the discretion of the foreign minister (Ito to Mutsu, Hiroshima, Oct. 10, 1894, JA, TEL 1894/3411).

14. Mutsu to Sugimura, no. 161, Tokyo, Oct. 18, 1894, JA, TEL 1894/1436–1437; Mutsu to Nishi, no. 28, to Aoki, no. 16, and to Uchida, no. 43, Tokyo, Oct. 14, 1894/1423–1424. Villetard de Laguérie, who interviewed Inoue in March 1895, gave a vivid description of his appearance. "Small of stature, with slender limbs, and a large head topped by a shaggy mane of coarse hair atop a high skull; looking as if the cerebellum had been pulled down over the brains, with small, very black and bridled eyes, concealed under heavy eyelids pleated like Venetian blinds, Inoue looked more like a Kalmyk than a Japanese," he wrote. "An expression of cunning and of cold

insensitivity belied on the cheeks spangled with rigid tufts of a sparse and poorly planted beard the honeyed and sly benignity which was illuminated by a sinister smile on his face, disfigured by small pox scars and saber cuts" (Villetard de Laguérie, *La Corée, indépendante, Russe, ou Japonaise*, 214–15).

15. Lefèvre to Hanotaux, DP, no. 1, Seoul, Jan. 20, 1895, FA, CP, Korea, 6: 10–16.

16. Inoue to Mutsu, no. 139, Seoul, Nov. 8, 1894, JA, TEL 1894/117; Hayashi to Nabeshima for Ito, Tokyo, Nov. 8, 1894, JA, TEL 1894/3170–3171.

17. Inoue to Mutsu, no. 142, Nov. 16, 1894, JA, TEL 1894/1159–1160.

18. "Great Changes in the Korean Government," *Korean Repository*, 1895, 2: 111–18; Laguérie, 218–19. Hitrovo reported that the Japanese sought to strengthen their influence in Korea by reeducating Korean children "in a purely Japanese spirit." For a start, 113 boys and youth were brought from Korea to Japan to be remolded in the school of the noted educator and publicist Fukuzawa Yukichi (Hitrovo to Lobanov-Rostovskii, no. 44, Tokyo, June 4, 1895, RA, AVPR, Iaponskii stol, 1895, delo 900).

19. Inoue to Mutsu, no. 145, Seoul, Nov. 21, 1894, JA, TEL 1894/1175–1176; Inoue to Mutsu, no. 147, Seoul, Nov. 22, 1894, JA, TEL 1894/1183; Lefèvre to Hanotaux, DP, no. 1, Seoul, Jan. 20, 1895.

20. Lefèvre to Hanotaux, DP, no. 1, Seoul, Jan. 20, 1895; Conroy, *Japanese Seizure*, 274.

21. Hillier to O'Conor, Seoul, Dec. 7, 1894, EA, FO 405–62, pp. 76–77.

22. Inoue to Mutsu, no. 152, Seoul, Dec. 10, 1894, JA, TEL 1894/1297–1299, and *Nihon gaiko bunsho*, vol. 27, p. 2, pp. 119–20.

23. Hillier to O'Conor, Seoul, Dec. 11, 1894, EA, FO 405–62, pp. 76–77.

24. Inoue to Mutsu, no. 156, Seoul, Dec. 25, 1894, JA, TEL 1894/1282–1284, and *Nihon gaiko bunsho*, vol. 27, pt. 2, pp. 123–24.

25. Inoue to Mutsu, no. 156, Seoul, Dec. 25, 1894, JA, TEL 1894/1282–1284.

26. Inoue to Mutsu, no. 157, Seoul, Dec. 26, 1894, JA, TEL 1894/1287.

27. Ro, 43–44; Laguérie, 223; Hatada, 103–4.

28. Inoue to Mutsu, no. 161, Seoul, Jan. 8, 1895, JA, TEL 1895/0121–0123, and *Nihon gaiko bunsho*, vol. 28, pt. 1, pp. 315–16 and 380–81; Lefèvre to Hanotaux, DP, no. 1, Seoul, Jan. 20, 1895; Conroy, *Japanese Seizure*, 276–77.

29. Inoue to Mutsu, no. 164, Seoul, Jan. 11, 1895, JA, TEL 1895/0131–0132, and *Nihon gaiko bunsho*, vol. 28, pt. 1, p. 317; Conroy, *Japanese Seizure*, 277–78.

30. Inoue to Mutsu, no. 160, Seoul, Jan. 16, 1895, JA, TEL 1895/1682–1686, and *Nihon gaiko bunsho*, vol. 28, pt. 1, pp. 318–19.

31. Inoue to Mutsu, no. 166, Seoul, Jan. 26, 1895, JA, TEL 1895/1759–1760.

32. Nishi to Mutsu, no. 44, St. Petersburg, May 15, 1895, JA, TEL 1895/0422–0423, and *Nihon gaiko bunsho*, vol. 28, pt. 1, pp. 413–14.

33. Inoue to Mutsu, May 19, 1895, JA, TEL 1895/0427–0430, and *Nihon gaiko bunsho*, vol. 28, pt. 1, pp. 420–21.

34. Mutsu to Kato, Tokyo, May 18, 1895, JA, TEL 1895/0699–0700, and *Nihon gaiko bunsho*, vol. 28, pt. 1, p. 419.

35. Kato to Mutsu, London, May 19, 1895, JA, TEL 1895/0432, and *Nihon gaiko bunsho*, vol. 28, pt. 1, p. 420.

36. Mutsu to Nabeshima for Ito, Tokyo, May 17, 1895, JA, TEL 1895/0695–0698, and *Nihon gaiko bunsho*, vol. 28, pt. 1, pp. 415–16.

37. Mutsu to Nabeshima for Ito, Tokyo, May 25, 1895, JA, TEL 1895/0708–0709, and *Nihon gaiko bunsho*, vol. 28, pt. 1, pp. 434–35.

38. Nishi to Mutsu, no. 47, St. Petersburg, May 27, 1895, JA, TEL 1895/0443.

39. Saionji to Kato, no. 78, Tokyo, June 20, 1895, JA, TEL 1895/0738.

40. Kato to Saionji, no. 111, London, June 25, 1895, JA, TEL 1895/0503–0505.

41. The Japanese government had received word that the unity with which the three powers opposed Japanese entrenchment in southern Manchuria did not extend to Korea. Germany encouraged Japanese ambitions in that region. Minister Aoki had reported from Berlin that Foreign Secretary Marschall had told him in interviews on May 2 and May 4 that Japan could be "her own master of Corea." Aoki had persuaded Chancellor Hohenlohe indirectly a few days before, he cabled, that Japan should be allowed a free hand in Korea (Aoki to Mutsu via Nishi, no. 110, St. Petersburg, June 8, 1895, JA, TEL 1895/0463).

42. Lowther to Salisbury, no. 288, Tokyo, July 13, 1895, "Confidential," EA, FO 405–64, p. 120.

43. O'Conor to Salisbury, no. 265, Peking, July 13, 1895, "Confidential," EA, FO 405–64, pp. 152–53.

44. Hillier to O'Conor, Seoul, July 18, 1895, "Very Confidential," EA, FO 405–64, pp. 144–45.

45. *Nihon gaiko bunsho*, vol. 28, pt. 1, pp. 480–81; Saionji to Nishi, no. 135, to Inoue, no. 206, and to Hayashi, no. 16, Tokyo, Aug. 1, 1895, JA, TEL 1895/1119–1120. Premier Ito informed Sir Ernest Satow, the new British minister to Japan, of the above. He wished to know England's attitude, though the moment had not yet come, he thought, for proposing to the great powers a joint declaration respecting Korea. "Count Ito fears to inform Germany of the Japanese policy regarding Corea, lest it should be communicated to France and Russia, though the Japanese Minister at Berlin recommends this step," Satow reported (Satow to Salisbury, no. 77, tel., Tokyo, Aug. 1, 1895, EA, FO 405–64, pp. 84–85). Kato made a similar communication of the Russian declaration in London and solicited Salisbury's advice (Salisbury to Satow, no. 71, London, Aug. 7, 1895, "Confidential," EA, FO 405–64, p. 104).

46. Inoue to Saionji, no. 183, Seoul, Aug. 2, 1895, JA, TEL 1895/0890–0891.

47. Gutschmid to Hohenlohe-Schillingsfürst, no. A. 263, Tokyo, Aug. 9, 1895, GA, FSU/China, 20/56. In a conversation with the German ambassador in St. Petersburg, Count Hugo Lezczyc von Radolin-Radolinsky, Nishi hinted at the possibility of difficulties between Russia and Japan over Korea, as Japan hesitated to withdraw until the reforms she desired had been implemented. He remarked in this connection that the military forces which Russia had at Vladivostok were insignificant and did not arouse serious concern on the part of his country (Radolin to Hohenlohe-Schillingsfürst, no. 350, St. Petersburg, Sept. 19, 1895, FA, FSU/China, 20/57).

48. F. A. McKenzie, *Korea's Fight for Freedom*, 48.

49. X. Y. Z., "The Attack on the Top Knot," *Korean Repository*, 1896, 3: 263–72.

50. Inoue to Mutsu, Seoul, May 19, 1895, JA, TEL 1895/0427–0430.

51. Gutschmid to Hohenlohe-Schillingsfürst, no. A. 197, Tokyo, June 2, 1895, GA.

52. "The Downfall and Departure of the Minister of Home Affairs," *Korean Repository*, 1895, 2: 268–70; Hulbert, I: 283–84; Ro, 45–47.

53. Conroy, *Japanese Seizure*, 298–99; Kim and Kim, 84.

54. Lefèvre to Hanotaux, DP, no. 12, Seoul, Sept. 28, 1895, FA, CP, Korea, 6: 61–62. For an analysis of Japanese policy and the reason for Inoue's failure, see Synn, 103–16. The Japanese thought of the maintenance of Korean independence in collaboration with Russia as a temporary measure until Japan was stronger. Japanese ultrana-

tionalists clamored for the acquisition of Korea as a step in Japanese expansion on the continent. Arguments that Korea was necessary as a shield against Chinese or Russian aggression were not genuine. Miura himself favored the annexation of Korea (Synn, 156–59).

55. Gutschmid to Hohenlohe-Schillingsfürst, no. A. 293, Tokyo, Oct. 1, 1895, GA, FSU/China, 20/59. Hitrovo had been satisfied with Ito's explanation. He deemed it absolutely reasonable, he told Gutschmid, to grant Japan the necessary time to evacuate the two regions successively. (Hitrovo made no reference to his conversation with Ito, but said that Inoue had confidentially informed Waeber that Japan intended to withdraw from Korea once the Liaotung affair had been settled.) Hitrovo hoped, Gutschmid reported, that all questions pending between Russia and Japan would be regulated by the end of the year and that he intended to go to Moscow at the beginning of January 1896 to attend the coronation (Gutschmid to Hohenlohe-Schillingsfürst, no. A. 294, Tokyo, Oct. 2, 1895, GA, FSU/China, 20/59).

Chapter Eighteen

1. Conroy, *Japanese Seizure*, 313–14.
2. Lensen, *Russian Diplomatic*, 53.
3. *Korean Repository*, 1897, 4: 353.
4. Isabella Bird Bishop, *Korea and her Neighbors*, 280.
5. Account of Seredin-Sabatin printed in S. M., *Po Dal'nemu Vostoku*, pp. 71–74, and enclosed in Hillier to O'Conor, Seoul, Oct. 10, 1895, EA, FO 405–65, pp. 45–47. From his position in the palace, where he resided temporarily, the Russian architect A. J. Seredin-Sabatin, observed the machinations of the contending parties. He found that the progressive or "Japanese" party was favorably inclined toward the United States, the conservative or "Chinese" party to which Queen Min belonged, toward Russia. The Americans actually contrived to be on good terms with both parties, while the Russian representative favored the conservative party. Sabatin himself deemed the Russian policy better, because the conservative party stood for stability and seemed to have greater popular support. But he regretted that the amicable disposition of Waeber and the other representatives toward the Korean court had led the queen to drop her guard toward the Japanese.
6. Lefèvre to Hanotaux, DP, no. 13, Seoul, Sept. 26, 1895, FA, CP, Korea, 6: 63–64.
7. "The Assassination of the Queen of Korea," *Korean Repository*, 1895, 2: 386–92.
8. Harrington, 263; Ro, 48.
9. The civilian henchmen, described officially by the generic term *soshi*, were not political zealots but hired swords. Miura paid them 6,000 yen for the murder of the queen (Synn, 168).
10. "Official Report on Matters connected with the Events of October 8th, 1895, and the Death of the Queen," *Korean Repository*, 1896, vol. 8, no. 3, pp. 120–25; Hillier to O'Conor, Seoul, Oct. 10, 1895, EA, FO 405–65, p. 43; Conroy, *Japanese Seizure*, 314–18; "Assassination," 387.
11. Seredin-Sabitin's eyewitness account, related to Hillier, enclosed in Hillier to O'Conor, Seoul, Oct. 10, 1895, EA, FO 405–65, pp. 46–47; a slightly different

version, also in the first person, communicated perhaps directly to a visiting compatriot, is given in S. M., *Po Dal'nemu Vostoku*, 53–74.

12. F. A. McKenzie, *The Tragedy of Korea*, 62.

13. S. M., *Po Dal'nemu Vostoku*, 56; Wm. McE. Dye, Letter to the Editor, *Korean Repository*, 1896, 3: 219.

14. Dye, 218–19.

15. Laguérie, 240–43; "Assassination," 386–92.

16. Dye, 219.

17. Lefèvre to Hanotaux, DP, no. 16, Seoul, Oct. 22, 1895, FA, CP, Korea, 6: 81–88.

18. S. M., 57–65; Hillier to O'Conor, Oct. 10, 1895, EA, FO 405–65, pp. 43–47.

19. "Statement of Col. Hyun," enclosed in Allen to Olney, no. 157, DS, Oct. 11, 1895.

20. S. M., 57–65; Hillier to O'Conor, Oct. 10, 1895, EA, FO 405–65, pp. 43–47.

21. "Official Report," 126–27.

22. "Statement of Col. Hyun."

23. Bishop, *Korea and Her Neighbors*, 273–74; Allen to Olney, no. 156, Seoul, Oct. 10, 1895, *Korean-American Relations*, 2: 357–62.

24. "Official Report," 126.

25. "Official Report," 127–28; Hillier to O'Conor, Seoul, Oct. 10, 1895, EA, FO 405–65, p. 44.

26. Notification enclosed in Allen to Olney, no. 159.

27. Allen to secretary of state, no. 156, Seoul, Oct. 10, 1895, *Korean-American Relations*, 2: 357–62; Hillier to O'Conor, Seoul, Oct. 10, 1895, EA, FO 405–65, p. 44.

28. Hillier to O'Conor, Seoul, Oct. 10, 1895, EA, FO 405–65, p. 44; "Official Report," 120; Allen to secretary of state, no. 156, *Korean-American Relations*, 2: 360. Allen makes no mention of the conversation with Miura and asserts that they finally "went boldly into the king's apartments."

29. Hillier to O'Conor, Seoul, Oct. 10, 1895, EA, FO 405–65, p. 44–45.

30. Memorandum of the meeting of the foreign representatives at the Japanese legation on October 8, 1895, appended to Lefèvre to Hanotaux, DP, no. 15, Seoul, Oct. 14, 1895, FA, CP, Korea, 6: 70–80, and enclosed in Hillier to O'Conor, Seoul, Oct. 11, 1895, EA, FO 405–65, pp. 47–49, and in Allen to Secretary of State Richard Olney, no. 159, DS, Seoul, Oct. 14, 1895. A verbatim account of the conversation was sent by Allen earlier, apparently as an enclosure in no. 156. See USDD, Korea, 134/12.

31. Saionji to Nishi, no. 147, Tokyo, Oct. 9, 1895, JA, TEL 1895/1213–1214, and *Nihon gaiko bunsho*, vol. 28, pt. 1, pp. 496–97.

32. Hillier to O'Conor, Seoul, Oct. 11, 1895, "Confidential," EA, FO 405–65, pp. 49–50.

33. "Notes of a conversation held between Mr. Hillier, British Representative and the Minister of the Household, eldest son of Tai Wen Kun, very privately at the Palace, Oct. 13, 5 p.m., 1895," enclosed in Allen to Olney, no. 159.

34. Miura to Kim Yun-sik, undated, enclosed in Sill to Olney, no. 173.

35. Kim Yun-sik to Miura, Seoul, Oct. 10, 1895, enclosed in Sill to Olney, no. 173; Allen to Olney, no. 158, Seoul, Oct. 13, 1895, *Korean-American Relations*, 2: 362–64.

36. Miura to Kim, Seoul, Oct. 10, 1895, enclosed in Sill to Olney, no. 173.

37. Kim to Miura, Seoul, Oct. 12, 1895, enclosed in Sill to Olney, no. 173.

38. Saionji to Nishi, no. 146, Tokyo, Oct. 8, 1895, JA, TEL 1895/1211.

39. Saionji to Nishi, no. 147, Tokyo, Oct. 9, 1895.

40. Saionji to Nishi, no. 148, Tokyo, Oct. 9, 1895, JA, TEL 1895/1215. See also Saionji to Hayashi, no. 56, and Saionji to Chinda (Shanghai), Tokyo, Oct. 11, 1895, JA, TEL 1895/1224–1225.

41. Saionji to Nishi, no. 149, Tokyo, Oct. 9, 1895, JA, TEL 1895/1216, and *Nihon gaiko bunsho*, vol. 28, pt. 1, pp. 497–98.

42. Nishi to Saionji, no. 81, St. Petersburg, Oct. 11, 1895, JA, TEL 1895/0924, and *Nihon gaiko bunsho*, vol. 28, pt. 1, pp. 500–1.

43. Saionji to Nishi, no. 151, Tokyo, Oct. 12, 1895, JA, TEL 1895/1226–1228. Russian and American marines had been landed to guard the legations (Saionji to Nishi, no. 150, and to Hayashi, no. 58, Tokyo, Oct. 11, 1895, JA, TEL 1895/1223; Saionji to Chinda, Tokyo, Oct. 11, 1895, JA, TEL 1895/1225; Saionji to Kurino via Nishi, no. 27, Oct. 14, 1895, JA, TEL 1815/1234).

44. Nishi to Saionji, no. 85, St. Petersburg, Oct. 14, 1895, JA, TEL 1895/0928, and *Nihon gaiko bunsho*, vol. 28, pt. 1, p. 516.

45. Kim Yun-sik to Lefèvre, Seoul, Oct. 11, 1895, enclosed in Lefèvre to Hanotaux, DP, no. 16, Seoul, Oct. 22, 1895, FA, CP, Korea, 6: 81–88.

46. Allen to Olney, no. 157, Oct. 11, 1895, USDD, Korea, 134/12.

47. Allen to Olney, no. 159, DS, Seoul, Oct. 14, 1895, USDD, Korea, 134/12. In addition to their show of support for the monarch, the Western representatives gave asylum to a number of officials. The following Koreans took refuge in the United States legation: Yi Yun-ying, recent inspector of the palace; his brother, Yi Wan-ying, one-time chargé d'affaires in Washington and lately minister of education; Yi Chai-yun, governor of Seoul and also one-time chargé in Washington; Yi Ha-yeng, of late royal treasurer and also former chargé in Washington; Min Sang-ho, who had been educated in Washington under the care of an American admiral and who had been on the verge of being appointed secretary of the legation in Washington, and Col. Hyön In-tak, who had defended the palace on October 8. Min Ying-hwan, who had been appointed minister to Washington, was among those who had fled to the Russian legation. The officials had reason to go into hiding, for many followers of the queen had been arrested. Although the Western representatives had no way of ascertaining whether there was any truth to reports that a number of those apprehended had been executed in prison, it was evident that the foreign settlement was closely watched by the police and by detectives who waited for the opportunity to seize the refugees and those who communicated with them.

48. Kim Yun-sik to Lefèvre, Seoul, Oct. 11, 1895, enclosed in Lefèvre to Hanotaux, DP, no. 16, Seoul, Oct. 22, 1895, FA, CP, Korea, 6: 81–88.

49. Kim Yun-sik to Allen, Seoul, Oct. 11, 1895, enclosed in Allen to Olney, no. 157.

50. D'Anethan to Foreign Minister de Burlet, no. 140/48, Tokyo, Oct. 17, 1895, BA.

51. Lefèvre to Hanotaux, DP, no. 16, Seoul, Oct. 22, 1895.

52. Allen to Olney, no. 157, DS, Seoul, Oct. 11, 1895; Allen to Olney, no. 158, Seoul, Oct. 13, 1895, *Korean-American Relations*, 2: 362–64.

53. "Notes of a conversation held between the Minister for Foreign Affairs and Mr. Brown, Chief Commissioner of Customs, at the Foreign Office on Oct. 13, p.m., 1895," enclosed in Allen to Olney, no. 159.

54. Allen to Olney, no. 157, DS, Seoul, Oct. 11, 1895, USDD, Korea, 134/12.

55. *Ibid*.

56. Miura to Kim, Seoul, Oct. 12, 1895, enclosed in Allen to Olney, no. 173.

57. Allen to Olney, no. 159, DS, Seoul, Oct. 14, 1895.

58. Allen to Olney, no. 157, Seoul, Oct. 11, 1895, USDD, Korea, roll 12.

59. Allen to Olney, no. 159, DS, Seoul, Oct. 14, 1895.

60. Radolin to Hohenlohe-Schillingsfürst, no. 374, St. Petersburg, Oct. 13, 1895, GA, FSU/China, 20/58.

61. Saionji to Hisamidzu, Tokyo, Oct. 16, 1895, JA, TEL 1895/1239.

62. Kurino to Saionji, no. 36, Washington, Oct. 17, 1895, JA, TEL 1895/0935–0936. When the Russian Pacific Squadron left Hakodate on the seventeenth, the British minister to Japan supposed that the nine vessels were proceeding to Chemulpo in response to Waeber's summons (Satow to Salisbury, no. 93, tel., Tokyo, Oct. 19, 1895, EA, FO 405–65, p. 9). Eitaki telegraphed from Shanghai a week later that fifteen Russian men-of-war were said to have left Vladivostok for Chemulpo and Wonsan on the twenty-third (Eitaki to Saionji, Shanghai, Oct. 24, 1895, JA, TEL 1895/0965).

63. Lauenstein to German minister of war, no. 95, St. Petersburg, Oct. 18, 1895, GA, FSU/China, 20/58.

64. Allen to Olney, no. 161, DS, Seoul, Oct. 19, 1895, USDD, Korea, 134/12.

65. Satow to Salisbury, no. 288, Tokyo, Oct. 8, 1895, EA, FO 405–65, p. 66.

66. Saionji to Nishi, no. 153, Tokyo, Oct. 18, 1895, JA, TEL 1895/1245–1246, and *Nihon gaiko bunsho*, vol. 28, pt. 1, pp. 519–20. Identical telegrams were sent to the other Japanese ministers abroad.

67. Nishi to Saionji, no. 83, St. Petersburg, Oct. 20, 1895, JA, TEL 1895/0944–0945, and *Nihon gaiko bunsho*, vol. 28, pt. 1, p. 512.

68. Nishi to Saionji, no. 84, St. Petersburg, Oct. 25, 1895, JA, TEL 1895/0968–0969, and *Nihon gaiko bunsho*, vol. 28, pt. 1, pp. 527–28.

69. Saionji to Nishi, no. 157, Tokyo, Oct. 25, 1895, JA, TEL 1895/1262–1264. Similar instructions were sent to other Japanese ministers (JA, TEL 1895/1266–1267).

70. Nishi to Saionji, no. 85, St. Petersburg, Oct. 27, 1895, JA, TEL 1895/0982.

71. Saionji to Nishi, no. 160, Tokyo, Oct. 29, 1895, JA, TEL 1895/1280.

72. Allen to Olney, no. 162, DS, Seoul, Oct. 20, 1895, and Allen to Olney, no. 163, DS, Seoul, Oct. 22, 1895, USDD, Korea, 134/12.

73. Allen to Olney, no. 163, DS, Seoul, Oct. 22, 1895, USDD, Korea, 134/12.

74. *Ibid*.; Sill to Olney, no. 164, DS, Seoul, Oct. 26, 1895; Sill to Olney, no. 173, DS, Seoul, Nov. 20, 1895, USDD, Korea, 134/12.

75. "Réunion des Representants étrangers à la Legation des Etats-Unis le 25 octobre 1895," enclosed in Lefèvre to Hanotaux, DP, no. 17, Seoul, Nov. 1, 1895, FA, CP, Korea, 6: 89–95. Saionji informed Nishi that Waeber desired the disbandment of the *kunrentai* and the dismissal of the incumbent Korean minister of war. Komura had not gone along with the proposal, he cabled, because at the moment there was no other military force in Korea strong enough to cope with the *kunrentai* and an attempt to disband it could lead to another disturbance. "I think such a scheme is very dangerous unless it be carried out slowly and cautiously," Saionji commented. "I instructed Komura to take safe course by consulting Inoue on his arrival. Call [the] attention of [the] Russian Government to this matter" (Saionji to Nishi, no. 159, Tokyo, Oct. 26, 1895, JA, TEL 1895/1273).

76. Sill to Olney, no. 173, DS, Seoul, Nov. 20, 1895, USDD, Korea, 134/12.

77. Saionji to Nishi, no. 155, Tokyo, Oct. 25, 1895, JA, TEL 1895/1259.

78. Satow to Salisbury, no. 295, Tokyo, Oct. 26, 1895, EA, FO 405–65, pp. 72–73; Lefèvre to Hanotaux, DP, no. 17, Seoul, Nov. 1, 1895, FA, CP, Korea, 8: 89–95.

79. Sill to Olney, no. 164, DS, Seoul, Oct. 26, 1895, USDD, Korea, 134/12.

80. Lefèvre to Hanotaux, DP, no. 17, Seoul, Nov. 1, 1895.

81. Memorandum of the conversation at the Japanese legation on November 5 and copy of the paper prepared by Sill, Waeber, and Hillier, enclosed in Sill to Olney, no. 173, DS, Seoul, Nov. 20, 1895, USDD, Korea, 134/12; Hillier to Salisbury, no. 2, tel., Seoul, Nov. 5, 1895, EA, FO 405–65, p. 20.

82. Komura and Inoue to Saionji, no. 187, Seoul, Nov. 6, 1895, JA, TEL 1895/1005–1008.

83. French translation of the letter from the Japanese emperor to the Korean king, dated Oct. 24, 1895, enclosed in Lefèvre to Hanotaux, DP, no. 19, Seoul, Nov. 11, 1895, FA, CP, Korea, 6: 97–105.

84. Lefèvre to Hanotaux, DP, no. 19, Seoul, Nov. 11, 1895, FA, CP, Korea, 6: 97–105.

85. Summary of conversation between Inoue and Kim, taken down by Hillier from Allen's statement of the conversation between himself and Inoue and corrected by the latter, enclosed in Sill to Olney, no. 173, Seoul, Nov. 20, 1895. See also slightly different French resumé of the conversation, enclosed in Lefèvre to Hanotaux, DP, no. 19, Seoul, Nov. 11, 1895.

86. Enclosure no. 3 in Sill to Olney, no. 173, Seoul, Nov. 20, 1895; Lefèvre to Hanotaux, DP, no. 19, Seoul, Nov. 11, 1895.

87. Sill to Olney, Nov. 8, 1895, USDD, Korea, 134/12. Krien had agreed to the reply to Komura drafted by his colleagues, but he had declined to express an opinion.

88. Sill to Olney, no. 167, DS, Seoul, Nov. 9, 1895, USDD, Korea, 134/12.

89. Lefèvre to Hanotaux, DP, no. 19, Seoul, Nov. 11, 1895, FA, CP, Korea, 6: 97–105.

90. Sill to Olney, Seoul, Nov. 9, 1895, USDD, Korea, 134/12.

91. "Memorandum of conversation that took place at an interview at the Japanese Legation, November 12, 1895," taken down by Hillier at the time and corrected by Sill and Waeber, enclosed in Sill to Olney, no. 173, Seoul, Nov. 20, 1895, and in Lefèvre to Hanotaux, DP, no. 19, Seoul, Nov. 20, 1895, FA, CP, Korea, 6: 107–12; Komura to Saionji, no. 188, Seoul, Nov. 13, 1895, JA, TEl 1895/1027–1030.

92. "Memorandum of conversation that took place at an interview at the Japanese legation, November 12, 1895."

93. Saionji to Nishi, no. 169, and to Hayashi, no. 87, Tokyo, Nov. 15, 1895, JA, TEL 1895/1327–1329; Dun to Sill, Tokyo, Nov. 14, 1895, enclosed in Sill to Olney, no. 171, DS, Seoul, Nov. 15, 1895, USDD, Korea, 134/12.

94. Saionji to Nishi, no. 169, Tokyo, Nov. 15, 1895.

95. Saionji to Nishi, no. 170, and to Hayashi, no. 188, Tokyo, Nov. 15, 1895, JA, TEL 1895/1330.

96. Sill to Olney, no. 173, DS, Seoul, Nov. 20, 1895.

97. Saionji to Nishi, no. 170, Tokyo, Nov. 15, 1895.

98. Appropriate instructions were not telegraphed from Paris until November 17.

99. Lefèvre to Hanotaux, DP, no. 20 (misnumbered 19), Seoul, Nov. 20, 1895, FA, CP, Korea, 6: 113–14.

100. Olney to Sill, Washington, Nov. 11, 1895, enclosed in Sill to Olney, no. 174, DS, Seoul, Nov. 13, 1895, USDD, Korea, 134/12.

101. Sill to Olney, no. 173, DS, Seoul, Nov. 20, 1895, USDD, Korea, 134/12.

102. Olney to Sill, Washington, Nov. 20, 1895, enclosed in Sill to Olney, no. 174, DS, Seoul, Nov. 22, 1895, USDD, Korea, 134/12. Hillier had instructions not to join in any representations to Komura regarding Korean affairs without first referring home (Kato to Saionji, London, Nov. 22, 1895, JA, TEL 1895/1059).

103. "Memo of Conversation at Audience Nov. 26, 1895," enclosed in Sill to Olney, no. 175, DS, Seoul, Dec. 2, 1895, USDD, Korea, roll 12; "Audience du 26 Novembre 1895," enclosed in Lefèvre to Hanotaux, DP, no. 21, Seoul, Nov. 27, 1895, FA, CP, Korea, 6: 115–17; Saionji to Nishi, no. 174, and to Hayashi, no. 98, Tokyo, Nov. 29, 1895, JA, TEL 1895/1362. The rehabilitation of the queen and the dismissal of War Minister Cho and Seoul Police Chief Kwan Yon-chin had been taken on the advice of Komura and Inoue, who hoped that if this satisfaction were given to the foreign representatives, they might not persist in their demand for the removal of the *kunrentai* from the palace (Lefèvre to Hanotaux, DP, no. 21, Seoul, Nov. 27, 1895, FA, CP, Korea, 6: 115–17).

104. Saionji to Nishi, no. 174 and to Hayashi, no. 98, Tokyo, Nov. 29, 1895, JA, TEL 1895/1362.

105. Sill to Olney, no. 175, DS, Seoul, Dec. 2, 1895, USDD, Korea, 134/12; Saionji to Nishi, no. 174, and to Hayashi, no. 98, Tokyo, Nov. 29, 1895, JA, TEL 1895/1362.

106. Lefèvre to Berthelot, DP, no. 3, Seoul, Jan. 12, 1895, FA, CP, Korea, 6: 139–40.

107. Sill to Olney, no. 177, DS, Seoul, Dec. 3, 1895, and enclosed copy of letter from Sill to Komura, dated Seoul, Nov. 28, 1895, as well as enclosed unsigned letter to Sill, dated Seoul, Nov. 28, 1895, USDD, Korea, 134/12.

108. "Translation of a letter to the Japanese Minister in the name of the soldiers of the Royal Body Guard, dated 12th day of the 10th month of Korean calendar," enclosed in Sill to Olney, no. 177.

109. Sill to Olney, no. 177.

110. Sill to Olney, no. 175, DS, Seoul, Dec. 2, 1895; Saionji to Nishi, no. 174, Nov. 29, 1895; Lefèvre to Foreign minister, DD, no. 22, Seoul, Dec. 3, 1895, FA, CP, Korea, 6: 118–23. Yin Cheu-son and Yi To-chol eventually were condemned to death; four individuals were exiled for life; three others were sentenced to three years' imprisonment. This was surprisingly light punishment by Korean standards, considering the number of people involved in the conspiracy. The Western representatives believed that the Japanese legation had counseled moderation in this matter (Lefèvre to Berthelot, DP, no. 3).

111. Sill to Olney, no. 177.

112. Saionji to Nishi, no. 174, Tokyo, Nov. 29, 1895.

113. Sill to Olney, no. 175, DS, Seoul, Dec. 2, 1895, and no. 177.

114. *Ibid.*; Consul L. C. Hopkins to Beauclerk, Chefoo, Dec. 9, 1895, "Confidential," EA, FO 405–70, p. 61.

115. Sill to Olney, Dec. 1, 1895; Sill to Olney, no. 175.

116. Olney to Sill, Washington, Dec. 2, 1895, enclosed in Sill to Olney, no. 178, DS, Seoul, Dec. 4, 1895, USDD, Korea, 134/12.

117. Olney to Sill, tel., Washington, Jan. 11, 1895, enclosed in Sill to Olney, no. 188, DS, Seoul, Jan. 14, 1896, USDD, Korea, 134/12.

118. Sill to Olney, tel., Seoul, Jan. 13, 1895, enclosed in Sill to Olney, no. 188.

119. Sill to Olney, no. 189, DS, Seoul, Jan. 20, 1896, USDD, Korea, 134/12.

120. Lefèvre to Hanotaux, no. 22.

121. Sill to Olney, no. 176, Seoul, Dec. 2, 1895, and enclosures (Kim Yun-sik to Sill, no. 24, Seoul, Dec. 1, 1895, and Sill to Kim, no. 81, Seoul, Dec. 2, 1895), USDD, Korea, roll 12; Lefèvre to foreign minister, DP, no. 23, Seoul, Dec. 5, 1895, FA, CP, Korea, 6: 123–25, and enclosure (Kim to Lefèvre, Seoul, Dec. 1, 1895).

122. Lefèvre to foreign minister, DP, no. 23, Seoul, Dec. 5, 1895, FA, CP, Korea, 6: 123–25. The Japanese court went into mourning for seven days from December 5 (Saionji to Nishi, no. 176, Tokyo, Dec. 6, 1895, JA, TEL 1895/1375).

123. Extract of the official *Gazette* of Seoul of Dec. 29, 1895, enclosed in Lefèvre to Berthelot, DP, no. 26, Seoul, Dec. 31, 1895, FA, CP, Korea, 6: 129–32.

124. Sill to Olney, no. 187, DS, Seoul, Jan. 13, 1896, USDD, Korea, 134/12. The Korean people did not believe the story that a compatriot garbed in European dress had slain the queen. They took it as a maneuver to shift the blame away from the Japanese. So convinced were natives and foreigners alike that none of the crimes committed in the palace had been the handiwork of Koreans, that neither the conviction of the above three Koreans nor the acquittal of the Japanese conspirators in Hiroshima the following month could change their mind (Lefèvre to Berthelot, DP, no. 26. See also "Official Report on Matters connected with the Events of October 8th, 1895," 136–39).

125. "Copy of the Decision of the Japanese Court of Preliminary Inquiries," as cited in the "Official Report," 124–25. The *non sequitur* involved in the dismissal of charges aroused much surprise in Tokyo. Saionji admitted to Satow on January 23 that the result of the trial had appeared strange to him. The British minister voiced the conviction that the world in general "could not but take an unfavourable view of a Judgment that practically acquitted the criminals" (Satow to Salisbury no. 15, Jan. 28, 1896, EA, FO 405–70, pp. 93–99). "The judgment is the more iniquitous and scandalous, because it is clearly evident from the grounds which precede the sentence . . . that Miura has repeatedly and to a large number of persons given the order to kill the Queen," Baron d'Anethan, the Belgian minister, remarked (D'Anethan to Foreign Minister de Burlet, no. 11/6, Feb. 17, 1896, BA).

Chapter Nineteen

1. Lefèvre to Foreign Minister Pierre Eugène Marcelin Berthelot, DP, no. 25, Seoul, Dec. 22, 1895, FA, CP, Korea, 6: 127–28.

2. Extract from the official *Gazette* enclosed in Lefèvre to Berthelot, DP, no. 2, Seoul, Jan. 7, 1896, FA, CP, Korea, 7: 135–38.

3. Lefèvre to Berthelot, DP, no. 2; Collin de Plancy to foreign minister, DP, no. 139, Seoul, Jan. 31, 1896, FA, Korea, PE, 8: 133–36.

4. Lefèvre to Berthelot, DP, no. 2.

5. Saionji to Nishi, no. 8, Tokyo, Jan. 24, 1896, JA, TEL 1896/0135.

6. Lefèvre to Berthelot, DP, no. 1, Seoul, Jan. 5, 1896, FA, CP, Korea, 6: 134–35; decree of January 1, 1896, enclosed in Lefèvre to Berthelot, DP, no. 2.

7. Lefèvre to Hanotaux, DP, no. 14, Seoul, Oct. 1, 1895, FA, CP, Korea, 6: 66–68.

Actually Waeber was replaced to appease the Japanese who did not like him (Synn, 214).

8. Nikhamin, "Russko-iaponskie otnosheniia," 184; Nikhamin, "Diplomatiia russkogo tsarizma v Koree," 150.

9. Sill to Olney, no. 187, DS, Seoul, Jan. 13, 1896, USDD, Korea, 134/12.

10. Lefèvre to Berthelot, DP, no. 5, Seoul, Jan. 25, 1896, FA, CP, Korea, 6: 144–46.

11. Nikhamin, "Russko-iaponskie otnosheniia," 185.

12. Gutschmid to Schillingsfürst, no. A. 349, Tokyo, Dec. 8, 1895, GA, FSU/Korea, 1/20.

13. Nikhamin, "Russko-iaponskie otnosheniia," 184.

14. Nikhamin, "Russko-iaponskie otnosheniia," 185 and 187; Nikhamin, "Diplomatiia," 150–51.

15. Lefèvre to Berthelot, DP, no. 5, Seoul, Jan. 25, 1896.

16. Krien to Hohenlohe-Schillingsfürst, J. no. 47 (?), Seoul, Jan. 31, 1896, GA, FSU/Korea, 1/21; Saionji to Nishi, no. 7, Tokyo, Jan. 23, 1896, JA, TEL 1896/0133.

17. Nishi to Saionji, no. 7, St. Petersburg, Feb. 5, 1896, JA, TEL 1896/0050.

18. Hillier to Beauclerk, Seoul, Feb. 1, 1896, EA, FO 405–70, p. 127.

19. Nikhamin, "Russko-iaponskie otnosheniia," 177–79.

20. Sill to Olney, no. 195, DS, Seoul, Feb. 11, 1896, USDD, Korea, 134/12.

21. Nikhamin, "Russko-iaponskie otnosheniia," 185–86; Nikhamin, "Diplomatiia," 151.

22. Nikhamin, "Russko-iaponskie otnosheniia," 187. The published extract of Nikhamin's dissertation deletes the words "at the present time," which may or may not have been a conscious qualification on the part of Lobanov (Nikhamin, "Diplomatiia," 152).

23. Nikhamin, "Russko-iaponskie otnosheniia," 187–88.

24. Hitrovo to Lobanov, Tokyo, Jan. 15/27, 1896, as cited by Nikhamin.

25. Hitrovo was going back also to undergo medical treatment.

26. Nikhamin, "Russko-iaponskie otnosheniia," 185, 189; Nikhamin, "Diplomatiia," 152, based on Hitrovo to Lobanov, Jan. 12/27, 1896, and Jan. 30/Feb. 11, 1896.

27. Nikhamin, "Russko-iaponskie otnosheniia," 189; Nikhamin, "Diplomatiia," 152.

28. Nikhamin, "Russko-iaponskie otnosheniia," 190–91.

29. "Official Report," 140; Synn, 191.

30. Nikhamin, "Russko-iaponskie otnosheniia," 191.

31. Nikhamin, "Russko-iaponskie otnosheniia," 192; Nikhamin, "Diplomatiia," 153–54.

32. Nikhamin, "Russko-iaponskie otnosheniia," 192–93; "The King at the Russian Legation," 82.

33. Nikhamin, "Russko-iaponskie otnosheniia," 193.

34. Krien to Hohenlohe-Schillingsfürst, J. no. 74, Seoul, Feb. 16, 1896, GA, FSU/Korea, 1/21.

35. The exact number is not clear. Four officers and 100 sailors with the field-piece were landed by the *Admiral Kornilov* (Nikhamin, "Russko-iaponskie otnosheniia," 193; Hillier to Beauclerk, Seoul, Feb. 12, 1896, EA, FO 405–71, pp. 3–5). Krien reported that a total of about 120 sailors and the field-piece had been put ashore by the *Admiral Kornilov* and the *Bobr* (Krien to Hohenlohe-Schillingsfürst, J. no. 59, Seoul, Feb. 11, 1896, GA, FSU/Korea, 1/21). Komura telegraphed on October 10 that five

Russian naval officers and 107 marines had entered Seoul (Saionji to Nishi, no. 17, Tokyo, Feb. 13, 1896, JA, TEL 1896/0198).

36. Komura had confirmed this to Hillier on February 8. No Japanese officers had been sent with the Korean troops against the insurgents and no Japanese soldiers would intervene in the struggle, Komura explained, because the 500 Japanese, of whom the garrison was composed, were needed to protect the Japanese residents (Hillier to Beauclerk, Seoul, Feb. 9, 1896, EA, FO 405–71, p. 3).

37. The marines which Hillier and Sill had brought ashore after the disturbances of October 8 had been sent back once relative tranquility had settled over Seoul.

38. Hillier to Beauclerk, Seoul, Feb. 12, 1896. Sill asked Commander Houston of the U.S.S. *Macheas* to hold a guard of twenty men in readiness (Sill to Olney, no. 195, DS, Seoul, Feb. 11, 1896, USDD, Korea, 134/12).

39. Krien to Hohenlohe-Schillingsfürst, J. no. 59, Seoul, Feb. 11, 1896.

40. Krien to Hohenlohe-Schillingsfürst, Seoul, Feb. 16, 1896; "The King at the Russian Legation," 82; Nikhamin, "Russko-iaponskie otnosheniia," 193. Some sources state that only the crown prince wore women's clothes, the king being dressed as a coolie (Harrington, 289). According to information garnered by Hillier, Kojong and his son huddled behind two court ladies, seated in front of them, in the sedan chairs (Hillier to Beauclerk, Feb. 12, 1896, EA, FO 405–71, pp. 3–5). Since Hillier makes no mention of the disguise which the king and the crown prince had donned, it is possible that the two court ladies in this early report had been the king and the crown prince themselves.

41. "The King at the Russian Legation," 82; Lefèvre to Berthelot, DP, no. 7, Seoul, Feb. 15, 1896, FA, CP, Korea, 6: 144–46; Nikhamin, "Russko-iaponskie otnosheniia," 193.

42. Speyer to Sill, Seoul, Feb. 11, 1896, enclosed in Sill to Olney, no. 195, Seoul, Feb. 11, 1896, USDD, Korea, 134/12; Speyer to Hillier, Seoul, Feb. 11, 1896, enclosed in Hillier to Beauclerk, Seoul, Feb. 12, 1896; Krien to Hohenlohe-Schillingsfürst, J. no. 59, Seoul, Feb. 11, 1896; Speyer to Komura, Seoul, Feb. 11, 1896, *Nihon gaiko bunsho*, vol. 29, pp. 687–88.

43. Hillier to Beauclerk, Seoul, Feb. 12, 1896.

44. Yi Wan-yong to Sill, Feb. 11, 1896, enclosed in Sill to Olney, no. 195. Yi had attached the royal seal to the letter, because his own new seal had not yet been delivered.

45. Hillier to Beauclerk, Seoul, Feb. 12, 1896.

46. "Notes of remarks at Audience at the Quarters of the King, Russian Legation, Seoul, Korea, 12:30 noon, Feb. 11, 1896," initialled by Allen and enclosed in Sill to Olney, no. 195; Hillier to Beauclerk, Seoul, Feb. 12, 1896.

47. Komura to Saionji, Seoul, Feb. 16, 1896, JA, TEL 1896/0082.

48. Krien to Hohenlohe-Schillingsfürst, J. no. 59.

49. Lefèvre to Berthelot, DP, no. 7.

50. Nikhamin, "Russko-iaponskie otnosheniia," 193.

51. Nikhamin, "Diplomatiia," 153.

52. Synn, 191–92.

53. Lefèvre to Berthelot, DP, no. 7, Seoul, Feb. 15, 1896, FA, CP, Korea, 6: 144–46. According to the American scholar Dr. Fred Harvey Harrington, who studied the manuscripts of Dr. Horace Allen, secretary of the United States legation, Allen helped to arrange Kojong's flight to the Russian legation (Harrington, 292–93).

54. Nikhamin, "Russko-iaponskie otnosheniia," 220–21.

55. Synn, 193–94; Ro, 62; Harrington, 292–93; *Korean Repository*, 1896, 3: 91; Sill to Olney, no. 195; Krien to Hohenlohe-Schillingsfürst, Seoul, Feb. 16, 1896; Hillier to Beauclerk, Seoul, Mar. 2, 1896.

56. Special Supplement to the *Korean Repository*, 1896, 3: 83–4. A slightly different translation of the proclamation may be found in Sill to Olney, no. 195. See also Krien to Hohenlohe-Schillingsfürst, J. no. 74, Seoul, Feb. 16, 1896, GA, FSU/Korea, 1/21, and Lefèvre to Berthelot, DP, no. 8, Seoul, Feb. 22, 1896, FA, CP, Korea, 6: 157–64.

57. Lefèvre to Berthelot, DP, no. 8; Krien to Hohenlohe-Schillingsfürst, Seoul, Feb. 16, 1896; Special Supplement to the *Korean Repository*, 1896, 3: 84.

58. Special Supplement to the *Korean Repository*, 1896, 3: 84. The Japanese helped their puppets get away safely (Synn, 194).

59. Hillier to Beauclerk, Seoul, Feb. 12, 1896, EA, FO 405–71, pp. 3–5. According to some reports the mob had seized Kim and Chung from the police while they were being led to jail. For varying accounts of the gruesome affair, see Lefèvre to Bethelot, DP, no. 7, Seoul, Feb. 15, 1896, and no. 8, Seoul, Feb. 22, 1896; Krien to Hohenlohe-Schillingsfürst, Seoul, Feb. 16, 1896, GA, FSU/Korea, 1/21; Special Supplement to the *Korean Repository*, 1896, 3: 88–89.

60. Special Supplement to the *Korean Repository*, 1896, 3: 92.

61. Sill to Olney, no. 195.

62. According to one report the Japanese had gone to watch the execution of the Korean ministers (Saionji to Nishi, no. 19, Tokyo, Feb. 17, 1896, JA, TEL 1896/ 0204–0205).

63. Lefèvre to Berthelot, DP, no. 7.

64. Lefèvre to Berthelot, no. 8.

65. Special Supplment to the *Korean Repository*, 1896, 3: 89.

66. *Ibid.*, 82.

67. Sill to Olney, no. 195.

68. Francis N. Pelly to Vice-Admiral Buller, *Porpoise*, at Chemulpo, Feb. 13, 1896, EA, FO 405–71, p. 10.

69. Lefèvre to Berthelot, DP, no. 7.

70. Special Supplement to the *Korean Repository*, 1896, 3: 92.

71. Lefèvre to Berthelot, DP, no. 7, Seoul, Feb. 15, 1896.

72. Nikhamin, "Russko-iaponskie otnosheniia," 208–11.

73. Nikhamin, "Russko-iaponskie otnosheniia," 211–14.

74. Nikhamin, "Russko-iaponskie otnosheniia," 214. Grodekov wrote the above to the General Staff on June 18, 1896.

75. Nikhamin, "Russko-iaponskie otnosheniia," 214–15.

76. Nikhamin, "Russko-iaponskie otnosheniia," 202–3.

77. Nikhamin, "Russko-iaponskie otnosheniia," 214–15.

78. *Ibid.*, 215.

79. *Ibid.*, 216.

80. Lefèvre to Berthelot, DP, no. 9, Seoul, Feb. 28, 1896, FA, CP, Korea, 6: 165–67.

81. Krien to Hohenlohe-Schillingsfürst, no. A. 3920, Seoul, Mar. 2, 1896, GA, FSU/Korea, 1/21.

82. Hillier to Beauclerk, Seoul, Mar. 2, 1896, EA, FO 405–71, pp. 28–29; Sill to Olney, no. 200, DS, Mar. 1, 1896, USDD, Korea, 134/12.

83. Sill to Olney, no. 200.

84. Nikhamin, "Russko-iaponskie otnosheniia," 217–19.

85. Hillier to Beauclerk, Seoul, Mar. 2, 1896, EA, FO 405–71, pp. 28–29; Sill to Olney, no. 200, DS, Seoul, Mar. 1, 1896, USDD, Korea, 134/12. See also Krien to Hohenlohe-Schillingsfürst, J. no. 104, Seoul, Feb. 27, 1896, GA, FSU/Korea, 1/21.

86. Hillier to Beauclerk, Seoul, Mar. 2, 1896, EA, FO 405–71, pp. 28–29.

87. Sill to Olney, no. 200; Hillier to Beauclerk, Seoul, Mar. 2, 1896.

88. Olney to Sill, tel., Washington, Feb. 27, 1896, enclosed in Sill to Olney, no. 201, DS, Seoul, Mar. 2, 1896, USDD, Korea, 134/12.

89. Sill to Olney, tel., Mar. 2, 1896, USDD, Korean, 134/12.

90. Sill to Olney, no. 201, DS, Seoul, Mar. 2, 1896, USDD, Korea, 134/12.

91. Hillier to Beauclerk, Seoul, Mar. 2, 1896.

92. Vauvineux to Hanotaux, no. 34, St. Petersburg, Apr. 30, 1896, DDF, ser. 1, 12: 578–79.

93. Hillier to MacDonald, Seoul, July 28, 1896, "Confidential," EA, FO 405–72, pp. 54–55.

94. Sill to Olney, no. 226, DS, Seoul, July 17, 1896, USDD, Korea, 134/12.

95. Extract from *Novoe Vremia* of September 10/22, 1896, in O'Conor to Salisbury, no. 216, St. Petersburg, Sept. 24, 1896, EA, FO 405–72, pp. 56–57.

96. Plancy to Hanotaux, DP, no. 27, Seoul, Oct. 5, 1896, FA, CP, Korea, 6: 284–87.

97. Plancy to Hanotaux, DP, no. 15, Seoul, Aug. 1, 1896, FA, CP, Korea, 6: 250–53.

98. Allen to Olney, no. 245, Seoul, Nov. 13, 1896, USDD, Korea, 134/13. See also Plancy to Hanotaux, DP, no. 36, Seoul, Nov. 16, 1896, FA, CP, Korea, 6: 310-12.

Chapter Twenty

1. Nikhamin, "Russko-iaponskie otnosheniia," 197.

2. *Ibid.*, 198.

3. *Ibid.*, 199–201.

4. The date is not certain. Nikhamin, on the basis of a dispatch from Hitrovo to Lobanov, written on February 14, states that the meeting took place on February 11. Gutschmid in a report to Hohenlohe-Schillingsfürst, dated February 14, relates that Ito had called on Hitrovo "the day before yesterday," that is on the twelfth. As the telegraph line between Seoul and Pusan was out, word of the coup did not reach Tokyo until February 13 (*Nihon gaiko bunsho*, 29: 682–88).

5. Nikhamin, "Russko-iaponskie otnosheniia," 205–7. It soon became common knowledge in diplomatic circles in Seoul that the Japanese government planned to bring Komura to Tokyo to discuss the Korean question with Speyer there (Lefèvre to Berthelot, CP, no. 10 [misnumbered no. 9], Seoul, Mar. 1, 1896, FA, CP, Korea, 6: 167–68).

6. Saionji to Nishi, no. 16, Tokyo, Feb. 12, 1896, JA, TEL 1896/0194.

7. Hitrovo had a favorable reputation in both social and official circles in St. Petersburg and was regarded as a good diplomat ("The New Russian Representative in Japan," *Japan Weekly Mail*, Oct. 8, 1892, p. 431; Gutschmid to Caprivi, A. 7, Tokyo, Jan. 30, 1893, GA). Yet his appointment to Tokyo had elicited stories in the European and Japanese press about intrigues of which Hitrovo was said to have been guilty

during his service in Bucharest. Documents professing to be copies of correspondence between Hitrovo and Zinoviev, the director of the Asiatic Department, and said to have been sold to the Rumanian government for a sum of 30,000 francs by a former dragoman and bitter foe of Hitrovo represented the latter as having proposed that money be paid to kill Prince Ferdinand with dynamite. Zinoviev was alleged to have approved of the scheme so that both Hitrovo and he were depicted as "vulgar assassins and conspirators of the clumsiest type." The *Japan Weekly Mail* ridiculed this "mad tale" and complained that "many journalists make it their business to educate among the public the lowest possible estimate of the Russian Government and its methods" (Heard to Foster, no. 364, DS, Seoul, Feb. 10, 1893, "Confidential," USDD, Korea, 124/9).

8. Gutschmid to Hohenlohe-Schillingsfürst, no. A. 36, Tokyo, Feb. 14, 1896; GA, FSU/Korea, 1/21.

9. Gutschmid to Hohenlohe-Schillingsfürst, no. A. 37, Tokyo, Feb. 16, 1896, and Gutschmid to Hohenlohe-Schillingsfürst, no. 1, tel., Tokyo, Feb. 17, 1896, GA, FSU/Korea, 1/20. True to his word, Saionji showed to Gutschmid on the evening of February 17 a telegram from Komura filed at Fusan that forenoon, recounting events in Seoul. The Japanese minister telegraphed that the Russian legation, in which the king and the crown prince remained, was guarded on the outside by a ring of royal body guards and Korean police, on the inside by Russian marines. Gutschmid had learned as much from Krien, but he was pleased by the fact that Saionji had shared the information with him. "The communication of the minister of foreign affairs is a welcome sign of the confidence which the Japanese government has been markedly showing to us for some time," he observed (Gutschmid to Hohenlohe-Schillingsfürst, no. A. 41, Tokyo, Feb. 17, 1896, GA, FSU/Korea, 1/21). Gutschmid to Hohenlohe-Schillingsfürst, no. A. 42, Tokyo, Feb. 18, 1896, GA, FSU/Korea, 1/21. Waeber had informed Krien on February 10 that he would once again take charge of the affairs of the Russian legation, while Speyer would go to Tokyo to relieve Hitrovo, who was to return to Russia on leave (Krien to Hohenlohe-Schillingsfürst, J. no. 59, Feb. 11, 1896).

10. Unpublished diary of Sir Ernest Satow, Feb. 14, 1896, and Satow to Salisbury, no. 6, tel., Tokyo, Feb. 15, 1896, EA, FO 405–70, p. 60.

11. Satow diary, Feb. 17 and 19, 1896. For additional views of Satow, see Lensen (ed.), *Korea and Manchuria between Russia and Japan 1895–1904: The Observations of Sir Ernest Satow*.

13. *Nichi-Ro kosho-shi*, 259.

14. Nishi to Saionji, no. 10, St. Petersburg, Feb. 17, 1896, JA, TEL 1896/0088–0089.

15. Nikhamin, "Russko-iaponskie otnosheniia," 225.

16. Salisbury to Satow, no. 14 A, London, Feb. 19, 1896, "Confidential," EA, FO 405–70, p. 74; Saionji to Kato, no. 10, Tokyo, Feb. 17, 1896, JA, TEL 1896/0204–0205; Kato to Saionji, no. 13, London, Feb. 19, 1896, JA, TEL 1896/0098.

17. EA, FO 405–70, p. 77. In a conversation with Krien, Waeber disputed that there was any documentary foundation for the British position. It was based solely on an unauthorized remark made by Ladyzhenskii, who had since been dismissed from service, to Li Hung-chang over a glass of champagne. Hillier conceded to Krien that the British government had no written pledge from the tsarist government to that effect, merely an assurance on the part of the Chinese government that Russia had made such a commitment in connection with the return of Port Hamilton by the En-

glish (Krien to Hohenlohe-Schillingsfürst, J. no. 156, Seoul, Mar. 23, 1896, GA, FSU/ Korea, 1/22).

18. Lascelles to Salisbury, no. 43, Berlin, Feb. 20, 1896, "Confidential," EA, FO 405–70, p. 78.

19. Aoki to Saionji, no. 14, Berlin, Feb. 21, 1896, JA, TEL 1896/0104–0105.

20. Japanese chargé in Italy to Saionji, no. 99, via Nishi, Feb. 21, 1896, JA, TEL 1896/0421.

21. Japanese minister to Italy, Kurino Shinichiro, to Saionji, no. 5, via Nishi, Feb. 21, 1896, JA, TEL 1896/0103.

22. Japanese minister in France, Sone Arasuke, to Saionji, no. 3, via Nishi, Feb. 21, 1896, JA, TEL 1896/0418.

23. Kurino to Saionji, no. 2, via Nishi, Feb. 21, 1896, JA, TEL 1896/0419.

24. Kurino to Saionji, no. 3, via Nishi, Feb. 28, 1896, JA, TEL 1896/0440.

25. Nikhamin, "Russko-iaponskie otnosheniia," 225–26.

26. Numata Ichiro, *Nichi-Ro gaiko-shi*, 39–42; Nikhamin, 227.

27. Nikhamin, "Russko-iaponskie otnosheniia," 222.

28. Nikhamin, "Russko-iaponskie otnosheniia," 223.

29. *Ibid.*, 224.

30. Nishi to Saionji, no. 11, St. Petersburg, Feb. 19, 1896, JA, TEL 1896/0101–0102. Nishi gathered from remarks which Lobanov had dropped and from what he had heard from a "reliable source" that the Russian foreign minister was of the opinion that the principal cause of the troubles in Korea was the aversion of the inhabitants toward the Japanese who tried to impose on them unfamiliar reforms in the name of civilization by keeping troops in the land. This, plus Lobanov's earlier comments regarding the coup of October 8, and his "stubborn silence on the present situation" induced Nishi to warn Saionji on February 23 that the tsarist government might propose the withdrawal of all Japanese troops from Korea as a condition for a Russo-Japanese understanding (Nishi to Saionji, no. 14, St. Petersburg, Feb. 23, 1896, JA, TEL 1896/0427).

31. Saionji to Nishi, no. 23, Tokyo, Feb. 20, 1896, JA, TEL 1896/0214–0216; Saionji's record of his conversation with Hitrovo, Feb. 19, 1896, *Nihon gaiko bunsho*, vol. 29, pp. 731–36. Nikhamin gives February 20 as the date of the conversation (Nikhamin, "Russko-iaponskie otnosheniia," 227–28; *Nichi-Ro kosho-shi*, pt. 1: 259–60).

32. Saionji to Nishi, no. 24, Tokyo, Feb. 20, 1896, JA, TEL 1896/0218, and *Nihon gaiko bunsho*, 29: 699.

33. Saionji to Nishi, no. 29, and Saionji to Komura, no. 5, Tokyo, Feb. 23, 1896, JA, TEL 1896/0229; Nikhamin, "Russko-iaponskie otnosheniia," 228–29; *Nihon gaiko bunsho*, 29: 738; *Nichi-Ro kosho-shi*, pt. 1: 260.

34. *Nihon gaiko bunsho*, 29: 740–42; Saionji to Nishi, no. 31, and Saionji to Komura, no. 6, Tokyo, Feb. 25, 1896, JA, TEL 1896/0234–0235, and *Nihon gaiko bunsho*, 29: 742–43; Nikhamin, "Russko-iaponskie otnosheniia," 236. *Nichi-Ro kosho-shi* is mistaken in its assertion that the Japanese proposal was transmitted simultaneously in Tokyo and St. Petersburg (*Nichi-Ro kosho-shi*, pt. 1: 260–61).

35. Saionji to Nishi, no. 32, Tokyo, Feb. 25, 1896, JA, TEL 1896/0239–0241.

36. Nikhamin, "Russko-iaponskie otnosheniia," 229–30, based on Hitrovo to Lobanov, Feb. 20, 1896; Gutschmid to Hohenlohe-Schillingsfürst, no. A. 43, Tokyo, Feb. 20, 1896, GA, FSU/Korea, 1/21.

37. Saionji to Nishi, no. 30, Tokyo, Feb. 24, 1896, *Nihon gaiko bunsho*, 29: 808–9.

38. Gutschmid to Hohenlohe-Schillingsfürst, no. A. 48, Tokyo, Feb. 24, 1896, GA, FSU/Korea, 1/21.

39. Saionji to Nishi, no. 30.

40. Hitrovo to Lobanov, Feb. 20, 1896, cited in Nikhamin, "Russko-iaponskie otnosheniia," 229–30; Gutschmid to Hohenlohe-Schillingsfürst, no. A. 43.

41. Nikhamin, "Russko-iaponskie otnosheniia," 230. Gutschmid at first expressed doubt that Yamagata had been entrusted with so important a task as the negotiation of the Korean question, for he was neither a politician nor a diplomat. Rather, he thought, he was sufficiently highly placed to obtain from Lobanov a full exposition of the Russian program (Gutschmid to Hohenlohe-Schillingsfürst, no. A. 48, and no. A. 80, Tokyo, Apr. 19, 1896, GA, FSU/Korea, 1/22). But he reported on April 29 that Speyer, who had informed him of the provisions of the Waeber-Komura agreement, had told him that, as far as he knew, Yamagata carried with him extensive powers for the definitive settlement of the Korean question and that a final discussion on this subject could be expected almost certainly soon after the completion of the coronation festivities (Gutschmid to Hohenlohe-Schillingsfürst, no. A. 89, Tokyo, Apr. 29, 1896, GA, FSU/Korea, 1/22).

42. Nikhamin, "Russko-iaponskie otnosheniia," 230–31.

43. Nishi to Saionji, no. 15, St. Petersburg, Feb. 26, 1896, JA, TEL 1896/0435.

44. Saionji to Nishi, no. 34, Tokyo, Feb. 27, 1896, JA, TEL 1896/0247.

45. *Nichi-Ro kosho-shi*, pt. 1: 261.

46. Nishi to Saionji, no. 16, St. Petersburg, Feb. 29, 1896, JA, TEL 1896/ 0445–0446.

47. *Nihon gaiko bunsho*, 29: 747–48; *Nichi-Ro kosho-shi*, pt. 1: 261; Nikhamin, "Russko-iaponskie otnosheniia," 237–38.

48. *Nihon gaiko bunsho*, 29: 750; Saionji to Nishi, no. 36, Tokyo, Mar. 3, 1896, *ibid.*, 750–51; Nikhamin, "Russko-iaponskie otnosheniia," 240.

49. Saionji to Komura, no. 6, Tokyo, Mar. 3, 1896, JA, TEL 1896/1003–1005.

50. Nishi to Saionji, no. 19, St. Petersburg, Mar. 4, 1896, JA, TEL 1896/0462.

51. Nikhamin, "Russko-iaponskie otnosheniia," 240–41; *Nichi-Ro kosho-shi*, pt. 1: 262.

52. *Nihon gaiko bunsho*, 29: 758–65; *Nichi-Ro kosho-shi*, pt. 1: 267–68. Hitrovo never returned to his post. He died in July. His death was mourned in diplomatic as well as official Japanese circles. "The deceased had known how to win the confidence of the local government, in spite of the bad reputation which had preceded him and which had made him appear as not quite *persona grata* here at first," Gutschmid reported. "The mistrust which he encountered during the last twelve months of his stay was directed not so much at his person as at the policy which he had to represent. I do not think I am mistaken when I assert that the so far relatively smooth unfolding of the Korean question is due thanks primarily to the conciliatory and adroit behavior of Mr. Hitrovo, who until the very last tried to bring his benevolent intentions toward Japan to bear on the proper place in St. Petersburg" (Gutschmid to Hohenlohe-Schillingsfürst, no. A. 127, Tokyo, July 16, 1896, GA). Hitrovo's death evoked a variety of reflections in the Japanese press. A number of newspapers spoke well of his diplomatic ability and credited him in large part with the success of the Lobanov-Yamagata talks. He had equalled Sir Harry Parkes in energy; he had excelled him in knowing how to

garb the most unpleasant missions in an amiable guise (Gutschmid to Hohenlohe-Schillingsfürst, no. A. 132, Tokyo, July 20, 1896, GA). Gutschmid had been on friendly terms with Hitrovo, an "outspoken Anglophobe," skeptical also of the intimate relationship between Russia and France. Speyer told Gutschmid that the position of minister might remain unfilled for some time in order to make use of the salary funds freed by Hitrovo's death to pay off Hitrovo's numerous private debts. Hitrovo had received only one third of his salary in Japan, the other two thirds having been attached by his European creditors. As a result he owed over 30,000 rubles in Japan alone at the time of his demise (Gutschmid to Hohenlohe-Schillingsfürst, no. A. 127, Tokyo, July 16, 1896, GA). Over a year passed before Hitrovo was replaced in Tokyo by Baron Roman Romanovich Rosen (*Nihon gaiko nempyo*, vol. 2, appendix 2, p. 71).

53. Hitrovo to Saionji, Tokyo, Mar. 6, 1896, *Nihon gaiko bunsho*, 20: 767. Although Speyer's original orders to proceed to Tokyo had reached him on February 10 (Krien to Hohenlohe-Schillingsfürst, no. A. 3920, Seoul, Mar. 2, 1896, GA, FSU/Korea, 1/21), he had delayed his departure from Korea following the events of February 11 thinking that he might be *persona non grata* in Japan, but his government had renewed its order on the twenty-ninth for him to proceed to Tokyo forthwith (Sill to Olney, no. 200, DS, Seoul, Mar. 1, 1896, USDD, Korea, 134/12).

54. *Nichi-Ro kosho-shi*, pt. 1: 262; Komura to Saionji, no. 1, Seoul, Mar. 22, 1896, JA, TEL 1896/0532–0533.

55. Komura to Saionji, no. 1, Seoul, Mar. 22, 1896, JA, TEL 1896/0532–0533; Nikhamin, "Russko-iaponskie otnosheniia," 240–41; *Nichi-Ro kosho-shi*, pt. 1: 262. *Nichi-Ro kosho-shi* mistakenly states that the draft memorandum was presented on March 13. Japanese and Russian sources agree on the substance of the memorandum, but Nikhamin reverses the order of points 3 and 4.

56. Nikhamin, "Russko-iaponskie otnosheniia," 241–42.

57. *Nihon gaiko bunsho*, 29: 777–78.

58. Nikhamin, "Russko-iaponskie otnosheniia," 243.

59. Nikhamin, "Russko-iaponskie otnosheniia," 243–44; *Nichi-Ro kosho-shi*, pt. 1: 262–63. Nikhamin mistakenly states that Waeber's memorandum was transmitted on April 13. Synn, on the basis of an American dispatch, gives the date as April 5 (Synn, 203).

60. Nikhamin, "Russko-iaponskie otnosheniia," 244–47; Komura to Saionji, no. 2, Seoul, Apr. 4, 1896, JA, TEL 1896/0600–0601; *Nichi-Ro kosho-shi*, pt. 1: 262–63.

61. Gutschmid to Hohenlohe-Schillingsfürst, no. A. 73, Tokyo, Apr. 9, 1896, GA, FSU/Korea, 1/22.

62. Nikhamin, "Russko-iaponskie otnosheniia," 248–49; *Nichi-Ro kosho-shi*, pt. 1: 263.

63. Gutschmid to Hohenlohe-Schillingsfürst, no. A. 73, Tokyo, Apr. 9, 1896, GA, FSU/Korea, 1/22.

64. Satow to Salisbury, no. 87, Tokyo, Apr. 21, 1896, "Very Confidential," EA, FO 405–71, pp. 74–75. On May 6 Satow telegraphed that Japan and Russia were negotiating a *modus vivendi* (no. 19, tel., EA, FO 405–71, p. 48).

65. *Nichi-Ro kosho-shi*, 264.

66. Nikhamin, "Russko-iaponskie otnosheniia," 250.

67. Nikhamin, "Russko-iaponskie otnosheniia," 250–51.

68. Mutsu to Omae, no. 57, Tokyo, May 1, 1896, JA, TEL 1896/1170–1171, and *Nihon gaiko bunsho*, 29: 783.

69. Omae to Mutsu, no. 31, St. Petersburg, May 3, 1896, JA, TEL 1896/0634.

70. Nikhamin, "Russko-iaponskie otnosheniia," 251–52. In mid-April Japanese consuls had been authorized to deport from Korea any Japanese subjects for attempting to disturb the peace (Satow to Salisbury, no. 81, Tokyo, Apr. 16, 1896, EA, FO 405–71, pp. 66–67).

71. Gutschmid to German Foreign Ministry, no. 10, tel., Tokyo, Apr. 25, 1896, GA, FSU/Korea, 1/21.

72. Krien to Hohenlohe-Schillingsfürst, J. no. 236, Seoul, May 4, 1896, GA, FSU/Korea, 1/22.

73. Gutschmid to Hohenlohe-Schillingsfürst, no. A. 91, Tokyo, May 5, 1896, GA, FSU/Korea, 1/22.

74. Nikhamin, "Russko-iaponskie otnosheniia," 251; Nishi to Mutsu, no. 33, St. Petersburg, May 8, 1896, JA, TEL 1896/0643–0644.

75. Mutsu to Chargé d'Affaires Omae Taizo, no. 59, Tokyo, May 5, 1896, JA, TEL 1896/1180–1181, and *Nihon gaiko bunsho*, 29: 785–87.

76. Nishi to Mutsu, no. 33, St. Petersburg, May 8, 1896, JA, TEL 1896/0643–0644.

77. Nikhamin, "Russko-iaponskie otnosheniia," 253; Mutsu to Nishi, no. 61, Tokyo, May 12, 1896, JA, TEL 1896/1187, and *Nihon gaiko bunsho*, 29: 788–89; Nishi to Mutsu, no. 34, St. Petersburg, May 14, 1896, JA, TEL 1896/0657, and *Nihon gaiko bunsho*, 29: 792. Japanese documents state that the controversy was over the limitation of the number of Russian troops in Korea. According to Nikhamin the issue was partly one of wording, Waeber being willing to agree that Russian troops "not" exceed Japanese troops in number, but balking at the demand that they "never" do so. In view of the silence of Japanese sources on this subject, it is conceivable that the Japanese failed to comprehend the nature of Waeber's objections and unwittingly contributed to the delay.

78. Nikhamin, "Russko-iaponskie otnosheniia," 254.

79. "Where peace and order will have been restored sufficiently," the Russian text stated.

80. For the official, rather awkward, English translation published by both sides, see *Sbornik dogovorov i diplomaticheskikh dokumentov*, 147–48, and *Obzor snoshenii s Iaponiei po Koreiskim delam s 1895 g.*, 38–39; Komura to Mutsu, no. 3, May 14, 1896, JA, TEL 1896/0652–0653, and *Nihon gaiko bunsho*, 29: 802–3. A smoother, but unofficial rendering, is enclosed in Satow to Salisbury, no. 39, Tokyo, Mar. 1, 1897, EA, FO 405–73, pp. 50–52.

81. Nikhamin, "Russko-iaponskie otnosheniia," 256–57; Romanov, *Rossiia v Man'chzhurii*, 141. Nikhamin takes issue with Romanov's contention that the Seoul memorandum wiped out any advantages for Japan. He argues that while Russia never utilized the right to station troops in Korea, Japan kept her soldiers there without opposition and retained her strong position in the country's foreign trade. Plancy commented in March 1897 that although the Russians had received the same right as the Japanese to guard their legation and consulates with troops, they could not take advantage of the opportunity because they had only 100 marines in Korea (Plancy to Hanotaux, no. 66, Seoul, Mar. 18, 1897, FA, Korea, PE, 8: 31–41).

82. *Nichi-Ro kosho-shi*, pt. 1: 266.

83. Krien to Hohenlohe-Schillingsfürst, J. no. 236, Seoul, May 4, 1896, GA, FSU/Korea, 1/22. Plancy had served in Seoul as French commissar from 1888 to 1891. He

presented his credentials and assumed his position as chargé on April 28, 1896.

84. Plancy to French foreign minister, DP, no. 4, Seoul, May 30, 1896, FA, CP, Korea, 6: 203–6.

85. Krien to Hohenlohe-Schillingsfürst, J. no. 209, Seoul, Apr. 20, 1896, GA, FSU/Korea, 1/22.

86. Plancy to French foreign minister, DP, no. 3, Seoul, May 21, 1896, FA, CP, Korea, 6: 201–2.

87. Plancy to French foreign minister, DP, no. 4, Seoul, May 30, 1896, FA, CP, Korea, 6: 203–6.

88. Krien to Hohenlohe-Schillingsfürst, J. no. 267, Seoul, May 31, 1896, "Confidential," GA, FSU/Korea, 1/22.

89. Nikhamin, "Russko-iaponskie otnosheniia," 258–59.

90. Nishi to Saionji, no. 18, St. Petersburg, Mar. 3, 1896, JA, TEL 1896/0458.

91. Nishi to Saionji, no. 20, St. Petersburg, Mar. 4, 1896, JA, TEL 1896/0461.

92. *Nichi-Ro kosho-shi*, pt. 1: 268–71.

93. Nikhamin, "Russko-iaponskie otnosheniia," 263–64; *Nichi-Ro kosho-shi*, 271–72; Nishi to Mutsu, no. 2, St. Petersburg, May 26, 1896, JA, TEL 1896/0673–0676, and *Nihon gaiko bunsho*, 29: 812–13. The negotiations were slow in getting started, because the Japanese, considering any conversation as official and binding, did not want to talk until they were sure the Russians would listen to them. The French general Raoul Le Mouton de Boisdeffre, who was in Moscow at the time as ambassador extraordinary, sought to expedite the talks by obtaining the substance of the views of Yamagata from the latter's secretary and confidante and conveying the information to Lobanov through General Obruchev, urging Russia to come to an agreement with Japan (Boisdeffre to Hanotaux, letter no. 7, Paris, June 13, 1896, DDF, ser. 1, 12: 640–42).

94. *Nichi-Ro kosho-shi*, 272–73; Nishi to Saionji, July 8, 1896, *Nihon gaiko bunsho*, 29: 820–26.

95. Nikhamin, "Russko-iaponskie otnosheniia," 266–67. The right to string a telegraph line like the right to maintain a military force equal to that of Japan was never exploited by Russia.

96. Yamagata to Saionji, in Nishi to Saionji, no. 4, St. Petersburg, June 7, 1896, JA, TEL 1896/0691–0693; *Nichi-Ro kosho-shi*, 273; *Nihon gaiko bunsho*, 29: 836–37. The amendment was based on the proposal of the special Korean ambassador (Synn, 208).

97. Nikhamin, "Russko-iaponskie otnosheniia," 267–68; Nishi to Saionji, July 8, 1896, *Nihon gaiko bunsho*, 29: 820–22. Yamagata's proposal and Lobanov's evaluation thereof may have given rise to the assertion made in several Russian documents in 1903 and repeated by historians ever since that Yamagata had proposed the partition of Korea along the 38th parallel. No mention of the 38th parallel appears in the documents of 1896. Although it is possible that unofficial mention was made thereof in the talks, it is more likely, Nikhamin points out, that the later documents were in error. Speyer told Harmand that Yamagata had been optimistic about obtaining Russian assent to the partition of Korea, because Hitrovo had shown himself favorable to the idea. Harmand thought the notion to be "profoundly erroneous and dangerous" (Harmand to Hanotaux, DP, no. 25, Tokyo, Mar. 4, 1897, FA, Korea, PE, 8: 14–21). Saionji was not enthusiastic about the fifth article. "If this article is accepted by Russia, we must remember that it will impose upon us a heavy responsibility for the

future," he telegraphed to Yamagata. "If the Russian Government hesitate to accept our proposal on this point, I think there is no necessity to insist upon it" (Saionji to Nishi for Yamagata, no. 73, Tokyo, June 9, 1896, JA, TEL 1896/1219, and *Nihon gaiko bunsho*, 30: 814).

98. Nishi to Saionji, July 8, 1896, *Nihon gaiko bunsho*, 29: 823.

99. *Nichi-Ro kosho-shi*, 274–75; Nikhamin, "Russko-iaponskie otnosheniia," 268–70.

100. *Nichi-Ro kosho-shi*, 275–76.

101. *Sbornik dogovorov i diplomaticheskikh dokumentov*, 159–60; *Nihon gaiko bunsho*, 29: 815–17. The above has been translated from the Russian text. For a slightly different English translation of the public articles, see the enclosure in Satow to Salisbury, no. 39, Tokyo, Mar. 1, 1897, EA, FO 405–73, p. 52. The French text sent by Harmand was a translation of the translation into English (enclosed in Harmand to Hanotaux, DP, no. 25, Tokyo, Mar. 4, 1897, FA, Korea, PE, 8: 14–21). The French version published along with the Russian version differed from the latter in that a comma was inserted prior to "without foreign assistance" in article 2. As a result Waeber interpreted the clause to mean that the military force to be organized was to be sufficient to maintain internal order without foreign aid, while Kato argued that it stipulated that Korea organize the military force without foreign assistance (Jordan to MacDonald, no. 27, Seoul, Mar. 19, 1897, "Confidential," EA, FO 405–73, pp. 70–71). On November 1, 1896, the Meiji emperor expressed to Speyer his special pleasure at the brilliant and sincere reception accorded to Prince Fushimi and Marshal Yamagata in Russia. He asked him to thank Nicholas for the many marks of attention shown to the representatives of Japan during the Moscow festivities (Speyer to Shishkin, no. 35, Tokyo, Nov. 1, 1896, RA, AVPR, Iaponskii stol, 1896, delo 901).

102. Nikhamin, "Russko-iaponskie otnosheniia," 273–75.

103. Ki-tak Lee, 276.

104. Nikhamin, "Russko-iaponskie otnosheniia," 276. In his memoirs Witte asserts that the Moscow Protocol gave Russia the right to furnish Korea with military instructors and a financial adviser, the latter being tantamount to appointing a finance minister (Vitte, 2: 75).

105. Speyer confided to Gutschmid on June 4, 1896, that a *modus vivendi* had been reached between Waeber and Komura a few days earlier (Gutschmid to Hohenlohe-Schillingsfürst, no. 109, Tokyo, June 4, 1896, GA, FSU/Korea, 1/22). Saionji assured Satow that the Seoul memorandum did not violate British interests (Satow to Salisbury, no. 126, Tokyo, June 18, 1896, "Confidential," EA, FO 405–72, p. 12). Vice Minister of Foreign Affairs Komura Jutaro denied categorically to Gutschmid that the "definitive understanding" which was being negotiated between Lobanov and Yamagata constituted a joint protectorate over Korea (Gutschmid to Hohenlohe-Schillingsfürst, no. A. 115, Tokyo, June 19, 1896, GA, FSU/Korea, 1/22).

106. Nishi to Saionji, no. 40, St. Petersburg, June 10, 1896, JA, TEL 1896/0695; Nishi to Saionji, no. 49, St. Petersburg, Aug. 3, 1896, JA, TEL 1896/0767; Nishi to Saionji, no. 50, St. Petersburg, Aug. 5, 1896, JA, TEL 1896/0756; Harmand to French foreign minister, DP, no. 16, Tokyo, Feb. 6, 1897, FA, Korea, PE, 8: 4–8.

107. Okuma to Motono, no. 13, Tokyo, Feb. 16, 1897, JA, TEL 1897/2555.

108. Okuma to Motono, no. 16, Tokyo, Feb. 20, 1897, JA, TEL 1897/2566. Synn interprets the publication of the agreements by the Japanese government to have been an intrigue to exploit the growing coolness between Russia and Korea (Synn, 234).

109. Motono to Okuma, no. 12, St. Petersburg, Feb. 22, 1897, JA, TEL 1897/2822.

110. Satow to Salisbury, no. 39, Tokyo, Mar. 1, 1897, EA, FO 405–73, pp. 50–51; O'Conor to Salisbury, no. 3, St. Petersburg, Feb. 25, 1897, and no. 4, St. Petersburg, Feb. 26, 1897, EA, FO 405–73, p. 38; Harmand to Hanotaux, DP, no. 18, Tokyo, Feb. 18, 1897, FA, Korea, PE, 8: 9–10; Okuma to Motono, no. 22, Tokyo, Feb. 26, 1897, JA, TEL 1897/2588; Motono to Okuma, no. 13, St. Petersburg, Feb. 24, 1897, JA, TEL 1897/2833. The secret articles of the Moscow protocol were not revealed until 1915, when they were first published by B. E. Nolde in his book *Vneshniaia politika, Istoricheskie ocherki* (Nikhamin, "Russko-iaponskie otnosheniia," 271–72). The existence of secret articles was suspected from the very beginning because of the vagueness of the published agreements (Harmand to Hanotaux, DP, no. 25, Tokyo, Mar. 4, 1897, FA, Korea, PE, 8: 14–21).

11. *Nihon gaiko nempyo*, 2: appendix, 47.

112. Yi to Kato, Seoul, Mar. 9, 1897, printed in the Seoul *Independent*, Mar. 18, 1897, enclosed in Sill to Olney, no. 263, DS, Seoul, Mar. 18, 1897, USDD, Korea, 134/13, and in Plancy to Hanotaux, DP, no. 66, Seoul, Mar. 18, 1897, FA, Korea, PE, 8: 31–32; Jordan to MacDonald, no. 25, Seoul, Mar. 10, 1897, EA, FO 405–73, pp. 66–70; Plancy to Hanotaux, DP, no. 63, Seoul, Mar. 13, 1897, FA, Korea, PE, 8: 27–28.

113. Jordan to MacDonald, no. 27, Seoul, Mar. 19, 1897, FO 405–73, pp. 70–71; Plancy to Hanotaux, no. 66, Seoul, Mar. 18, 1897, FA, Korea, PE, 8: 31–41.

114. Jordan to MacDonald, no. 25, Seoul, Mar. 10, 1897, EA, FO 405–73, pp. 66–68.

Chapter Twenty-one

1. Plancy to Hanotaux, DP, no. 15, Seoul, Aug. 1, 1896, FA, CP, Korea, 6: 250–53.

2. Plancy to Hanotaux, DP, no. 19, Seoul, Aug. 26, 1896, FA, CP, Korea, 6: 263–65.

3. Plancy to French foreign minister, DP, no. 3, Seoul, May 21, 1896, FA, CP, Korea, 6: 201–2.

4. Saionji to Omae, no. 82, Tokyo, June 25, 1896, JA, TEL 1896/1236–1237.

5. Saionji to Omae, no. 92, Tokyo, Aug. 21, 1896, JA, TEL 1896/1297–1298.

6. Nishi to Saionji, no. 53, St. Petersburg, Aug. 24, 1896, JA, TEL 1896/0784–0785.

7. Saionji to Omae, no. 93, Tokyo, Aug. 29, 1896, JA, TEL 1896/1305–1306. Rumors that the Russian government had resolved to send military officers to organize a royal guard and a number of civilian advisers to take charge of affairs in the various ministries pleased the French representative in Seoul. "If this information is accurate," Plancy remarked, "it would indicate that Russia comprehends at last the role she has to play and that she will hear no longer of letting things drift so as to relinquish to the English and the Americans who staff the Korean administration the influence which they have held too long and which she is in a position of claiming today for herself" (Plancy to Hanotaux, DP, no. 19, Seoul, Aug. 26, 1896, FA, CP, Korea, 6: 263–65).

8. "Funeral of Her Majesty, the Late Queen," *Korean Repository*, 1897, 4: 443.

9. Plancy to Hanotaux, DP, no. 19, Seoul, Aug. 26, 1896.

10. Sill to Olney, no. 231, Seoul, Sept. 1, 1896, USDD, Korea, 134/13; Plancy to Hanotaux, DP, no. 20, Seoul, Sept. 5, 1896, FA, CP, Korea, 6: 267–68.

11. Plancy to Hanotaux, DP, no. 33, Seoul, Nov. 3, 1896, FA, CP, Korea, 6: 306–7.

12. Plancy to Hanotaux, DP, no. 40, Seoul, Dec. 4, 1896, FA, CP, Korea, 6: 317–18; Sill to Olney, no. 264, DS, Seoul, Mar. (n.d.), 1897, USDD, Korea, 134/13.

13. Afanas'ev I and Grudzinskii, "Zapiski russkikh instruktorov v Koree," 231: 19; Okuma to Motono, no. 17, Tokyo, Feb. 22, 1897, JA, TEL 1897/2568.

14. Sill to Olney, no. 258, DS, Feb. 22, 1897, USDD, Korea, 134/13. The legations of Russia and Japan both had retained their guards; these were the only foreign troops then in Seoul.

15. Sill to Olney, no. 258, DS, Seoul, Feb. 22, 1897. Waeber was outraged when a proclamation posted by agitators in various parts of Seoul in May alleged that Kojong's move to the tsarist legation had been the work of "traitors-conspirators" who had blinded the king and brought disorder to the government of the country. Had the events of the autumn of 1895 and of the following winter already been forgotten? Had not the horrors regarding the queen and the explanations issued by the government at the beginning of the previous year clearly indicated the reasons which had forced the king and all the Korean ministers to seek refuge in the Russian legation, he berated Foreign Minister Yi Wan-yong in a stiff protest (Waeber to Yi, no. 28, Seoul, May 9/21, 1897, "A Weon-an").

16. "Her Majesty's Funeral," *Korean Repository*, 1897, 4: 30; Allen to Sherman, no. 3, DS, Seoul, Sept. 17, 1897, USDD, Korea, 134/13.

17. "The Whang-chei of Dai-Han, or the Emperor of Korea," *Korean Repository*, 1897, 4: 385–90.

18. Nikhamin, "Russko-iaponskie otnosheniia," 399–400.

19. Text of memorial, as cited in "The Whang-chei of Dai Han," 387–88.

20. "The Whang-chei of Dai Han," 385–90.

21. Nikhamin, "Russko-iaponskie otnosheniia," 400–401.

22. Allen to Sherman, no. 18, DS, Seoul, Oct. 14, 1897, and Allen to Sherman, no. 14, DS, Seoul, Oct. 5, 1897, USDD, Korea, 134/13.

23. "The Whang-chei of Dai Han," 385–86.

24. "Coronation Ceremony," *The Independent*, Nov. 14, 1897; "The Whang-chei of Dai Han," p. 386; "Notes and Comment," *Korean Repository*, 1897, 4: 399.

25. Allen to Sherman, no. 18, DS, Seoul, Oct. 14, 1897, USDD, Korea, 134/13; Okuma to Hayashi, no. 87, Tokyo, Oct. 22, 1897, JA, TEL 1897/1270.

26. Text of edict as cited in "The Whang-chei of Dai Han," 388–90.

27. Korean foreign minister to Jordan, Oct. 16, 1897, EA, FO 405–73, p. 166.

28. Jordan to MacDonald, no. 87, Seoul, Oct. 21, 1897, EA, FO 405–74, p. 166.

29. Allen to Denby, no. 12, L. & C., Seoul, Nov. 9, 1897, USDD, Korea, 134/13.

30. Rosen to Muraviev, no. 46, Tokyo, Oct. 2/14, 1897, RA, AVPR, Iaponskii stol, 1897, delo 902.

31. Allen to Sherman, no. 50, DS, Seoul, Dec. 23, 1897, and enclosed copy of telegram from Nicholas to Kojong, USDD, Korea, 134/14.

32. Okuma to Hayashi, no. 87, Oct. 22, 1897, JA, TEL 1897/1270.

33. Allen to Sherman, no. 54, DS, Seoul, Jan. 2, 1898, USDD, Korean, 134/14.

34. Jordan to Foreign Office, no. 24, Seoul, Feb. 25, 1898, EA, FO 405–80, p. 87; Jordan to MacDonald, no. 29, Seoul, Mar. 9, 1898, EA, FO 405–80, p. 91.
35. Allen to Olney, no. 25, DS, Seoul, Oct. 21, 1897, USDD, Korea, 134/13.
36. Allen to Sherman, no. 39, DS, Nov. 27, 1897, USDD, Korea, 134/13.
37. "Her Majesty's Funeral," *Korean Repository*, 1897, 4: 30–31; Allen to Sherman, no. 3, DS, Seoul, Sept. 17, 1897, USDD, Korea, 134/13.
38. "Funeral of Her Majesty, the Late Queen," *Korean Repository*, 1897, 4: 433–34.
39. Allen to Sherman, no. 39, DS, Seoul, Nov. 27, 1897.
40. "Funeral of Her Majesty, the Late Queen," *Korean Repository*, 1897, 4: 433–34. The remains of Queen Min were moved once more in 1919, upon the death of Kojong, to Hong-nung near the town of Kumgok.
41. Allen to Sherman, no. 39, DS, Seoul, Nov. 27, 1897.
42. *Ibid.*

Chapter Twenty-two

1. Nikhamin, "Russko-iaponskie otnosheniia," 277–78.
2. Sill to Olney, no. 203, Seoul, Mar. 18, 1896 USDD, Korea, 134/12.
3. Lefèvre to Berthelot, DP, no. 12, Seoul, Mar. 14, 1896, FA, CP, Korea, 6: 170–71.
4. Lefèvre to Berthelot, no. 15, Seoul, Apr. 4, 1896, FA, CP, Korea, 6: 174–75; Krien to Hohenlohe-Schillingsfürst, J. no. 209, Seoul, Apr. 20, 1896, GA, FSU/Korea, 1/22; Lensen, *Russian Diplomatic*, 46.
5. Krien to Hohenlohe-Schillingsfürst, J. no. 209, Seoul, Apr. 20, 1896, GA, FSU/Korea, 1/22.
6. Nikhamin, "Russko-iaponskie otnosheniia," 279–83.
7. Tschirschky to Hohenlohe-Schillingsfürst, no. A 8670, St. Petersburg, Aug. 10, 1896, GA.
8. Romanov, *Rossiia v Man'chzhurii*, 144–45. According to Soviet historiography the five-point reply was an example of the "duplicity" (*dvoistvennost'*) of tsarist policy in Korea. On one hand it did not comply with the proposals of the Korean government and in view of its vagueness was bound to arouse doubt on the part of the latter about the sincerity of Russian professions to be willing to protect and assist Korea. On the other hand, despite its qualifications, the Russian answer conflicted with the Lobanov-Yamagata protocol. Although the promise to send advisers and instructors did not violate any specific article of the Moscow protocol, it was contrary to the spirit of the agreement, which envisaged concerted action by Russia and Japan in Korea. The reference to the possibility of a Russian loan was in direct violation of the first article of the Moscow protocol, which obligated Russia to act jointly with Japan if Korea had to resort to a foreign loan (Nikhamin, "Diplomatiia," 162–63). B. A. Romanov asserts that Lobanov had signed the protocol of June 9 "with the firm intention not to pay heed to the obligations taken upon himself" (Romanov, *Rossiia v Man'chzhurii*, 144). Witte, who had participated in the negotiations with Yamagata in a secondary role, contended that in accordance with the secret agreement with Japan Russia had the right to maintain military instructors and several hundred Russian soldiers in Korea so that "in a military and financial respect, in the sense of managing the state finances, Russia was given sufficient, one can say dominant, rights; since accord-

ing to the agreement we were to appoint a financial adviser to the Korean emperor [sic]" (Vitte, 1: 59–60). Boris Borisovich Glinskii, who had access to the Witte archives, gave the same appraisal of the Lobanov-Yamagata agreement. In a confidential letter to Waeber, Lobanov reasoned that Korea as a completely independent country retained absolute freedom of action in all questions of domestic and foreign policy and was not subject to any restrictions in the selection of foreign advisers and military instructors to whom she might resort. Lobanov's successor, Mikhail Nikolaevich Muraviev, also considered that the agreement with Japan did not stand in the way of the dispatch of instructors to Korea (Lobanov to Waeber, St. Petersburg, July 2/14, 1896, and memorandum signed by Muraviev, cited in Nikhamin, "Diplomatiia," 163, footnote). The Japanese interpreted the Moscow protocol differently. They were to regard Russia's separate attempts to solve the military instructors and adviser question as a violation of the agreement (*Nichi-Ro kosho-shi*, pt. 1: 278–79). Thus the reduction in tension between Russia and Japan in Korea due to the moderation shown by both sides in Moscow was bound to be transitory (Nikhamin, "Russko-iaponskie otnosheniia," 277).

9. A civil service rank equivalent to lieutenant colonel.

10. Nikhamin, "Diplomatiia," 164–65; Plancy to Hanotaux, DP, no. 18, Seoul, Aug. 18, 1896, FA, CP, Korea, 6: 258–62; "Memorandum respecting the proposed Russian Loan," enclosed in Hillier to MacDonald, Seoul, Aug. 22, 1896, "Confidential, EA, FO 405–72, pp. 58–59; Lensen, *Russian Diplomatic*, 41. Pokotilov was to serve as Russian minister to China in 1906–1907.

11. According to the French minister in St. Petersburg, Putiata had been military attaché at Seoul (Montebello to Hanotaux, DP, no. 22, St. Petersburg, Mar. 5, 1897, FA, Korea, PE, 8: 21–23).

12. Nikhamin, "Diplomatiia," 165–66; Acting Consul General J. N. Jordan to MacDonald, no. 87, Seoul, Oct. 27, 1896, EA, FO 405–72, p. 81.

13. Speyer to Muraviev, no. 18, Tokyo, Mar. 12/24, 1897, RA, AVPR, Iaponskii stol, 1897, delo 902. Lamsdorff's German nephew, Gustav Count von Lamsdorff, states in his memoirs that Uncle Vladimir Nikolaevich spelled the family name as "Lamsdorf" (Gustav Graf von Lamsdorff, *Die Militärbevollmächtigten Kaiser Wilhelms II am Zarenhofe 1904–1914*, 62). However, since the tsarist statesman signed the telegrams he sent in foreign languages as "Lamsdorff," the latter version has been used in this work. Lamsdorff had been director of the Office of the Foreign Ministry from 1880 to 1897. He was vice minister of foreign affairs from 1897 to 1900, and was to serve as foreign minister from 1900 to 1906. A modest, self-educated individual who had joined the Foreign Ministry in a lowly position, Lamsdorff had climbed to the top by hard work and familiarity with the documents of the Foreign Ministry, within whose walls he spent his entire career. In Witte's words, Lamsdorff was a "walking archive" (Vitte, 2: 112–13).

14. Afans'ev I and Grudzinskii, no. 231, pp. 15–19; Acting Consul General J. N. Jordan to Sir Claude MacDonald, no. 87, Seoul, Oct. 27, 1896, EA, FO 405–72, p. 81.

15. Jordan to MacDonald, no. 87.

16. Afanas'ev I and Grudzinskii, no. 231, pp. 15–19. The low estimate of the traditional Korean soldiers expressed by the Russians was shared by other Europeans. The British acting consul general regarded the Korean army as "rabble." (J. N. Jordan to MacDonald, no. 89, Seoul, Nov. 14, 1896, "Confidential," EA, FO 4–5–73, pp. 2–3.)

In addition to the drill instructors and the noncoms in charge of the legation guard, there was also a Russian military agent, Colonel Strelbitskii, in Seoul. (Allen to Olney, no. 240, DS, Seoul, Oct. 27, 1896, USDD, Korea, roll 13; Plancy to Hanotaux, DP, no. 34, Seoul, Nov. 7, 1896, FA, CP, Korea, 6: 308–9.)

17. Plancy to Hanotaux, DP, no. 50, Seoul, Jan. 17, 1897, FA, Korea, PE, 8: 2–4; Jordan to MacDonald, no. 3, Seoul, Jan. 14, 1897, EA, FO 404–73, pp. 22–23.

18. J. N. Jordan to MacDonald, no. 89, Seoul, Nov. 14, 1896, "Confidential," EA, FO 405–73, pp. 2–3. Waeber told Jordan that he had not heard from his government for many months and that he was apprehensive that his conduct might be disavowed at any moment. Although Min seemed "closely identified" with the Russian legation and the Russian military mission in Seoul, he did not get along with Colonel Putiata. It was perhaps for this reason, Plancy speculated, that Min was shortly appointed minister plenipotentiary to the six European treaty powers—Great Britain, Germany, Russia, Italy, France, and Austria. "He is comparatively a young man, of pleasing manners, who professes to have been greatly impressed by his experiences abroad, but his desire to serve his country in a European post may possibly be based upon a prudent resolve to avoid the risks of official life in Seoul," Jordan reflected. (Plancy to Hanotaux, DP, no. 50, Seoul, Jan. 17, 1897, FA, Korea, PE, 8: 2–4; Jordan to MacDonald, no. 3, Seoul, Jan. 14, 1897, EA, FO 405–73, pp. 22–23). McLeavy Brown counseled against the dispatch of the mission, which seemed to be a revival of the abortive attempts made by Kojong in the days of Chinese domination to enter into direct relations with the courts of Europe, arguing that it would be an act of folly in view of Korea's impecuniosity. But Waeber, whose advice was also sought, seemed to have raised no objections. Jordan wondered why. "The attitude of the Russian Minister in this, as in many other matters, is far from clear," he observed. "He seems at times to be so indulgent towards the King's love of extravagance as to give rise to the perhaps ungenerous criticism that Russia's object is to encourage reckless expenditure, and to create the necessity for the loan which she is known to be pressing upon the Corean Government." It was possible, he conceded, that Waeber considered the appointment to be only a formal one. The arrangements were so indefinite as to strengthen the suspicion that the actual purpose of the appointment was to offer "a safe retreat in case of difficulty" (Jordan to MacDonald, no. 3, Seoul, Jan. 14, 1897). In a subsequent dispatch, classified "very confidential," Jordan related that Brown had sought Waeber's support in dissuading Kojong from embarking on the costly and useless undertaking. Waeber had defended the mission, saying that it would be useful for the Korean government to have an agent in Europe, because of the glass and paper-making industries which it was planning to establish. When Brown pressed the king for the real motives, Kojong confided to him in a low voice that there was reason to believe that the Russian government was about to replace Waeber with Speyer; as this was not in Korea's interest, he wanted to send Min to St. Petersburg to request the retention of Waeber. Brown was indignant that the scant resources of the country should be wasted on what to him seemed the personal interests of the Russian minister, but he promised to consider Kojong's request for funds, conscious that the appointment of Speyer might make his own position untenable (Jordan to MacDonald, no. 4, Seoul, Jan. 18, 1897, "Very Confidential," EA, FO 405–73, pp. 23–24).

19. Plancy to Hanotaux, DP, no. 27, Seoul, Oct. 5, 1896, FA, CP, Korea, 6: 284–87.

20. Sill to Olney, no. 266, DS, Seoul, July 17, 1896, USDD, Korea, 134/13.

21. *Nihon gaiko nempyo*, 1: 123, 2: appendix, 47.

22. Plancy to Hanotaux, DP, no. 11, Seoul, July 16, 1896. In later years Hara was to become president of the *Osaka Mainichi* newspaper, minister of communications, home minister, and finally prime minister. In 1921 he was stabbed to death by a young ultranationalist who had punned to friends that he was about to commit "Hara-kiri."

23. Gutschmid to Hohenlohe-Schillingsfürst, no. A. 172, Tokyo, Oct. 6, 1896, GA, FSU/Korea, 1/23.

24. Plancy to Hanotaux, DP, no. 11, Seoul, July 16, 1896, FA, CP, Korea, 6: 234–36.

25. Sill to Olney, no. 226, DS, July 17, 1896.

26. Allen to Olney, no. 236, DS, Seoul, Oct. 5, 1896, USDD, Korea, 134/13; Gutschmid to Hohenlohe-Schillingsfürst, no. A. 172, Tokyo, Oct. 6, 1896, GA, FSU/ Korea, 1/23. When it was rumored that Oishi, a member of Okuma's party, was being considered as successor to Hara, Speyer objected strongly, because Oishi, during his past service in Seoul, had shown a propensity for violent means and had agitated for direct Japanese intervention in the affairs of the peninsular kingdom (Gutschmid to Hohenlohe-Schillingsfürst, no. A. 172, Tokyo, Oct. 6, 1896, GA, FSU/Korea, 1/23; Plancy to Hanotaux, DP, no. 35, Seoul, Nov. 18, 1896, FA, CP, Korea, 6: 309–10). Kato remained chargé until Nov. 29, 1898, when he was promoted to minister (*Nihon gaiko nempyo*, 2: appendix, 47).

27. Nikhamin, "Diplomatiia," 166–68; Jordan to MacDonald, no. 87, Seoul, Oct. 27, 1896, EA, FO 405–72, p. 81.

28. Speyer to Shishkin, no. 36, Tokyo, Nov. 1/13, 1896, RA, AVPR, Iaponskii stol, 1896, delo 901. Thus the Japanese did not openly oppose the training of Korean troops by Russian instructors at this time, counting upon a reaction of popular feeling caused by the king's continued stay in the Russian legation when the situation no longer warranted it to swing the pendulum of influence back in their favor. "With some 15,000 of their people settled on Corean soil, and fully one-half of the total trade in their hands, they naturally consider that their interests here are not inferior to those of Russia, whose chief claim to a voice in Corean affairs rests upon her being a conterminous State with 11 miles of frontier," Jordan commented. "On the other hand, Russia has the advantage of being able to draw warm supporters and active agents for the propagation of her policy from the 16,000 Corean emigrants settled in Russian Manchuria, and from the inhabitants of the northern province of Corea, which has come largely under her influence," he reflected (Jordan to MacDonald, no. 4, Seoul, Jan. 18, 1897, "Very Confidential," EA, FO 405–73, pp. 23–24).

29. Muraviev was not yet firmly established in his position. He had become director of the Foreign Ministry only on January 1, 1897, and was not appointed foreign minister until April 13 of that year. Muraviev owed his appointment partly to his acquaintance with Nicholas, who knew him from Copenhagen where the imperial family frequently visited because the Tsarina Maria Federova was the daughter of Christian IX and where Muraviev had served as Russian minister from 1893 to 1897. Like Lobanov, Muraviev was a worldly and entertaining person, but of a different type. While Lobanov had been elegant in his words and conversation and interesting for cultured people, Muraviev was amusing because of his stories and manners. Lobanov was well-read and polished, while Muraviev was little-read, if not downright ignorant, according to Witte. Furthermore, Muraviev liked to eat well and to drink a great deal with his meal. Consequently Muraviev did not feel like getting back to work after dinner, and usually did not do so. It was because of his personal indolence that

Muraviev chose as his vice minister a very industrious individual, Count Lamsdorff, the councilor of the Foreign Ministry (Vitte, 2: 112–13; *Holstein Papers*, 4: 1–2).

30. Nikhamin, "Diplomatiia," 169–70.

31. Putiata himself was not employed by Korea, but the lieutenants and noncoms of the military mission all were in the service of the Korean government (Jordan to Mac-Donald, no. 25, Seoul, Mar. 10, 1897, EA, FO 405–73, pp. 66–68).

32. Plancy to Hanotaux, DP, no. 62, Seoul, Mar. 10, 1897, FA, Korea, PE, 8: 25–27.

33. Nikhamin, "Russko-iaponskie otnosheniia," 360–61.

34. Nikhamin, "Russko-iaponskie otnosheniia," 361–62; *Nichi-Ro kosho-shi*, pt. 1: 278; Motono to Okuma, no. 20, St. Petersburg, Mar. 25, 1897, JA, TEL 1897/2922–2923.

35. Nikhamin, "Russko-iaponskie otnosheniia," 362.

36. *Ibid.*, 362–63.

37. Muraviev, according to Motono's telegram and *Nichi-Ro kosho-shi*; Vice Minister Shishkin, according to Nikhamin.

38. Motono to Okuma, no. 20, St. Petersburg, Mar. 25, 1897, JA, TEL 1897/2922–2923; *Nichi-Ro kosho-shi*, pt. 1: 279; Nikhamin, "Russko-iaponskie otnosheniia," 362.

39. Okuma to Motono, no. 31, Tokyo, Mar. 27, 1897, JA, TEL 1897/2665.

40. Motono to Okuma, no. 26, St. Petersburg, Apr. 15, 1897, JA, TEL 1897/0073.

41. Nikhamin, "Russko-iaponskie otnosheniia," 363–66.

42. Okuma to Motono, no. 44, Tokyo, Apr. 27, 1897, JA, TEL 1897/0830–0831. For proposed pay and housing arrangements, see the agreement enclosed in Jordan to Salisbury, no. 40, Apr. 28, 1897, "Confidential," EA, FO 405–73, p. 84. Japanese documents speak of 160 officers. Actually plans called for the engagement of 27 officers out of a total of 161 military instructors. The breakdown was as follows: 18 infantry officers, 97 infantry noncoms, 1 artillery officer, 1 director of the arsenal, 8 artillerymen, 4 grooms for the artillery horses, 4 farriers and saddlers, 1 cavalry officer, 4 cavalry noncoms, 1 fortifications officer, 4 noncoms for diverse other services, 1 professor of military science for the cadet academy, 1 professor of military science for the school for officers, 1 director of the military mission, 1 commandant, 1 assistant commandant, 1 chief surgeon, 1 surgeon, 5 hospital attendants, 1 musical director, 3 musicians, 2 extras (see contract enclosed in Plancy to French foreign minister, DP, no. 108, Seoul, Oct. 4, 1897, FA, Korea, PE, 8: 89–95).

43. Jordan to MacDonald, no. 38, Seoul, Apr. 27, 1897, "Confidential," EA, FO 405–73, pp. 83–84.

44. In communicating his conversation with Kojong to Jordan, Kato did not mention the king's reference to the Min-Lobanov agreement. Instead he asserted that the king pleaded his inability to resist the strong pressure being brought to bear on him by Waeber (Jordan to MacDonald, no. 38, Seoul, Apr. 27, 1897, "Confidential"). Kato may have used this version in an attempt to enlist Jordan's support.

45. According to Jordan, the idea for a reduction in the number of Russian personnel had been suggested as a compromise by the acting minister of the Board of War, whom he regarded, perhaps for that reason, as "of a peculiarly unstable character even for a Korean" (Jordan to MacDonald, Seoul, May 7, 1897, EA, FO 405–73, p. 88).

46. Kato told Jordan that he had assured the king that the Japanese government would assume full responsibility of guaranteeing him against the consequences of the

rejection of the entire Russian scheme. No mention of this declaration is made in Okuma's account of the conversation.

47. Okuma to Motono, no. 45, Tokyo, Apr. 28, 1897, JA, TEL 1897/0835–0836; Jordan to MacDonald, no. 38, Seoul, Apr. 27, 1897, "Confidential." "The minister resident in Korea reports [that the] King of Korea seemed anxious and repentant concerning the matter," Okuma telegraphed to Motono. "The minister resident in Korea is doing his best to prevent [the] consummation of [the] project."

48. Plancy to Hanotaux, DP, no. 79, Seoul, May 20, 1897, FA, Korea, PE, 8: 70–73.

49. Okuma to Motono, no. 46, Tokyo, Apr. 30, 1897, JA, TEL 1897/0840.

50. Nikhamin, "Russko-iaponskie otnosheniia," 370–71.

51. Okuma to Motono, no. 44, Tokyo, Apr. 27, 1897, JA, TEL 1897/0830–0831.

52. *Nichi-Ro kosho-shi*, pt. 1: 279; Nikhamin, "Russko-iaponskie otnosheniia," 366–67.

53. Nikhamin, "Russko-iaponskie otnosheniia," 367–68.

54. *Ibid.*, 368–69.

55. Motono to Okuma, no. 34, St. Petersburg, May 5, 1897, JA, TEL 1897/0159; *Nichi-Ro kosho-shi*, pt. 1: 279.

56. Okuma to Motono, no. 48, Tokyo, May 4, 1897, JA, TEL 1897/0853.

57. Okuma to Motono, no. 49, Tokyo, May 4, 1897, JA, TEL 1897/0857. Okuma informed Motono of the developments. In a telegram, dated May 4, he instructed him to use his "best endeavors" to obtain deferment of the Russian military adviser project pending adjustment of the general question of Korean military organization between the Japanese government and Rosen (Okuma to Motono, no. 48, Tokyo, May 4, 1897, JA, TEL 1897/0853).

58. Nikhamin, "Russko-iaponskie otnosheniia," 370–72. The various dispatches disagree on the exact number and functions of personnel involved. Kato telegraphed at first that Kojong had sanctioned the employment of seventeen officers, then that it was a matter of only ten officers, the other seven probably being engineers for the arsenal (Okuma to Motono, no. 49, Tokyo, May 4, 1897). Jordan too wrote of seventeen Russians; three officers, ten noncommissioned officers, one doctor, three musicians, and a saddler (Jordan to MacDonald, Seoul, May 7, 1897, EA, FO 405–73, p. 88). Muraviev told Motono that Waeber had arranged for the engagement of some seventeen officers and three musicians (Motono to Okuma, no. 38, May 19, 1897, JA, TEL 1897/0223–0224), but the request handed to Waeber on May 5 was for twenty-one Russian instructors, according to Nikhamin (Nikhamin, "Russko-iaponskie otnosheniia," 370–72). This seems to be the most accurate figure, for it corresponds to the breakdown given by Waeber himself in a letter to Foreign Minister Yi: three officers and ten noncoms as instructors, as well as a professor of military science, a personnel director, a musical director, two assistant directors, and three artillerymen (Letter enclosed in Plancy to French foreign minister, DP, no. 108, Seoul, Oct. 4, 1897, FA, Korea, PE, 8: 89–95. See also Motono to Okuma, no. 40, Tokyo, May 24, 1897, JA, TEL 1897/0246–0247; *Nichi-Ro kosho-shi*, pt. 1: 279).

59. Nikhamin, "Russko-iaponskie otnosheniia," 372.

60. C. G. von Treutler to Hohenlohe-Schillingsfürst, no. A. 74, Tokyo, May 5, 1897, with a postscript dated May 6, 1897, GA.

61. Sill to Sherman, no. 270, DS, May 10, 1897, and no. 269, May 8, 1897, USDD, Korea, 134/13.

62. Okuma to Nishi, no. 22, Tokyo, May 5, 1897, JA, TEL 1897/0862–0863.

63. Sherman to Sill, Washington, May 8, 1897, and Sill to Sherman, Seoul, May 8, 1897, USDD, Korea, 134/13; Sill to Sherman, no. 270, DS, Seoul, May 10, 1897. To the British consul general, on the other hand, Kato revealed that he keenly resented American interference and related that he had warned Sill to stand aloof from the contest. He had hinted to Sill, Kato told Jordan, that otherwise he might be obliged to take official notice of his conduct (Jordan to MacDonald, Seoul, May 7, 1897, EA, FO 405–73, pp. 87–88).

64. Harmand to Hanotaux, DP, no. 47, Tokyo, May 12, 1897, FA, Korea, PE, 8: 61–66.

65. Motono to Okuma, no. 38, May 19, 1897, JA, TEL 1897/0223–0224.

66. E. de Cartier de Marchienne to Foreign Minister de Favereau, no. 93/32, Tokyo, May 19, 1897, BA, CPL, série reliée, 3: 17.

67. Motono to Okuma, no. 40, Tokyo, May 24, 1897, JA, TEL 1897/0246–0247; *Nichi-Ro kosho-shi*, pt. 1: 279.

68. Nikhamin, "Russko-iaponskie otnosheniia," 373–77.

69. *Ibid.*, 378–79; Afanas'ev I and Grudzinskii, no. 230, p. 20.

70. Nikhamin, "Russko-iaponskie otnosheniia," 379–80; Okuma to Hayashi, no. 65, Tokyo, July 28, 1897, JA, TEL 1897/1094.

71. Okuma to Hayashi, no. 66, Tokyo, Aug. 4, 1897, JA, TEL 1897/1101–1102. The question of the relative responsibility of Waeber, the tsarist government, and King Kojong for the dispatch of Russian military instructors had exercised the Japanese for some time. Believing that Waeber personally had been behind the Min mission and that he wished to remain in Korea as the Russian representative or, failing that, to resign his post and become adviser to the Korean Household Department, Okuma had instructed Motono on April 8 of that year to hint to the tsarist government confidentially at a favorable opportunity that Waeber's continued stay in Korea in either capacity was "highly undesirable." Motono was to suggest also confidentially that inasmuch as the Japanese government had appointed a minister resident for Korea, the naming by the tsarist government of an official of equal rank would be "highly desirable in adjusting all matters of joint interest" (Okuma to Motono, no. 34, Tokyo, Apr. 8, 1897, JA, TEL 1897/0763). Motono discussed the above with the vice minister of foreign affairs and the director of the Asiatic Department. Both declared that it was improbable that Waeber would remain in Korea in any capacity. The matter of the appointment of a minister resident, they said, would probably be submitted to the tsar (Motono to Okuma, no. 25, St. Petersburg, Apr. 12, 1897, JA, TEL 1897/0066). On May 7 Okuma instructed Motono to renew his efforts to secure the removal of Waeber from Korea. Foreign Minister Yi Wan-yong had privately asked Kato if there was a way to acquaint the tsarist government with the true situation. He was afraid that the Korean government might yield to Waeber's efforts to succeed Le Gendre as adviser to the Household Department and that St. Petersburg might consent without realizing that the king and the Korean government disliked Waeber and did not want him to remain (Okuma to Motono, no. 50, Tokyo, May 7, 1897, JA, TEL 1897/0868). Motono replied that in Kapnist's opinion Speyer would never allow that Waeber should remain in Korea in any capacity. Motono advised that Okuma hint at the matter to Speyer (Motono to Okuma, no. 36, St. Petersburg, May 9, 1897, JA, TEL 1897/0179). As speculation about the pending employment of Waeber by the Korean government was renewed in the Japanese press in July, Speyer revealed to Treutler the exchange of

telegrams between Tokyo and St. Petersburg. According to Speyer, Muraviev himself, rather than Kapnist, had remarked that Speyer would oppose Waeber's stay and would hardly be inclined to assume the post in Seoul if Waeber became adviser of the Korean government. In view of the well-known jealousy between the two representatives, Muraviev regarded such an arrangement as impracticable. More talkative than usual during an excursion to the mountains with his German colleague, Speyer implied that he had had something to do with the foundering of the project. He voiced his opposition to Waeber becoming an adviser to the Korean government on the ground that it would necessarily arouse public opinion, especially in Japan. The Russian representative in Seoul, he said, had enough influence to carry out his mission without such help, which would constantly keep awake the mistrust of all of Russia's opponents. Believing that Speyer's point of view corresponded to that of St. Petersburg, Treutler suspected that the alarming rumors about Korea were being spread by the Okuma administration, which was resorting to any means to beat back the attempts of its political rivals to bring down the government. It hoped to impress the public by creating professed difficulties and then overcoming them, he explained (Treutler to Hohenlohe-Schillingsfürst, no. A. 98, Tokyo, July 27, 1897, GA).

72. Nikhamin, "Russko-iaponskie otnosheniia," 380–81.

73. Plancy to Hanotaux, DP, no. 98, Seoul, Aug. 12, 1897, FA, Korea, PE, 8: 84–87.

74. Okuma to Hayashi, no. 66, Tokyo, Aug. 4, 1897, JA, TEL 1897/1101–1102, *Nichi-Ro kosho-shi*, pt. 1: 279.

75. Hayashi to Okuma, no. 60, St. Petersburg, Aug. 5, 1897, JA, TEL 1897/0474; Nikhamin, "Russko-iaponskie otnosheniia," 382.

76. On the tenth according to Nikhamin, on the fifteenth or perhaps the day before, judging from a telegram dispatched by Hayashi on August 15.

77. A compromise suggested by Vice Minister of Foreign Affairs Komura to Speyer that several Japanese officers be given administrative positions in the Korean War Ministry did not find favor in St. Petersburg (Nikhamin, "Russko-iaponskie otnosheniia," 383).

78. Hayashi to Okuma, no. 61, St. Petersburg, Aug. 15, 1897, JA, TEL 1897/ 0504–0505; Nikhamin, "Russko-iaponskie otnosheniia," 383.

79. Plancy to French foreign minister, DP, no. 100, Aug. 24, 1897, FA, Korea, PE, 8: 87–88.

80. Plancy to French foreign minister, DP, no. 108, Oct. 4, 1897, FA, Korea, PE, 8: 89–95; Sill to Sherman, no. 279, DS, Seoul, Aug. 3, 1897, and no. 286, Seoul, Sept. 9, 1897, USDD, Korea, 134/13.

81. Baron von Waecker-Gotter to Hohenlohe-Schillingsfürst, no. 57, Belgrad, Apr. 14, 1897, GA.

82. Nikhamin, "Russko-iaponskie otnosheniia," 388. See also Baron Rosen, 1: 143–46.

83. Hanotaux to Harmand, no. 55, Paris, June 29, 1897, DDF, ser. 1, 13: 436–37. Hanotaux was alluding to Marquis Ito, who had spoken to Captain de Labry, former French military attaché in Tokyo, and himself of the inevitable breakup of China and her apportionment into political and especially commercial spheres of interest (above and Hanotaux to Harmand, no, 61, Paris, July 23, 1897, "Confidential," DDF, ser. 1, 13: 465–66). The Japanese minister to France, Kurino, confided to Labry that Japan wished to take part in whatever measures the European powers might take in regard to

China. In the event of discord in the concert, Japan would side with the stronger side, which at the moment was Russia (Labry's note of his conversation with Kurino, enclosed in Hanotaux to Harmand, no. 58, Paris, July 13, 1897, "Very Confidential," DDF, ser. 1, 13: 459–60). Marquis Ito, who had also stopped over in Paris on his way to the Diamond Jubilee of Queen Victoria, spoke to Hanotaux of a similiar desire on the part of his government to avoid any complications with Russia, notably on the Korean issue. In case of need, he said, Tokyo might solicit the friendly mediation of Paris with St. Petersburg (Hanotaux to Harmand, no. 61, Paris, July 23, 1897, "Confidential," DDF, ser. 1, 13: 465–66). Ito had been ordered to visit Austria, France, Germany, Italy, and Russia "in a private capacity" (Okuma to Hayashi, no. 54, Tokyo, June 23, 1897, JA, TEL 1897/0956). However, he did not go to Russia, because the tsarist government was preoccupied with festivities in connection with the visits of the emperor of Germany and the president of France, and he skipped Berlin, partly because he did not wish to offend St. Petersburg by missing it alone, partly because he was averse to meeting with the German authorities (Kato to Okuma, no. 60, London, Aug. 9, 1897, JA, TEL 1897/0478). Harmand, to whom Hanotaux wrote of his conversation with Rosen, questioned that the Russian minister, whatever his professional qualifications and patriotic will might be, could obtain an entente with Japan in the face of Anglo-Saxon influence and British opposition. For it to be otherwise, he wrote, one would have to assume that the entente which Rosen had in mind would go so far as the drawing up of a precise document with reciprocal engagements and mutual guarantees directed more or less against England. "But can one believe," Harmand asked rhetorically, "that the Russian imperial government, with the prudence which distinguishes it and the long patience which characterizes its aims, would be disposed to go that far, to enter into [an agreement] at the price of evident and undoubted dangers, with a state so megalomaniac, launched on a path of scabrous experiences and a very uncertain future, with a nation so ardent, capricious, [and] impressionable, whose demographic conditions are such, moreover, that expansion beyond its insular limits, in view of the constitution of a "Greater Japan," constitutes for it still less of an ambition, perhaps, than a necessity of life or death?" He predicted that "all the defects of the government and of the race of Japan . . . would be exaggerated and would show themselves without restraint the moment the government and people knew themselves assured of the obligatory support of a European great power." Harmand admitted that the Japanese desired an alliance with a European great power "despite the natural antipathies which separate the two races." Yet in his mind few of them could think of an alliance with Russia, who, he believed, was regarded by almost the entire nation as the "unavoidable enemy" (*l'ennemie nécessaire*). He dismissed Rosen's views of Japan as illusions derived from his memories of the country where he had served as a young secretary and predicted that they would be dissipated upon contact with New Japan. Although he agreed that Russia and Japan could arrive at an entente limited to Korean affairs, Harmand remarked that this would not be easy because the notions of Speyer and Rosen were far apart. Speyer had frequently confided to Harmand that it was his ambition, if he were left the time, to let whatever influence the Japanese still exercised disappear from the entire peninsula. Speyer wanted to exclude even the Americans from Korea, chasing them at first from the official and semi-official positions which they occupied in the government and forcing them subsequently by a system of annoyances and impediments of all sorts to abandon their commercial and industrial enterprises in the country. Harmand commented that Speyer had apparently failed to grasp the causes which explained and justified the American expansion, a social phenomenon involving an intricacy of facts too great to be limited by his will and zeal. According to information confided by Speyer to Harmand, Rosen had not accepted the Tokyo post until assured by the tsarist government of the acceptance of his own views regarding Russo-Japanese relations, expounded in a long memorial to Nicholas. Going beyond a mere rapprochement with Japan, Rosen advocated "an *entente* on all points, *cost what it may*" (*coûte que coûte*). He did so on two grounds: the progress achieved by Japan in recent years and the fact that if war between Japan and Russia was inevitable, as Speyer claimed, one should try to delay it until Russia was ready to sustain it in the Far East. which was not the case at present. Relating that he had received new instructions enjoining him to conform scrupulously to Rosen's policy, Speyer did not conceal his sadness at the curtailment of his ambitions. His job would be easier, he said, but less interesting. Ever suspicious, Harmand speculated that Rosen might have different instructions from those he had communicated to Hanotaux and that Rosen and Speyer might be conspiring to lull the attention of the French and of the Japanese by pacific declarations while pursuing in reality the opposite. France could not be too vigilant, he remarked, in view of the grave consequences which could befall her because of her ties with the tsarist government and the obligations which could ensue therefrom (Harmand to Acting Foreign Minister Jules Meline, no. 68, Tokyo, Aug. 18, 1897, "Confidential," DDF, ser. 1, 13: 499–505).

84. Treutler to Hohenlohe-Schillingsfürst, no. A. 108, Tokyo, Aug. 25, 1897, GA.
85. Nikhamin, "Russko-iaponskie otnosheniia," 388–89.
86. Okuma to Hayashi, no. 70, Tokyo, Aug. 26, 1897, JA, TEL 1897/1138; *Nichi-Ro kosho-shi*, pt. 1: 280.
87. Nikhamin, "Russko-iaponskie otnosheniia," 389–90. Rosen's recollection in his memoirs that he received this answer after the replacement of Okuma is incorrect.
88. Okuma to Hayashi, no. 70, Tokyo, Aug. 26, 1897.
89. Hayashi to Okuma, no. 63, St. Petersburg, Sept. 2, 1897, JA, TEL 1897/0527–0528.
90. Okuma to Hayashi, no. 75, Tokyo, Sept. 9, 1897, JA, TEL 1897/1174–1175.
91. Nikhamin, "Russko-iaponskie otnosheniia," 391–94.
92. Plancy to Hanotaux, DP, no. 32, Seoul, Oct. 28, 1896, FA, CP, Korea, 6: 304–6; Radolin to Hohenlohe-Schillingsfürst, no. 88, St. Petersburg, Feb. 26, 1896, GA, FSU/Korea, 1/20.
93. Treutler to Hohenlohe-Schillingsfürst, no. A. 90, Tokyo, June 17, 1897, GA.
94. Synn, 247.
95. Waeber turned over the legation on September 7 (Sill to Sherman, no. 285, DS, Seoul, Sept. 7, 1897, USDD, Korea, 134/13).
96. Nikhamin, "Russko-iaponskie otnosheniia," 394; Plancy to French foreign minister, DP, no. 108, Seoul, Oct. 4, 1897, FA, Korea, PE, 8: 89–95.
97. Afanas'ev I and Grudzinskii, no. 231, pp. 20–21; Nikhamin, "Russko-iaponskie otnosheniia," 396.
98. Allen to Sherman, no. 20, DS, Seoul, Oct. 14, 1897, USDD, Korea, 134/13.
99. Allen to Sherman, no. 27, DS, Seoul, Oct. 25, 1897, USDD, Korea, 134/13.
100. Plancy to French foreign minister, DP, no. 114, Seoul, Oct. 30, 1897, FA, Korea, PE, 8: 101–2; Nikhamin, "Russko-iaponskie otnosheniia," 396.
101. Nikhamin, "Russko-iaponskie otnosheniia," 399.
102. Plancy to Hanotaux, DP, no. 18, Seoul, Aug. 18, 1896, FA, CP, Korea, 6:

258–62. The sending of Pokotilov had been hastened by word that the French had secretly offered a loan to Korea (Romanov, *Rossiia v Man'chzhurii*, 149).

103. "Memorandum respecting the proposed Russian loan," composed by Wilkinson and enclosed in Hillier to MacDonald, Seoul, Aug. 22, 1896, "Confidential," EA, FO 405–72, pp. 58–59; Allen to Olney, no. 243, DS, Seoul, Nov. 4, 1896, USDD, Korea, 134/13; J. N. Jordan to MacDonald, no. 9, Seoul, Feb. 10, 1897, "Confidential," EA, FO 405–73, p. 55. Chargé Kato warned the Korean Foreign Office toward the end of January 1897 that under the agreement concluded between their countries, the Korean customs revenue could not be pledged as security for any other purpose until the Japanese loan had been paid off.

104. Nikhamin, "Russko-iaponskie otnosheniia," 402–9; *Nichi-Ro kosho-shi*, pt. 1: 280; Romanov, *Rossiia v Man'chzhurii*, 159; Motono to Okuma, no. 17, St. Petersburg, Mar. 8, 1897, JA, TEL 1897/2874; Allen to Sherman, no. 12, DS, Seoul, Oct. 5, 1897, USDD, Korea, 134/13. Alekseev and his staff were quartered in one of several brick buildings which had been constructed that summer, ostensibly for the use of Kojong, Due to a large influx of Russians into Seoul during 1897, all the houses suitable for European residence in the foreign quarter were occupied (Jordan to MacDonald, no. 109, Seoul, Dec. 4, 1897, "Confidential," EA, FO 405–80, pp. 33–34).

105. Allen to Sherman, no. 12, DS, Seoul, Oct. 5, 1897, and Allen to Alfred E. Buck, no. 11, L. & C., Seoul, Nov. 9, 1897, USDD, Korea, 134/13.

106. Nikhamin, "Russko-iaponskie otnosheniia," 408–9; Speyer to Min, no. 59, Seoul, Sept. 24 (Oct. 6), 1897, "A-Weon-An." See also *Ku Han'guk oegyo munso*, 17: 469–70; Allen to Sherman, no. 17, Seoul, Oct. 8, 1897, USDD, Korea, 134/13; and EA, FO 405–73, p. 152.

107. Nikhamin, "Russko-iaponskie otnosheniia," 409. The question of Alekseev's appointment as financial adviser was not supposed to have been raised until later and the taking over of the Customs Service, not at all. In his report to St. Petersburg on October 7 Speyer made no mention of his attempts to obtain control of the customs revenues for Alekseev, thereby depriving the tsarist government of the opportunity to stop him.

108. Allen to Sherman, no. 17, DS, Seoul, Oct. 9, 1897, USDD, Korea, 134/13. According to information which the American minister obtained from Korean acquaintances, the monarch was allegedly "so hedged in by the Russian party as to be unable to speak privately to his friends." One of three Russian interpreters was said to be on duty in Kojong's rooms at all times. The whole situation was practically in the hands of the Russian chief interpreter, Allen added, because the new representative and his staff were unfamiliar with the Korean language, Korean affairs, and Korean individuals.

109. Jordan to MacDonald, no. 79, Seoul, Oct. 8, 1897, EA, FO 405–73, pp. 153–54. Brown had been appointed by Waeber. His removal was directed less at Brown himself than at Waeber, whom Speyer disliked and whose policy he sought to reverse.

110. Allen to Sherman, no. 19, DS, Seoul, Oct. 14, 1897, USDD, Korea, 134/13. Jordan confided to Allen that he would try to obtain the removal of Min for having denied him an audience with the monarch.

111. Translations of the letter from the Korean finance minister to and of Speyer's note, enclosed in Jordan to Salisbury, no. 86, Seoul, Oct. 18, 1897, "Confidential," EA, FO 405–73, pp. 161 and 165–66; the Seoul *Independent*, Oct. 30, 1897.

112. Nikhamin, "Russko-iaponskie otnosheniia," 410–12.

113. Allen to Sherman, no. 27, DS, Seoul, Oct. 25, 1897, and no. 29, DS, Seoul, Nov. 7, 1897, USDD, Korea, 134/13; Min to MacDonald, Seoul, Oct. 28, 1897, and MacDonald to Min, Peking, Oct. 29, 1897, enclosed in Allen to Sherman, no 29; Nikhamin, "Russko-iaponskie otnosheniia," 413.

114. Nikhamin, "Russko-iaponskie otnosheniia," 412–15; Allen to Sherman, no. 29, DS, Seoul, Nov. 7, 1897, USDD, Korea, 134/13. As will be recalled, Min Chong-muk had become foreign minister when Yi Wan-yong had refused to sign the contracts of the Russian military instructors. His own removal for obstructing Russian wishes was the more ironical, because Min had the reputation of being genuinely pro-Russian. His lack of cooperation with Speyer had been due less to political opposition than to timidity of soul and the disinclination to shoulder responsibility.

115. Translation of the agreement, enclosed in Allen to Sherman, no. 29. A slightly different wording will be found in the translation published in the *Independent* on November 16, 1897. See also MacDonald to Salisbury, no. 77, tel., Peking, Dec. 3, 1897, EA, FO 405–73, p. 153. The above agreement together with control of the Korean army gave Russia a virtual protectorate over Korea, the American minister noted. Attributing the development primarily to the weakness and desire for personal safety of Kojong, he opined that the condition of the Korean people could not be worse than it was already and that they would welcome Russian control. Allen comprehended that the tsarist government did not desire to incorporate Korea into the Russian empire. Not only would it be difficult and expensive to protect the peninsula, but an independent Korea would form "a useful buffer between the real Russian domain and the rising and warlike Empire of Japan" (Allen to Sherman, no. 29, DS, Seoul, Nov. 7, 1897, USDD, Korea, 134/13).

116. Nikhamin, "Russko-iaponskie otnosheniia," 415–16. In a letter to Alfred E. Buck, who had succeeded Dun as American minister in Japan, Allen remarked that Speyer had such power that he could "make and unmake cabinets at his discretion" (Allen to Buck, no. 11, L. & C., Seoul, Nov. 9, 1897, USDD, Korea, 134/13).

117. "Here and There," *Independent*, Seoul, Nov. 11, 1897; "Editorial Notes," *Independent*, Nov. 18, 1897; Allen to Sherman, no. 30, DS, Seoul, Nov. 9, 1897, USDD, Korea, 134/13; Nikhamin, "Russko-iaponskie otnosheniia," 417. Pak was eventually replaced by Min Chong-muk, who had been removed as foreign minister for "lack of energy" in dismissing Brown (Allen to Sherman, no. 45, DS, Seoul, Dec. 17, 1897, USDD, Korea, 134/14). While the American minister had with reason attributed Pak's removal to the influence of Speyer, Pak's courageous protest was ascribed by some people to Allen's prodding, for he had been a good friend of Pak and had conducted his legation to Washington in 1888. Allen assured the State Department that he had not been involved in any way. In view of the "Russian complications," he had made a point of keeping away from all the Koreans concerned with the "difficult question"; he had not seen Pak since it had become known that he was to reenter the cabinet and had not communicated with him either directly or indirectly (Allen to Sherman, no. 32, DS, Seoul, Nov. 11, 1897, USDD, Korea, 134/13).

118. Nikhamin, "Russko-iaponskie otnosheniia," 421–23.

119. "An Approaching Crisis," *The Kobe Chronicle*, Nov. 1, 1897.

120. Okuma to Hayashi, no. 90, Tokyo, Nov. 6, 1897, JA, TEL 1897/1309–1310; Nishi to Hayashi, no. 99, Tokyo, Dec. 16, 1897, JA, TEL 1897/1433–1434.

121. Nikhamin, "Russko-iaponskie otnosheniia," 442–46, 455–56.

122. Jordan to MacDonald, no. 11, Seoul, Jan. 22, 1898, "Confidential," EA, FO

405–80, p. 60; Jordan to MacDonald, no. 6, Seoul, Jan. 9, 1898, "Confidential," EA, FO 405–80, pp. 57–58. In a conversation with Muraviev on January 19, 1898, O'Conor observed that the moral of such incidents as the removal of Brown, the rumored dismissal of Kinder (an English railroad engineer in China), and the entry of British ships into Port Arthur was to show how England and Russia could thwart and annoy each other and how much more sensible it would be for them to come to a friendly understanding reconciling their respective interests. "I completely agree with you on this," Muraviev declared (O'Conor to Salisbury, no. 21, St. Petersburg, Jan. 20, 1898, "Confidential," EA, FO 405–76, p. 67*, and FO 405–80, p. 39).

123. Speyer to Cho Pyong-sik, no. 4, Seoul, Jan. 15 (27), 1898, *Ku Han'guk oegyo munso*, 17: 509–10. See also enclosure in Jordan to MacDonald, no. 14, Seoul, Jan. 31, 1898, "Confidential," EA, FO 405–80, pp. 70–71. On February 22 Speyer informed the Korean government that the Russo-Korean Bank would commence transactions on March 1 (Speyer to Acting Foreign Minister Min Chong-muk, no. 7, Seoul, Feb. 10 [22], 1898, *Ku Han'guk oegyo munso*, 17: 516).

124. Jordan to MacDonald, no. 14, Seoul, Jan. 31, 1898, "Confidential," EA, FO 405–80, pp. 70–71. In addition to the Russo-Korean Bank there were three or four Japanese banks and an agency of the Hong Kong and Shanghae Bank in Korea.

125. Plancy to French foreign minister, DP, no. 139, Seoul, Jan. 31, 1898, FA, Korea, PE, 8: 133–36. Yi To-chai, the new minister of foreign affairs, had been a provincial governor in 1894. Appointed minister of education following the murder of Queen Min, he had resigned in 1896 as a protest against the hair-cutting ordinance. The French representative foresaw that Yi To-chai would not remain in office long, partly because of his timidity and ignorance of foreign affairs, partly because he was not likely to succeed in regulating the questions which interested St. Petersburg. Yi Yong-in, who succeeded as minister of justice, had come into Kojong's good graces as a fortuneteller. He was fond of alcohol and when intoxicated committed foolish acts.

126. Allen to Sherman, no. 70, DS, Seoul, Feb. 2, 1898, USDD, Korea, 134/14.

127. Nikhamin, "Russko-iaponskie otnosheniia," 465–66.

128. Jordan to MacDonald, no. 21, Seoul, Feb. 24, 1898, EA, FO 405–80, pp. 82–83.

129. Extract from the *Independent* of Feb. 24, 1898, enclosed in Jordan to MacDonald, no. 21, Seoul, Feb. 24, 1898, EA, FO 405–80, pp. 82–84, and in Allen to Sherman, no. 76, DS, Seoul, Feb. 24, 1898, USDD, Korea, 134/14. A French version of the memorial is enclosed in Plancy to French foreign minister, DP, no. 148, Seoul, Mar. 3, 1898, FA, Korea, PE, 8: 152–53.

130. *Independent*, Feb. 26, 1898, enclosed in Allen to Sherman, no. 77, DS, Seoul, Feb. 26, 1898, USDD, Korea, 134/14.

131. Allen to Sherman, no. 86, DS, Seoul, Mar. 14, 1898, USDD, Korea, 134/14; Jordan to MacDonald, no. 22, Seoul, Feb. 24, 1898, EA, FO 405–80, p. 84; Plancy to French foreign minister, DP, no. 148, Seoul, Mar. 3, 1898, FA, Korea, PE, 8: 149–51.

132. Krien to Hohenlohe-Schillingsfürst, no. 26, Seoul, Feb. 27, 1898, GA.

133. Allen to Sherman, no. 77, DS, Seoul, Feb. 26, 1898, USDD, Korea, 134/14.

134. With a sword-cane, according to Krien.

135. Jordan to MacDonald, no. 22, Seoul, Feb. 24, 1898, and enclosed extract from the *Independent* of Feb. 24, EA, FO 405–80, pp. 84–85. See also enclosure in Allen to Sherman, no. 76, DS, Seoul, Feb. 24, 1898.

136.   Speyer to Min Chong-muk, no. 8, Seoul, Feb. 11 (23), 1898, *Ku Han'guk*

oegyo munso, 17: 517; *Independent*, Feb. 25, 1898, enclosed in Allen to Sherman, no. 77, DS, Feb. 26, 1898.

137. *Ibid.*

138. Plancy to French foreign minister, DP, no. 148, Seoul, Mar. 3, 1898.

139. Allen to Sherman, no. 77, DS, Seoul, Feb. 26, 1898, USDD, Korea, 134/14. Ironically the Russian legation under Waeber had much to do with starting the *Independent* and encouraging the Independence Club, which Jaisohn headed. In a later dispatch Allen remarked that Jaisohn's naturalization seemed to have been in violation of the Revised Statutes as quoted in Diplomatic Instructions, Par. 140, but that Jaisohn had been accepted as an American citizen by Sill when he had shown his passport, issued by Secretary Olney, and that he himself had not raised the question when Jaisohn's case had demanded consideration (Allen to Sherman, no. 101, DS, Seoul, Apr. 27, 1898, USDD, Korea, 134/14).

140. Nikhamin, "Russko-iaponskie otnosheniia," 472–73. Bülow was known as a skillful intriguer. Even his mother-in-law, Donna Laura Minghetti, complained that he made a secret of everything. "He takes you by the arm, leads you to the window and says: Don't say anything, but there's a little dog down there who's pissing" (Cecil, 282).

141. Krien to Hohenlohe-Schillingsfürst, no. 26, Seoul, Feb. 27, 1898, GA; Jordan to MacDonald, no. 26, Mar. 3, 1898, "Confidential," EA, FO 405–80, pp. 87–88; Plancy to foreign minister, DP, no. 148, Seoul, Mar. 3, 1898, FA, Korea, PE, 8: 149–51; Allen to Sherman, no. 89, DS, Seoul, Mar. 19, 1898, USDD, Korea, 134/14.

142. Jordan to MacDonald, no. 26, Seoul, Mar. 3, 1898, "Confidential," EA, FO 405–80, pp. 87–88. According to Synn, Kojong actually ordered Yi Chai-sun to assassinate Kim in an effort to weaken the Russian position in his country (Synn, 264).

143. Plancy to French foreign minister, DP, no. 151, Seoul, Mar. 5, 1898, FA, Korea, PE, 8: 156–57.

144. Jordan to MacDonald, no. 26, Seoul, Mar. 3, 1898, "Confidential," EA, FO 405–80, pp. 87–88.

145. Jordan to Salisbury, no. 26, Seoul, Mar. 3, 1898, "Confidential."

146. Ye of Yangkeun, Joung of Chungju Joung, Kim of Andong, Ho of Jungpeng, and Ye and Im of Kangneung.

147. Extract from the Seoul *Independent* of Mar. 10, 1898, enclosed in Jordan to MacDonald, no. 30, Seoul, Mar. 10, 1898, EA, FO 405–80, pp. 91–92.

148. Allen to Sherman, no. 87, DS, Seoul, Mar. 14, 1898, USDD, Korea, 134/14.

149. Jordan to MacDonald, no. 35, Seoul, Apr. 20, 1897, "Confidential," EA, FO 405–73, p. 79; Jordan to MacDonald, no. 70, Seoul, Sept. 10, 1897, "Confidential," Brown to Hunt, Seoul, Aug. 26, 1897, tel., Hunt to Jordan, Pusan, Aug. 30, 1897, "Private," and Hunt to Jordan, Pusan, Sept. 1, 1897, EA, FO 405–73, pp. 135–38.

150. Allen to Sherman, no. 8, DS, Seoul, Oct. 1, 1897, and enclosed protocol of Sept. 22, as well as Allen to Sherman, no. 16, DS, Seoul, Oct. 8, 1897, USDD, Korea, 134/13.

151. Plancy to Hanotaux, DP, no. 115, Seoul, Oct. 21, 1897, FA, Korea, PE, 8: 103–5.

152. Jordan to MacDonald, no. 93, Seoul, Oct. 29, 1897, EA, FO 405–73, p. 173.

153. Jordan to MacDonald, no. 110, Seoul, Dec. 5, 1897, "Confidential," EA, FO 405–80, p. 24. Jordan gave the vice admiral's name incorrectly as "Dubaroff."

154. Allen to Sherman, no. 48, DS, Seoul, Dec. 20, 1897, USDD, Korea, 134/14.

"There has been much comment here of late over the report that the Russian Government was acquiring a very large portion of the ground allotted to the General Foreign Settlement at Chemulpo," Allen recounted. "I was fortunate enough to see the plan of this land, made for Mr. de Speyer by a Russian officer, and saw for myself, that while they have acquired a tract of land just outside the Settlement limits but within the treaty area, larger than the Settlement itself, their purchase within the Settlement limits is not greatly in excess of that of the Japanese, though both are larger than the Municipal Council will probably care to allow." Speyer himself had shown the plan to Allen because he was eager to secure a piece of ground secured by the American firm of Townsend and Co. in the middle of the tract. Mr. Townsend, who did a large rice mill business in Chemulpo, did not care to antagonize the Russians and exchanged the land for another site to the great satisfaction of the Russian legation.

155. J. H. Hunt to Jordan, Pusan, Jan. 23, 1898, "Confidential," Kamni at Pusan to Cho Pyong-sik, undated, and Jordan to MacDonald, no. 12, Seoul, Jan. 28, 1898, "Confidential," EA, FO 405–80, pp. 61–62.

156. Korean Foreign Office to the Kamni of Pusan, undated, "Confidential," and Jordan to MacDonald, no. 13, Seoul, Jan. 30, 1898, "Confidential," EA, FO 405–80, pp. 69–70.

157. Jordan to MacDonald, no. 18, Seoul, Feb. 12, 1898, "Confidential," EA, FO 405–80, p. 73.

158. Plancy regarded Yi as a prisoner of the anti-Russian party. He suspected that the English and German representatives had counseled him against granting the coaling station to Russia. When Speyer refused to attend the meeting called by Yi for February 14, Plancy excused himself on the pretext of another engagement (Plancy to French foreign minister, DP, no. 145, Seoul, Feb. 19, 1898, FA, Korea, PE, 8: 139–41). Speyer told Allen that he had suggested the change because Cho had begun dealing with the Japanese (Allen to Sherman, no. 87, DS, Seoul, Mar. 14, 1898, USDD, Korea, 134/14).

159. Plancy to French foreign minister, DP, no. 145, Seoul, Feb. 19, 1898, FA, Korea, PE, 8: 139–41, and DP, no. 152, Seoul, Mar. 9, 1898, FA, Korea, PE, 8: 157–62; Allen to Sherman, no. 87, DS, Seoul, Mar. 14, 1898, USDD, Korea, 134/14.

160. Plancy to French foreign minister, DP, no. 152, Mar. 9, 1898, FA, Korea, PE, 8: 157–62; Allen to Sherman, no. 87, DS, Seoul, Mar. 14, 1898, USDD, Korea, 134/14; Jordan to MacDonald, no. 32, Mar. 12, 1898, EA, FO 405–80, pp. 94–95.

161. *Independent*, Mar. 8, 1898, enclosed in Allen to Sherman, no. 87, DS, Seoul, Mar. 14, 1898.

162. Plancy to French foreign minister, DP, no. 152, Mar. 9, 1898, FA, Korea, PE, 8: 157–62.

163. Allen to Sherman, no. 86, DS, Seoul, Mar. 14, 1898, USDD, Korea 134/14.

164. Jordan to MacDonald, no. 30, Seoul, Mar. 10, 1898.

165. Krien to Hohenlohe-Schillingsfürst, no. 34, Seoul, Mar. 18, 1898, GA.

166. For data on the consular sites question, see Plancy to French foreign minister, DP, no. 145, Seoul, Feb. 19, 1898, FA, Korea, PE, 8: 139–41; Nishi to Hayashi, no. 23, St. Petersburg, Mar. 1, 1898, JA, TEL 1898/1649–1650; Allen to Sherman, no. 81, DS, Seoul, Mar. 7, 1898, USDD, Korea, 134/14; Jordan to Salisbury, no. 28, Seoul, Mar. 7, 1898, "Confidential," EA, FO 405–880, p. 88.

167. Jordan to MacDonald, no. 32, Seoul, Mar. 12, 1898, EA, FO 405–80, pp. 94–95.

168. Jordan to MacDonald, no. 30, Seoul, Mar. 10, 1898.

169. Nikhamin, "Russko-iaponskie otnosheniia," 475–76; Plancy to French foreign minister, DP, no. 148, Seoul, Mar. 3, 1898, and DP, no. 152, Mar. 9, 1898; Synn, 265.

170. Nikhamin, "Russko-iaponskie otnosheniia," 476–79; Hayashi to Nishi, no. 25, St. Petersburg, Mar. 9, 1898, JA, TEL 1898/0287; Synn, 265. The other, more pressing, Far Eastern problems to which Muraviev referred are traced in the following two chapters.

171. Plancy to French foreign minister, DP, no. 156, Seoul, Mar. 14, 1898, FA, Korea, PE, 8: 166–72.

172. Nikhamin, "Russko-iaponskie otnosheniia," 479–80.

173. Speyer to Min, no. 11, Seoul, Feb. 23 (Mar. 7), 1898, "A Weon-an," and *Ku Han'guk oegyo munso*, 17: 521–22. The text published in the *Independent* on March 12, 1898, and transmitted by the American and German representatives differed in wording somewhat; it had been rendered into English from a Korean translation of the Russian note (Allen to Sherman, no. 89, DS, Seoul, Mar. 19, 1898; Krien to Hohenlohe-Schillingsfürst, no. 34, Mar. 18, 1898, GA). The version prepared by the British legation sounded more threatening (Jordan to MacDonald, no. 32, Seoul, Mar. 11, 1898, EA, FO 405–80, pp. 94–95). The French translation relayed by Plancy was elegant and temperate. While the text dispatched by Jordan declared that if Korea no longer needed the Russian military instructors and the financial adviser, "the Russian Government will act accordingly, and make such arrangement as may be considered to be necessary in its own interests," Speyer wrote to Min in the French version that if his emperor and government considered the military instructors and financial adviser of no importance to them, "the Russian government would take all measures necessary to conform to your desire, but in that case your government will have to assure its independence all by itself in the future." There was no implied threat, no mention of Russian interests. See also Nishi to Hayashi, no. 27, Tokyo, Mar. 14, 1898, JA, TEL 1898/1684–1685. For a copy of the Chinese text, see *Nihon gaiko bunsho*, vol. 31, pt. 1, pp. 155–56, and *Ku Han'guk oegyo munso*, 17: 522–53.

174. Plancy to French foreign minister, DP, no. 152, Seoul, Mar. 9, 1898, and DP, no. 156, Seoul, Mar. 14, 1898, FA, Korea, PE, 8: 166–72; Treutler to Hohenlohe-Schillingsfürst, no. A. 31, Tokyo, Mar. 14, 1898, GA.

175. Krien to Hohenlohe-Schillingsfürst, no. 34, Seoul, Mar. 18, 1898, GA.

176. Plancy to French foreign minister, DP, no. 156, Seoul, Mar. 14, 1898, FA, Korea, PE, 8: 166–72; Nikhamin, "Russko-iaponskie otnosheniia," 481–82.

177. Plancy to French foreign minister, DP, no. 155, Seoul, Mar. 12, 1898, FA, Korea, PE, 8: 162–65.

178. *Independent*, Mar. 12, 1898, enclosed in Allen to Sherman, no. 89, DS, Mar. 19, 1898.

179. Plancy to French foreign minister, DP, no. 155, Seoul, Mar. 12, 1898, FA, Korea, PE, 8: 162–65.

180. Plancy to French foreign minister, DP, no. 155, Seoul, Mar. 12, 1898; *Independent*, Mar. 10, 1898, enclosed in Allen to Sherman, no. 86, DS, Mar. 14, 1898. Nothing was done to Kim at this time, but on September 14, when Speyer was no longer in Korea, he was arrested on charges of having tried to poison the emperor and crown prince, was banished without a trial, and later executed (Synn, 281).

181. Allen to Sherman, no. 89, DS, Seoul, Mar. 19, 1898; Nishi to Hayashi, no. 25, Mar. 8, 1898, JA, TEL 1898/1667–1668.

182. Plancy to French foreign minister, DP, no. 156, Seoul, Mar. 14, 1898, FA, Korea, PE, 8: 166–72.

183. Krien to Hohenlohe-Schillingsfürst, no. 36, Seoul, Mar. 19, 1898, GA, FSU/ Korea, 1/26; Synn, 267.

184. According to *Nichi-Ro kosho-shi* the reply had been drafted by Kato and used by the Korean government verbatim (1: 282).

185. *Independent*, Mar. 15, 1898, enclosed in Allen to Sherman, no. 89, DS, Mar. 19, 1898, and in Krien to Hohenlohe-Schillingsfürst, no. 34, Seoul, Mar. 18, 1898. Slightly different translations will be found enclosed in Jordan to MacDonald, no. 34, Seoul, Mar. 15, 1898, EA, FO 405–80, pp. 98–99, and in Plancy to French foreign minister, DP, no. 156, Seoul, Mar. 14, 1898, FA, Korea, PE, 8: 166–72. In the present version Min began by apologizing for an unavoidable delay in his answer; in the two other translations he stated that he had written Speyer requesting him to wait three days for a definite reply.

186. Krien to Hohenlohe-Schillingsfürst, no. 36, Seoul, Mar. 29, 1898, GA, FSU/ Korea, no. 1/26.

187. Nikhamin, "Russko-iaponskie otnosheniia," 483–85.

188. Jordan to MacDonald, no. 34, Seoul, Mar. 15, 1898, and no. 35, Seoul, Mar. 18, 1898, "Confidential," EA, FO 405–80, pp. 98–99, 101. The "ulterior purpose" was, of course, to free Russian hands in Manchuria and facilitate an agreement with Japan.

189. Jordan to MacDonald, no. 34, Seoul, Mar. 15, 1898, EA, FO 405–80, pp. 98–99, and Krien to Hohenlohe-Schillingsfürst, no. 34, Seoul, Mar. 18, 1898.

190. Allen to Sherman, no. 90, DS, Seoul, Mar. 22, 1898, USDD, Korea, 134/14. Allen was as bewildered as his colleagues by what seemed to him "a sudden change of policy by the Russian Government in direct opposition to that pursued by the Russian Representative" (Allen to Sherman, no. 89, DS, Seoul, Mar. 19, 1898).

191. Plancy to Hanotaux, DP, no. 158, Seoul, Mar. 17, 1898, FA, Korea, PE, 8: 173–75.

192. Speyer to Min, no. 12, Mar. 5 (17), 1898, "A-Weon An," and *Ku Han'guk oegyo munso*, 17: 526–27. Two slightly different translations of Speyer's note may be found in Jordan to MacDonald, no. 35, Seoul, Mar. 18, 1898, EA, FO 405–80, p. 100, and in the *Independent* of Mar. 19, 1898, enclosed in Allen to Sherman, no. 89, DS, Seoul, Mar. 19, 1898. They concur with the above translation, made straight from the original Russian document, that Speyer alluded only indirectly to the employment of other foreign officers when he congratulated Korea on her ability to do without any foreign assistance. According to the French rendition, prepared from a Korean version of the note, Speyer stated that the tsarist government was relieving the military instructors and financial adviser of their duties with the understanding that the promise had been made that Korea would administer herself "without having recourse to the assistance of foreigners, whoever they might be" (Plancy to French foreign minister, DP, no. 159, Seoul, Mar. 24, 1898, FA, Korea, PE, 8: 192–97). The French translation was in line with what Speyer had told Jordan and corresponded to the statement published in the *Official Gazette* (see below).

193. Plancy to Hanotaux, DP, no. 158, Seoul, Mar. 17, 1898, FA, Korea, PE, 8: 173–75; Allen to Sherman, no. 89, DS, Seoul, Mar. 19, 1898. According to Plancy, six lieutenants and twenty noncoms were involved; Jordan gives a figure of six commissioned and twenty-one noncommissioned officers (Jordan to MacDonald, no. 37,

Seoul, Mar. 23, 1898, EA, FO 405–80, p. 105). The legation guard now totalled 150 men according to Plancy, 130 according to Jordan. *Nichi-Ro kosho-shi* asserts that the military instructors left on March 22, the legation guards on the twenty-third (1: 283).

194. Plancy to Hanotaux, DP, no. 158, Seoul, Mar. 17, 1898, FA, Korea, PE, 8: 173–75.

195. *Ibid.*

196. Allen to Sherman, no. 89, DS, Seoul, Mar. 19, 1898.

197. Montebello to Hanotaux, no. 73, tel., St. Petersburg, Mar. 18, 1898, FA, Korea, PE, 8: 177–78, and DDF, ser. 1, 14: 155; O'Conor to Salisbury, no. 109, St. Petersburg, Mar. 19, 1898, EA, FO 405–80, pp. 65–66.

198. Montebello to Hanotaux, DP, no. 30, St. Petersburg, Mar. 18, 1898, FA, Korea, PE, 8: 180–85; Hanotaux to Plancy, no. 9, Paris, Mar. 25, 1898, FA, Korea, PE, 8: 199–200.

199. O'Conor to Salisbury, no. 102, St. Petersburg, Mar. 16, 1898, EA, FO 405–80, p. 65.

200. O'Conor to Salisbury, no. 115, St. Petersburg, Mar. 23, 1898, EA, FO 405–80, pp. 66–67.

201. Kato to Nishi, London, Mar. 19, 1898, as relayed by Hayashi to Nishi, no. 40, St. Petersburg, Mar. 19, 1898, JA, TEL 1898/0345–0346. "Have [the] Japanese Government had any share in the affairs and what does this semi-official communication signify?" Kato queried of Nishi in reporting the above.

202. Jordan to MacDonald, no. 36, Seoul, Mar. 21, 1898, "Confidential," EA, FO 405–80, pp. 102–3.

203. Extract from the *Journal de Saint-Petersbourg* of Mar. 11/23, 1898, enclosed in O'Conor to Salisbury, no. 115, St. Petersburg, Mar. 23, 1898, EA, FO 405–80, pp. 66–68.

204. Geoffray to Hanotaux, DP, no. 159, London, Mar. 21, 1898, "Confidential," FA, Korea, PE, 8: 190–92.

205. Min Chong-muk to Speyer, Mar. 18, 1898, enclosed in Jordan to MacDonald, no. 36, Mar. 21, 1898, "Confidential," Seoul, Mar. 21, 1898, and in Plancy to French foreign minister, DP, no. 159, Seoul, Mar. 24, 1898, FA, Korea, PE, 8: 192–97.

206. Speyer to Min, no. 14, Seoul, Mar. 7 (19), 1898, *Ku Han'guk oegyo munso*, 17: 529. See also enclosure in Plancy to French foreign minister, DP, no. 159, Seoul, Mar. 24, 1898, FA, Korea, PE, 8: 192–97.

207. Plancy to French foreign minister, DP, no. 159, Seoul, Mar. 24, 1898, FA, Korea, PE, 8: 192–97.

208. Plancy to French foreign minister, DP, no. 160, Seoul, Mar. 25, 1898, FA, Korea, PE, 8: 200–2.

209. Jordan to MacDonald, no. 37, Seoul, Mar. 23, 1898, EA, FO 405–80, p. 105. Alekseev went to Japan accompanied by his interpreter, a Mr. Garfield. He settled down in Yokohama, where the Russian military attaché and the navy attaché and his adjutant lived also. Alekseev's position was that of a commercial agent. Count von Leyden, who had succeeded Treutler as German minister, was convinced that Alekseev's task would be to wait quietly until he could be used again at a given moment, without losing touch with conditions in Japan (Leyden to Hohenlohe-Schillingsfürst, no. A. 59, Tokyo, May 10, 1898, "Confidential," GA).

210. Cho Pyong-sik to Speyer, Apr. 1, 1898, EA, FO 405–80, p. 112.

211. Allen to Sherman, no. 41, DS, Seoul, Dec. 1, 1898, USDD, Korea, 134/14;

Jordan to MacDonald, no. 107, Seoul, Dec. 1, 1897, EA, FO 405–80, p. 29; Mac-Donald to Salisbury, no. 162, Peking, Dec. 1, 1897, EA, FO 405–76, pp. 39–40.

212. Allen to Sherman, no. 90, DS, Seoul, Mar. 22, 1898, USDD, Korea, 134/14; Jordan to MacDonald, no. 37, Seoul, Mar. 23, 1898, EA, FO 405–80, p. 105.

213. Leyden to Hohenlohe-Schillingsfürst, no. A. 42, Tokyo, Apr. 6, 1898, GA, FSU/Korea, 1/26.

214. Allen to Sherman, no. 90, DS, Seoul, Mar. 22, 1898; Jordan to MacDonald, no. 37, Seoul, Mar. 23, 1898.

215. Matiunin, who had been commissioner of trade on the Russo-Korean frontier for about a decade, came as chargé d'affaires. Except for Waeber who had been promoted in conjunction with his appointment to another country, Russia posted chargés rather than ministers to Korea. Matiunin had traveled to Seoul by way of Tokyo, where he had conferred with Rosen and the Japanese vice minister of foreign affairs (Plancy to French foreign minister, DP, no. 161, Seoul, Mar. 28, 1898, FA, Korea, PE, 8: 203).

216. Allen to Sherman, no. 96, DS, Seoul, Apr. 12, 1898, USDD, Korea, 134/14. The Deer Island affair dragged on so long partly because the minister of the navy in St. Petersburg did not have on hand the large sum needed for the purchase of the coaling depot site and was scrounging for the required funds (Plancy to French foreign minister, DP, no. 145, Seoul, Feb. 19, 1898, FA, Korea, PE, 8: 139–41). It was settled eventually by a conference of all the foreign representatives except Speyer, who nonetheless sanctioned the proposals there made. At the suggestion of Allen, who had secured Speyer's approval of his proposition, the whole low-lying end of Deer Island, some 900,000 square meters in all, was allotted for a general foreign settlement, with the Russian coaling station forming part of the general foreign settlement. "As all ground within these limits will be subject to Municipal Regulations, it seemed to offer the best solution of a vexed question," Allen commented (Allen to Sherman, no. 111, DS, Seoul, June 3, 1898, USDD, Korea, 134/14; Jordan to Salisbury, no. 5, tel., Seoul, June 1, 1898, EA, FO 405–80, p. 112).

Chapter Twenty-three

1. Schrecker, 1–35; Oscar Rosen, 148–65.

2. Foreign Secretary Marschall to Navy Secretary Vice Admiral von Hollmann, no. 1628, Berlin, Mar. 11, 1895, "Top Secret," *Grosse Politik*, 14: 5–7.

3. *Briefe Wilhelms II and den Zaren*, 291.

4. The response itself is not available, but Nicholas told Hohenlohe about it on September 11, 1895, When Hohenlohe replied that Wilhelm had informed him of the correspondence and had warned him that it must be kept secret, Nicholas nodded in confirmation. As Lobanov had not mentioned anything about the exchange, Hohenlohe concluded that Nicholas had kept the matter to himself (Hohenlohe to Wilhelm II, St. Petersburg, Sept. 13, 1895, *Grosse Politik*, 14: 12, note **. See Hohenlohe Schillingsfürst, 2: 521 ff).

5. Hollman to Marschall, Berlin, Apr. 17, 1895, "Secret," *Grosse Politik*, 14: 7–11.

6. Hohenlohe-Schillingsfürst to Marschall, no. 15, tel., Werki, Sept. 1, 1895, and Marschall to Hohenlohe-Schillingsfürst, no. 62, Berlin, Sept, 2, 1895, *Grosse Politik*, 14: 11–14.

7. Memorandum of Rotenhan, Berlin, Sept. 9, 1895, *Grosse Politik*, 14: 14–15.

8. Memorandum by Gesselin of conversation with Aoki on Mar. 14, 1896, dated Mar. 15, 1896, EA, FO 405–70, pp. 129–30.

9. Memorandum of Rotenhan, Berlin, Sept. 9, 1895.

10. Wilhelm II to German Foreign Ministry, Theerbude, Sept. 23, 1895, *Grosse Politik*, 14: 16–17.

11. Generaloberst (Lieutenant Colonel) Helmuth von Moltke, *Erinnerungen, Briefe, Dokumente 1877–1916*, 187–92; Arthur Diósy, *The New Far East*, frontispiece.

12. Wilhelm II to Nicholas II, Jagdhaus Rominten, September 26, 1895, in *Briefe Wilhelms II and den Zaren*, 294–95.

13. Moltke, 187–92.

14. Radolin to Hohenlohe-Schillingsfürst, no. 374, St. Petersburg, Oct. 13, 1895, GA, FSU/China, 20/58. Yet Nicholas did not share Wilhelm's apprehension of a Sino-Japanese alliance. Although he agreed that the yellow race might imperil Europe, he realized that the hatred between the Chinese and the Japanese was too great for them to unite in a dangerous brotherhood.

15. Marschall to Radolin, no. 656, Berlin, Oct. 25, 1895, *Grosse Politik*, 14: 17–18.

16. Radolin to Hohenlohe-Schillingsfürst, no. 415, St. Petersburg, Oct. 29, 1895, *Grosse Politik*, 14: 18–20. When Kaiser Wilhelm read Radolin's dispatch, he scribbled on the margin next to the assertion that Germany was probably the only great power who had not demanded anything for herself, "*Kommt noch*" (yet to come).

17. Schenck to German Foreign Ministry, no. 64, tel., Peking, Oct. 29, 1895, *Grosse Politik*, 14: 20.

18. Schenck to German Foreign Ministry, no. 77, tel., Peking, Nov. 30, 1895, *Grosse Politik*, 14: 21–22.

19. Schenck to Hohenlohe-Schillingsfürst, no. 269, Peking, Dec. 15, 1895, *Grosse Politik*, 14: 23.

20. Marschall to Schenck, no. 4, tel., Berlin, Feb. 1, 1896, *Grosse Politik*, 14: 24.

21. Radolin to Hohenlohe-Schillingsfürst, no. 69, St. Petersburg, Feb. 15, 1896, and memorandum of Councilor Klehmet in the German Foreign Ministry, Berlin, Mar. 18, 1896, *Grosse Politik*, 14: 24–26.

22. Memorandum of Klehmet, Berlin, Mar. 18, 1896, *Grosse Politik*, 14: 25–26.

23. Marschall's record of his conversation with Li, Berlin, June 19, 1896, *Grosse Politik*, 14: 27–34.

24. Heyking to Hohenlohe-Schillingsfürst, no. 102, Peking, Aug. 22, 1896, "Secret," *Grosse Politik*, 14: 34–36.

25. Memorandum of Knorr, Berlin, Nov. 9, 1896, "Top Secret," *Grosse Politik*, 14: 36–39.

26. Radolin to Hohenlohe-Schillingsfürst, no. 514, St. Petersburg, Nov. 19, 1896, "Secret," *Grosse Politik*, 14: 39–41.

27. *Ibid.*

28. "*Es ist doch deprimierend, dass ein chinesischer Gesandter uns dämlichen Deutschen erst klar machen muss, was zu unserem Nutzen und Frommen wir in China zu tun haben*" (Wilhelm II to Hohenlohe-Schillingsfürst, Altona, Nov. 27, 1896, and Hohenlohe-Schillingsfürst to Wilhelm II, Berlin, Nov. 23, 1896, *Grosse Politik*, 14: 42–43).

29. Memorandum of Klehmet, Berlin, Nov. 28, 1896, *Grosse Politik*, 14: 43–46.

30. Hollman to Marschall, Berlin, Dec. 6, 1896, "Secret," Marschall to Wilhelm II, Berlin, Feb. 19, 1897, Heyking to Hohenlohe-Schillingsfürst, no. A. 69, Peking, May 1897, and Rotenhan to Radolin, no. 660, Berlin, June 22, 1897, "Secret," *Grosse Politik*, 14: 47, 49–54. Francius and Zeye were accompanied by Francius's nephew and by Navy Lieutenant *Graf* Zeppelin.

31. Kuo-chi Lee, *Die chinesische Politik*, 128–29.

32. *Ibid.*, 130.

33. Heyking to German Foreign Office, no. 64, Peking, Dec. 16, 1896, and footnotes, *Grosse Politik*, 14: 48; Marschall to Wilhelm II, Berlin, Feb. 19, 1897, *Grosse Politik*, 14: 49–50; Kuo-chi Lee, 131.

34. Radolin to Hohenlohe-Schillingsfürst, no. 590, St. Petersburg, Dec. 18, 1896, *Grosse Politik*, 14: 48–49.

35. Marschall to Wilhelm II, Berlin, Feb. 19, 1897, *Grosse Politik*, 14: 49–50.

36. Memorandum of the German Foreign Office, dated Mar. 19, 1897, as cited in footnote * of *Grosse Politik*, 14: 46.

37. Heyking to Hohenlohe-Schillingsfürst, no. A. 69, Peking, May 5, 1897, "Secret," *Grosse Politik*, 14: 50–54.

38. Rotenhan to Radolin, no. 660, Berlin, June 22, 1897, "Secret," *Grosse Politik*, 14: 54.

39. Radolin to Hohenlohe-Schillingsfürst, no. 286, St. Petersburg, July 3, 1897, *Grosse Politik*, 14: 55.

40. Hohenlohe-Schillingsfürst to Rotenhan, no. 9, Alt-Aussee, July 12, 1897, *Grosse Politik*, 14: 57.

41. Radolin to Hohenlohe, no. 294, St. Petersburg, July 8, 1897, *Grosse Politik*, 14: 56–57. When Wilhelm read about the regret expressed by Cassini at the time lost by Germany, he remarked that he himself had wanted to obtain a harbor three years ago. Councilor Alfred von Kiderlen-Wächter commented that the clever Russian said so afterwards to veil his negative attitude.

42. Bülow to German Foreign Ministry, no. 10, St. Petersburg, Aug. 11, 1897, and memorandum of Bülow, Berlin, Aug. 17, 1897, *Grosse Politik*, 14: 58–60.

43. Heyking to German Foreign Office, no. 56, Peking, Oct. 1, 1897, and a detailed report, dated Oct. 3, 1897, *Grosse Politik*, 14: 61–62.

44. Tschirschky to Hohenlohe-Schillingsfürst, no. 382, St. Petersburg, Oct. 14, 1897, *Grosse Politik*, 14: 62–64.

45. *Grosse Politik*, 14: 62–63. The Russians raised and then dropped the question of priority of anchorage, admitting that it would require an agreement with China regarding the bay, which did not exist. The recollections of Wilhelm concerning the background of the Kiaochow action in his book, *Ereignisse und Gestalten*, are marred by many slips of memory.

46. Schrecker, 31–33; Oscar Rosen, 148–65; MacDonald to Salisbury, no. 161, Peking, Dec. 1, 1897, EA, FO 405–76, pp. 37–39. Kuo-chi Lee gives the name of the village as Chang-chia-chuang (Kuo-chi Lee, 138). MacDonald described the governor as "an ignorant and bigoted anti-foreign official of the old-fashioned type."

47. Wilhelm II to German Foreign Office, Neues Palais, Nov. 6, 1897, *Grosse Politik*, 14: 67.

48. Hohenlohe-Schillingsfürst to Wilhelm II, Berlin, Nov. 6, 1897, *Grosse Politik*, 14: 68.

49. Wilhelm II to Bülow, no. 137, Neues Palais, Nov. 7, 1897, and Wilhelm II to Hohenlohe-Schillingsfürst of the same date, *Grosse Politik*, 14: 69–71. The statement

allegedly made by Muraviev to Baron Hayashi, the Japanese minister, that Germany had merely informed Russia of the seizure of Kiaochow after the act (Pooley, *Secret Memoirs*, 97) is incorrect.

50. Wilhelm II to Hohenlohe-Schillingsfürst, Neues Palais, Nov. 7, 1897, *Grosse Politik*, 14: 69.

51. Wilhelm II to Bülow, no. 137, Neues Palais, Nov. 7, 1897, *Grosse Politik*, 14: 69–71.

52. Hohenlohe-Schillingsfürst to Wilhelm II, Berlin, Nov. 7, 1897, *Grosse Politik*, 14: 71.

53. Rotenhan to Tschirschky, no. 324, Berlin, Nov. 8, 1897, *Grosse Politik*, 14: 72–73.

54. Rotenhan to Wilhelm II, Berlin, Nov. 10, 1897 (actually dispatched during the night of November 9 to 10), and Tschirschky to German Foreign Ministry, no. 300, Nov. 9, 1897, *Grosse Politik*, 14: 73–74.

55. *Ibid.*

56. Rotenhan to Bülow, no. 140, Berlin, Nov. 9, 1897, *Grosse Politik*, 14: 75–76. Bishop Anzer happened to be in Berlin at the time of the Kiaochow incident. According to a memorandum by Rotenhan of November 7, Anzer expressed to him the hope that Germany would take advantage of the opportunity to occupy Kiaochow, which he described as by far the best base for Germany in every respect. In an audience with the Kaiser on November 16 the bishop argued that this was the last opportunity for the German empire to acquire any territory in Asia and to strengthen its weakened prestige. "Whatever it may cost, we must under no circumstances give up Kiaochow," Anzer declared. Contending that Kiaochow had a future that would be greater from a commercial and industrial point of view than that of Shanghai, Anzer asserted that the occupation of Kiaochow would surprise no one in the Orient, as everyone had been expecting it already for a long time (*Grosse Politik*, 14: 76, footnote).

57. Wilhelm II to German Foreign Ministry, as relayed by Rotenhan to Bülow, no. 146, tel., Berlin, Nov. 11, 1897, *Grosse Politik*, 14: 77–78.

58. Hohenlohe-Schillingsfürst to Wilhelm II, Berlin, Nov. 11, 1897, tel., *Grosse Politik*, 14: 78–79.

59. *Grosse Politik*, 14: 78 and 79 footnotes.

60. Hohenlohe-Schillingsfürst to Wilhelm II, Berlin, Nov. 11, 1897, tel., *Grosse Politik*, 14: 79–81.

61. *Grosse Politik*, 14: 80–81, footnotes.

62. Hohenlohe-Schillingsfürst to Hatzfeldt, no. 1429, Berlin, Nov. 13, 1897, tel., "Top Secret," *Grosse Politik*, 14: 81–83.

63. Hohenlohe-Schillingsfürst to Hatzfeldt, no. 326, Berlin, Nov. 16, 1897, tel., "Secret," *Grosse Politik*, 14: 86–87.

64. Muraviev to Osten-Sacken, St. Petersburg, Nov. 13, 1897, *Grosse Politik*, 14: 83–84.

65. Hohenlohe-Schillingsfürst to Osten-Sacken, Berlin, Nov. 14, 1897, *Grosse Politik*, 14: 84.

66. Schrecker, 34; Oscar Rosen, 148–65; Nishi to Odagiri, Tokyo, Nov. 21, 1897, JA, TEL 1897/1348; Memorandum by Gosselin of conversation with Aoki on Mar. 14, 1896. Governor Li Ping-heng had wished to resist the German encroachment, but Peking had not given the necessary permission, lest the Kiaochow affair escalate into a much wider conflict (Schulman, "China's Response," 199–200).

67. The word "*Besitzergreifung*" could be translated as "occupation" as well as

"seizure." Translated literally it means "taking possession." "Seizure" seems more appropriate, because elsewhere the Kaiser wrote of the *"Besetzung"* (occupation) and subsequent *"Besitzergreifung"* (seizure) of Kiaochow.

68. Memorandum dated Berlin, Nov. 15, 1897, *Grosse Politik*, 14: 85–86.

69. Holstein to Bülow, no. 31, Berlin, Nov. 18, 1897, *Grosse Politik*, 14: 89.

70. *Grosse Politik*, 14: 89–90, footnote.

71. Muraviev to Osten-Sacken, St. Petersburg, Nov. 4/16, 1897, tel., *Grosse Politik*, 14: 90.

72. Hohenlohe-Schillingsfürst to Wilhelm II, Berlin, Nov. 18, 1897, *Grosse Politik*, 14: 90–91.

73. Comment of Wilhelm II, dated Nov. 18, 1897, *Grosse Politik*, 14: 91. Seeking for some common action by Germany and England to disconcert Russia, Hatzfeldt proposed to Lord Salisbury that their governments make a joint démarche in Washington regarding the American annexation of Hawaii. Salisbury replied that there was particular irritation with Britain in the United States at the moment and that in view of the character of Secretary of State John Sherman (the brother of General William Tecumseh Sherman), if he were to make representations concerning Hawaii now, he would have to be prepared for no less than insults, which he would prefer to avoid. Besides, he thought that such a step would actually hasten the annexation. Since Salisbury said that he was not in a position to make any concessions in Africa without equivalent compensation, Hatzfeldt remarked that one might then seek in Asia a way in which England could show her obligingness. As Salisbury knew, Hatzfeldt proceeded, Germany had been forced by recent developments in China to occupy Kiaochow Bay to compel the Chinese to make due reparations. The German government had no other purpose in occupying the place, but he personally doubted, in view of his knowledge of conditions in Germany, that public opinion, which had long blamed the government for not having obtained any benefits from its intervention in the Sino-Japanese War, would allow Germany to withdraw. It was here, he declared, that Germany would see where to find her friends and that England, if she wished and if she understood her own interests, could accommodate Germany. Should London not be prepared to do so, he warned, Germany might have to come to terms with another power, should the latter raise objections, even at the risk of a high price. Salisbury understood Hatzfeldt's hint. He observed that he could not give a binding reply without studying the matter; offhand, however, he saw no reason why England should raise any objections to German occupation of a point on the Chinese coast. Hatzfeldt got the impression from this very confidential conversation that Salisbury, "though fearful and irresolute," realized that the occupation of Kiaochow by Germany did not run counter to English interests, indeed was required by them to prevent exclusive Russian domination of the northern coast of China. He thought it possible, therefore, that Salisbury's consent could be obtained for the permanent occupation of Kiaochow or of another place, so long as the latter was not too close to the English sphere of interest (Hatzfeldt to German Foreign Ministry, no. 219, London, Nov. 17, 1897, "Secret," *Grosse Politik*, 14: 92–94). Although Hatzfeldt faithfully hinted that Germany might have to make a deal with Russia regardless of the price if England failed to cooperate with her and although he asked his government for permission to bring further pressure on Salisbury by informing him that Germany had been invited to join the Franco-Russian alliance, he personally disagreed with the notion that an agreement with Russia was desirable at any cost. "If the price is too high, the deal remains bad, whatever

the position of England may be," he remarked. To set German policy in accordance with Russian wishes appeared to him as "the worst of all solutions." Not even "the possession of half of China" could make up for its disadvantages (Hatzfeldt to German Foreign Ministry, London, Nov. 18, 1897, "Secret, Private for Baron von Holstein," *Grosse Politik*, 14: 94–95).

74. Heyking had wanted to demand that the construction of a railway between Kiaochow and Peking and mining operations along the line be reserved exclusively for German entrepreneurs but had been directed by the German Foreign Ministry to proceed cautiously on this point lest the Chinese be driven into Russian arms (*Grosse Politik*, 14: 98–99, footnote). Nonetheless the British, Japanese and other members of the diplomatic corps presumed that Germany had asked for a monopoly on the building of railroads and adjoining mines in Shantung (Yano to Nishi, no. 53, Peking, Nov. 25, 1897, no. 57, Peking, Nov. 28, 1897, and no. 58 of same date, JA, TEL 1897/ 0671, 0679–0681). According to Chinese sources, Germany demanded the formation of a joint Sino-German company to construct the railroad and adjoining mines in Shantung (Schulman, "China's Response," 202). Informing Satow of the substance of the German demands telegraphed by Yano, Vice Minister Komura expressed doubt that China would ever consent to the construction of railways in Shantung province, which she regarded as sacred because it contained the birthplace of Confucius. Komura surmised that Germany had put forward the demand with the expectation that it would be refused in order to obtain something else, possibly a coaling station. Komura told Satow that the Japanese government would not send any warships to Kiaochow. He gave the same assurance to Chargé Treutler, adding that Japan had no intention of protesting against the German action and that the critical language of the Japanese press did not represent the views of the Japanese cabinet (Satow to Salisbury, no. 246, Tokyo, Dec. 2, 1897, EA, FO 405–76, p. 3).

75. Heyking to German Foreign Ministry, no. 73, Peking, Nov. 21, 1897, *Grosse Politik*, 14: 98–99.

76. Hohenlohe-Schillingsfürst to Wilhelm II, Berlin, Nov. 21, 1897, *Grosse Politik*, 14: 99–100.

77. Heyking to German Foreign Ministry, no. 77, Peking, Nov. 22, 1897, *Grosse Politik*, 14: 102. Full name of Count de Sercey supplied by his daughter-in-law, the Countess Ellen de Sercey of Monticello, Florida.

78. Rotenhan to Osten-Sacken, Berlin, Nov. 22, 1897, *Grosse Politik*, 14: 97–98. "This is the sort of tone I like toward foreign states," Wilhelm had declared when he had read the original draft of the note, drawn up by Hohenlohe (*Grosse Politik*, 14: 97 footnote).

79. Wilhelm II to Hohenlohe-Schillingsfürst, no. 2, Kiel, Nov. 22, 1897, *Grosse Politik*, 14: 100–101.

80. Wilhelm II to Hohenlohe-Schillingsfürst, unnumbered, Kiel, Nov. 22, 1897, *Grosse Politik*, 14: 101.

81. *Grosse Politik*, 14: 100 footnote.

82. Yano to Nishi, no. 51, Peking, Nov. 22, 1897, "Special," JA, TEL 1897/ 0061–0063; Nishi to Yano, no. 48, Tokyo, Nov. 24, 1897, JA, TEL 1897/1362. The Japanese minister in Vienna deemed it desirable from the point of view of treaty revision with Austria-Hungary that Japan take no hostile attitude toward Germany "at least for the present," since Austria-Hungary was always influenced by German politics. "If I may be permitted to make my suggestion," Takahira Kogoro telegraphed, "it

appears to me advisable to induce China to settle [the] German trouble without any delay, as it has been generally presumed here, that [the] political interest of [the] European countries is being rapidly transferred to Eastern Asia from South Eastern Europe, and this presumption is being well [?] proved by recent events (Kogoro to Nishi, Vienna, Nov. 21, 1897, relayed in Hayashi to Nishi, no. 58, St. Petersburg, Nov. 21, 1897, JA, TEL 1897/0659–0660).

83. Nishi to Hayashi, no. 94, Tokyo, Nov. 20, 1897, JA, TEL 1897/1342; Nishi to Yano, no. 43, Tokyo, Nov. 21, 1897, JA, TEL 1897/1349; Nishi to Hayashi, no. 96, Tokyo, Nov. 24, 1897, JA, TEL 1897/1356. The British under secretary of state told the Japanese minister as his "purely personal opinion" that he could hardly believe that Germany had occupied Kiaochow without some understanding with Russia, as the latter had secured Chinese consent to use the bay as winter station for her fleet (Japanese minister in England, Kato, to Japanese Foreign Office, no. 84, London, Nov. 13 [23?], 1897, relayed in Hayashi to Nishi, St. Petersburg, Nov. 25, 1897, JA, TEL 1897/0672–0673).

84. Nishi to Yano, no. 47, Tokyo, Nov. 24, 1897, JA, TEL 1897/1361. It was generally felt in Japan that the German action in China had been unnecessarily hasty and that a prolonged or possibly permanent occupation of such a strategically important place as Kiaochow Bay by a Western power would imperil the peace of the Far East (Satow to Salisbury, no. 245, Tokyo, Dec. 1, 1897, EA, FO 405–76, p. 2).

85. Yano to Nishi, no. 55, Peking, Nov. 26, 1897, JA, TEL 1897/0675.

86. Hayashi to Nishi, no. 83, St. Petersburg, Nov. 24, 1897, JA, TEL 1897/ 0670–0671.

87. Miyaoka to Japanese Foreign Office, no. 52, Nov. 26, 1897, relayed in Hayashi to Nishi, St. Petersburg, Nov. 27, 1897, JA, TEL 1897/0678–0679; Nishi to Yano, no. 57, Nov. 28, 1897, JA, TEL 1897/1383.

88. Yano to Nishi, no. 53, Peking, Nov. 25, 1897, JA, TEL 1897/0671.

89. Nishi to Yano, Special 59, Tokyo, Nov. 30, 1897, JA, TEL 1897/1387. Li Hung-chang, whom Yano saw on December 5, praised the wisdom of the above suggestions, so that Yano was led to believe that he had more or less influenced the Chinese statesmen (Yano to Nishi, no. 61, Peking, Dec. 5, 1897, JA, TEL 1897/ 0692–0693).

90. Note of Hanotaux, Nov. 24, 1897, DDF, ser. 1, 13: 605–6. When Hanotaux asked whether this meant deflecting the Germans to the south where the French were, Mohrenheim protested animatedly that that was not the case; the place under consideration was in the neighborhood of the English possessions or claims. Mohrenheim told Kurino that the occupation of Kiaochow did not greatly alarm Russia or France, because the bay was relatively distant from areas in which the two powers were interested. England might be more sensitive, Mohrenheim added, but he thought that instead of seeking to block the German move, she might find it much easier to counterbalance it by occupying some port herself (Kurino to Nishi, no. 66, Paris, Nov. 29, 1897, JA, TEL 1897/0682–0683).

91. *Grosse Politik*, 14: 104–5 footnote. According to his memoirs, Witte was consistently opposed to German retention of Kiaochow (Vitte, 2: 132–33).

92. Memorandum of Bülow, Berlin, Nov. 30, 1897, *Grosse Politik*, 14: 102–6.

93. Japanese chargé in Berlin to Japanese Foreign Office, no. 53, Nov. 30, 1897, relayed in Hayashi to Nishi, St. Petersburg, Dec. 1, 1897, JA, TEL 1897/0686–0687.

94. Tschirschky to the German Foreign Ministry, no. 313, tel., St. Petersburg, Dec. 1, 1897, *Grosse Politik*, 14: 106.

95. Bülow to Radolin, no. 333, tel., Berlin, Dec. 2, 1897, *Grosse Politik*, 14: 107.
96. Radolin to German Foreign Ministry, no. 317, tel., St. Petersburg, Dec. 4, 1897, *Grosse Politik*, 14: 107–8.
97. *Grosse Politik*, 14: 111–12. footnote.
98. Kato to Japanese Foreign Office, no. 76, Dec. 2, 1897, relayed in Hayashi to Nishi, St. Petersburg, Dec. 2, 1897, JA, TEL 1897/0689–0690. The English consoled themselves with the thought that Germany would profit little from the possession of Kiaochow because she had no intermediate station between the homeland and China. "In peace time it was harmless, and in war time it could be easily disposed of by her enemy. Thus [the] present enterprise would have little result but to satisfy [the] vanity of the Emperor," the British under secretary of state told the Japanese minister. He believed that Germany would remain in Kiaochow until she got something better. The British government had pointed out to Peking, he related, that the most-favored nation clause precluded the granting of exclusive railroad construction and mining concessions to Germany (Kato to Japanese Foreign Office, no. 80, Dec. 18, 1897, relayed in Hayashi to Nishi, St. Petersburg, Dec. 19, 1897, JA, TEL 1897/0719–0720).
99. Vauvineux to Hanotaux, no. 324, tel., St. Petersburg, Dec. 5, 1897, DDF, ser. 1, 13: 621–22. Vauvineux reported that General Obruchev shared Muraviev's optimism ("*Parbleu*! [Indeed!]," Hanotaux commented in the margin). Vauvineux added that he had learned from a reliable source that Germany's unwonted action in China had been due to the initiative of the Kaiser, prodded by the chief of his naval ministry, and that Hohenlohe and Bülow harbored some misgivings about the consequences of this attitude.
100. Radolin to German Foreign Ministry, nos. 318 and 319, St. Petersburg, Dec. 6, 1897, *Grosse Politik*, 14: 111.
101. Radolin to German Foreign Ministry, no. 321, tel., St. Petersburg, Dec. 8, 1897, *Grosse Politik*, 14: 112–13.
102. Romanov, *Rossiia v Man'chzhurii*, 190–91.
103. Schulman, "China's Response," 203–4. Robert Hart had favored such a move. As he explained in a private letter: "Li is for invoking Russian protection—and sooner or later it must come to this, but the others see in that a farewell to independence and oppose it. I advise them to concede Von Heyking's demands and finish with it, as the least damaging solution. Of course the German procedure is, internationally speaking, disgraceful: but, on the other hand, the Chinese officials when dealt with as comity suggests have been too slow to do their duty and have rather interpreted politeness and comity as a confession of inferiority and weakness—they are only reaping what they have sown!" (Hart to Campbell, no. Z/775, Nov. 28, 1897, *The I. G. in Peking*, 1144–45).
104. *Grosse Politik*, 14: 110, footnote; Schulman, "China's Response," 208.
105. Heyking to German Foreign Ministry, no. 88, tel., Peking, Dec. 4, 1897, *Grosse Politik*, 14: 110–11.
106. Heyking to German Foreign Ministry, no. 92, tel., Peking, Dec. 7, 1897, *Grosse Politik*, 14: 113–14.
107. Heyking to German Foreign Ministry, no. 90, Peking, Dec. 6, 1897, as quoted in *Grosse Politik*, 14: 114, footnote.
108. Heyking to German Foreign Ministry, no. 92, tel., Peking, Dec. 7, 1897, *Grosse Politik*, 14: 113–14.
109. Schulman, "China's Response," 211–12.
110. *Grosse Politik*, 14: 114, footnote.

111. Bülow to Hatzfeldt, no. 17, tel., Berlin, Jan. 12, 1898, *Grosse Politik*, 14: 145.

112. Bülow to Heyking, no. 71, tel., Berlin, Dec. 2, 1897, *Grosse Politik*, 14: 115. In a conversation with Salisbury, Hatzfeldt asserted that France's close association with Russia in East Asia was England's doing. England had made the mistake of not participating in the tripartite intervention after the Sino-Japanese War and had left Germany alone with Russia and France. Salisbury did not deny that this had been a mistake, but said that it had been made by Lord Rosebery, not by himself. "Very convenient," Wilhelm commented sarcastically (Hatzfeldt to Hohenlohe-Schillingsfürst, no. 489, London, Dec. 11, 1897, *Grosse Politik*, 14: 116–17). The draft treaty concerning Kiaochow, which was dispatched to Heyking at the same time as Bülow's telegram of the twelfth, had originated with Brandt, the former German minister to China (*Grosse Politik*, 14: 117).

113. Heyking to German Foreign Ministry, no. 98, tel., Peking, Dec. 16, 1897, *Grosse Politik*, 14: 123–24; Schulman, "China's Response," 213–14. Heyking reported that he was in possession of a secret Chinese document, a report to the throne, according to which Pavlov had recently censured the German occupation of Kiaochow as contrary to international law and had held out the prospect of Russian help against Germany, provided that China first granted to Russia the right of mining and railroad construction in the northern provinces and pledged the employment exclusively of Russian military instructors in China. The report pointed to the danger for China of throwing herself in the arms of Russia and noted that the course of negotiations with the German representative offered hope that an amicable understanding could be reached with Germany without the risky intervention of other powers. The same source from which Heyking had obtained the above document alleged that the Belgian and Dutch minister residents had also communicated to the Tsungli Yamen their regret and disapproval of German violation of international law. When Heyking questioned MacDonald, the latter denied categorically that he had talked to the Chinese about the cession of a harbor to England and that he was delighted that Germany did not want a harbor in the south. The Belgian and Dutch ministers likewise insisted that the information Heyking had received was untrue (*Grosse Politik*, 14: 124 footnote). One wonders whether the allegations or the denials were honest and, if the latter was the case, whether the document pertaining to Russian designs was genuine or a fabrication on the part of the Chinese as part of their general strategy of playing the foreign powers against each other.

114. Schrecker, 37–38; Langer, *Diplomacy of Imperialism*, 459.

115. Schulman, "China's Response," 217–18.

116. *Grosse Politik*, 14: 133, footnote.

117. Radolin to German Foreign Ministry, no. 341, tel., St. Petersburg, Dec. 29, 1897, *Grosse Politik*, 14: 133. Muraviev was convinced that Japan would not move, but he deemed it better, he told Radolin, not to reveal this to the Chinese and to leave them in fear of Japanese action. He expressed full agreement with Bülow that Germany and Russia should cooperate in the commercial and financial questions of the Far East.

118. Schulman, "China's Response," 218–21; *Grosse Politik*, 14: 141 footnote; Maximilian Müller-Jabusch, *Fünfzig Jahre Deutsch-Asiatische Bank 1890–1939*, 99–100; Yano to Nishi, no. 81, Peking, Jan. 6, 1898, no. 83, Jan. 9, 1898, and no. 88, Jan. 12, 1898, JA, TEL 1898/0011–0012, 0031–0032, 0044–0045; Miyaoka to Nishi, no. 60, Berlin, Jan. 5, 1898, JA, TEL 1898/0014.

119. Although the arrangement was similar to that Great Britain had at Hong Kong,

it had not been contemplated originally, because the actual exercise of German authority inside the narrowly circumscribed territory would have been the same with or without the suspension of Chinese sovereign rights. But as Bülow explained to Radolin, those who knew conditions in China had insisted that it was impossible for Germany as for any other civilized power to leave to the mandarins the formal right to torture and execute people inside the German orbit (Bülow to Radolin, no. 1131, Berlin, Dec. 18, 1897, "Secret," *Grosse Politik*, 14: 125–27). Unlike other German protectorates which were placed under the Colonial Section of the Foreign Ministry, Kiaochow was to be administered by the Navy Ministry (Müller-Jabusch, 99–100).

120. "Vertrag zwischen Deutschland und China über die Abtretung von Kiaot-schau, Peking, 6 März 1898," *Sbornik dogovorov*, 325–30.

121. Japanese chargé d'affaires in Germany to Japanese Foreign Office, no. 62, Berlin, Jan. 25, 1898, relayed in Hayashi to Nishi, St. Petersburg, Jan. 26, 1898, JA, TEL 1898/0115.

122. Bülow to Hatzfeldt, no. 26, Berlin, Jan. 23, 1898, *Grosse Politik*, 14: 148–50. In an earlier telegram to Hatzfeldt, Bülow had observed for British consideration that there was no reason why England now, anymore than in 1895, should exclude herself from this community of interest. Germany's action in East Asia did not infringe on the interests of any other power, and in the event of a conflict, which he deemed unlikely because Formosa was to occupy Japan both financially and militarily for quite some time, Germany would have a defensive role and a good conscience (Bülow to Hatzfeldt, no. 1541, Berlin, Dec. 19, 1897, *Grosse Politik*, 14: 127–29).

Chapter Twenty-four

1. Glinskii, 43.

2. There were two vice admirals by the name of Tyrtov: Pavel Petrovich and his younger brother Sergei Petrovich, who was occasionally called Tyrtov II. Sergei Petrovich (1839–1903) had been commander of the Pacific squadron and then commander of the combined squadrons in the Pacific Ocean in 1895; Pavel Petrovich was director of the Naval Ministry in 1896–1902, that is, at the time of Muraviev's writing.

3. Memorandum of Muraviev to Nicholas II, Nov. 11/23, 1897, in "Pervye shagi," 103–8. "*Wan*" means "bay" in Chinese. Strictly speaking, "Talienwan" should be used for Talien Bay only, and "Talien" for the city. However, few of the documents cited made the distinction.

4. Nicholas to Muraviev, Nov. 11/23, 1897, "Pervye shagi," 102.

5. Glinskii, 43–46.

6. Vitte, 2: 136–37. As Wilhelm remarked in his memoirs concerning Nicholas's vacillating character, "the last one to be with him was right" (Wilhelm II, *Ereignisse und Gestalten 1878–1918*, 268).

7. Vitte, 2: 136–38.

8. O'Conor to Salisbury, no. 12, St. Petersburg, Jan. 23, 1898, "Secret," EA, FO 405–76, p. 52.

9. Vitte, 2: 138–39.

10. Hayashi to Nishi, no. 1, "Special," St. Petersburg, Jan. 4, 1898, JA, TEL 1898/0008–0009.

11. Tsyvinskii interpreted the German occupation of Kiaochow as a provocation on

the part of Wilhelm II to push Nicholas II into the Far East in order to deflect his attention from the Bosphorus and the Near East, in which he himself was interested, building a railroad from Baghdad to the Persian Gulf (Admiral G. Tsyvinskii, *50 let v Imperatorskom flote*, 166, footnote 1). The bitter rivalry between Russia and England did not preclude amicable personal relations between the officers of the Russian and British naval vessels at Nagasaki. They joined in excursions, competed at the Bowling Club, and dined on each other's ships. Christmas was celebrated aboard the Russian squadron with fir trees, a lottery, and gifts. Two volunteer ships, which stopped en route to Vladivostok with guards for the Chinese Eastern Railroad, had two dozen Georgian dancers aboard, who entertained the seamen.

12. Tsyvinskii, 165–67. A footnote in Tsyvinskii's memoirs identifies the Russian vessels as the *Sysoi Velikii*, *Navarin*, and *Dmitrii Donskoi*. Semen Semenovich Fabritskii, on the other hand, gives them as the cruiser *Admiral Nakhimov* (Reunov's flagship), the cruiser Admiral Kornilov, the gunboat *Otvazhnyi* (his own vessel), and several boats. According to Fabritskii the British naval unit, consisting of two cruisers and one boat, appeared some two hours later and took up a similar position, but between the Russian ships and the land, as if protecting Port Arthur from the Russians (Semen Semenovich Fabritskii, *Iz proshlago*, 41–42).

13. Salisbury to O'Conor, no. 31, London, Jan. 26, 1898, "Confidential," EA, FO 405–76, p. 55; Salisbury to O'Conor, no. 19, tel., London, Jan. 23, 1898, EA, FO 405–76, p. 51. Salisbury told Kato that the British men-of-war had been sent to Port Arthur by the English admiral, not himself, with Chinese consent; the action had no political significance (Kato to Nishi, no. 84, London, Jan. 5, 1898, transmitted by Hayashi on Jan. 6, 1898, JA, TEL 1898/0018–0019). Reporting that Pavlov had informed the Tsungli Yamen that Russia did not intend to occupy Port Arthur permanently, MacDonald cast some doubt on the meaning of Staal's language, though he personally believed that Russia was merely biding her time until Japan evacuated Weihaiwei and she herself was otherwise ready. He remarked that if Staal's words regarding the adoption of more practical measures to protect Russian interests in her sphere of influence were to be construed as an avowed occupation of Port Arthur, British interests would be best served "by compelling Russia to show her hand." "As it is," MacDonald complained, "By inviting us to withdraw our ships for the sake of 'avoiding friction,' Russia now enjoys the advantages of an occupation without incurring any of the odium attached to it. She represents herself here as the friend of China, and her Agents spread the report that it was orders from St. Petersburgh that frustrated the designs which they declare the British fleet had on Port Arthur" (MacDonald to Salisbury, no. 31, Peking, Jan. 29, 1898, "Secret," EA, FO 405–76, p. 58). MacDonald recommended that unless St. Petersburg issued an official denial of the abovementioned announcement of the Russian Telegraph Bureau, the *Iphigenia*, if she was still in Port Arthur, be instructed to remain there a while longer to prevent the Chinese from believing that the British ships were withdrawn from there out of fear of Russia "at a moment when China is hesitating as to which of the two Powers she has most reason to fear" (MacDonald to Salisbury, no. 29, tel., Peking, Jan. 29, 1898, EA, FO 405–76, p. 58).

14. Fabritskii, 41–42.

15. Muraviev to Osten-Sacken, St. Petersburg, Dec. 2/14, 1897, *Grosse Politik*, 14: 121.

16. Bülow to Osten-Sacken, private letter, Berlin, Dec. 17, 1897, *Grosse Politik*, 14: 122–23.

17. Glinskii writes that the Russian vessels occupied Port Arthur and Talien Bay "in the early days of December." Since Glinskii went by the old calendar, this could mean anywhere on or after December 13 (Glinskii, 48). Romanov states that news of the entry of the Russian vessels into Port Arthur was received in St. Petersburg on December 2/14 (Romanov, *Rossiia v Man'chzhurii*, 193 footnote 3). The newspaper *Novoe Vremia* reported that the vessels had occupied Port Arthur on the fifteenth (Hayashi to Nishi, no. 87, St. Petersburg, Dec. 19, 1897, *Nihon gaiko bunsho*, 30: 406). According to Efimov the vessels entered Port Arthur and Talienwan on December 4/16; according to a telegram by MacDonald on or before the seventeenth (Arthur J. Marder, *The Anatomy of British Sea Power 1880–1905*, 30); according to the *Grosse Politik* on the eighteenth (14: 151 footnote); according to Malozemoff on December 19 (p. 102); and according to Spendelow on the twenty-ninth (p. 149)! The announcement which Rosen made to Nishi on December 17 concerning the dispatch of the Russian squadron was dated December 1/13 (*Nihon gaiko bunsho*, 30: 404).

18. Glinskii, 48–49.

19. Bülow to Osten-Sacken, private letter, Berlin, Dec. 17, 1897, *Grosse Politik*, 14: 122–23. Bülow remarked that Germany wished to replace in its region the Chinese Maritime Customs, a primarily English institution, with an analagous organization, directed by a German chief with Chinese subordinates. He also mentioned very confidentially that ultimately Germany would like to see the merchants of all countries placed on a footing of equality in the Yangtze valley (which then was in the English sphere of influence). On December 16 the Kaiser telegraphed to the tsar from Kiel on the occasion of Prince Heinrich's departure: "Henry just leaving for China sends his best love and farewell wishes. He is happy to meet your officers and ships out in the East, on whose side he has my orders to place himself if ever serious danger threatens them or your interests." Nicholas replied the same day thanking Wilhelm "for giving such clear instructions to Henry" (*Grosse Politik*, 14: 126 footnote).

20. *Grosse Politik*, 14: 129–30 footnote.

21. Wilhelm II to Nicholas II, pr., Dec. 19, 1897, *Grosse Politik*, 14: 129–30. On January 4, 1898, Wilhelm sent Nicholas a sketch he had drawn by the lights of the Christmas tree, showing, as he explained, "the Symbolising figures of Russia and Germany as sentinels at the Yellow Sea for the proclaiming of the Gospel of Truth and Light in the East" (Wilhelm II to Nicholas II, Neues Palais, January 4, 1898, *Briefe Wilhelms II an den Zaren*, 306).

22. Malozemoff, 101–2. Malozemoff comments that by sending the message through the Russian chargé, Wilhelm did not bind Germany the way Nicholas had bound Russia through his direct telegram to him on November 7, which had made it possible for Germany to ignore Russian prior claims to Kiaochow.

23. Japanese chargé in Germany to Nishi, no. 59, Berlin, Dec. 21, 1897, relayed by Hayashi, St. Petersburg, Dec. 22, 1897, JA, TEL 1897/0727. The newspapers were nervous about the eventual attitude of Japan. Their uneasiness was increased by word of the departure of a Japanese squadron from Nagasaki.

24. The French ambassador in London, Courcel, testified that the German initiative at Kiaochow and the subsequent entry of the Russian fleet into Port Arthur had "manifestly surprised and disconcerted England." "I am told that the Marquis of Salisbury under his serene mask is in reality perplexed; and this is easily believable," he wrote. "His accurate feeling as statesman and his perspicacity show him how many hard tasks already lie heavily on England, how much she is thoroughly engaged in a series of undertakings which can turn into adventures." Courcel speculated that if England

were to oppose directly both Germany and Russia in regard to Chinese affairs, the temptation would be great for Russia to take advantage of her rival's vulnerability in northern India to push towards the breach which the insurrection (of the Afridi in Afghanistan) had made in the natural defenses of the vast empire that had so often changed masters and to support the martial tribes whose resistance England had not been able to overcome so far (Courcel to Hanotaux, no. 547, London, Dec. 23, 1897, DDF, ser. 1, 13: 640–43).

25. Memorandum of Bülow, Berlin, Dec. 21, 1897, *Grosse Politik*, 14: 130–31. At his reception on December 22, Muraviev explained that the Russian vessels had gone to Port Arthur merely because of the difficulty of keeping more than a certain number of warships in Japanese ports at one time (Goschen to Salisbury, no. 103, tel., St. Petersburg, Dec. 23, 1897, EA, FO 405–75, p. 203). Muraviev and Witte both asserted that Russia had no intention of moving her Far Eastern center from Vladivostok, which was now kept open all year by an exceptionally powerful icebreaker. Goschen warned his government that the assurances would hold true only "as long as it suits Russia not to precipitate matters and show her full hand in the Far East." He was convinced that as soon as her railroads had been completed and her military strength built up sufficiently, "Russia will endeavour to establish herself definitely in a port free from ice in the winter, either Port Arthur, or some equally convenient and commanding position in the vicinity" (Goschen to Salisbury, no. 295, St. Petersburg, Dec. 26, 1897, EA, FO 405–76, pp. 3–4).

26. Announcement of Rosen to Nishi, Dec. 1/13, 1897, *Nihon gaiko bunsho*, 30: 404–5. Nishi informed Yano of the above and instructed him to ascertain at the Tsungli Yamen whether the Chinese government had indeed consented to the Russian anchorage and to telegraph immediately the result of his inquiry (Nishi to Yano, no. 72, Tokyo, Dec. 17, 1897, JA, TEL 1897/1418, and *Nihon gaiko bunsho*, 30: 404–5).

27. Nishi to Hayashi, no. 101, "Special," Tokyo, Dec. 20, 1897, JA, TEL 1897/1422–1423; Nishi to Yano, no. 73, Tokyo, Dec. 20, 1897, *Nihon gaiko bunsho*, 30: 406.

28. Nishi to Hayashi, no. 104, Tokyo, Dec. 28, 1897, *Nihon gaiko bunsho*, 30: 416–17.

29. *Grosse Politik*, 14: 131–32 footnote.

30. Bülow to Treutler, no. 22, Berlin, Dec. 28, 1897, *Grosse Politik*, 14: 131–32.

31. Nishi to Hayashi, no. 105, Tokyo, Dec. 31, 1897, JA, TEL 1897/1460.

32. Yano to Nishi, no. 75, Peking, Dec. 27, 1897, JA, TEL 1897/0736.

33. Nishi to Yano, no. 77, Tokyo, Dec. 28, 1897, JA, TEL 1897/1453, and *Nihon gaiko bunsho*, 30: 417.

34. Hayashi to Nishi, no. 91, St. Petersburg, Dec. 29, 1897, JA, TEL 1897/0741, and *Nihon gaiko bunsho*, 30: 422–23. Nishi informed Hayashi on January 6 that the diplomatic circle in Peking likewise thought that the Russian occupation of Port Arthur might turn out to be permanent (Nishi to Hayashi, no. 2, Jan. 6, 1898, JA, TEL 1898/1492).

35. Tei to Nishi, Tientsin, Dec. 31, 1897, JA, TEL 1897/0742, and *Nihon gaiko bunsho*, 30: 425.

36. Yano to Nishi, no. 84, "Special," Peking, Jan. 10, 1898, JA, TEL 1898/0035, and *Nihon gaiko bunsho*, 30: 222–23. Muraviev repeated to foreign representatives at his reception on January 12 that the wintering of the Russian fleet at Port Arthur was a temporary measure taken with the free consent of the Chinese government because of

the difficulty of harboring many vessels in Japanese ports. Alluding to the German seizure of Kiaochow, he reiterated that the Russians had received from the Chinese after wintering there the prior right of anchorage (O'Conor to Salisbury, no. 13, St. Petersburg, Jan. 12, 1898, EA, FO 405–76, p. 40).

37. The Chinese Eastern Railroad Company originally thought of running the main line from Chita to Vladivostok along a more southerly route than was actually done. Although the Chinese government, after protracted negotiations, had agreed to the plan in the summer of 1897, it had refused to give written permission. For that reason Witte now sought categorical confirmation.

38 Glinskii, 46–47; Romanov, *Rossiia v Man'chzhurii*, 190–93.

39. Yano to Nishi, no. 76, Peking, Dec. 29, 1897, JA, TEL 1897/0741.

40. Russian memorandum as cited in *Grosse Politik*, 14: 134–35. The Russian demands had been revealed to Heyking by Pavlov on December 24. The chargé remarked that he hoped that the German minister would not object if also German instructors active in the regions in question would be dismissed with full compensation or transferred to other provinces in China. Bülow, to whom Heyking reported the conversation, agreed to go along with the Russians provided they supported the German demands concerning Kiaochow (Heyking to German Foreign Ministry, no. 111, Dec. 24, 1897, and Bülow to Tschirschky, no. 348, Dec. 26, 1897, *Grosse Politik*, 14: 134 footnote).

41. Memorandum of Bülow, Berlin, Jan. 2, 1898, *Grosse Politik*, 14: 135–37.

42. Bülow to Radolin, no. 6, Berlin, Jan. 3, 1898, *Grosse Politik*, 14: 137–38.

43. Memorandum of Bülow, Berlin, Jan. 1898, *Grosse Politik*, 14: 138–40. Germany mistrusted Russia to the same extent that Russia and France mistrusted her. Russian attempts in negotiations with the Chinese and the Germans to limit the Kiaochow trade to Germany and prevent its extension to foreigners in general surprised her because of the insignificance of Russian trade. She believed that Russia sought to maneuver Germany into a policy of prohibition in order to impair relations between Germany and England. It was Bülow's intention to resort to free trade as a means of making Kiaochow into one of the more significant centers of commerce in East Asia. He wished to assure the British that Germany planned to adhere to the principle of free trade in commerce outside Europe, but in order not to put Russia into a worse mood than necessary, he planned to delay any public statement to that effect until after the conclusion of the entire Chinese agreement, including the railroad and coal mining concessions (Bülow to Hatzfeldt, no. 3, Berlin, Jan. 5, 1898, "Secret," *Grosse Politik*, 14: 140–41). In a letter to the Marquis de Noailles, the French ambassador in Berlin, François-Auguste-Armand Nisard, the director of political affairs of the French Foreign Ministry, remarked that the conjectures of Noailles concerning "the tendency of John Bull to take again the strong arm of the German Michael" were being confirmed every day a little more. It would be rather curious, he pondered, if the Kiaochow expedition which should have fanned the hostility among the two rivals "of the same race and of the same appetite" would on the contrary become the point of departure of a *connubio* [marriage] whose children France would have to fear singularly (Nisard to Noailles, Paris, Jan. 14, 1898, DDF, ser. 1, 14: 26–27).

44. Yet Li continued to intrigue against Russia. He told Yano that Pavlov had told him that Russia could not aid China against Germany, because she wanted the latter's cooperation against Japan (Yano to Nishi, no. 17, Peking, Jan. 15, 1898, JA, TEL 1895/0068–0069).

45. Howard R. Spendelow, "Russia's Lease of Port Arthur and Talien," 148–50.

46. Glinskii, 48–49.

47. Efimov, *Vneshniaia politika*, 238–39.

48. Romanov, *Rossiia v Man'chzhurii*, 193–97; Glinskii, 49–50.

49. Kato to Nishi, no. 4, London, Jan. 17, 1898, JA, TEL 1898/0080–0081; Stanley F. Wright, 664.

50. MacDonald to Salisbury, no. 19, tel., Peking, Jan. 16, 1898, EA, FO 405–76, p. 24.

51. MacDonald to Salisbury, no. 31, St. Petersburg, Jan. 26, 1898, EA, FO 405–76, p. 68.

52. O'Conor to Salisbury, no. 30, St. Petersburg, Jan. 26, 1898, "Confidential," EA, FO 405–76, p. 68.

53. Hatzfeldt to German Foreign Ministry, no. 19, London, Jan. 22, 1898, *Grosse Politik*, 14: 147–48. While Hatzfeldt did not presume to judge whether such a Russian program corresponded to German interests, he gave vent to the impression that "the Russian action at this moment, when Russia did not yet have on the spot the necessary means of resistance against England, still less against an Anglo-Japanese fleet, reinforced possibly by a Japanese army, had been rash and unreflecting [*übereilt und unüberlegt*]."

54. Courcel to Hanotaux, no. 10, tel., London, Jan. 23, 1898, "Confidential," DDF, ser. 1, 14: 43–44. Yet the British government was peaceably disposed toward Russia and regarded her action toward Port Arthur as correct so far, Salisbury asserted to Hatzfeldt on January 26 (Hatzfeldt to German Foreign Ministry, no. 24, London, Jan. 26, 1898, "Secret," *Grosse Politik*, 14: 150–51).

55. Kato to Nishi, no. 5, London, Jan. 18, 1898, relayed by Hayashi, St. Petersburg, Jan. 19, 1898, "Special," JA, TEL 1898/0088–0089.

56. See chapter 29 for the Anglo-Russian deal concerning China.

57. Romanov, *Rossiia v Man'chzhurii*, 197–204; Glinskii, 50–53; Müller-Jabusch, 94–98. The Chinese committed themselves in this connection not to alienate the Yangtze valley to any foreign power, to leave the directorship of the Maritime Customs in the hands of a British subject so long as British trade in China would exceed the volume of trade of other powers, and to open Chinese inner waters to British steamships. As security for the loan the Chinese government pledged the unencumbered portion of the Maritime Customs revenue and fixed quotas from the general *likin* and salt *likin* taxes of specified regions (Stanley F. Wright, 665–66). Some of the clauses of the agreement, Witte told O'Conor on March 12, contravened the stipulations of the Russo-Chinese loan, which had given the Russians a prior lien on any increase of revenue and a collateral charge on the *likin* tax. He said that Russia would exact compensation from the Chinese for violating the contract and that Muraviev was "quite right to pull their ears," O'Conor reported (O'Conor to Salisbury, no. 92, St. Petersburg, Mar. 13, 1898, EA, FO 405–76, pp. 165–66). For the text of the telegrams exchanged by Witte with Pokotilov and Pavlov concerning the attempted bribery of the Chinese officials in connection with the loan question, see Romanov, "Perepiska o podkupke kitaiskikh sanovnikov Li Khun-chzhana i Chzhan In-khuana."

58. *Sovetskaia istoricheskia entsiklopediia*, 8: 318.

59. Glinskii, 53–55.

60. MacDonald to Salisbury, no. 66, tel., Peking, Mar. 9, 1898, EA, FO 405–76, p. 143; Yano to Nishi, no. 51, Peking, Mar. 9, 1898, "Special," JA, TEL 1898/0283–0285, and *Nihon gaiko bunsho*, vol. 31, pt. 1, pp. 257–58; Yano to Nishi,

no. 52, Peking, Mar. 10, 1898, JA, TEL 1898/0288–0289, and *Nihon gaiko bunsho*, vol. 31, pt. 1, pp. 258–59; Nishi to Kato, no. 28, Tokyo, Mar. 10, 1898, JA, TEL 1898/1673–74.

61. Salisbury to O'Conor, no. 63, tel., London, Mar. 8, 1898, EA, FO 405–76, p. 142; Kato to Nishi, no. 29, London, Mar. 7, 1898, JA, TEL 1898/0273; Kato to Nishi, no. 30, London, Mar. 8, 1898, JA, TEL 1898/0280.

62. Hayashi to Nishi, no. 19, St. Petersburg, Feb. 16, 1898, "Special," JA, TEL 1898/0195; O'Conor to Salisbury, no. 78, St. Petersburg, Mar. 8, 1898, "Secret," EA, FO 405–76, p. 155; Salisbury to O'Conor, no. 63, tel., London, Mar. 8, 1898.

63. O'Conor to Salisbury, no. 40, tel., St. Petersburg, Mar. 9, 1898, EA, FO 405–76, p. 146; Kato to Nishi, no. 32, London, Mar. 11, 1898, via Hayashi, St. Petersburg, same date, JA, TEL 1898/0300. When Radolin reported likewise that the Russians did not intend to send troops into Manchuria, Wilhelm remarked sarcastically, "*Weil sie schon da sind*" (Because they are there already). (Radolin to German Foreign Ministry, no. 60, St. Petersburg, Mar. 12, 1898, *Grosse Politik*, 14: 155–56).

64. O'Conor to Salisbury, no. 81, St. Petersburg, Mar. 8, 1898, EA, FO 405–76, p. 156.

65. MacDonald to Salisbury, no. 71, tel., Peking, Mar. 1898, EA, FO 405–76, pp. 147–48.

66. MacDonald to Salisbury, no. 46, tel., Peking, Mar. 17, 1898, EA, FO 405–77, pp. 114–15.

67. MacDonald to Salisbury, no. 66, tel., Peking, Mar. 9, 1898, EA, FO 405–76, p. 143; Glinskii, 55.

68. Spendelow, 151.

69. Li Hung-chang had told Yano on March 7 that he regarded Pavlov's demand for a reply within five days as "extraordinary" and that the Chinese government had no intention of answering in haste (Yano to Nishi, no. 50, Peking, Mar. 7, 1898, JA, TEL 1898/0275; Nishi to Hayashi, no. 26, Tokyo, Mar. 10, 1898, "Special," JA, TEL 1898/1671).

70. Yano to Nishi, no. 56, Peking, Mar. 18, 1898, *Nihon gaiko bunsho*, vol. 31, pt. 1, p. 266.

71. Spendelow, 152–53.

72. Glinskii, 55.

73. Spendelow, 152–54. By requiring China's assent to broad principles and leaving details to subsequent negotiation, Spendelow comments, St. Petersburg forced China at each step "to commit herself further and further to the goals which Russia sought, while the specific arrangements, where China might get a guarantee of some concession, were further and further removed from the original commitment."

74. Montebello to Hanotaux, St. Petersburg, Mar. 15, 1898, FA, NS 30, Mf, 1: 36–40.

75. Précis of article in *Novoe Vremia* of March 1/13, enclosed in O'Conor to Salisbury, no. 97, St. Petersburg, Mar. 15, 1898, EA, FO 405–76, pp. 167–77.

76. Salisbury to MacDonald, no. 67, tel., London, Mar. 11, 1898, "Very Confidential," EA, FO 405–76, p. 149.

77. Kato to Nishi, no. 33, London, Mar. 12, 1898, JA, TEL 1898/0306.

78. Salilsbury to O'Conor, no. 70, tel., London, Mar 12, 1898, EA, FO 405–76, p. 151.

79. Nishi to Yano, no. 40, Tokyo, Mar. 15, 1898, JA, TEL 1898/1689–1690.

80. Salisbury to O'Conor, no. 69, tel., London, Mar. 11, 1898, EA, FO 405–76, p. 149.

81. O'Conor to Salisbury, no. 93, St. Petersburg, Mar. 13, 1898, EA, FO 405–76, pp. 166–67; O'Conor to Salisbury, no. 45, tel., St. Petersburg, Mar. 13, 1898, EA, FO 405–76, pp. 152–53.

82. O'Conor to Salisbury, no. 46, St. Petersburg, Mar. 13, 1898, EA, FO 405–76, pp. 153–54.

83. MacDonald to Salisbury, no. 75, tel., Peking, Mar. 13, 1898, EA, FO 405–76, p. 154. In another dispatch, on March 17, MacDonald remarked that should the British government demand the cession of territory in the event that Russia obtained a lease on Port Arthur and Talienwan, it would be easy to include the extension of Hong Kong. However, he did not deem this important enough to countervail Russian gains, while it might, at the same time, serve as a pretext for the French to make territorial acquisitions in the south (MacDonald to Salisbury, no. 46, Peking, Mar. 17, 1898, EA, FO 405–77, pp. 113–14).

84. See EA, FO 405–76, p. 154.

85. Kato to Nishi, no. 36, London, Mar. 13, 1898, via Hayashi, St. Petersburg, Mar. 14, 1898, JA, TEL 1898/0317–0318.

86. MacDonald to Salisbury, no. 76, tel., Peking, Mar. 13, 1898, EA, FO 405–76, p. 155.

87. MacDonald to Salisbury, no. 79, Peking, Mar. 15, 1898, "Very Confidential," EA, FO 405–76, p. 159. The idea of an Anglo-Japanese-Chinese alliance seemed to have originated with Chang Chih-tung, the viceroy of Hankow, MacDonald reported three days later. "It has met with much favour, the fact that China contributes nothing to the strength of the alliance being left out of the account," he observed (MacDonald to Salisbury, no. 47, Peking, Mar. 18, 1898, EA, FO 405–77, pp. 114–15).

88. Salisbury to MacDonald, no. 71, London, Mar. 15, 1898, "Secret," EA, FO 405–76, p. 159.

89. O'Conor to Salisbury, no. 99, St. Petersburg, Mar. 16, 1898, EA, FO 405–76, pp. 184–85.

90. O'Conor to Salisbury, no. 112, St. Petersburg, Mar. 21, 1898, "Confidential," EA, FO 405–76, pp. 227–28; MacDonald to Salisbury, no. 53, Peking, Mar. 22, 1898, "Very Confidential," EA, FO 405–76, p. 190. MacDonald doubted that the occupation, even the fortification, of Port Arthur would give Russia a hold on the Chinese government. "Russia's influence at Peking is determined entirely by the nearness of her frontier to the capital, and by the facility with which she can invade Manchuria and strike at Peking from that frontier," he observed (MacDonald to Salisbury, no. 90, tel., Peking, Mar. 21, 1898, EA, FO 405–76, p. 188).

91. O'Conor to Salisbury, no. 55, tel., St. Petersburg, Mar. 22, 1898, EA, FO 405–76, p. 191.

92. Salisbury to O'Conor, no. 90, tel., London, Mar. 22, 1898, EA, FO 405–76, p. 191.

93. Salisbury to MacDonald, no. 45, London, Mar. 23, 1898, EA, FO 405–76, pp. 198–99.

94. O'Conor to Salisbury, no. 121, St. Petersburg, Mar. 23, 1898, EA, FO 405–76, pp. 229–30. As O'Conor noted in a telegraphic summary of the situation, Russia was prepared to open both Port Arthur and Talienwan to trade as well as to ships of war (O'Conor to Salisbury, no. 57, tel., St. Petersburg, Mar. 23, 1898, EA, FO 405–76, p. 197).

95. O'Conor to Salisbury, no. 62, tel., St. Petersburg, Mar. 26, 1898, EA, FO 405–76, p. 209.

96. Salisbury to O'Conor, no. 76A, London, Mar. 28, 1898, EA, FO 405–76, pp. 236–37.

97. Glinskii, 55.

98. The French had already demanded that the Chinese not cede the three southwestern provinces of Yunnan, Kwangsi, and Kwangtung and that they make some customs modifications in regard to their postal administration. They also wanted a railroad concession in Yunnan and a coaling station (Yano to Nishi, no. 58, Peking, Mar. 19, 1898, "Special," JA, TEL 1898/0335–0336).

99. Yano to Nishi, no. 60, Peking, Mar. 19, 1898, "Special," JA, TEL 1898/0342–0343.

100. Glinskii, 55–56.

101. Spendelow, 155.

102. Glinskii, 56; Vitte, *Vospominaniia*, 2: 140–42.

103. Pokotilov to Witte, Peking, Mar. 9/21, 1898, and telegram by Pavlov of the same date, in Romanov, "Perepiska o podkupe kitaiskikh sanovnikov," 290.

104. Spendelow, 155–56; Glinskii, 156.

105. Glinskii, 56.

106. Pavlov to Witte, Peking, Mar. 12/24, 1898, in B. A. Romanov, "Perepiska o podkupe kitaiskikh sanovnikov," 281.

107. Witte to Pokotilov, St. Petersburg, Mar. 13/25, 1898, *Ibid.*, 291.

108. Pokotilov to Witte, Peking, Mar. 14/26, 1898, Pavlov to Witte, Peking, Mar. 15/27, 1898, and Witte to Pokotilov, St. Petersburg, Mar. 16/28, 1898, *Ibid.*, 291–92.

109. Romanov, *Rossiia v Man'chzhurii*, 203–5; Vitte, 2: 142.

110. Spendelow, 156.

111. *Sbornik dogovorov i diplomaticheskikh dokumentov*, 331–37; Cordier, *Histoire des rélations*, 3: 362–64. Li Hung-chang and Pavlov both revealed the terms of the lease to the Japanese (Yano to Nishi, no. 67, Peking, Mar. 28, 1898, JA, TEL 1898/0394–0395). "I must congratulate you most heartily at the successful issue of your action at Port Arthur," Wilhelm wrote to Nicholas on March 28; "we two will make a good pair of sentinels at the entrance of the gulf of Petchili, who will be duly respected especially by the Yellow Ones!" (*Briefe Wilhelms II an den Zaren*, 307–9).

112. Tsyvinskii, 67; Glinskii, 57. According to Tsyvinskii, Dubasov left Nagasaki on March 10/22, arrived at the Port Arthur roadstead on March 13/25, and went ashore on March 14/26. However, Glinskii's assertion that the landing occurred the day the agreement was signed, that is on the twenty-seventh, appears more reasonable.

113. Glinskii, 57. Baron Rosen informed Nishi of the conclusion of the convention and of the military occupation of the leasehold in a note dated Mar. 17/29 (*Nihon gaiko bunsho*, vol. 31, pt. 1, pp. 288–90).

114. *Sbornik dogovorov*, 338–39; Hayashi to Nishi, no. 35, St. Petersburg, Mar. 29, 1898, JA, TEL 1898/0399–0400 and *Nihon gaiko bunsho*, vol. 31, pt. 1, pp. 290–91.

115. Salisbury to O'Conor, no. 83, London, Apr. 4, 1898; O'Conor to Salisbury, no. 71, tel., St. Petersburg, Apr. 4, 1898; and O'Conor to Salisbury, no. 71A, St. Petersburg, Apr. 4, 1898, EA, FO 405–77, pp. 16–17 and 50–51; Kato to Nishi, no. 52, London, Apr. 5, 1898, via Hayashi, St. Petersburg, Apr. 6, 1898, "Special," JA, TEL 1898/0448–0449. Münster, the German ambassador in Paris, exhorted his English colleague that Britain ought to send a ship of war into Port Arthur without

delay, lest the Russians be encouraged at a later time to deny the validity of her right to do so (Monson to Salisbury, no. 168, Paris, Apr. 5, 1898, "Confidential," EA, FO 405–77, p. 20).

116. Montebello to Hanotaux, no. 33, St. Petersburg, Mar. 30, 1898, DDF, ser. 1, 14: 177–80.

117. Extracts from the "Official Messenger" of March 28/April 9, 1898, and from the *Journal de Saint-Pétersbourg* of March 29/April 10, 1898, enclosed in O'Conor to Salisbury, no. 150, St. Petersburg, Apr. 9, 1898, EA, FO 405–77, pp. 58–59; Hayashi to Nishi, no. 50, St. Petersburg, Apr. 10, 1898, JA, TEL 1898/0469; Glinskii, 57.

118. Salisbury to MacDonald, no. 152, tel., Peking, Apr. 18, 1898, and MacDonald to Salisbury, no. 131, tel., Peking, Apr. 19, 1898, "Confidential," EA, FO 405–77, pp. 65–66.

119. Glinskii, 58; Cordier, *Histoire des rélations*, 3: 365–66.

120. The acquisition of the Liaotung leasehold slowed down construction of the trunk line of the Chinese Eastern Railroad, as engineers were transferred to work on the new projects.

121. Glinskii, 60–61. Work was conducted simultaneously on the main line of the Chinese Eastern Railroad and on the South Manchurian branch. The administration of the construction of the railroad was moved from Vladivostok to Harbin, where the two lines joined.

122. Report of H. J. van Sittat Neale, sent by the British Admiralty to the Foreign Office, Apr. 2, 1898, "Secret," EA, FO 405–77, p. 7.

123. Tsyvinskii, 167–70. L. C. Hopkins, the British consul general at Chefoo, reported on November 16 that engineers' plans for Talienwan showed ambitious harbor works, including a breakwater and a bund allowing ocean steamers to come alongside in twenty-eight or thirty feet of water (Hopkins to MacDonald, no. 44, Chefoo, Nov. 16, 1898, EA, FO 405–84, p. 23).

124. Tayui to Japanese Foreign Ministry, Chefoo, Sept. 7, 1898, JA, TEL 1898/1063; Hayashi to Foreign Minister Okuma Shigenobu, no. 157, Peking, Sept. 8, 1898, JA, TEL 1898/1070; Okuma to Hayashi, no. 67, Tokyo, Sept. 10, 1898, JA, TEL 1898/2141–2142; Hayashi to Okuma, no. 76, St. Petersburg, Sept. 12, 1898, JA, TEL 1898/1094; Tayui to Japanese Foreign Ministry, Chefoo, Sept. 15, 1898, JA, TEL 1898/1103; Hayashi to Okuma, no. 80, St. Petersburg, Oct. 1, 1898, JA, TEL 1898/1171; Okuma to Kato, no. 113, Tokyo, Oct. 10, 1898, JA, TEL 1898/2221; Okuma to Hayashi, no. 77, Tokyo, Oct. 20, 1898, JA, TEL 1898/2250–2251; Hayashi to Okuma, no. 87, St. Petersburg, Oct. 29, 1898, JA, TEL 1898/1308–1309; Okuma to Yano, no. 146, Tokyo, Nov. 1, 1898, JA, TEL 1898/2277–2278; Okuma to Hayashi, no. 82, Tokyo, Nov. 1, 1898, JA, TEL 1898/2280–2281; Yano to Okuma, no. 224, Peking, Nov. 8, 1898, JA, TEL 1898/1353; Foreign Minister Aoki Shuzo to Hayashi, no. 85, St. Petersburg, Nov. 18, 1898, JA, TEL 1898/2303.

125. MacDonald to Salisbury, no. 47, Peking, Mar. 18, 1898, EA, FO 405–77, pp. 114–15.

126. Li received 500,000 liang according to the weight used in Peking in daily life; this amounted to 486,500 liang according to the weight used in banks.

127. Pokotilov to Witte, Peking, Mar. 16/28 and Mar. 27/Apr. 8, 1898, in Romanov, "Perepiska o podkupe," 292.

128. Hummel, 1: 63; Pokotilov to Witte, Peking, Sept. 9/21, 1898, in Romanov "Perepiska o pudkupe," 292. The intervention of the Japanese chargé, Hayashi Gon-

suke, had saved Chang from execution at this time. He was put to death, however, two years later, at the height of the xenophobic mania in Peking.

129. Pokotilov to Witte, Peking, Sept. 9/21, 1898.

130. Pokotilov to Privy Councilor P. M. Romanov, Peking, Sept. 22/Oct. 4, 1898; Vice Minister of Foreign Affairs Vladimir Nikolaevich Lamsdorff to Pavlov, no. 217, St. Petersburg, Sept. 26/Oct. 8, 1898, "Secret," and Pavlov to Lamsdorff, Peking, Sept. 28/Oct. 10, 1898, "Top Secret," in Romanov, "Perepiska o podkupe," 293.

131. "*Spravka*" (statement) listing disbursements from the special fund of the Finance Ministry in Romanov, "Likhunchangskii fond," 124–26. According to the statement Chang received money in May and November (old style), despite Pokotilov's assertion of September 21 that he had not paid him anything yet.

132. Spendelow, 162.

Chapter Twenty-five

1. Baron Rosen, 1: 156–57; Synn, 269–70; Kajima Morinosuke, *The Emergence of Japan as a World Power, 1895–1925*, 67; Conroy, *Japanese Seizure*, 327–28; Borton, 253. For the Chishima-Karafuto *kōkan* see Lensen, *Russian Push Toward Japan*, 443–44. Russian gains in China appeared less disconcerting than those of Germany. As Aoki had told Gosselin in March 1896, "he would infinitely prefer to see Port Arthur and the whole of the Liaotung in Russian hands: that would indeed be bad enough from a Japanese point of view, but not half so dangerous as a permanent occupation of the Shantung Peninsula" (Gosselin's memorandum of his conversation with Aoki on March 14, 1896, enclosed in Lascelles to Salisbury, no. 77, Berlin, Mar. 18, 1896, "Confidential," EA, FO 405–70, pp. 129–30).

2. Plancy to Hanotaux, DP, no. 18, Seoul, Aug. 18, 1896, FA, CP, Korea, 6: 258–62.

3. Hanotaux to Montebello, no. 964, tel., Paris, Dec. 21, 1897, "Confidential," and no. 967, tel., Paris, Dec. 23, 1897, DDF, ser. 1, 13: 638–39; Kurino to Nishi, no. 70, Paris, Dec. 22, 1898, via Hayashi, St. Petersburg, Dec. 23, 1898, JA, TEL 1898/0730–0731.

4. Montebello to Hanotaux, no. 102, St. Petersburg, Dec. 24, 1897, DDF, ser. 1, 13: 643–44.

5. Nishi to Kurino, no. 78, Dec. 28, 1898, JA, TEL 1898/1454.

6. Kurino to Nishi, no. 72, Paris, Dec. 26, 1897, via Hayashi, St. Petersburg, Dec. 27, 1897, JA, TEL 1897/0737–0738.

7. Nishi to Kurino, no. 78, Dec. 28, 1898. Nishi instructed Hayashi that day, in the wake of the Russian anchorage at Port Arthur, to "exhaust [his] best efforts to maintain [the] most friendly relations possible with [the] Russian Government" and keep him fully informed of its attitude and prospective action (Nishi to Hayashi, no. 104, Tokyo, Dec. 28, 1898, JA, TEL 1898/1446).

8. Radolin to German Foreign Ministry, no. 325, tel., St. Petersburg, Dec. 12, 1897, *Grosse Politik*, 14: 118. Radolin promised to be careful not to let the Russians catch on that he knew their secret plans.

9. Bülow remarked that although a large part of the Japanese army was tied down in Formosa for the time being, the Japanese navy was strong enough to require in the event of war such efforts on the part of the German navy and of German finances as

could not be recouped by victory, because a real success was bound to be prevented by the other powers, who would let the Germans and the Japanese fight it out and then would intervene at the psychological moment. So unfavorable were the prospects for the outcome of a German-Japanese war that German policy must do what it could to prevent a worsening in German-Japanese relations, Bülow continued. This could readily be done by letting the Japanese notice that Germany no longer, as in 1895, opposed in principle and everywhere their entrenchment on the East Asian continent, but was inclined rather to extend the justification of "live and let live" to Japan as well. He asked for imperial permission to indicate to the Japanese representative Chargé Miyaoka Tsunejiro, directly and through entrusted middle persons, that in the view of the German government there was no conflict of interest between Germany and Japan, indeed that Germany was inclined to recognize the Japanese as coheirs (*Miterben*) in China. No harm could be done by Japanese use of such utterances in St. Petersburg, a possibility with which they must reckon, because the object of their talk was not Korea, but China as a whole. By such a step Bülow hoped to paralyze the work of Germany's "enemies and questionable friends" who were trying to set Japan against Germany. The Kaiser approved of the policy proposed by Bülow. "We can also give moral support to Japan's protest regarding Hawaii and thereby to draw her away from America," he suggested (Bülow to Wilhelm II, Berlin, Dec. 13, 1897, *Grosse Politik*, 14: 118–21).

10. Treutler to Hohenlohe-Schillingsfürst, no. A. 5, Tokyo, Jan. 7, 1898, GA. The French chargé, Pourtalès-Gorgier, confirmed that the Japanese general staff favored the negotiation of a *modus vivendi* with Russia, but *only*, he underlined, because Japan was not ready to shed her reserve for at least two years (Pourtalès-Gorgier to Hanotaux, no. 8, Tokyo, Jan. 26, 1898, DDF, ser. 1, 14: 54–55).

11. Mohrenheim to Hanotaux, Paris, Dec. 29, 1897, FA, Korea, PE, 8: 126–27.

12. Hanotaux to Montebello, no. 979, Paris, Dec. 29, 1897, FA, Korea, PE, 8: 125.

13. Montebello to Hanotaux, no. 4, St. Petersburg, Jan. 6, 1898, DDF, ser. 1, 14: 2–3.

14. Hayashi to Nishi, no. 4, St. Petersburg, Jan. 7, 1898, "Special," JA, TEL 1898/0028–0030, and *Nihon gaiko bunsho*, vol. 31, pt. 1, pp. 109–10; Nishi to Kato, no. 5, Tokyo, Jan. 19, 1898, JA, TEL 1898/1545–1546, and *Nihon gaiko bunsho*, vol. 31, pt. 1, pp. 117–18; *Nichi-Ro kosho-shi*, 1: 288.

15. Montebello to Hanotaux, no. 4, St. Petersburg, Jan. 6, 1898.

16. Hayashi to Nishi, no. 4, St. Petersburg, Jan. 7, 1898.

17. Montebello to Hanotaux, no. 4, St. Petersburg, Jan. 6, 1898. Pourtalès-Gorgier reported that there were several persons in the Japanese cabinet who favored reaching a *modus vivendi* with Russia, among them Foreign Minister Nishi, Finance Minister Inoue Kaoru, and Justice Minister Sone Arasuke (Pourtalès-Gorgier to Hanotaux, no. 8, Tokyo, Jan. 26, 1898, DDF, ser. 1, 14: 54–55).

18. Hayashi to Nishi, no. 4, St. Petersburg, Jan. 7, 1898, "Special," JA, TEL 1898/0028–0030, and *Nihon gaiko bunsho*, vol. 31, pt. 1, pp. 109–10.

19. Hayashi to Nishi, no. 6, St. Petersburg, Jan. 11, 1898, JA, TEL 1898/0048, and *Nihon gaiko bunsho*, vol. 31, pt. 1, p. 116.

20. Nishi to Hayashi, no. 8, Tokyo, Jan. 18, 1898, JA, TEL 1898/1538, and *Nihon gaiko bunsho*, vol. 31, pt. 1, p. 117; Nishi to Kato, no. 5, Tokyo, Jan. 19, 1898, JA, TEL 1898/1545–1546, and *Nihon gaiko bunsho*, vol. 31, pt. 1, pp. 117–18; *Nichi-Ro kosho-shi*, 1: 288–89. Kato commented that he fully agreed with the opinion ex-

pressed by Nishi to Rosen. He thought that Russia might accept the Japanese proposition without difficulty, because she was beginning to feel that she was gradually losing influence in Korea and because she intended, if possible, to take advantage of their friendship and form an alliance with Japan in the East. Although it might be hard in consideration of her prestige to make Russia cancel the contract for the financial adviser and abandon the drilling of the Korean army entirely, it might be possible to modify the contract restricting the power of the financial adviser and fixing a reasonable term. Similarly the number of Russian military officers could be limited and their powers restricted to educational matters, terminating their relations with the army corps. At any rate, Japan had nothing to lose by making the proposition. Kato remarked that the Russian offer of assistance in commercial and industrial matters was too vague; he wondered whether it was merely a contrivance to keep Japan from drawing toward England (Kato to Nishi, no. 1, Seoul, Jan. 21, 1898, JA, TEL 1898/0091, and *Nihon gaiko bunsho*, vol. 31, pt. 1, p. 119).

21. Hayashi to Nishi, no. 7, St. Petersburg, Jan. 20, 1898, "Special," JA, TEL 1898/0096–0097, and *Nihon gaiko bunsho*, vol. 31, pt. 1, p. 118.

22. Hayashi to Nishi, no. 10, St. Petersburg, Jan. 27, 1898, "Special, Strictly Confidential," JA, TEL 1898/0121–0122, and *Nihon gaiko bunsho*, vol. 31, pt. 1, pp. 120–21. Hayashi added that England did not oppose Russia in everything. Not only were her interests in Korea not in conflict with those of Japan, but England would like to see Russian influence divided by the Japanese, he asserted.

23. Nishi to Hayashi, no. 10, Tokyo, Jan. 26, 1898, JA, TEL 1898/1558–1559, and *Nihon gaiko bunsho*, vol. 31, pt. 1, pp. 288–89. Nicholas was said to have declared at a reunion of Russian officers toward the end of May that he had been gravely preoccupied with the events in the Far East and especially with the difficulties which had arisen with Japan, but that, thank God, the situation had been cleared up (Plancy to French foreign minister, DP, no. 149, Seoul, Mar. 3, 1898, FA, Korea, PE, 8: 154–55).

24. Nishi to Hayashi, no. 13, Tokyo, Jan. 31, 1898, *Nihon gaiko bunsho*, vol. 31, pt. 1, p. 129.

25. Hayashi to Nishi, no. 13, St. Petersburg, Jan. 29, 1898, JA, TEL 1898/0131–0132, and *Nihon gaiko bunsho*, vol. 31, pt. 1, pp. 128–29; *Nichi-Ro kosho-shi*, 1: 289.

26. Hayashi to Nishi, no. 14, St. Petersburg, Feb. 2, 1898, "Special," JA, TEL 1898/0152, and *Nihon gaiko bunsho*, vol. 31, pt. 1, pp. 129–30.

27. Nishi to Hayashi, no. 14, Tokyo, Feb. 5, 1898, "Special," JA, TEL 1898/1576, and *Nihon gaiko bunsho*, vol. 31, pt. 1, p. 130.

28. *Nihon gaiko bunsho*, vol. 31, pt. 1, p. 138; *Nichi-Ro kosho-shi*, 1: 292.

29. Glinskii, 66–67.

30. Nikhamin, "Russko-iaponskie otnosheniia," 487–88.

31. Hayashi to Nishi, no. 26, St. Petersburg, Mar. 10, 1898, "Special," JA, TEL 1898/0294–0295, and *Nihon gaiko bunsho*, vol. 31, pt. 1, p. 146. Hayashi told O'Conor, with whom he was well acquainted from Peking, that the gist of his instructions was to insist on Russian adherence to the Lobanov-Yamagata convention, from which Russia had deviated in a number of instances, notably in the appointment of a financial adviser. "Public opinion in Japan is easily but very strongly moved by events in Corea, and while the Japanese public may possibly submit to what may seem to them the inevitable development of Russian policy in the Liaotung Peninsula, I can hardly think that they will exhibit equal forbearance in face of Russian action in the

Hermit Kingdom," O'Conor commented. There was little doubt, he reported, that the tsarist government felt that it was treading on dangerous ground and was not without anxiety regarding the possible consequences. "I was struck with this during two recent conversations, when Count Lamsdorff seemed to me to go out of his way to assure me that his Government considered that the Russian Representative in Seoul and M. Alexieff, the Financial Adviser to the Corean Government, had been far too energetic, and had committed the diplomatic mistake of showing 'trop de zèle' [too much zeal]," O'Conor related. "Russia only desired, he said, the independence of Corea. But when he went on to complain of the difficulty of understanding what was going on in that country, and to tell that he had only just become aware of the conditions of the Convention between the Corean Government and the Russian Financial Adviser, I confess that my faith in his previous assurances was put to a severe test" (O'Conor to Salisbury, no. 76, St. Petersburg, Mar. 5, 1898, "Confidential," EA, FO 405–80, pp. 60–61).

32. Nikhamin, "Russko-iaponskie otnosheniia," 489–90.

33. Nishi to Hayashi, no. 25, Tokyo, Mar. 8, 1898, *Nihon gaiko bunsho*, vol. 31, pt. 1, p. 144.

34. Nishi to Hayashi, no. 27, Tokyo, Mar. 14, 1898, *Nihon gaiko bunsho*, vol. 31, pt. 1, pp. 147–48.

35. Hayashi to Nishi, no. 27, St. Petersburg, Mar. 16, 1898, JA, TEL 1898/0322–0323, and *Nihon gaiko bunsho*, vol. 31, pt. 1, pp. 147–48. See also Satow to Salisbury, no. 16, tel., Tokyo, Mar. 19, 1898, EA, FO 405–80, p. 64.

36. Hayashi to Nishi, no. 28, St. Petersburg, Mar. 18, 1898, *Nihon gaiko bunsho*, vol. 31, pt. 1, p. 152.

37. Nishi to Hayashi, no. 30, Mar. 20, 1898, "Special," JA, TEL 1898/1703–1704; *Nichi-Ro kosho-shi*, 1: 290; Nikhamin, "Russko-iaponskie otnosheniia," 491. Kato confirmed to Speyer that the recall of Alekseev and of the military instructors removed the sole serious obstacle to the achievement of an understanding between their governments regarding the Korean peninsula (Plancy to French foreign minister, DP, no. 161, Seoul, Mar. 28, 1898, FA, Korea, PE, 203–4).

38. Baron Rosen, 1: 157–58; Nikhamin, "Russko-iaponskie otnosheniia," 491–92.

39. Nishi to Rosen, Tokyo, Mar. 19, 1898, *Nihon gaiko bunsho*, vol. 31, pt. 1, p. 152; *Nichi-Ro kosho-shi*, 1: 290–91. In communicating the proposal to Hayashi, Nishi instructed him to transmit it to the Japanese ministers in England and France for their "strictly confidential information" (Nishi to Hayashi, no. 30, Tokyo, Mar. 20, 1898, JA, TEL 1898/1703–1704).

40. Nishi to Hayashi, no. 31, Tokyo, Mar. 21, 1898, JA, TEL 1898/1706–1708, and *Nihon gaiko bunsho*, vol. 31, pt. 1, pp. 158–59; *Nichi-Ro kosho-shi*, 1: 291–92. Kurino informed Hanotaux of the Russo-Japanese negotiations (Hanotaux to Montebello, no. 217, Paris, Mar. 31, 1898, FA, Korea, PE, 8: 210–11).

"I think the way you managed to soothe the feelings of the 'fretful Japs' by the masterly arrangement at Korea a remarkable fine piece of diplomacy and a great show of foresight," Wilhelm wrote to Nicholas. Attributing the tsar's success to the personal knowledge he had acquired of the Far Eastern situation during his Asian tour of 1891, the Kaiser flattered the tsar that he was now "morally speaking the Master of Peking!" (Wilhelm II to Nicholas II, Berlin, March 28, 1898, *Briefe Wilhelms II an den Zaren*, 307–9).

41. Nishi to Kato, no. 39, Tokyo, Mar. 22, 1898, JA, TEL 1898/1713–1715, and *Nihon gaiko bunsho*, vol. 31, pt. 1, pp. 160–61.

42. Kato to Nishi, no. 44, London, Mar. 23, 1898, JA, TEL 1898/0357–0358, and *Nihon gaiko bunsho*, vol. 31, pt. 1, pp. 161–62. When Nishi did not answer his telegram, Kato concluded that his views were unacceptable to him and offered to resign because of ill health and Nishi's "negative attitude towards Great Britain" (Kato to Nishi, no. 48, London, Mar. 30, 1898, via Hayashi, St. Petersburg, Mar. 31, 1898, "Special," JA, TEL 1898/0410). Nishi replied that no response had been made to his telegram because the whole subject was still under consideration; no definite course of action could be adopted regarding Korea until Russia's answer had been obtained. "Moreover," Nishi cabled, "[the] Japanese Government are unwilling to commit themselves finally to any fixed line of policy until after [the] receipt of [the] Chinese indemnity, the immediate payment of which they have used every effort to secure and are apparently about to be successful owing, in no small degree, to your valuable assistance. Under these circumstances, and in view also of [the] present situation, your continued presence in London is of utmost importance to Japan and I sincerely trust that, unless your illness is of such grave nature as to render your immediate return imperative, you will be able to remain at your post at least until Far Eastern affairs assume [a] more settled condition" (Nishi to Kato, no. 43, Tokyo, Apr. 1, 1898, "Special," via Hayashi, JA, TEL 1898/1740–1742).

43. Hayashi to Nishi, no. 29, St. Petersburg, Mar. 23, 1898, "Special," JA, TEL 1898/0364–0365, and *Nihon gaiko bunsho*, vol. 31, pt. 1, pp. 162–63. Hayashi believed that Manchuria formed a natural *Hinterland* for the Russian railroad to open up and that it was destined to become eventually a Russian province whether the tsarist government wished it or not (Charles S. Scott to Salisbury, no. 243, St. Petersburg, Aug. 9, 1899, EA, FO 405–86, pp. 137–38).

44. Synn, 270. The Korea-Manchuria exchange did not look like a fair deal to many Russians. While Russia could leave Korea to Japan, the latter was not in a position to leave Manchuria to Russia, for Great Britain, not Japan, was Russia's main rival in that region at that time. The elimination of Japan from Manchuria would not of itself have made it into a Russian sphere of influence (Nikhamin, "Russko-iaponskie otnosheniia," 493).

45. Muraviev to Rosen, St. Petersburg, Mar. 29, 1898, transmitted by Nishi on Apr. 2, *Nihon gaiko bunsho*, vol. 31, pt. 1, pp. 163–64; Nikhamin, "Russko-iaponskie otnosheniia," 493–94. See also Nishi to Kato, no. 11, Tokyo, Apr. 1, 1898, JA, TEL 1898/1378, and *Nihon gaiko bunsho*, vol. 31, pt. 1, p. 175; *Nichi-Ro kosho-shi*, 1: 292–93.

46. Hayashi to Nishi, no. 37, St. Petersburg, Mar. 30, 1898, JA, TEL 1898/0407, and *Nihon gaiko bunsho*, vol. 31, pt. 1, pp. 172–74. The introductory paragraphs of the French text handed to Hayashi differed somewhat from the English version presented by Rosen. They asserted that throughout the negotiations which had arisen as the result of developments in Korea since the Sino-Japanese War, the tsarist government had shown itself ever desirous of dealing with successive questions "in a spirit of amicable understanding" with Japan. It added in regard to the notice which Nishi had recently remitted to Rosen about the attitude to be observed by the two empires vis-à-vis Korea, that it was of the opinion that "in the new phase of the question, the establishment of an accord to this effect would be of great practical utility."

47. Nishi to Hayashi, no. 37, Tokyo, Apr. 5, 1898, "Special," JA, TEL 1898/1757–1759, and *Nihon gaiko bunsho*, vol. 31, pt. 1, pp. 177–78; Hayashi to Nishi, no. 46, St. Petersburg, Apr. 7, 1898, JA, TEL 1898/0451, and *Nihon gaiko bunsho*, vol. 31, pt. 1, p. 178; *Nichi-Ro kosho-shi*, 1: 293.

48. Hayashi to Nishi, no. 42, St. Petersburg, Apr. 3, 1898, "Special," JA, TEL 1898/0433–0434, and *Nihon gaiko bunsho*, vol. 31, pt. 1, pp. 176–77.

49. Baron Rosen, 1: 158–59. The idea of a division of spheres of influence was shelved, but not that of an agreement concerning Korea. "Justified as the refusal to recognize Korea as an exclusively Japanese sphere of influence may have been," comments Nikhamin, "the attempt to insist on the recognition of Manchuria as lying outside the Japanese sphere of interest was absolutely without foundation and bore a patently adventurous character" (Nikhamin, "Russko-iaponskie otnosheniia," 496).

50. Kato to Nishi, no. 55, London, Apr. 5, 1898, via Hayashi, St. Petersburg, Apr. 9, 1898, "Special," JA, TEL 1898/0470–0471.

51. For the full text of the Japanese proposal see *Nihon gaiko bunsho*, vol. 31, pt. 1, pp. 178–79, and Nishi to Hayashi, no. 38, Tokyo, Apr. 8, 1898, "Special," *Nihon gaiko bunsho*, vol. 31, pt. 1, pp. 179–80; also *Nichi-Ro kosho-shi*, 1: 293–94. The proposal had been approved by Premier Ito the previous day, on April 7.

52. Nikhamin, "Russko-iaponskie otnosheniia," 499–500.

53. Nishi to Hayashi, no. 41, Tokyo, Apr. 16, 1898, JA, TEL 1898/1787–1789, and *Nihon gaiko bunsho*, vol. 31, pt. 1, pp. 181–82; *Nichi-Ro gaiko-shi*, 1: 294. See also the statement handed by Rosen to Nishi on the twelfth, *Nihon gaiko bunsho*, vol. 31, pt. 1, p. 180.

54. Nikhamin, "Russko-iaponskie otnosheniia," 501–2; telegram from Rosen to Muraviev shown to Nishi on April 16, 1898, *Nihon kosho bunsho*, vol. 31, pt. 1, pp. 180–81; *Nichi-Ro kosho-shi*, 1: 294–95.

55. Nikhamin, "Russko-iaponskie otnosheniia," 502.

56. For the full text of the Nishi-Rosen Protocol, see *Nihon gaiko bunsho*, vol. 31, pt. 1, pp. 182–84; *Sbornik dogovorov i diplomaticheskikh dokumentov*, 346–48; and *Nichi-Ro kosho-shi*, 1: 295.

57. Nikhamin, "Russko-iaponskie otnosheniia," 503–4.

58. Kato to Nishi, no. 62, London, Apr. 29, 1898, via Hayashi, St. Petersburg, Apr. 30, 1898, JA, TEL 1898/0543. Hayashi speculated that Russia had insisted on secrecy; Harmand believed that the request had emanated from Japan, who wanted to delay revelation of the agreement at least until the opening of the Diet. At any rate, Harmand reported, the tsarist legation and Premier Ito were acting in perfect accord at the moment (O'Conor to Salisbury, no. 185, St. Petersburg, May 3, 1898, "Confidential," EA, FO 405–80, p. 105; Harmand to Hanotaux, no. 29, Tokyo, May 10, 1898, FA, Korea, PE, 8: 219–24, and DDF, ser. 1, 14: 274–76; Harmand to Hanotaux, DP, no. 34, Tokyo, May 23, 1898, FA, Korea, PE, 8: 239–42).

59. The *Messager officiel*, St. Petersburg, May 12, 1898, enclosed in Montebello to Hanotaux, DP, no. 44, St. Petersburg, May 12, 1898, FA, Korea, PE, 8: 226–28. See also *Sbornik dogovorov i diplomaticheskikh dokumentov*, 345–46.

60. Hayashi to Nishi, no. 56, St. Petersburg, May 14, 1898, JA, TEL 1898, and *Nihon gaiko bunsho*, vol. 31, pt. 1, p. 185.

61. French analysis of the article, enclosed in Montebello to Hanotaux, DP, no. 61, St. Petersburg, June 13, 1898, FA, Korea, PE, 8: 252–56. "The Moscow Protocol of 1896 had already tied the freedom of action of Russia in Manchuria to a certain extent; the Tokyo Protocol of 1898, however, confined our policy in this country still further," complained Boris Borisovich Glinskii in his historical review of the period (Glinskii, 68).

62. Allen to Sherman, no. 109, DS, Seoul, May 26, 1898, USDD, Korea, roll 14.

63. Treutler to Hohenlohe-Schillingsfürst, no. A. 31, Tokyo, Mar. 14, 1898, GA. In reading the dispatch, Wilhelm scribbled *"Richtig"* (Correct) in the margin next to Treutler's supposition that there must be a direct connection between the Russian occupation of Port Arthur and the Korean episode. "Very well observed and correctly judged," he commented at the end of the dispatch. The counselor of the tsarist embassy in London, Lessar, who passionately followed Asian affairs, told his French colleague that Port Arthur and Talienwan met the Russian *desiderata* in these parts. All that Russia wanted in Korea, he asserted, was that no power assume any preponderant influence there. The accord which she had reached with Japan gave Russia full guarantee and full security in regard to Korea, he believed (Geoffray to Hanotaux, DP, no. 159, London, Mar. 21, 1898, "Confidential," FA, Korea, PE, 8: 190–92).

64. Harmand to Hanotaux, no. 44, Tokyo, July 15, 1898, FA, NS 30, MF, 1: 41–42; Baron Rosen, 1: 159–61.

Chapter Twenty-six

1. Salisbury to MacDonald, no. 55, tel., London, Mar. 7, 1898, "Secret," EA, FO 405–76, p. 137.

2. Admiralty to Foreign Office, London, Apr. 2, 1898, "Secret," EA, FO 405–77, p. 7.

3. Salisbury to MacDonald, no. 68, tel., London, Mar. 12, 1898, EA, FO 405–76, p. 151.

4. Sanderson suggested that if Japan wished to know the attitude of his government in the matter of Weihaiwei, she might address inquiries to the latter. "He seemed to feel eager interest in the question," Kato observed (Kato to Nishi, no. 33, London, Mar. 12, 1898, JA, TEL 1898/0306–0309).

5. Bülow to Radolin, no. 51, Berlin, Mar. 15, 1898, *Grosse Politik*, 14: 156–57. Bülow remarked that while Japan, if given a choice, would probably prefer to retain Weihaiwei rather than receive the 13 million pounds, it would make a great difference for the quicker or slower progress of Japanese arming and consequently for the *Kriegslust* (bellicosity) of Japan whether or not she would possess the additional funds. At the moment Japan was trying to obtain both the indemnity and the naval base. Satow reported, on the other hand, that it appeared quite certain from what Ito and Nishi had said to him that Japan would evacuate Weihaiwei if China paid the indemnity (Satow to Salisbury, no. 14, tel., Tokyo, Mar. 16, 1898, EA, FO 405–76, p. 161).

6. O'Conor to Salisbury, no. 56, tel., St. Petersburg, Mar. 23, 1898, "Very Confidential," EA, FO 405–76, p. 196.

7. Nishi to Kato, no. 38, Tokyo, Mar. 22, 1898, JA, TEL 1898/1712.

8. Salisbury to MacDonald, no. 109, tel., London, Mar. 25, 1898, and to Lascelles, no. 38, tel., London, Mar. 26, 1898, "Special," EA, FO 405–76, pp. 209–10.

9. Salisbury to MacDonald, no. 116, tel., London, Mar. 29, 1898, EA, FO 405–76, p. 238.

10. Salisbury to MacDonald, no. 119, tel., London, Mar. 30, 1898, EA, FO 405–76, p. 442. To support MacDonald's demands for the lease of Weihaiwei and to check Russian opposition, the British admiralty ordered its commander-in-chief on the China Station to collect a force in the Gulf of Pechili "fairly superior to [the] Russian

force there" (Admiralty to the Commander-in-chief on the China Station, no. 49, tel., London, Mar. 26, 1898, EA, FO 405–76, p. 234. See also Odagiri to Nishi, Shanghai, Mar. 28, 1898, and Taiyui to Japanese Foreign Office, Chefoo, Apr. 12, 1898, JA, TEL 1898/0390 and 0479).

11. Nishi to Kato, no. 44, and to Yano, no. 49, Tokyo, Apr. 2, 1898, JA, TEL 1898/1745–1746; Satow to Salisbury, no. 21, tel., Tokyo, Apr. 2, 1898, EA, FO 405–77, p. 8. Nishi instructed Yano that the Japanese reply was to be regarded as strictly confidential and that if the Tsungli Yamen or others should ask questions about this matter, he was not to make any answer without checking with him. MacDonald told Yano that Russia had promised England three days before the conclusion of the Liaotung lease that both Talien and Port Arthur would be opened and not fortified. Finding now that Port Arthur was to be closed and fortified, the British were determined to occupy and fortify Weihaiwei if Port Arthur remained a fortified Russian port. "Have [the] Russian Government sent an answer regarding Corea?" Yano inquired of Nishi. "If not, it will be better to secure [the] desired end before it is too late. When both England and Russia are satisfied and the situation begins to settle down, I am afraid, it will be too late" (Yano to Nishi, no. 72, Peking, Apr. 2, 1898, JA, TEL 1898/0423–0424).

12. Nishi to Hayashi, no. 36, Tokyo, Apr. 4, 1898, JA, TEL 1898/1748.

13. Hanotaux to Montebello, no. 232, Paris, Apr. 4, 1898, "Urgent, Confidential," DDF, ser. 1, 14: 195.

14. Bülow to Hatzfeldt, no. 98, Berlin, Apr. 4, 1898, "Confidential," *Grosse Politik*, 14: 163.

15. Yano to Nishi, no. 74, Peking, Apr. 4, 1898, JA, TEL 1898/0437; Francis Bertie to Admiralty, London, Apr. 4, 1898, "Confidential," EA, FO 405–77, p. 17.

16. Bertie to Admiralty, London, Apr. 4, 1898, "Confidential," and Salisbury to MacDonald, no. 131, tel., London, Apr. 4, 1898, EA, FO 405–77, pp. 16–17.

17. Balfour to Lascelles, no. 44, tel., London, Apr. 2, 1898, EA, FO 405–77, p. 8.

18. Miyaoka to Nishi, no. 14, Berlin, Apr. 4, 1898, "Special," JA, TEL 1898/0444–0445.

19. Bülow to Hatzfeldt, no. 99, Berlin, Apr. 4, 1898, *Grosse Politik*, 14: 162. Balfour agreed to give such a guarantee (Hatzfeldt to Bülow, no. 77, London, Apr. 5, 1898, *Grosse Politik*, 14: 163–64). See also Salisbury to Lascelles, no. 52, tel., London, Apr. 7, 1898, EA, FO 405–77, p. 21.

20. Wilhelm II to Bülow, tel., Homburg v. d. Höhe, Apr. 6, 1898, *Grosse Politik*, 14: 164.

21. Metternich to Bülow, private letter, Schloss Homburg v. d. Höhe, Apr. 5, 1898, *Grosse Politik*, 14: 164–65.

22. Bülow to Wilhelm II, tel., Berlin, Apr. 7, 1898, *Grosse Politik*, 14: 165–67.

23. Wilhelm II to Bülow, tel., Schloss Homburg, Apr. 8, 1898, *Grosse Politik*, 14: 167–68.

24. Wilhelm II to Bülow tel., Homburg, v. d. Höhe, Apr. 8, 1898, *Grosse Politik*, 14: 168–69.

25. Bülow to Wilhelm II, tel., Berlin, Apr. 21, 1898, *Grosse Politik*, 14: 171; Salisbury to Lascelles, no. 73, tel., London, Apr. 19, 1898, EA, FO 405–77, p. 66.

26. *"Das Tränkchen ging ihm glatt hinunter*," reported Bülow.

27. *Grosse Politik*, 14: 172 footnote*.

28. Bertie to Admiralty, London, Apr. 14, 1898, "Confidential," EA, FO 405–77, p. 57.

29. *Nihon gaiko nempyo*, 1: 130.

30. Satow to Salisbury, no. 34, tel., Tokyo, May 9, 1898, EA, FO 405–77, p. 149.

31. Morse, 3: 118.

32. Satow to Salisbury, no. 103, Tokyo, June 11, 1898, EA, FO 405–78, p. 41.

33. Montebello to Hanotaux, no. 90, tel., St. Petersburg, Apr. 5, 1898, DDF, ser. 1, 14: 205.

34. Hayashi to Nishi, no. 45, St. Petersburg, Apr. 6, 1898, JA, TEL 1898/0453. In reporting the above, Hayashi related that the diplomatic circle in St. Petersburg was surprised at Japan's "complaisance" in handing over Weihaiwei to Britain without compensation. Although Staal did not conceal from the French undersecretary of state the discontent that the Anglo-Chinese agreement had aroused in St. Petersburg, Sanderson alleged to the French representative in London that Russia preferred to have the English rather than the Japanese in the Gulf of Pechili (Hanotaux to Montebello, no. 245, Paris, Apr. 6, 1898, DDF, ser. 1, 14: 206).

35. *Grosse Politik*, 14: 165 footnote*.

36. Kato to Nishi, no. 54, London, Apr. 6, 1898, via Hayashi, St. Petersburg, Apr. 7, 1898, JA, TEL 1898/0454–0455.

37. Editorial comment added to E. H. Parker, "The Conscience of Corea," in the *Imperial and Asiatic Quarterly Review* 1896, vol. 2, no. 4, pp. 291–97.

38. Extract from *Novoe Vremia* of July 9/21, 1897, enclosed in O'Conor to Salisbury, no. 168, St. Petersburg, July 24, 1897, EA, FO 405–73, p. 101.

39. Salisbury to O'Conor, no. 184 A, London, Aug. 13, 1897, EA, FO 405–73, p. 106.

40. Salisbury to O'Conor, no. 7, London, Jan. 17, 1898, "Secret," EA, FO 405–76, p. 42.

41. O'Conor to Salisbury, no. 10, St. Petersburg, Jan. 20, 1898, "Secret," EA, FO 405–76, p. 48; A. Popov, "Anglo-russkoe soglashenie o razdele Kitaia (1899 g.)," 114–15.

42. O'Conor to Salisbury, no. 12, St. Petersburg, Jan. 23, 1898, "Secret," EA, FO 405–76, p. 52. Reporting that Witte had expressed nervousness at the idea of an Anglo-Japanese alliance, O'Conor remarked: "I thought it advisable not to exclude from his political vision the possibility of such an alliance."

43. Salisbury to O'Conor, no. 22, London, Jan. 25, 1898, "Secret," EA, FO 405–76, pp. 53–54.

44. Popov, "Anglo-russkoe," 114–15.

45. O'Conor to Salisbury, no. 16, St. Petersburg, Feb. 2, 1898, "Secret," EA, FO 405–76, p. 73. Reporting that he was to see Muraviev on the afternoon of February 2, O'Conor added that it seemed "desirable for many reasons to preserve the utmost secrecy on the subject of these negotiations."

46. O'Conor to Salisbury, no. 17, St. Petersburg, Feb. 2, 1898, "Secret," EA, FO 405–76, p. 77. Like O'Conor, Muraviev thought it most desirable to keep the negotiations regarding an Anglo-Russian entente as secret as possible.

47. O'Conor to Salisbury, no. 27, tel., St. Petersburg, Feb. 9, 1898, "Secret," EA, FO 405–76, p. 92; A. Popov, "Anglo-russkoe," 115–16. In the margin of the report of the above conversation, Nicholas jotted, "Our negotiations with England at the present time can only touch the affairs of the Far East." O'Conor perceived the objection to including Persia. "Can we, if we leave it out, induce any reference to Afghanistan, or may it be taken for granted that the common apprehensions as to the North-west Frontier will disappear as soon as a cordial entente is established," he queried Salis-

bury. Russian reluctance to consider a comprehensive settlement entailing mutual assistance put Salisbury on his guard. "Some interchange of friendly language has taken place at St. Petersburgh in regard to an understanding with Russia, but their language is ambiguous, and they are insincere," he cabled to MacDonald (Salisbury to MacDonald, no. 34, London, Feb. 11, 1898, "Secret," EA, FO 405–76, p. 94*).

48. Popov, "Anglo-russkoe," 115–16.

49. O'Conor to Muraviev, St. Petersburg, Feb. 12, 1898, "Confidential," EA, FO 405–76, pp. 101–2.

50. Popov, "Anglo-russkoe," 117.

51. O'Conor to Salisbury, no. 33, St. Petersburg, Feb. 22, 1898, "Secret," EA, FO 405–76, p. 117*.

52. O'Conor to Salisbury, no. 34, St. Petersburg, Feb. 22, 1898, "Secret," EA, FO 405–76, p. 117A; Popov, "Anglo-russkoe," 117–18.

53. Salisbury to O'Conor, no. 56, tel., London, Feb. 25, 1898, and O'Conor to Salisbury, no. 71, St. Petersburg, Mar. 3, 1898, "Secret," EA, FO 405–76, pp. 120 and 127*.

54. O'Conor to Salisbury, no. 78, St. Petersburg, Mar. 8, 1898, "Secret," EA, FO 405–76, pp. 155–56.

55. Salisbury to O'Conor, no. 75, London, Mar. 24, 1898, EA, FO 405–76, p. 207; Chargé Geoffray to Hanotaux, no. 59, tel., London, Mar. 26, 1898, "Very Confidential," DDF, ser. 1, 14: 163–64.

56. Geoffray to Hanotaux, no. 265, London, May 7, 1898, "Confidential," DDF, ser. 1, 14: 265–68. In the House of Lords Salisbury asserted on May 18 that Weihaiwei had been occupied by Britain "in order to strengthen and encourage China against her enemies and also to show Japan and Corea that England did not mean to throw up the game in northern China," Kato Takaaki reported. He applauded the action of the late government in not joining the Tripartite Intervention against Japan and remaining instead on good terms with "the rising power of Japan with whom England had so many grounds of sympathy and co-operation" (Kato to Nishi, no. 69, London, May 18, 1898, via Hayashi, St. Petersburg, May 19, 1898, "Special," JA, TEL 1898/0644–0645).

57. Kato to Nishi, no. 67, London, May 14, 1898, via Hayashi, St. Petersburg, May 15, 1898, "Special," JA, TEL 1898/0630. In a subsequent speech in mid-November Chamberlain identified the countries with whom Britain should make common cause in maintaining the open door in China as Japan, Germany, and the United States (Kato to Aoki, no. 92, London, Nov. 17, 1898, via Hayashi, St. Petersburg, Nov. 18, 1898, JA, TEL 1898/1388–1389). For a discussion of the importance of an alliance with Japan for Great Britain in the event of the outbreak of hostilities in China, see Harmand to Delcassé, no. 97, Tokyo, Dec. 3, 1898, DDF, ser. 1, 14: 845–49.

58. Montebello to Hanotaux, no. 49, St. Petersburg, May 25, 1898, FA, Corée, PE, 8: 242–46.

59. O'Conor to Salisbury, no. 240, St. Petersburg, June 15, 1898, EA, FO 405–77, pp. 250–51.

60. Geoffray to Delcassé, no. 437, London, Aug. 20, 1898, "Confidential," DDF, ser. 1, 14: 464–66.

61. Scott to Muraviev, St. Petersburg, Aug. 16/28, 1898, "Private," EA, FO 405–78, pp. 203–4.

62. Scott to Salisbury, no. 300, St. Petersburg, Sept. 6, 1898, "Confidential," EA, FO 405–78, pp. 202–3. See also Geoffray to Delcassé, no. 491, London, Sept. 22,

1898, DDF, ser. 1, 14: 571–73; Pichon to Delcassé, no. 73, Peking, Sept, 25, 1898, DDF, ser. 1, 14: 583–85; and Scott to Salisbury, no. 325, St. Petersburg, Oct. 6, 1898, "Very Confidential," EA, FO 405–79, p. 33.

63. Popov, "Anglo-russkoe," 121–23.

64. Scott to Salisbury, no. 355, St. Petersburg, Nov. 2, 1898, "Very Confidential," EA, FO 405–79, pp. 62–63; Romanov, *Rossiia v Man'chzhurii*, 220.

65. Scott to Salisbury, no. 361, St. Petersburg, Nov. 8, 1898, "Very Confidential," EA, FO 405–79, pp. 82–83.

66. Salisbury to Scott, no. 320, tel., London, Nov. 24, 1898, EA, FO 405–79, p. 105.

67. Scott to Salisbury, no. 381, St. Petersburg, Nov. 286, 1898, "Very Confidential," EA, FO 405–79, pp. 133–36.

68. Popov, "Anglo-russkoe," 123; Romanov, *Rossiia v Man'chzhurii*, 221–22.

69. Private letter of Lessar, dated Nov. 24/Dec. 6, 1898, as cited in Popov, "Anglo-russkoe," 124.

70. Popov, "Anglo-russkoe," 126–27.

71. *Ibid.*, 128; Romanov, *Rossiia v Man'chzhurii*, 229–31; Scott to Salisbury, no. 114, St. Petersburg, Apr. 18, 1899, and no. 115, "Confidential," of the same date, EA, FO 405–85, pp. 94–96.

72. French text of the identic notes, enclosed in Scott to Salisbury, no. 121, St. Petersburg, Apr. 20, 1899, and Salisbury to Scott, no. 63, tel., London, Apr. 22, 1899, EA, FO 405–85, pp. 94–97.

73. Great Britain, Foreign Office, *State Papers* 1898–1899, 91: 91–93. The agreement was officially communicated to the Chinese government by the British chargé d'affaires on May 8 (Yano to Aoki, no. 79, Peking, May 10, 1899, JA, TEL 1899/1045).

74. Great Britain, Foreign Office, *State Papers* 1898–1899, 91: 93–94.

75. Inoue Katsunosuke to Aoki, no. 26, Berlin, May 4, 1899, via Hayashi, St. Petersburg, May 5, 1899, JA, TEL 1899/1025–1026.

76. Pichon to Delcassé, no. 53, Peking, Apr. 24, 1899, "Confidential," and Delcassé to Montebello, no. 192, Paris, Apr. 27, 1899, DDF, ser. 1, 15: 241–46.

Conclusion: The Policy of Russia in East Asia

1. Commodore Matthew C. Perry declared in 1855 that "the freedom or the slavery of the world" would depend on the mighty battle which would eventually be fought in East Asia between "the Saxon and the Cossack" (Lensen, *Russia's Japan Expedition*, 128–29).

2. For a witty description of the Russians, as perceived by the Americans at the turn of the century, see William Franklin Sands, *Undiplomatic Memories*, 212–15.

3. For example, many authors relied on F. A. McKenzie's anti-Russian generalizations, without noting that they were at variance with his narrative. Writing of 1895, McKenzie asserted in *The Tragedy of Korea* that the Russians had adopted "a bold and aggressive policy" in Seoul (p. 55) and that Waeber's action in giving asylum to Kojong was "in keeping with the new aggressive policy of the Russian Government in the Far East" (p. 89). Yet in the same book McKenzie depicted Waeber as "a kindly, simple, straight-forward man," whose policy was "as open as the day." Conceding

that "even the other foreign representatives were amazed at the disinterestedness of his action," McKenzie related that Waeber "regarded the King as his guest, and he placed the big Russian Legation at the Royal disposal, asking for nothing in return, not even attempting to secure those concessions for his country which almost any other man of whatever nationality would have obtained under the circumstances" (p. 82). He damned Russian expansion while admitting that St. Petersburg's quest for an ice-free outlet to the Pacific was "a very natural and praiseworthy ambition" (p. 90).

4. Alexis Krausse predicted at the turn of the century that once the shoddily constructed Trans-Siberian Railroad had been repaired and completed, Russia would "like a giant refreshed, . . . once more gird up her loins and set forth on a renewed campaign for the conquest of the world" (Krausse, *Russia in Asia*, xxiv).

5. Malozemoff, 1–19; Fabritskii, 40.

6. Solov'ev, 18–19, 34–35; Cordier, *Histoire des rélations*, 3: 66–67. Cassini had obtained the position in Peking through the protection of friends in the Foreign Ministry. He had incurred heavy debts during a stormy youth in St. Petersburg and needed the money that went with the position in Peking—45,000 rubles a year—to meet his obligations. Far from young, Cassini was a diplomat of the old school which was becoming outmoded already then. He spoke and wrote almost exclusively in French, knew German well, and some English. He avoided writing in Russian. During the two years that Soloviev worked with him, he saw only one paper penned by Cassini in his own language. Cassini's predecessors had let the prestige of the Russian legation in Peking decline greatly. Popov had been too old; Kumani had been preoccupied with philological studies; and Chargé Konstantin Vasil'evich Kleimenov had merely followed the views of his Western colleagues. Furthermore, the Russian legation was rent by internal dissension. Determined to restore the respect due to a minister of his country, Cassini adopted a firm line both toward the Chinese and his subordinates. At his request First Secretary Kleimenov and Second Secretary Ivan Iakovlevich Korostovets were transferred to other posts against their will, and Aleksandr Ivanovich Pavlov, a former naval officer attached to the legation but actually Cassini's personal secretary, was promoted to second and then to first secretary of the legation. Iurii Iakovlevich Soloviev was brought in from the Asiatic Department as Second Secretary. Cassini lived with a young niece and her governess. He eventually married the governess and adopted the girl.

7. James Mavor, *An Economic History of Russia*, 2: 224–29; Romanov, *Ocherki*, 23–25.

8. Hitrovo to Lobanov-Rostovskii, no. 33, Tokyo, Apr. 28/May 10, 1895, RA, AVPR, Iaponskii stol, delo 900.

9. Moulin to Billot, no. 1531, St. Petersburg, Mar. 27, 1898, "Confidential," DDF, ser. 1, 14: 166–70.

10. Fabritskii, 37–39.

11. Moulin to Billot, no. 1531, St. Petersburg, Mar. 27, 1898, "Confidential," DDF, ser. 1, 14: 166–70.

12. According to Nikhamin, the Tonghak upheaval and the intervention of China and Japan removed the restraint placed on Russian policy toward Korea by apprehension of a Sino-Japanese rapprochement and the isolation of St. Petersburg. Confronted instead by the far greater threat of the absorption of Korea by the victor in a Sino-Japanese war, the tsarist government sought to forestall such conflict and maintain the *status quo* in order to keep China and Japan at a distance and leave her own options in Korea open (Nikhamin, "Russko-iaponskie otnosheniia," 27).

13. The subsequent occupation of Port Arthur might not have occurred had Germany not persisted, despite Russian objections (*not* prodding) in the occupation of Kiaochow. The opportunism of German policy was clearly revealed by Bülow in a top-secret review of the situation at the close of the nineteenth century. It was in Germany's interest, he wrote, to delay the further partition of China temporarily, partly in the interest of peace, partly because her own position in East Asia was steadily improving, but above all to allow for the development of her naval forces. Germany sought for the present to avoid conflicts of her own and to keep a free hand in the case of conflicts between third powers, particularly in the clash of interests between Russia and England. She wished to maintain the excellent relations with her Russian neighbor, due to the personal friendship of the two sovereigns, yet continue at the same time the good relations existing with England. "In this way we do not bind our hands prematurely and can at a given moment go to the side which then best corresponds to our interests," Bülow declared (Memorandum of Bülow, Berlin, Mar. 14, 1899, "Top secret," *Grosse Politik*, 14: 181–89). The prospect of Russia becoming deeper engaged in China appealed to Britain no less than to Germany, so long as her own interests were not violated. As Salisbury pointed out in a confidential conversation with Hatzfeldt on October 25, 1895, Russia's attention would thereby be drawn away from the Near East and she would not be strong enough with the remaining force to move out of the Black Sea (Hatzfeldt to German Foreign Office, Oct. 25, 1895, as cited in *German Diplomatic Documents*, 2: 345).

14. Hitrovo to Lobanov-Rostovskii, no. 54, Tokyo, Aug. 10/22, 1895, RA, AVPR, Iaponskii stol, 1895, delo 900. Contains seven enclosures with excerpts from the Japanese press.

15. Nishi to Saionji, no. 4, St. Petersburg, Jan. 13, 1896.

16. *Ibid.*; Saionji to Nishi, no. 172, Tokyo, Nov. 22, 1895, JA, TEL 1895/1350–1352; Nishi to Saionji, no. 91, St. Petersburg, Nov. 25, 1895, JA, TEL 1895/1067–68; Saionji to Nishi, no. 175, Tokyo, Nov. 29, 1895, JA, TEL 1895/1363; Nishi to Saionji, no. 93, St. Petersburg, Dec. 8, 1895, JA, TEL 1895/1088; Nishi to Saionji, no. 94, St. Petersburg, Dec. 11, 1895, JA, TEL 1895/1096; Nishi to Saionji, no. 2, St. Petersburg, Jan. 3, 1896, JA, TEL 1896/0005.

17. Saionji to Nishi, no. 33, Tokyo, Feb. 27, 1896, JA, TEL 1896/0246; Nishi to Saionji, no. 17, St. Petersburg, Mar. 1, 1896, JA, TEL 1896/0447–0448; Nishi to Saionji, no. 39, St. Petersburg, June 7, 1896, JA, TEL 1896/0690.

18. Gutschmid to Hohenlohe-Schillingsfürst, no. A 18, Tokyo, Jan. 18, 1896, GA.

19. Gutschmid to Hohenlohe-Schillingsfürst, no. A 27, Tokyo, Feb. 5, 1896, GA, FSU/Korea, no. 1/21. Hitrovo confided to Gutschmid that Foreign Minister Lobanov had listened to his counsel and had instructed Waeber and Speyer to curb their excessive zeal and exercise restraint. In spite of all good intentions, Gutschmid commented, it appeared from statements by Hitrovo and the minister of foreign affairs that Speyer upon his arrival in Seoul had fallen under the influence of Waeber, who lingered there, and was filled with the ambition to equal the political style of the latter, which in no way corresponded to the present policy of Russia, represented by Hitrovo, in this part of East Asia.

20. Kung-chuan Hsiao, *A Modern China and a New World*, 209.

21. Nikhamin, "Russko-iaponskie otnosheniia," 232.

22. Rosen had abandoned his customary reserve after extracting from Harmand the promise to keep his remarks in strictest confidence and not make use of them. Harmand broke his word and reported everything that Rosen had told him to Delcassé,

938 . *Notes to pages 851–53*

though he in turn insisted that Rosen's comments, particularly his appraisals of certain individuals in St. Petersburg and the Far East, not be transmitted to the French representative in Russia.

23. Note, appended to Harmand to Delcassé, no. 119, Tokyo, Nov. 18, 1899, "Very Confidential," FA, Korea, PE 9: 64–73, not published in DDF. He had succeeded, Rosen related, in lulling the mistrust and the suspicions of Japanese chauvinists and dispelling the alarmist predictions which had spread among the public in the wake of the Sino-Japanese War and Russia's "maladroit" intervention in Liaotung. But the attitude recently displayed by his countrymen had revived these alarms. The Japanese knew that England could not aid them at the moment. Those who were rational understood, he thought, that a conflict with Russia would end in their ultimate defeat. Nevertheless Japan would go to war, he predicted, if Russia continued on the dangerous road she had taken, making people believe that she harbored bad intentions which, he was convinced, did not exist except in the minds of young greenhorns eager to hurt and impede him and in the process to win imaginary glory for themselves. The Japanese Council of Ministers had discussed the situation at length. Marquis Ito, upon being consulted, had replied that nothing ought to be neglected to appease Russia and that no pretext must be given for aggression, but that should the government of St. Petersburg really show the intention of establishing itself in Korea to the detriment of Japan, the latter must bravely accept the consequences of the situation and oppose such encroachment by every means. All this, Rosen confessed, did not augur well for the future. But he expressed the hope that the counsels of prudence and moderation would prevail over the excitations of the inexperienced, bellicose group whose impetuous desire seemed to be to put fire to the powder. Might it please God, he invoked, that no new incident would arise in Korea.

24. Harmand to Delcassé, no. 134, Tokyo, Dec. 17, 1899, FA, NS 30, Mf 1: 71–74, and DDF, ser. 1, 16: 48–50. Although Aoki, in a conversation with Harmand, blamed the Russian seamen for enflaming the situation, he conceded that all sailors, Japanese no less than European, were "terrible" people.

25. Motono to Okuma, no. 72 and no. 73 ("Special"), St. Petersburg, Sept. 1, 1898, JA, TEL 1898/1045 and 1053–1054; Florinsky, 2: 1260–61; Jelavich, 224. Noting that no vital questions currently separated Germany from Russia, Foreign Secretary Bülow wrote in a review of the Far Eastern situation in the spring of 1899: "The traditional dynastic bonds of the two mutual ruling houses, which restrain possible fits [*Velleitäten*] of unreliable Russian statesmen, still form the strongest safeguard for European peace. For that reason we did not deny a benevolent reception to the Russian peace manifesto, however doubtful we are inwardly about the practical benefit of this notice" (Memorandum of Bülow, Berlin, Mar. 14, 1899, "Top Secret," *Grosse Politik*, 14: 181–89).

26. Langer, *Diplomacy of Imperialism*, 581–92; Edward McNall Burns and Philip Lee Ralph, *World Civilizations*, 2: 947.

27. Horace Rumbold to Salisbury, no. 70, Vienna, Mar. 13, 1898, "Confidential," EA, FO 405–76, pp. 185–86.

28. Sir Charles S. Scott to Salisbury, no. 361, St. Petersburg, Nov. 8, 1898, "Very Confidential," EA, FO 405–79, pp. 82–83.

29. Scott to Salisbury, no. 344, St. Petersburg, Nov. 2, 1898, "Very Confidential," EA, FO 405–79, pp. 62–63.

30. Liang Ch'i-ch'ao, *Likhunchzhan ili politicheskaia istoriia Kitaia za posledniia 40 let*, xii–xiii.

31. As Vice Admiral Hamilton reported in the fall of 1886, after a visit to the Korean and Russian ports in the Sea of Japan and the Gulf of Tatary, "whatever may be the wishes of Russia as to the occupation of any of the Corean ports, they have not now the power to take them, nor will have for many years to come under the changed circumstances of China and Japan." The changed circumstances to which Hamilton alluded, included "comparatively powerful navies," built by both China and Japan. (The dispatch of four Chinese men-of-war to Vladivostok in 1886 to fetch several Chinese commissioners had been in the nature of a naval demonstration to impress Russia with China's power. [Sienkiewicz to Freycinet, DP, no. 5, undated, received by cabinet on Oct. 18, 1886, FA, CP, Japan, 32: 208–11]). Hamilton related that a high authority on Eastern Siberia had told him that "every Russian from the Governor-General [of the Amur Region] downwards lived in fear of Chinese aggression." General I. G. Baranov himself had unmistakably shown to Hamilton his fear of China, asking him whether he did not think the European powers should combine against China rather than lend her officers and drill her troops. "In my opinion," Hamilton wrote, "the power of Russia on the sea-coast of Siberia is very weak; they know it, and play the game of brag to hide it. Moreover, it is an expensive toy, and must be neglected when more serious calls on their service arise elsewhere." Vladivostok was no threat to Great Britain economically because of its position. Nor was it a military menace. It was inadequately fortified and was ice-bound or fogged-in much of the year. "Before Vladivostok can become even a third-rate naval port, much money must be spent on it," Hamilton remarked. He doubted that the Russians would take a more advanced position, for it would be weaker than Vladivostok and would undermine their position in the Far East further. Above all, Hamilton noted, the Russian fleet wintered in Japanese ports—"Japan is practically their headquarters now." If Russia were to alienate Japan by seizing a Korean harbor, she would lose use of the Japanese ports. Japan would be "sealed" to her ships (Hamilton to Walsham, "Confidential," *Audacious*, Hakodate, Sept. 29, 1886, EA, FO 405–36, p. 80).

Bibliography

I was so fortunate as to obtain from the Historical Archives of the Foreign Ministry of the U.S.S.R. microfilms of Russian diplomatic dispatches from the Far East in exchange for microfilms of Japanese dispatches from St. Petersburg. Russian documents preserved in Seoul, Soviet doctoral dissertations with extensive quotes from tsarist manuscripts, and the unpublished dispatches of the French representatives in Korea (with whom the Russian diplomats shared their thoughts and often their instructions) helped to fill in some of the gaps. The diplomatic archives of Germany, Japan, Great Britain, the United States, and Belgium provided balancing data. I have made little direct use of Chinese sources, but have gleaned the Chinese point of view from dissertations written by Chinese and Korean doctoral candidates in German, French, and English on the basis of published collections of Chinese and Korean documents. Though I had acquired over the past thirty years copies, at least on microfilm, of practically everything ever printed on Russian relations with East Asia, I shelved most secondary sources until I had reconstructed the above story, because their authors had not had access to the treasure trove of unpublished dispatches. Instead of harnessing the original documents to a preconceived theme based on traditional interpretations, I let the new material guide me. I did not go beyond 1899 in this work, which had already grown to inordinate length, because detailed studies exist on the period from 1900 to 1917.

Since the footnote citations, for the sake of brevity, are confined to the author's name or in case of several publications by the same author to his name and an abbreviated title, readers may have to refer back to the bibliography from time to time. To simplify the task, works are listed in the bibliography in one alphabetic grouping the way they are cited in the footnotes. For example, series of documents are to be found under the title of the collection rather than under the name of the country and ministry or institute that compiled them. The following abbreviations are used in the source notes:

BA—Belgian Archives
EA—English Archives
FA—French Archives
GA—German Archives
JA—Japanese Archives
KA—Korean Archives
RA—Russian Archives
USDD—United States Diplomatic Dispatches

G.A.L.

"Abdication, Acclamation, Assassination!" *Korean Repository* 1898, 5: 342–49.
Abe Kozo. "Nisshin kowa to sangoku kansho." In Nihon Kokusai Seiji Gakkai, comp., *Nihon gaikoshi kenkyu: Nisshin Nichi-Ro senso*, 52–70. Tokyo, 1961.
Adams, Edward B. *Through Gates of Seoul: Trails and Tales of Yi Dynasty*. 2 vols. 2d ed. Seoul, 1974–1977.
Afanas'ev I and Grudzinskii, S. "Zapiski russkikh instruktorov v Koree." *Priamurskiia vedomosti* 1898, 230: 9–19, and 231: 17–24.
Africa, Philip. "Russian-Chinese Relations and the American Presence in Eastern Asia: 1898–1905." Undated offprint from *Asian Studies* (Bombay), vol. 1.
"The Agreement between Russia and Japan." *Korean Repository* 1897, 4: 108–10.
Akagi, Roy Hidemichi. *Japan's Foreign Relations*. Tokyo, 1936.
Aleksandrenko, V. N. "Ocherki vneshnikh snoshenii Iaponii s inostrannymi derzhavami." *Zhurnal Ministerstva iustitsii* 1904, 5: 95–132.
———, comp. *Sobranie vazhneishikh traktatov i konventsii, zakliuchennykh Rossii s inostrannymi derzhavami (1774–1906)*. Warsaw, 1906.
Al'ftan, Lieutenant Colonel. "Poezdka v Koreiu Gen. Sht. podpolkovnika Al'ftana v dekabre 1895 i ianvare 1896 g." *Sbornik geograficheskikh, topograficheskikh i statisticheskikh materialov po Azii* 1896, 69: 8–96.
Allen, James. *Under the Dragon Flag: My experiences in the Chino-Japanese War*. London, 1898.
Allgemeine Deutsche Biographie. 65 vols. München, 1875–1912.
"Along Progressive Lines." *Korean Repository* 1896, 3: 368–70.
Anosov, Semen D. *Koreitsy v Ussuriiskom krae*. Khabarovsk, 1928.
Anschel, Eugene, ed. *The American Image of Russia, 1775–1917*. New York, 1974.
Aoki Hatsuzaburo. *Taigai kosho shifu*. Tokyo, 1945.
Aoyagi Atsutsune. *Kyokuto gaikoshi gaikan*. Tokyo, 1938.
Appenzeller, Rev. H. G. "The Opening of Korea: Admiral Shufeldt's Account of It." *Korean Repository* 1892, 1: 57–62.
Aprelev, V. P. "Snosheniia Rossii s Kitaem. Istoricheskaia spravka." MS in three notebooks in the collection of the American Society for Russian Naval History.

Ariga, Nagao. *La guerre sino-japonaise au point de vue du droit international.* Paris, 1896.

Armstrong, Terence. *Russian Settlement in the North.* Cambridge, 1965.

Asahi Shimbunsha, comp. *Meiji Taisho-shi.* 6 vols. 1930–1931.

Asakawa, K. *The Russo-Japanese Conflict: Its Causes and Issues.* Westminster, 1904.

"The Assassination of the Queen of Korea." *Korean Repository* 1895, 2: 386–92.

Aston, W. G. "Hideyoshi's Invasion of Korea." *Transactions of the Asiatic Society of Japan* 1878, ser. 1, vol. 6, pt. 2, pp. 227–48.

"The Attempt on the Life of Kim Hongyuk." *Korean Repository* 1898, 5: 107–9.

Atteridge, A. Hilliard. "The Battle of the Yalu River: Sept. 17, 1894." In *Battles of the Nineteenth Century,* 2: 79–89. London, 1897.

Avarin, V. Ia. *Bor'ba za Tikhii Okean: Iapono-amerikanskie protivorechie.* Moscow, 1947.

—————. *Bor'ba za Tikhii Okean: Agressiia SShA i Anglii, ikh protivorechiia i osvoboditel'naia bor'ba narodov.* Moscow, 1952.

—————. *Imperializm i Manchzhuriia: Etapy imperialisticheskoi bor'by za Manchzhuriiu.* Moscow, 1931.

—————. *Imperializm v Manchzhurii: Imperializm i proizvoditel'nye sily Manchzhurii.* Moscow, 1934.

Azbelev, I. P. *Iaponiia i Koreia. Zametki iz krugosvetnago plavaniia s 15-iu risunkami.* Moscow, 1895.

Badmaev, P. A. *Rossiia i Kitai.* St. Petersburg, 1905.

Baedecker, Karl. *Russland nebst Teheran, Port Arthur, Peking: Handbuch für Reisende.* 7th ed. Leipzig, 1912.

Bagashev, I. V. "Ob ispravlenii Russko-Kitaiskoi granitsy v Nerchinskom krae i o torgovle s Mongoliei i Mandzhuriei." *Trudy obshchestva dlia sodeistviia russkoi promyshlennosti i torgovle* 1881, 12: 57–81.

Balkashin, N. N. "Torgovoe dvizhenie mezhdu Zapadnoi Sibir'iu, Srednei Aziei i kitaiskimi vlastiiami." *Zapiski Zapodnosibirskogo otdela Russkogo geograficheskogo ob-va* 1881, 2: 1–32

Balz, Toku, ed. *Erwin Bälz: Das Leben eines deutschen Arztes im erwachenden Japan.* Stuttgart, 1930.

"Baron von Möllendorff." *Korean Review* 1901, 1: 247.

Barsukov, Ivan. *Graf Nikolai Nikolaevich Murav'ev-Amurskii po ego pis'mam, offitsial'nym dokumentam, razskazam sovremennikov i pechatnym istochnikam.* 2 vols. in 1. Moscow, 1891.

Bartlett, Sir Ellis Ashmead. "The War between China and Japan." *The Imperial and Asiatic Quarterly Review, an Oriental and Colonial Record* 1895, 2nd ser., 9: 1–20.

Bartol'd, V. *Istoriia izucheniia Vostoka v Evrope i Rossii.* Leningrad, 1925.

Battistini, Lawrence H. "The Korean Problem in the Nineteenth Century." *Monumenta Nipponica* 1952, 8: 47–66.

Beasley, W. G. *The Modern History of Japan.* New York, 1963.

Becker, Robert Dean. "Anglo-Russian Relations 1898–1910." Ph.D. dissertation, University of Colorado, 1972.

Beckmann, George M. *The Modernization of China and Japan.* New York, 1962.

Bee, Minge C. (Benjamin Ming-chu). "The Leasing of Kiaochow: A Study in Diplomacy and Imperialism," Ph.D. dissertation, Harvard University, 1935.

————. "Origins of German Far Eastern Policy." *Chinese Social and Political Science Review* 1937–38, 21: 65–97.

————. "The Peterhof Agreement." *Chinese Social and Political Science Review* 1937, 20: 231–50.

Beisner, Robert L. *From the Old Diplomacy to the New, 1865–1900*. New York, 1974.

Belgium, Foreign Ministry Archives.

Bell, John. *Travels from St. Petersburg in Russia to Diverse Parts of Asia*. 2 vols. Glasgow, 1763.

Bérard, V. *La revolte de l'Asie. (L'Asie et l'Europe. Le Japon et l'Europe. La descente russe. L'expansion japonaise. Le rôle de l'Angleterre.)* Paris, 1904.

Beresford, Lord Charles. *The Break-up of China*. London, 1899.

————. *The Memoirs of Admiral Lord Charles Beresford Written by Himself*. 2 vols. London, 1914.

Bernstein, Hermann, ed. *The Willy-Nicky Correspondence: Being the Secret and Intimate Telegrams Exchanged between the Kaiser and the Tsar*. New York, 1918.

Beskrovnyi, L. G. *Russkaia armiia i flot v XIX veke*. Moscow, 1973.

Beskrovnyi, L. G. and Narochnitskii, A. L. "K istorii vneshnei politiki Rossii na Dal'nem Vostoke v XIX veke." *Voprosy istorii* 1974, 6: 14–36.

Beveridge, Albert J. *The Russian Advance*. New York, 1904.

Bigham, Clive. *A Year in China, 1899–1900*. London, 1901.

Bikle, George B. Jr. "An Essay on the Authorities for Sino-Russian Relations, 1850–1905." Unpublished essay, 1959.

————. "The Russian Role in the Triplice Intervention against Japan." Unpublished paper, 1960.

Bilof, Edwin George. "The Imperial Russian General Staff and China in the Far East 1880–1888: A Study of the Operations of the General Staff." Ph.D. dissertation, Syracuse University, 1974.

Bing, Edward J., ed. *The Secret Letters of the Last Tsar*. New York, 1938.

Bingham, Woodbridge; Conroy, Hilary; and Iklé, Frank W. *A History of Asia*. 2d ed. vol. 2. Boston, 1974.

Bishop, Isabella Bird. *Korea and Her Neighbors: A Narrative of Travel, with an Account of the Recent Vicissitudes and Present Position of the Country*. New York, 1898.

————. "Koreans in Russian Manchuria." *Korean Repository* 1897, 4: 41–44.

Bix, Herbert Philip. "Japanese Imperialism and Manchuria, 1890–1931." PhD. dissertation, Harvard University, 1972.

Blaker, Michael. *Japanese International Negotiating Style*. New York, 1977.

Bland, J. O. P. *Li Hung-chang*. London, 1917.

Bodley, R. V. C. *Admiral Togo: The Authorized Life of Admiral of the Fleet, Marquis Heihachiro Togo, O. M.* London, 1935.

Bogdanovich, E. V. *Russiia na Dal'nem Vostoke*. St. Petersburg, 1901.

Bogdanovich, T. *Ocherki iz proshlago i nastoiashchago Iaponii*. St. Petersburg, 1905.

————. *Sovremennyi Kitai: Istoriko-kulturnyi ocherk*. St. Petersburg, 1901.

Bogoiavlenskii, N. V. *Zapadnyi zastepnyi Kitai: Ego proshloe, nastoiashchee sostoianie i polozhenie v nem russkikh poddanykh*. St. Petersburg, 1906.

"Bokserskoe vostanie." Edited by A. Popov. *Krasnyi Arkhiv* 1926, 14: 1–49.

Bolkhovitinov, L. M. "Kolonizatory Dal'nego Vostoka." In *Velikaia Rossiia: Sbornik statei*, 217–35. Moscow, 1910.

————. "Rossiia na Dal'nem Vostoke." In *Velikaia Rossiia: Sbornik statei*, 195–216. Moscow, 1910.

Borton, Hugh. *Japan's Modern Century*. 2d ed., New York, 1970.

Boulger, D. C. "Li Hung-chang." *Contemporary Review* 1896: 18–29.

Bounds, Marcella. "The Sino-Russian Secret Treaty of 1896." In Harvard East Asian Research Center, *Papers on China* 1970, 23: 109–25.

Brahm, Heinz. *Die Chinapolitik Russlands und der Sowjetunion*. Köln, 1969. (Berichte des Bundesinstituts für Ostwissenschaftliche und Internationale Studien, no. 40.)

Brandenburg, Erich. *Von Bismarck zum Weltkriege: Die deutsche Politik in den Jahrzehnten vor dem Kreige. Dargestellt auf Grund der Akten des Auswärtigen Amtes*. Berlin, 1924.

Brandt, Maximilian August von. *China und seine Handelsbeziehungen zum Auslande*. Berlin, 1899.

————. *Drei Jahre Ostasiatischer Politik—1894–1897*. Stuttgart, 1897.

————. *Dreiunddreissig Jahre in Ost-Asien: Erinnerungen eines deutschen Diplomaten*. 3 vols. Leipzig, 1901.

————. *Die Zukunft Ostasiens: Ein Beitrag zur Geschichte und zum Verhältniss der ostasiatischen Frage*. 3d ed. Stuttgart, 1903.

Brennan, William Howard. "The Russian Foreign Ministry and the Alliance with Germany, 1878–84." Ph.D. dissertation, University of Oregon, 1971.

Bridgham, Philip Low. "American Policy Toward Korean Independence, 1866–1910." Ph.D. dissertation, Fletcher School of Law and Diplomacy, Tufts College, 1951.

Briefe Wilhelms II an den Zaren 1894–1914. Edited by Dr. Walter Goetz. Berlin, 1920.

British Documents on the Origins of the War, 1898–1914. Edited by G. P. Gooch and Harold Temperley for the British Foreign Office. 11 vols. London, 1926–1938.

Brodskii, R. M. *Amerikanskaia ekspansiia v severno-vostochnom Kitae, 1898–1905*. Lvov, 1965.

Brown, Delmer M. *Nationalism in Japan: An Introductory Historical Analysis*. Berkeley, 1955.

Bruce, Maurice. *The Shaping of the Modern World*. New York, 1958.

Bujac, E. *La guerre sino-japonaise*. Paris, 1896.

Buksgevden, A. *Russkii Kitai: Ocherki diplomaticheskikh snoshenii Rossii s Kitaem*. Port Arthur, 1902.

Bulgakov, F. I. *Port Artur: Iaponskaia osada i russkaia obornoa ego s moria i sushi*. vol. 1. St. Petersburg, 1905.

Bülow, Bernhard Fürst von. *Denkwürdigkeiten*. Edited by F. von Stockhammern. vol. 1 Berlin, 1930.

Bülow, H. v. *Russland-Japans Handelspolitik und Industrie*. Dresden, 1904.

Bunakov, E. V. "Iz istorii russko-kitaiskikh otnoshenii v pervoi polovine XIX v." *Sovetskoe vostokovedenie* 1956, 2: 96–104.

Burns, Edward McNall, and Ralph, Philip Lee. *World Civilizations*. 5th ed. 2 vols. New York, 1955.

Cady, John F. *The Roots of French Imperialism in Eastern Asia*. Ithaca, N.Y., 1954.

Cambon, Paul. *Correspondence, 1870–1924*. 2 vols. Paris, 1940–1946.

Campbell, C. W. "Report by Acting Vice-Consul Campbell of a Journey in North

Corea in September and October 1889." Confidential Correspondence of the British Foreign Office, English Archives, 405–48, pp. 1–37, plus map.

Carles, W. R. *Life in Korea*. London, 1888.

Cassey, John W. "The Mission of Charles Denby and International Rivalries in the Far East, 1885–1898." Ph.D. dissertation, University of Southern California, 1959.

Cecil, Lamar. *The German Diplomatic Service, 1871–1914*. Princeton, N.J., 1976.

Chang, Chung-fu. *The Anglo-Japanese Alliance*. Baltimore, 1931.

Chang, Kia-ngau. *China's Struggle for Railroad Development*. New York, 1943.

Chang, Tao Shing. "International Controversies over the Chinese Eastern Railway." Ph.D. dissertation, University of Iowa, 1934.

Chay, Jongsuk. "The United States and the Closing Door in Korea: American-Korean Relations, 1894–1905." Ph.D. dissertation, University of Michigan, 1965.

Chen, Changbin. *La presse francaise et les questions Chinoises (1894–1901). Étude sur la rivalité des puissances étrangères en Chine*. Paris, 1941.

Ch'en, Jerome. *Yüan Shih-k'ai 1859–1916: Brutus Assumes the Purple*. Stanford, 1961.

Ch'en, Tieh-ming. "The Sino-Japanese War, 1894–95: Its Origin, Development and Diplomatic Background." Ph.D. dissertation, University of California, Berkeley, 1944.

Cheng, Lin. *The Chinese Railways: A Historical Survey*. Shanghai, 1935.

Cheng, Tien-fong. *A History of Sino-Russian Relations*. Washington, 1957.

Cherevkov, V. "Iz noveishei istorii Iaponii 1854–1894." *Vestnik Evropy* 1894, 170: 227–72, 478–524.

Cherevkova, A. A. "Iz vospominanii o Iaponii." *Istoricheskii vestinik* 1893, 51: 262–80, 540–58, 850–74; 52: 187–206, 473–89, 801–25; 53: 202–22, 469–83.

———. *Ocherki sovremennoi Iaponii*. St. Petersburg, 1898.

Cherkasova, Mariia Aleksandrovna. "Zapiski russkoi missionerki v Iaponii Marii Aleksandrovny Cherkasovoi." *Missioner* 1879, 43: 366–70; 44: 375–78.

Chien, Frederick Foo. *The Opening of Korea: A Study of Chinese Diplomacy 1876–1885*. Hamden, Conn., 1967.

The China Review: or, Notes and Queries on the Far East. 25 vols. Hong Kong, 1872–1901.

"China, Russia and the Liaotung Peninsula." *Japan Weekly Mail* 1895, p. 637.

Chirol, Valentine. *The Far Eastern Question*. London, 1896.

———. *Fifty Years in a Changing World*. London, 1927.

Choe, Ching Young. *The Rule of the Taewon Gun, 1864–73; Restoration in Yi Korea*. Cambridge, 1972.

Choi, Soo Bock. "Political Dynamics in Hermit Korea: The Rise of Royal Power in the Decade of the Taewonkun, 1864–1873." Ph.D. dissertation, University of Maryland, 1963.

Choi, Woonsang. *The Fall of the Hermit Kingdom*. Dobbs Ferry, N.Y., 1967.

Chow, Jen-hwa. *China and Japan: The History of Chinese Diplomatic Missions in Japan, 1877–1911*. Singapore, 1975.

Christie, Mrs. Dugald, ed. *Thirty Years in Moukden, 1883–1913: Being the Experiences and Recollections of Dugald Christie, C. M. G., F. R. C. S., F. R. C. P. Edin*. London, 1914. (Published in the United States as *Thirty Years in the Manchu Capital*.)

Chun, Chung-whan. "La France et la guerre russo-japonaise (1895–1905)." Ph.D. dissertation, Université de Paris, 1970.

Chun, Hae-jong. *Kankoku kinsei taigai kankei bunken biyo.* Seoul, 1966.

————. "Sino-Korean Relations in the Ch'ing Period." In John K. Fairbank, ed. *The Chinese World Order: Traditional China's Foreign Relations.* Cambridge, Mass., 1968.

Clark, Allen D. and Clark, Donald N. *Seoul Past and Present: A Guide to Yi T'aejo's Capital.* Seoul, 1969.

Clubb, O. Edmund. *China and Russia: The "Great Game."* New York, 1971.

Clyde, Paul H. *International Rivalries in Manchuria, 1689–1922.* 2d ed. rev. Columbus, 1928.

Clyde, Paul H. and Beers, Burton F. *The Far East: A History of Western Impacts and Eastern Responses, 1830–1975.* 6th ed. Englewood Cliffs, N.J., 1975.

Colquhoun, Archibald R. *China in Transformation.* New York, 1898.

————. *The 'Overland' to China.* London, 1900.

The Columbia Lippincott Gazetteer of the World. New York, 1961.

Conroy, Hilary. "Chôsen mondai: The Korean Problem in Meiji Japan." In American Philosophical Society, *Proceedings* 1956, 100: 443–54.

————. *The Japanese Seizure of Korea, 1868–1910: A Study of Realism and Idealism in International Relations.* Philadelphia, 1960.

————. "Lessons from Japanese Imperialism." *Monumenta Nipponica* 1966, 21: 334–45.

Cook, Harold F. *Korea's 1884 Incident, Its Background and Kim Ok-Kyun's Elusive Dream.* Seoul, 1972. (Royal Asiatic Society, Korea Branch, Monograph Series, no. 4.)

Coquin, Francois-Xavier. *La Siverie: Peuplement et immigration paysanne au XIXᵉ siècle.* Paris, 1969. (Collection historique de l'Institut d'Études slaves, vol. 20.)

Cordier, Henri. *Histoire des relations de la Chine avec les puissances occidentales 1860–1902.* 3 vols. Paris, 1901–2.

————. *Histoire Générale de la Chine et de ses relations avec les pays étrangers depuis les temps les plus anciens jusqu'à la chute de la dynastie Manchoue.* Vol. 4. Paris, 1920.

Cornwall, Peter George. "The Meiji Navy: Training in an Age of Change." Ph.D. dissertation, University of Michigan, 1970.

"Coronation Ceremony." *The Independent.* Nov. 14, 1897.

Corrigan, Francis P. "The Early Years of Chinese Intervention in Korea, 1882–87." Certificate essay, East Asian Institute, Columbia University, New York, 1956.

Coucheron-Aamont, W. *Die Geschichte Ostasiens nach dem Frieden von Schimonoseki.* Translated from the Norwegian by Kathe Robolsky. Leipzig, 1899.

Courant, Maurice. "La Coree et les puissances étrangères." *Annales des sciences politiques* 1904, 19: 253–67.

————. "Un siècle et demi des relations russe-japonaises." *Journal des Debats* 1904, Feb. 5–12.

Craig, Albert M. and Shively, Donald H., eds. *Personality in Japanese History.* Berkeley, 1970.

Cramer, Anneliese. *Die Beziehungen zwischen England und Japan von 1894–1902.* Zeulenroda, 1935.

Creelman, James. *On the Great Highway: The Wanderings of a Special Correspondent.* Boston, 1901.

Crist, David Scott. "Russia's Manchurian Policy, 1895–1905." Ph.D. dissertation, University of Michigan, 1941.

Curzon, George N. *Problems of the Far East. Japan—Korea—China.* New York, 1896.

Cyon, E. de. M. *Witte et les Finances Russes d'après des documents officiels et inédits.* 4th ed. Paris, 1895.

Dai jimmei jiten. 10 vols. Tokyo, 1953–1955.

Dallet, Charles. *Histoire de l'église de Corée.* 2 vols. Paris, 1874.

Dallin, David J. *The Rise of Russia in Asia.* New Haven, 1949.

Dal'nii Vostok. Compiled by the Russian General Staff. 3 vols. St. Petersburg, 1911.

D'Anethan, Baroness Albert. *Fourteen Years of Diplomatic Life in Japan.* London, 1912.

Daniels, Gordon. "Sir Harry Parkes: British Representative in Japan 1865–1883." Ph.D. dissertation, Oxford University, 1967.

Davidov, D. A. *Kolonizatsiia Man'chzhurii i severo-vostochnoi Mongolii. (Oblasti Tao-Nan-Fu.)* Vladivostok, 1911.

Davidson-Houston, J. V. *Russia and China From the Huns to Mao Tse-tung.* London, 1960.

Dawson, Wm. H. "Foreign Encroachments in China, 1885–1898." In A. M. Ward and G. P. Gooch eds. *Cambridge History of British Foreign Policy*, vol. 3, chpt. 3. Cambridge, 1923.

De Bary, Wm. Theodore, ed. *Sources of the Japanese Tradition.* Compiled by Ryusaku Tsunoda, Wm. Theodore de Bary, and Donald Keene. New York, 1958.

"The Deer Island Episode." *Korean Repository* 1898, 5: 109–13.

De Laguérie, R. Villetard. *La Corée, indépendante, Russe, ou Japonaise.* Paris, 1898.

De Lima, Jude. "La question d'Extrême-Orient vue par la diplomatie française (1894–1904)." Ph.D. dissertation, Université de Paris, 1974.

Demchinskii, Boris. *Rossiia v Manchzhurii. (Po neopublikovannym dokumentam).* St. Petersburg, 1908

Denby, Charles. *China and Her People: Being the Observations, Reminiscences, and Conclusions of an American Diplomat.* 2 vols. Boston, 1906.

————. "How Peace was made between China and Japan." *Forum* 1900, 29: 713–19.

Denikin, A. I. *Russko-kitaiskii vopros. Voenno-politicheskii ocherk.* Warsaw, 1908.

Denisov, V. I. *Rossiia na Dal'nem Vostoke.* St. Petersburg, 1913.

Dennett, Tyler. "American Choices in the Far East in 1882." *American Historical Review* 1924–1925, 30: 84–98.

————. *Americans in Eastern Asia: A Critical Study of the Policy of the United States with Reference to China, Japan and Korea in the 19th Century.* New York, 1922.

————. "Early American Policy in Korea, 1883–7." *Political Science Quarterly* 1923, 38: 82–103.

————. *John Hay: From Poetry to Politics.* New York, 1933.

Denny, O. N. *China and Korea.* Shanghai, 1888.

Deuchler, Martina. "The Opening of Korea, 1875–1884." Ph.D. dissertation, Harvard

University, 1967. (Published since the writing of this book as *Confucian Gentlemen and Barbarian Envoys*. Seattle, 1977.)

Diósy, Arthur. *The New Far East*. London, 1905.

Diplomaticheskii Slovar'. Edited by A. A. Gromyko and others. 2d ed. 3 vols. 1971–73.

Djang, Chu. "Chinese Suzerainty: A Study of Diplomatic Relations between China and her Vassal States (1870–1896)." Ph.D. dissertation, Johns Hopkins University, 1935.

Djang, F. D. *The Diplomatic Relations between Germany and China since 1898*. Shanghai, 1936.

Dmitriev-Mamonov, A. I. *Ot Volgi do Velikago okeana: Putevoditel' po velikoi sibirskoi zheleznoi doroge s opisaniem Shilko-Amurskago vodnago puti i Manchzhurii*. St. Petersburg, 1900.

"Dnevnik ministerstva inostrannykh del za 1915–1916 gg." *Krasnyi Arkhiv* 1928, 31: 3–50; 32: 3–87.

Dnevnik Imperatora Nikolaia II. Berlin, 1923.

"Dnevnik Nikolaia Romanova," *Krasnyi Arkhiv* 1927, 20: 123–52; 21: 79–96.

Dnevnik V. N. Lamzdorfa, 1886–1890. Compiled by Tsentrarkhiv. Moscow, 1926.

Dnevnik V. N. Lamzdorfa, 1891–1892. Moscow, 1934.

Dobrynin, Anatolii Fedorovich. "Dal'nevostochnaia politika SShA v period russko-iaponskoi voiny (1904–1905 gg.)." Ph.D. dissertation, Moscow, 1947.

————. "SShA i nezavisimost' Korei 1904–1905 gg." In Academy of Sciences of the USSR, *Izvestiia*, Historical and Philosophical Series, 1947, 4: 342–54.

Documents diplomatiques français, 1871–1914. Compiled by the French Foreign Ministry. 41 vols. Paris, 1929–59.

"Dogovor s Koreei, 25 iiunia 1884 goda." In *Sbornik torgovykh dogovorov i drugikh vytekaiushchikh iz nikh soglashenii, zakliuchennykh mezhdu Rossiei i inostrannymi gosudarstvami*, 370–92. St. Petersburg, 1915.

"Doku-Ro no Koshuwan oyobi Ryojun-ko soshaku mondai narabi ni Kankoku hozen ni kansuru Nichi-Ro kyotei teiyo." Document MT 1.4.1.25 (reel 58) of microfilmed Japanese Ministry of Foreign Affairs Archives.

Dong, Chong. "Japanese Annexation of Korea: A Study of Korean-Japanese Relations to 1910." Ph.D. dissertation, University of Colorado, 1955.

————. "The United States Attitude towards the Sino-Russian-Japanese Policies in Korea, 1891–1898." In Hanguk Yongu Tosogwan, Seoul, *Bulletin of the Korean Research Center: Journal of the Social Sciences and Humanities* 1965, 23: 1–28.

Dorwart, Jeffrey Michael. "The Pigtail War: The American Response to the Sino-Japanese War of 1894–1895." Ph.D. dissertation, University of Massachusetts, 1971.

Dotson, Lillian Ota. "The Sino-Japanese War of 1894–95: A Study in Asian Power Politics." Ph.D. dissertation, Yale University, 1951.

Douglas, Sir Robert K. *Europe and the Far East, 1506–1912*. Revised and corrected with an additional chapter (1904–1912) by Joseph H. Longford. Cambridge, 1913.

————. *Li Hung-chang*. London, 1895.

Driault, Edouard. *La Question d'Extrême Orient*. Paris, 1908.

Du Boulay, N. W. H. *An Epitome of the Chino-Japanese War, 1894–1895*. London, 1896.

Dulles, Foster Rhea. *Yankees and Samurai: America's Role in the Emergence of Modern Japan, 1791–1900.* New York, 1965.
Duncan, Chesney. *Corea and the Powers: A Review of the Far Eastern Question.* Shanghai, 1889.
Dye, William McE. Letter to the Editor, *Korean Repository* 1896, 3: 219.

Eastlake, F. Warrington and Yamada, Yoshi-aki. *Heroic Japan: A History of the War between China and Japan.* Yokohama, 1896.
Eastman, Lloyd E. *Throne and Mandarins: China's Search for a Policy During the Sino-French Controversy, 1880–1885.* Cambridge, Mass., 1967
Eckardstein, Hermann Freiherr von. *Lebenserinnerungen und politische Denkwürdigkeiten.* 3 vols. Leipzig, 1920–1921.
Edwardes, Michael. *Asia in the European Age, 1498–1955.* New York, 1961.
Efimov, G. V. "Germanskii imperializm v Kitae (1894–1902)." *Uchenye zapiski Tikhookeanskogo instituta* 1947, 1: 51–84.
————. "Pervye shagi germanskogo imperilizma v Kitae." *Uchenye zapiski LGU*, seriia gumanitarnykh nauk, 1943, 87: 67–91.
————. *Vneshniaia politika Kitaia 1894–1899 gg.* Moscow, 1958.
————. "Vneshniaia politika Tsinskogo pravitel'stva vo vremia Kitaisko-Iaponskoi voiny 1894–1895 godov." *Sovetskoe vostokovedenie* 1957, 3: 17–31.
Eidus, Kh. T. *Istoriia Iaponii s drevneishikh vremen do nashikh dnei.* Moscow, 1968.
Eikichi, Endo, and Shigesaburo, Ikazaki. *Nisshin senso shimatsu.* Tokyo, 1895.
"The Emperor of Korea," *Korean Repository* 1895, 2: 435–38.
"The Emperor of Russia." *Japan Weekly Mail* 1893, pp. 229–30.
"England and Russia in the East." *Japan Weekly Mail* 1895, p. 667
Entsiklopedicheskii slovar'. 86 vols. St. Petersburg, 1890–1907.
Entsiklopediia voennykh i morskikh nauk. 8 vols. St. Petersburg, 1883–1897.
Erdmann, Ada v. *Nikolaj Karlovič Giers, russischer Aussenminister 1882–1895: Eine politische Biographie.* Berlin, 1936.
Esthus, Raymond. "Changing Concepts of the Open Door, 1899–1910." *Mississippi Valley Historical Review* 1959, 46: 435–54.
Eyre, James K. Jr. "Russia and the American Acquisition of the Philippines." *Mississippi Valley Historical Review* 1942, 28: 539–62.

Fabritskii, Semen Semenovich. *Iz proshlago: Vospominaniia fligel'-adiutanta gosudaria imperatora Nikolaia II.* Berlin, 1926.
Fairbank, John K., ed. *The Chinese World Order: Traditional China's Foreign Relations.* Cambridge, Mass., 1968.
Fairbank, John K.; Reischauer, Edwin O.; and Craig, Albert M., eds. *East Asia: The Modern Transformation.* Boston, 1965.
Falk, Edwin Albert. *From Perry to Pearl Harbor: The Struggle for Supremacy in the Pacific.* Garden City, N.Y., 1943.
"The Far Eastern Situation." *Japan Weekly Mail* 1898, p. 263.
"The Fate of the Queen." *Korean Repository* 1895, 2: 431–35.
Fedorov, M. P. *Sopernichestvo torgovykh interesov na Vostoke.* St. Petersburg, 1903.
"First Steps of Russian Imperialism in the Far East (1888–1903)." *Chinese Social and Political Science Review* 1934–35, 18: 236–81, 572–94. (Translation of "Pervye shagi russkogo imperializma na Dal'nem Vostoke [1888–1903 gg.]").

Fistié, Pierre. *Le reveil de l'Extrême-Orient: Guerres et revolutions, 1834–1954.* Avignon, 1956.

Florinsky, Michael T. *Russia: A History and an Interpretation.* 2 vols. New York, 1953.

Fo, Y. S. *An Illustrated History of Sino-Russian Relations.* Hong Kong, 1951.

Fochler-Hauke, Gustav. *Der Ferne Osten: Macht- und Wirtschaftskampf in Ostasien.* Leipzig, 1938.

Foner, Philip S. *The Spanish-Cuban-American War and the Birth of American Imperialism.* 2 vols. New York, 1972.

Ford, Harold P. "Russian Far Eastern Diplomacy: Count Witte and the Penetration of China, 1895–1904." Ph.D. dissertation, University of Chicago, 1950.

————. "The Foreign Imperial Body Guard." *Korean Repository* 1898, 5: 352–53.

Foster, John W. *Diplomatic Memoirs.* 2 vols. Boston, 1909.

Foulk, Edwin A. *Togo and the Rise of Japanese Sea-Power.* London, 1936.

Fox, Grace. *Britain and Japan, 1858–1883.* Oxford, 1969.

France, Foreign Ministry Archives. Correspondence politique.

Frank, V. and Schule, E. "Graf Pavel Andreevič Šuvalov, Russischer Botschafter in Berlin, 1885–1894." *Zeitschrift für Osteuropäische Geschichte*, new series, 1933, 3: 525–59.

Franke, Otto. *Die Grossmächte in Ostasien von 1894 bis 1914.* Braunschweig, 1923.

————. *Ostasiatische Neubildungen: Beiträge zum Verständnis der poltischen und kulturellen Entwicklungs-Vorgänge im Fernen Osten.* Hamburg: C. Boysen, 1911.

Frazar, Everett. *Korea and Her Relations to China, Japan and the United States.* Orange, N.J., 1884.

Freitag, Adolf, "Die Japaner im Urteil der Meiji-Deutschen." In *Deutsche Gesellschaft fur Natur und Völkerkunde Ostasiens, Mitteilungen* 1939, vol. 31, pt. C.

Friedjung, Heinrich. *Das Zeitalter des Imperialismus 1884–1914.* 3 vols. Berlin, 1911–1922.

Frost, Michael B. "Russian Penetration of China from the Tripartite Intervention to the Boxer Uprising." Seminar paper, Florida State University, n.d.

Fujii Matsuichi. *Nisshin Nichi-Ro senso.* Tokyo, 1969.

Fujimura Michio. *Nisshin senso.* Tokyo, 1973.

Fukaya Hiroshi, *Nisshin senso to Mutsu gaiko: Mutsu Munemitsu no "Kenkenroku."* Tokyo, 1940.

Funaoka, Seigo. *Japan im Sternbild Ostasiens: Darbietung einer geschichtlichen Grundlage für die Aussenpolitik Japans in der Neuzeit.* 2 vols. Tokyo, 1941–1942.

"Funeral of Her Majesty, the Late Queen." *Korean Repository* 1897, 4: 443.

Fung, Edmund S. K., "Peace Efforts of Li Hung-chang on the eve of the Sino-Japanese War (June–July 1894)." *Papers on Far Eastern History* (Canberra), 1971, 3: 131–66.

Fursenko, A. A. *Bor'ba za razdel Kitaia i amerikanskaia doktrina "otkrytykh dverei," 1895–1900 gg.* Moscow, 1956.

Gaimusho no hyakunen. Compiled by Gaimusho Hyakunenshi Hensen Iinkai. 2 vols. Tokyo, 1969.

Gale, Jas. S., "The Fate of the 'General Sherman,' From an Eye Witness." *Korean Repository* 1895, 2: 252–54.

————. "The Korean Gentleman." *Korean Repository* 1895, 2: 1–6.

Gal'perin, A. L. *Anglo-iaponskii soiuz, 1902–1921 gody*. Moscow, 1947.

————. "Russko-Kitaiskaia torgovlia v XVIII—pervoi polovine XIX veka. (Opyt sravneniia kiakhtinskogo torga s torgovlei cherez Guanchzhou)," *Problemy vostokovedeniia*, 1959, 5: 215–227.

Gapanovich, Ivan Ivanovich. *Rossiia v Severo-Vostochnoi Azii*. 2 vols. Peking, 1933–1934.

————. "Sino-Russian Relations in Manchuria, 1892 till 1906." *Chinese Social and Political Science Review* 1939, 17: 283–306, 457–479. (Summary of B. A. Romanov's *Rossiia v Man'chzhurii [1892–1906]*.)

Gardner, Lloyd C. *Imperial America: American Foreign Policy Since 1898*. New York, 1976.

Garin, N. G. *Po Koree, Manchzhurii i Liaodunskom poluostrove: Karandashom s natury*. St. Petersburg, 1904. (Republished in abridged form as *Iz dnevnikov krugosvetnogo puteshestviia [Po Koree . . .]*, Moscow, 1950.)

Georgievskii, Sergei. *Vazhnost' izucheniia Kitaia*. St. Petersburg, 1890.

Gérard, Auguste. *Ma mission en Chine (1893–1897)*. Paris, 1918.

————. *Mémoires d'Auguste Gérard, Ambassadeur de France. La vie d'un diplomate sous la troisième republique*. Paris, 1928.

German Diplomatic Documents 1871–1914. Translated by E. T. S. Dugdale. vol. 2. New York, 1929.

Germany, Foreign Ministry Archives, 1867–1920. Microfilms at Florida State University of documents kept at Whaddon Hall, England.

————. Original documents in Bonn.

Gilbert, Lucien. *Dictionnaire Historique et Géographique de la Mandchourie*. Hongkong, 1934.

Gippius, A. I. *O prichinakh nashei voiny s Iaponiei*. St. Petersburg, 1905. (Includes appendix of trade statistics compiled by M. P. Fedorov.)

Girault, René. *Emprunts russes et investissement français en Russie 1887–1914; recherches sur l'investissement international*. Paris, 1973.

Glazik, Joseph. *Die Russisch-Orthodoxe Heidenmission seit Peter dem Grossen: Ein missions geschichtlicher Versuch nach russischen Quellen und Darstellungen*. Münster, 1954.

Gleason, John Howes. *The Genesis of Russophobia in Great Britain: A Study of the Interaction of Policy and Opinion*. Cambridge, Mass., 1950.

Glinskii, Boris Borisovich. *Prolog russko-iaponskoi voiny: Materialy iz arkhiva grafa S. Iu Vitte*. Petrograd, 1916.

Goll, Eugene Wilhelm. "The Diplomacy of Walter Q. Gresham, Secretary of State, 1893–1895." Ph.D. dissertation, Pennsylvania State University, 1974.

Gollwitzer, Heinz. *Die Gelbe Gefahr: Geschichte eines Schlagworts. Studien zum imperialistischen Denken*. Göttingen, 1962.

Golovachev, P. *Rossia na Dal'nem Vostoke*. St. Petersburg, 1904.

Golovnin, D. "Iaponiia prezhde i teper'." *Russkaia mysl'* 1903, 7: 35–65.

Goodman, Grant, comp. *Imperial Japan and Asia: A Reassessment*. New York, 1967.

Gordenev, M. Iu. "Dal'nii Vostok i Sibirskaia flotiliia." In S. V. Gladkii and Iu. K. Dvorzhitskii, eds. *S. Beregov Ameriki, iubileinyi istoricheskii sbornik O-va Russkikh Morskikh Ofitserov v Amerike 1923–1938*. New York, 1939.

Gorelik, S. B. *Politika SShA v Man'chzhurii v 1898–1903 gg. i doktrina "Otkrytykh dverei."* Moscow, 1960. (Based on Gorelik's doctoral dissertation, "Agressivnaia politika SShA v Man'chzhurii v kontse XIX—nachale XX vekov," Institut Vosto-kovedeniia, Moscow, 1952.)

Gottschalk, Louis, and Lach, Donald. *The Transformation of Modern Europe*. Chicago, 1954. (Vol. 2 of *Europe and the Modern World*.)

Gould, F. Carruthers. *Political Caricatures*. London, 1904.

Gradalin, Yohann Athanasius. "Russian Expansion in the Far East: the Case of the Ussuri Region, 1860–1900." Master's thesis, University of Washington, 1950.

Grand Larousse encyclopedique. Rev. ed. 24 vols. Paris, 1970–1976.

Great Britain, Foreign Office. *British Foreign and State Papers*.

————. Confidential Correspondence. (Popularly know as Confidential Prints.)

————. General Correspondence.

"Great Changes in the Korean Government." *Korean Repository* 1895, 2: 111–18.

Greaves, Rose Louise. *Persia and the Defense of India, 1884–1892: A Study in the Foreign Policy of the Third Marquis of Salisbury*. London, 1959.

Grebenshchikov, M. G. *Po Dal'nemu Vostoku: Putevye zapiski i vospominaniia*. St. Petersburg, 1887.

Grebnitskii, N. "Znachenie kitaiskago elementa v dele kolonizatsii Iuzhno-Ussurii-skago kraia." In Russkoe geograficheskoe obshchestvo, Sibirskii Otdel, *Izvestiia* 1877, 8: 155–162.

Grenville, John. *Lord Salisbury and Foreign Policy: The Close of the Nineteenth Century*. London, 1964.

Grew, E. Sharpe. *War in the Far East: A History of the Russo-Japanese Struggle*. vol. 1. London, 1905 (?).

Griffis, William Elliot. *Corea, the Hermit Nation*, Rev. ed., New York, 1907.

————. *The Mikado's Empire*. 2 vols. New York, 1906.

Grigor'ev A. M. *Antiimperialisticheskaia programma kitaiskikh burzhuaznykh revoliutsionerov (1895–1905)*. Moscow, 1966.

Grimm, E. D. "Kitaiskii vopros ot Simonosekskogo mira do morovoy voiny, 1895–1914." *Novyi Vostok* 1924, 6: 43–62.

Griswold, A. Whitney. *Far Eastern Policy of the United States*. New York, 1938.

Die grosse Politik der europäischen Kabinette, 1871–1914. Compiled by the German Foreign Ministry. 40 vols. Berlin, 1922–27.

Grulev, M. *Zapiski generala-evreia*. Paris, 1930.

Grulew, M. *Das Ringen Russlands und Englands in Mittelasien*. Berlin, 1909.

Grünfeld, Ernst. *Hafenkolonien und Kolonieähnliche Verhältnisse in China, Japan und Korea; eine kolonialpolitische Studie*. Jena, 1913.

Grüning, Irene. *Die russische öffentliche Meinung und ihre Stellung zu den Grossmächten 1878 bis 1894*. Berlin, 1929.

Grunt, A. Ia. and Firstova, V. N. *Rossiia v epokhu imperializma, 1890–1907 gg*. Moscow, 1959.

Guber, A. A. *Filippinskaia respublika 1898 g. i amerikanskii imperializm*. Moscow, 1948.

————. "Mezhdunarodnye otnosheniia na Dal'nem Vostoke, 1894–1904 gg." *Ucheniye zapiski Tikhookeanskogo Instituta* 1947, 1: 3–50.

Guide to the Great Siberian Railway. Published by the (Tsarist) Ministry of Ways of Communication. Edited by A. I. Dmitriev-Mamonov and A. F. Zdziarski. English translation by L. Kukol-Yasnopolsky, revised by John Marshall. St. Petersburg, 1900.

Gurko, V. I. *Features and Figures of the Past. Government and Opinion in the Reign of Nicholas II.* Edited by J. E. Wallace Sterling, Xenia Joukoff Eudin and H. H. Fisher. Translated by Laura Matveev. Stanford, 1939.

Guzanov, V. G. *Odissei s Beloi Rusi.* Minsk, 1969.

Hackett, Roger. *Yamagata Aritomo in the Rise of Modern Japan, 1838–1922.* Cambridge, Mass., 1970.

Hallgarten, George W. F. *Imperialismus vor 1914: Die soziologischen Grundlagen der Aussenpolitik europäischer Grossmächte vor dem Ersten Weltkrieg.* 2 vols. 2d ed. München, 1963.

Halot, Alexandre. *L'Extrême-Orient: Études d'hier, événements d'aujourdhui.* Bruxelles, 1905.

Hamada, Kengi. *Prince Ito.* Tokyo, 1936.

Hamada, Yoshizumi. *Nichi-Ro gaiko nenshi.* Tokyo, 1904.

Hamilton, Angus. *Korea.* New York, 1904.

Hammann, Otto, *Deutsche Weltpolitik, 1890–1912.* Berlin, 1925.

Han, Woo-keun. *The History of Korea.* Translated by Lee Kyung-shik, edited by Grafton K. Mintz. Honolulu, 1970.

Hanabusa Nagamichi. *Meiji gaikoshi.* Tokyo, 1960.

Hanai Tokuzo. *Otsu jiken temmatsu roku.* Tokyo, 1931.

Harbison, Larry J. "Korea's Request for American Advisors and the Dual Role of Foote and Foulk as Diplomats and Personal Advisor to the King of Korea (1883–1887)." Seminar paper, Florida State University, 1974.

Harrington, Fred Harvey. *God, Mammon, and the Japanese: Dr. Horace N. Allen and Korean-American Relations, 1884–1905.* Madison, 1961.

Harvey, Ted G. "Russia, Japan and Korea, 1899 and 1900." Seminar paper, Florida State University, 1964.

Hashagen, Justus. *England und Japan seit Schimonoseki.* Essen, 1915.

Hatada, Takashi. *A History of Korea.* Translated and edited by Warren W. Smith, Jr. and Benjamin H. Hazard. Santa Barbara, California, 1969.

Hatano Yoshihiro. "Ri Kosho sen-happyaku-hachijunendai ni okeru tai-Nichi seisaku ni tsuite." *Rekishigaku kenkyu* 1961, 253: 38–42.

Hattori Shiso. *Kindai Nihon gaikoshi.* Tokyo, 1954

Hauser, Oswald. *Deutschland und der englisch-russische Gegensatz 1900–1914.* Göttingen, 1958.

Haushofer, Karl von. *Dai Nihon: Betrachtungen über Gross-Japans Wehrkraft, Weltstellung und Zukunft.* Berlin, 1913.

—————. *Japans Reichserneuerungen, Strukturwandlungen von der Meiji-Ära bis heute.* Berlin, 1930.

Hayase, Yukiko. "Japanese Diplomacy during the Sino-Japanese War up to the Signing of the Treaty of Shimonoseki." Seminar paper, Florida State University, 1970.

Hayit, Baymirza. *Turkestan zwischen Russland und China.* Amsterdam, 1971.

Heki Shoichi, comp. *Kokushi dai-nempyo.* 6 vols. Tokyo, 1935.

Henderson, W. O. *The Industrial Revolution on the Continent: Germany, France, Russia, 1900–1914.* London, 1963.

Hendrix, Bishop E. R. "Russia in the Far East." *Korean Repository 1897,* 4: 401–6.

"Her Majesty's Funeral." *Korean Repository* 1897, 4: 30.

Hesse, Kurt. *Die Schicksalstunde der alten Mächte: Japan und die Welt.* Hamburg, 1933.

Hewlett, Sir Meyrick. *Forty Years in China.* London, 1943.

Hillgruber, Andreas. *Deutsche Grossmacht- und Weltpolitik im 19. und 20. Jahrhundert.* Düsseldorf, 1977.

————. *Kontinuität und Diskontinuität in der deutschen Aussenpolitik von Bismarck bis Hitler.* Düsseldorf, 1969.

Hiratsuka Atsushi, ed. *Ito Hirobumi hiroku.* Tokyo, 1929.

————. *Shishaku Kurino Shinichiro den.* Tokyo, 1942.

Hiroe, Sawajiro. *Kankoku jidai no Roshia katsuyakushi.* Tokyo, 1932.

"His Majesty, the King of Korea." *Korean Repository* 1896, 3: 422–30.

A Historical Summary of United States-Korean Relations, With a Chronology of Important Developments, 1834–1962. Compiled by the Historical Office of the U.S. Department of State. Washington, 1962.

History of the Peace Negotiations, Documentary and Verbal, between China and Japan, March-April, 1895. With Text of the Treaty of Peace. Officially rev. Tientsin, 1895.

Ho Han-wen. *Chung O wai chiao chih.* Shanghai, 1936.

Ho Takushu, "Koshin jihen o meguru Inoue gaimukyo to Furansu koshi to no kosho." *Rekishigaku kenkyu* 1963, 282: 34–44.

————. "Shimonoseki joyaku ni tsuite." *Nihonshi kenkyu* 1961, 56: 27–48.

————. "Shin-Futsu sensoki ni okeru Nihon no tai-Kan seisaku." *Shirin* 1960, 43: 124–43.

Hoare, James Edward. "The Japanese Treaty Ports 1868–1899: A Study of the Foreign Settlements." Ph.D. dissertation, University of London, 1971.

Höcker, Gustav. *Ruszland und Japan im Kampf um die Macht in Ostasien.* vol. 1. Leipzig, 1905.

Hoetzsch, Otto. *Russland in Asien: Geschichte einer Expansion.* Stuttgart, 1966.

Hohenlohe-Schillingsfürst, Prince Chlodwig zu. *Memoirs of Prince Chlodwig of Hohenlohe-Schillingsfuerst.* Edited by Friedrich Curtius; English edition supervised by George W. Chrystal. 2 vols. New York, 1906.

Holstein, Friedrich von. *The Holstein Papers.* Edited by Norman Rich and M. H. Fisher. 4 vols. Cambridge, 1955–1963.

Hölzle, Erwin, *Geschichte der zweigeteilten Welt: Amerka und Russland.* Reinbek bei Hamburg, 1961.

Hoo, Chi-Tsai. *Les bases conventionelles des relations modernes entre la Chine et la Russie.* Paris, 1918.

Hori Makoto. *Nichi-Ro senso zeneki.* Tokyo, 1940.

Horikawa Takeo. *Nihon gaiko hyakunenshi.* 2 vols. Tokyo, 1941.

Hosie, Alexander. *Manchuria: Its People, Resources, and Recent History.* New York, 1904.

Hosokawa Kameichi. *Kindai Nihon gaikoshi kenkyu.* Tokyo, 1942.

Houang, Tschang Sin. *Le Problème du Chemin de Fer Chinois de l'Est.* Paris, 1927.

Hsiao, Kung-chuan. *A Modern China and a New World.* Seattle, 1975.

Hsieh, Pao Chao. *The Government of China (1644–1911).* Baltimore, 1925.

Hsü, Immanuel C. Y. *The Ili Crisis: A Study of Sino-Russian Diplomacy 1871–1881.* Oxford, 1965.

————. "Russia's Special Position in China during the early Ch'ing period." *Slavic Review* 1964, 23: 688–700.

————. The Rise of Modern China. 2d ed. New York, 1975.

Hsü, Shu-hsi. *China and Her Political Entity: A Study of China's Foreign Relations with Reference to Korea, Manchuria, and Mongolia.* New York, 1926.

Hsü, Yungtai. "Procedure and Perception in the Making of Chinese Foreign Policy: A Study of the 1896 Treaty with Russia." B. Litt. thesis, St. John's College, Oxford University, 1974.

Hu Sheng. *Imperialism and Chinese Politics.* Peking, 1955.

Hudson, G. F. *The Far East in World Politics.* Oxford, 1937.

Hulbert, Homer B. *The History of Korea.* 2 vols. Seoul, 1905. (This edition used as source of illustrations only; for text used the revised edition prepared by C. N. Weems, New York, 1962.)

————. *The Passing of Korea.* New York, 1909.

Hummel, Arthur W., ed. *Eminent Chinese of the Ch'ing Period (1644–1912).* 2 vols. Washington, 1943–44.

Hunt, Michael H. *Frontier and the Open Door: Manchuria in Chinese-American Relations, 1895–1911.* New Haven, 1973.

"Iaponiia." *Vsemirnaia illiustratsiia* 1877, 454: 182.

The I. G. in Peking: Letters of Robert Hart, Chinese Maritime Customs, 1868–1907. Edited by John King Fairbank, Katherine Frost Bruner, and Elizabeth MacLeod Matheson. 2 vols. Cambridge, Mass., 1976.

Iiams, Thomas M., Jr. *Dreyfus, Diplomatists, and the Dual Alliance: Gabriel Hanotaux at the Quai d'Orsay (1894–1898).* Geneva, 1962.

Ikeda Kiyoshi. *Nihon no kaigun.* Vol. 1. Tokyo, 1966.

Iklé, Frank W. "The Triple Intervention: Japan's Lesson in the Diplomacy of Imperialism." *Monumenta Nipponica* 1967, 1–2: 122–30.

The Illustrated London News.

Illustratsiia. Ezhenedel'noe obozrenie.

Illustrierte Zeitung. Wochentliche Nachrichten über alle wesentlichen Zeitereignisse, Zustände und Persönlichkeiten der Gegenwart, öffentliches und gesellschaftliches Leben, Wissenschaft und Kunst.

"Imennoi vysochaishii ukaz. Ob utverzhdenii vremennago polozheniia ob upravlenii kvantunskoi oblasti i sego upravlennia," *Priamurskiia Vedomosti* 1899, 304: 2–4; 305: 2–5.

"The Independence Club." *Korean Repository* 1898, 5: 28–87.

The Independent. Seoul.

Ino Tentaro. "Kinsei Nihon ni okeru shinrosetsu no keifu." *Kokushigaku* 1953, 60: 44–59.

Inoguchi, Takashi. "Wars as International Learning: Chinese, British and Japanese in East Asia." Ph. D. dissertation, Massachusetts Institute of Technology, 1974.

"Inostrannye iazyki v vysshem kommercheskom uchilishche v Tokio." *Priamurskiia Vedomosti* 1894, 49: 11.

"Inostrantsy v Priamurskom krae." *Priamurskiia Vedomosti* 1896, 143: 15–16; 144: 12–13.

Inoue Kaoru Ko Denki Hensankai, comp. *Segai Inoue ko den.* 5 vols. Tokyo, 1933–1934.

Inouye, Jukichi. *The Japan-China War from the Battle of Haiyang to the Fall of Wei-Hai-Wei.* Yokohama, 1895.

————. *The Japan-China War: On the Regent's Sword: Kinchow, Port Arthur, and Talienwan.* Yokohama, 1895.

————. *The Fall of Weihaiwei.* Yokohama, 1895.

Inozemtsev, N. *Venshniaia politika SShA v epokhu imperializma.* Moscow, 1960.

International Military Tribunal for the Far East. "Analyses of Documentary Evidence." Mimeographed, Tokyo, 1946–1947.

————. "Documents Presented in Evidence." Mimeographed. Tokyo, 1946–1948.

Iriye, Akira. *Across the Pacific: An Inner History of American-East Asian Relations.* New York, 1967.

————. *Pacific Estrangement: Japanese and American Expansion, 1897–1911.* Cambridge, Mass., 1972.

Irmer, Arthur Julius. *Die Erwerbung von Kiautschou 1894–1898.* Cologne, 1930.

Istoricheskaia spravka o vazhneishikh dlia Rossii sobytiiakh na Dal'nem Vostoke v trekhletie 1898–1900 g. St. Petersburg, 1902.

Istoricheskii obzor Kitaiskoi Vostochnoi zheleznoi dorogi, 1896–1923 gg. Compiled by the Chinese Eastern Railroad Company. Harbin, 1923.

Istoriia diplomatii. 2d ed. 5 vols. Moscow, 1959–1974.

Istoriia Sibiri. Compiled by the Institute of History, Philology, and Philosophy of the Siberian Branch of the Academy of Sciences of the USSR under the editorship of A. P. Okladnikov and others. vol. 3. Leningrad, 1968.

Ito Hirobumi, ed., and Hiratsuka Atsushi, rev. *Hisho ruisan: gaiko hen.* vol. 3. Tokyo, 1935.

Ito Hirobumi-den. Compiled by Shumpo Ko Tsuishokai. 3 vols. Tokyo, 1940.

Iuzhakov, S. "Mimokhodom v Iaponii. Iz putevykh vpechatlenii." *Russkoe bogatstvo* 1893, 9: 88–110.

Iuzhnyi Krai.

Iwakura Tomomi kankei bunsho. Edited by Otsuka Takematsu. 8 vols. Tokyo, 1927–1935.

"Iz epokhi iapono-kitaiskoi voiny 1894–95 gg." Edited by B. G. Veber and S. R. Dimant. *Krasnyi arkhiv* 1932, 50–51: 3–63. (Translated as "Russian Documents Relating to the Sino-Japanese War, 1894–95," *Chinese Social and Political Science Review* 1933–1934, 17: 480–515, 632–70.)

Jackson, W. A. Douglas. *The Russo-Chinese Borderlands: Zone of Peaceful Contact or Potential Conflict?* Princeton, N.J., 1962.

Jakobs, Peter. *Das Werden des französich-russischen Zweibunds, 1890–1894.* Wiesbaden, 1968.

Jan, Cecilia Osteen. "The East Asian Diplomatic Service and Observations of Sir Ernest Mason Satow." Ph.D. dissertation, Florida State University, 1976.

Jansen, Marius B. *Japan and China: From War to Peace, 1894–1972.* Chicago, 1975.

Japan, Foreign Office. *Nichi-Ei gaiko-shi.* Classified "Secret." Vol. 1. Tokyo, 1937.

Japan, Foreign Office Archives. Original documents in Tokyo as well as the material microfilmed for the Library of Congress.

Japan, Kwantung Bureau. *Manshu-shi.* 15 vols. Dairen, 1911–1912.

"Japan and Russia in Korea." *Japan Weekly Mail* 1899, p. 517.

The Japan Daily Mail.

"Japan's Answer to Russia." *Japan Weekly Mail* 1898, p. 311.
"Japan's Relations with Russia." *Japan Weekly Mail* 1891, p. 595.
The Japan Times.
The Japan Weekly Mail.
Jelavich, Barbara. *A Century of Russian Foreign Policy, 1814–1914.* Philadelphia, 1964.
Jelavich, Charles and Barbara, eds. *The Education of a Russian Statesman: The Memoirs of N. K. Giers.* Berkeley, 1962.
Jemetel, Maurice. "La Chine et les Puissances Européenes." *L'Economiste français* 1882, 446–48.
Jensen, Gustav. *Japans Seemacht, 1853–1937.* Berlin, 1938.
Jerrussalimski, Arkadij Samsonovič. *Die Aussenpolitik und Diplomatie des deutschen Imperialismus Ende des 19. Jahrhunderts.* Berlin, 1954.
Jiji Shimpo.
Johnson, Donald. D. "The United States in the Pacific: Private Interests and Public Policies." Mimeographed, n.d.
Jones, Francis Clifford. *Extraterritoriality in Japan and the Diplomatic Relations Resulting in its Abolition, 1853–1899.* New Haven, 1931.
————. "Foreign Diplomacy in Korea, 1866–1894." Ph.D. dissertation, Harvard University, 1935.
Jones, Geo. Herber. "Chemulpo." *Korean Repository* 1897, 4: 374–84.
————. "The Taiwon Kun." *Korean Repository* 1898, 5: 241–50.
Jones, Hazel J. "The Meiji Government and Foreign Employees, 1868–1900." Ph.D. dissertation, University of Michigan, 1967.
Joseph, Philip. *Foreign Diplomacy in China 1894–1900: A Study in Political and Economic Relations with China.* London, 1928.
Joyaku isan. Compiled by the Japanese Foreign Office. 9 vols. Tokyo, 1926–29.
Jue, Kam B. "The Korean Independence Question and George C. Foulk, 1883–1887." Seminar paper, Florida State University, 1974.
Jung, Yong Suk. "The Rise of American National Interest in Korea: 1848–1950." Ph.D. dissertation, Claremont Graduate School, 1970.
Junkin, William M. "The Tong Hak." *Korean Repository* 1895, 2: 56–60.

Kabonov, P. I. *Amurskii vopros.* Blagoveshchensk, 1959.
Kai, Miwa and Yampolsky, Philip B., comp. *Political Chronology of Japan 1885–1957.* New York, 1957.
Kaigun Yushu Kai, comp. *Taiheiyo nisenroppyakunen-shi.* Edited by Hirose Hikota. Tokyo, 1940.
Kajima Heiwa Kenkyujo, comp. *Nisshin senso to sangoku kansho.* Tokyo, 1970. (Vol. 6 of *Nihon gaikoshi.*)
Kajima Morinosuke. *The Diplomacy of Japan, 1894–1922.* 2 vols. Tokyo, 1976–1978.
————. *The Emergence of Japan as a World Power, 1895–1925.* Rutland, Vt., 1968.
————. *Nichi-Ei gaiko-shi.* Tokyo, 1957.
————. *Nihon gaiko-shi.* Tokyo, 1965.
————. *Teikoku gaiko no kihon seisaku.* Tokyo, 1938.

Kamikawa, Hikomatsu. *Japan-American Diplomatic Relations in the Meiji-Taisho Era*. Translated by Kimura Michiko. Tokyo, 1958.

Kang, Soon Heung. "The Problems of Autonomy for Korea amid Rivalries of Great Powers: the Search for a New Order." Ph.D. dissertation, University of Iowa, 1974.

"Kankoku ni kansuru Nichi-Ro kyoyaku zakken," Feb. 1896–July1898. Japanese Archives doc. MT 2.1.1.2 (reel 277).

Kantorovich, A. Ia. *Amerika v borbe ze Kitai*. Moscow, 1935.

Kase Toshikazu. *Gaikokan*. Tokyo, 1957.

Kato Kanji Denki Hensankai, ed. *Kato Kanji taisho den*. Tokyo, 1941.

Keene, Donald. "The Sino-Japanese War of 1894–95 and Its Cultural Effect on Japan." In D. H. Shively, ed., *Tradition and Modernization in Japanese Culture*, 121–75. Princeton, 1971.

Keeton, George Williams. *China, the Far East and the Future*. Rev. ed. London, 1949.

Kelly, John S. *The Negotiations at Peking, 1900–1901*. Geneva, 1963.

Kemuyama, Sentaro. "Nichi-Ro no gaiko." In Japan, Ministry of Education, *Rokoku Kenkyu*, 399–443. Tokyo, 1917.

—————. *Nisshin Nichi-Ro no eki*. Tokyo, 1931. (Vol. 9 of *Iwanami koza Nihon rekishi*.)

Kent, Percy Horace. *Railway Enterprise in China: An Account of Its Origin and Development*. London, 1907.

Kharbinskii, St. *Chto takoe Kitaiskaia Vostochnaia zheleznaia doroga i kuda idut eia milliony?* St. Petersburg, 1908.

Khu Shen, *Agressiia imperialisticheskikh derzhav v Kitae*. Translated from the Chinese by L. P. Deliusin and A. V. Kotov. Moscow, 1951.

Kh—v. "Russko-poddanye koreitzy v Primorskoi oblasti." *Priamurskiia vedomosti* 1897, 181: 16–19; 182: 13–19.

Khva, Kim Syn. *Ocherki po istorii sovetskikh koreitsev*. Alma Alta, 1965.

Kim, C. I. Eugene and Kim Han-kyo. *Korea and the Politics of Imperialism 1876–1910*. Berkeley, 1968.

Kim, Chang Hoon. "Relations internationales de la Corée de la seconde moitié du XIXe siecle à la perte de son independence (1910)." Ph. D. dissertation, Université de Paris, 1959.

Kim Chong-myong, ed. *Nikkan gaiko shiryo shusei*. Vols. 5 and 8. Tokyo, 1967 and 1964.

Kim, Han-gu. "Tonghak: Revitalization Movement in Korea." Ph.D. dissertation, University of Toronto, 1970.

Kim, Han-Kyo. "The Demise of the Kingdom of Korea: 1882–1910." Ph.D. dissertation, University of Chicago, 1962.

Kim, Young Hum. *East Asia's Turbulent Century: With American Diplomatic Documents*. New York, 1966.

Kim, Yung Chung. "Great Britain and Korea, 1883–1887." Ph.D. dissertation, Indiana University, 1965.

—————, ed. and transl. *Women of Korea: A History from Ancient Times to 1945*. Seoul, 1977.

Kimase, Seizo. *Mitsuru Toyama kämpft fur Grossasien*. Munich, 1941.

Kindermann, Gottfried-Karl. *Der Ferne Osten in der Weltpolitik des industrialen Zeitalters.* Munich, 1970.

"The King at the Russian Legation." Special supplement to the *Korean Repository* 1896, no. 3.

Kiniapina, N. S. *Vneshniaia politika Rossii vtoroi poloviny XIX veka.* Moscow, 1974.

Kitaiskaia-Vostochnaia zheleznaia doroga: Istoricheskii ocherk. Compiled by the Chinese Eastern Railroad Company. vol.1 (1896–1905). St. Petersburg, 1914.

Kitaisko-iaponskaia voina: Kratkoe opisanie voennykh deistvii, s planami kartami i rissunkami. St. Petersburg, 1895.

"Kitaisko-iaponskaia voina." *Morskoi sbornik* 1894, no. 12, naval chronicle section, 1–11.

Kiuner, N. V. *Snosheniia Rossi s Dal'nim Vostokom na protiazhenii tsarstvovannia Doma Romanovykh. (Rech, proiznesennaia na torzhestvonnom akte v Vostochnom Institute 22-go fevralia 1913 goda, po sluchaiu trekhsotletiia tsarstvovannia Doma Romanovykh.)* Vladivostok, 1913.

Kiyosawa Kiyoshi. *Nihon gaikoshi.* 2 vols. Tokyo, 1942.

Klado, N. L. "Voennyia deistviia na more vo vremia iapono-kitaiskoi voiny." *Morskoi sbornik* 1896, no. 4, unofficial section, pp. 1–28; no. 5, unofficial section, pp. 1–20; no. 7, unofficial section, pp. 43–55.

Klein, Albert. *Der Einfluss des Grafen Witte auf die deutschrussischen Beziehungen.* Münster, 1932.

Klein, Donald W. "The Chinese Foreign Ministry." Ph.D. dissertation, Columbia University, 1974.

Kleinbort, L. *Russkii imperializm v Azii.* St. Petersburg, 1906.

The Kobe Chronicle.

Kochan, Lionel. "Sergei Witte: The Last Statesman of Imperial Russia." *History Today*, 1968, pp. 102–8.

Kokushi dai-nempyo. 9 vols. Tokyo, 1940–41.

Komatsu Midori. *Meiji gaiko hiwa.* Tokyo, 1936.

Kolonial'naia politika kapitalisticheskikh derzhav (1870–1914). Compiled by Iu. I. Kopelova, P. I. Ostrikov, E. E. Iurovskaia (ed.), and Z. P. Iakhimovich. Moscow, 1967.

Komura gaiko-shi. Compiled by the Japanese Foreign Office. 2 vols. Tokyo, 1953.

Kononov, Rear Admiral I. A. *Puti k golgofe russkago flota (istoricheskii ocherk) i morskie razskazy.* New York, 1961.

Korea, Government-General of Chosen. *Chosen-shi.* 37 vols. Seoul, 1931–1940.

"Korea, Japan and Russia." *Japan Weekly Mail* 1899, p. 468.

"Korea, Russia and Japan." *Japan Weekly Mail* 1886, p. 57; 1896, p. 548.

Korean-American Relations: Documents Pertaining to the Far Eastern Diplomacy of the United States. Vol. 1 (The Initial Period, 1883–1886), edited by George M. McCune and John A. Harrison; vol. 2 (The Period of Growing Influence, 1887–1895), edited by Spencer J. Palmer. Berkeley, 1951 and 1963.

Korean Foreign Ministry Archives, deposited at the Central Library of the Seoul National University. "A-Weon-an" (original Russian documents, 1886–1903) and "Ju-a lae-geo an" (documents of the comings and goings of Russians, 1886–1903).

"The Korean Question." *Japan Weekly Mail*, Aug. 6, 1892, p. 168.

The Korean Repository.

"Korea's New Responsibility." *Korean Repository* 1898, 5: 146–48.

"Koreitsy Priamurskago kraia." *Trudy Priamurskago otdela Imperatorskago russkago geograficheskago obshchestva* 1895, pp. 1–36.

Korff, Baron S. A. "Russia in the Far East." *The American Journal of International Law* 1923, 17: 252–84.

————. *Russia's Foreign Relations during the Last Half Century.* New York, 1922.

Korostovets, Ivan. *Kitaitsy i ikh tsivilizatiia.* St. Petersburg, 1896.

————. *Von Cinggis Khan zur Sowjetrepublik: Eine Kurze Geschichte der Mongolei unter besonderer Berüchsichtigung der neuesten Zeit.* Berlin, 1926.

Korostowetz, W. von. *Graf Witte, der Steuermann in der Not.* Translated and edited by Heing Stratz. Berlin, 1929.

Kostylev, Vasilii Iakovlevich. *Ocherk istorii Iaponii.* St. Petersburg, 1888.

Kotvich and Borodovskii. *Liaodun i ego porty: Port-Artur i Dalian-wan', istoriko-geograficheskii ocherk.* St. Petersburg, 1898.

Krahmer, Gustav. *Die Beziehungen Russlands zu Japan (mit besonderer Berücksichtigung Koreas).* Leipzig, 1904.

————. *Russland in Ost-Asien (mit besonderer Berücksichtigung der Mandschurei).* Leipzig, 1899.

Krakowski, Edouard. *Chine et Russie: L'Orient contre la civilisation occidentale.* Paris, 1957.

Krasnov, A. "U iapontsev. (Iz poezdki po ostrovam Dalekogo Vostoka)." *Knizhki nedeli* 1893, 10: 126–50.

"Kratkii ocherk sovremennogo sostoianniia Korei kniazia Dadeshkaliani." In G. D. Tiagai, ed., *Po Koree,* 48–95. Moscow, 1958.

Krausnick, Helmut. *Holstein's Geheimpolitik in der Ära Bismarcks, 1886–1890.* Hamburg, 1942.

Krausse, Alexis. *The Far East and Its Question.* London, 1900.

————. *Russia in Asia: A Record and a Study, 1558–1899.* New York, 1901.

Krestovskii, Vsevolod Vladimirovich. *Sobranie sochinenii.* Edited by Iu. L. El'ts. Vols. 6 and 7. St. Petersburg, 1899–1900.

Krupinski, Kurt. *Russland und Japan, ihre Beziehungen bis zum Frieden von Portsmouth.* Berlin, 1940.

Ku Han' guk oegyo munso. Compiled by the Asiatic Research Center of Korea University (Koryo Taehakkyo Munje Yon'guso). 22 vols. Seoul, 1965–1973.

Kublin, Hyman. "A Century of Port Arthur." In United States Naval Institute *Proceedings* 1957, 83: 505–14.

Kulomzin, A. "Krugovye reisy po Iaponii iz Vladivostoka." *Priamurskiia vedomosti* 1894, 12: 11–13; 13: 13–15.

————. "Po Iaponii, putevye zametki." *Priamurskiia vedomosti* 1894, 16: 10–13; 17: 10–14; 18: 12–15.

————, ed. *Sibirskaia zheleznaia dorgoa v proshlom i nastoiashchem.* St. Petersburg, 1903.

Kun, Joseph C. "North Korea: Between Moscow and Peking," *The China Quarterly* 1967, 31: 48–58.

Kuno, Yoshi S. *Japanese Expansion on the Asiatic Continent: A Study in the History of Japan with Special Reference to Her International Relations with China, Korea, and Russia.* 2 vols. Berkeley, 1937–1940.

Kuo, Sung-ping. "Chinese Reaction to Foreign Encroachment: With Special Reference to the First Sino-Japanese War and Its Immediate Aftermath." Ph.D. dissertation, Columbia University, 1953.

Kurgan van Hentenryk, G. *Léopold II et les groups financiers belges en Chine: La politique royale et ses prolongements (1895–1914)*. Bruxelles, 1972.

Kuropatkin, General (Aleksei N.). *The Russian Army and the Japanese War, Being Historical and Critical Comments on the Military Policy and Power of Russia and on the Campaign in the Far East*. 2 vols. New York, 1909.

―――――. *Russko-kitaiskii vopros*. St. Petersburg, 1913.

Kutuzov, P. *Zhelatel'nye osnovy russko-kitaiskago soglasheniia: Vozrazheniia na mysli kn. S. N. Trubetskogo o razdele Kitaiskoi imperii*. St. Petersburg, 1900.

Kuzuu Yoshihisa. *Nikkan gappo hishi*. 2 vols. Tokyo, 1930.

―――――. *Nisshi kosho gaishi*. 2 vols. Tokyo, 1936.

"Kvantun: Bytovye ocherki Kvatunskoi Oblasti." *Novyi krai* 1900, nos. 9, 12, 15.

"K voprosu o razvitii nashikh snoshenii s Iaponiei i Amerikoi, v sviazi so stroiushcheisia zheleznoi dorogoi." *Priamurskiia vedomosti* 1894, 19: 11.

Kwan, Siu-hing. "Japanese and Chinese Attitudes toward the Idea of a Sino-Japanese Special Relationship, 1895–1911." Ph.D. dissertation, University of London, 1974.

La Feber, Walter. *The New Empire: An Interpretation of American Expansion 1860–1898*. Ithaca, 1963.

Laguérie, Villetard. *La Corée, independante, russe, ou japonaise*. Paris, 1898.

Lakshevits, K. "Naselenie po poberezh'iu ot koreiskoi granitsy do Imperatorskoi gavani." *Priamurskiia vedomosti* 1894, 33: 13–15.

La Mazelière, Marquis de. *Le Japon: Histoire et civilisation*. 8 vols. Paris, 1907–1923.

Lamsdorff, Gustav Graf von. *Die Militärbevollmächtigten Kaiser Wilhelms II am Zarenhofe 1904–1914*. Berlin, 1937.

Langer, William L. *The Diplomacy of Imperialism 1890–1902*. 2d ed. New York, 1951.

―――――. *The Franco-Russian Alliance 1890–1894*. Cambridge, Mass., 1929.

Langford, Joseph Henry. *The Story of Korea*. New York, 1911.

Latourette, Kenneth Scott. *The Chinese, Their History and Culture*. 2 vols. New York, 1934.

Lattimore, Owen. *Manchuria, Cradle of Conflict*. New York, 1935.

Laue, Theodore H. von. *Sergei Witte and the Industrialization of Russia*. New York, 1963.

―――――. "The 'Vitte System' in Mid-Passage, 1896–1899." *Jahrbücher für Geschichte Osteuropas* 1960, 8: 195–229.

Lee, Ki-tak. "Un aspect de la politique Russe en Extrême-Orient—La Russie et la Corée (1860–1904)." Ph.D. dissertation, Université de Paris, 1968 (?).

Lee, Kuo-chi. *Die chinesische Politik zum Einspruch von Shimonoseki und gegen die Erwerbung der Kiautschou-Bucht: Studien zu den chinesisch-deutschen Beziehungen von 1895 bis 1898*. Münster, 1966.

Lee, Robert H. G. *The Manchurian Frontier in Ch'ing History*. Cambridge, Mass., 1970.

Lee, Yur-bok. *Diplomatic Relations between the United States and Korea, 1866–1887*. New York, 1970.

Leger, François. *Les influences occidentales dans la revolution de l'Orient: Inde-Ma-*

laisie-Chine, 1850–1950. 2 vols. Paris, 1955.

Lensen, George Alexander. "The Attempt on the Life of Nicholas II in Japan," *The Russian Review* 1961, 20: 232–53.

————. *The Damned Inheritance: The Soviet Union and the Manchurian Crises, 1924–1935*. Tallahassee, 1974.

————. "Japan and Tsarist Russia—The Changing Relationships, 1875–1917." *Jahrbücher für Geschichte Osteuropas* 1962, 10: 337–48.

————. "The Russian Impact on Japan." In Wayne S. Vucinich, ed., *Russia and Asia: Essays on the Influence of Russia on the Asian Peoples*, 338–68 and 457–65. Stanford, 1972.

————. *The Russian Push Toward Japan: Russo-Japanese Relations, 1697–1875*. Princeton, N.J., 1959.

————. *Russia's Japan Expedition of 1852 to 1855*. Gainesville, 1955.

————. *The Russo-Chinese War*. Tallahassee, 1967.

————. "Yalta and the Far East." In John L. Snell, ed. *The Meaning of Yalta: Big Three Diplomacy and the New Balance of Power*, 127–66. Baton Rouge, 1956.

————, comp. *Japanese Diplomatic and Consular Officials in Russia: A Handbook of Japanese Representatives in Russia from 1874 to 1968, Compiled on the Basis of Japanese and Russian Sources with a Historical Introduction*. Tokyo, 1968.

————, comp. *Russian Diplomatic and Consular Officials in East Asia: A Handbook of the Representatives of Tsarist Russia and the Provisional Government in China, Japan and Korea from 1858 to 1924 and of Soviet Representatives in Japan from 1925 to 1968, Compiled on the Basis of Russian, Japanese and Chinese Sources with a Historical Introduction*. Tokyo, 1968.

————, ed. *Korea and Manchuria Between Russia and Japan, 1895–1904: The Observations of Sir Ernest Satow, British Minister Plenipotentiary to Japan (1895–1900) and China (1900–1906)*. Tallahassee, 1966.

————, ed. *Revelations of a Russian Diplomat: The Memoirs of Dmitrii I. Abrikossow*. Seattle, 1964.

————, ed. *Russia's Eastward Expansion*. Englewood Cliffs, N.J., 1964.

————, transl. and ed. *The d'Anethan Dispatches from Japan, 1894–1910: The Observations of Baron Albert d'Anethan, Belgian Minister Plenipotentiary and Dean of the Diplomatic Corps*. Tokyo, 1967.

Leroy-Beaulieu, Pierre. *The Awakening of the East: Siberia—Japan—China*. New York, 1900.

Levi, Werner. *Modern China's Foreign Policy*. Minneapolis, 1953.

Levine, Isaac Don. *Letters from the Kaiser to the Tsar*. New York, 1920.

Levitov, Il'ia Semonovich. *Zheltaia rasa*. St. Petersburg, 1900.

————. *Zheltorossiia, kak bufernaia koloniia*. St. Petersburg, 1905.

Li, Chi. "Manchuria in History." *Chinese Social and Political Science Review* 1932–33, 16: 226–58.

Li, Chien-nung. *The Political History of China, 1840–1928*. Translated and edited by Ssu-yu Teng and Jeremy Ingalls. Princeton, N.J., 1956.

Li, Dun J. *The Ageless Chinese: A History*. 2d ed. New York, 1971.

Li, Ting-i. *A History of Modern China*. Translated by L. Bennett and Hsüeh-feng Yang. Hanover, N.H., 1970.

Liang, Chia-pin. "History of the Chinese Eastern Railway. A Chinese Version." *Pacific Affairs* 1930, 3: 188–211.

Liang, Ch'i-ch'ao. *Likhunchzhan ili politicheskaia istoriia Kitaia za posledniia 40 let.* Translated from the Chinese by A. N. Voznesenskii and Chang Chih-tung. St. Petersburg, 1905.

Liem, Channing. *America's Finest Gift to Korea: The Life of Philip Jaisohn.* New York, 1952.

Likhachev, I. "K istorii politiki nashei v Kitae i uchastiia v nei nashego flota— broshiura Ignat'eva, iun'1902 g." *Morskoi sbornik* 1913, 379: 11: 25–31.

L'Illustration.

Lin, T. C. "Li Hung-chan: His Korean Policies, 1870–1885." *Chinese Social and Political Science Review* 1935–36, 19: 202–33.

Little, Mrs. Archibald. *Li Hung-chang His Life and Times.* London, n.d.

Liu, Hsien-Tung. "Border Disputes between Imperial China and Tsarist Russia." Ph.D. dissertation, Claremont Graduate School, 1967.

Lo, H. M. "The Battle of the Concessions in China, 1895–1900." Ph.D. dissertation, Harvard University, 1957.

Lobanov-Rostovsky, Prince A. *Russia and Asia.* New York, 1933.

Longford, Joseph H. *The Story of Korea.* New York, 1911.

Lowell, Percival. *Chosön: The Land of the Morning Calm.* Boston, 1888. (The preface and copyright date back to 1885.)

————. "A Korean Coup d'État," *Atlantic Monthly* 1886, 58: 599–618.

Lubentsov, A. "Ussuriiskaia zheleznaia doroga i kul'turnoekonomicheskii rost Ussuriisko-Primorskago kraia so vremeni eia postroiki." *Priamurskiia vedomosti* 1901, 392: 15–20; 393: 15–19; 395: 15–19; 399: 14–20.

Ludwig, Albert Philip. "Li Hung-chang and Chinese Foreign Policy, 1870–1885." Ph.D. dissertation, University of California, 1936.

Lung, Chang. *La Chine à l'aube du XXᵉ siècle: Les relations diplomatiques de la Chine avec les puissances depuis la guerre sino-japonaise jusqu'à la guerre russo-japonaise.* Paris, 1962.

M., S. *Po Dal'nemu Vostoku; putevyia zametki.* With illustrations by N. N. Karazin. St. Petersburg, 1899.

Macdonald, Donald Ross Hazelton. "Russian Interest in Korea, to 1895: The Pattern of Russia's Emerging Interest in the Peninsula From the Late Seventeenth Century to the Sino-Japanese War." Ph.D. dissertation, Harvard University, 1957.

MacKinnon, Stephen R. "The Peiyang Army, Yüan Shih-k'ai, and the origins of modern Chinese warlordism." *Journal of Asian Studies* 1973, 32: 405–23.

MacNair, Harley Farnsworth. "Some Aspects of China's Foreign Relations in Long Retrospect." *Chinese Social and Political Review* 1938–39, 22: 346–62.

————, ed. *Modern Chinese History: Selected Readings.* Shanghai, 1927.

Madrolle. *North-Eastern China, Manchuria, Mongolia, Vladivostock, Korea, With Maps and Plans.* Paris, 1912.

Maejima Shozo. "Ro-Shin mitsuyaku no Kato gaiko." *Ritsumeikan hogaku* 1960, 34: 239–81.

Mahan, A. T. *The Problem of Asia and Its Effect upon International Policies.* London, 1900.

Mai, Joachim. *Das deutsche Kapital in Russland, 1850–1894.* Berlin, 1970.

Maître, Cl. E. "Les origines du conflit russo-japonais." *Bulletin de l'École Française d'Extrême Orient à Hanoi* 1904, 4: 499–522.

Maki, John McGilvrey, ed. *Conflict and Tension in the Far East: Key Documents, 1894–1960.* Seattle, 1961.

Makino Yoshitomo. *Shina gaikoshi.* Tokyo, 1914.

Maksimov, A. Ia. *Na Dal'nem Vostoke.* St. Petersburg, 1894.

————. *Nashi zadachi na Tikhom Okeane: Politicheskie etiudy.* St. Petersburg, 1894.

————. "Nemtsy-instruktory v kitaiskoi armii." *Russkii vestnik* 1890, June, 234–43.

————. "Ussuriiskii krai: Inorodcheskoe naselenie kraia." *Russkii vestnik* 1888, Dec., 19–46.

Malozemoff, Andrew. *Russian Far Eastern Policy 1881–1904, With Special Emphasis on the Causes of the Russo-Japanese War.* Berkeley, 1958.

Mancall, Mark. *Russia and China: Their Diplomatic Relations to 1728.* Cambridge, Mass., 1971.

Mannix, William Francis. *Memoirs of Li Hung Chang. With the Story of a Literary Forgery, by Ralph D. Paine.* Boston, 1923.

Marder, Arthur J. *The Anatomy of British Sea Power: A History of British Naval Policy in the pre-dreadnought era 1880–1905.* New York, 1940.

"Marquis Ito in Korea." *Korean Repository* 1898, 5: 350–52.

Martin, Rudolf. *Die Zukunft Russlands und Japans: Die deutschen Milliarden in Gefahr.* Berlin, 1905.

Masanori Ito. *Kato Takaaki.* 2 vols. Tokyo, 1929.

Materialy k istorii voprosa o Sibirskoi zheleznoi dorogi. St. Petersburg, 1891.

Materialy po istorii Vladivostoka. Compiled by Dal'nevostochnyi Filial Imeni V. L. Komarova, Sibirskoe otdelenie Akademii Nauk SSSR. vol. 1 (1860–1917). Vladivostok, 1960.

Matiunin, N. B. "Ob otnosheniiakh Korei k inostrannym gosudarstvam," *Sbornik geograficheskikh, topograficheskikh i statisticheskikh materialov po Azii* 1894, 58: 1–32.

Matsokin. "K rasovoi bor'be v Priamurskom krae." *Priamurskiia vedomosti* 1901, 376: 16–19.

Matsugawa Kametaro. "Nichi-Ro-Shi gaiko no sanju-nen." *Toyo* 1928, 31: 7–49.

Matsumoto Shigeharu, Oka Yoshitake, Nishi Haruhiko, Kawagoe Shigeru, and Kase Toshikazu. *Kindai Nihon no gaiko.* Tokyo, 1962.

Matsumoto Tadao. *Kinsei Nihon gaikoshi kenkyu.* Tokyo, 1942.

Matsushita Yoshio. *Nisshin senso zengo.* Tokyo, 1949.

Matveev, N. P. *Kratkii istoricheskii ocherk Vladivostoka* (1860–1910). Vladivostok, 1910.

Mavor, James. *An Economic History of Russia.* 2 vols. London, 1914.

May, Ernest R., and Thomson, James C., Jr. *American-East Asian Relations: A Survey.* Cambridge, Mass., 1972.

Mayo, Marlene J. "The Korean Crisis of 1873 and Early Meiji Foreign Policy." *Journal of Asian Studies* 1972, 31: 793–820.

McCarthy, Michael J. F. *The Coming Power: A Contemporary History of the Far East 1898–1905.* London, 1905.

McCordock, R. Stanley. *British Far Eastern Policy, 1894–1900.* New York, 1931.

McCormick, Thomas J. *China Market: America's Quest for Informal Empire, 1893–1901.* Chicago, 1967.

McCune, George McAfee. "Korean Relations with China and Japan, 1800–1864." Ph.D. dissertation, University of California, 1941.

————. "Russian Policy in Korea: 1895–1898." *Far Eastern Survey* 1946, 14: 272–74.

McKenzie, F. A. *Korea's Fight for Freedom.* New York, 1920.

————. *The Tragedy of Korea.* New York, 1908 (?).

McLaren, Walter Wallace. *A Political History of Japan during the Meiji Era, 1867–1912.* London, 1916.

Meissner, Kurt. *Deutsche in Japan 1639–1960.* Tokyo, 1961.

Melgunoff, S., ed. *Das Tagebuch des letzten Zaren von 1890 bis zum Fall nach den unveröffentlichten Russischen Handschriften.* Berlin, 1923.

Mezhdunarodnye otnosheniia na Dal'nem Vostoke. Compiled by A. L. Narochnitskii, A. A. Guber, M. I. Sladkovskii, I. Ia. Burlingas under the auspices of the Institut Dal'nego Vostoka Akademii Nauk SSSR. Edited by E. M. Zhukov, M. E. Sladkovskii, and A. M. Dubinskii. 2 vols. Moscow, 1973.

Mezhdunarodnye otnosheniia na Dal'nem Vostoke (1870–1945 gg). Compiled by G. N. Voitinskii, A. L. Gal'perin, A. A. Guber, A. M. Dubinskii, E. M. Zhukov, L. I. Zubok, and A. L. Narochnitskii under the auspices of the Institut Vostokovedeniia Akademii Nauk SSSR. Edited by E. M. Zhukov. Moscow, 1951.

Michael, Franz H. *Der Streit um die Mandschurei; die chinesisch-japanischen Rechtsbeziehungen in den "Drei Östlichen Provinzen" Chinas vor Ausbruch des Konfliktes im September 1931.* Leipzig, 1933.

Michaelis, Georg. *Für Staat und Volk: Eine Lebensgeschichte.* Berlin, 1922.

Michon, Georges. *L'Alliance Franco-Russe, 1891–1917.* Paris, 1927.

"Min Yong-whan." *Korean Review* 1906, 6: 406–12.

Minrath, Paul. *Das englisch-japanische Bündnis von 1902: Die Grundlegung der Ententepolitik im Fernosten.* Stuttgart, 1933.

Mitsukawa Kametaro. *Sangoku kansho igo.* Tokyo, 1935.

Miura Goro. *Kanki shokun kaiko roku.* Tokyo, 1925.

Moellendorff, Rosalie von. *P. G. von Moellendorff: Ein Lebensbild.* Leipzig, 1930.

Moltke, Helmuth von. *Erinnerungen, Briefe, Dokumente 1877–1916.* Stuttgart, 1922.

Moore, John Bassett. *Collected Papers.* vols. 1 and 2. London, 1944.

Morley, James W., ed. *Japan's Foreign Policy, 1868–1941; A Research Guide.* New York, 1974.

Morrison, G. E. *Correspondence.* Edited by Lo Hui-min. Vol. 1: 1895–1912. Cambridge, 1976.

Morse, Hosea Ballou. *The International Relations of the Chinese Empire.* 3 vols. Shanghai, 1910–1918.

Morse, Hosea Ballou, and MacNair, Harley Farnsworth. *Far Eastern International Relations.* New York, 1931.

Mörsel, F. H. "Chinampo and Mokpo." *Korean Repository* 1897, 4: 334–38.

————. "Events Leading to the Emeute of 1884." *Korean Repository* 1897, 4: 95–98, 135–40, 212–19.

Morskoi sbornik. Compiled by the Naval Scientific Section of the Russian Ministry of the Navy. St. Petersburg, 1848–1917.

Mosely, Philip E. "Aspects of Russian Expansion." *The American Slavic and East European Review* 1948, 7: 197–213.

Moskovskiia vedomosti.

Mosolff, Hans. *Die chinesische Auswanderung. (Ursachen, Wesen und Wirkungen).* Rostock, 1932.

Moulin, Henri Alexis. *La politique russe et la politique japonaise en Asie.* Dijon, 1905.

Müller-Jabusch, Maximilian. *Fünfzig Jahre Deutsch-Asiatische Bank 1890–1939.* Berlin, 1940.

Müller-Link, Horst. *Industrialisierung und Aussenpolitik: Preussen, Deutschland und das Zarenreich, 1860–1890.* Göttingen, 1977.

Muradian, A. A. *Amerikanskie missionery v stranakh Dal'nego Vostoka, Iugo-Vostochnoi Azii i Okeanii v XIX v.* Moscow, 1971.

Murakawa Kengo. *Nihon gaiko shi.* Tokyo, 1940.

Muskatblit, F. *Rossiia i Iaponiia na Dal'nem Vostoke. Istorikopoliticheskii etiud.* Odessa, 1904.

Mutsu Hirokichi, ed. *Hakushaku Mutsu Munemitsu iko.* Tokyo, 1929.

Mutsu Munemitsu. *Kenken-roku.* Tokyo, 1946.

—————. Manuscript translation of the above in the Shidehara Peace Library, Tokyo.

N., A. "Iaponiia i Rossiia." In *Drevniaia i novaia Rossiia* 1897, vol. 15, no. 2.

Naberfeld, P. Emil. *Grundriss der japanischen Geschichte zum memorieren, orientieren und repetieren.* Tokyo, 1940.

Nadarov, I. P. "Puteshestvie po Koree s dekabria 1885 po mart 1886 goda P. M. Delotkevicha." In Russkoe geograficheskoe obshchestvo, *Izvestiia* 1889, 25: 295–315.

Nagoka Shinjiro. "Yamagata Aritomo no Rokoku haken to Nichi-Ro kyotei." *Nihon rekishi* 1953, 59: 16–19.

Nahm, Andrew Changwoo. "Kim Ok-kyun and the Korean Progressive Movement, 1882–1884." Ph.D. dissertation, Stanford University, 1961.

—————. "Reaction and the Response to the Opening of Korea, 1876–1884." In Yung-hwan Jo, ed. *Korea's Response to the West,* 141–62. Kalamazoo, Mich., 1970. (Reprinted from Robert K. Sakai, ed. *Studies in Asia: 1965,* 61–80. Lincoln, Neb., 1965.)

Naito Chishu, Hanaoka Shiro, Murakami Shoji, and Kurihara Ken. *Roshia no toho seisaku.* Tokyo, 1942.

Nakada Sempo. *Nihon gaiko hiwa.* Tokyo, 1940.

Nakamura Kikuo. *Ito Hirobumi.* Tokyo, 1958.

Nakatsuka Akira. *Nisshin senso no kenkyu.* Tokyo, 1968.

Narochnitskii, A. L. "Angliia, Kitai i Iaponiia nakanune iaponokitaiskoi voiny 1894–1895 gg." *Istoricheskie zapiski* 1946, 19: 189–214.

—————. "Angliia, Rossiia i koreiskii vopros nakanune napadeniia Iaponii na Kitai letom 1894 g." *Istoricheskie zapiski* 1947, 24: 160–83.

—————. "Ekspansiia SShA na Dal'nem Vostoke v 1886–1894 gg." *Uchenye zapiski* 1953, 25: 3–108.

—————. "K voprosu o iaponskoi agressii v Koree i prichinakh iapono-kitaiskoi voiny 1894–1895 gg." *Voprosy istorii* 1950, 5: 51–76.

—————. *Kolonial'naia politika kapitalistcheskikh derzhav na Dal'nem Vostoke 1860–1895.* Moscow, 1956.

Nasekin, N. A. "Koreitsy Priamurskago kraia." In Russia, Ministerstvo Narodnago Prosveshcheniia, *Zhurnal* 1904, 370: 1–61.

Nasha zheleznodarozhnaia politika po dokumentam arkhiva Komiteta Ministrov. vol. 3. St. Petersburg, 1902.

"Nashi pochtovyia i telegrafnyia snosheniia s Iaponiei i Kitaem." *Priamurskiia vedomosti* 1894, 15: 9–11.

Nebol'sin, Lt. A. "Morskaia voina Iaponii s Kitaem." *Morskoi sbornik* 1895, no. 9, unofficial section, pp. 1–19.

Nedachin, S. V. "Koreitsy-kolonisty; k voprosu o sblizhenii koreitsev s Rossiei." *Vostochnyi sbornik* 1913, 1: 183–204.

"Nedovol'stvo russko-iaponskim soglasheniem. (Politicheskoe obozrenie.)" *Niva* 1891, 30: 538.

Nelson, M. Frederick. *Korea and the Old Orders in Eastern Asia.* Baton Rouge, 1945.

Neskol'ko slov po voprosu o Sibirskoi zheleznoi doroge. Moscow, 1882.

"The New Ports." *Korean Repository* 1897, 4: 345–48.

Nichi-Ro kosho-shi. Compiled by Tanaka Bunichiro for the use of the Japanese Foreign Ministry in 1944; published in 1969.

Nihon gaiko bunsho. Compiled by the Japanese Foreign Office. Tokyo, 1936–   .

Nihon gaiko nempyo to shuyo bunsho. Compiled by the Japanese Foreign Office. 2 vols. Tokyo, 1965–1966.

Nihon Kokusai Seiji Gakkai, comp. *Nichi-Ro Nisso kankei no tenkai.* Tokyo, 1966.

————. *Nihon gaiko shi kenkyu: Nisshin Nichi-Ro senso.* Tokyo, 1961.

————. *Nikkan kankei no tenkai.* Tokyo, 1963.

Nihon rekishi daijiten. 20 vols. and 2 supplementary vols. Tokyo, 1956–1960.

Nikhamin, V. P. "Diplomatiia russkogo tsarizma v Koree posle iapono-Kitaiskoi voiny (1895–1896 gg.), Po dokumentam Arkhiva vneshnei politik Rossii." In *Uchenye zapiski: Istoriia mezhdunerodnykh otnoshenii, istoriia zarubezhnykh stran,* 137–72. Moscow, 1957.

————. "Russko-iaponskie otnosheniia i Koreia 1894–1898 gg." Candidate dissertation, Vysshaia diplomaticheskaia shkola Ministerstva inostrannykh del SSSR, 1948.

Nilus, E. Kh. *Istoricheskii obzor Kitaiskoi Vostochnoi zheleznoi dorogi, 1896–1923.* Harbin, 1923.

Nish, Ian H. *The Anglo-Japanese Alliance. The Diplomacy of Two Island Empires 1894–1907.* London, 1966.

————. *Japanese Foreign Policy 1869–1942: Kasumigaseki to Miyakezaka.* London, 1977.

————. "Korea, Focus of Russo-Japanese Diplomacy." *Asian Studies* 1966, 4: 1: 70–83.

"The Nishi-Rosen Convention." *Korean Repository* 1898, 5: 189–92.

Nishi Tokujiro. *Danshaku Nishi Tokujiro den.* Tokyo, 1932.

————. *Sankoku kansho.* Tokyo, 1932.

Niva. Illiustrirovannyi zhurnal literatury i sovremennoi zhizni.

Noble, Harold Joyce. "Korea and her Relations with the United States before 1895." Ph.D. dissertation, University of California, 1931.

————. "The United States and Sino-Korean Relations, 1885–1887." *Pacific Historical Review* 1933, 2: 292–304.

Nohara, W. K. *Die "Gelbe Gefahr."* Stuttgart, 1936.

Nolde, Baron Boris E. *L'Alliance Franco-Russe: Les origines du systeme diplomatique d'avant-guerre.* Paris, 1936.

————. *Vneshniaia politika: istoricheskie ocherki*. Petrograd, 1915.

Nomura Hideo, ed. *Meiji-Taisho-shi*. 6 vols. Tokyo, 1930–1931.

The North-China Herald and Supreme Court and Consular Gazette.

North Manchuria and the Chinese Eastern Railway. Compiled by the Chinese Eastern Railroad Company. Harbin, 1924.

"Notes on the Japan-China War." In United States Office of Naval Intelligence, *General Information Series*, no. 14, pp. 9–25. Washington, 1895.

Notes on the War between China and Japan. Bulletin no. 11 of the Military Information Division of the United States Adjutant-General's Office. Washington, 1896.

Novaia istoriia stran zarubezhnoi Azii i Afriki. Edited by G. V. Efimov and D. A. Ol'derogge. Leningrad, 1959.

Novoe Vremia.

Novyi Krai.

Nozikov, N. *Iapono-kitaiskaia voina 1894–1895 gg*. Moscow, 1939.

Numata Ichiro. *Nichi-Ro gaiko-shi*. Tokyo, 1943.

"Ob otkrytii Korei dlia vneshnei morskoi torgovli." Compiled by D. M. *Morskoi sbornik* 1883, 196: 5: 67–82.

Obzor snoshenii s Iaponiei po Koreiskim delam s 1895 g. Compiled by the Russian Ministry of Foreign Affairs. St. Petersburg, 1906.

Ocherk istorii ministerstva inostrannykh del 1802–1902. Compiled by the Russian Foreign Ministry. St. Petersburg, 1902.

"Official Report on Matters connected with the Events of October 8th, 1895, and the Death of the Queen." *Korean Repository* 1896, 8: 3: 118–42.

Ogasawara, Vice Admiral Viscount Nagayo. *Life of Admiral Togo*. Translated by Jukichi Inouye and Tozo Inouye. Tokyo, 1924.

Ogg, Frederick A. "The Lion and the Bear in the Far East." *Chautauquan* 1903, 37: 14–25.

————. "Russia's Quest of the Pacific." *Chautauquan* 1903, 36: 358–69.

————. "Two Imperial Creations: A Comparison." *Chautauquan* 1903, 37: 131–43.

Ogiso Teruyuki, Sakurai Toshiteru, Fujimura Michio, and Yoshii Hiroshi. "Nisshin Nichi-Ro senso kenkyushi." In Nihon Kokusai Seiji Gakkai, comp., *Nihon gaikoshi kenkyu—Nisshin Nichi-Ro senso*, 151–69. Tokyo, 1961.

Oh, Bonnie Bongwan. "The Background of Chinese Policy Formation in the Sino-Japanese War of 1894–1895." Ph.D. dissertation, University of Chicago, 1974.

Ohata Tokujiro. *Kokusai kanyo to Nihon gaikoshi*. Tokyo, 1966.

Okamoto, Shumpei. *The Japanese Oligarchy and the Russo-Japanese War*. New York, 1970.

Oka Yoshitake. *Yamagata Aritomo*. Tokyo, 1958.

"O Likhunch zhane." *Priamurskiia vedomosti* 1901, 417: 16–20.

Oncken, Hermann. *Das Deutsche Reich und die Vorgeschichte des Weltkrieges*. 2 vols. Leipzig, 1933.

Ono, Giichi. *Expenditures of the Sino-Japanese War*. New York, 1922.

Opisanie Korei. Edited by the Institut Narodov Azii Akademii Nauk SSSR. Moscow, 1960. (Abridged edition of the 3 vol. work compiled by the Russian Finance Ministry in 1900.)

Oppert, Ernst. *A Forbidden Land: Voyages to Corea*. London, 1880.

Osatake Takeshi. *Konan jiken.* Tokyo, 1950.
Ostwald, Paul. *Ostasien und die Weltpolitik.* Bonn, 1928.
"O torgovle Iaponii s Rossieiu." *Priamurskiia vedomosti* 1894, no. 8, supplement.
"O torgovle Kitaia s Rossieiu." *Priamurskiia vedomosti* 1894, no. 12, supplement.
Oudendyk, William J. *Ways and By-ways in Diplomacy.* London, 1939.
Owens, Rameth Richard. "A Century at Vladivostok, 1860–1960." Master's thesis, Florida State University, 1961.
Oyama Azusa, ed. *Yamagata Ikensho.* Tokyo, 1966.
Ozawa Yonezo. *Kaikoku hachijunen-shi.* Tokyo, 1931.

"Pacific Russia." *Japan Weekly Mail* 1889, pp. 61–62.
Pak. "Koreitsy v Man'chzhurii." *Materialy po natsional'no-kolonial'nym problemam* 1932, 3(4): 111–120.
Palais, James B. *Politics and Policy in Traditional Korea.* Cambridge, Mass., 1975.
Paléologue, Maurice. *Guillaume II et Nicholas II.* Paris, 1934.
Palmer, A. W. "Lord Salisbury's Attempts to Reach an Understanding with Russia, June 1895–November 1900." B. Litt. thesis, Oxford University, 1953.
P'an, Stephen Chao-ying. *American Diplomacy Concerning Manchuria.* Washington, 1938.
Panikkar, K. M. *Asia and Western Dominance: A Survey of the Vasco Da Gama Epoch of Asian History 1498–1945.* New York, 1959.
Panov, A. A. "Zheltyi vopros v Priamur'e. Istoriko-statisticheskii ocherk." *Voprosy kolonizatsii* 1910, 7: 53–116.
Panov, V. "Istoricheskaia oshibka." Vladivostok, 1908. (Reprinted from *Dal'nii Vostok* 1908, nos. 23–47.)
Pantzer, Peter. *Japan und Österreich-Ungarn. Die diplomatische, wirtschaftliche und kulturelle Beziehungen von ihrer Aufnahme bis zum ersten Weltkrieg.* Vienna, 1973. (Beiträge zur Japanologie, vol. 11).
Papers Relating to the Foreign Relations of the United States. Compiled by the Department of State. Washington.
Parker, E. H. "The Conscience of Corea." *Imperial and Asiatic Quarterly Review* 1896, 2: 4: 291–97.
———. "The Manchu Relations with Korea." *Transactions of the Asiatic Society of Japan* 1887, 15: 96–102.
———. "Russia and China." *Imperial and Asiatic Quarterly Review* 1905, 19: 11–47.
———. "Russia's sphere of influence, or a thousand years of Manchuria." *Imperial and Asiatic Quarterly Review* 1900, 9: 287–313.
Pasvolsky, Leo. *Russia in the Far East.* New York, 1922.
Paullin, C. O. "The Opening of Korea by Commodore Shufeldt." *Political Science Quarterly* 1910, 25: 470–99.
Peip'ing Ku-kung Po-wu Yüan, comp. *Ch'ing Kuang-hsü ch'ao chung-jih chiao-she shih-liao.* Peiping, 1932.
Pelcovits, N. *Old China Hands and the Foreign Office.* New York, 1948.
Pelikan, A. *Progressiruiushchaia Iaponiia.* St. Petersburg, 1895.
Penson, Lillian M. "The Principles and Methods of Lord Salisbury's Foreign Policy." *Cambridge Historical Journal* 1935–37, 5: 87–106.
Perepiska Vil'gelma II s Nikolaem II, 1894–1914. Moscow, 1923.

Perry, John Curtis. "Great Britain and the Emergence of Japan as a Naval Power." *Monumenta Nipponica* 1966, 21: 305–21.

"Pervye shagi russkogo imperializma na Dal'nem Vostoke (1888–1903 gg.)." Edited by A. Popov and S. R. Diamant. *Krasnyi arkhiv* 1932, 52: 34–124. (Translated by X as "First Steps of Russian Imperialism in the Far East [1888–1903]" in the *Chinese Social and Political Science Review* 1934–1935, 18: 236–81, 572–94.)

Petrov, D. V. *Kolonialnaia ekspansiia soedinennykh shtatov Ameriki v Iaponii v seredine XIX veka.* Moscow, 1955.

Petrov, Victor P. "Manchuria as an Objective of Russian Foreign Policy." Ph.D. dissertation, American University, 1953.

Petrov-Baturich, S. V. "Istoricheskii ocherk vozniknoveniia i razvitiia koreiskogo voprosa." *Russkii vestnik* 1894, 234: 212–37.

Philip, Joseph. *Foreign Diplomacy in China 1894–1900.* London, 1928.

"Piatiletnee upravlenie Priamurskim kraem general-leitenantom Sergeem Mikhailovichem Dukhovskim." *Priamurskiia vedomosti* 1898, 224: 13–17; 225: 12–17; 226: 12–14.

Pinon, René. "La Chine et les puissances européennes, 1894–1904." *Revue des Deux Mondes* 1904.

—————. *La Chine qui s'ouvre.* Paris, 1900.

Podzhio, M. A. *Ocherki Korei. Sostavleno po zapiskam.* St. Petersburg, 1892.

"Poezdka general'nogo shtaba polkovnika Karneeva i poruchika Mikhailova po Iuzhnoi Koree v 1895–1896 gg." *Sbornik geograficheskikh, topograficheskikh i statisticheskikh materialov po Azii* 1901, no. 75.

"Poezdka v Koreiu gen. sht. podpolkovnika Vebelia letom 1889 g. s marshrutnoiu s'emkoiu." *Sbornik geograficheskikh, topograficheskikh i statisticheskikh materialov po Azii* 1890, 41: 143–252.

Poidevin, Raymond. *Finances et relations internationales, 1887–1914.* Paris, 1970.

Pokotilov, D. D. *Kitaiskie porty imeiushchie Znachenie dlia russkoi torgovli na dal'nem vostoke.* St. Petersburg, 1895.

—————. *Koreia i Iaponno-Kitaiskoe stolknovenie.* St. Petersburg, 1895.

Pokrovskii, Mikhail N. *Diplomatiia i voiny tsarskoi Rossii v XIX siecle.* Moscow, 1924.

Pollard, Robert T. "American Relations with Korea, 1882–1895." *Chinese Social and Political Science Review* 1932, 16: 425–71.

Polovtsov, A. A. ed. *Russki biograficheskii slovar'.* 25 vols. St. Petersburg, 1896–1918.

Pooley, A. M. *Japan's Foreign Policies.* London, 1920.

—————, ed. *The Secret Memoirs of Count Tadasu Hayashi.* New York, 1915.

Popov, A. "Angliiskaia politika v Indii i russko-indiiskie otnosheniia v 1897–1905 gg." *Krasnyi arkhiv* 1926, 19: 53–63.

—————. "Anglo-russkoe soglashenie o razdele Kitaia (1899)." *Krasnyi arkhiv* 1927, 25: 111–34.

—————. "Dal'nevostochnaia politika tsarizma v 1894–1901 godakh." *Istorik-Marksist* 1935, 11: 38–57.

—————. "Ot Bosfora k Tikhomu okeanu: Vneshniaia politika Rossiia v 80-kh i 90-kh godakh XIX veka." *Istorik Marksist* 1934, 3: 37: 3–28.

Popov, I. I. *Ot Nebesnoi imperii k Seredonnoi respubliki. Ocherki po istorii Kitaia, Man'chzhurii, Mongolii i Tibeta so stat'iami: "Istoriia torgovykh otnoshenii mezhdu Rossiei i Kitaem,"* "*Russko-kitaiskii torgovyi dogovor i Transmongol'skaia zheleznaia doroga.*" Moscow, 1912.

Popov, Konstantin. *Japan: Essays on National Culture and Scientific Thought.* Moscow, 1969.

Powell, Ralph L. *The Rise of Chinese Military Power, 1895–1912.* Princeton, N.J., 1955.

Pozdneev, Dimitrii. *Opisanie Man'chzhurii.* vol. 1. St. Petersburg, 1897.

"Pravila dlia inostrannykh kontsessii v Tsinampo i Mokpo." *Priamurskiia vedomosti* 1899, 309: 2–6.

"Prebyvanie chrezvychainago Koreiskago posol'stva v Khabarovske." *Priamurskiia vedomosti* 1895.

"Preliminary Notes on China-Japan War." Compiled by H. M. Witzel and Lincoln Karmany. In United States Naval Intelligence Office, *General Information Series*, no. 14, pp. 215–34. Washington, 1895.

Preller, Hugo. *Die Weltpolitik des 19. Jahrhunderts.* Berlin, 1923.

"The Press on the Situation." *Korean Repository* 1897, 4: 468–71.

Presseisen, Ernest L. *Before Aggression: Europeans Prepare the Japanese Army.* Tucson, 1965.

Priamurskiia vedomosti. Khabarovsk.

Price, Don C. *Russia and the Roots of the Chinese Revolution, 1896–1911.* Cambridge, Mass., 1974.

Prokhorov, A. *K voprosu o sovetsko-kitaiskoi granitse.* Moscow, 1975.

Punch, or the London Charivari.

Purcell, Victor. *The Boxer Uprising; A Background Study.* Cambridge, 1963.

Putiata, D. V. *Kitai. Ocherki geografii, ekonomicheskago sostoianiia, administrativnago i voennage ustroistva Seredinnoi Imperii i voennago znacheniia pogranichnoi s Rossiei polos.* St. Petersburg, 1895.

Quested, Rosemarie. *The Expansion of Russia in East Asia, 1857–1860.* Kuala Lumpur, 1968.

————. *The Russo-Chinese Bank.* Birmingham, England, 1977. (Birmingham Slavonic Monographs, no. 2.)

"The Question of Korea." *Japan Weekly Mail* 1894, pp. 461–64.

Rader, Ronald Ray. "Decline of the Afghan Problem as a Crisis Factor in Russian Foreign Policy, 1892–1907." Ph.D. dissertation, Syracuse University, 1965.

Ramming, Martin. *Deutschland und Japan: 100 Jahre einer Völkerfreundschaft.* Berlin, 1961.

————. "Geschichtlicher Rückblick auf die deutsch-japanischen Beziehungen der älteren Zeit." *Zeitschrift für Politik* 1942, 32: 602–20.

Rawlinson, John L. *China's Struggle for Naval Development.* Cambridge, Mass., 1967.

Reisner, I. M. and Rubtsov, B. K. ed. *Novaia istoriia stran zarubezhnogo vostoka.* 2 vols. Moscow, 1952.

"Reminiscences of July 23, 1894." *Korean Repository* 1896, 3: 293–97.

Remmey, Paul B., Jr. "British Diplomacy and the Far East, 1892–1898." Ph.D. dissertation, Harvard University, 1965.

Renouvin, Pierre. *La question d'Extrême-Orient, 1840–1940.* Paris, 1946.

"A Retrospect,—1894." *Korean Repository* 1895, 2: 29–30.

Reventlow, Graf Ernst zu. *Deutschlands auswärtige Politik 1888–1914*. Berlin, 1916.

"Right About Face." *Korean Repository* 1898, 5: 113–17.

Ritchie, Galen Blaine. "The Asiatic Department during the reign of Alexander II, 1855–1881." Ph.D. dissertation, Columbia University, 1970.

Ro, Kwang Hai. "Power Politics in Korea and its Impact on Korean Foreign and Domestic Affairs, 1882–1907." Ph.D. dissertation, University of Oklahoma, 1966.

Rockhill, William Woodville. *China's Intercourse with Korea from XVth Century to 1895*. London, 1905.

—————. "The United States and the Future of China." *Forum* 1900, 29: 324–31.

Romanov, B. A. "Likhunchangskii fond" (Iz istorii imperialisticheskoi politiki na Dal'nem Vostoke) *Bor'ba klassov* 1924, 1–2: 77–126.

—————. *Ocherki diplomaticheskoi istorii russko-iaponskoi voiny, 1895–1907–*. 2d ed. Moscow, 1955.

—————. "Osnovnye momenty v russkoi politike na D. Vostoke v 1892–1925 gg." *Sibirskie ogni* 1926, 4: 98–116.

—————. "Perepiska o podkupe kitaiskikh sanovnikov Li Khun-chzana i Chzhan In-khuana." *Krasnyi arkhiv* 1922, 2: 287–93.

—————. *Rossiia v Man'chzhurii (1892–1906): Ocherki po istorii vneshnei politiki samoderzhaviia v epokhu imperializma*. Leningrad, 1928.

Rosen, Baron (Roman Romanovich). *Forty Years of Diplomacy*. 2 vols. London, 1922.

Rosen, Oscar. "German-Japanese Relations, 1894–1902: A Study of European Imperialism in the Far East." Ph.D. dissertation, University of Wisconsin, 1956.

Rosenbaum, Arthur Lewis. "China's First Railway: The Imperial Railways of North China, 1880–1911." Ph.D. dissertation, Yale University, 1972.

Rossiia na Dal'nem Vostoke. St. Petersburg, 1901.

Rossov, P. "Opisanie vstrechi kniazia Ukhtomskago v Pekine i audientsii ego u Kitaiskago Imperatora." *Priamurskiia vedomosti* 1897, 118: 8–11.

—————. "Pis'ma iz Kitaia." *Priamurskii vedomosti* 1897, 197: 13–17.

—————. *Russkii Kitai. Ocherki zaniatiia Kvantuna i byta tuzemnago naseleniia*. Port Arthur, 1901.

—————. "Vstrecha kniazia Ukhtomskago v Tian'tszine." *Priamurskiia vedomosti* 1897, 190: 8–10.

Rothstein, F. A. *Mezhdunarodyne otnosheniia v kontse XIX veka*. Moscow, 1960.

Rozental', E. M. *Diplomaticheskaia istoriia russko-frantsuzskogo soiuza v nachale XX veka*. Moscow, 1960.

Runin, Sergei. *V Man'chzhurii*. St. Petersburg, 1904.

Russia, Ministry of Foreign Affairs. *Annuaire diplomatique de l'Empire de Russie (Ezhegodnik Ministerstva Inostrannykh Del)*. 25 vols. 1862–1909.

"Russia and China." *Japan Weekly Mail* 1898, p. 337.

"Russia and Japan." *Japan Weekly Mail* 1891, pp. 650, 734; 1895, p. 732; 1899, p. 536.

"Russia and Japan in Korea." *Japan Weekly Mail* 1896, pp. 267, 501.

"Russia and Korea." *Japan Weekly Mail* 1888, p. 540; 1895, p. 584.

"Russia in Eastern Asia." *Japan Weekly Mail* 1899, p. 58.

"Russia in Korea." *Japan Weekly Mail* 1898, pp. 289, 312, 339, 388.

"Russia in Manchuria." *Japan Weekly Mail* 1898, p. 274.

"Russia in the Far East." *Japan Weekly Mail* 1899, pp. 339, 493.

"Russia, Japan, and Korea." *Japan Weekly Mail* 1898, p. 419.
"Russia on the Pacific." *Japan Weekly Mail* 1895, pp. 191–92.
"The Russian Admiral in Kagoshima." *Japan Weekly Mail* 1894, p. 205.
"Russian Ascendency in Korea." *Korean Repository* 1897, 4: 231–35.
"Russian Documents Relating to the Sino-Japanese War." *Chinese Social and Political Science Review* 1933–1934, 17: 480–515, 632–70. (Translation of "Iz epokhi iapono-kitaiskoi voiny 1894–1895 gg.")
"The Russian Minister in Japan." *Japan Weekly Mail* 1894, p. 235.
"The Russian Navy." *Japan Weekly Mail* 1895, p. 479.
"Russians and Japanese in Korea." *Japan Weekly Mail* 1897, pp. 497–98.
"Russian Supremacy in Northeast Asia." *Japan Weekly Mail* 1891, pp. 153–54.
"Russia's Peace Proposals." *Japan Weekly Mail* 1898, p. 435.
"Russia's View of the Protocol." *Japan Weekly Mail* 1898, p. 646.
"Russkaia shkola v Tokio." *Priamurskiia vedomosti* 1894, 18: 9–10.
"Russkii beregovoi lazaret v Nagasaki dlia komand plavaiushchikh v Tikhom okeane sudov." *Morskoi sbornik* 1887, 200: 5: 91–154.
Russkii biograficheskii slovar'. 25 vols. St. Petersburg, 1896–1918.
"Russko-iaponskii torgovyi dogovor." *Priamurskiia vedomosti* 1896, 112: 14–15; 119: 14–15; 120: 13–14.
"Russko-kitaiskie otnosheniia." *Dal'nevostochnoe obozrenie* 1911, nos. 8–9, 10–11, pp. 43–130; no. 12, pp. 64–101.
Russko-kitaiskie otnosheniia 1689–1916: Ofitsial'nye dokumenty. Compiled by Institut Kitaevediniia Akademii Nauk SSSR. Moscow, 1958.
"Russland, Grossbritannien und Deutschland in Nord-China." *Der Ferne Osten* 1902, 1: 67–101.
"Russland und China." *Ostasien* 1898–1899, 1: 51–55.
"The Russo-Chinese Secret Treaty." *Japan Weekly Mail* 1895, p. 518.
"Russo-Japanese Commerce." *Japan Weekly Mail* 1895, p. 302.
"Russo-Japanese Protocol." *Japan Weekly Mail* 1898, p. 530.
Rzhevuskii, Lt., comp. *Iaponsko-kitaiskaia voina 1894–1895 gg*. St. Petersburg, 1896.

S., A. "Chetyrnadtsat' mesiatsev v Koree." *Knizhki nedeli* 1898, 1: 110–37; 2: 54–72.
Sabey, John Wayne. "The Gen'yosha, the Kokuryukai, and Japanese Expansionism." Ph.D. dissertation, University of Michigan, 1972.
Sabler, S. V. and Sosnovskii, I. V. *Sibirskaia zheleznaia doroga v ee proshlom i nastoiashchem*. St. Petersburg, 1903.
Saito Yoshie. *Kinsei toyo gaikoshi josetsu*. Tokyo, 1927.
Sakatani Yoshiro, ed. *Segai Inoue-ko den*. 5 vols. Tokyo, 1934.
Sakharov, K. V. *Istoriia Iaponii*. Tokyo, 1920.
Samoilov, Captain. *Opisanie zaniatoi nami territorii na Liaodunskom poluostrove*. St. Petersburg, 1898.
Sands, William Franklin. *Undiplomatic Memories: The Far East, 1896–1904*. New York, 1930.
Sanktpeterburgskiia Vedomosti.
Sarkisyanz, Emanuel. *Geschichte der orientalischen Völker Russlands bis 1917*. Munich, 1961.
Sauvage, Maxime Joseph Marie. *La guerre sino-japonaise 1894–1895*. Paris, 1897.

Savvin, V. P. *Vzaimootnosheniia tsarskoi Rossii i SSSR s Kitaem.* Moscow, 1930.
Sbornik dogovorov i diplomaticheskikh dokumentov po delam Dal'niago Vostoka, 1895–1905. Compiled by the Russian Ministry of Foreign Affairs. St. Petersburg, 1906.
Sbornik dogovorov i drugikh dokumentov po istorii mezhdunarodnykh otnoshenii na Dal'nem Vostoke, 1842–1925. Edited by E. D. Grimm. Moscow, 1927.
Sbornik dokumentov otnosiashchikhsia k Kitaiskoi Vostochnoi zheleznoi doroge. Compiled by the Chinese Eastern Railroad Company. Harbin, 1922.
Sbornik geograficheskikh, topograficheskikh i statisticheskikh materialov po Azii. Compiled by the Russian General Staff. 87 issues. St. Petersburg, 1883–1914.
Schierbrand, Wolf von. *America, Asia and the Pacific; With Special Reference to the Russo-Japanese War and its Results.* New York, 1904.
Schmidt, Vera. *Die deutsche Eisenbahnpolitik in Shantung, 1898–1914: Ein Beitrag zur Geschichte des deutschen Imperialismus in China.* Wiesbaden, 1976.
Schön, Major Joseph. *Die Russischen Kriegshafen in Ostasien.* Vienna, 1904.
————. Über die Ziele Russlands in Asien. 2d ed. Vienna, 1900.
Schrameier, Dr. W. *Kiautschou, Seine Entwicklung und Bedeutung: Ein Rückblick.* Berlin, 1915.
Schrecker, John E. *Imperialism and Chinese Nationalism: Germany in Shantung.* Cambridge, Mass., 1971.
Schulman, Irwin J. "China's Response to Imperialism, 1895–1900." Ph.D. dissertation, Columbia University, 1967.
————. "Sino-Russian Relations, 1895–1896: A Political Study in Late Ch'ing Foreign Relations." Certificate essay, East Asian Institute, Columbia University, 1958.
Schulthess' Europäischer Geschichtskalender. vols. 23–40. Nördlingen and Munich, 1882–1899.
Schüssler, Wilhelm. *Deutschland zwischen Russland und England.* Leipzig, 1940.
Schwartz, Harry. *Tsars, Mandarins, and Commissars: A History of Chinese-Russian Relations.* Philadelphia, 1964.
Schwarz, von, and Romanowski. *Die Verteidigung von Port Arthur.* Translated from the Russian by Ullrich. 2 vols. Berlin, 1910.
Schweinitz, Hans Lothar von. *Denkwürdigkeiten des Botschafters General v. Schweinitz.* 2 vols. Berlin, 1927.
Schwertfeger, Generalmajor Bernhard. *Deutschland und Russland im Wandel der europäischen Bundnisse.* Hanover, 1939.
"The Secret Treaty between Russia and China." *Japan Weekly Mail* 1895, p. 464.
Selby, John. *The Paper Dragon: An Account of the China War, 1840–1900.* London, 1968.
Semenoff, E. "Le role mondial du Japon predit par un grand écrivain russe." *La Grande Revue* 1904, 1: 519–28.
Serevianov, A. "V Nagasaki i obratno sredi zimy." *Priamurskiia vedomosti* 1895, 61: 14–16.
Sergii, Archimandrite. *Na Dal'nem Vostoke (Pis'ma iaponskago missionera).* Arzamas, 1897.
————. *Po Iaponii (Zapiski missionera).* Sv. Troitskaia Lavra, 1903.
Seton-Watson, Hugh. *The Russian Empire 1801–1917.* Clarendon Press, 1967.
Seuberlich, Wolfgang. "Amtliches Kartenmaterial von 1911 zu nordmandschurischen

Grenzfragen." *Oriens Extremus* 1977, 24: 229–54.

Severnaia Man'chzhuriia i kitaiskaia vostochnaia zheleznaia doroga. Compiled by the Chinese Eastern Railroad Company. Harbin, 1922.

"Severo-Amerikanskie Soedinennye Shtaty i tsarskaia Rossiia v 90-kh godakh XIX v." *Krasnyi arkhiv* 1932, 52: 125–42.

Sh., A. S. "Sovremennaia Koreia i eia emigranty v Priamurskom kraie." *Vostochnoe obozrenie* 1886, no. 5.

Shanghai Mercury. *The Story of Russia and the Far East: Being a Series of Papers Contributed to the "Shanghai Mercury" During the Latter Part of the Year 1899.* Shanghai, 1899.

Shestunov, N. *Vdol' po Iaponii.* St. Petersburg, 1882.

Shidehara Taira. *Nichi-Ro-kan no Kankoku.* Tokyo, 1905.

Shimada Saburo. *Nihon to Roshia.* Tokyo, 1900.

Shimonaka Yasaburo, ed. *Shinsen dai-jimmei jiten.* 7 vols. Tokyo, 1937.

Shin, K. S. "The Diplomatic Relations between Russia and China on the Korean Problem 1884–1890." *Journal of National Academy of Sciences* (Seoul) 1959, 1: 155–66.

Shinobu, Jumpei. *Komura Jutaro.* Tokyo, 1942.

―――――. *Nidai gaiko no shinso.* Tokyo, 1928.

Shinobu Seizaburo. *Kindai Nihon gaiko-shi.* 2 vols. Tokyo, 1974.

―――――. *Mutsu gaiko: Nisshin senso no gaiko shiteki kenkyu.* Tokyo, 1935. (First published as *Nisshin senso.* Tokyo, 1934.)

―――――. *Mutsu Munemitsu.* Tokyo, 1938.

―――――, ed. *Nihon no gaiko.* Tokyo, 1961.

Shinobu Seizaburo and Nakayama Jiichi, eds. *Nichi-Ro senso shi no kenkyu.* Tokyo, 1959.

Shively, Donald H., ed. *Tradition and Modernization in Japanese Culture.* Princeton, N.J., 1971.

Shlomin, V. S., ed. *S. O. Makarov: Dokumenty.* vol. 2. Moscow, 1960.

Shoemaker, Michael Myers. *The Great Siberian Railway from St. Petersburg to Pekin.* New York, 1903.

Shreider, D. I. *Iaponiia i iapontsy: Putevye ocherki sovremennoi Iaponii.* St. Petersburg, 1895.

Shteinfel'd, Nikolai. *Russkoe delo v Man'chzhurii: S XVII veka do nashikh dnei.* Harbin, 1910.

"The Siberian Railway." *Japan Weekly Mail* 1895, p. 9.

Sibir' i velikaia Sibirskaia zheleznaia doroga. 2d ed. St. Petersburg, 1896.

Sibirtsev, M. "Po stranam dal'niago Vostoka v zimu 1896/97 gg." *Priamurskiia vedomosti* 1897, 170: 12–16; 171: 13–17; 172: 11–13; 173: 9–13.

Siemers. Bruno. *Japans Kampf gegen den U.S.A.-Imperialismus; ein Abriss der japanisch-U.S. amerikanischen Beziehungen, 1854–1942.* Berlin, 1943.

Sil'nitskii, A. *Kul'turnoe vliianie Ussuriiskoi zheleznoi dorogi na iuzhno-ussuriiskii krai.* Khabarovsk, 1901.

Simkin, Arnold P. "Anglo-Russian Relations in the Far East, 1897–1904." Ph.D. dissertation, University of London, 1967.

Simmons, Robert R. *The Strained Alliance: Peking, P'yongyang, Moscow and the Politics of the Korean Civil War.* New York, 1975.

"Sir Rutherford Alcock on Russia and Korea." *Japan Weekly Mail* 1886. pp. 253, 255.

Skachkev, K. A. "O znachenii dlia russkoi torgovli novago dogovora Rossii s Kitaem." *Russkii vestnik* 1881, 156: 361–71.

Skal'kovskii, K. A. *Russkaia torgovlia v Tikhom Okeane.* St. Petersburg, 1883.

————. *Vneshnaia politika Rossii i polozhenie inostrannykh derzhav.* 2d ed. St. Petersburg, 1901.

Skrine, F. H. *Expansion of Russia, 1815–1900.* Cambridge, 1903.

Sladkovskii, M. I. *Istoriia torgovo-ekonomicheskikh otnoshenii narodov Rossii s Kitaem (do 1917 g.).* Moscow, 1974.

————. *Kitai i Iaponiia.* Moscow, 1971.

Slovar' sovremennogo russkogo literaturnogo iazyka. Compiled by the Institut russkogo iazyka Akademii Nauk SSSR. 17 vols. Moscow, 1950–1965.

"Slovesnye peregovory o zakluchenii mira, vedennye v Simonoseki upolnomochennymi Kitaia i Iaponii v marte 1895 g." Translated from English by Cpt. Marchenko. *Sbornik geograficheskikh, topograficheskikh i statisticheskikh materialov po Azii.* 1897, 71: 42–97.

Smirnov, Dmitrii. "Gorod Ootsu v Iaponii." *Niva* 1891, pp. 457–58.

Sokovnin, M. "Kratkii ocherk iaponsko-kitaiskoi kampanii 1894/95 gg." *Priamurskiia vedomosti* 1895, 76: 1014.

Solov'ev, Iurii. *25 let moei diplomaticheskoi sluzhby 1893–1918.* Moscow, 1928.

South Manchuria Railroad Company (Minami Manshu Tetsudo Kabushiki Kaisha). *Kindai Ro-Shi kankei no kenkyu.* Compiled by Miyazaki Masayoshi. Dairen, 1922.

Sovetskaia istoricheskaia entsiklopediia. Compiled by Institut Istorii Akademii Nauk SSSR. 16 vols. Moscow, 1961–1976.

Soyeda, J. "The Adoption of Gold Monometallism in Japan." *Political Science Quarterly* 1898, 13: 60–90.

Spector, Stanley. *Li Hung-chang and the Huai Army.* Seattle, 1964.

Spendelow, Howard Randall. "Russia's Lease of Port Arthur and Talien. The Failure of China's Traditional Foreign Policy." *Papers on China* 1917, 24: 146–69.

Staal, G. G. *Correspondence diplomatique de M. de Staal, Ambassadeur de Russie à Londres 1884–1900.* 2 vols. Paris, 1929.

Staton, David Wayne. "Russia's Far Eastern International Relations, 1894–1898: A Study of Issues and Russian Attitude toward Asia as Reflected in Russo-Chinese and Russo-Japanese Negotiations." Honors thesis, Florida State University, 1962.

Stauffer, Robert Burton. "Manchuria as a political entity: Government and politics of a major region of China, including its relations to China proper." Ph.D. dissertation, University of Minnesota, 1954.

Stead, Alfred. "Conquest by Bank and Railways, with examples from Russia and Manchuria." *The Nineteenth Century* 1903.

————, ed. *Japan by the Japanese: A Survey by Its Highest Authorities.* London, 1904.

Steiger, George Nye. *China and the Occident. The Origin and Development of the Boxer Movement.* New Haven, 1927.

————. *History of the Far East.* Boston, 1944.

Steinberg, David I. *Korea: Nexus of East Asia. An Inquiry into Contemporary Korea in Historical Perspective.* Rev. ed., New York, 1970.

Steinmann, Friedrich von. *Russlands Politik im Fernen Osten und der Staatssekretär Bezobrazov. Ein Beitrag zur Vorgeschichte des russisch-japanischen Krieges.* Leipzig, 1931.

Stoddart, Anna M. *The Life of Isabella Bird (Mrs. Bishop), Hon. Member of the Oriental Society of Pekin, F.R.G.S., F.R.S.G.S.* London, 1907.
Stoecker, Helmuth. *Deutschland und China im 19. Jahrhundert.* Berlin, 1858.
Stults, Taylor. "Imperial Russia through American Eyes, 1894–1904: A Study in Public Opinion." Ph.D. dissertation, University of Missouri, 1970.
Sugawara, Takamitsu. "Japanese Interests in Korea and the Yalu Issue 1903–1904." Master's thesis, University of Hawaii, Honolulu, 1963.
————. "Nisshin senso chokuzen ni okeru Roshia Kyokuto seisaku no kicho. Chosen mondai wo chushin to shite." Undated reprint from *Seiyo-shi kenkyu*, no. 9, pp. 26–47.
Suh, Byung Han. "Die internationalen Beziehungen Koreas von der Mitte des 19. Jahrhunderts bis zum Ende der Unabhängigkeit." Ph.D. dissertation, University of Vienna, 1967.
Sumiya Mikio. *Dai Nihon teikoku no shiren.* Tokyo, 1966. (vol. 22 of Nihon no rekishi.)
Sumner, B. H. "Tsardom and Imperialism in the Far East and Middle East, 1880–1914." *Proceedings of the British Academy* 1941, 27: 25–65.
Sun, E-tu Zen. *Chinese Railways and British Interests 1898–1911.* New York, 1954.
Susaki Yoshisaburo. *Rokoku shinryaku-shi.* Tokyo, 1904.
Sviiagin, N. S. *Po russkoi i kitaiskoi Man'chzhurii ot Khabarovska do Ninguty. Vpechatleniia i nabliudeniia.* St. Petersburg, 1897.
————. *Svod mezhdunarodnykh postanovlenii, opredeliaiushchikh vzaimnyia otnosheniia mezhdu Rossieiu i Kitaem, 1689–1897.* Compiled by the Russian Foreign Ministry. St. Petersburg, 1900.
Swisher, Earl. *Early Sino-American Relations, 1841–1912.* Collected articles edited by Kenneth W. Rhea.
Sydacöff, Bresnitz von. *Aus dem Reiche des Mikado und die asiatische Gefahr.* Leipzig, n.d. (about 1904 or 1905.)
Synn, Seung Kwon. "The Russo-Japanese Struggle for Control of Korea, 1894–1904." Ph.D. dissertation, Harvard University, 1967.

T., T. von. *Russland am Stillen Ocean: Eine zeitgemässe Studie.* Berlin, 1896.
Tabohashi Kiyoshi. *Kindai Nissen kankei no kenkyu.* 2 vols. Tokyo, 1929.
————. *Meiji gaikoku kankei-shi.* Rev. ed. Tokyo, 1931.
————. *Nisshin seneki gaikoshi no kenkyu.* Tokyo, 1951.
Takahashi Yoshio. *Meiji keisatsushi kenkyu.* vol. 2. Tokyo, 1963.
————. *Sanko iretsu.* Tokyo, 1925.
Takeuchi, Tatsuji. *War and Diplomacy in the Japanese Empire.* Chicago, 1935.
Takizawa, Roberta. "Russo-Japanese Rivalry in Korea, 1894–1898." Honor's thesis, Florida State University, 1965.
Tan, Chester C. *The Boxer Catastrophe.* New York, 1967.
Tang, Peter S. H. *Russian and Soviet Policy in Manchuria and Outer Mongolia 1911–1931.* Durham, N.C., 1959.
Tansill, C. C. *The Foreign Policy of Thomas F. Bayard, 1885–1897.* New York, 1940.
Tarsaïdzé, Alexandre. *Czars and Presidents: The Story of a Forgotten Friendship.* New York, 1958.
Tatsumi Raijiro. *Nisshin seneki gaikoshi.* Tokyo, 1902.
Taylor, A. J. P. *The Struggle for Mastery in Europe, 1848–1918.* Oxford, 1954.

Tchen, Hohshien. *Les relations diplomatiques entre la Chine et le Japon de 1871 à nos jours*. Paris, 1921.

Teng, Ssy-yu, and Fairbank, John K., eds. *China's Response to the West: A Documentary Survey,, 1839–1923*. Cambridge, Mass., 1954.

Teplov, V. "Problemy Dal'nego Vostoka." *Russkii vestnik* 1903, Nov., 382–433; 1904, Jan., 414–455.

Teters, Barbara Joan. "The Conservative Opposition in Japanese Politics, 1877–1894." Ph.D. dissertation, University of Washington, 1955.

————. "The Otsu Affair: The Formation of Japan's Judicial Conscience." In David Wurfel, ed. *Meiji Japan's Centennial: Aspects of Political Thought and Action*, 36–62. Lawrence, Kansas, 1971.

Thompson, Richard Austin. "The Yellow Peril, 1890–1924." Ph.D. dissertation, University of Wisconsin, 1957.

Thorn, William Henry III. "Russia and the British Periodical Press 1856–1903: A Study of Attitudes Toward Russian Internal Affairs." Ph.D. dissertation, University of Rochester (New York), 1968.

Tiagai, G. D. *Krest'ianskoe vosstanie v Koree 1893–1895 gg*. Moscow, 1953.

————. *Narodnoe dvizhenie v Koree vo vtoroi polovine XIX veka*. Moscow, 1958.

————. "O planakh zheleznodorozhnogo stroitel'stva inostrannykh derzhav v Koree v kontse XIX v." In Institut Vostokovedeniia Akademii Nauk SSSR, *Kratkie soobshcheniia* 1957, 25: 78–84.

————. *Ocherk istorii Korei vo vtoroi polovine XIX v*. Moscow, 1960.

————, ed. *Po Koree: Puteshestviia 1885–1896*. Moscow, 1958.

Tikhomirov, Mikhail, and Gafurov, Babadjan. *The Slavs and the East*. Paris, 1965.

Timkovskii, Egor. *Puteshestvie v Kitai cherez Mongoliiu v 1820 i 1824 godakh*. 3 parts, St. Petersburg, 1824.

Timkowski, George. *Travels of the Russian Mission through Mongolia to China, and Residence in Peking, in the Years 1820–1821*. Translated with corrections and notes by Julius Klaproth. 2 vols. London, 1827.

Tirpitz, Alfred von. *Erinnerungen*. Leipzig, 1919.

Todt, Manfred. *Die Beurteilung der deutschen Politik 1894–1900 und ihrer leitenden Persönlichkeiten durch schweizerische Diplomaten*. Tübingen, 1964.

Tokutomi Iichiro and Hamada Yoshizumi. *Nich-Ro gaiko junenshi*. Tokyo, 1904.

Tolmachev, S. E. *Nuzhna li nam Vostochnaia Sibir? Zapiska o Sibiri i Dal'nem Vostoke*. Moscow, 1911.

Tomimas, Shutaro. *The Open-Door Policy and the Territorial Integrity of China; With Verses in Japanese*. New York, 1919.

"Torgovlia Rossii s Iaponiei cherez Kobe v 1895 godu." *Priamurskiia vedomosti* 1896, 139: 19.

"Torgovye interesy Rossii v Kitae." *Priamurskiia vedomosti* 1895, 96: 14–15.

Trautmann, Oskar P. *Die Sängerbrücke: Gedanken zur russischen Aussenpolitik von 1870–1914*. Stuttgart, 1940.

Treat, Payson J. "The cause of the Sino-Japanese War 1894." *Pacific Historical Review* 1939, 8: 149–57.

————. "China and Korea, 1885–1894." *Political Science Quarterly* 1934, 49: 506–43.

————. *Diplomatic Relations between the United States and Japan 1853–1895*. 2 vols. Stanford, 1932.

————. *Diplomatic Relations between the United States and Japan: 1895–1905.* Stanford, 1938.

————. "The Good offices of the United States during the Sino-Japanese War." *Political Science Quarterly* 1932, 47: 547–75.

Treaties and Agreements with and Concerning China, 1894–1918. Compiled by John Van A. MacMurray. 2 vols. New York, 1921.

"Treaties between Japan and Russia." Reels TR1-3 of Japanese Ministry of Foreign Affairs Archives microfilms.

"The Treaty of Tientsin." *Japan Weekly Mail* 1886, pp. 38–39.

Treue, Wilhelm. "Russland und die Eisenbahnen im Fernen Osten." *Historische Zeitschrift* 1938, 158: 504–40.

Trubetskoi, Count G. "Kitai, Iaponiia i Rossiia." *Moskovskii Ezhenedel'nik* 1909, 37: 7–20.

"Tsarskaia diplomatiia o zadachakh Rossii na Vostoke v 1900 g." Edited by M. Pokrovskii. *Krasnyi arkhiv* 1926, 18: 3–29.

Tseng, You-ho. *Chinese Diplomatic History.* Shanghai, 1928.

Tsiang, T. F. "Sino-Japanese Diplomatic Relations, 1870–1894." *Chinese Social and Political Science Review* 1933, 17: 1–106.

Tsuboi Kumazo. *Saikin seiji gaiko-shi.* 4 vols. Tokyo, 1928–1929.

Tsuzuki Keiroku den. Edited by Keikokai. Tokyo, 1926.

Tsyvinskii, Admiral G. *50 let v Imperatorskom flote.* Riga, n.d. (ca. 1923).

Tung, William L. *China and the Foreign Powers: The Impact of and Reaction to Unequal Treaties.* Dobbs Ferry, N.Y., 1970.

Tyler, William Ferdinand. *Pulling Strings in China.* New York, 1930.

Udovenko, V. G. *Dal'nii Vostok. Ekonomiko-geograficheskaia kharakteristika.* Moscow, 1957.

Ueda Toshio, ed. *Kindai Nihon gaiko-shi no kenkyu.* Tokyo, 1956.

Ukhtomskii, E. E. *Puteshestvie Gosudaria Imperatora Nikolaia II na Vostok (v 1890–1891).* 3 vols. St. Petersburg, 1897.

Umetani, Noboru. *The Role of Foreign Employees in the Meiji Era in Japan.* Tokyo, 1971. (Institute of Developing Economies Occasional Papers, no. 9.)

Underwood, L. H. *Fifteen Years among the Top-Knots; Or Life in Korea.* New York, 1904.

Unger, Frederic William. Assisted by Charles Morris. *Russia and Japan, and a Complete History of the War in the Far East.* Philadelphia, 1904.

Union of Soviet Socialist Republics. Foreign Ministry Historical Archives. Arkhiv vneshnei politiki Rossii.

United States Army Japan, Headquarters, Assistant Chief of Staff, G3, Foreign Histories Division. "Imperial Japanese Army in Manchuria 1894–1945." Mimeographed. Vol. 2 of "Japanese Studies on Manchuria." Tokyo, 1959.

United States, National Archives. United States Diplomatic Despatches.

Unterberg, P. F. *Primorskaia oblast', 1856–1898 gg.* St. Petersburg, 1900.

"Ustav russko-kitaiskogo banka." *Priamurskiia vedomosti* 1896, supplement to nos. 126–127.

"Ustav russko-koreiskago banka." *Priamurskiia vedomosti* 1898, 224: 204; 225: 2–4; 226: 2–4.

Uyehara, George E. *The Political Development of Japan, 1867–1909.* London, 1910.

Vagin, V. "Koreitsy na Amure." *Sbornik istoriko-statisticheskikh svedenii o Sibiri i sopredel'nykh ei stranakh* 1875, vol. 1, chpt. 9.

Valliant, Robert Britton. "Japan and the Trans-Siberian Railroad, 1885–1905." Ph.D. dissertation, University of Hawaii, 1974.

——. "The Selling of Japan." *Monumenta Nipponica* 1974, 29: 4: 415–38.

Varg, Paul A. *The Making of a Myth: The U.S. and China, 1897–1912.* East Lansing, 1968.

Vart, E. "Armiia Korei: pis'mo ochevidtsa." *Niva* 1894, 38: 907–8.

Vebel', F. D. "Poezdka v Koreiu." *Russkii Vestnik* 1894, 234: 115–53.

Verchau, Ekkard. "Europa und der Ferne Orient 1894 bis 1898." Ph.D. dissertation, Universität Tübingen, 1957.

Vern, M. *Sovremennaia Iaponiia.* (Iz zapisnoi knizhki moriaka). Moscow, 1882.

Viallate, Achille. *Economic Imperialism and International Relations during the Last Fifty Years.* New York, 1923.

"Vil'gel'm II o zaniatii tsarskoi Rossii Port-Artura." *Krasnyi arkhiv* 1933, 3 (58): 150–55.

Villenoisy, F. de. *La guerre sino-japonaise et ses consequences pour l'Europe.* Paris, 1895.

Vinacke, Harold M. *A History of the Far East in Modern Times.* 6th ed. New York, 1959.

Vitgeft, Captain V. "Obzor voenno-morskikh deistvii v nyneshniuiu Kitaisko-Iaponskuiu voinu." *Morskoi sbornik* 1895, no. 1, unofficial section, pp. 19–50; no. 5, unofficial section, pp. 13–36.

Vitte, Sergei Iul'evich. *Vospominaniia.* Annotated ed. 3 vols. Moscow, 1960.

Vladimir (Volpicelli, Zinone [?]). *The China-Japan War.* New York, 1896.

——. *Russia on the Pacific and the Siberian Railway.* London, 1899.

"Vladivostok." *Japan Weekly Mail* 1889, pp. 62–63.

Vladivostok. (Sbornik istoricheskikh dokumentov. 1860–1907 gg.). Compiled by G. M. Voronkova, Z. I. Dvinskikh, T. V. Kashirina, I. F. Kulakova, A. I. Novikova, and Z. F. Fedotova. Vladivostok, 1960.

"Voennyia deistviia v Koree." *Morskoi sbornik* 1894, no. 9, naval chronicle section, pp. 20–26; no. 10, naval chronicle section, pp. 1–25; no. 11, naval chronicle section, pp. 1–27.

Vogak, K. I. "Doneseniia russkogo voennogo agenta v Kitae i Iaponii Vogaka, 1893–1895." *Sbornik geograficheskikh, topograficheskikh i statisticheskikh materialov po Azii* 1895, 60: 1–204; 61: 1–60.

Vogel, Barbara. *Deutsche Russlandpolitik: Das Scheitern der deutschen Weltpolitik unter Bülow 1900–1906.* Hamburg, 1973. (Studien zur modernen Geschichte, vol. 11.)

Volkonskii, Prince A. "Russkie instruktora v Seulie." *Sankt Peterburgskiia vedomosti,* Oct. 17, 1887.

Vollan, Grigorii de. "V gorakh Iaponii." *Russkii vestnik* 1898, 11: 124–41.

——. "V strane voskhodiashchego solntsa." *Russkoe obozrenie* 1895, 9: 93–109.

——. *V strane voskhodiashchego solntsa: Ocherk i zametki o Iaponii.* St. Petersburg, 1903.

Vostochnoe obozrenie.

Vsemirnaia illiustratsiia. St. Petersburg.

Walder, David. *The Short Victorious War: the Russo-Japanese Conflict, 1904–5.* London, 1973.

Waldersee, Alfred Graf von. *Denkwürdigkeiten.* Edited by Heinrich Otto Meissner. 3 vols. Stuttgart, 1922.

Wang, C. C. "The Chinese Eastern Railway." *Annals of the American Academy of Political and Social Sciences* 1925, 122: 57–69.

Warner, Denis and Peggy. *The Tide at Sunrise: A History of the Russo-Japanese War, 1904–1905.* New York, 1974.

Watanabe Ikujiro. *Gaiko to gaikoka.* Tokyo, 1939.

———. *Nihon kinsei gaikoshi.* Tokyo, 1938.

———. *Nisshin Nich-Ro senso shiwa.* Tokyo, 1937.

Weale. B. L. Putnam. *Manchu and Muscovite: Being Letters from Manchuria Written during the Autumn of 1903 With an Historical Sketch Entitled "Prologue to the Crisis."* London, 1904.

Weems, Clarence N., ed. *Hulbert's History of Korea.* 2 vols. New York, 1962.

———. "The Korean Reform and Independence Movement, 1881–1898." Ph.D. dissertation, Columbia University, 1954.

———. "Reformist Thought of the Independence Program (1896–1898)." In Yung-hway Jo, ed. *Korea's Response to the West,* 163–218. Kalamazoo, Mich., 1970.

Wegener, Georg. "Das Kiautschougebiet." In Hans Meyer, ed. *Das Deutsche Kolonialreich: Eine Länderkunde der deutschen Schutzgebiete,* 2: 499–542. Leipzig, 1910.

Wehler, Hans-Ulrich. *Der Aufstieg des amerikanischen Imperialismus: Studien zur Entwicklung des Imperium Americanum 1865–1900.* Göttingen, 1974.

Wehrle, Edmund S. *Britain, China, and the Antimissionary Riots, 1891–1900.* Minneapolis, 1966.

Wei, Ying-Pang. "Les relations diplomatiques en la Chine et la Russie de 1881 à 1924." Ph.D. dissertation, Université de Paris, 1946.

Weicker, Hans. *Kiautschou: Das deutsche Schutzgebiet in Ostasien.* Berlin, 1908.

Weigh, Ken Shen. *Russo-Chinese Diplomacy.* Shanghai, 1928.

Westwood, J. N. *Endurance and Endeavour: Russian History, 1812–1971.* Oxford, 1973.

———. *A History of Russian Railways.* London, 1964.

———. *Witnesses of Tsushima.* Tallahassee, 1970.

"The Whang-chei of Dai-Han, or the Emperor of Korea." *Korean Repository* 1897, 4: 385–90.

White, John Albert. "Bezobrazov and the Coming of the Russo-Japanese War." Mimeographed essay, n.d.

———. *The Diplomacy of the Russo-Japanese War.* Princeton, 1964.

White, Trumbull. *The War in the East: Japan, China, and Corea.* Philadelphia, 1895.

"Why Russia Went to War with Japan: The Story of the Yalu Concession." *Fortnightly Review,* 1910, 87: 1030–1044.

Wiese, Gertrud. *Der Einspruch von Schimonoseki; ein Beitrag zur deutschen Aussenpolitik.* Poznan, 1924.

Wilberforce, Archibald, ed. *The Great Battles of all Nations from Marathon to the Surrender of Cronje in South Africa 490 B. C. to the Present Day.* vol. 2. New York, 1900.

Wilhelm II. *Ereignisse und Gestalten aus den Jahren 1878–1918.* Leipzig, 1922.

Wilkison, W. H. "The Korean Government." *Korean Repository* 1897, 4: 1–13, 45–56.

Williams, William Appleman. *American-Russian Relations, 1781–1947.* New York, 1952.

Willoughby, Westel W. *Foreign Rights and Interests in China.* Baltimore, 1920.

Witham, Wallace Fernald, Jr. "A Study of Meiji Japan's Foreign Policy Decision-Making Structure: Japanese Attitudes Pertaining to the Expansion of the United States in the Pacific, 1888–1898." Ph.D. dissertation, University of Minnesota, 1974.

"Wonsan and Across the Peninsula." By H. G. A. *Korean Repository* 1898, 5: 401–3.

Wright, Mary C. "The Adaptability of Ch'ing Diplomacy: The Case of Korea." *Journal of Asian Studies* 1958, 17: 363–81.

Wright, Stanley F. *Hart and the Chinese Customs.* Belfast, 1950.

Wu, Aitchen K. *China and the Soviet Union: A Study of Sino-Soviet Relations.* New York, 1950.

Wu, Hsiang-hsiang. *O-ti ch'in-lüeh Chun-Kuo shih.* Taipei, 1954.

X. Y. Z. "The Attack on the Top Knot." *Korean Repository* 1896, 3: 263–72.

Yakhontoff, Victor A. *Russia and the Soviet Union in the Far East.* London, 1932.

Yamabe Kentaro. "Chosen kaikaku undo to Kin Gyokukin: Koshin jihen ni kanren shite." *Rekishigaku kenkyu* 1960, 247: 31–46.

———. "Itsubi no hen ni tsuite." In Nihon Kokusai Seiji Gakkai, comp. *Nikkan kankei no tenkai,* 69–81. Tokyo, 1962.

———. "Jingo gunran ni tsuite." *Rekishigaku kenkyu* 1961, 257: 13–25.

———. "Nisshin Tenshin joyaku ni tsuite." *Ajia kenkyu* 1960, 7: 2: 1–46.

Yanaga, Chitoshi. "Biographies of Japanese Historical Figures." Unpublished compilation given by Dr. Yanaga to the author for his use.

———. *Japan Since Perry.* New York, 1949.

Yano, Jinichi. *Manshu kindai-shi.* Tokyo, 1941.

Yoneda Minoru. *Gendai gaiko kowa.* Tokyo, 1926.

Young, C. Walter. *The International Relations of Manchuria: A Digest and Analysis of Treaties, Agreements, and Negotiations Concerning the Three Eastern Provinces of China.* Chicago, 1929.

Young, Ernest P. "A Study of Groups and Personalities in Japan Influencing Events Leading to the Sino-Japanese War (1894–1895)." In *Papers on Japan,* 2: 229–75. Cambridge, Mass., 1963.

Young, L. K. *British Policy in China, 1895–1902.* London, 1970.

Young, Marilyn B. "American Expansion, 1870–1900: The Far East." In Barton J. Bernstein, ed. *Towards a New Past: Dissenting Essays in American History,* 176–201. New York, 1968.

———. *The Rhetoric of Empire: American China Policy, 1895–1901.* Cambridge, Mass. 1968.

Yu, Te-jen. *The Japanese Struggle for World Empire.* New York, 1967.

Yun, T. H. "The Korean Abroad." *Korean Repository* 1897, 4: 104–7, 180–3.

Zabriskie, Edward H. *American-Russian Rivalry in the Far East: A Study in Diplomacy and Power Politics, 1895–1914.* Philadelphia, 1946.

Zabugin, N. P. *O sudokhodstve na russkom Dal'nem Vostoke.* St. Petersburg, 1896.

Zaichikov, V. T. *Koreia*. Moscow, 1951.

Zaionchkovskii, P. A. *Samoderzhavie i russkaia armiia na rubezhe XIX–XX stoletii, 1881–1903*. Moscow, 1973.

Zakharov, S. E.; Zakharov, M. N.; Bagrov, V. N.; and Kotukhov, M. P. *Tikhookeanskii flot*. Moscow, 1966.

"Zapiski russkikh instruktorov v Koree." *Priamurskiia vedomosti* May 31, 1898.

Zarina, L. L. and Livshits, S. G. *Britanskii imperializm v Kitae (1896–1901 gg.)*. Moscow, 1970.

Zepelin, C. von. *Der russische Ferne Osten und seine Besiedelung*. Berlin, 1909.

"Zheltyi vopros v Priamure. (Istoriko statisticheskii ocherk.)" *Voprosy kolonizatsii* 1910, 7: 53–116.

Zischka, Anton. *Japan in der Welt: Die japanische Expansion seit 1854*. Leipzig, 1936.

Zubok, L. I. *Ekspansionistskaia politika SShA v nachale XX veka*. Moscow, 1969.

Zühlke, H. *Die Rolle des Fernen Osten in den politischen Beziehungen der Mächte, 1895–1905*. Berlin, 1929.

Index

Adachi Kenzo, Japanese adventurer in
Korea, 533
Adamoli, Giulio, Italian undersecretary of
state for foreign affairs (1893–96), 312
Afanas'ev I, Russian military instructor in
Korea, 652, 673
Aleksandr Mikhailovich, Russian grand
duke, 755
Alekseev [Alexeieff], Adm. Evgenii
Ivanovich, assistant chief of Russian
naval general staff (1892–95), Pacific
Fleet commander (1895–97), Black Sea
Squadron commander (1897–99), com-
mander-in-chief of Russian troops in
Kwantung region and Russian naval
forces in the Pacific (1899–1903), 662,
illus. 663, 722, 729, 740, 839, 845
Alekseev [Alexeieff], Kir Alekseevich,
Russian Finance Ministry agent, senior
counselor of state, 675–81 passim,
700–703 passim, 706, 905n.209
Aleksei Aleksandrovich, Grand Duke, admiral of the Russian fleet: described,
215–16; and Russian policy during
Sino-Japanese War, 218, 219, 220; and
Russo-Japanese relations, 283–85;
mentioned, 772
Alexander III, tsar of Russia (1881–94):
and Russian policy during Sino-
Japanese War, 195, 205, 206; mentioned, 36, 133, 153, 160, 841, 843

Alexeieff, Adm. Evgenii Ivanovich. See
Alekseev, Adm. Evgenii Ivanovich
Alexeieff, Kir Alekseevich. See Alekseev,
Kir Alekseevich
Al'ftan, Lieutenant Colonel, Russian general staff officer, 579, 593
Allen, Dr. Horace N., American mission-
ary and diplomat in Korea, chargé
(1893–94), minister (1897–1901): and
safeguarding Kojong, 534, 547; and
Japanese involvement in Queen Min
murder, 541–43 passim, 550–53 passim; and Russian aid to Korea, 665,
675, 681–92 passim, 698, 702, 706;
mentioned, 74, 86, 92, 93, 94, 104–5,
121, 642–47 passim
Andreevskii, Capt. Étienne, Russian military officer, 505
An Keiju, Korean war minister, 433, 586
Anzer, Bishop Johann, German bishop in
China, 712, 736, 909n.56
Aoki Shuzo, Viscount, Japanese foreign
affairs vice minister (1886–89), foreign
minister (1889–91, 1898–1900), minister to Germany (1892–97) and to Great
Britain (1894–95): and British prewar
peace efforts, 156–57, 158, 165, 173;
and Anglo-Russian mediation efforts in
Sino-Japanese War, 202, 208; and Japanese peace terms, 257, 265–73 passim; and Japan's response to Tripartite

Index

Index

Curzon, George Nathaniel, British under-secretary of foreign affairs, 819
Cyril, Russian grand duke, 813

D'Anethan, Baron Albert, Belgian minister to Japan (1893–1901), 176, 185, 237, 548
Davydov, Aleksandr Petrovich, Russian minister to Japan (1883–85): and Tientsin Convention, 28–30; and Möllendorff, 33–44 passim; mentioned, 55, 57, 58
de Courcel, Baron Alphonse Chodron. *See* Courcel, Baron Alphonse Chodron de
Decrais, Pierre-Louis-Albert, French ambassador to Great Britain (1893–94), 197
Denby, Charles, Jr., American chargé in Peking, 159, 183
Denby, Col. Charles, U.S. minister to China (1885–98): as peace negotiator for Chinese, 209, 230–31, 232, 233; and American intervention, 397n.44; mentioned, 89, 210, 237, 238, 313, 321
Denison, Henry Willard, American legal adviser to Japanese Foreign Office (1880–1914), 111, 112, 232, 233, 236
Denny, Owen N., American adviser of Kojong, Korean Home Office vice minister: *China and Korea* author, 88–89; mentioned, 74–75, 83, 86, 93
Depasse, Dr., French legation physician in China, 406n.44
Derby, Edward Henry Smith Stanley, Earl of, British foreign secretary (1874–78), 54
Detring, Gustav, German customs commissioner at Tientsin, 229–30, 403n.6, 494, 716–18 passim
Diederichs, Otto von, German rear admiral in China (1892–97), vice admiral (1897), 727, 728, 732, 734
Dimant, S. R., Soviet scholar, 291
Dinsmore, Hugh A., U.S. minister resident and consul general in Seoul (1887–90), 69, 88, 89, 90, 688
Dmitrevskii [Dmitrevsky], Pavel An-dreevich, Russian consul in Hankow (1883–92) and in Tientsin (1893–96), acting chargé in Korea (1891, 1893), 84, 93, 100–106 passim, 123, 141, 143
Dowell, Sir William, British admiral, 37, 60, 366n.10
Drew, E. B., Chinese Maritime Customs Service employee, 494
Dubasov, Fedor Vasil'evich, Russian admiral: and Russian occupation of Port Arthur, 757, 758, 789, 793; mentioned, 689, 690, 839
Dudgeon, Dr., physician and unofficial private secretary to Marquis Tseng, 82
Dukhovskoi, Sergei Mikhailovich, Amur Region governor general (1893–98), 489, illus. 490, 491–93, 846
Dun, Edwin, U.S. minister to Japan (1893–97): and American mediation in Sino-Japanese War, 208, 209, 210; mentioned, 231, 238, 321
Dye, Gen. William McE., American military instructor in Korea: and Queen Min murder, 534–36, 543; mentioned, 541, 547, 570

Empress dowager. *See* Tz'u-hsi
Enomoto Takeaki [Buyo], Adm., Japanese minister to China (1882–85), foreign minister (1891–92), agriculture and commerce minister (1894–97), 24, 95, 96, 97, 247, 362n.8
Eulenburg-Hertefeldt, Count Philipp zu, German ambassador to Austria-Hungary (1894–1902), 276–77

Faure, Félix, French president (1895–99), 292, 294
Fel'dgauzen, Rear Adm. A. F., military governor of Vladivostok (1880–87), 72
Foote, Lucius H., U.S. minister to Korea (1883–85), 24, 25, 47, 74, 360n.78
Foster, John W., American secretary of state (1892–93): in Treaty of Shimonoseki negotiations, 231–39 passim, 244, 248, 249, 255, 409n.84; and Li Hung-chang, 245; appointment of, 404n.16

Index

Index

256, 314, 317, 347–51 passim, 523,
551–52, 605, 607, 639, 847
Lobanov-Yamagata protocol (1896),
627–37
Lo Feng-loh, secretary to Li Hung-chang
(1895), Chinese minister to Great Britain (1896–1901), 239, 255, 406n.47,
494, 502, 721, 783
Loftus, Lord Augustus, British minister to
Russia, 15
Low, Frederick, U.S. minister to China
(1869–74), 6
Lowther, Gerard Augustus, British chargé
in Tokyo, 305–6, 419n.80, 526

MacDonald, Sir Claude Maxwell, British
minister to China (1896–1900): and
Russian lease of Port Arthur, 768–84
passim, 791, 916n.13; and British lease
of Weihaiwei, 814–18 passim; mentioned, 508, 510, 677, 725, 746, 779,
793
McGiffen, Commander, U.S. naval officer,
186
Ma Chien-chung, Chinese commissioner in
Korea, 21, 22
Malet, Sir Edward B., British ambassador
to Germany (1884–95), 205, 479
Malozemoff, Andrew, American historian,
291
Marschall, Adolf Hermann, Baron von
Bieberstein, German state secretary of
foreign affairs (1890–97): and German
policy during Sino-Japanese War, 205,
207–8, 228; and proposed intervention
over Japanese peace terms, 265–76 passim, 282; and Tripartite Intervention,
293–94, 296–97, 305; and Japan's response to Tripartite Intervention, 318–
24 passim; and indemnity negotiations,
327, 328, 329, 339–44 passim, 424n.5,
426n.31; and German base in China,
708–12, 721; on Sino-German relations,
713–16; mentioned, 332, 346, 479, 480
Martino, Renato de, Italian minister to
Japan (1885–95), 203
Matiunin, Nikolai Gavrilovich, Russian
consul and chargé in Seoul (1898), 706

Matsukata, Masayoshi, Japanese premier
(1891–92, 1896–98), finance minister
(c. 1894), 97, 247, 310, 311, 611
Meckel, Maj. Gen. Klemens Wilhelm
Jakob, German adviser to Japanese
army general staff, 185, 265
Meiji [Mutsuhito], emperor of Japan
(1868–1912), 189, 265, 310, 561
Merrill, Henry F., American chief commissioner of Korean Customs Service,
74
Metternich, Count Paul von Wolff-
Metternich zur Bracht, German ambassador to Great Britain, 817
Michie, Alexander, London *Times* special
correspondent, 229
Min Chong-muk, Korean Foreign Office
president (1889–92), foreign minister
(1897, 1898), acting foreign minister
(1898): and Russian aid to Korea, 676–
78 passim, 690, 691, 692, 695–701 passim, 705; mentioned, 669, 684, 688
Min Myongsong, queen of Korea: and
power struggle with taewongun, Kojong, 18–21; renewed influence of,
531–32; assassination of, chap. 18 passim, 595, 847, 874n.124; funeral of,
641, 645–47; mentioned, 25, 27, 73,
119, 518, 520, 522, 580
Min Sang-ho, acting Korean foreign minister (1898), 870n.47
Min Sung-ho, brother of Queen Min,
18–19
Min Ying-hwan, Korean minister to U.S.,
870n.47
Min Yong-hwan, Prince, Korean war minister: and appeal for Russian aid, 648–
54 passim, 658, 660, 849; mentioned,
601, 676
Min Yong-ik, Prince, head of Korean diplomatic mission to U.S., 24, 25, 73, 75,
88, 89, 532
Min Yong-jun, Korean statesman, 99
Min Yong-ton, Korean minister to Russia,
France, and Austria-Hungary (1898–
99), 890n.8
Min Yung-chün, favorite of Queen Min,
119

Index

secretary in Tokyo, minister to Japan (1884–87), 13, 55, 57, 60–61, 68

Pokotilov, Dmitrii Dmitrievich, Russo-Chinese Bank director: and Peking Convention negotiations, 763, 787, 794; mentioned, 495, 511, 652, 674, 771

Polianovskii, Zinovii Mikhailovich, Russian student, 608

Popov, A. L., Soviet scholar, 291

Popov, Sergei Ivanovich, Russian minister to China (1884–86), 58, 70, 78

Putiata, Colonel, Russian military instructor in Korea, 652–64 passim, 667, 673

Putiatin, Evfimii Vasil'evich, Russian vice admiral, 8

Radolin-Radolinski, Hugo Leszczyc, Prince von, German ambassador to Russia (1895–1900): on indemnity negotiations with Japan, 335–43 passim; and German base in China, 709, 710, 711; on dealing with China, 718–24 passim, 741–44 passim; mentioned, 276, 325–32 passim, 346, 348, 717, 733, 734, 756, 817

Raspopov, Nikolai Aleksandrovich, Russian legation secretary in Seoul (1890–95), vice-consul (1896–98), 527

Read, Sheridan P. H., American consul in Tientsin, 159

Reunov, Rear Admiral, Russian officer, 757, 758, 759

Ribot, Alexandre Félix Joseph, French foreign minister (1890–93), premier and finance minister (1895), 292, 294

Rodgers, John, American rear admiral, 6

Romanov, B. A., Soviet historian, 512

Romanov, P. A., Russian privy councilor, director of Finance Ministry general office, 510

Rosebery, Archibald Philip Primrose, Earl of, British foreign secretary (1886, 1892–94), 158, 208, 266, 290, 315

Rosen, Baron Roman Romanovich, Russian chargé in Tokyo (1877–83), minister to Japan (1897–99): and Russian military instructors in Korea, 666, 674, 849; career of, 669; on Russian policy in Korea, 670, 672; on Russian lease of Port Arthur, 760–61; as negotiator of Nishi-Rosen Protocol, chap. 25 passim; on Russia's East Asian policy, 851–52, 938n.23; mentioned, 645, 656, 659, 667, 673, 698, 816, 850

Rotenhan, Baron Wolfram von, German undersecretary of state for foreign affairs: and indemnity negotiations with Japan, 332–33, 345; and German base in China, 708, 722, 727–38 passim; mentioned, 264, 335, 338

Rothstein [Rotshtein], A. Iu., Russian director of Russo-Chinese Bank, 498–511 passim

Roze, Rear Admiral, French officer, 5

Ryder, Sir Alfred Phillips, British admiral, 54

Sabatin. See Seredin-Sabatin, A. J.

Saigo Tsugumichi, Japanese navy minister (1885–86, 1887–90, 1893–1900), 247, 310

Saionji Kimmochi, Japanese minister to Austria-Hungary (1885–87) and to Germany and Belgium (1887–91), acting foreign minister (1895–96), foreign minister (1896): as indemnity negotiator, 331, 337–54 passim; on Japanese involvement in Queen Min murder, 545–46, 550–53 passim; and Russo-Japanese entente, 602–21 passim; and Kojong's move to palace, 638–39; mentioned, 527, 561, 567–68, 577, 579, 628, 848

Saito, Japanese Foreign Office first secretary, 109

Sakharov, Gen. Victor Viktorovich, Russian army chief of staff, 772

Sakuma Samata, Japanese general, 354

Salisbury, Lord Robert Gascoyne-Cecil, British prime minister (1885–86, 1886–92, 1895–1902), foreign secretary (1885–86, 1887–92, 1895–1900): and Russian occupation of Port Arthur, 757–58, 770, 775, 779–90 passim; and Anglo-Russian agreement on China, chap. 26 passim; mentioned, 61, 526,

Index

DATE DUE